the OPEN ROAD

50 BEST ROAD TRIPS in the USA

From Weekend Getaways
to Cross-Country Adventures

JESSICA DUNHAM

CONTENTS

Although every effort was made to make sure the information in this book was accurate when going to press, research was impacted by the COVID-19 pandemic. Some things may have changed during this crisis and the recovery that followed. Be sure to confirm specific details when making your travel plans.

TOP TO BOTTOM: CANYONLANDS NATIONAL PARK; STINSON BEACH; LA JOLLA BEACH; CRATER LAKE; ROUTE 66

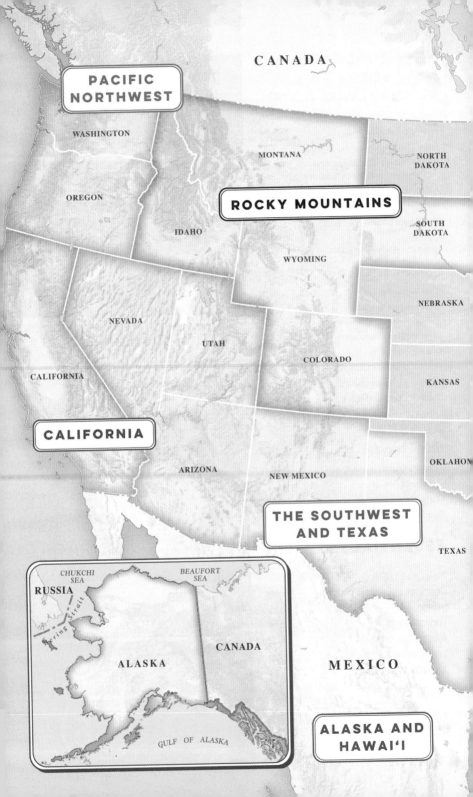

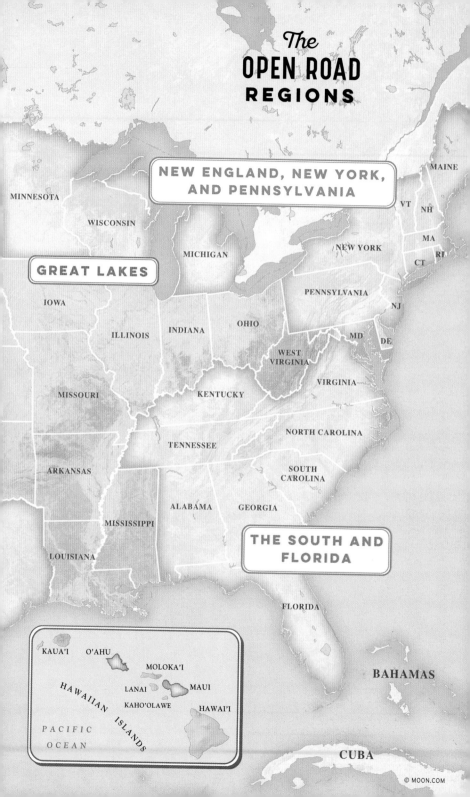

HIT THE ROAD

Even if you've never taken to the highway—elbow hooked over the open window, favorite song blaring, horizon unfurling ahead—you *feel* something when you hear the words "road trip." An adrenaline rush. A shot of exhilaration. The anticipation of discovering something new. About the world or perhaps about yourself.

American road trips are rooted in a deep mythology that connects to our country's westward expansion and the optimism for new beginnings. Captured poetically in books by Steinbeck and Kerouac, and thrillingly in movies like *Thelma and Louise,* road trips embody the ultimate expression of freedom. All you need is a set of wheels and you can go anywhere, do anything, and meet anyone.

When we travel, we pack more than just a change of clothes and a toothbrush. We bring with us grand expectations for life-changing experiences and soul-stirring sights. We want to relax and unwind, yes. But we also believe that once untethered from our daily routines, we'll be transformed.

The 50 trips in this guide meet such a tall order. The vast expanse of the Loneliest Road in Nevada lures you into meditation. The vivid colors of Vermont's fall foliage take your breath away. The mysterious Marfa Lights blinking over a black desert call into question everything you think you know about the universe. And the speed limit on the Blue Ridge Parkway forces you to slow down in the best way possible.

For this journey, you only need a set of wheels. The rest is up to you. Be free.

◀ HIGHWAY 1 IN CALIFORNIA

Top ⑩ **EXPERIENCES**

① SUMMIT DIAMOND HEAD

The 560-foot climb to the top of this dormant volcano on Oʻahu leads you to views of Waikiki, the Koʻolau Mountains, and the teal-blue waters of the Pacific Ocean (PAGE 690).

② DRINK IN DESERT VISTAS ON THE APACHE TRAIL

State Route 88, just outside of Phoenix, Arizona, traverses cactus-studded land-scapes and canyon-walled lakes. Drive it during spring and you'll be rewarded with colorful desert blooms, from the yellow palo verde to the deep orange tips of the ocotillo (PAGE 312).

①

3

3 HEAR THE WAVES CRASHING IN BIG SUR

There's a reason why the Big Sur Coast Highway is so storied. As you drive the cliff-hugging road, you'll be accompanied by the sounds of the Pacific Ocean crashing into the shore (**PAGE 130**).

4 ADMIRE AN EPIC WATERFALL ON MICHIGAN'S UPPER PENINSULA

When road-tripping through the U.P., a stretch-your-legs stop at Tahquamenon Falls State Park is essential. It's home to the second most powerful waterfall east of the Mississippi River, bested only by Niagara Falls (**PAGE 437**).

⑤ WATCH FOR WILDLIFE IN YELLOWSTONE

Driving through the stark wilderness of Yellowstone brings you face to face with an abundance of wildlife. Bison and elk roam the valleys, coyotes, foxes, and wolves skirt the hills, and bears lumber below the trees (**PAGE 360**).

⑥ NOSH YOUR WAY ALONG LAKE CHAMPLAIN SCENIC BYWAY

Vermont's western border along Lake Champlain is a plethora of farms, dairies, orchards, and maple houses that offer endless ways to savor local flavor, from fresh cheese and just-churned ice cream to ripe blueberries and sweet syrup (**PAGE 510**).

⑦ CRUISE DOWN ICONIC ROUTE 66

Relish the kitschy fun and Instagram-worthy neon signs on historic Route 66, which stretches from Chicago to Los Angeles (**PAGE 60**).

8

8 CROSS OVER TO THE KEYS

Florida's most famous and longest bridge connects the Florida Keys, a string of tropical islands south of Miami. The bridge spans turquoise waters as far as the eye can see and gifts motorists with 360-degree horizon views (PAGE 638).

9 FEAST YOUR EYES ON FALL FOLIAGE

Take an impressive fall drive along the Blue Ridge Parkway from Virginia to Tennessee. It offers everything you want in a road trip: zero billboards, a cruising speed of 45mph, and a dramatic conclusion in Great Smoky Mountains National Park (PAGE 562).

10 GAWK AT NORTH AMERICA'S TALLEST MOUNTAIN

Denali rises grandly in the distance on Alaska's Parks Highway, which serves as the main artery to the eponymous national park (PAGE 664).

Best VIEWS

BEST OF THE GOLDEN STATE

Enjoy golden views in California and beyond: sunrise at the Grand Canyon, sunset on the Santa Monica Pier, and midnight gazing down at the glittering lights of Las Vegas (**PAGE 108**).

NORTHERN CALIFORNIA LOOP

See towering redwoods, the rolling vineyards of wine country, the snow-covered peak of Mount Shasta, Yosemite's sequoias, and the ocean waves crashing into Big Sur (**PAGE 156**).

CALIFORNIA DESERTS

There is nothing like seeing a Joshua tree for the first time. At Joshua Tree National Park, prepare to be astounded by forests of this gnarled yucca and hulking boulders (**PAGE 194**).

SANTA FE, TAOS, AND THE ENCHANTED CIRCLE

See the red mesas, green valleys, and mountainous backcountry of New Mexico—including the looming Wheeler Peak—along the Enchanted Circle drive (**PAGE 304**).

▼ ROAD TO HANA

ROCKY MOUNTAIN NATIONAL PARK

WEST TEXAS AND BIG BEND NATIONAL PARK

Big Bend offers unobstructed sightlines of the winding Rio Grande, the forested Chisos Mountains, and the stark desert landscape that stretches for miles (PAGE 346).

DENVER, BOULDER, AND ROCKY MOUNTAIN NATIONAL PARK

The Rocky Mountains encircle Estes Park, so no matter where you are in town or in what direction you look, you're rewarded with resplendent, snowcapped mountain vistas (PAGE 388).

THE APPALACHIAN TRAIL

From the peak of Mount Greylock you can see the Berkshires, and from the top of Spruce Mountain you have unparalleled views of the forests and lakes of Maine's backcountry (PAGE 494).

LAKE CHAMPLAIN SCENIC BYWAY

To grasp just how big the sixth-largest lake in the country is, walk or drive to the top of Mount Philo, where Adirondack chairs and wooden benches invite you to stay awhile (PAGE 510).

ADIRONDACKS AND CATSKILLS

This region boasts an abundance of state parks and preserves, with thousands of acres of vista-packed wild spaces and natural lands to explore (PAGE 530).

ROAD TO HANA

You'll have a hard time deciding which views are more memorable—those of rushing waterfalls that plunge into secluded swimming holes or the endless expanse of the sparkling Pacific Ocean (PAGE 698).

Best COASTAL DRIVES

PACIFIC COAST HIGHWAY: CALIFORNIA

Whether it's a cliff jutting over the ocean in Big Sur or the warm sands of Huntington Beach or San Diego, this highway keeps you linked to Pacific Ocean views at all times (**PAGE 124**).

PACIFIC COAST HIGHWAY: WASHINGTON AND OREGON

Staring at the deep-blue hue and unruly waves of the Pacific Ocean never gets old. Thankfully, this trip affords plenty of secluded beaches from which to gaze at the coastal horizon (**PAGE 236**).

MICHIGAN'S GOLD COAST

No matter if you're lunching at a family-owned restaurant or staying at a charming bed-and-breakfast, you're never far from water views thanks to the route's 300 miles of coastline (**PAGE 450**).

BEST OF NEW ENGLAND

Lighthouses line the rugged Maine coast, linking quaint towns and lovely beaches, most of which lie dormant in winter only to come alive with the crowds in summer (**PAGE 476**).

▼ OREGON COAST BEACH

WILD HORSES IN NORTH CAROLINA'S OUTER BANKS

CHESAPEAKE BAY

The Chesapeake Bay hugs Maryland's shoreline. This drive drive hops from yacht-filled marinas and bustling bayside towns to peaceful beaches sometimes populated only by a morning walker and his golden retriever (PAGE 612).

NORTH CAROLINA'S OUTER BANKS

This drive straddles Pamlico Sound to the west and the Atlantic Ocean to the east. Breathe in the sea air, and linger in the coastal villages that line the barrier islands (PAGE 620).

O'AHU COASTAL LOOP

The quiet beaches and pounding surf of the North Shore tempt you to pull over. Make time for frequent stops so you don't to miss a chance to watch surfers navigate the 30-story waves (PAGE 688).

ROAD TO HANA

Hairpin curves wind around Maui's eastern coastline, where the only thing that stands between you and the view is a palm tree or a banana stand (PAGE 698).

RAINBOW EUCALYPTUS TREE ON O'AHU

Best FOODIE ADVENTURES

COLUMBIA RIVER GORGE AND WINE COUNTRY

No trip to Washington State is complete without sampling the goods of the grape—cabernet franc, merlot, syrah—at tasting rooms in the region's wine country (PAGE 264).

WISCONSIN'S DOOR COUNTY

Ever downed a shot of bitters, dined on pickled herring and lingonberries, or eaten a potato pancake? On this Scandinavian culinary tour, you can (PAGE 460).

BEST OF NEW ENGLAND

Roadside vegetable stands and u-pick farms are plentiful, but the real treats are the lobster rolls and clam cakes in Maine or the pizza pies in Boston (PAGE 476).

LAKE CHAMPLAIN SCENIC BYWAY

The syrup is tapped from the maple trees that shade the road, and the cheese in the markets comes from nearby dairy farms. Then there are the orchards, which offer u-pick fresh fruit and hard ciders (PAGE 510).

▼ KENTUCKY BOURBON TRAIL

FARMERS MARKET IN MAINE

HUDSON RIVER VALLEY

Home of the Culinary Institute of America, this region invites you to explore the gastronomy of its renowned restaurants, often owned and operated by top chefs (PAGE 540).

THE NATCHEZ TRACE: NASHVILLE TO NEW ORLEANS

From Nashville hot chicken to gumbo, beignets, and po'boys in New Orleans, you'll get a true taste of regional flavors along the Natchez Trace (PAGE 582).

CHARLESTON TO SAVANNAH

These are just a few of the dishes you must try: slow-smoked pork (pulled, shredded, or chopped), shrimp and grits, fried green tomatoes, low-country boil, pimento cheese on bread, and pralines (PAGE 600).

KENTUCKY'S BOURBON TRAIL

Have your designated driver ready so you can indulge in bourbon tastings at some of the most notable distilleries in the world, including Jim Beam, Maker's Mark, Evan Williams, and Buffalo Trace (PAGE 628).

NASHVILLE, TENNESSEE

Best GLIMPSES OF AMERICANA

THE LONELIEST ROAD

As it travels through small town after small town, Route 50 shows you what Main Street U.S.A. looks like from coast to coast; hence its secondary nickname, "the Backbone of America" (PAGE 36).

ROUTE 66

The retro neon signs, kitschy tourist traps, and vintage motor courts found on the Mother Road provide a captured-in-time image of American life (PAGE 60).

GOLD COUNTRY RAMBLE

The gold rush and the West's growth are intrinsically linked. Step back into the dusty, rowdy, hopeful, pioneering history of the Old West on this California road trip (PAGE 202).

AUSTIN, SAN ANTONIO, AND THE HILL COUNTRY

Expect big hats, cowboy boots, and a friendly welcome. From Austin to San Antonio, and everywhere in between, the Texas spirit runs strong and proud (PAGE 336).

▼ HISTORIC ROUTE 66

AMISH BUGGY

PHILADELPHIA, PITTSBURGH, AND PENNSYLVANIA DUTCH COUNTRY

Find Americana treasures in the heart of Amish country, where buggies share the road with cars, shops sell handmade quilts, and restaurants serve chicken pot pie (PAGE 518).

BLUE RIDGE PARKWAY

Dig into the fascinating world of bluegrass music and Appalachian folk arts, then pay a visit to Dollywood, an amusement park owned by the one and only Dolly Parton (PAGE 562).

THE NATCHEZ TRACE: NASHVILLE TO NEW ORLEANS

With destinations like Elvis Presley's Graceland, a studio where the greatest musicians of all time recorded hits, and civil rights landmarks, this trip offers a crash course in all things American (PAGE 582).

HATS FOR SALE IN SAN ANTONIO

Best FOR KIDS

ROUTE 66

Along the Mother Road, the quirky roadside attractions in small towns and kid-friendly museums in big cities keep the whole family entertained (PAGE 60).

OREGON TRAIL

Ideal for older kids, this trip offers a hands-on, interactive education on America's westward expansion, including a chance to ride on a real pioneer wagon (PAGE 78).

SOUTHERN CALIFORNIA AND ROUTE 66 LOOP

Children will never be bored by the rides and shows at Disneyland and California Adventure, nor by the family-friendly offerings in Newport Beach and San Diego (PAGE 178).

BEST OF THE SOUTHWEST

There's family fun to be had in the Southwest, whether it's riding the rails to the Grand Canyon, taking in a PG-rated show in Las Vegas, or standing in four states at once at the Four Corners Monument (PAGE 288).

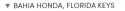

▼ BAHIA HONDA, FLORIDA KEYS

MOUNT RUSHMORE

RENO TO THE RUBIES

If children aren't mesmerized by the stalagmites in the Lehman Caves, they'll love the steam-train ride in Ely and the Chollar Mine tour in Virginia City (**PAGE 318**).

MOUNT RUSHMORE AND THE BLACK HILLS

Every child should see the rock-carved faces of past presidents at Mount Rushmore. At Custer State Park, bring carrots so the kids can feed the burros, then saddle up for a family horseback ride (**PAGE 404**).

THE JERSEY SHORE

Bring swimsuits, sunscreen, and a lot of energy for the beach and boardwalk activities—such as arcades, games, and amusement rides—along the Jersey Shore (**PAGE 548**).

SOUTH FLORIDA AND THE KEYS

Kiddos can build sand castles and frolic in the warm water at Daytona Beach, then enjoy the amusements at Disney World's theme parks (**PAGE 638**).

HISTORIC COLORFUL BUILDINGS ALONG ROUTE 66

Best FOR OUTDOOR EXPLORERS

PACIFIC CREST TRAIL: CALIFORNIA

Pack your hiking boots for numerous opportunities to pull off to the side of the road and hit the trail on California's segment of the PCT, which runs from Mexico to Canada (**PAGE 140**).

PACIFIC CREST TRAIL: OREGON AND WASHINGTON

Summit rocky peaks, balance on the caldera's edge of Crater Lake, and camp in the shadow of Mount Rainier. Then cap off your adventures with a locally brewed craft beer (**PAGE 250**).

HIGH ADVENTURE IN BEND

Bend's craggy volcanic peaks draw high-adrenaline thrill seekers, from downhill skiers and mountain bikers to rock climbers, rafters, and kayakers (**PAGE 274**).

SALT LAKE CITY, PARK CITY, AND THE WASATCH RANGE

You'll find four-season outdoor fun in this region. In winter, bundle up for skiing and snowboarding; come summer, there's hiking and mountain biking (**PAGE 328**).

▼ PACIFIC CREST TRAIL, YOSEMITE NATIONAL PARK

ALASKA'S PARKS HIGHWAY

YELLOWSTONE TO GLACIER NATIONAL PARK

When you're finished hiking glacier trails and summiting steep mountains, walk to a waterfall or take a dip in the healing hot springs (PAGE 360).

IDAHO'S RIVERS AND MOUNTAINS: BOISE TO COEUR D'ALENE

Hook up with a river guide to embark on a float trip or rafting tour down the Salmon River. For something tamer, rent a canoe to paddle the placid waters of Payette Lake (PAGE 396).

MINNEAPOLIS TO VOYAGEURS NATIONAL PARK

Outdoors adventures come by way of water: fish for trout, camp on a houseboat, paddle the Boundary Waters, or hike to lake and river views (PAGE 420).

THE APPALACHIAN TRAIL

The Appalachian Trail is well marked and heavily traveled, making it easy to hop on at various points for a sunset hike or a vigorous day trek that leads to 360-degree views (PAGE 494).

ALASKA'S PARKS HIGHWAY

Calling all birders and wildlife-watchers: Keep your binoculars out and your eyes open for caribou, moose, beavers, and migratory waterfowl (PAGE 664).

THE KENAI PENINSULA

With its boat tours, glacier cruises, and gentle nature trails, the Kenai Peninsula is perfect for outdoor lovers who don't want high-intensity adventure (PAGE 674).

Best ON TWO WHEELS

THE LONELIEST ROAD

Motorcyclists will see nary another vehicle on the empty stretches through Utah and Nevada, and bicyclists can jump on the scenic, 239-mile Katy Trail through Missouri (PAGE 36).

ROUTE 66

Thousands of motorcyclists and bicyclists ride this historic route. Complete the end-to-end journey—from Chicago to Santa Monica—or join the road somewhere in the middle (PAGE 60).

BEST OF THE PACIFIC NORTHWEST

Not only are the rural areas of this region welcoming to two-wheeled travelers, but so are the cities; Seattle, Portland, Vancouver, and Victoria all cater to bicyclists (PAGE 216).

THE APACHE TRAIL

Motorcyclists take to this road on the weekends to enjoy the slow and scenic ride through the Sonoran Desert, complete with one or two saloon stops and dinner overlooking Apache Lake (PAGE 312).

RENO TO THE RUBIES

The ride from Reno to bawdy Virginia City is popular with motorcyclists—mostly for the epic views and wild-horse sightings, but also for the lively saloons that await at the end of the trip (PAGE 318).

▼ MOTORCYCLE ON ROUTE 66

WILD WYOMING

The big skies and open spaces—not to mention the striking scenery—of Wyoming make it an ideal road trip for motorcyclists and bicyclists alike (PAGE 378).

MICHIGAN'S UPPER PENINSULA

Heritage trails, historic stops, picnic areas, and welcoming B&Bs make it easy to explore Michigan's Upper Peninsula on two wheels (PAGES 430 AND 440).

BISON IN WYOMING

MAKE IT A *Greener Road Trip*

Taking a road trip requires the use of a vehicle, which increases your carbon footprint. Below are some tips to help offset that increase and lighten your environmental impact.

GETTING AROUND

- Pack your vehicle as light as possible so as not to weight down the car, which decreases fuel efficiency.

- Plan your driving route thoroughly to avoid wasting gas by backtracking.

- Get a vehicle tune-up before you launch. It helps increase fuel efficiency when your car operates at peak performance.

- Rent a hybrid or electric car. If you opt for an electric car, you'll be pleased to know there are more than 20,000 charging stations throughout the United States. Find specific locations at the **U.S. Department of Energy's website** (https://afdc.energy.gov/stations/#/find/nearest).

- Keep your vehicle's tire pressure at its optimum level to aid with fuel efficiency.

- Use public transportation in cities.

REDUCE, REUSE, RECYCLE

- Save your recyclables until you get to a recycling center in a town or city, or at a rest stop. **Google Maps** can help locate recycling centers near you.

- Pack reusable grocery sacks and utilize them when making purchases on the road, even at gas stations or mini-marts.

- Conserve water by re-wearing clothing when possible, using dry shampoo, and doing a full load of laundry instead of several smaller loads.

- Bring your own toiletries rather than using those provided in individual bottles at hotels and motels.

FOOD AND DRINKS

- Bring a reusable water bottle instead of buying individual plastic bottles.

- Save food by planning meals ahead of time and buy in bulk when possible.

- Pack snacks and meals for the road and keep them in a small cooler in the vehicle.

- Bring reusable food containers, so you can store restaurant leftovers in a sustainable manner that doesn't involve Styrofoam or throwaway plastic.

CROSS-COUNTRY ROUTES

These trips thread from coast to coast. They carry you deep into America's heartland, stopping in some of the nation's biggest cities and taking you far back in time. There's Route 66, one of the most famous highways in the United States, which offers roadside attractions and a glimpse at a bygone era from Chicago to Santa Monica. The Oregon Trail is a route carved in history by the intrepid pioneers heading west from Missouri to Oregon. And then there's the Loneliest Road, a quiet two-lane stretch that starts in Sacramento, California, wanders through America's small towns, and finishes in Maryland, at the Atlantic Ocean.

◄ HISTORIC ROUTE 66

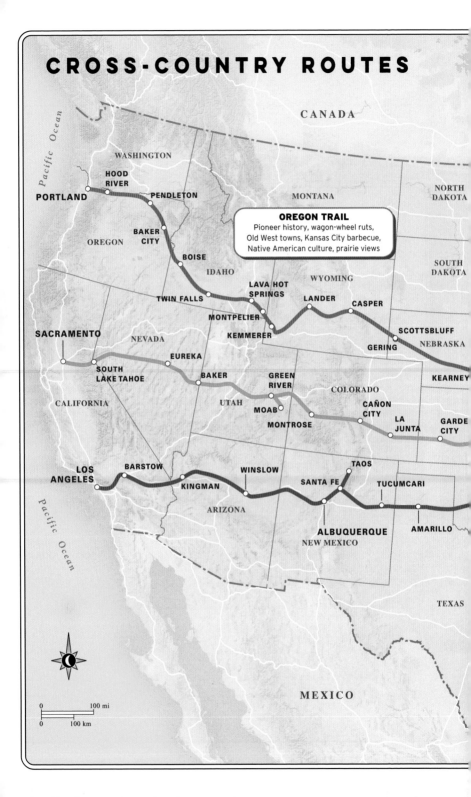

CROSS-COUNTRY ROUTES

CANADA

WASHINGTON

MONTANA

NORTH DAKOTA

HOOD RIVER

PORTLAND

PENDLETON

OREGON

BAKER CITY

BOISE

SOUTH DAKOTA

IDAHO

WYOMING

OREGON TRAIL
Pioneer history, wagon-wheel ruts,
Old West towns, Kansas City barbecue,
Native American culture, prairie views

LAVA HOT SPRINGS

LANDER

CASPER

TWIN FALLS

MONTPELIER

KEMMERER

SCOTTSBLUFF

GERING

NEBRASKA

SACRAMENTO

NEVADA

EUREKA

SOUTH LAKE TAHOE

BAKER

GREEN RIVER

COLORADO

KEARNEY

CALIFORNIA

UTAH

MOAB

MONTROSE

CAÑON CITY

LA JUNTA

GARDE CITY

LOS ANGELES

BARSTOW

KINGMAN

WINSLOW

TAOS

SANTA FE

TUCUMCARI

ARIZONA

ALBUQUERQUE
NEW MEXICO

AMARILLO

TEXAS

Pacific Ocean

Pacific Ocean

MEXICO

0   100 mi

0   100 km

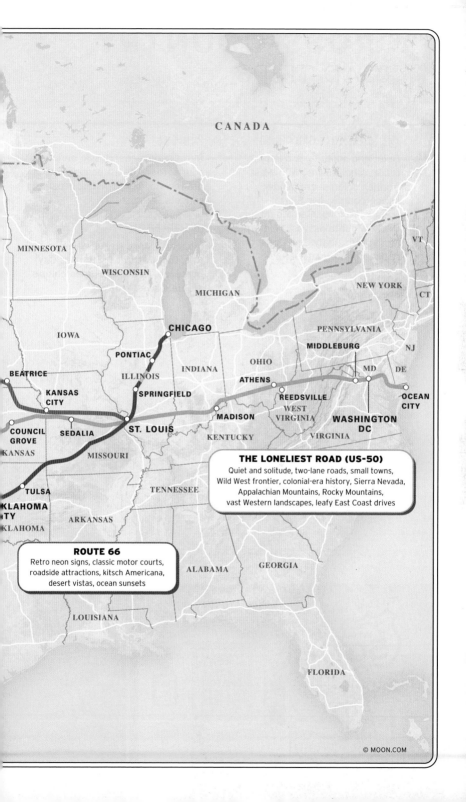

CANADA

MINNESOTA

WISCONSIN

MICHIGAN

IOWA

PONTIAC

CHICAGO

ILLINOIS

INDIANA

OHIO

PENNSYLVANIA

MIDDLEBURG

NEW YORK

VT

CT

NJ

MD

DE

BEATRICE

KANSAS
CITY

SPRINGFIELD

ATHENS

REEDSVILLE

OCEAN
CITY

COUNCIL
GROVE

SEDALIA

ST. LOUIS

MADISON

WEST
VIRGINIA

WASHINGTON
DC

KANSAS

MISSOURI

KENTUCKY

VIRGINIA

THE LONELIEST ROAD (US-50)
Quiet and solitude, two-lane roads, small towns,
Wild West frontier, colonial-era history, Sierra Nevada,
Appalachian Mountains, Rocky Mountains,
vast Western landscapes, leafy East Coast drives

TULSA

TENNESSEE

KLAHOMA
TY

ARKANSAS

KLAHOMA

ROUTE 66
Retro neon signs, classic motor courts,
roadside attractions, kitsch Americana,
desert vistas, ocean sunsets

ALABAMA

GEORGIA

LOUISIANA

FLORIDA

© MOON.COM

CROSS-COUNTRY
ROAD TRIPS

THE LONELIEST ROAD (US-50)
Quiet and solitude, two-lane roads, small towns, Wild West frontier, colonial-era history, beach boardwalks, Sierra Nevada, Appalachian Mountains, Rocky Mountains, vast Western landscapes, leafy East Coast drives, regional eats (PAGE 36)

ROUTE 66
Retro neon signs, classic motor courts, roadside attractions, kitsch Americana, desert vistas, ocean sunsets (PAGE 60)

OREGON TRAIL
Pioneer history, wagon-wheel ruts, Old West towns, Kansas City barbecue, Native American culture, prairie views (PAGE 78)

LEFT TO RIGHT: SIGN ON ROUTE 50; TOWER STATION AND U-DROP INN CAFÉ ON ROUTE 66; CHIMNEY ROCK, NEBRASKA

Best of THE ROAD TRIPS

1 Stare into a canyon formed by the oldest rocks on earth at **Black Canyon of the Gunnison National Park** in Colorado (PAGE 46).

2 Drive the spiny ridges of the remote **Allegheny Mountains** in West Virginia's mining country (PAGE 54).

3 Soak up the history of the Mother Road at the **Illinois Route 66 Hall of Fame & Museum** (PAGE 62).

4 Indulge in roadside kitsch and good eats at **Delgadillo's Snow Cap Drive-In** in Seligman, Arizona (PAGE 75).

Black Canyon of the Gunnison National Park, Colorado

Allegheny Mountains, West Virginia

Illinois Route 66 Hall of Fame & Museum

Delgadillo's Snow Cap Drive-In, Seligman

National Historic Oregon Trail Interpretive Center, Baker City

5 Follow the arduous trek of pioneers at the **National Historic Oregon Trail Interpretive Center** in Baker City, Oregon (PAGE 96).

THE LONELIEST ROAD (US-50)

WHY GO: Quiet and solitude, two-lane roads, small towns, Wild West frontier, colonial-era history, beach boardwalks, Sierra Nevada, Appalachian Mountains, Rocky Mountains, vast Western landscapes, leafy East Coast drives, regional eats

TOTAL DISTANCE: 3,655 miles/ 5,880 kilometers

NUMBER OF DAYS: 21

SEASONS: Spring through fall

START: Sacramento, California

END: Ocean City, Maryland

▶ ROUTE 50, NEVADA

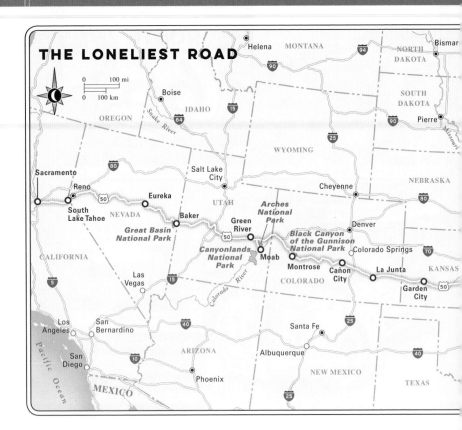

THE LONELIEST ROAD

Route 50 is a road of many names. It has been coined the "Backbone of America" for its path through the country's small towns, populated by hardworking citizens. It is also referred to as the "Loneliest Road" because of the route's breathtaking isolation in Nevada, where motorists encounter not a single gas station, stoplight, or another soul for hundreds of miles. The 3,000-plus-mile, two-lane blacktop runs from Sacramento, California, to the shores of the Atlantic in Ocean City, Maryland. Route 50 is a slow, deep breath of fresh air.

DAY 1: Sacramento, California

MORNING AND AFTERNOON

① In Sacramento, order locally roasted coffee and from-scratch banana-blackberry pancakes at the delightful **Orphan Breakfast House** (3440 C St., 916/442-7370, www.orphan-breakfast.com, 7am-2pm daily, $7-13).

② At the **California State Railroad Museum** (125 I St., 916/323-9280, www.parks.ca.gov, 10am-5pm daily, $12 adults, $6 children 6-17) in Old Sacramento, the history of the gold rush and the golden era of the railroad come alive.

③ Your final destination of Ocean City, Maryland, is thousands of miles away, so you're probably not expecting to see road signage for this oceanside town yet. But! At the junction of I-80 and US-50 just west of downtown, you'll see the famous **Ocean City distance sign** (right side of eastbound I-80, just before US-50). It reads: "Placerville 46, South Lake Tahoe 107, Ocean City, MD 3,037." Because it's a highway sign, it's difficult to get a picture, but it's worth a drive-by glimpse.

EVENING

④ Enjoy a relaxed and locally sourced dinner at **The Waterboy** (2000 Capitol Ave., 916/498-9891, www.waterboy-restaurant.com, 5pm-9pm Sun.-Mon., 5pm-9:30pm Tues.-Thurs., 5pm-10:30pm Fri.-Sat., $10-35).

⑤ Settle in for the night at **Amber House Inn of Midtown** (1315 22nd St., 916/444-8085, www.amberhouse.com, $179-300). It offers 10 classically appointed rooms.

DAY 2: Sacramento to South Lake Tahoe, California

120 miles/193 kilometers | 3 hours

ROUTE OVERVIEW: US-50

① Get up early and hit the road for **Placerville,** a former gold rush town at the foothills of the Sierra Nevada. Learn about Placerville's gold mining history and watch blacksmiths at work at **Gold Bug Park and Mine** (2635 Gold Bug Ln., 530/642-5207, www.goldbugpark.org, 10am-4pm daily summer, 10am-4pm Sat.-Sun. fall-spring, $9 adults, $5 children 6-17),

CALIFORNIA STATE RAILROAD MUSEUM

Top 5 THE LONELIEST ROAD

1. See the gravity-defying natural sandstone arches at **Arches National Park** in Utah (PAGE 44).

2. Stare into a canyon formed by the oldest rocks on earth at **Black Canyon of the Gunnison National Park** in Colorado (PAGE 46).

3. Walk in the footsteps of pioneers at the well-preserved frontier town of **Council Grove,** Kansas (PAGE 49).

4. Drive the spiny ridges of the remote **Allegheny Mountains** in West Virginia's mining country (PAGE 54).

5. Tour the renowned **Smithsonian museums** in Washington DC (PAGE 56).

the only municipally owned gold mine in the country.

> *Go east on US-50 to Placerville (41 mi/66 km).*

❷ As you continue into the Sierra Nevada, take a break to stretch your legs on a hike to **Horsetail Falls** on the **Pyramid Creek Trail** (3.1 mi/5 km roundtrip, 1.5 hours, moderate). Dropping 500 feet, the falls cut through the rocky escarpment of the mountain. The trail can be tough to spot on the way up, so bring a map. There's a $5 parking fee at the trailhead.

> *To get to Horsetail Falls, take US-50 east for 41 miles (66 km) to the parking lot on the north side of the road.*

❸ Soon you'll arrive at the sparkling, deep-blue oasis of **Lake Tahoe,** the second-deepest lake in the country. When you arrive in **South Lake Tahoe,** get your lake photos at the pristine **Lakeside Beach** (4081 Lakeshore Blvd., 530/542-2314, http://lakesideparkassociation.org, sunrise-sunset daily, $10 adults, $5 children under 18).

> *Continue east on US-50 to South Lake Tahoe (16 mi/26 km).*

❹ Your lodging for the night is the **Coachman Hotel** (4100 Pine Blvd., 530/545-6460, http://coachmantahoe.com, $260-370), an inviting boutique hotel within steps of the lake and downtown South Lake Tahoe.

❺ For pizza and local brews, walk to **Base Camp Pizza Co.** (1001 Heavenly Village Way, 530/544-2273, http://basecamppizzaco.com, 11am-9pm Sun.-Thurs., 11am-10pm Fri.-Sat., $9-27). Return to The Coachman for complimentary s'mores by the fire pit.

DAY 3: South Lake Tahoe to Eureka, Nevada

275 miles/440 kilometers | 5-6 hours

ROUTE OVERVIEW: US-50 • NV-341 • NV-79 • US-50

❶ Wake up early and hit the road for **Carson City.** A worthy stop is the **Nevada State Museum** (600 N. Carson St., 775/687-4810, www.carsonnvmuseum.org, 8:30am-4:30pm Tues.-Sun., $8). The museum showcases exhibits on mining, Nevada history, geology and geography of the area, and Native American culture.

> *Follow US-50 E for 28 miles (45 km) to Carson City.*

❷ Before you leave, snap a selfie in front of the nearby **Carson City Nugget** (507 N. Carson St., 775/882-1626, http://ccnugget.com, 24 hours daily), a 1950s-era casino that's still going strong.

❸ Continue on to **Virginia City,** a former mining boomtown that's now a tourist hot spot, perched on the side of a mountain. Ride the rails of the **Virginia & Truckee Railroad** (165 F St., 775/847-0380, www.virginiatruckee.com, 10:30am-4pm daily late May-late Oct., $12-14 adults, $6-7 children

LAKESIDE BEACH, LAKE TAHOE

VIRGINIA CITY, NEVADA

5-10) past mines, over bridges, and through tunnels.

> Drive 5 miles (8 km) to NV-341. Turn left and take NV-341 to Virginia City (7 mi/11 km).

④ Enjoy a self-guided tour along the half-mile loop at **Hickison Petroglyph Recreation Area** (US-50, 775/635-4062, www.blm.gov, 24 hours daily, free), where ancient petroglyphs are etched into the rocks of the Hickison Summit. The easy trail winds through sagebrush and junipers and leads to a breathtaking view of the Great Basin and the 7,000-foot mountain ranges that surround it.

> From Virginia City, take NV-79 for 6 miles (10 km), then continue onto Six Mile Canyon Rd. In 2 miles (3 km), turn left on US-50 and stay on it to Fallon (44 mi/71 km). Drive east on US-50 to Hickison Petroglyph Recreation Area (135 mi/217 km).

⑤ The mines in **Eureka** are operational, which means this little Great Basin town is still a thriving community. Centuries-old buildings line Main Street and house restaurants, city offices, and even a restored opera house from 1880. Bed down for the night at the historic **Eureka Gold Country Inn** (251 N. Main St., 775/237-5247, www.eurekagoldcountryinn.com, $108-113).

> Follow US-50 E for 45 miles (72 km) to Eureka.

DAY 4: Eureka to Baker, Nevada

150 miles/240 kilometers | 3 hours

ROUTE OVERVIEW: US-50 • NV-487 • NV-488

① Before leaving town, grab a hot coffee and tasty breakfast burrito from the **Pony Express Deli** (101 Bullion St., 775/237-7665, 6am-2pm Mon.-Sat., $5-9).

② US-50 stretches long and desolate between Eureka and Ely; now you'll understand why it's nicknamed "the Loneliest Road." Once in **Ely**, another former mining town, make a quick-but-interesting stop at the **Nevada Northern Railway Museum** (1100

LEHMAN CAVES, GREAT BASIN NATIONAL PARK

Ave. A, 775/289-2085, www.nevadanorthernrailway.net, 8am-5pm daily, $33 adults, $15 children 4-12).

> It's 78 miles (126 km) from Eureka to Ely going east on US-50.

③ Continue on to **Great Basin National Park** (www.nps.gov/grba, free), an hour east of Ely. Don't miss a guided tour of the **Lehman Caves** (5500 W. NV-488, 775/234-7331, ext. 242, visitors center 8am-5pm daily summer, shorter hours fall-spring, $9-11 adults, $5-6 children 5-15), where you'll see fascinating stalagmite and stalactite formations. Tours depart every two hours in summer; there are less frequent departures the rest of the year. Near the visitors center is a short, easy path to an orchard of 100-year-old apricot trees, which ripen in mid-August.

> Continue east on US-50 for 57 miles (92 km) to NV-487. Turn right on NV-487, which leads to the town of Baker. In 5 miles (8 km), turn right on NV-488. Follow NV-488 W to the Lehman Caves Visitor Center (5 mi/8 km).

④ Next, head back into **Baker** to check out the **Great Basin Visitor Center** (57 N. NV-487, 775/234-7331, www.nps.gov/grba, 11am-5pm daily Apr.-Oct.), which offers orientation exhibits and videos.

> Take NV-488 east into Baker (5 mi/8 km).

⑤ Check into the **Stargazer Inn** (115 Baker Ave., 775/234-7323, www.stargazernevada.com, $72-98), where you can dine at the on-site restaurant, **Kerouac's** (7am-10am and 5pm-10pm Wed.-Mon. mid-Apr.-mid-Nov., $15-30).

EAT LIKE A *Local*

As the landscape changes with every mile you drive, so too does the regional food. Break out of your culinary comfort zone and try the local fare of each new place you visit. When in Rome, right?

CALIFORNIA

Cioppino: An iconic Italian fish stew popularized in San Francisco, cioppino is made with mussels, crab, clams, and whitefish in a base of tomato and wine sauce.

NEVADA

Steak: The best version is a juicy, bone-in rib eye served with a classic baked potato at an old-school cowboy steak house.

UTAH

Navajo tacos: Fry bread—dough that's been deep fried—serves as the base for beef, cheese, shredded lettuce, ranchero sauce, and pinto beans.

COLORADO

Chile relleno burrito: This tasty dish features a breaded and fried chile stuffed into a tortilla with beans and rice, then smothered in green chile sauce.

KANSAS

Barbecue hot wings: It doesn't get better than this: jumbo wings covered in a spice rub, marinated in hot sauce, and smoked to perfection.

MISSOURI

St. Louis-style pizza: The cracker-thin crust is layered with provel (a blend of provolone, swiss, and white cheddar) and sweet red sauce.

ILLINOIS

The Horseshoe: This open-faced sandwich is made with thick-cut bread topped with a slice of horseshoe-shaped ham, French fries, and a sharp white cheddar sauce.

INDIANA

Pork sandwich: For this dish, pork tenderloin is pounded, breaded, deep fried, and served on a small, soft bun—a chewy complement to the crispy pork.

OHIO

Cincinnati chili: For this regional take on chili, a thin, mildly spiced meat sauce is poured over hot dogs or spaghetti and capped with shredded cheddar.

WEST VIRGINIA

Pepperoni rolls: Hunks of pepperoni are stuffed into a warm, fluffy roll, often with cheese. Italian immigrants invented these hand-held treats as a nonperishable snack to take underground in the mines.

VIRGINIA

Oysters: As the "Oyster Capital of the East Coast," Virginia's oyster industry dates to the 1600s. Eight regions harvest oysters, with flavors that range from salty to creamy to sweet.

MARYLAND

Blue crab: You'll find this succulent, tender crab everywhere in Maryland. Try it in a crab cake or, if you don't mind a little work, crack it out of the shell yourself.

CIOPPINO, AN ICONIC SAN FRANCISCO DISH

DAY 5: Baker to Green River, Utah

315 miles/510 kilometers | 6 hours

ROUTE OVERVIEW: US-50/US-6 • US-6 • US-6/US-191 • I-70

❶ Pop by the adorable **Baker's Bean** (40 S. Baker Ave., 719/237-5725, http://saltandsucre.com, 7am-3pm daily, $5) for espresso drinks and egg-and-cheese paninis. Fill up, because you've got a long drive ahead this morning.

❷ As you drive over **Soldier Summit,** which peaks at nearly 8,000 feet, you'll pass stands of cottonwood and pine trees, steep sandstone canyons, and the hulking mountains of the Wasatch Range. When you reach the railroad town of **Helper,** visit the **Western Mining & Railroad Museum** (294 S. Main St., 435/472-3009, 10am-5pm Mon.-Sat. summer, 11am-4pm Tues.-Sat. fall-spring, free) to learn how the "helper" engines pushed the trains over Solider Summit—the very one you just traversed. The museum offers displays on railroading, coal mining, and real-life stories of the people who worked in the mines from 1880 to 1950.

> Drive east on US-50/US-6 for 92 miles (148 km), then turn left onto US-6. Stay on US-6 for 143 miles (230 km) to Helper.

❸ Grab a quick bite to eat in **Price,** the largest city in eastern Utah, then continue to **Green River.** Here, take in the

KEY RESERVATIONS

- For tours of the **Lehman Caves** at **Great Basin National Park,** reservations are strongly recommended. Make them **two weeks** in advance.

- Book a room at the **Magnolia Hotel** in St. Louis, Missouri, a **month** early. Its location next to the Gateway Arch makes it a popular choice for lodging.

- At **Gateway Arch National Park** in St. Louis, go online to buy tickets for the tram ride to the top of the Arch **a few days** ahead of your arrival.

- Reserve tickets to visit **Blennerhassett Island Historical State Park** in Parkersburg, West Virginia, a **few days** in advance. Access to the park is by boat only.

- **Modern Homestead** in Reedsville, West Virginia, offers the only accommodations for miles around in a very remote part of West Virginia. Reserve one of their five rooms a **month** ahead of your arrival.

- **The Red Fox Inn and Tavern** in Middleburg, Virginia, gets booked up quickly on the weekends. Reserve a room **3-4 weeks** in advance.

collection at the **John Wesley Powell River History Museum** (1765 E. Main St., 435/564-3427, http://johnwesleypowell.com, 9am-7pm Mon.-Sat., noon-5pm Sun. summer, 9am-5pm Tues.-Sat. fall-spring, $6). The repository of artifacts tells the tale of explorer Powell and his team, as well as other explorers whose daring adventures helped shape the West.

> Continue on US-6/US-191 to Price (8 mi/13 km).

❹ Stay at the hip riverfront hotel **Skyfall Guestrooms** (1710 E. Main St., 435/564-8109, www.skyfallguestrooms.com, from $250). The themed rooms are bright and stylish, plus the

STATUE OF A COAL MINER IN HELPER, UTAH

SACRAMENTO, CALIFORNIA, TO PUEBLO, COLORADO

9 days; 1,162 miles/1,870 kilometers

From Sacramento, take **nine days** to follow Route 50 through California's gold country, over the Sierra Nevada to **Lake Tahoe,** across the desolate stretch of Nevada to **Arches and Canyonlands** in Utah, and into the outdoors wonderland of Colorado's Rocky Mountains.

Pueblo sits in the eastern foothills of the Rockies and is a short drive south of Denver. You can return home by flying out of the Denver airport. For more details, see Days 1–9.

KANSAS CITY, MISSOURI, TO MOAB, UTAH

7 days; 1,019 miles/1,640 kilometers

Fly into **Kansas City,** and then launch west on Route 50. This trip requires only **seven days** to see the frontier towns of Kansas, the **Tallgrass Prairie Preserve,** the Rocky Mountains of Colorado, and **Arches and Canyonlands National Parks** just outside of Moab.

You can fly home out of Salt Lake City, a four-hour drive north of Moab. For more details, see Days 6–12, but note that you'll need to reverse the direction of travel.

CINCINNATI, OHIO, TO OCEAN CITY, MARYLAND

6 days; 643 miles/1,035 kilometers

Fly into Cincinnati, then hit the road heading east. This trip offers **six days** to drive through West Virginia's mining country, the beautiful and remote **Allegheny Mountains,** through the colonial villages of Virginia, and then on to **Washington DC** and **Annapolis, Maryland,** to conclude with the bayside trek along Maryland's Eastern Shore to the beach community of **Ocean City.**

See Days 16–21 for more details; note that you can skip the full day in Washington DC to make this a five-day trip.

hotel offers complimentary breakfast at the on-site **Tamarisk Restaurant** (www.tamariskrestaurant.com, 7am-8:30pm daily, $9-14).

> Continue on US-6/US-191 to I-70 (60 mi/97 km). Merge onto I-70 E and follow it for 3 miles (5 km) to Green River.

⑤ Opt for beers and burgers at the low-key **Ray's Tavern** (25 S. Broadway, 435/564-3511, 11am-9:30pm daily, $8-12).

DAY 6: Green River to Moab, Utah

140 miles/225 kilometers | 3-4 hours

ROUTE OVERVIEW: I-70 • US-191 • UT-313 • US-191

① After filling up at the hotel's complimentary breakfast, head to **Moab,** the gateway to Arches and Canyonlands. Check in to **The Gonzo Inn** (100 W. 200 S., 435/259-2515 or 800/791-4044, www.gonzoinn.com, $199-249), a colorful boutique hotel.

> Take I-70 E to US-191 (17 mi/27 km). Turn right on US-191 and drive 32 miles (51 km) to Moab.

② After you drop off your bags, make your way to **Arches National Park** (435/719-2299, www.nps.gov/arch, $30 per vehicle, $25 per motorcycle, $15 bicyclists and pedestrians), which is just 5 miles (8 km) away.

> Get back on US-191 and drive north for 5 miles (8 km) to the park entrance.

ARCHES NATIONAL PARK

❸ Drive to **The Windows Section** (2.5 mi/4 km past Balanced Rock) and walk along the short paths that lead to four arches. Crowds can be heavy, as this is the park's most popular attraction. But the views and the photo ops are worth it.

❹ From Arches, it's a 40-minute drive to **Canyonlands National Park** (435/719-2313, www.nps.gov/cany, $30 per vehicle, $25 per motorcycle, $15 bicyclists and pedestrians). See how water, gravity, and time have shaped the mesas, buttes, spires, and canyons of this primitive wilderness area.

> Take US-191 N to UT-313 (7 mi/11 km). Turn left and follow UT-313 west to Grand View Point Road/Island in the Sky Rd. (15 mi/24 km). Continue for another 5 miles (8 km) to Canyonlands National Park.

❺ At the end of the main road in the park, in the Island in the Sky District, visit **Grand View Point** (12 mi/19 km south of the visitors center). Monument Basin lies below in the distance, and in between, you can see the Colorado River, The Needles, canyons, and mountains. Hike the short **Grand View Trail** (1 mi/1.6 km, 1 hour, easy) along slickrock cliffs, which captures the essence of the Island in the Sky. Return to **Moab** and enjoy dinner in town.

> Follow UT-313 back to US-191, turn right and drive south on US-191 back to Moab (30 mi/48 km).

DAY 7: Moab to Montrose, Colorado

290 miles/470 kilometers | 6 hours

ROUTE OVERVIEW: US-191 • I-70 • US-50 • Million Dollar Hwy./US-550

❶ Rise and shine early. You have a lot of ground to cover. Take in breakfast at the buzzy **Moab Diner** (189 S. Main St., 435/259-4006, www.moabdiner.com, 6am-9pm Mon.-Tues., 6am-10pm Wed.-Thurs., 6am-11pm Fri.-Sat., $7-10), then drive east to Colorado.

❷ Cruise through the rivers, red-rock canyons, and dinosaur fossils of Grand Junction and Delta on your way to **Montrose**. This farming town encircled by the San Juan Mountains and Black Canyon is your home base for the night. Check into one of the clean and tidy chain hotels along US-50.

> Go north from Moab on US-191 to I-70 (32 mi/52 km). Merge onto I-70 and drive east for 75 miles (121 km), then join US-50 E. Stay on US-50 to Montrose (65 mi/105 km).

❸ Now it's time to embark on one of the best drives in the United States: the **Million Dollar Highway.** So named for the million-dollar fortunes earned and lost in this Wild West mining country, this two-lane road zigzags along hairpin curves through the jagged peaks of the San Juan Mountains, past historic small towns, and through beautiful, steep, stark countryside.

> From Montrose, go south on the Million Dollar Hwy./US-550 for 59 miles (95 km) to Silverton.

❹ Once you reach **Silverton**, grab an early dinner at the Old West-themed **Handlebars Food & Saloon** (1323 Greene St., 970/387-5395, http://handlebarssilverton.com, 10:30am-8pm daily, $12-29), then make the drive back to your hotel in **Montrose.**

> Return to Montrose via US-550 (59 mi/95 km).

MILLION DOLLAR HIGHWAY

DAY 8: Montrose to Cañon City, Colorado

200 miles/320 kilometers | 4-5 hours

ROUTE OVERVIEW: US-50 • CO-347 • US-50

1 First on today's agenda: **Black Canyon of the Gunnison National Park** (9800 CO-347, 970/641-2337, ext. 205, www.nps.gov/blca, 24 hours daily, $25 per vehicle, $20 per motorcycle, $15 bicyclists and pedestrians), where two million years of erosion formed the hardest and oldest rocks on earth. The 2,000-foot-deep gorge is so steep and the bottom so rugged that no humans are allowed inside it. Instead, see the magnificent sight from the rim's edge.

> *Leave Montrose by driving east for 8 miles (13 km) on US-50. At CO-347, turn left and follow it to Black Canyon of the Gunnison National Park (5 mi/8 km).*

2 Stop in **Salida,** a former railroad town, for lunch at **Boathouse Cantina** (228 N. F St., 719/539-5004, www.boathousesalida.com, 11am-8pm Sun.-Thurs., 11am-9pm Fri.-Sat., $8-30). This Mexican restaurant sits right on the Arkansas River in Salida's historic downtown.

> *Return to US-50 via CO-347 (5 mi/ 8 km). Turn left on US-50 and go 121 miles (195 km) to Salida.*

3 Follow up lunch with a dip at the **Salida Hot Springs Aquatic Center** (410 W. Rainbow Blvd./US-50, 719/539-6738, 6am-8pm Mon.-Thurs., 6am-9pm Fri.-Sat., noon-6pm Sun., $11), the largest hot springs in the state.

4 Arrive in mile-high **Cañon City,** where 14,000-foot Rocky Mountain peaks enclose the town. Even though it's known for its 12 prisons, including a maximum-security penitentiary, it's a perfectly safe and lovely spot to spend the night. Try the Victorian, gingerbread-style **Jewel of the Canyons Bed & Breakfast** (429 Greenwood Ave., 719/275-0378, www.jewelofthecanyons.com, $149).

> *From Salida, it's 58 miles (93 km) east on US-50 to Cañon City.*

5 Plenty of worthy restaurants are within walking distance of the B&B. **Pizza Madness** (509 Main St., 719/276-3088, http://www.mypizzamadness.com, 11am-9pm Sun.-Thurs., 11am-9:30pm Fri.-Sat., $10-20) pairs creative pizza pies with funky local art.

DAY 9: Cañon City to La Junta, Colorado

130 miles/209 kilometers | 3 hours

ROUTE OVERVIEW: US-50 • I-25 • US-50

1 Set out for **Royal Gorge Bridge & Park** (4218 County Rd. 3A, 888/333-5597, http://royalgorgebridge.com, 10am-7pm daily summer, shorter hours fall-spring, $25 adults, $20 children 6-12). The red-granite Royal Gorge is a six-mile canyon that drops 1,000 feet down to the Arkansas River. This spot, which is like an amusement park for the outdoorsy type, invites visitors to experience the gorge in myriad ways. Take an aerial tram, an incline railroad, or a gondola, or walk across a vertigo-inducing suspension bridge—all thrilling options for gazing down into the canyon.

> *Backtrack west on US-50 for 9 miles (14 km) to County Rd. 3A. Turn left and follow this to Royal Gorge Bridge & Park (4 mi/6 km).*

BLACK CANYON OF THE GUNNISON NATIONAL PARK

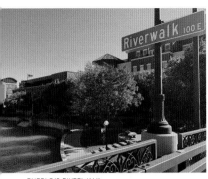

PUEBLO'S RIVERWALK

2 See the Arkansas River in tamer fashion along the **Riverwalk** (entrance at Union Ave. and Grand Ave., 719/595-1589, www.puebloriverwalk.org, 24 hours daily, free), a one-mile promenade in **Pueblo**. The town was founded by a fur trapper in 1842, and grew exponentially in the 1870s after the railroad came through. Today, Pueblo is artsy and pretty, with bookstores, galleries, cafés, and funky boutiques.

> Return to US-50 (4 mi/6 km), turn right, and drive east to I-25 (44 mi/71 km). Merge south on I-25 to Pueblo (4 mi/6 km).

3 Next stop is **La Junta**. Visit the **Koshare Museum** (115 W. 18th St., 719/384-4411, http://koshares.com, noon-5pm daily June-Aug., noon-5pm Wed.-Sat. Sept.-May, $5), founded in 1949 by the Boy Scout Indian Club. Today it features art and artifacts of Pueblo and Plains tribal members.

> From Pueblo, take Northern Ave. east to US-50 (1 mi/1.6 km), then follow US-50 E to La Junta (61 mi/98 km).

4 Have dinner at **El Azteca Mexican Restaurant** (710 W. 3rd St., 719/384-4215, 5pm-8pm Tues.-Sat., $5-10). The green chile soup with pinto beans is a standout.

5 Stay at the clean and simple **Midtown Motel** (215 E. 3rd St., 719/384-7741, $50-75).

DAY 10: La Junta to Garden City, Kansas

260 miles/420 kilometers | 5 hours

ROUTE OVERVIEW: CO-194 • US-50 • US-287 • CO-96 • US-287 • US-50

1 As you leave La Junta, make a detour to **Bent's Old Fort National Historic Site** (35110 CO-194, 719/383-5010, www.nps.gov/beol, 9am-4pm daily, $3). Built by fur traders in the 1840s, this adobe trading post was considered an important outpost of the West, as it was a peaceful stopover place for trappers, explorers, Native Americans, and other travelers. Step back to the early days of the frontier at this living history museum; rangers dress in period clothing and reenact activities from that time.

> Drive east on CO-194 to Bent's Old Fort (7 mi/11 km).

BENT'S OLD FORT NATIONAL HISTORIC SITE IN LA JUNTA, COLORADO

❷ Descend across the Rocky Mountain foothills into **Lamar**. Make sure to stop at the town's **visitors center** (109 E. Beech St., 719/336-3483, www.colorado.com, 8am-6pm daily), housed in a historic train depot. You'll get great info from the helpful staff and free coffee, plus you'll see the 20-foot-tall **Madonna of the Trail memorial**. During the 1920s, the Daughters of the American Revolution headed up the installation of 12 of these statues along Route 66.

> *Leave the fort by heading east on CO-194 to US-50 (14 mi/23 km). Continue onto US-50 for 35 miles (56 km) to Lamar.*

❸ Take a moment to learn about and reflect on the horrific events that took place in 1864 at **Sand Creek Massacre National Historic Site** (55411 County Rd. W, 719/729-3003, 9am-4pm daily Apr.-Sept., 9am-4pm Mon.-Fri. Oct.-Mar., free). It was here that volunteer U.S. soldiers fired on a camp of Cheyenne and Arapahoe people, killing more than 100 unarmed women and children.

> *Take US-50/US-287/Main St. north out of town and continue for 8 miles (13 km). Merge onto US-287 N and continue for 25 miles (40 km). Turn right onto CO-96 and follow this for 12 miles (19 km). Turn left onto County Rd. 54 and head north for 7 miles (11 km). Turn right onto County Rd. W to reach Sand Creek.*

❹ It's time to head east once again. After you cross into Kansas, you'll pass through **Holcomb**, site of the murders documented by Truman Capote in his book *In Cold Blood*. Continue east to **Garden City**. Here, swing by the pleasant **Lee Richardson Zoo** (312 E. Finnup Dr., 620/276-1250, www.leerichardsonzoo.org, 8am-7pm daily Apr.-Labor Day, 8am-5pm daily Labor Day-Mar., $10 per vehicle, free for pedestrians). The zoo is home to 100 species of animals, including rhinos, lions, pythons, birds, and more.

> *Retrace your path back to Lamar via CO-96 and US-287 (53 mi/85 km). Head east on US-50 for 99 miles (159 km) to reach Holcomb. It's another 6 miles (10 km) east on US-50 to reach Garden City.*

❺ Check into your room at Garden City's **Sunnyland B&B** (501 N. 5th St., 620/276-0500, www.sunnylandbandb.com, $89-135), a 1909 Queen Anne house with private bathrooms and Wi-Fi, and then enjoy the leisurely stroll to dinner at **Pho Hoa One Restaurant** (713 E. Fulton St., 620/276-3393, 10am-2pm and 4:30pm-8pm Mon.-Sat., 10am-3pm Sun., $7-10). The place isn't much to look at, but the pho is amazing.

DAY 11: Garden City to Council Grove, Kansas

280 miles/450 kilometers | 5-6 hours

ROUTE OVERVIEW: US-50 • K-177

❶ After an early breakfast, head east to **Dodge City**. This frontier town was once home to notorious gunfights, cattle drives, and Wyatt Earp. Known as "Hell on the Plains" during its 1800s heyday, Dodge City is now a law-abiding place. You can't see the original Boot Hill Cemetery, but you can spend a fun hour or two at **Boot Hill Museum** (500 W. Wyatt Earp Blvd., 620/227-8188, www.boothill.org, 8am-8pm daily Memorial Day-Labor Day, 9am-5pm Mon.-Sat., 1pm-5pm Sun. Labor Day-Memorial Day, $12). It's a re-created Old West town with interactive displays, artifacts, live shows, staged gunfights, building replicas, and a nice souvenir shop.

DODGE CITY, KANSAS

TALLGRASS PRAIRIE NATIONAL PRESERVE

> It's 50 miles (81 km) east to Dodge City on US-50.

❷ This part of the drive is flat, empty, and lonely. Maybe that explains the disproportionate level of excitement you'll feel when you get to **Kinsley**, aka Midway USA. Kinsley sits equidistant (1,561 miles, to be exact) from New York City and San Francisco. You're smack-dab in the middle of the country! A big sign—perfect for a photo—indicates this fact on the grounds of the **Edwards County Historical Society Museum** (US-50/US-56, 620/659-2420, www.edwardscountymuseum.com, 9am-5pm Mon.-Sat., 1pm-5pm Sun. May-Oct., free).

> Continue for another 36 miles (58 km) east on US-50 to Kinsley.

❸ Tallgrass once covered large swaths of North America, but now only a small fraction remains. See this delicate ecosystem in the Kansas Flint Hills at the **Tallgrass Prairie National Preserve** (2480B K-177, 620/273-8494, www.nps.gov/tapr, trails 24 hours daily, visitors center 8:30am-4:30pm daily, free). Here, you can engage in interactive exhibits, tour historic buildings, and walk among the remaining tallgrass prairieland on dedicated trails. Keep your eye out for bison, who wander throughout the park's 11,000 acres.

> Continue east on US-50 to K-177 (170 mi/274 km). Go north on K-177 to Tallgrass Prairie National Preserve (2 mi/3 km).

❹ As you enter **Council Grove**, you'll feel as though you're driving back in time. This frontier stop is where travelers made final repairs on their covered wagons before continuing west on the Santa Fe Trail. Download a map of the self-guided historical tour from the town's website (www.councilgrove.com), or pick up a hard copy from one of the businesses along Main Street. For dinner, head to the **Hays House** (112 W. Main St., 620/767-5911, www.hayshouse.com, 11am-8pm Tues.-Thurs., 11am-9pm Fri.-Sat., 11am-7pm Sun., $10-32), the oldest restaurant west of the Mississippi.

> Leave the preserve by turning left onto K-177. Drive 17 miles (27 km) north to Council Grove.

DAY 12: Council Grove to Sedalia, Missouri

220 miles/350 kilometers | 4-5 hours

ROUTE OVERVIEW: US-56 • I-35 • I-435 • MO-78 • MO-291 • US-50

❶ Start your drive through the rocky and beautiful Flint Hills, named for the flint that's eroded from the bedrock near the earth's surface. Soon you'll come to the friendly town of **Baldwin City**, where trees line the brick-paved streets. Stop for lunch at the always-busy **Homestead Kitchen & Bakery** (719 8th St., 785/766-3442, http://www.homestead.cafe, 6am-6pm Mon.-Thurs., 6am-8pm Fri.-Sat., 10am-3pm Sun., $5-12).

> Head east on US-56 to Baldwin City (80 mi/129 km).

❷ After you cross into Missouri, head to **Independence,** the official start of the Oregon Trail. Visit the **National Frontier Trails Museum** (318 W. Pacific Ave., 816/325-7575, www.ci.independence.mo.us, 9am-4:30pm Mon.-Sat., 12:30pm-4:30pm Sun., $6), which commemorates the westward expansion trails that began in Independence: the Santa Fe, Oregon, and California Trails.

> Drive 12 miles (19 km) east on US-56 to I-35. Merge north onto I-35 and in 17 miles (27 km) go east and north on I-435 to MO-78 (22 mi/35 km). Turn right on MO-78 and drive 5 miles (8 km) to Independence.

Playlist

THE LONELIEST ROAD

SONGS

- **"Crazy" by Patsy Cline:** Legendary country singer Cline was born in Winchester, Virginia, a town on US-50. Sadly, she passed away in a plane crash in Tennessee in 1963 when she was only 30 years old. Celebrate her life and talent by listening to this song when you drive through Winchester.

PODCASTS

- *NoSleep:* Not for the faint of heart, this scary-story podcast suits the desolate stretches of US-50 through Nevada and West Virginia. A perfect mix of spooky tales as told by voice actors, this podcast features themes that range from paranormal encounters to monsters under the bed.

- *Wait Wait... Don't Tell Me!* You'll need entertainment—and news—throughout this three-week journey. Enter National Public Radio. They host this weekly current events and trivia quiz podcast. The humorous format tests your news knowledge while also giving you a chance to decide what's factual and what's been made up.

SEDALIA

❸ Continue to **Sedalia,** home of ragtime musician Scott Joplin and a happening stop on the Katy Trail (a popular cycling route through Missouri). The whole town evokes a distinctly 1920s feel, especially your accommodations for the night, **Hotel Bothwell** (103 E. 4th St., 660/826-5588, www.hotelbothwell.com, from $115). Harry S. Truman, Bette Davis, and Clint Eastwood have all been guests.

> *Turn left on MO-78 and follow it to MO-291 (2 mi/3 km). Turn right on MO-291. Drive 13 miles (21 km) to US-50. Turn left and stay on US-50 into Sedalia (65 mi/105 km).*

DAY 13: Sedalia to St. Louis, Missouri

190 miles/300 kilometers | 3-4 hours

ROUTE OVERVIEW: US-50

❶ In the morning, check out the modern art scene in Sedalia. Specifically, make time to tour the **Daum Museum of Contemporary Art** (3201 W. 16th St., 660/530-5888, www.daummuseum.org, 11am-5pm Tues.-Fri., 1pm-5pm Sat.-Sun., free). The museum's permanent collection features 1,500 works by prominent artists from the last 50 years.

❷ Drive east to Missouri's state capital of **Jefferson City,** a peaceful little place on the banks of the Missouri River. Take a 45-minute guided tour of the **state capitol** (201 W. Capitol Ave., 573/751-2854, http://mostateparks.com, 8am-5pm daily, free), which was

JEFFERSON CITY

❷ Next, walk over to **Gateway Arch National Park** (11 N. 4th St., 314/655-1600, www.gatewayarch.com, 8am-10pm daily summer, 9am-6pm daily fall-spring, free). Made of steel and concrete, the arch rises 630 feet, and is the tallest constructed monument in the country. The on-site museum shares the history of westward expansion. The **tram ride** ($16) to the top offers a bird's-eye view of the city.

AFTERNOON

❸ Get your fix of St. Louis barbecue with lunch at the nearby **Sugarfire Smoke House** (605 Washington Ave., 314/394-1720, http://sugarfiresmokehouse.com, 11am-9pm daily, $13).

❹ Spend the afternoon at **Forest Park** (5595 Grand Dr., 314/367-7275, 24 hours daily, free), one of the largest urban parks in the United States, and one of the loveliest. Some 500 acres larger than New York's Central Park, Forest Park offers much to pass the time. Stroll the trails that ramble past ponds and under leafy trees or pop into one of park's cultural centers: St. Louis Art Museum, St. Louis Science Center, St. Louis Zoo, The Muny, or the Missouri History Museum.

EVENING

❺ Toast the day's adventure with an artisan cocktail and dinner at **Robie's Restaurant Lounge** (421 N. 8th St., 314/436-9000, www.magnoliahotels.com, 6:30am-1am daily, $10-34), which is conveniently located at the Magnolia. Save room for gooey butter cake, a regional dessert.

built in 1917 and acts as the centerpiece of the city.

> *Follow US-50 E to Jefferson City (60 mi/97 km).*

❸ Stop into **Central Dairy** (610 Madison St., 573/635-6148, http://centraldairy.biz, 8am-6pm Mon.-Sat., 10am-6pm Sun., $2.50-4) for a treat. Options include hand-churned ice cream, sodas, malts, shakes, and sundaes.

❹ In **St. Louis,** check into the elegant **Magnolia Hotel** (421 N. 8th St., 314/436-9000, www.magnoliahotels.com, $151-312), a regal 18-story landmark where Cary Grant once stayed. You'll have your pick of restaurants for dinner within steps of the hotel.

> *Continue east on US-50 to St. Louis (126 mi/203 km).*

DAY 14: St. Louis, Missouri

MORNING

❶ Start the day off right—with the award-winning Bloody Marys and crepes at **Rooster** (1104 Locust St., 314/241-8118, www.roosterstl.com, 8am-3pm daily, $8-11). Keep it regional with a savory crepe stuffed with spiced apples, cheddar, and Missouri sausage.

ST. LOUIS ART MUSEUM IN FOREST PARK

DAY 15: St. Louis to Madison, Indiana

285 miles/460 kilometers | 6 hours

ROUTE OVERVIEW: I-64 • US-50 • IN-60 • IN-56

❶ Today includes a lot of driving, so start early. As you leave St. Louis and cross into Illinois, US-50 takes you past miles of cornfields. There's not much to see until you get to **Salem,** birthplace of politician William Jennings Bryan. See pictures, newspaper clippings, furniture, and other artifacts from his early life at the **William Jennings Bryan Boyhood Home** (408 S. Broadway Ave., 618/547-2222, by appointment, free).

> *Take I-64 E to US-50 (21 mi/34 km), then continue on US-50 to Salem (54 mi/87 km).*

❷ Have lunch in Salem at **Mamma Antonia's** (114 W. Main St., 618/548-6130, 11am-9pm Tues.-Sun., $10-20). This trattoria serves up traditional Italian favorites like spaghetti Bolognese and cannelloni.

❸ Continue east to **Olney,** home to grand mansions and albino squirrels. To see the snow-white critters frolic, visit **City Park** (502 White Squirrel Cir., 618/395-7302, www.ci.olney.il.us, 6am-11pm daily, free). This is a good opportunity to stretch your legs with a walk around the green lawns.

> *Follow US-50 E for 48 miles (77 km) to County Rd. 1150. Turn left and drive 1 mile (2 km) to Olney.*

ALBINO SQUIRREL IN OLNEY'S CITY PARK

❹ Cross the Wabash River into Indiana and follow the pastoral countryside along the Ohio River to **Madison.** Eat a burger at **Hinkle's Sandwich Shop** (204 W. Main St., 812/265-3919, www.hinkleburger.com, 6am-10pm Mon.-Thurs., 6am-1am Fri.-Sat., $2-6), a 1930s diner with 1930s prices.

> *Drive east on US-50 for 85 miles (137 km). Continue onto IN-60 for 31 miles (50 km). Turn left onto IN-56. Drive east on IN-56 for 44 miles (71 km) to Madison.*

❺ Spend the night at the **Riverboat Inn & Suites** (906 E. 1st St., 812/265-2361, www.riverboatinnandsuites.com, $70-295), a quaint hotel boasting river views galore.

DAY 16: Madison to Athens, Ohio

260 miles/420 kilometers | 5-6 hours

ROUTE OVERVIEW: US-421 • US-50 • OH-73 • OH-32 • OH-104 • US-35 • US-50

❶ Grab coffee and a pastry at **The Attic Coffee Mill & Café** (631 W. Main St., 812/265-5781, www.atticmadison, 7am-5pm Mon.-Sat., $8-12), then stroll the blocks and blocks of photo-worthy architecture in Madison's business district.

❷ Drive to **Lawrenceburg,** just west of the Indiana-Ohio-Kentucky border. Head downtown to the waterfront. The best views of the Ohio River are from the paved **Dearborn Trail** (2 mi/3.2 km round-trip, 1 hour, easy), a nature trail that runs along the levee. Get onto the trail near the **Lawrenceburg Event Center** (Walnut St.). As you leave town, you'll notice the giant whiskey distillery at the north end of Main Street. It's among the oldest in the country, and was once owned by Seagram's.

> *Drive north on US-421 to US-50 (26 mi/42 km). Turn right on US-50 and drive to Lawrenceburg (25 mi/40 km).*

❸ US-50 meanders through the rolling farmlands of Ohio. In the middle of this bucolic scenery, you'll come to **Serpent Mound** (3850 OH-73,

SERPENT MOUND

800/752-2757, http://arcofappalachia. org, grounds dawn-dusk daily, museum 10am-4pm daily Apr.-Oct., Sat.-Sun. Mar. and Nov.-Dec., $8 per vehicle). Forming the shape of a snake, this long, curving mound of earth was created 1,000-2,000 years ago by ancient indigenous peoples. It's the largest and most impressive effigy mound in the country, spanning some 1,300 feet with an oval-shaped head at one end and a coiled tail at the other.

> Continue east on US-50 to OH-73 (82 mi/132 km). Turn right on OH-73. Drive 18 miles (29 km) to Serpent Mound.

4 Near Chillicothe, a quick detour north of US-50 brings you to the **Hopewell Culture National Historical Park** (16062 OH-104, 740/774-1126, www.nps.gov/hocu, 8:30am-5pm daily, free). Colloquially referred to as **Mound City,** the two dozen prehistoric earthworks that the park protects were built by the Hopewell culture, and take the form of circles, squares, and other geometric shapes. Some have earthen walls that stretch up to 12 feet high and span 1,000 feet across. The mounds are reachable via a one-mile trail that starts at the visitors center.

> Head south on OH-73 from Serpent Mound for 7 miles (11 km) to OH-32. Turn left and follow OH-32 to OH-104 (19 mi/31 km). Turn left on OH-104 and follow it for 6 miles (10 km). At US-23, turn

left and go 13 miles (21 km), then turn left to get back on OH-104. Head north for 4 miles (6 km) to Chillicothe. Continue another 3 miles (5 km) north on OH-104 to reach the park.

5 Head east on US-50 once more. The welcoming college town of **Athens** is the home of Ohio University. Eat dinner and be sure to save room for dessert from **Whit's Frozen Custard** (49 S. Court St., 740/594-7375, www.whitscustard.com, 8am-10pm daily, $5). Overnight at one of the chain hotels located near US-50.

> Take OH-104 S for 2 miles (3 km), then turn left onto US-35. Head east for 4 miles (6 km), then continue onto US-50. From here, it's 52 miles (84 km) on US-50 E to reach Athens.

ATHENS, OHIO

DAY 17: Athens to Reedsville, West Virginia

155 miles/250 kilometers | 3-4 hours

ROUTE OVERVIEW: US-50 • US-119 • WV-92

① Before you hit the road, pop over to **Union Street Diner** (70 W. Union St., 740/594-6007, http://unionstreetdiner.com, 24 hours daily, $8-18) for a hearty breakfast.

INTERNATIONAL MOTHER'S DAY SHRINE, GRAFTON

② From Athens, US-50 ambles toward the West Virginia border, passing abandoned coal-mining towns and inching toward the rural, rugged hill country of the Allegheny Mountains. First stop: **Parkersburg.** Here, in the middle of the Ohio River, is the **Blennerhassett Island Historical State Park** (137 Juliana St., 304/420-4800, http://wvstateparks.com, 10am-5pm Tues.-Sun. May-Oct., $4). The park is located on an island, and via self-guided walking tours and carriage rides, it offers insight into local history. The island is only accessible via a **ride on a sternwheeler** (round-trip $10), which departs from **Point Park** (2nd St.) in town.

> Drive east on US-50 from Athens to Parkersburg (36 mi/58 km).

③ Continue winding through West Virginia's mining country; canopies of thick trees drape over the road and white-water rivers snake by. But its empty towns and rural poverty are evidence of the hardships endured by the people living here. A former B&O railroad city, **Grafton** is dotted with architectural gems, but most of them are boarded up or run-down. Grafton does offer a bright spot, though: It's the birthplace of Mother's Day, first celebrated here in 1908. See the **International Mother's Day Shrine** (11 E. Main St., 304/265-1589, call for hours, $5) in an old church.

> Continue east on US-50 to Grafton (92 mi/148 km).

④ You're now fully committed to the hairpin curves and steep climbs of the **Allegheny Mountains.** Isolated mountain villages pop up every now and then, but you likely won't see a soul. Cell service is nonexistent and service stations are few and far between. The neighboring towns of **Arthurdale** and **Reedsville** are a welcome sight. These homestead communities were part of the rural resettlement projects initiated during the Depression-era New Deal. Stay the night at the idyllic **Modern Homestead** (52 S. Robert Stone Way, Reedsville, 304/864-4333, www.mymodernhomestead.com, $85-165), which offers five guest suites, a coffee shop, and a farmers market.

> From Grafton, head north on US-119 for 13 miles (21 km) to Gladesville Rd. Turn right on Gladesville and in 6 miles (10 km), turn left on WV-92. Go north for 3 miles (5 km) to Reedsville; you'll pass through Arthurdale on the way.

⑤ Grab dinner at **Prime Thyme** (82 Cedar Dr., Reedsville, 304/980-2214, 3pm-8:30pm Tues.-Sat., 11am-3pm Sun., $13-20), a homey spot for comfort food.

MODERN HOMESTEAD IN REEDSVILLE

DAY 18: Reedsville to Middleburg, Virginia

170 miles/275 kilometers | 4-5 hours

ROUTE OVERVIEW: WV-92 • US-50

1 After breakfast, take in the landscape with an easy hike on the nearby **Deckers Creek Trail** (access at Morgan Mine Road, http://montrails.org, free parking). The trail runs 19 miles from Morgantown to Reedsville, but you can do an out-and-back hike at a distance of your choice. Launch from the trailhead in Reedsville, off Morgan Mine Road.

2 Continue to navigate the tight turns and treacherous climbs of the Alleghenies. Go slowly to soak up the 3,000-foot views that erupt in sudden breaks in the tree line. When you reach civilization again in **Romney**, stop for lunch.
> *Follow WV-92 S from Reedsville to US-50 (15 mi/24 km). Turn left on US-50 and head to Romney (76 mi/122 km).*

3 Once in Virginia, drive through the apple orchards of **Winchester**—also the hometown of 1960s country singer Patsy Cline—and into the stately colonial village of **Middleburg.** Here is where you'll encounter the multimillion-dollar estates of politicians and aristocrats. The downtown district offers elegant restaurants, upscale shops, and art galleries to peruse. But first, check in to your room at **The Red Fox Inn & Tavern** (2 E. Washington St., 540/687-6301, www.redfox.com, from $195), built in 1728 as a coach house.

THE RED FOX INN & TAVERN IN MIDDLEBURG

> *Continue east on US-50 to Middleburg (72 mi/116 km).*

4 A short drive outside of Middleburg brings you to **Cana Vineyards and Winery** (38600 John Mosby Hwy., 703/348-2458, http://canavineyards.com, noon-6pm Thurs.-Mon., $12). Sip fine wines, recline in an Adirondack chair, and unwind after a day navigating mountain roads.
> *Take US-50 E for 4 miles (6 km) to reach the winery.*

5 Return to Middleburg for dinner at **King Street Oyster Bar** (1 E. Washington St., 540/883-3156, http://kingstreetoysterbar.com, 11am-9:30pm Mon.-Thurs., 11am-11pm Fri.-Sat., 10:30am-9:30pm Sun., $11-33), across the street from your hotel.
> *Follow US-50 W back into Middleburg (4 mi/6 km).*

DAY 19: Middleburg to Washington DC

45 miles/72 kilometers | 1-1.5 hours

ROUTE OVERVIEW: US-50

1 Enjoy breakfast in Middleburg at **Cuppa Giddy Up** (8 E. Washington St., 540/687-8122, www.cuppagiddyup.com, 7am-5:30pm daily, $5-8), then depart for the nation's capital.

2 Just before you reach Washington DC, pay your respects at **Arlington National Cemetery** (across Memorial Bridge from the Lincoln Memorial, Arlington, Virginia, 877/907-8585, www.arlingtoncemetery.mil, 8am-7pm daily Apr.-Sept., 8am-5pm daily Oct.-Mar., free, parking $2/hour). The second-oldest national cemetery contains the Tomb of the Unknown Soldier and the gravesite of JFK, among its monuments to patriotic sacrifice.
> *Drive east on US-50 for 39 miles (63 km). Follow signs for Memorial Bridge/George Washington Pkwy., then take the exit for Arlington Cemetery (1 mi/1.6 km).*

3 Check in to your hotel room, then strike out on foot to visit DC's iconic monuments along the **National Mall,** such as the **Washington Monument** (2 15th St. NW, 877/444-6777, tickets

WASHINGTON MONUMENT

877/559-6777, www.nps.gov/wamo, 9am-10pm daily Memorial Day-Labor Day, 9am-5pm daily Labor Day-Memorial Day, free, tickets required), **Lincoln Memorial** (2 Lincoln Memorial Cir. NW, 202/426-6841, www.nps.gov/linc, 24 hours daily, free), and **Vietnam Veterans Memorial** (5 Henry Bacon Dr. NW, 202/426-6841, www.nps.gov/vive, 24 hours daily, free).

> *Cross Arlington Memorial Bridge into Washington DC (3 mi/5 km).*

④ For dinner, head to **Rasika** (633 D St. NW, 202/637-1222, www.rasikarestaurant.com, 11:30am-2:30pm and 5:30pm-10:30pm Mon.-Thurs., 11:30am-2:30pm and 5pm-11pm Fri., 5pm-11pm Sat., $20-28), a restaurant serving flavorful Indian cuisine.

DAY 20: Washington DC

MORNING AND AFTERNOON

① Spend the day checking out the Smithsonian's roundup of impressive museums. Start at the **National Air and Space Museum** (Independence Ave. and 6th St. SW, 202/633-2214, www.airandspace.si.edu, 10am-5:30pm daily, free), then move on to the **National Portrait Gallery** (8th St. and F St. NW, 202/633-8300, www.npg.si.edu, 11:30am-7pm daily, free), and finish up at the **National Museum of Natural History** (10th St. and Constitution Ave., 202/633-1000, www.mnh.si.edu, 10am-5:30pm daily, free).

② In between museums, break for lunch at **Ben's Chili Bowl** (1213 U St. NW, 202/667-0909, www.benschilibowl.com, 6am-2am Mon.-Thurs., 6am-4am Fri., 7am-4am Sat., 11am-midnight Sun., $4-9), a DC institution.

NATIONAL MUSEUM OF NATURAL HISTORY

Best BIG-CITY DETOURS

US-50 is known—and beloved—for connecting America's tiny towns. But when the lights of the big city beckon, here are several cosmopolitan detours to take.

CALIFORNIA

San Francisco: Just 90 miles southwest of Sacramento is San Francisco, a hub of culture, history, museums, food, art, and big-city nightlife.

NEVADA

Reno: The "Biggest Little City in the World" boasts 24-hour casinos, affordable lodging, classic-car culture, and a relaxed vibe.

UTAH

Salt Lake City: Detour north to Utah's biggest city. With a metro area population of over 1 million, this place has plenty of urbane offerings.

COLORADO

Denver: Sports fans, outdoors enthusiasts, and foodies will find much to do in this Rocky Mountain city, 100 miles north of US-50.

MISSOURI

Kansas City: From barbecue and jazz to history and sports, KC keeps visitors of all ages and interests entertained. This city is right on US-50, so you can stop here before visiting Independence.

INDIANA

Louisville, KY: Head south across the Indiana border to the bustling home of the Kentucky Derby and the Louisville Slugger Museum.

OHIO

Cincinnati: Situated on the Ohio River, this city appeals to art lovers, history geeks, and sports fans. You won't even need a detour to get here—it's right on US-50.

MARYLAND

Baltimore: Catch an Orioles game, dine on fresh seafood, and tour the Inner Harbor. This city is just 30 miles north of Annapolis and US-50.

▼ SAN FRANCISCO'S GOLDEN GATE BRIDGE

EVENING

❸ Sneak in a quick nap at your hotel, then dress for dinner at **Sfoglina** (4445 Connecticut Ave. NW, 202/450-1312, www.sfoglinadc.com, 4pm-10pm Mon., 11:30am-10pm Tues.-Thurs., 11:30am-10:30pm Fri., 10:30am-10:30pm Sat., 10:30am-9pm Sun., $19-24), one of the best Italian restaurants in the city.

❹ Stay up late to take in a jazz show at **Columbia Station** (2325 18th St. NW, 202/462-6040, 5pm-2am Tues.-Thurs., 5pm-3am Fri.-Sun.), a cozy space with great live music and no cover charge.

OCEAN CITY, MARYLAND

DAY 21: Washington DC to Ocean City, Maryland

170 miles/270 kilometers | 4 hours

ROUTE OVERVIEW: US-50 • MD-322 • MD-33 • Easton Pkwy. • US-50

① Your first stop today is Maryland's state capital: **Annapolis.** Explore the **Annapolis City Dock** (Dock St. on the waterfront) in downtown. Annapolis boasts more 18th-century beaux arts buildings than any other American city, and many of these charming structures line the dock area.

> *Depart Washington DC by driving east on US-50. Continue for 32 miles (51 km) to Annapolis.*

② Drive over the **Chesapeake Bay Bridge** and across Kent Island to the historic and sleepy town of **St. Michaels** on Maryland's Eastern Shore. Walk the brick-paved streets to browse the antiques shops and boutiques.

> *Follow US-50 east and south to MD-322 (38 mi/61 km). Turn right and in 2 miles (3 km), make another right onto MD-33 W. Drive MD-33 into St. Michaels (9 mi/14 km).*

③ Once you land in **Ocean City,** head straight to the **Ocean City Boardwalk** (2nd St. to 27th St.) to celebrate your epic achievement on the shores of the Atlantic Ocean. Congratulations— you made it! Take in the festive vibe of the boardwalk, then order the famous fries at **Thrasher's French Fries** (410/289-7232, www.thrashersfries.

com, 10am-10pm daily Memorial Day-Labor Day, 10am-5pm daily Labor Day-Memorial Day). You'll have to wait in line for these crispy french fries doused in apple cider vinegar and Old Bay seasoning, but it's worth it.

> *Take MD-33 E for 9 miles (14 km) to Easton Pkwy. Turn right and follow this to US-50 (3 mi/5 km). Merge onto US-50 and head east to Ocean City (73 mi/117 km).*

④ Wind down the day on the white sands of **Ocean City Beach** (5am-10pm daily). You'll find beach access nearly everywhere along the 10-mile shoreline, but the main entrance is at **Division Street and Baltimore Avenue.** Linger until the sun sets and turns the skies pink and orange.

⑤ Your final accommodation on this journey is the 1927 **Atlantic House Bed and Breakfast** (501 N. Baltimore Ave., 410/289-2333, www.atlantichouse.com, $190-270). Sleep well. In the morning, you'll be treated to coffee and a home-cooked breakfast on the front porch. You deserve it.

OCEAN CITY BOARDWALK

GETTING THERE

AIR

The closest airport to the start of the trip is **Sacramento International Airport** (SMF, 6900 Airport Blvd., 916/929-5411, www.sacramento.aero), which is served by several major airlines and offers on-site car rental facilities.

There's also **San Francisco International Airport** (SFO, 800/435-9736 www.flysfo.com), located about 90 miles southwest of Sacramento, a two-hour drive via I-80.

TRAIN

The Capitol Corridor route run by **Amtrak** (800/872-7245, www.amtrak.com) runs from the **Sacramento train station** (401 I St.) to San Francisco, which connects to major destinations throughout the United States via the California Zephyr service. Major stops on the California Zephyr include Salt Lake City, Denver, Omaha, and Chicago. From the Chicago hub, you can connect to most East Coast destinations.

BUS

The **Greyhound bus station** (420 Richards Blvd., 800/231-2222, www.greyhound.com, $7.50-48) is north of downtown. The long-distance carrier offers service throughout the country.

CAR

In addition to sitting at the western terminus of US-50, Sacramento lies at the nexus of two other major freeways: I-80 (east-west) and I-5 (north-south).

To get to Midtown from the **Sacramento airport,** it's a 15-mile (24-km) drive of 20-30 minutes. Take I-5 S to Q Street. Make a left on Q Street, following it to 20th Street. Make a left and you're in Midtown.

To reach Sacramento from the **San Francisco airport,** it's a 100-mile (160-km) drive that takes around two hours. Take US-101 N to I-80 E. Continue east onto US-50, then to I-5. At the intersection of I-80 and US-50, keep an eye out for the famous mileage sign that reads "Ocean City: 3,037 miles." From US-50, head north on I-5 into town.

GETTING BACK

To return to **Sacramento** from Ocean City, the fastest route is 2,860 miles (4,610 km), which totals 44 hours of drive time. Follow US-50, I-70, and I-80 through Maryland, Pennsylvania, Ohio, Indiana, Illinois, Iowa, Nebraska, Wyoming, Utah, and Nevada.

There are three airports close to Ocean City, so it's easy to fly out of this area after a one-way drive. **Baltimore/Washington International Airport** (BWI, 7050 Friendship Rd., 410/859-7111, www.bwiairport.com) is in Baltimore, Maryland, which is 140 miles (225 km) from Ocean City. The drive to the airport takes 2.5-3 hours via US-50 and I-97.

Reagan National Airport (DCA, 2401 Smith Blvd., Arlington, 703/417-8000, www.flyreagan.com) is in Arlington, Virginia, 150 miles (245 km) from Ocean City. The drive to the airport takes about three hours via US-50.

Dulles International Airport (IAD, 1 Saarinen Circle, Dulles, 703/572-2700, www.flydulles.com) is 175 miles (280 km) from Ocean City, and is located in Virginia near Washington DC. The drive to Dulles takes around three hours via US-50 and I-495.

CONNECT WITH

- At Moab: **Best of the Southwest** (PAGE 288)
- At Washington DC: **Blue Ridge Parkway** (PAGE 562)
- At Annapolis: **Chesapeake Bay** (PAGE 612)
- At Sacramento: **Gold Country Ramble** (PAGE 202)
- At Lake Tahoe: **Northern California Loop** (PAGE 156)
- At Baker, Ely, and Virginia City: **Reno to the Rubies** (PAGE 318)
- At St. Louis: **Route 66** (PAGE 60)

ROUTE 66

WHY GO: Retro neon signs, classic motor courts, roadside attractions, kitsch Americana, desert vistas, ocean sunsets

TOTAL DISTANCE: 2,570 miles/ 4,140 kilometers

NUMBER OF DAYS: 14

SEASONS: Late spring through early summer; early fall

STARTING POINT: Chicago, Illinois

END: Santa Monica, California

▶ HACKBERRY, ARIZONA

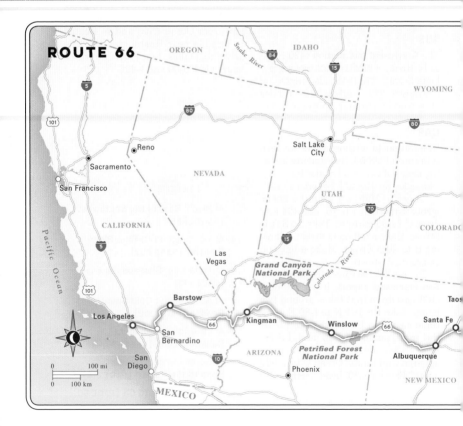

Route 66 cuts a swath through the heart of America. Plan to explore leisurely and get to know the locals—a lot of the people who live and work on Route 66 run family-owned businesses that have been in operation for decades. Get ready for an up-close view of many of the cultures, dialects, and traditions that comprise America, from past to present. Note: Much of the route was realigned along the interstate highways, so if you need to make up time, you can jump on and off the freeway to reach your next destination quickly.

DAY 1: Chicago to Pontiac, Illinois

100 miles/161 kilometers | 3-4 hours

ROUTE OVERVIEW: Ogden Ave./US-34 • IL-53 • Historic US-66

❶ Have lunch at **The Green Door Tavern** (678 N. Orleans St., 312/664-5496, www.greendoorchicago.com, 11:30am-2am daily, $8-15) in **Chicago.** The city's oldest tavern was constructed in 1872, one year after the Great Chicago Fire. Opt for the corned beef with gooey swiss cheese and sauerkraut.

❷ After lunch, head to **Pontiac** to see the **Illinois Route 66 Hall of Fame & Museum** (110 W. Howard St., 815/844-4566, www.il66assoc.org, 9am-5pm daily Apr.-Oct., 10am-4pm daily Nov.-Mar., free), where the world's largest mural of the Route 66 road sign is emblazoned outside—a perfect photo op. Spend at least an hour exploring the artifacts inside.

BEGINNING OF ROUTE 66 IN CHICAGO

ILLINOIS ROUTE 66 HALL OF FAME & MUSEUM

> Head west on Ogden Ave./US-34 to join Joliet Rd. Follow this to IL-53. Continue for 38 miles (61 km). West of Gardner, follow Historic US-66 as it branches off IL-53 to head south, paralleling I-55, to Pontiac (26 mi/42 km).

❸ Stretch your legs by walking across one of Pontiac's **swinging footbridges** over the Vermillion River—the oldest is from 1898.

❹ Enjoy dinner at Pontiac's **Old Log Cabin Inn & Restaurant** (18700 Old Rte. 66, 815/842-2908, 5am-8pm Mon.-Sat., $8-15). Opened in 1926, it symbolizes Route 66's historic past, and was even turned around to continue facing Route 66 after the Mother Road was reconfigured. Walk behind the restaurant today to see the original Route 66 alignment along the railroad tracks.

❺ Spend the night in Pontiac at **Three Roses Bed & Breakfast** (209 E. Howard St., 630/999-0420, www.threerosesbedandbreakfast.org, $100-160), a Victorian home with a lovely front porch. Look forward to homemade breakfast in the morning.

Top **5** ROUTE 66

1. Soak up Mother Road history at the **Illinois Route 66 Hall of Fame & Museum** in Pontiac, IL (PAGE 62).

2. Walk through the mouth of the **Blue Whale** in Catoosa, OK (PAGE 68).

3. See the inventive **art installation** at **Cadillac Ranch** in Amarillo, TX (PAGE 70).

4. Indulge in roadside kitsch and good eats at **Delgadillo's Snow Cap Drive-In** in Seligman, AZ (PAGE 75).

5. Watch the sun set off the **Santa Monica Pier** in Santa Monica, CA (PAGE 76).

The story of Route 66 isn't complete without the illustrious women who've contributed to the road's growth, success, and preservation. This list highlights the women who made a profound impact on the Mother Road.

ILLINOIS

- **Hazel Funk** inherited and ran **Funks Grove Pure Maple Sirup** (5257 Old Route 66, Funks Grove, 309/874-3360, www.funksmaplesirup.com, 9am-5pm Mon.-Fri., 10am-5pm Sat., 1pm-5pm Sun. Mar.-Aug.), the family maple syrup business.

- **Sally Rand** was an early pioneer of burlesque, hosting shows at several iconic places on Route 66, like the **Coleman Theatre** (103 N. Main St., 918/550-2425, www.colemantheatre.org, tours 10am-4pm Tues.-Fri., 10am-2pm Sat., free) in Miami, Oklahoma, and the **KiMo Theatre** (423 Central Ave. NW, 505/768-3544, www.kimotickets.com, 9am-4pm Tues.-Sat.) in Albuquerque, New Mexico.

MISSOURI AND KANSAS

- **Julia Chaney** and her husband owned and ran the now-closed Red's Giant Hamburg, one of the first drive-through restaurants in the country. See a replica of the famous sign at the **Birthplace of Route 66 Roadside Park** (1200 Block W. College St., 24 hours daily, free) in Springfield, Missouri.

- **Allyne Earls** owned the (now demolished) Midway Café in Cuba, Missouri, keeping it open 24/7 for Route 66 travelers in need of a bite.

- **Elaine Graham Estes** worked at her family's motel and restaurant in Springfield, Missouri, the Graham Rib Station, which appeared in the *Negro Motorist Green Book* and welcomed all visitors.

- **Melba Rigg** was one of four women who restored an abandoned gas station that now operates as the popular **Cars on the Route** (119 N. Main St., 620/783-1366, www.

CARS ON THE ROUTE, GALENA, KANSAS

kansastravel.org, 10am-4pm Wed.-Sat., 1pm-3pm Sun., free) in Galena, Kansas.

OKLAHOMA

- **Gladys Cutberth,** aka "Mrs. Route 66," fought to keep Route 66 in small towns.

- **Lucille Hamons** was known as "Mother of the Mother Road." She and her husband ran **Lucille's Service Station** (Route 66, west of OK-58) in Hydro.

- **Dawn Welch** is the owner of Stroud's popular **Rock Cafe** (114 W. Main St., 918/968-3990, www.rockcafert66.com, 7am-9pm daily, $6-12.50). She's also the inspiration for the character Sally Carrera in Pixar's *Cars*.

TEXAS

- **Fran Houser** owned the **MidPoint Café** (305 W. Route 66, 805/536-6379, 8:30am-5pm daily, $8-14), welcoming travelers to the halfway point in Adrian.

NEW MEXICO

- **Mary Colter** is the famed architect who designed many places along Route 66, including **La Posada Hotel** (303 E. 2nd St., 928/289-4366, www.laposada.org, $129-169) in Winslow, Arizona, and **La Fonda** (100 E. San Francisco St., 800/523-5002, www.lafondasantafe.com, $240-475) in Santa Fe, New Mexico.

- **Lillian Redman** and her husband owned the iconic **Blue Swallow Motel** (815 E. Rte. 66, 575/461-9849, www.blueswallowmotel.com, $85-140) in Tucumcari.

- **Fabiola Cabeza de Baca** was a teacher and activist who traveled Route 66 to teach rural New Mexicans new techniques for agriculture and homemaking.

ARIZONA

- **Susie Woo** immigrated to Winslow from China in the 1930s and ran a grocery store.

- **Andrea Arizaga Limon** was a Harvey Girl, one of many young women hired to meet and greet train travelers at Harvey Houses.

- **Joy Nevin** drove Route 66 countless times as the owner and operator of Stockmen's Supply Service, a traveling sales company.

CALIFORNIA

- **Minerva Hoyt** founded the International Desert Conservation League in 1930.

- **Lucia Rodriguez** opened **Mitla Café** (602 N. Mount Vernon Ave., 909/888-0460, www.mitlacafesb.com, 9am-8pm Tues.-Thurs. and Sat.-Sun., 9am-9pm Fri., $12-17) in San Bernardino to support the town's Mexican American residents.

- **Cynthia Hare Troup** came up with the catchy title for her husband Bobby's famous song, "(Get Your Kicks on) Route 66."

DAY 2: Pontiac to St. Louis, Missouri

210 miles/340 kilometers | 4-5 hours

ROUTE OVERVIEW: Historic US-66 • I-55 • Old Route 66 • IL-4 • IL-157 • I-55

❶ Start the day early and drive along Route 66 to **Funk's Grove Pure Maple Sirup** (5257 Old Route 66, 309/874-3360, www.funksmaplesirup.com, 9am-5pm Mon.-Fri., 10am-5pm Sat., 1pm-5pm Sun. Mar.-Aug.), a Mother Road landmark where the Funk family has been producing and selling gallons of maple syrup every year for three generations. For a fun souvenir, pick up some "sirup" of your own.

> *Take Historic US-66 S as it parallels I-55 for 50 miles (81 km) to the syrup shop.*

❷ Have lunch at **Ariston Café** (413 Old Route 66 N., 217/324-2023, www.ariston-cafe.com, 11am-9pm Wed.-Fri., 4pm-8pm Sat., 11am-3pm Sun., $7-24), one of the oldest operating restaurants on Route 66, in **Litchfield,** about 1.5 hours away. When Ariston Café opened in the 1930s, a porterhouse steak cost just $0.85.

> *Continue for 102 miles (164 km) to Litchfield, using I-55.*

❸ Head to **Staunton** to say hello to the lovable rabbits at **Henry's Rabbit Ranch** (1107 Old Route 66, 618/635-5655, www.henrysroute66.com, 9am-4pm Mon.-Fri., 9am-1pm Sat., free).

HENRY'S RABBIT RANCH

ST. LOUIS

Inside what appears to be an old filling station is a Route 66 information center—albeit one with rabbits. As you check out the memorabilia, owner Rich Henry will bring out a rabbit, set him or her on the counter, and let you pet the furry friend while you chat it up.

> Follow Old Route 66 for 15 miles (24 km) to Staunton.

❹ In **Edwardsville,** have dinner at **Cleveland-Heath** (106 N. Main St., 618/307-4830, www.clevelandheath. com, 11am-10pm Mon.-Thurs., 11am-11pm Fri., 10am-11pm Sat., 10am-8pm Sun., $10-35). The fare at this James Beard-nominated eatery is a much-needed break from the standard road trip eats.

> Follow IL-4 and IL-157 to reach Edwardsville in 20 miles (32 km).

❺ From Edwardsville, it's a short jaunt to **St. Louis,** Missouri. Check into the **Magnolia Hotel** (421 N. 8th St., 314/436-9000, www.magnoliahotels.com, $151-312), an upscale 18-story landmark that's housed the likes of Cary Grant, John Barrymore, and Douglas Fairbanks.

> Follow IL-157 and I-55 for 23 miles (37 km) to reach St. Louis.

DAY 3: St. Louis to Springfield, Missouri

215 miles/350 kilometers | 4-5 hours

ROUTE OVERVIEW: I-44

❶ Savor a hearty meal at **Fitz's** (6605 Delmar Blvd., 314/726-9555, 11am-9pm Sun.-Thurs., 11am-10pm Fri.-Sat., $8-20) in **St. Louis,** where you can taste more than a dozen flavors of craft soda on tap, from sassafras root to vanilla bean.

❷ Spend a few hours playing at St. Louis's **City Museum** (750 N. 16th St., 314/231-2489, www.citymuseum.org, 9am-5pm Mon.-Thurs., 9am-midnight Fri.-Sat., 10am-5pm Sun., $14 pp), a wildly innovative playground made from scrapped pieces of America's infrastructure.

❸ In the afternoon, drive to **Cuba** to see the 12 murals depicting the town's heritage that line the Mother Road. One painting shows Amelia Earhart when she landed outside Cuba in 1928; another depicts Bette Davis's 1948 visit to the town in her Packard station wagon.

> From Market St. (near the Gateway Arch) in St. Louis, turn south on Tucker Blvd. As the road passes under I-44 and over I-55, Route 66 turns into MO-30 (Gravois Ave.). In less than 3 miles (5 km), turn right on MO-366, joining I-44 W. It's 68 miles (109 km) to Cuba.

❹ Stop in nearby **Fanning** to get a picture of the **World's Largest Rocking Chair on Route 66** (5957 Hwy. ZZ, 573/885-1474).

> Take Historic US-66 W/Hwy. ZZ for 4 miles (6 km) to Fanning.

❺ Head to **Springfield,** the birthplace of Route 66, and spend the night at the **Best Western Route 66 Rail Haven** (203 S. Glenstone Ave., 417/866-1963, www.bwrailhaven.com, $88-165), a historic, pet-friendly hotel with a 1950s-style lobby.

> Follow I-44 W for 121 miles (195 km) to reach Springfield.

WORLD'S LARGEST ROCKING CHAIR ON ROUTE 66 IN FANNING

DAY 4: Springfield to Tulsa, Oklahoma

200 miles/320 kilometers | 4-5 hours

ROUTE OVERVIEW: MO-266 • MO-96 • MO-43 • Route 66 • Sidewalk Highway • US-69 • US-60 • Route 66

❶ Start the day with locally sourced eats at **The Order** (305 E. Walnut St., 417/851-5299, 7am-2pm and 5pm-10pm Mon.-Fri., 8am-2pm and 5pm-10pm Sat., 8am-2pm and 5pm-9pm Sun., $9-45) before driving about 75 miles (121 km) to the Missouri state line at **Joplin.**

> *Depart Springfield via West College St. When it joins West Chestnut Expy. (Bus. I-44), turn left and keep straight as the road turns into MO-266 (Route 66). Follow this for 16 miles (26 km). MO-266 dips south and turns right onto MO-96. Follow this for 34 miles (55 km) to Carthage, where you'll take E. Main St. 2 miles (3 km) to Webb City. Take MO-43 4 miles (6 km) south to Joplin.*

❷ Continue for a quick jaunt through Kansas, checking out **Cars on the Route** (119 N. Main St., 620/783-1366, www.kansastravel.org, 10am-4pm Wed.-Sat., 1pm-3pm Sun., free) in **Galena.** Here you can see the 1951 International boom truck that inspired Tow Mater, the beloved character from Pixar's *Cars* movie. It sits in front of this historic service station, a former Kan-O-Tex gas station turned tourist attraction.

> *Follow Route 66 west for 7 miles (11 km) to Galena.*

CARS ON THE ROUTE, GALENA, KANSAS

3 Cross into Oklahoma and plan to drive one of the oldest roadbeds on the journey: the **Sidewalk Highway,** between **Miami** and **Afton.** This 3-mile (5-km), 9-foot-wide stretch predates Route 66 by about 15 years. The rough and narrow patch of road is covered with dirt and gravel, and the original curbing is still visible in some places. Go slow, and don't drive the Sidewalk Highway if it's wet.

> As you leave Miami, go south on Main St./OK-125. The road curves right to become East St. SW. Continue heading south. Once you reach East 120 Rd./20th Ave. SW, keep going straight for 1 mile (1.6 km). Turn right onto East 130

Rd. Drive 1.5 miles (2.5 km), then turn left onto South 540 Rd. and make a right on East 140 Rd. After 1 mile (1.6 km), turn left on US-69/Route 66. In Afton, the road becomes US-60/US-69.

4 In **Catoosa,** see an iconic Route 66 roadside attraction, the **Blue Whale** (2680 N. SR-66, www.bluewhaleroute66.com, 8am-dusk daily, free). Featured on the History Channel's *American Pickers,* and as part of Snapchat's Spectacles marketing campaign, the concrete-and-pipe Blue Whale draws visitors from near and far.

> Take US-60 out of Afton. In 20 miles (32 km), pick up Route 66 again and follow it for 43 miles (69 km) to Catoosa.

5 From Catoosa, it's not far to **Tulsa,** where you'll spend the night at the **Campbell Hotel** (2636 E. 11th St., 855/744-5500, www.thecampbellhotel. com, $139-209). Built in 1927, this boutique hotel boasts 26 impeccably appointed rooms that overlook Route 66.

> Take Route 66 for 16 miles (26 km) as it parallels I-44 into Tulsa.

DAY 5: Tulsa to Oklahoma City, Oklahoma

120 miles/193 kilometers | 3 hours

ROUTE OVERVIEW: Route 66 • OK-66 • Route 66 • US-77

1 In Tulsa, have breakfast at **Corner Café** (1103 S. Peoria Ave., 918/587-0081, www.cornercafetulsa.com, 6am-9pm daily, $6-14), where you'll enjoy a no-frills, belly-filling, delicious breakfast fit for a day on the road. Bonus: The coffee is amazing.

2 Visit Tulsa's **Greenwood Cultural Center** (322 N. Greenwood Ave., 918/596-1020, www.greenwoodculturalcenter.com, 9am-5pm Mon.-Fri., free), where you'll learn about the Tulsa Race Massacre, considered to be the worst racial violence event in U.S. history. The center showcases an important collection of memorabilia about the event, including photos of the Greenwood District before,

▶ Playlist

ROUTE 66

SONGS

- **"Meet Me in Chicago" by Buddy Guy:** Blues crooner Buddy Guy sings about iconic spots in Chicago, capturing the live-wire spirit of the city with his electric blues melodies.

- **"Amarillo by Morning" by George Strait:** No self-respecting road-trip playlist through Texas omits George Strait. Play this twangy tune as you roll into Amarillo.

- **"Take It Easy" by the Eagles:** This is easily the most popular song about Winslow, Arizona. The melody will stick in your head for miles.

- **"New Slang" by The Shins:** You'll want to whistle along with the windows down when you hear this 2002 breakout song from Albuquerque-based indie darlings The Shins.

during, and after the riots, when it was burned to the ground.

❸ Afterward, head west to **Arcadia** and stop at **Pops** (660 SR-66, 405/928-7677, www.pops66.com, 6am-10pm daily, restaurant 10:30am-9pm Mon.-Fri., 7am-9pm Sat.-Sun., $8-13), a futuristic gas station and soda pop heaven. Not only can you fill the car's tank and stock up your soda supply, but you can also take a photo of the 66-foot-tall (20-m), LED-lit sculpture of a soda bottle.

> *Follow Route 66 south before joining OK-66 to Sapulpa (14 mi/23 km), then cross I-44 into Bristow and Stroud (23 mi/37 km). Continue on Route 66 south through Chandler and Warwick (39 mi/63 km), where you'll head west to reach Luther (12 mi/19 km). Leaving Luther, Route 66 turns into E. Danforth Rd. on its way to Arcadia (8 mi/13 km).*

❹ Drive 30 minutes to **Oklahoma City** and check out the **Gold Dome Building** (1112 NW 23rd St.), a 1958 structure with a roof of 625 gold panels. When it was originally constructed as a Citizens State Bank, the building was considered one of the most innovative bank designs of the time.

> *As you travel west, Route 66 ends at I-35 (6 mi/10 km). Keep heading west and follow US-77 into Edmond. After 3 miles (5 km), turn left on Broadway/US-77 and drive to the exit for Memorial Rd./Kelley Ave. Turn left on Kelley and join I-44 W. Take exit 128A for Lincoln Blvd. Turn left and head south into Oklahoma City.*

❺ Tuck in for the night at **Skirvin Hilton Hotel** (1 Park Ave., 405/272-3040, www.skirvinhilton.com, $208-355). The historic 1911 hotel has hosted presidents, actors, politicians, and athletes during its 100-year life span.

DAY 6: Oklahoma City to Amarillo, Texas

260 miles/420 kilometers | 4-5 hours

ROUTE OVERVIEW: Route 66

❶ Get on the road early, because it's a long drive to your first stop, the beautifully restored **Tower Station and U-Drop Inn Café** (1242 N. Main

TOWER STATION AND U-DROP INN CAFÉ, SHAMROCK

St., www.shamrockedc.org/u-drop-inn, 806/256-2501, free) in **Shamrock,** Texas. Not only is this former Conoco station a landmark—architecturally and historically—but the 1936 art deco marvel is also the town's Route 66 visitors center.

> *Travel west on Route 66/I-40 out of Oklahoma City. This will take you through Hydro in 63 miles (101 km). Keep to the I-40 frontage road for 5 miles (8 km) into Weatherford. In 3 miles (5 km), join I-40 BUS into Clinton. Leaving Clinton, follow Route 66 as it crisscrosses I-40 from Canute to Elk City. The I-40 frontage road (Route 66) takes you to Sayre, Erick, and the border town of Texola. From Texola, it's 14 miles (23 km) west to reach Shamrock.*

❷ Drive to **McLean** to tour the **Devil's Rope Museum** (100 Kingsley St., 806/779-2225, www.barbwiremuseum.com, 9am-4pm Mon.-Sat., free). It

DEVIL'S ROPE MUSEUM, MCLEAN

houses the world's largest collection of published material about barbed wire. Hyper niche; super fascinating.

> *Continue west for 20 miles (32 km) to reach McLean.*

❸ Head 70 miles (113 km) to **Amarillo** and stay overnight at the **Courtyard by Marriott Amarillo Downtown** (724 S. Polk St., 806/553-4500, www.marriott.com, $159-190), located in the historic Fisk Building.

> *Continue west into Amarillo (70 mi/113 km).*

❹ Dinner is right across the street at **Crush Wine Bar** (701 S. Polk St., 806/418-2011, www.crushdeli.com, 11am-9pm Mon.-Thurs., 11am-10pm Fri.-Sat., $15-30). Skip the wait for a table and instead grab a seat at the bar to mingle with a diverse crowd of local cowboys and traveling business professionals. The steak frites is to die for.

DAY 7: Amarillo to Tucumcari, New Mexico

115 miles/185 kilometers | 2-3 hours

ROUTE OVERVIEW: Route 66 • I-40 BUS • Route 66 • I-40 • Route 66

❶ Tour **Amarillo's Route 66 Historic District** (6th Ave. between Georgia St. and Western St.). The 13-block area was added to the National Register of Historic Places in 1994 and offers an insightful look at the city's Route 66 heritage.

❷ Don't miss **Cadillac Ranch** (I-40 frontage road near exit 60, dawn-dusk daily, free), about 10 miles (16 km) west as you leave Amarillo. In a Texas field, you'll find 10 graffiti-splattered Cadillacs—each manufactured between 1948 and 1964—planted nose-first in the soil. Public art at its best.

> *Drive west on Amarillo Blvd. Route 66 heads south and turns into I-40 BUS as it crosses TX-335. About 1.5 miles (2.5 km) after passing TX-335, turn right, then make a left onto Indian Hill Rd. Turn left on S. Blessen Dr. and take the next right on the I-40 frontage road. Follow*

MIDPOINT MARK IN ADRIAN

Route 66 for 10 miles (16 km) to Cadillac Ranch.

❸ Stop for lunch, a slice of pie, and a photo op at **MidPoint Café** (305 W. Route 66, 805/536-6379, 8:30am-5pm daily, $8-14) in **Adrian**—this marks the halfway point of your Route 66 road trip.

> *Follow Route 66 along the frontage road for 40 miles (64 km) to Adrian.*

❹ After crossing the New Mexico border, drive to **Tucumcari** and tour the murals. Artists Sharon and Doug Quarles painted 40 murals throughout the city that, when taken as a whole, tell the complicated story of the country's westward migration.

> *Head west from Adrian for 23 miles (37 km) on Route 66. As you enter New Mexico, join I-40, then take exit 369 after several miles. Turn right and then take the first left on Quay Rd. to follow N. Frontage Rd. As the road curves west, turn left on NM-469, cross I-40 heading south, and then turn right in San Jon to rejoin Route 66 on S. Frontage Rd (20 mi/32 km). Follow Route 66 west for the next 20 miles (32 km) to Tucumcari.*

❺ Stay overnight at the legendary **Blue Swallow Motel** (815 E. Rte. 66, 575/461-9849, www.blueswallowmotel.com, $85-140). The Blue Swallow's bird-in-flight symbol harkens back to the classic sailor tattoo: When sailors saw this bird, they knew land—and home—was near.

DAY 8: Tucumcari to Santa Fe, New Mexico

180 miles/290 kilometers | 3-4 hours

ROUTE OVERVIEW: I-40 • US-84 • I-25 frontage road • NM-63 • NM-50 • I-25/US-85 • Old Las Vegas Hwy. • Old Pecos Trail • Old Santa Fe Trail

❶ Start the day with breakfast at **Comet II Drive-In** (1257 E. Rte. 66, 575/472-3663, 11am-9pm Tues.-Sun., $10-15) in **Santa Rosa,** which is about an hour from Tucumcari.

> Follow I-40 W to Santa Rosa (54 mi/87 km).

❷ Take the road's pre-1937 alignment for the beautiful 120-mile (193-km) drive to **Santa Fe.** See the impressive art collection at the **Georgia O'Keeffe Museum** (217 Johnson St., 505/946-1000, www.okeeffemuseum.org, 9am-5pm Sat.-Thurs., 9am-7pm Fri., $13), which houses the largest repository of her art, including personal notes and books from her own collection.

> Take I-40 W for 16 miles (26 km). Take exit 256 and head north on US-84, then cross I-25 (42 mi/68 km). Turn left on the frontage road. Near Rowe, turn right to cross under US-84 (32 mi/52 km). Turn left on NM-63. In 6 miles (10 km), at Pecos, turn left on NM-50. In 6 miles (10 km), join I-25 W/US-85 and drive 5 miles (8 km) to exit 294 for Cañoncito. Turn left on Old Las Vegas Hwy./NM-300, which parallels I-25. Stay on this for 10 miles (16 km), then turn right on NM-466/Old Pecos Trail. Drive north 1 mile (1.6 km), then bear right to follow Old Pecos Trail north. The road merges with Old Santa Fe Trail, which leads to Santa Fe.

❸ In Santa Fe, stroll the shops on **The Plaza** and tour **The Palace of the Governors** (105 W. Palace Ave.,

THE PALACE OF THE GOVERNORS, SANTA FE

Neon PHOTO OPS

This road trip boasts some of the country's best retro neon signs, many of them more than half a century old. Here are a few you should build into your itinerary.

- **The Berghoff** (17 W. Adams St., Chicago, IL)
- **Dell Rhea's Chicken Basket** (645 Joliet Rd., Willowbrook, IL)
- **Munger Moss Motel** (1336 East Rte. 66, Lebanon, MO)
- **66 Drive-in Theater** (17321 Old 66 Blvd., Carthage, MO)
- **Waylan's Ku-Ku** (915 N. Main St., Miami, OK)
- **Meadow Gold** (11th St. and Quaker Ave., Tulsa, OK)
- **Tee Pee Curios** (924 E. Rte. 66, Tucumcari, NM)
- **Blue Swallow Motel** (815 E. Rte. 66, Tucumcari, NM)
- **Wigwam Motel** (811 W. Hopi Dr., Holbrook, AZ)
- **The World Famous Sultana Bar** (301 W. Rte. 66, Williams, AZ)
- **Roy's Motel & Café** (87520 National Trails Hwy., Amboy, CA)

WIGWAM MOTEL, HOLBROOK

505/476-5100, www.palaceofthegovernors.org), the oldest continuously occupied public building in the United States. It predates the White House by 200 years.

④ Toast a predinner cocktail on the rooftop of the historic **La Fonda** (100 E. San Francisco St., 800/523-5002, www.lafondasantafe.com, $240-475), which is a former Harvey House that opened in 1922. As soon as the sun sets on the horizon, the bar takes last call, so be ready to head out after your drink.

⑤ Dine at **Tomasita's** (500 S. Guadalupe St., 505/983-5721, www.tomasitas.com, 11am-9pm Mon.-Thurs., 11am-10pm Fri.-Sat., $10-20). The restaurant specializes in northern New Mexican food and has won awards for its green and red chile sauces. The bottle of honey on your table is for the complimentary *sopaipillas* that arrive post-meal.

DAY 9: Santa Fe to Taos, New Mexico

80 miles/129 kilometers | 2 hours

ROUTE OVERVIEW: US-84/US-285 • NM-76 • NM-75 • NM-68

① Head north on the **High Road to Taos.** On the way, have lunch at **Sugar Nymphs Bistro** (15046 NM-75, 505/587-0311, www.sugarnymphs.com, 11am-4pm Mon.-Thurs., 4pm-8pm Fri.-Sat., and 10:30am-3pm Sun. summer, call for winter hours, $10-18), near **Peñasco.** Order a fresh-as-can-be salad with locally sourced ingredients.

EARTHSHIP BIOTECTURE, TAOS

> Go north on US-84/US-285 for 23 miles (37 km) to its junction with NM-68 near Española. Turn north onto NM-68, then go east onto NM-76 for 30 miles (48 km). After driving through the towns of Chimayo, Cordova, Truchas, and Las Trampas, NM-76 dead-ends into NM-75. Turn right onto NM-75 and continue for 2 miles (3 km) to Peñasco.

② Complete the drive to **Taos** and tour **Earthship Biotecture** (2 Earthship Way, 575/751-0462, www.earthship.com, 9am-5pm daily June-Aug., 10am-4pm daily Sept.-May, $8-18), the world's largest off-the-grid community. The "earthships" are sculptural homes with curved walls made from compacted earth, tires, and cans in order to create efficient insulation.

> Follow NM-75 E for 6 miles (10 km), then go north on NM-518 through Talpa (16 mi/26 km) to NM-68, where you will turn right and continue for 4 miles (6 km) to Taos.

③ In Taos, eat dinner at **La Cueva** (135 Paseo del Pueblo Sur, 575/758-7001, www.lacuevacafe.com, 10am-9pm daily, $10-15), a vegetarian heaven with delicious enchiladas.

④ Stay in an earthship overnight; if they're fully booked, spend the night at the **El Pueblo Lodge** (412 Paseo del Pueblo Norte, 800/433-9612 www.elpueblolodge.com, $100-190) in Taos.

DAY 10: Taos to Albuquerque, New Mexico

175 miles/280 kilometers | 3-4 hours

ROUTE OVERVIEW: US-64 • US-285 • US-84 • NM-599 • I-25/Route 66

① Drive 150 miles (242 km) south to **Albuquerque** and have lunch at **Loyola's Family Restaurant** (4500 Central Ave. SE, 505/268-6478, www.loyolasfamilyrestaurant.com, 6am-2pm Tues.-Fri., 6am-1pm Sat., $6-10). If the dining room looks familiar, that's because commercials, movies, and scenes from TV shows like *Breaking Bad* have all been filmed here.

OLD TOWN ALBUQUERQUE

DAY 11: Albuquerque to Winslow, Arizona

310 miles/500 kilometers | 6 hours

ROUTE OVERVIEW: Route 66 • NM-23 • Route 66 • I-40 • Petrified Forest National Park Road • US-180 • I-40

> *Head north on US-64 out of Taos. Drive 28 miles (45 km) to Tres Piedras and take US-285 S. Follow this for 48 miles (77 km) to US-84 and turn left. Drive through Española (8 mi/13 km). Continue for 20 miles (32 km). Just north of Santa Fe, take NM-599/Veterans Memorial Hwy. south for 13 miles (21 km) to join I-25 S. From I-25, you'll follow Route 66 south to Albuquerque (50 mi/81 km).*

❷ Tour **Old Town Albuquerque** and its more than 150 shops and galleries, all in adobe buildings clustered along flower-lined brick paths. It's a great place to stretch your legs and enjoy a glimpse into the city's past.

❸ Before dinner, catch a movie at the historic **KiMo Theatre** (423 Central Ave. NW, 505/768-3544, www.kimo-tickets.com, 9am-4pm Tues.-Sat.). Built in the 1920s, it was the first theater to fuse art deco and American Indian architectural styles.

❹ Have dinner at the **Standard Diner** (320 Central Ave. SE, 505/243-1440, www.standarddiner.com, 8am-9pm Sun.-Thurs., 8am-9pm Fri.-Sat., $8-16), a hip and modern eatery in a refurbished 1938 Texaco station. Go for the bacon-wrapped meat loaf.

❺ Spend the night at the lovely **Los Poblanos Inn** (4803 Rio Grande Blvd., 505/344-9297, www.lospoblanos.com, $175-570) a 25-acre organic lavender farm and boutique hotel.

❶ Start the day with a visit to **Acoma Pueblo** (Pueblo of Acoma, 800/747-0181, www.acomaskycity.org, 9am-5pm daily, $25 adults, $17 children), west of Albuquerque. It's the oldest continuously inhabited settlement in North America, with a village of 250 structures set on a sandstone bluff.

> *Take Route 66 as it parallels I-40 for 50 miles (81 km). Turn left onto NM-23 and follow this for 12 miles (19 km) to reach Acoma Pueblo.*

❷ Stop in **Gallup** to shop the trading posts and explore the city's murals before crossing the border into Arizona. Gallup is one of the most significant trading centers in the Southwest and is known as the "Indian Capital of the World." Navajo Nation land wraps around the northwestern edge of Gallup; the Zuni Reservation sits just to the south.

> *Retrace your path back to Route 66/I-40 via NM-23 (12 mi/19 km). Head west on Route 66 for 85 miles (137 km) to reach Gallup.*

GALLUP, NEW MEXICO

❸ About 45 miles after crossing into Arizona, drive through the **Painted Desert** and **Petrified Forest National Park** (Exit 311 off I-40 in Navajo, 928/524-6228, www.nps.gov/pefo, 8am-5pm daily, hours vary seasonally, $25 per vehicle). See badlands, mesas, ancient petroglyphs, petrified wood, and fossils that date back 200 million years.

> Continue west from Gallup. On the eastern side of Arizona, much of the original Route 66 alignment from Lupton to Winslow is not continuous or intact; you will have to take I-40 to get around. It's 68 miles (109 km) from Gallup to the exit for Petrified Forest National Park. Follow the park road for 28 miles (45 km) and exit the park at US-180. Take US-180 west for 17 miles (27 km) to Holbrook to rejoin I-40. It's another 29 miles (47 km) west on I-40 to reach Winslow.

❹ Spend the evening at **La Posada Hotel & Gardens** (303 E. 2nd St., 928/289-4366, www.laposada.org, $129-169) in **Winslow.** Designed by famed architect Mary Colter as a Harvey House in 1929, the 11-acre Spanish Colonial hotel was said to be Colter's favorite work.

❺ For an upscale experience featuring Southwestern cuisine, dine in Winslow at the **Turquoise Room** (305 E. 2nd St., 928/289-2888, www.theturquoiseroom.net, 7am-2pm and 5pm-9pm daily, $10-42). Reservations are highly recommended, but if you decide to pop in on a whim, no worries: The bar offers a smaller version of the restaurant's award-winning menu.

DAY 12: Winslow to Kingman, Arizona

220 miles/355 kilometers | 4-5 hours

ROUTE OVERVIEW: I-40 • Townsend Winona Rd. • US-89 • I-40 • Old Route 66 • I-40 • AZ-64 • Historic Route 66 • I-40 • Route 66

❶ In the morning, drive to **Flagstaff.** Walk the picturesque streets of the historic downtown and get a bite to eat at **Miz Zips** (2924 E. Rte. 66, 928/526-0104, 6am-9pm Mon.-Sat., 7am-2pm Sun, $6-10, cash only). This is the place to get all of your comfort food needs met.

> Drive I-40 W from Winslow. In 40 miles (64 km), take exit 211, turn right and follow Townsend Winona Rd./County Rd. 394 for 10 miles (16 km). Keep west and turn left onto US-89 W; continue for 3 miles (5 km) into Flagstaff.

❷ Drive to **Williams.** Stop by **Pete's Gas Station Museum** (101 E. Rte. 66, 928/635-2675, 10am-8pm daily summer, call ahead, free). Not only is it a great photo op, but it's a fascinating museum. The restored gas station, with its bright orange paint, tall cylindrical gas pumps, and classic Ford sedan, offers an impressive collection of car culture memorabilia.

> From Flagstaff, drive west on I-40 BUS/Route 66 for 4 miles (6 km) to join I-40 W. Continue for 13 miles (21 km) and take exit 178 to Parks. Turn right and take the next left onto Old Route 66. Continue west on Old Route 66 for 6 miles

PAINTED DESERT

PETE'S GAS STATION MUSEUM, WILLIAMS

(10 km). Jump back onto I-40 W. Drive 6 miles (10 km) to exit 165. Turn left onto AZ-64, cross under I-40, and continue for 2.5 miles (4 km) to Williams on Historic Route 66.

❸ Head to **Seligman** for lunch at **Delgadillo's Snow Cap Drive-In** (301 W. Rte. 66, 928/422-3291, 10am-6pm daily spring-fall, $10). Make sure to end your meal with a soft-serve ice cream and don't leave without asking to meet owner Angel Delgadillo. His life stories inspired John Lasseter, the producer of the Pixar film *Cars.*

> *Go west on I-40, through Ash Fork, for 21 miles (34 km), then take exit 139. Turn right onto Route 66. From here, it's 18 miles (29 km) to Seligman.*

❹ Take the two-lane drive to Kingman, passing through **Peach Springs** and **Hackberry.** Peach Springs is the tribal headquarters for the Hualapai Indian Reservation. In the 1880s, the peach trees in the area led people to the water source that was eventually used to power steam locomotives.

> *Continue west on Route 66 for 87 miles (140 km) to Kingman.*

❺ Spend the night in **Kingman** at **El Trovatore Motel** (1440 E. Andy Devine Ave., 928/753-6520, www.eltrovatoremotel.com, $60). Built in 1937 as a service station, this Route 66-themed motel is one of the few pre-WWII Kingman motels still standing.

DAY 13: Kingman to Barstow, California

210 miles/340 kilometers | 4-5 hours

ROUTE OVERVIEW: Route 66 • Oatman Hwy. • AZ-95 • I-40 • National Trails Hwy./Route 66 • I-40

❶ As you leave Kingman, drive the 1926 alignment via **Oatman Highway,** a scenic winding road through the Black Mountains. Take your time—the road has hairpin turns, steep mountain grades, and tight switchbacks.

> *Leave Kingman via Route 66 (W. Andy Devine Ave.). You'll be driving next to I-40; keep an eye out for exit 44. Turn right onto Shinarump Rd. and cross under*

NEEDLES, CALIFORNIA

I-40. Turn left on Oatman Hwy. and drive for 29 miles (47 km) to Oatman.

❷ In **Oatman,** have lunch at **The Oatman Hotel & Restaurant** (181 Main St., 928/768-4408, 10:30am-6pm daily, $8-15), where the walls are papered with one-dollar bills, a reference to a time when miners started getting paid with paper rather than coins. The mines were so filthy that paper money got destroyed, so miners needed a safe place to stash their cash. They set up a system with the local bartender to put a dollar bill behind the bar with their name on it to cover their drinking tab.

❸ As you cross the border into California, gas up in **Needles** because you'll soon be driving through the desolate Mojave Desert. Visit the dusty desert town of **Amboy** to see **Roy's Motel and Café** (87520 National Trails Hwy.). Though the motel is closed, gas is available and the café sells soft drinks. But the real draw is the iconic Roy's signage—it features the mid-century "Googie" style, a type of futuristic architecture influenced by the post-WWII space age and car culture.

> *Go west from Oatman for 14 miles (23 km). Turn left onto AZ-95 and take it south for 9 miles (15 km) over the Arizona-California border to Needles. Take I-40 W for 36 miles (58 km) out of Needles to Fenner. From here, join the National Trails Hwy./Route 66 for 28 miles (45 km), crossing Kelbaker Rd. and continuing to Amboy. (Note: Route 66 from Needles to Barstow is notorious for road closures due to fierce desert storms and monsoons. For areas that are closed, I-40 is your alternative route.)*

ROUTE 66, CALIFORNIA

❹ In **Barstow,** spend a peaceful night at **Route 66 Motel** (195 W. Main St., 760/256-7866, www.route66motelbarstow.com $50-60). Guest rooms are simple, but the retro neon sign, vintage cars, and funky Route 66 memorabilia keeps things interesting.

> Continue west on National Trails Hwy./Route 66 for 28 miles (45 km). Here, join back up with I-40 and continue west for another 50 miles (81 km) to reach Barstow.

DAY 14: Barstow to Los Angeles, California

155 miles/250 kilometers | 4-5 hours

ROUTE OVERVIEW: Route 66/ National Trails Hwy. • I-15 • CA-210 • surface streets • I-10

❶ From Barstow, head to **Fair Oaks Pharmacy** (1526 Mission St., South Pasadena, 626/799-1414, www.fairoakspharmacy.net, 9am-9pm Mon.-Thurs., 9am-10pm Fri.-Sat., 10am-8pm Sun.) in **Pasadena,** a good place for a late breakfast or an early lunch. After your meal, browse the vintage goodies at this 1915 soda fountain.

> Take Route 66 south, following the National Trails Hwy. and paralleling I-15 to Victorville (30 mi/48 km). Take I-15 S for 34 miles (55 km). Take exit 115A for CA-210 W. Follow this for 38 miles (61 km) to Pasadena.

❷ Time your arrival into downtown **Los Angeles** before 3pm to avoid traffic. The **original Route 66 terminus** is at 7th and Broadway. There were actually three endings to Route 66 in Los Angeles. The second terminus extended farther west to Santa Monica at the intersection of Olympic and Lincoln Boulevards. Then, in 2009, the terminus was moved to the Santa Monica Pier.

> To follow the original Route 66 from Pasadena into Los Angeles, drive south on Fair Oaks Ave. to where it dead-ends at Huntington Dr. Turn right and drive 3 miles (5 km) on Huntington Dr. Continue on N. Mission Rd. for less than a mile, then take a right onto N. Broadway. In 1.5 miles (2.5 km), stay right (don't follow Spring St.) to continue on Broadway. Drive 2.5 miles (4 km) down Broadway to 7th St.

❸ Check into nearby **Hotel Figueroa** (939 S. Figueroa St., 866/723-9381, www.hotelfigueroa.com, $130-290) to stay in oh-so-cool DTLA for the night.

❹ Spend a few hours at LACMA, the **Los Angeles County Museum of Art** (5905 Wilshire Blvd., 323/857-6000, www.lacma.org, 11am-5pm Mon.-Tues. and Thurs., 11am-8pm Fri., 10am-7pm Sat.-Sun., $25 pp). It features some of the most compelling modern art exhibitions in the country, as well as offers art classes, film screenings, live music, and tours.

> Take I-10 W for 5 miles (8 km). Take exit 7B and turn right onto S. Fairfax Ave. Follow this for 2 miles (3 km) to reach the museum.

❺ In **Santa Monica,** greet the end of the Mother Road at the edge of the Pacific Ocean on the **Santa Monica Pier** (200 Santa Monica Pier, 310/458-8901, www.santamonicapier.org, daily, hours of businesses vary). Walk to the pier's edge over the ocean, stopping first to take a picture of the famous **"End of the Trail" sign.** Before you leave, visit the End of the Trail information booth to sign your name in the log of travelers who've successfully completed Route 66.

END OF THE TRAIL, SANTA MONICA

> *Retrace your path back to I-10 (2 mi/3 km). Continue west on I-10 for 8 miles (13 km) to reach Santa Monica Pier. Note: If you head to Santa Monica on a weekday, try not to leave after 2pm; the drive can take 1.5 hours during rush hour. It's a 15-mile (24-km) drive back to the hotel from Santa Monica.*

GETTING THERE

This road trip begins in Chicago, Illinois, and heads west for 2,570 miles (4,140 km) to Los Angeles, California.

AIR

There are two major airports in Chicago. **O'Hare International Airport** (ORD, 10000 W. O'Hare Ave., 800/832-6352, www.flychicago.com) hosts 47 airlines, including American, British Airways, JetBlue, and United. **Midway International Airport** (MDW, 5700 S. Cicero Ave., 773/838-0600, www.flychicago.com) is a smaller, more manageable airport hosting five airlines, including Delta and Southwest. O'Hare International Airport is 19 miles (31 km) from the start of Route 66; Midway is 12 miles (19 km) from the start.

TRAIN

Since part of Route 66 parallels the Santa Fe train route, **Amtrak** (800/872-7245, www.amtrak.com) offers easy access to the Mother Road. Chicago's **Union Station** (210 S. Canal St., 5am-1am daily) is the third-busiest rail station in the United States and is a major hub for Amtrak, with service to cities throughout the country.

Amtrak also offers a 14-day **Route 66 by Rail** tour (800/268-7252, www.amtrakvacations.com, fares vary) that starts in Chicago, with stops in St. Louis, Albuquerque, Williams, the Grand Canyon, and Los Angeles.

BUS

Greyhound Bus (www.greyhound.com) lines don't follow Route 66 exactly, but there are stations located along the way. The Greyhound station in **Chicago** (630 W. Harrison St., 312/408-5821) offers service to all major U.S. cities.

CAR

Midway International Airport is 12 miles (19 km) from the start of Route 66 in Chicago, a 30-minute drive via I-55. **O'Hare International Airport** is 19 miles (31 km) from the start of Route 66, a drive of 30-45 minutes via I-90.

GETTING BACK

A quicker, more direct route from Santa Monica back to **Chicago** runs 2,032 miles and totals approximately 30 hours of driving. Follow I-15, I-70, I-76, and I-80 through Nevada, Utah, Colorado, Nebraska, Iowa, and Illinois.

It's also possible to book a one-way fare home from one of the Los Angeles-area airports. The largest airport serving Los Angeles is **Los Angeles International Airport** (LAX, 1 World Way, Los Angeles, 855/463-5252, www.flylax.com). It offers direct flights from around the world, but with constant traffic congestion and long lines from check-in to security, you must arrive two hours ahead of departure time—three for international or holiday flights. To get from Santa Monica to LAX, it's a 10-mile (16-km) drive of less than an hour via CA-1.

For a less-crowded airport, seek flights to or from **Hollywood Burbank Airport** (BUR, 2627 N. Hollywood Way, Burbank, 818/840-8840, http://hollywoodburbankairport.com). To get from Santa Monica to BUR, it's a 30-mile (48-km) drive of about an hour via I-10, I-405, and I-5.

CONNECT WITH

- At Kansas City: **Oregon Trail** (PAGE 78)

- At Santa Fe: **Santa Fe, Taos, and the Enchanted Circle** (PAGE 304)

- At Los Angeles: **Southern California and Route 66 Loop** (PAGE 178), **Best of the Golden State** (PAGE 108), and **Pacific Coast Highway: California** (PAGE 124)

OREGON TRAIL

WHY GO: Pioneer history, wagon-wheel ruts, Old West towns, Kansas City barbecue, Native American culture, prairie views

TOTAL DISTANCE: 2,510 miles/ 4,040 kilometers

NUMBER OF DAYS: 20

SEASONS: Spring through fall

START: St. Louis, Missouri

END: Portland, Oregon

▶ SCOTTS BLUFF NATIONAL MONUMENT

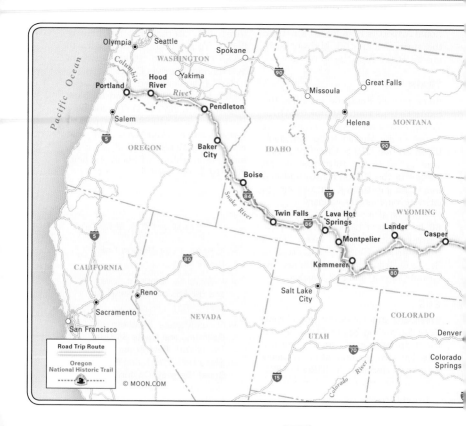

OREGON TRAIL

While the Oregon Trail isn't a literal sea-to-sea trip, it's one of the most historically significant routes in the United States. Before the Civil War, nearly 500,000 people journeyed westward on this path, crossing what is today six states: Missouri, Kansas, Nebraska, Wyoming, Idaho, and Oregon. Historians believe it to be the largest land migration ever; the pioneers' daring expedition doubled the size of the United States. As you travel the Trail—climbing mountains, dipping in hot springs, walking along wheel ruts—you'll understand where our country's plucky pioneer spirit was born.

DAY 1: St. Louis, Missouri

MORNING

❶ While not the initial starting point for Oregon Trail pioneers, **St. Louis**, Gateway to the West, is a fun and convenient place to begin. First, try a local specialty: the gooey butter cake at **Park Avenue Coffee** (417 N. 10th St., 314/231-5282, http://parkavenuecoffee.com, 7am-6pm Mon.-Sat., 7:30am-6pm Sun., $5). Park Avenue makes over 70 varieties, but most folks agree that Mom's Traditional is the best.

❷ Next, head to **Gateway Arch National Park** (11 N. 4th St., 314/655-1600, www.gatewayarch.com, 8am-10pm daily summer, 9am-6pm daily winter, free). Made of steel and concrete, the arch rises 630 feet, and is the tallest constructed monument in the country. The **Museum at the Gateway Arch** offers a perfect introduction to the history of the country's westward expansion. The **Tram Ride to the Top** ($16) gives you a bird's-eye view of the city.

AFTERNOON

❸ For lunch, walk over to **Sugarfire Smoke House** (605 Washington Ave., 314/394-1720, http://sugarfiresmokehouse.com, 11am-9pm daily, $13) to get your fix of St. Louis barbecue. Order at the counter, then drench your brisket or pulled pork in the range of sauces kept on each table.

❹ Visit to the fantastically fun **City Museum** (750 N. 16th St., 314/231-2489, www.citymuseum.org, 9am-5pm Mon.-Thurs., 9am-midnight Fri.-Sat., 11am-5pm Sun., $15), which is more like a giant playground than a museum. Housed in an old shoelace factory, this quirky attraction repurposes architectural and industrial materials from around the city, transforming them into slides, tunnels, and cave systems. Dress wisely: Long pants and closed-toe shoes.

EVENING

❺ Head out for a night of live music. At **BB's Jazz, Blues, and Soups** (700 N. Broadway, 314/436-5222, www.bbsjazzbluessoups.com, 6pm-3am Sun.-Fri., 6pm-1:30am Sat., $10 cover), you can listen to the blues and feast on Cajun and Creole food in a historic building that dates back to the mid-1800s.

GATEWAY ARCH NATIONAL PARK

Top 5 OREGON TRAIL

1. Savor the tasty burnt ends at **Arthur Bryant's Barbeque** in Kansas City (PAGE 82).

2. Learn about the Walla Walla, Cayuse, and Umatilla peoples at the **Tamástslikt Cultural Institute** (PAGE 98).

3. Follow the pioneers' arduous trek at the **National Historic Oregon Trail Interpretive Center** (PAGE 96).

4. Stand in the deep wagon-wheel ruts at **Guernsey Ruts** (PAGE 88).

5. Celebrate the conclusion of the Oregon Trail at the **End of the Trail Interpretive Center** (PAGE 100).

@CHICKERYSTRAVELS

DAY 2: St. Louis to Kansas City, Missouri

270 miles/430 kilometers | 4.5-5 hours

ROUTE OVERVIEW: I-70 • MO-41 • K Hwy. • I-70 • I-435 • US-71

① Today, you'll cover the entire state of Missouri. Stop at the midpoint of **Arrow Rock** for an early lunch at the historic **J. Huston Tavern** (305 Main St., 600/837-3200, www.hustontavern.com, 11am-2pm Sun. and Wed.-Thurs., 11am-2pm and 5pm-8pm Fri.-Sat. June-Sept., 11am-2pm and 4:30pm-8pm Fri.-Sat., 11am-2pm Sun. Mar.-May and Oct.-Dec., $13), the oldest continuously operating restaurant west of the Mississippi.

> *Leave St. Louis by heading west on I-70. In 151 miles (243 km), turn right on MO-41, then drive for 13 miles (21 km) to Arrow Rock.*

② Continue on to **Independence,** the official starting point of the Oregon Trail. Wander through **Independence Courthouse Square** (bordered by W. Maple Ave., N. Main St., W. Lexington Ave., and N. Liberty St.), where emigrants stocked up on supplies before setting off. Make sure to snap a photo with the **plaque** marking the start of the Oregon Trail on the west side of the **Historic Truman Courthouse** (112 W. Lexington Ave.).

> *Head back south on MO-41 for 6 miles (10 km), then turn right on K Hwy. In 3 miles (5 km), turn left to continue on K Hwy. for another 3 miles (5 km) to I-70. Continue west on I-70 to Noland Rd. (77 mi/124 km). Turn right and follow Noland to Independence (3 mi/5 km).*

NATIONAL FRONTIER TRAILS MUSEUM

③ Visit the **National Frontier Trails Museum** (318 W. Pacific Ave., 816/325-7575, www.ci.independence.mo.us, 9am-4:30pm Mon.-Sat., 12:30pm-4:30pm Sun., $6), which commemorates the three westward expansion trails that began in Independence: the Santa Fe, Oregon, and California Trails. You'll find covered wagons and artifacts like pioneer diaries.

④ Head south of Independence to see your first **wagon ruts** at **85th and Manchester** (7558 E. 85th St., Kansas City). Sometimes referred to as the **Wieduwilt Swales,** these are some of the state's best ruts, deep and easy to see, dramatically cutting into the ground.

> *Take I-435 S for 8 miles (13 km), exiting at 87th St. Follow 87th St. for 1 mile (1.6 km), then turn left onto Oldham Rd. In less than a mile, turn right onto E. 85th St. to reach the wagon ruts.*

⑤ Loop north to **Kansas City** proper, where you can eat at **Arthur Bryant's Barbeque** (1727 Brooklyn Ave., 816/231-1123, www.arthurbryantsbbq.com, 10am-9pm Mon.-Sat., 11am-8pm Sun., $11), the legacy of one of the most popular pit masters in history. Spend the night in the historic neighborhood of **Westport.**

> *Head west and get onto Oldham Rd. Follow this northwest for 2 miles (3 km), then continue on E. Gregory Blvd. for another 2 miles (3 km). Turn right onto US-71 N. Follow this for 5 miles (8 km) to the exit for 29th St./27th St. and central Kansas City.*

INDEPENDENCE SQUARE COURTHOUSE

DAY 3: Kansas City, Missouri

MORNING AND AFTERNOON

❶ Explore Westport, the oldest neighborhood in Kansas City and another jumping-off point for the Oregon Trail. Then tour the sunken cargo of an 1856 riverboat at the **Arabia Steamboat Museum** (400 Grand Blvd., 816/471-1856, www.1856.com, 10am-5pm Mon.-Sat., noon-5pm Sun., $14.50). Visits start with a guided tour and an introductory video, then you're allowed to tour the display rooms freely.

❷ In the afternoon, head to **The Nelson-Atkins Museum of Art** (4525 Oak St., 855/830-1482, www.nelson-atkins.org, 10am-5pm Wed., 10am-9pm Thurs.-Fri., 10am-5pm Sat.-Sun., free). Admire the giant badminton birdie sculpture outside, then pop inside to enjoy European paintings and Imperial Chinese art.

EVENING

❸ Dinner is back in Westport with modern Mexican cuisine at **Port Fonda** (1414 Pennsylvania Ave., 816/216-6462, www.portfonda.com, 11am-10pm Mon.-Wed., 11am-1am Thurs.-Fri., 9am-1am Sat., 9am-10pm Sun., $12). Vegetarians will find plenty to love, like the jackfruit al pastor, and omnivores will love the barbacoa and drool-worthy carnitas.

ARABIA STEAMBOAT MUSEUM

KEY RESERVATIONS

- At **Gateway Arch National Park** in St. Louis, go online to buy tickets for the tram ride to the top of the Arch **a few days** ahead of your arrival.

- On weekends during the summer, book a table **two weeks** in advance at **J. Huston Tavern** in Arrow Rock, Missouri.

- Reservations are recommended for the cocktail bar **SoT** in Kansas City, Missouri.

- Make reservations **a week** early for the tour of **Carissa Mine** in South Pass City, Wyoming.

- Reservations are required for the **Pendleton Underground Tour** in Pendleton, Oregon.

---

❹ Find your new favorite cocktail at **SoT** (1521 Grand Blvd., 816/842-8482, www.sotkc.com, 4pm-11pm Tues.-Wed., 4pm-1:30am Thurs.-Sat.), which uses unusual ingredients in creative ways.

DAY 4: Kansas City to Beatrice, Nebraska

220 miles/350 kilometers | 4-4.5 hours

ROUTE OVERVIEW: I-70 • KS-99 • KS-9 • US-77 • US-36 • KS-148 • NE-112 • NE-8 • US-77

❶ Get an early start today. Cross the border into Kansas and stop in **Topeka,** the state capital, to visit the **Kansas Museum of History** (6425 SW 6th Ave., 785/272-8681, www.kshs.org, 9am-5pm Tues.-Sat., 1pm-5pm Sun., $10). Its informative exhibits include displays on the Oregon Trail. The large museum houses a wagon, biplane, soda fountain, log cabin, and even an entire train.

> Use I-670 W to connect to I-70 (2 mi/3 km). Drive west on I-70 to Topeka (60 mi/97 km).

❷ Back on the trail, find **Alcove Spring** (off US-77, E. River Rd., 785/363-7721,

PONY EXPRESS STATUE, MARYSVILLE

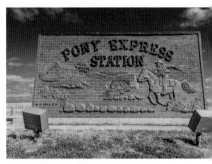

HOLLENBERG PONY EXPRESS STATION

dawn-dusk daily, free), a lush green spot that was a favorite of the pioneers. Stretch your legs with a short hike (0.25 mi/0.4 km) that takes you by dramatic wagon swales.

> *Continue west on I-70 to KS-99 (35 mi/56 km). Turn right on KS-99 to KS-9 (46 mi/74 km). Make a left on KS-9 and drive 12 miles (19 km) to US-77. Turn right on US-77 and in 3 miles (5 km) follow signs to Alcove Spring.*

❸ Have lunch at the **Wagon Wheel Café** (703 Broadway St., 785/562-3784, www.wagonwheelks.com, 6am-9pm Mon.-Sat., $13), the best place to eat in **Marysville.**

> *Make your way back to US-77 (3 mi/5 km), turn left, and follow US-77 to Wagon Wheel Café (4 mi/6 km).*

⏱ WITH LESS TIME

KANSAS CITY, MISSOURI, TO KEMMERER, WYOMING

7 days; 1,246 miles/2,005 kilometers

Fly into Kansas City and then venture to Independence, the official start of the Oregon Trail. From here, spend **one day** exploring Kansas City before taking the next **six days** to drive from Missouri through Kansas, Nebraska, and Wyoming. You'll see a Pony Express station, Buffalo Bill Cody's mansion, and original wagon wheel ruts, including the impressive ones at Guernsey. This route concludes in Kemmerer, at which point you can drive back to Kansas City or fly home from Salt Lake City.

---

❹ Head west to **Hanover** to visit the **Hollenberg Pony Express Station** (2889 23rd Rd., 785/337-2635, 10am-5pm daily Mar.-Oct., $6). Originally built in 1857, this is the only Pony Express barn still in its original location along the route.

> *Go west on US-36 to KS-148 (11 mi/18 km). Turn right and drive KS-148 for 4 miles (6 km) to KS-234. Turn left and stay on KS-234 to Hanover.*

❺ Drive north into Nebraska and end your day in **Beatrice** with dinner at **The Black Crow** (405 Court St., 402/228-7200, www.blackcrowrestaurant.com, 11:30am-2pm and 5:30pm-10pm Tues.-Sun., $20). Order oysters Rockefeller or roast duck, and savor a glass of wine from the surprisingly robust list. Stay at a hotel in town.

> *Follow KS-234 for less than a mile back to KS-148. Turn left and drive KS-148 for 8 miles (13 km) to where it turns into NE-112. Continue north on NE-112 and follow it to NE-8 (3 mi/5 km). Turn right on NE-8. Drive 7 miles (11 km) to US-77. Turn left and take US-77 to Beatrice (9 mi/14 km).*

DAY 5: Beatrice to Kearney, Nebraska

180 miles/290 kilometers | 3-3.5 hours

ROUTE OVERVIEW: US-136 • NE-4 • surface streets • US-136 • surface streets • NE-15 • US-136 • US-81 • NE-74 • NE-10 • NE-50A • NE-44

❶ Learn about the Homestead Act, a primary motivator for the movement west, at the **Homestead National Monument of America** (8523 W. NE-4,

402/223-3514, www.nps.gov/home, 8:30am-5pm Mon.-Fri., 9am-5pm Sat.-Sun., free). The monument is spread out on 150 acres of prairie grasses and woodlands, and houses the Heritage Center, which features exhibits on the impact of homesteading. Don't skip the thoughtful film *Land of Dreams—Homesteading America,* which gives voice to Native American nations who were displaced by the Homesteading Act.

> Take US-136 W for 2 miles (3 km) to NE-4. Turn right on NE-4. Drive 4 miles (6 km) northwest to Homestead National Monument of America.

② Hike along the wagon ruts at **Rock Creek Station Historical Park** (57426 710th Rd., Fairbury, 402/729-5777, http://outdoornebraska.gov, 9am-5pm daily, $6-8 per vehicle). Get a map for a self-guided tour from the **visitors center** (9am-5pm daily May-Sept., 1pm-5pm Sat.-Sun. Apr. and Oct., $2 adults, $1 children 3-13), then hike your way up the hill to wander past some covered wagons and along the ruts.

> Head west on NE-4 to 117th Rd. (3 mi/5 km). Turn left on 117th Rd. and drive 6 miles (10 km) to US-136. Turn left and follow US-136 to 573rd Ave. (12 mi/19 km). Take a left and drive south for 5 miles (8 km) to 710th Rd. Turn left and follow signs to Rock Creek Station Historical Park (1 mi/1.6 km).

③ From here, the route winds along rural highways through the Nebraska farmland. Once in **Kearney,** eat award-winning pizza for lunch at **The Flippin Sweet** (3905 2nd Ave., 308/455-4222, http://theflippinsweet.squarespace.com, 11am-9pm Mon.-Thurs., 11am-10pm Fri.-Sat., 11am-8pm Sun., $13).

> Return to 573rd Ave., turn right, drive 1 mile (1.6 km) to 711th Rd., turn left, and follow it for 5 miles (8 km) to NE-15. Go right on NE-15. At US-136, turn left and drive for 21 miles (34 km). At US-81, turn right and follow US-81 N to NE-74 (20 mi/32 km). Go left and follow NE-74 for 75 miles (121 km). Follow signs for NE-10 and go north for 10 miles (16 km) to NE-50A. Turn left. Drive 7 miles (11 km) to NE-44. Turn right on NE-44 and take it into Kearney (4 mi/6 km).

THE ARCHWAY

④ Head to **The Archway** (I-80 Exit 275, 308/237-1000, http://archway.org, 9am-6pm Mon.-Sat., noon-6pm Sun. Memorial Day-Labor Day, 9am-5pm Mon.-Sat., noon-5pm Sun. Labor Day-Memorial Day, $12 adults, $6 ages 6-12, free for children 5 and under) to learn about the Great Platte River Road and the many journeys along it, including the Oregon Trail. As you walk through The Archway, dedicated rooms present stories of the people who traveled this corridor.

⑤ Get out on the **Kearney Water Trail** (Yanney Park to Central Ave.) with a late-afternoon paddle. This 2.3-mile (3.7 km) route flows to the North Platte River and takes about 45 minutes. **Kearney Paddle Sports** (535 M Ave., 308/708-0792, Thurs.-Sun. Apr.-Sept.) will rent you a kayak, or you can join one of their tours. Have dinner and settle in for the night in town.

DAY 6: Kearney to Scottsbluff and Gering, Nebraska

280 miles/450 kilometers | 4.5-5 hours

ROUTE OVERVIEW: I-80 • US-83 • I-80 • US-26/NE-61 • US-26 • NE-92

① Head west to **North Platte** to wander the former ranch of famous Western personality Buffalo Bill Cody. The **Buffalo Bill Ranch State Historical Park** (2921 Scouts Rest Ranch Rd., 308/535-8035, www.outdoornebraska.gov,

FRONT STREET, OGALLALA

CHIMNEY ROCK

9am-5pm daily Memorial Day-Labor Day, 10am-4pm Sept. and Apr.-Memorial Day, $2 mansion tour, $8 state park entry) is where Cody rested when he wasn't touring with his Wild West Show. You can explore Cody's house, built in 1886 at the height of the show's popularity.

> Take 2nd Ave. south to I-80 (2 mi/3 km). Turn right and drive I-80 to US-83 N (95 mi/153 km). Turn right and follow US-83 into North Platte (3 mi/5 km).

❷ Continue to the cowboy town of **Ogallala,** where you can stretch your legs on **Historic Front Street** (519 E. 1st St./US-30, 308/284-6000, www.ogallalafrontstreet.com, 11am-8pm Mon.-Wed., 6:30am-9pm Thurs.-Sat., 8am-2pm Sun.). It's not a true "street," but instead a kitschy block-long replica town that evokes the Wild West. Behind the building facades are a fun museum (free), jail, general store, and barber shop.

> Return to I-80 via US-83, then continue west for 50 miles (80 km). Take the exit for US-26/NE-61, driving north 1 mile (1.6 km) to Ogallala.

❸ Drive northwest to **Ash Hollow State Historical Park** (4055 US-26, Lewellen, 308/778-5651, www.outdoornebraska. gov, 8am-sunset daily, $5). When pioneers came to this place, it would have had some of the first trees they'd seen in 100 miles (161 km), as well as fresh spring water. On the **Windlass Hill Trail** (0.5 mi/0.8 km loop, 30 minutes, moderate), you can see deep wagon ruts;

this was where travelers would have descended into the surrounding valley. Find the trailhead at the bottom of Windlass Hill, near a sod house and a covered wagon exhibit.

> Head north for 3 miles (5 km) on US-26/NE-61. Turn left on NE-61; in 2 miles (3 km) it turns into US-26. Continue on US-26 for 22 miles (35 km) to Ash Hollow State Historical Park.

❹ Back on the road, you'll drive by the pioneer landmark **Chimney Rock.** The 325-foot spire stands tall over the prairie, so it's no surprise that it was recorded in hundreds of pioneer diaries. If you've played the Oregon Trail computer game, you'll recognize Chimney Rock as a wagon party stop. Today, you can only see Chimney Rock from a distance; in order to preserve it, there is no access to its base. If you'd like to get slightly closer, you can get a good view from the **Chimney Rock Visitor Center** (9822 County Rd. 75, www. nps.gov, 9am-5pm daily, $3), which has telescopes pointed right at the rock.

> Continue for another 74 miles (119 km) on US-26 to Chimney Rock.

❺ Continue to the sister towns of **Scottsbluff** and **Gering,** where you can eat dinner and sleep at the **Barn Anew Bed and Breakfast** (170549 County Road L, Mitchell, 308/632-8647, www. barnanew.com, $140-150), a renovated homestead.

> Turn left onto NE-92 and drive west for 17 miles (27 km) to the towns of Scottsbluff and Gering.

DAY 7: Scottsbluff and Gering, Nebraska

15 miles/24 kilometers | 30 minutes

ROUTE OVERVIEW: Surface streets

1 In Gering, fortify yourself with breakfast from **The Mixing Bowl** (1945 10th St., 308/633-1288, www.mixingbowlgering.com, 7am-3pm Mon. and Wed.-Sat., 9am-2pm Sun., $12). Choose from a breakfast burrito, Swedish pancakes, and a chile relleno grilled cheese.

2 Learn more about prairie history at the **Legacy of the Plains Museum** (2930 Old Oregon Trail, Gering, 308/436-1989, www.legacyoftheplains. org, $10). At this museum on a working farm, the highlights are historical farm implements, but it also displays items like a bull boat from the Sioux, a tub-shaped boat lined with furs that once floated down the Platte River.

> *Take 9th St./Old Hwy. 92 west for 1.5 miles (2.5 km) to Legacy of the Plains Museum.*

3 Spend a few hours at the nearby **Scotts Bluff National Monument** (308/436-9700, www.nps.gov/scbl, 8am-6pm daily Memorial Day-Labor Day, 8am-4:30pm daily Labor Day-Memorial Day, $5 per vehicle). The highway drives straight through Mitchell Pass, where wagons found a route through the rocky terrain to the west, on its way through the monument. Stop at the **Oregon Trail Museum and Visitor Center** (Old Oregon Trail) to see a collection of artifacts from Oregon Trail pioneers on display such as weapons, diaries, and children's toys. From the visitors center, there are several trails you can take to walk in the footsteps of Oregon Trail pioneers and gain views from the summit of Scotts Bluff.

> *Continue west on Old Hwy. 92/Old Oregon Trail for 1 mile (1.6 km) to the Oregon Trail Museum and Visitor Center and Scotts Bluff National Monument.*

4 Head back into town and order a taster flight from **Flyover Brewing Company** (1824 Broadway, Scottsbluff, 308/575-0335, www.flyoverbrewingcompany.com, 3pm-11pm Wed.-Fri., 11am-11pm Sat.-Sun., $13), the Nebraska Panhandle's only craft brewery, where you can also feast on a tasty wood-fired pizza.

> *Return to town via the same route (2 mi/3 km). At Five Rocks Rd., turn left. Stay on Five Rocks for 2 miles (3 km) to Beltline Hwy. W. Turn right, then make a left on Avenue B. Stay on Avenue B for 1 mile (1.6 km) to 19th St. Turn right and follow 19th Street to Flyover Brewing Company. It's a straight shot west on W. 20th St./NE-92 to return to your B&B.*

DAY 8: Scottsbluff to Casper, Wyoming

185 miles/300 kilometers | 3.5-4 hours

ROUTE OVERVIEW: US-26 • I-25

1 Shortly after crossing the border into Wyoming, stop at **Fort Laramie** (965 Gray Rocks Rd., 307/837-2221, www.nps.gov/fola, sunrise-sunset daily, free), previously a trading post on the Oregon Trail. Today you can wander the fort's structures and visit a museum. The Commissary Storehouse—follow signs up the road from the parking lot—serves as the headquarters and **visitors center** (307/837-2221, 9am-7pm daily Memorial Day-Labor Day, 8am-4:30pm daily Labor Day-Memorial Day).

SCOTTS BLUFF NATIONAL MONUMENT

GUERNSEY RUTS

> From Scottsbluff, go north on Avenue B to US-26 (1 mi/1.6 km). Turn left on US-26 and drive west to Fort Laramie (51 mi/82 km).

❷ Next, step into some of the most dramatic wagon ruts along the trail at **Guernsey Ruts** (off S. Guernsey Rd., no phone, dawn-dusk daily, free). The ruts are up to four feet deep in places. To see them, follow the trail from the parking lot.

> Continue west on US-26 to Guernsey (13 mi/21 km). Make a left on Wyoming Ave., which turns into Guernsey Rd.; after 1 mile (1.6 km), turn right to reach the Guernsey Ruts.

❸ A short drive east along Guernsey Road will let you glimpse pioneer signatures at **Register Cliff Historic Site** (off S. Guernsey Rd., no phone, http://wyoparks.wyo.gov, dawn-dusk daily, free). Hundreds of emigrants carved their names into the sandstone. As you approach the cliff you'll see numerous names; most of these are actually modern graffiti. Turn left and head to the cliff's east end to find a section protected by a fence. These are the historical signatures. Some of the earliest date to the 1820s, when fur trappers passed through.

> Turn right on Guernsey Rd. to get to Register Cliff Historic Site (2 mi/3 km).

❹ Just past Guernsey, in **Casper**, visit the **National Historic Trails Interpretive Center** (1501 N. Poplar St., 307/261-7700, www.blm.gov, 8am-5pm Tues.-Sun. late May-early Sept., 9am-4:30pm Tues.-Sat. early Sept.-late

May, free), which focuses on the historic trails that once passed through town. The exhibits are well designed and interactive.

> Follow Guernsey Rd. back to US-26 (3 mi/5 km). Turn left and go west on US-26 for 15 miles (24 km) to I-25. Head north on I-25 to Casper (96 mi/154 km).

❺ Take an epic covered-wagon ride with **Historic Trails West** (307/266-4868, www.historictrailswest.com, from $65). The tour takes you away from town, so you get a good sense of what traveling might have felt like for the pioneers. Owner Morris Carter has actually taken a wagon on a six-month journey along the Oregon Trail, and has a keen understanding of the struggles of pioneers. You'll meet your wagon party at the parking lot of the National Historic Trails museum. From there, you'll follow in your car to the tour starting point, about 10 minutes away. You'll be tuckered out after your arduous journey, so find a hotel in Casper and get a good night's rest.

DAY 9: Casper to Lander, Wyoming

155 miles/250 kilometers | 2.5-3 hours

ROUTE OVERVIEW: WY-220 • US-287

❶ Travel southwest to see **Independence Rock State Historic Site** (off WY-220, no phone, http://wyoparks.wyo.gov, 24 hours daily, free), a major landmark

INDEPENDENCE ROCK STATE HISTORIC SITE

MORMON HANDCART HISTORIC SITE AT MARTIN'S COVE

for pioneers. The monolith stands 136 feet above the ground, and measures about a mile around. If your wagon train made it to Independence Rock by July 4, your group was likely to make it to Oregon before any risk of winter snow. Follow the trail around the rock, see if you can spot some of the pioneer signatures carved into the stone, and, if you're brave, climb to the top.

> *Use 1st St. to get to Poplar St., then head south on Poplar to WY-220 (1 mi/1.6 km). Take WY-220 southwest for 52 miles (84 km). At Oregon Trail Rd., turn left and follow signs to Independence Rock State Historic Site (1 mi/1.6 km).*

❷ Visit the **Mormon Handcart Historic Site at Martin's Cove** (47600 W. US-200, 307/328-2953, 9am-9pm daily Memorial Day-Labor Day, 9am-7pm daily Labor Day-Oct., 9am-4pm daily Nov.-Memorial Day, free). Here, learn how Mormons traveled the trail while marveling at the rugged landscape. While the distance to Utah was shorter, the going was arguably tougher for emigrants, about 10 percent of whom pulled their belongings on handcarts. Try out one of the center's handcarts to get a feel for what it was like. Bring a picnic lunch, as there's not much to eat along the way.

> *Return to WY-220, turn left, and follow WY-220 to US-287 (19 mi/31 km). Turn right and follow US-287 north and west to Mormon Handcart Historic Site (41 mi/66 km).*

❸ Continue west to the pretty, outdoorsy town of **Lander,** where the Wind River Mountains provide stunning scenery as you creep closer to the Continental Divide. Eat at the casual

Gannet Grill (126 Main St., 307/332-8228, www.landerbar.com, 11am-9pm daily, $12), the best place in town for burgers.

> *Continue north on US-287 into Lander (39 mi/63 km).*

❹ Save room for a chokecherry shake at **The Scream Shack** (126 Main St., 307/332-8228, www.landerbar.com/scream-shack.html, 11am-10pm daily June-Aug., $4), a ramshackle structure built from recycled materials.

❺ Stay at **The Inn at Lander** (260 Grandview Dr., 307/332-2847, www.innatlander.com, $93-158), just a 10-minute walk from downtown.

DAY 10: Lander to Kemmerer, Wyoming

230 miles/370 kilometers | 3.5-4 hours

ROUTE OVERVIEW: US-287 • WY-28 • WY-372 • I-80 • WY-414 • WY-412 • US-189

❶ Grab breakfast at **The Middle Fork** (351 Main St., 307/335-5035, www.themiddleforklander.com, 7am-2pm Mon.-Sat., 9am-2pm Sun., $10). Delicious options include blueberry corn bread French toast and a perfectly crispy Monte Cristo.

❷ Your first stop today is the mining ghost town of **South Pass City,** population 4. Check out the historic buildings and tour the old **Carissa Mine**

CARISSA MINE

(125 South Pass Main St., 307/332-3684, www.southpasscity.com, 2pm Thurs.-Sun., $5). On this two-hour tour, you'll learn how gold is separated from ore, see processing facilities, and enter the old shaft.

> Follow US-287 S to WY-28 (9 mi/14 km). Continue straight onto WY-28 to South Pass City Rd. (23 mi/37 km). Turn left and follow this to South Pass City (2 mi/3 km).

❸ Continue down the highway and you'll soon join the pioneers in

▶ Playlist

OREGON TRAIL

SONGS

- **"Oregon Trail" by Woody Guthrie:** This folk song, which Guthrie penned for the *Columbia River Ballads* album, was inspired by his 1940s trip to Oregon and Washington. The famous folk singer traveled the Pacific Northwest as part of a never-made documentary about the construction of public works dams.

AUDIOBOOKS

- ***The Oregon Trail: A New American Journey* by Rinker Buck:** An audiobook is a commitment, to be sure. But on this 20-day trip, you'll have the time. This book, narrated energetically by the author himself, tells the riveting tale of walking in the footsteps—or rather, riding in the wagon-wheel ruts—of the Oregon Trail pioneers when Buck and his brother traveled it in a covered wagon with a team of mules.

crossing the Continental Divide at the surprisingly gentle **South Pass.** Stop for lunch and a sweet treat at **Farson Mercantile** (4048 US-191, Farson, 307/273-9511, www.farsonmerc.com, 10am-9pm daily summer, 10am-7pm daily fall-spring, $6), famous for its giant scoops of ice cream.

> Return to WY-28, turn left, and drive to Farson Mercantile (43 mi/69 km).

❹ Keep on trucking to **Fort Bridger State Historic Site** (37000 I-80BL, http://wyoparks.wyo.gov, visitors center 9am-5pm daily May-Sept., 9am-5pm Fri.-Sun. Oct.-Apr., grounds dawn-dusk daily, $3-5 adults, free for children under 18), an old supply stop and military fort. Structures include a schoolhouse, an ice house, a Pony Express barn, and a carriage house.

> Continue southwest on WY-28 to WY-372 (29 mi/47 km). Turn left on WY-372 and drive 27 miles (43 km) to I-80. Head west on I-80 to Fort Bridger State Historic Site (48 mi/77 km).

❺ Loop up north to **Kemmerer,** and grab dinner at **Scroungy Moose Pizza** (179 WY-233, 307/877-4233, 4pm-9pm Mon.-Sat., $16). You can't go wrong with the Frontier Bar pie, which features pepperoni and Italian sausage. It's take-out only, so call ahead to avoid a wait.

> Follow WY-414 N for 3 miles (5 km) to WY-412. Continue north on WY-412 to US-189 (22 mi/35 km). Turn right to drive north on US-189 to Kemmerer (15 mi/24 km).

FORT BRIDGER STATE HISTORIC SITE

DAY 11: Kemmerer to Montpelier, Idaho

75 miles/121 kilometers | 1.5 hours

ROUTE OVERVIEW: US-30

❶ On your way west out of Wyoming, stop at **Fossil Butte National Monument** (www.nps.gov/fobu) to check out the impressive fish fossils. Start at the **visitors center** (864 Chicken Creek Rd., 307/877-4455, 8am-6pm daily late May-early Sept., shorter hours early Sept.-late May, free), which has a **gallery and interpretive space** showcasing over 300 fossils discovered in the buttes; many are casts, but there are plenty of real ones, too.

> Go west on US-30 to Fossil Butte National Monument (10 mi/16 km).

❷ As you head west into Idaho, you'll end up in **Montpelier** at the **National Oregon/California Trail Center** (320 N. 4th St., 208/847-3800, http://oregontrailcenter.org, 9am-5pm Mon.-Sat., 9am-3pm Sun. May 15-Sept., $12 adults, $9 ages 8-17, $5 ages 4-7, free for children under 4). Here, take a simulated wagon ride and enjoy a living history tour. The six-month trip will be condensed into an hour, but you'll come away with a sense of the daily life of pioneers.

> Continue west on US-30 out of Wyoming into Montpelier, Idaho (63 mi/101 km).

❸ Enjoy dinner at the 24-hour favorite **Ranch Hand Trail Stop** (23200 US-30, 208/847-1180, www.ranchhandtrailstop.com, 24 hours daily, $9), a greasy-spoon diner at a truck stop. But don't be deterred—the food here is homemade and delicious.

DAY 12: Montpelier to Lava Hot Springs, Idaho

55 miles/89 kilometers | 1 hour

ROUTE OVERVIEW: US-30

❶ Today is short on driving and big on fun. Stop in the city of **Soda Springs,** where you can drink the same water as the pioneers. Dip a cup into the springs and see how you like the mineral taste (it's perfectly safe). Check out the world's only "captive geyser" in **Geyser Park** (39 W. 1st St.). The city controls the geyser by letting it off once an hour, on the hour, for 4-5 minutes. It reaches a height of 100 feet.

> Drive north on US-30 from Montpelier to Soda Springs (30 mi/48 km).

❷ Continue west to **Lava Hot Springs** (430 E. Main St., 208/776-5221, http://lavahotsprings.com, 8am-11pm daily May-Sept., 9am-10pm Sun.-Thurs., 9am-11pm Fri.-Sat. Oct.-Apr., $6-8). This is where Oregon Trail travelers enjoyed a hot bath—and you can take a soak here, too. The pools range

EXHIBIT AT FOSSIL BUTTE NATIONAL MONUMENT

GEYSER PARK, SODA SPRINGS

Best OVERNIGHT STOPS

MISSOURI

- **St. Louis:** This lively Midwestern city makes an accessible and lively starting point with its delicious food, jazzy tunes, unique museums, and luxurious hotels.
- **Kansas City:** The biggest city in Missouri is located conveniently near the official start of the Oregon Trail in Independence. Enjoy fantastic barbecue, impressive museums, historical neighborhoods, and a thrilling nightlife.

KANSAS

- **Topeka:** Trail ruts, a museum focused on the state's history, and a monument to desegregation are all great reasons to stop for a night in Kansas's capital city.
- **Marysville:** This charming small town near Kansas's border with Nebraska was also on the Pony Express Trail and offers excellent (and free!) RV camping in its downtown city park.

NEBRASKA

- **Kearney:** Kearney is a major stop on I-80. Its hotels are mostly chains, but there are a couple of good campgrounds and several food options to satisfy your hunger.
- **Scottsbluff and Gering:** These neighboring towns sit right beside Scotts Bluff National Monument, where Oregon Trail pioneers navigated tricky terrain.

WYOMING

- **Casper:** The city of Casper offers plenty of history and fun to last a few days.

- **Lander:** A short detour from the route, this outdoorsy town near the Wind River Mountains is a nice place to spend a night, with excellent food and good camping and lodging options.

IDAHO

- **Lava Hot Springs:** Soak your troubles away in this small town that offered respite to emigrants and today features a hot springs complex, eateries, and hotels.
- **Twin Falls:** With a historic downtown offering good restaurants and located near sights like Shoshone Falls, this is an ideal stopping point before Boise.
- **Boise:** The capital and biggest city in Idaho, Boise is a vibrant place full of restaurants, nightlife, outdoor activities, and lodgings.

OREGON

- **Baker City:** A Victorian city in the high desert, Baker City has one of the best hotels on the route, a thriving food scene, and a fantastic trail interpretive center.
- **Pendleton:** Steeped in the Old West, this city embraces its wild cowboy heritage.
- **The Dalles:** The place where East Oregon meets the Columbia River Gorge, this is a growing destination with dozens of wineries and hiking trails.
- **Hood River:** This hot spot of activity has water recreation, great hotels, and too many restaurants to choose from.
- **Portland:** At the end of the trail, Portland offers boutique hotels, killer food, and live music.

in temperature 102-112°F (39-44°C), have ledges to sit on, and umbrellas shading them. Towels and lockers are available to rent, and there are dressing rooms and showers.

> Follow US-30 W to Lava Hot Springs (22 mi/35 km).

❸ Eat at the **Riverwalk Thai Restaurant** (695 E. Main St., 208/776-5872, 1pm-9pm Tues.-Sun., $13), which is set in an old gas station. It's a busy, family-run place with a familiar menu of curries, noodles, and fried rice.

❹ Stay at **Aura Soma Lava** (196 E. Main St., 208/776-5800, www.aurasomalava.com, $85-250) downtown. A private outdoor mineral hot spring for hotel guests is a block away.

DAY 13: Lava Hot Springs to Twin Falls, Idaho

170 miles/275 kilometers | 3-3.5 hours

ROUTE OVERVIEW: US-30 • I-15 • I-86/US-30 • I-84 • ID-50 • US-30

❶ Head west out of town, then north. In **Pocatello,** learn how to do laundry pioneer-style at the quirky **Museum of Clean** (711 S. 2nd Ave., 208/236-6906, www.museumofclean.com, 10am-5pm Tues.-Sat., $6). The whole place, as you might expect, is spotless.

> Leave Lava Hot Springs by going west on US-30 for 12 miles (19 km), then merge north onto I-15 to Pocatello (22 mi/35 km).

❷ Nearby, visit the **Bannock County Historical Museum** (3000 Ave. of the Chiefs, 208/233-0434, www.bchm-id.org, 10am-6pm Mon.-Sat., 1pm-5pm Sun. Memorial Day-Labor Day, 10am-4pm Tues.-Sat. Labor Day-Memorial Day, $5), where the highlight is the **Fort Hall Replica,** a re-creation of what was once a major stop on the Oregon Trail. In the early days, it was also the point at which parties abandoned their wagons and continued on foot. Inside the log doors are replica living quarters, clothing, pioneer wagons, blacksmith tools, old recipes, letters, and maps.

❸ North of town is the **Shoshone-Bannock Fort Hall Reservation,** where the original fort once stood. Though it's no longer there, the **Shoshone-Bannock Tribal Museum** (I-15 exit 80, Simplot Rd., 208/327-9791, www2.sbtribes.com, 9:30am-5pm Mon-Fri. Sept.-May, 9:30am-5pm daily June-Aug., $3.50) is a worthwhile stop. On a trail that's dominated by stories from white settlers, this museum is an honest look from an indigenous perspective, offering insight into how ancestors of the Shoshone-Bannock peoples moved across the land, what they hunted, and with whom they traded. Exhibits showcasing the beautiful craft- and artwork for which Shoshone artists are internationally renowned are also on display, including excellent beadwork and porcupine quill work.

> Return to I-15 (2 mi/3 km) and drive north to the Shoshone-Bannock Fort Hall Reservation (10 mi/16 km).

SHOSHONE-BANNOCK FORT HALL RESERVATION

❹ Continue west to **Twin Falls**. Enjoy fine dining and Snake River views at **Elevation 486** (195 River Vista Pl., 208/737-0486, http://elevation486.com, 11am-close daily, $20). The perfectly prepared Idaho ruby red trout comes straight from the river below.

> *Head back south on I-15 to I-86/US-30 (7 mi/11 km). Turn right and drive west on I-86/US-30 for 64 miles (103 km) to I-84. Continue onto I-84, heading west to ID-50 (39 mi/63 km). Follow ID-50 S for 5 miles (8 km) to US-30, then drive west on US-30 into Twin Falls (5 mi/8 km).*

❺ Settle into the **Blue Lakes Inn** (952 Blue Lakes Blvd., 208/933-2123, www.bluelakesinn.com, Apr.-Sept., $125-169) for the night. Local art adorns the spacious rooms at this renovated motel.

DAY 14: Twin Falls to Boise, Idaho

150 miles/240 kilometers | 2.5-3 hours

ROUTE OVERVIEW: Surface streets • US-93 • surface streets • US-30 • I-84 • US-20

❶ Make your way to **Shoshone Falls Park** (4155 Shoshone Falls Grade, www.tfid.org, dawn-dusk daily Mar.-Sept., $5 per vehicle). Called the Niagara of the West, the falls also dazzled Oregon Trail pioneers. Enjoy hiking trails and picnic sites before or after stepping onto the viewing platform to admire the falls, which are at their best during high flow in spring.

WATERFALLS ALONG THE THOUSAND SPRINGS SCENIC BYWAY

HAGERMAN FOSSIL BEDS NATIONAL MONUMENT

> *Drive east on Addison Ave. to Champlin Rd. (3 mi/5 km). Make a right on Champlin and follow it to Shoshone Falls Park (3 mi/5 km).*

❷ Depart Twin Falls for the **Thousand Springs Scenic Byway**. After about an hour, you'll reach **Hagerman Fossil Beds National Monument** (www.nps.gov/hafo, free). The area has turned up fossils that are renowned for their quality and completeness. Though there aren't any archaeological digs here anymore, you can find a set of well-preserved wagon ruts and beautiful views of the Snake river valley. Stop at the monument's **visitors center** (221 N. State St., 208/933-4105, 9am-5pm daily Memorial Day-Labor Day, 9am-5pm Thurs.-Mon. Labor Day-Memorial Day) in **Hagerman** for tips on where to find the best overlooks.

> *Head back south on Champlin Rd. to Falls Ave. (2 mi/3 km). Turn right and take Falls Ave. for 2 miles (3 km) to Eastland Dr. Turn right and in 1 mile (1.6 km) veer left. Eastland Dr. becomes US-93. Stay west on US-93 for 6 miles (10 km). Make a slight right onto Pole Line Rd. In 6 miles (10 km), turn left onto N. 1900 E, then make a quick right onto US-30. Drive west and north on US-30 for 25 miles (40 km) to Hagerman.*

❸ Have lunch in Hagerman at the **Snake River Grill** (611 Frogs Landing, 208/837-6227, www.snakeriver-grill.com, 7am-2pm Mon., 7am-9pm Tues.-Sun., $17), which pulls its trout right from the nearby river.

❹ Head north, then west to **Glenns Ferry**, where you can check out a Snake River fording spot at **Three Island Crossing State Park** (1083 S. Three

Island Park Dr., 208/366-2394, http://parksandrecreation.idaho.gov, 9am-5pm Sun.-Wed., 9am-6pm Thurs.-Sat., free). The shady park is situated in view of three islands the pioneers used to cross the Snake River. You can walk down to the river, where you can see the trail the wagons took.

> *Continue north on US-30 to Bliss (9 mi/14 km), then merge onto I-84. Head west on I-84 to Glenns Ferry (19 mi/31 km).*

❺ Keep going to **Boise,** and end your day with dinner at **Bittercreek Alehouse** (246 N. 8th St., 208/429-6360, www.bittercreekalehouse.com, 11am-midnight Sun.-Thurs., 11am-2am Fri.-Sat., $13). The restaurant is smack downtown and deservedly popular for its great food and beer. All leftovers are composted on-site by worms in the basement—this is the only restaurant using worm composting in the continental United States.

> *Take I-84 for 65 miles (105 km) to US-20. Follow US-20 into Boise (3 mi/5 km).*

DAY 15: Boise, Idaho

MORNING

❶ Head to **Julia Davis Park** (700 S. Capitol Blvd., 208/608-7600, www.cityofboise.org, sunrise-midnight daily), the city's oldest green space and home to many of its major museums. The large park has gardens, walking and biking paths, pavilions, ponds, and playgrounds.

❷ Dive into history at the **Idaho State Museum** (610 Julia Davis Dr., 208/334-2120, http://history.idaho.gov, 10am-5pm Mon.-Sat., noon-5pm Sun., $10) at Julia Davis Park. With interactive elements including games, videos, and touchable displays, the museum celebrates the state and its people. Other highlights are a life-sized Oregon Trail wagon, a 1980s-era computer—a callback to the iconic trail game—and a chance to guide your own pixel-raft across the Snake River.

AFTERNOON

❸ Get a burger from **Westside Drive-In** (1929 W. State St., 208/342-2957,

WESTSIDE DRIVE-IN'S ICE CREAM POTATO

www.westsidedrivein.com, 11am-10pm Mon.-Sat., 11am-9pm Sun., $8). Be sure to save room for the famous Idaho Ice Cream Potato (vanilla ice cream in the shape of a potato rolled in cocoa dust and topped with whipped cream).

❹ Venture beyond the city to take a tour of the **Old Idaho Penitentiary** (2445 Old Penitentiary Rd., 208/334-2844, http://history.idaho.gov, 10am-5pm daily, $6), which was established two decades before Idaho was a state. The prison was in use until 1972 and held more than 13,000 inmates: desperadoes, murderers, bounty hunters, train robbers, and bandits. You can wander the buildings at your own pace, but the prison's stories of murders, escapes, and executions are best experienced on one of the daily guided tours (hours vary seasonally).

EVENING

❺ Back in the city, go to the **Basque Block** (600 block of Grove St., www.thebasqueblock.com) to learn about the Basque people, a cultural group that has its own enclave in downtown Boise. For a taste of Basque cuisine, try **Bar Gernika** (202 S. Capitol Blvd., 208/344-2175, www.bargernika.com, 11am-11pm Mon., 11am-midnight Tues.-Thurs., 11am-1am Fri., 11:30am-1am Sat., $5-10). The Spanish-style pub serves *pintxos* (Basque tapas). Order the traditional *kalimoxto*—red wine and Coke—and sink your teeth into the fried crust of a croquette (fritter made with chicken stock and roux) while you wait for your *tortilla de patatas* (egg, potatoes, and onions with bread) to arrive.

DAY 16: Boise to Baker City, Oregon

150 miles/240 kilometers | 2.5-3 hours

ROUTE OVERVIEW: I-184 • I-84 • OR-86 • I-84

❶ Continue your journey west—you've made it to Oregon! But you're not done yet. Wave goodbye to the Snake River at **Farewell Bend State Recreation Area** (US-30 Bus., off I-84, 541/869-2365, http://oregonstateparks.org, dawn to dusk daily, $5 per vehicle for day-use pass). This is where pioneers rested before pushing on and bidding farewell to their dependable water source for the last 330 miles of the journey. At the park, restored covered wagons welcome visitors, along with informational kiosks about the pioneers' experiences.

> Take I-184 W to I-84 W (3 mi/5 km). Drive I-84 northwest into Oregon (74 mi/119 km). Take the exit for US-30 BUS and follow it for 1 mile (1.6 km) to Farewell Bend State Recreation Area.

❷ Drive northwest to reach the **National Historic Oregon Trail Interpretive Center** (22267 OR-86, Baker City, 541/523-1843, http://oregontrail.blm.gov, $8), possibly the best museum on the Oregon Trail. Spend a few hours following the story of the pioneers' long journey, illustrated with a life-size display of wagons, artifacts, and maps. Outside the museum are trails that allow you to take in acres of sagebrush, including the remnants of an old gold mine, wagon ruts carved into the prairie ground, and vistas of the Blue Mountains and Wallowa Mountains.

> Return to I-84 and head northwest to OR-86 (50 mi/80 km). Turn right on OR-86 and drive to the National Historic Oregon Trail Interpretive Center (6 mi/10 km).

❸ Loop back to **Baker City.** Grab a pint and a meal at **Barley Brown's Brew Pub** (2190 Main St., 541/523-4266, www.barleybrownsbeer.com, 4pm-10pm Mon.-Sat., $15), then head across the street for more beer and live music at sister property **Barley Brown's Taphouse** (2200 Main St., 541/523-2337, 2pm-close daily).

> Take OR-86 back to I-84 (6 mi/10 km), turn left to merge onto I-84, and follow it to Baker City (2 mi/3 km).

❹ Find your room at the historic **Geiser Grand Hotel** (1996 Main St., 541/523-1889, www.geisergrand.com, $229). Built in 1889 at the height of the gold boom, the Geiser catered to bankers, cattle barons, opera singers, and even Teddy Roosevelt. It's since been painstakingly restored to its elegant glory.

DAY 17: Baker City to Pendleton, Oregon

120 miles/193 kilometers | 2-2.5 hours

ROUTE OVERVIEW: I-84 • US-30 • I-84 • OR-331 • I-84 • US-30

❶ Check out the well-preserved ruts at the **Oregon Trail Interpretive Park** (Forest Rd. 1843, off Old Emigrant Hill Scenic Frontage Rd., no phone, www.fs.usda.gov, 9am-7pm Tues.-Sun. Memorial Day-Labor Day, $5 per vehicle) at **Blue Mountain Crossing.** The Blue Mountains were a tough challenge for the already-tired pioneers, driving their exhausted livestock up and over the mountain pass. This interpretive park houses a covered wagon and logging exhibit, and offers short hiking trails.

NATIONAL HISTORIC OREGON TRAIL INTERPRETIVE CENTER

Best HIKES

NEBRASKA

- **Windlass Hill Trail, Ash Hollow State Historical Park** (0.5 mi/0.8 km loop, 30 minutes, moderate): See deep ruts in a hillside that Oregon Trail wagons once descended.

- **Oregon Trail Pathway, Scotts Bluff National Monument** (0.5 mi/0.8 km one-way, 30 minutes, easy): Hike Mitchell Pass on the path of the pioneers, right on the Oregon Trail.

- **Daemonelix Trail, Agate Fossil Beds National Monument** (1 mi/1.6 km round-trip, 30 minutes, easy): Learn about some of the animals that roamed the land before the pioneers with this trek through the fossil-rich hills of the panhandle.

WYOMING

- **Oregon Trail Ruts Loop, Guernsey Ruts** (0.4 mi/0.6 km loop, 30 minutes, easy): A short hike leads you to the best wagon ruts of the Oregon Trail, cut deep into the rock.

- **Garden Creek Waterfall, Rotary Park** (1.3 mi/2 km round-trip, 1 hour, moderate): Get splashed by a waterfall on this trail on Casper Mountain.

- **Historic Quarry Trail, Fossil Butte National Monument** (2.5 mi/4 km round-trip, 1.5 hours, strenuous): Explore fossil beds in a prehistoric lake on this hike.

IDAHO

- **Box Canyon Hike, Box Canyon Springs Nature Preserve** (4 mi/6.4 km round-trip, 2 hours, moderate): This short hike has a big payoff, concluding at a cool blue pool deep in the canyon.

- **Emigrant Trail Hike, Hagerman Fossil Beds National Monument** (6 mi/9.7 km round-trip, 3-4 hours, strenuous): Walk in the path of the pioneers alongside impressive ruts.

- **Bruneau Dunes, Bruneau Dunes State Park** (6 mi/9.7 km round-trip, 3-4 hours, strenuous): Summit the state park's highest dune, then slide all the way back down on a sandboard.

- **Table Rock Trail, Old Idaho State Penitentiary** (3.7 mi/6 km round-trip, 1.5 hours, moderate): Hike up Table Rock for sparkling city views of Boise.

OREGON

- **Multnomah Falls, Historic Columbia River Highway** (2.4 mi/3.9 km round-trip, 2 hours, moderate): The most photographed waterfall in the state boasts a steep but spectacular hike to the top.

- **Pioneer Woman's Grave, Mount Hood** (2.2 mi/3.5 km round-trip, 1 hour, easy): Hike along the old wagon route to place a rock on the grave of this unknown pioneer woman.

- **Trillium Lake Loop, Mount Hood** (1.9 mi/3.1 km loop, 1 hour, easy): Admire the majesty of white-capped Mount Hood from this lakeside loop.

- **Angel's Rest, Bridal Veil** (4.8 mi/7.7 km round-trip, 2.5 hours, strenuous): Make the tough scramble up basalt boulders to catch a stunning view of the Columbia River Gorge.

THE RAINBOW CAFÉ

> *Get on I-84, heading northwest for 55 miles (89 km). Take exit 248, then turn right onto Old Emigrant Hill Scenic Frontage Rd. to reach the Oregon Trail Interpretive Park (3 mi/5 km).*

❷ Descend into **Pendleton.** Have lunch at **The Rainbow Café** (209 S. Main St., 541/276-4120, 6am-2am daily, $10), one of the oldest restaurants in the state. The old saloon is now a modern diner serving big portions. The walls are a veritable museum of western memorabilia, including a giant buffalo head and photographs of past Round-Up rodeo winners.

> *Return to I-84 and continue northwest for 35 miles (56 km). Take the exit for US-30 and follow US-30 into Pendleton (3 mi/5 km).*

❸ Next up is a visit to the **Tamástslikt Cultural Institute** (47105 Wildhorse Blvd., 541/429-7700, www.tamastslikt.org, 10am-5pm Mon.-Sat.), a history center owned and run by the Walla Walla, Cayuse, and Umatilla Tribes, offering perspective on their peoples' history. Take a seat around the fire in the lodge to hear the story of how Spilyay vanquished the forces of darkness, then check out the exhibits about the interactions between the tribes and the arriving pioneers. In the summer, enjoy the Living Cultural Village and its live demonstrations.

> *Take US-30 back to I-84 (3 mi/5 km). Follow I-84 E to OR-331 (3 mi/5 km). Head north on OR-331 for 1 mile (1.6 km) to Wildhorse Blvd. Turn right and follow this to the institute (1 mi/1.6 km).*

❹ Back in Pendleton proper, learn about the seedy underbelly of this pioneer town on the 90-minute **Pendleton Underground Tour** (31 SW Emigrant Ave., 541/276-0730, www.pendletonundergroundtours.org, 10am-5pm Mon. and Wed.-Sat., $15). The tour is led by knowledgeable and passionate local historians who walk you through the centuries of history running through the tunnels under the city. You'll see a Chinese bathhouse, an opium den, a Prohibition-era saloon, and more. Above ground, you'll peek into one of the longest-running brothels in the town's history.

> *Take Wildhorse Blvd. and OR-331 back to I-84 (2 mi/3 km). Go west on I-84 for 2.5 miles (4 km), then continue onto US-30 W for 3 miles (5 km) to get back to Pendleton.*

❺ Shop for a classic blanket at **Pendleton Woolen Mills** (1307 SE Court Pl., 541/276-6911, www.pendleton-usa.com, 8am-6pm Mon.-Sat., 9am-5pm Sun.). The company has been weaving its iconic blankets since 1909. If you're here on a weekday, take a free tour of the mill. You'll see how workers process the raw wool, then dye, card, spin, and weave the fabric. Spend the night in town.

DAY 18: Pendleton to Hood River, Oregon

160 miles/260 kilometers | 3-3.5 hours

ROUTE OVERVIEW: I-84 • Oregon Trail Rd. • OR-207 • I-84/US-30 • Fruit Loop

❶ On the way out of Pendleton, swing through the tiny town of **Echo** to check out the wagon ruts in **Echo Meadows** (Oregon Trail Rd., 541/376-8411, www.echo-oregon.com/meadows.html, dawn-dusk daily). A path leads you to preserved trail ruts, where pioneers faced a dry and dusty route through sagebrush. Follow another path up the hill for prairie views.

> *Drive west on Westgate out of Pendleton for 2 miles (3 km) to I-84. Follow I-84 W for 13 miles (21 km) to Echo Rd. Go left on Echo Rd. and follow it into the town of Echo (4 mi/6 km). Continue west on Oregon Trail Rd. for 6 miles (10 km) to reach Echo Meadows.*

COLUMBIA RIVER GORGE

2 Continue west to find yourself along the scenic **Columbia River Gorge.** Stop in **The Dalles,** where you can enjoy lunch at the **Sunshine Mill Artisan Plaza & Winery** (901 E. 2nd St., 541/298-8900, www.sunshinemill.com, noon-6pm daily, $8), located in an old wheat mill. After you eat, explore the winery grounds.

> *Return to I-84 by going north on OR-207 (5 mi/8 km). Turn left and merge onto I-84/US-30, driving for 97 miles (156 km) to The Dalles.*

3 Just outside of town, drive the winding **Historic Columbia River Highway** to **Rowena Crest Viewpoint** (off US-30, Mosier), for a breathtaking perspective on the landscape from a bluff high above the gorge. A popular photo op of a looping bend in the road can be snagged at the south side of the viewpoint.

> *Continue west on I-84 for 9 miles (15 km). Take exit 76 and follow US-30 W for 3 miles (5 km) to Rowena Crest Viewpoint.*

VIEW FROM ROWENA CREST VIEWPOINT

4 Roll into the charming town of **Hood River,** where you can spend a few hours touring the **Fruit Loop** (OR-35 to OR-281/Dee Hwy., www.hoodriverfruitloop.com). It's a roughly 30-mile (48-km) loop made up of farms, orchards, vineyards, and lavender fields. Depending on the season, you'll find u-pick orchards ripe with peaches, cherries, apples, or blueberries. The loop makes for a beautiful drive or bike ride: March through May the fruit trees and flower fields blossom, while September through November see stunning fall colors and pumpkin festivals.

> *Take US-30 back to I-84 (3 mi/5 km), then head west on I-84 for 13 miles (21 km) to Hood River. From here, you can drive the Fruit Loop, taking OR-281 back into Hood River.*

DAY 19: Hood River to Portland, Oregon

95 miles/153 kilometers | 2-2.5 hours

ROUTE OVERVIEW: I-84 • Historic Columbia River Hwy. • I-84 • I-205 • OR-213 • I-205 • I-5

1 It's the final stretch! Continue west along the Columbia River and stop at the waterfalls that dot the way. The most iconic is the 635-foot **Multnomah Falls.** While you can easily see the falls from Benson Bridge, challenge yourself by hiking to the top to view them from above via the **Multnomah Falls Trail** (2.4 mi/3.9 km round-trip, 2 hours, moderate). Switchbacks help gain elevation quickly, but the

MULTNOMAH FALLS

DAY 20: Portland, Oregon

MORNING

① From your hotel downtown, walk to the legendary **Powell's City of Books** (1005 W. Burnside St., 808/878-7323, www.powells.com, 9am-11pm daily). You could spend several lifetimes browsing the nine rooms of books in this massive independent bookstore.

② Take public transportation to **Washington Park** to explore the **International Rose Test Garden** (850 SW Rose Garden Way, www.portlandoregon.gov/parks, 7:30am-9pm daily). Free tours of the garden are offered daily at 1pm. Portland's love affair with roses goes back to Georgiana Pittock, an Oregon Trail pioneer. She started the Portland Rose Society, inviting her friends to showcase their roses beside her mansion, which lies just north of the park. Today the test garden showcases 10,000 bushes that grow more than 600 varieties of roses.

AFTERNOON

③ For lunch, head across the Willamette River to the east side of town and eat Russian dumplings at **Kachka** (960 SE 11th Ave., 503/235-0059, http://kachkapdx.com, 11:30am-2pm and 4pm-10pm daily, $14). The sour cherry *vareniki* dumplings with cream are drool-worthy.

④ Venture farther east and walk through the lovely **Lone Fir Cemetery** (SE 26th Ave. and SE Stark St., 503/797-1709, www.friendsoflonefircemetery.org, dawn-dusk daily), where some early pioneers are buried. Visit the northwest corner to see the oldest headstones as well as the cemetery's namesake Douglas fir tree.

well-maintained path is wide enough for breaks. Follow signs to the upper viewpoint.

> *Go west on I-84 for 26 miles (42 km). Take the exit for the Historic Columbia River Hwy. and follow it west to Multnomah Falls (4 mi/6 km).*

② Once in **Oregon City**, it's official: You've reached the end of the trail. Celebrate with a visit to the **End of the Trail Interpretive Center** (1726 Washington St., 503/657-9336, http://historicoregoncity.org, 9:30am-5pm Mon.-Fri., 10:30am-5pm Sun., $13). Using diary excerpts and historical information, the center gives an overview of the epic journey. It's especially great for kids, with lots of hands-on activities. You can practice loading your wagon in the Missouri frontier store, try on pioneer clothing, or make a candle to take home with you.

> *Continue west on the Historic Columbia River Hwy. for 3 miles (5 km). At Bridal Veil Rd., turn right, then merge onto I-84. Head west on I-84 for 20 miles (32 km) to I-205. Go south on I-205 to OR-213 (12 mi/19 km). Follow OR-213 south to Washington St., which takes you to the End of the Trail Interpretive Center (1 mi/1.6 km).*

③ Order bangers and mash at **The Highland Stillhouse** (201 S. 2nd St., 503/723-6789, www.highlandstillhouse.com, 11am-midnight Tues.-Sat., 11am-10pm Sun., $12). This is also one of the best places in the region for single malt scotch. Spend the night in downtown **Portland**.

> *Return to I-205 and drive south for 9 miles (14 km) to I-5. Merge onto I-5 and follow it north to Portland (11 mi/18 km).*

POWELL'S CITY OF BOOKS

EVENING

⑤ Kick back at some brewpubs, then catch a live show at the **Doug Fir Lounge** (830 E. Burnside St., 503/231-9663, www.dougfirlounge.com, bar 7am-late daily, showtimes and tickets vary by performance) to end your trip with a bang. You did it!

GETTING THERE

AIR

St. Louis Lambert International Airport (STL, 10701 Lambert International, 314/426-8000, www.flystl.com) offers nonstop service all over the United States, as well as service from Canada and Mexico. Airlines include Air Canada, Alaska Airlines, American Airlines, Delta, Frontier, Southwest, and United. The airport is located about 15 miles (24 km) northwest of St. Louis and 230 miles (370 km) east of Independence.

The closest major airport to Independence is **Kansas City International Airport** (MCI, 1 International Square, 816/243-5237, www.flykci.com), offering nonstop service to 56 cities in the United States, Canada, Mexico, and even Iceland. It's served by Air Canada, Alaska Airlines, Allegiant, American Airlines, Delta, Frontier, Icelandair, Southwest, Spirit, and United Airlines. The airport is located 15 miles (24 km) northwest of Kansas City and 30 miles (48 km) northwest of Independence. From St. Louis, it's 268 miles (431 km) due west on I-70.

TRAIN AND BUS

The **St. Louis Gateway Station** (430 S. 15th St., 800/872-7245, 24 hours daily) is in a central downtown location and offers train and bus services. **Amtrak** (800/872-7245, www.amtrak.com) has daily service from St. Louis to Kansas City on its Missouri River Runner route (from $36), while its Texas Eagle route serves Chicago, Dallas, San Antonio, and Los Angeles. The station also has **Greyhound** (800/231-2222, www.greyhound.com) connections to anywhere in the country. Popular routes travel four times a day from Chicago, Indianapolis, and Kansas City.

CAR

St. Louis, Missouri, east of Independence, is a convenient place to start your trip. It's served by the major interstate highways of I-55, I-70, and I-64. Downtown St. Louis is a 25-minute (14-mi/23-km) drive via I-70 from the **St. Louis airport.**

Independence, Missouri, is the official start of the Oregon Trail, and **Kansas City,** Missouri—10 miles (16 km) east—is the closest large city to the town, a 20-minute drive west via I-70.

Some sites along the Oregon Trail are served by dirt roads, which are passable (though bumpy) even for trailers and RVs, but take caution if it's been rainy because they can get extremely muddy.

GETTING BACK

If you're doing a one-way drive, you can return home by flying out of **Portland International Airport** (PDX, 7000 NE Airport Way, 877/739-4636, www.pdx.com). The airport is a 15-mile (24-km), 30-minute drive northeast of the city via I-5 and US-30B.

To return to **St. Louis** by car, the most direct route is 2,040 miles (3,290 km) long and takes approximately 30 hours. Follow I-84, I-80, and I-70 through Oregon, Idaho, Wyoming, Nebraska, and Missouri.

⌂ **CONNECT WITH**

- At Portland: **Best of the Pacific Northwest** (PAGE 216) and **Pacific Coast Highway: Washington and Oregon** (PAGE 236)

- At Hood River: **Columbia River Gorge and Wine Country** (PAGE 264) and **Pacific Crest Trail: Oregon and Washington** (PAGE 250)

- At Boise: **Idaho's Rivers and Mountains: Boise to Coeur d'Alene** (PAGE 396)

- At Kansas City: **Route 66** (PAGE 60)

- At Casper: **Wild Wyoming** (PAGE 378)

CALIFORNIA

The Golden State is one of those places you could spend a lifetime exploring without ever seeing all of its wonders. Northern California shows off the state's giant redwood trees, Yosemite's wild backcountry, and the coastal towns along the Pacific Coast Highway. In California's deserts you can soak up the mid-century vibe of Palm Springs before venturing into Joshua Tree National Park. Outdoorsy travelers shouldn't miss the Pacific Crest Trail, which traces the popular backpacking route, whose full length runs nearly 3,000 miles from Mexico to Canada.

◀ TAFT POINT, YOSEMITE NATIONAL PARK

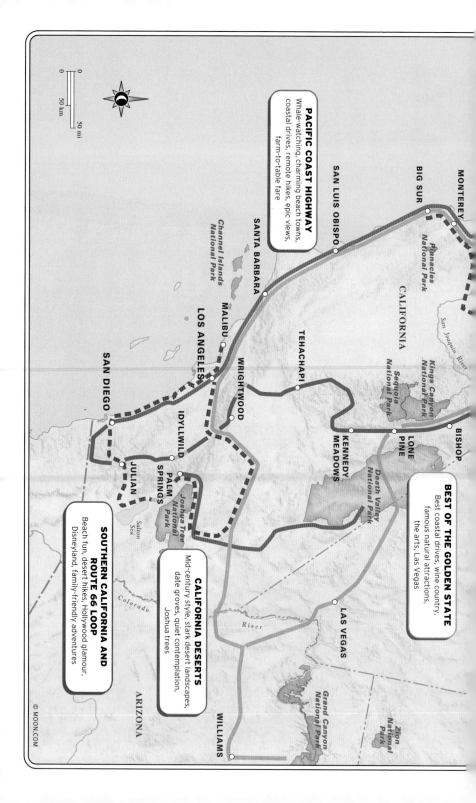

PACIFIC COAST HIGHWAY
Whale-watching, charming beach towns, coastal drives, remote hikes, epic views, farm-to-table fare

BEST OF THE GOLDEN STATE
Best coastal drives, wine country, famous natural attractions, the arts, Las Vegas

SOUTHERN CALIFORNIA AND ROUTE 66 LOOP
Beach fun, desert hikes, Hollywood glamour, Disneyland, family-friendly adventures

CALIFORNIA DESERTS
Mid-century style, stark desert landscapes, date groves, quiet contemplation, Joshua trees

MONTEREY
BIG SUR
SAN LUIS OBISPO
SANTA BARBARA
MALIBU
LOS ANGELES
SAN DIEGO
WRIGHTWOOD
IDYLLWILD
JULIAN
PALM SPRINGS
TEHACHAPI
KENNEDY MEADOWS
LONE PINE
BISHOP
LAS VEGAS
WILLIAMS

CALIFORNIA
ARIZONA

Channel Islands National Park
Pinnacles National Park
Kings Canyon National Park
Sequoia National Park
Death Valley National Park
Joshua Tree National Park
Grand Canyon National Park
Zion National Park

San Joaquin River
Colorado River
Salton Sea

0   50 km
0   50 mi

© MOON.COM

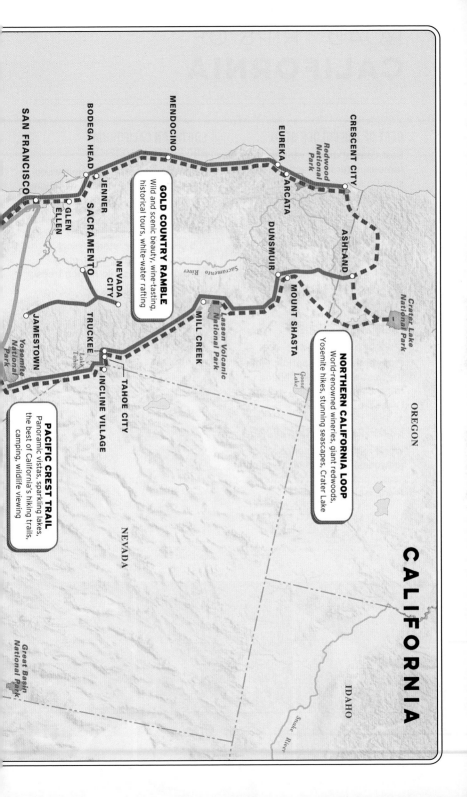

CALIFORNIA

San Francisco

Bodega Head

Mendocino

Eureka

Arcata

Crescent City

Redwood National Park

Ashland

Dunsmuir

Mount Shasta

Crater Lake National Park

OREGON

Jenner

Glen Ellen

Sacramento

Nevada City

Sacramento River

Lassen Volcanic National Park

Mill Creek

Goose Lake

Jamestown

Yosemite National Park

Truckee

Lake Tahoe

Incline Village

Tahoe City

NEVADA

IDAHO

Snake River

Great Basin National Park

GOLD COUNTRY RAMBLE
Wild and scenic beauty, wine-tasting, historical tours, white-water rafting

NORTHERN CALIFORNIA LOOP
World-renowned wineries, giant redwoods, Yosemite hikes, stunning seascapes, Crater Lake

PACIFIC CREST TRAIL
Panoramic vistas, sparkling lakes, the best of California's hiking trails, camping, wildlife viewing

ROAD TRIPS OF
CALIFORNIA

BEST OF THE GOLDEN STATE

Best coastal drives, wine country, famous natural attractions, the arts, side trips to the Grand Canyon and Las Vegas (PAGE 108)

PACIFIC COAST HIGHWAY: CALIFORNIA

Whale-watching, charming beach towns, coastal drives, remote hikes, epic views, farm-to-table fare (PAGE 124)

PACIFIC CREST TRAIL: CALIFORNIA

Panoramic vistas, sparkling lakes, the best of California's hiking trails, camping, wildlife viewing (PAGE 140)

NORTHERN CALIFORNIA LOOP

World-renowned wineries, giant redwoods, Yosemite hikes, stunning seascapes, side trip to Crater Lake (PAGE 156)

SOUTHERN CALIFORNIA AND ROUTE 66 LOOP

Beach fun, desert hikes, Hollywood glamour, Disneyland, family-friendly adventures (PAGE 178)

CALIFORNIA DESERTS

Mid-century style, stark desert landscapes, dates groves, quiet contemplation, iconic Joshua trees (PAGE 194)

GOLD COUNTRY RAMBLE

Wild and scenic beauty, wine-tasting, historical tours, white-water rafting (PAGE 202)

LEFT TO RIGHT: VERNAL FALL IN YOSEMITE NATIONAL PARK; MONO LAKE TUFA STATE NATURAL RESERVE; SURFERS IN HUNTINGTON BEACH

1 Drive into Yosemite National Park via the highest highway pass in California—the 9,900-foot **Tioga Pass** (PAGE 150).

2 Keep company with towering redwood trees—the tallest in the world—at **Redwood National Park** (PAGE 164).

3 Surf the Pacific Ocean in dreamy **Malibu** (PAGE 180).

Tioga Pass, Yosemite National Park

Redwood National Park

surfer in Malibu

La Jolla Cove

Mojave National Preserve

4 Snorkel in San Diego's **La Jolla Cove** (PAGE 185).

5 Soak up the otherworldly landscape of the desert during the **Mojave National Preserve's** scenic drive (PAGE 199).

BEST OF THE GOLDEN STATE

WHY GO: Best coastal drives, wine country, famous natural attractions, the arts, side trips to the Grand Canyon and Las Vegas

TOTAL DISTANCE: 1,770 miles/ 2,860 kilometers

NUMBER OF DAYS: 14

SEASONS: Spring, summer, and fall

START/END: San Francisco, California

▶ YOSEMITE VALLEY

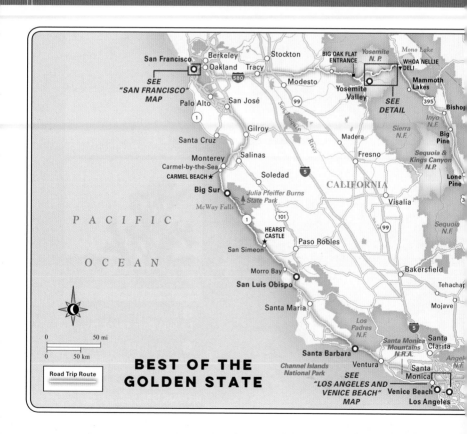

BEST OF THE GOLDEN STATE

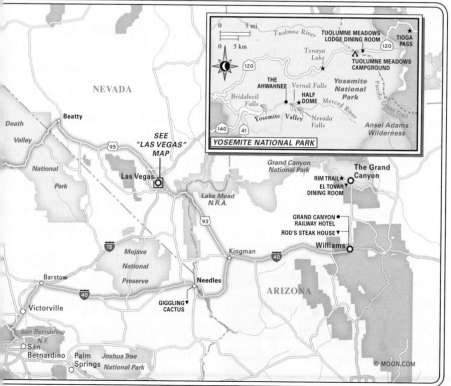

SEE "LAS VEGAS" MAP

NEVADA

Death Valley National Park

Beatty

Las Vegas

Lake Mead N.R.A.

Mojave National Preserve

Barstow

Victorville

San Bernardino N.F.

San Bernardino

Palm Springs

Joshua Tree National Park

Needles

GIGGLING CACTUS

Kingman

ARIZONA

Grand Canyon National Park

The Grand Canyon

RIM TRAIL
EL TOVAR DINING ROOM

GRAND CANYON RAILWAY HOTEL
ROD'S STEAK HOUSE

Williams

YOSEMITE NATIONAL PARK

0   5 mi
0   5 km

Tuolmne River

TUOLUMNE MEADOWS LODGE DINING ROOM

TIOGA PASS

120

Tenaya Lake

TUOLUMNE MEADOWS CAMPGROUND

THE AHWAHNEE

Vernal Falls

Yosemite National Park

Bridalveil Falls

HALF DOME

Yosemite Valley

Nevada Falls

Merced River

Ansel Adams Wilderness

Pacific Crest Trail

140
41

© MOON.COM

Whether you're a culinary pilgrim, a desert rat, a beach bum, an avid outdoorswoman, or a party animal, this road trip offers something for you. It traverses California's renowned vineyards and wild beaches, its cosmopolitan cities and rich arts and culture scene. When you set off from San Francisco, you'll find yourself in astonishing backcountry, only to end up in picturesque small towns that act as gateways to legendary natural landmarks. Prepare to be amazed at all that the Golden State has to offer.

DAY 1: San Francisco

MORNING AND AFTERNOON

❶ It's easy to fill two days with fun in San Francisco. On your first day, visit the foodie-friendly **Ferry Building** (1 Ferry Bldg., 415/983-8030, www.ferrybuildingmarketplace.com, 10am-7pm Mon.-Fri., 8am-6pm Sat., 11am-5pm Sun., check with businesses for individual hours). The 1898 building has been reimagined as the epicurean mecca of San Francisco. The thrice-weekly farmers market is not to be missed.

❷ Walk 1.5 miles down the Embarcadero to the ferry that will take you to **Alcatraz** (www.nps.gov/alcatraz). The incredible stories of this famous former maximum-security penitentiary in the middle of San Francisco Bay will blow your mind. Tours, offered by **Alcatraz Cruises** (Pier 33, 415/981-7625, www.alcatrazcruises.com, adults from $37, children from $24), typically sell out, so reserve tickets at least two weeks in advance.

EVENING

❸ For dinner, indulge in the old-school elegance of **Tadich Grill** (240

SAN FRANCISCO

California St., 415/391-1849, www.tadichgrill.com, 11am-9:30pm Mon.-Fri., 11:30am-9:30pm Sat., $15-38), which claims to be the oldest restaurant in the city. Since the mid-1800s, it's been serving an extensive menu that includes sensational Italian seafood stew.

❹ Rest your head at the tech-savvy **Hotel Zetta** (55 5th St., 415/543-8555, www.viceroryhotelsandresorts.com/zetta, $299-1,214), which embraces the region's tech side by filling guest rooms with a gaggle of gadgets.

DAY 2: San Francisco

MORNING

❶ Head west to **Golden Gate Park,** where you can delve into the art of the **de Young Museum** (50 Hagiwara Tea Garden Dr., 415/750-3600, http://deyoung.famsf.org, 9:30am-5:15pm Tues.-Sun., $15 adults, free for children). View paintings, sculpture, and ceramics from all over the world. Climb the museum's tower (free) for 360-degree views of the city.

❷ Visit the **Japanese Tea Garden** (75 Hagiwara Tea Garden Dr., 415/752-4227, www.japaneseteagardensf.com, 9am-5:45pm daily Mar.-Oct., 9am-4:45pm daily Nov.-Feb., $9 adults, $7 children 12-17, $3 children 5-11) for tea and a snack before leaving the park.

AFTERNOON AND EVENING

❸ Spend the afternoon at the **San Francisco Museum of Modern Art** (SFMOMA, 151 3rd St., 415/357-4000, www.sfmoma.org, 10am-5pm Sun.-Tues. and Fri., 10am-9pm Thurs.,

Top ⑤ BEST OF THE GOLDEN STATE

① Make a date with Lady Luck on a side trip to **Las Vegas** (PAGE 116).

② On another detour, trundle into the Grand Canyon Old West-style on the **Grand Canyon Railway** (PAGE 117).

③ See acclaimed artwork at the hilltop **Getty Center** (PAGE 119).

④ People-watch for hours at **Venice Beach** (PAGE 120).

⑤ Summit **Cone Peak** in **Big Sur** for 360-degree ocean views (PAGE 122).

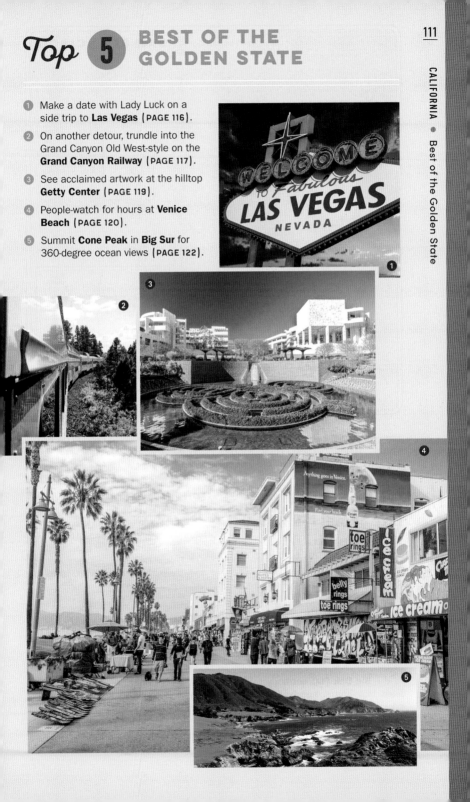

10am-8pm Sat. summer, 10am-9pm Thurs., 10am-5pm Fri.-Tues. winter, $25 adults, free for children) before dining at its touted on-site restaurant **In Situ.**

DAY 3: San Francisco to Yosemite

190 miles/305 kilometers | 5 hours

ROUTE OVERVIEW: I-80 • I-580 • I-205 • CA-120

❶ Grab a coffee for the long drive to **Yosemite National Park** (209/372-0200, www.nps.gov/yose, 24 hours daily, $35 per vehicle, $30 motorcyclists, $20 pedestrians or bicyclists). The drive to the **Big Oak Flat entrance** takes at least four hours; however, traffic, especially in summer and on weekends, can make it much longer.

> Take US-101 S out of San Francisco to I-80 E, then I-580 E. Follow I-580 E for 46 miles (74 km) to I-205 E. Continue on I-205 E for 15 miles (23 km) to CA-120 E. Stay on CA-120 E for 96 miles (154 km) to the Big Oak Flat entrance of Yosemite National Park.

❷ The 620-foot **Bridalveil Fall** (Southside Dr. past Tunnel View) makes a great first stop in the park. Reach it by following a 0.5-mile round-trip trail—more of a pleasant walk than a hike.

> Follow CA-120 E/Big Oak Flat Rd. from the park entrance for 20 miles (32 km) to reach the parking lot for Bridalveil Fall.

❸ Make reservations ahead of time to spend the night in the comfort of **The Ahwahnee** (888/413-8869, outside U.S. 602/278-8888, www.travelyosemite.com, $482-1,178). With its rock facade and superb Yosemite Valley views, this luxury hotel is a quintessential national parks property.

> It's another 5 miles (8 km) on the park road to reach The Ahwahnee.

For oenophiles, no trip to California is complete without an excursion to the state's renowned wine country. Napa and Sonoma Valleys offer multiple ways to spoil yourself, including spas, fine hotels, revered restaurants, and understated natural beauty. Both are less than 100 miles north of San Francisco, about an hour's drive if traffic is light.

WINERIES

A multitude of vineyards are strung along the Silverado Trail and CA-29, two roads that head north out of the city of Napa and into serious wine country. Grapevines braid the scenic valley as you drive through Rutherford, St. Helena, and Calistoga.

Grgich Hills Winery (1829 St. Helena Hwy., Rutherford, 800/532-3057, www.grgich.com, 9:30am-4:30pm daily, tasting $25) put Napa Valley on the map with a win at the Paris Wine Tasting of 1976. It's still known for its chardonnay.

Mumm (8445 Silverado Trail, Rutherford, 800/686-6272, www.mummnapa.com, 10am-6pm daily, tasting $20-35) produces sparkling varietals worth a taste even for those who typically prefer still wine.

Clos Pegase (1060 Dunaweal Ln., Calistoga, 707/942-4981, www.clospegase.com, 10:30am-5pm daily, tasting $30-55) showcases over 100 artworks on its grounds, including sculptor Henry Moore's *Mother Earth* and a painting by Francis Bacon.

FOOD

The city of Napa is located on the southern end of Napa Valley, with a scenic downtown perched on the Napa River. For an introduction to the area's vibrant food and wine scene, visit the **Oxbow Public Market** (610 and 644 1st St., 707/226-6529, www.oxbowpublicmarket.com, 9am-8pm Tues., 9am-7pm Wed.-Mon.), which has food vendors, produce markets, and cafés.

ACCOMMODATIONS

There is a range of options for staying overnight (and sleeping off an afternoon of wine-tasting). One of the more luxurious is **Auberge du Soleil** (180 Rutherford Hill Rd., St. Helena, 707/963-1211, www.aubergedusoleil.com, $875-5,200).

Less expensive options include St. Helena's **El Bonita Motel** (195 Main St./CA-29, 800/541-3284, www.elbonita.com, $140-320), which is within walking distance of the historic downtown and has a 1950s motel charm, and Calistoga's **Dr. Wilkinson's Hot Springs Resort** (1507 Lincoln Ave., 707/942-4102, www.drwilkinson.com, $229-350), with an on-site spa.

GETTING THERE

From San Francisco, take **I-80 East** across the Bay Bridge toward **Oakland**. Follow I-80 for about 30 miles (48 km) and cross the Carquinez Bridge. Take the exit for **CA-37 West** to **Napa**. After 1 mile (1.6 km), jump on **CA-29 (Sonoma Blvd.) North.** Continue on CA-29 for 13 miles (21 km) until you reach **downtown Napa**. CA-29 will take you as far as **Calistoga,** 25 miles (40 km) north of Napa.

NAPA VALLEY VINEYARDS

DAY 4: Yosemite

MORNING AND AFTERNOON

❶ Explore Yosemite Valley to see iconic attractions like **Half Dome,** the giant granite rock formation that rises 4,737 feet above the floor of the valley.

❷ Hike the famous **Mist Trail** (5.4 mi/8.7 km round-trip, 5-6 hours, strenuous), which will take you to two waterfalls. You'll trek up 600 stairsteps to the top of **Vernal Fall,** then continue on to **Nevada Fall.** Take a lightweight parka; this aptly named trail drenches intrepid visitors in the spring and early summer months.

EVENING

❸ Reward yourself for the hard work with dinner at **The Ahwahnee Dining Room** (209/372-1489, www.travelyosemite.com, 7am-10am, 11:30am-3pm, and 5:30pm-9pm Mon.-Sat., 7am-3pm and 5:30pm-9pm Sun., $12-21). You'll need to make reservations in advance to enjoy the fine cuisine in this grand space, complete with floor-to-ceiling windows and a magnificent high-beamed ceiling.

VIEW OF HALF DOME

DAY 5: Yosemite

MORNING AND AFTERNOON

❶ Pack a picnic lunch, then hike around **Tenaya Lake** (2.5 mi/4 km loop, 1-2 hours, easy). This trail offers possibly the most picturesque views in all of Yosemite. The only difficult part is fording the outlet stream at the west end of the lake, because the water gets chilly and can be high in the spring and early summer.

> *Follow the park road back toward the entrance for 7 miles (11 km). Turn onto Big Oak Flat Rd. and continue for 10 miles (16 km). Turn right to get onto CA-120 E. From here, it's 32 miles (52 km) to the trailhead, along Tioga Pass Road. There are parking lots at either end of the lake.*

EVENING

❷ Pitch your tent at the **Tuolumne Meadows Campground** (Tioga Pass Rd. at Tuolumne Meadows, 877/444-6777, www.recreation.gov, July-late Sept., $26), which sprawls among trees and boulders.

> *Follow CA-120 E/Tioga Pass Rd. for 8 miles (13 km) to reach the campground.*

❸ Food options in this part of the park are limited. **Tuolumne Meadows Lodge Dining Room** (Tuolumne Meadows Lodge, 209/372-8413, www.travelyosemite.com, 7am-9am and 5:45pm-8pm daily mid-June-mid-Sept., $10-28) is close to the campground. Be sure to make reservations for dinner.

WITH LESS TIME

SAN FRANCISCO, YOSEMITE, AND LOS ANGELES

6 days; 500 miles/805 kilometers

In just **six days,** you can devote two days each to **San Francisco** and **Los Angeles,** as well as **Yosemite National Park,** but you'll be doing a lot of driving most days.

LOS ANGELES, LAS VEGAS, AND THE GRAND CANYON

5-7 days; 560 miles/900 kilometers

In just **five days,** and with a lot of driving, you can experience a day each in **Los Angeles** and **Las Vegas,** along with the West's most famous natural attraction, the **Grand Canyon.** With a full **seven days,** add a day to each city to experience them more fully.

DAY 6: Yosemite to Las Vegas

390 miles/630 kilometers | 7 hours

ROUTE OVERVIEW: **CA-120** • **US-395** • **CA-136** • **CA-190** • **NV-374** • **US-95**

❶ You have a long drive ahead of you, so fuel up with a stop at the **Whoa Nellie Deli** (22 Vista Point Dr., CA-120 and US-395, 760/647-1088, www.whoanelliedeli.com, 6:30am-9pm daily, $8-12) at the Tioga Gas Mart, just east of the park's Tioga Pass entrance. What other gas station deli counter serves sashimi, lobster taquitos, or fish tacos with mango salsa and ginger coleslaw?

> *Follow CA-120 E for 19 miles (31 km) to the gas station.*

❷ For most of the year, the best way to Las Vegas from here is via **Tioga Pass.** (If you're traveling in winter or spring, check to make sure that it's open before heading out.) I recommend taking the scenic **California route** over the

KEY RESERVATIONS

- Book your **Alcatraz tour** at least **two weeks** in advance.

- Secure camping reservations at least **a month** in advance for **Tuolumne Meadows Campground.**

- At **The Ahwahnee Hotel,** book both your room and your reservations for **The Ahwahnee Dining Room** at least several months ahead.

- At the **California Science Center,** call ahead **a day or two** before your visit to book a tour for the **Space Shuttle *Endeavour*** exhibit.

more direct **Nevada route.** It's only 45 minutes longer and travels through the quaint towns of Mammoth Lakes, Bishop, and Lone Pine. Stop in **Beatty, Nevada,** for lunch.

> *Get on US-395 S and drive for 141 miles (227 km) to Lone Pine. Take CA-136 E for 18 miles (28 km) until it becomes CA-190. From here, you'll wind 68 miles (126 km) east through Death Valley. Take a left onto Scotty's Castle Rd., then an immediate right onto Daylight Pass Rd. This road will take you across the Nevada border after 13 miles (21 km). Continue on NV-374 N for 13 more miles (21 km) to Beatty.*

3 In Las Vegas, check into the luxe **Waldorf Astoria** (3752 Las Vegas Blvd. S., 702/590-8888, www.waldorfastorialasvegas.com, $295-399), which looks down on the bright lights of the Strip from a peaceful remove.

> *Follow US-95 S for 115 miles (185 km) to Las Vegas.*

DAY 7: Las Vegas

MORNING AND AFTERNOON

1 The glitz of the Las Vegas Strip makes it a surreal stopover between the natural wonders of Yosemite and the Grand Canyon. Fortify yourself with a rich but right croque madame from famed chef Thomas Keller's **Bouchon** (3355 Las Vegas Blvd. S., www.venetian.com, 702/414-6200, 7am-1pm and 5pm-10pm Mon.-Thurs., 7am-2pm and 5pm-10pm Sat.-Sun., $30-65) at **The Venetian.**

THE VENETIAN

2 Slough off the grime of the road with a decadent pool party at the **Palms Casino Resort** (4321 W. Flamingo Rd., 702/942-7777, www.palms.com), where the expression "party like a rock star" could have been invented.

EVENING

3 Watch the sun set from the 550-foot-tall **High Roller** (The Linq, 3545 Las Vegas Blvd. S., 702/777-2782 or 866/574-3851, www.caesars.com/linq/high-roller, 11:30am-2:30am daily, $25-37, youth $10-20), the world's largest observation wheel.

4 Sample the tapas-style menu at **Rose. Rabbit. Lie.** (Cosmopolitan, 3708 Las Vegas Blvd. S., 702/698-7440, www.cosmopolitanlasvegas.com, 6pm-midnight Wed.-Sat., $70-125), equal parts supper club, nightclub, and jazz club.

DAY 8: Las Vegas to Williams, Arizona

220 miles/355 kilometers | 4 hours

ROUTE OVERVIEW: US-93 • I-40

1 Before the drive across the high desert, you'll want to get in a good breakfast. At **The Egg & I** (4533 W. Sahara Ave., Ste. 5, 702/364-9686, http://theeggworks.com, 6am-3pm daily, $10-20), you can order something other than eggs—but given the name, why would you?

2 Drive over the Hoover Dam Bypass, and stop in **Kingman, Arizona.** Find the best burger in town at **Mr. D'z Route 66 Diner** (105 E. Andy Devine Ave., 928/718-0066, 7am-9pm daily, $9-18). If you're still full from breakfast, just pop in to check out the cool old jukebox.

> *Take US-93 S for 107 miles (172 km) to Kingman.*

3 Continue east to **Williams** and overnight at the **Grand Canyon Railway Hotel** (235 N. Grand Canyon Blvd., 928/635-4010, www.thetrain.com, $205-370), the highest-end accommodation in town.

> *Follow I-40 E for 114 miles (184 km) to Williams.*

Seligman, a tiny roadside settlement west of Williams, holds tightly to its Route 66 heritage. There are fewer than 500 full-time residents and often twice that number of travelers. Don't be surprised to see European visitors, classic-car aficionados, and motorcyclists passing through town. John Lasseter, codirector of the 2006 Disney-Pixar film *Cars,* has said that he based the movie's fictional town of Radiator Springs partly on Seligman.

FOOD

Stop at **Delgadillo's Snow Cap Drive-In** (301 E. Chino Ave., 928/422-3291, 10am-6pm daily spring-fall, $5-10), off Route 66 on the east end of town, a famous food shack dedicated to feeding and entertaining Route 66 travelers. The restaurant serves a mean chili burger, a famous "cheeseburger with cheese," hot dogs, malts, ice cream, and much more. Expect a wait—and to be teased, especially if you have a question that requires a serious answer. That's half the fun!

DELGADILLO'S SNOW CAP DRIVE-IN

ACCOMMODATIONS

There are a few motels in Seligman. The **Supai Motel** (134 W. Chino St., 928/422-4153, www.supaimotelseligman.com, $69-82), named for the nearby Grand Canyon village inhabited by the Havasupai people, has comfortable guest rooms at a fair price.

The **Historic Route 66 Motel** (928/422-3204, www.route66seligmanarizona.com, $69-82) offers free Wi-Fi and refrigerators in tidy guest rooms.

The **Canyon Lodge** (114 E. Chino St., 928/422-3255, www.route66canyonlodge.com, $69-82) has free Wi-Fi, free breakfast, and refrigerators and microwaves in themed guest rooms.

GETTING THERE

From **Williams** to Seligman, the drive takes about 45 minutes. Leave Williams by heading west on Historic Route 66 to I-40 (2 mi/3 km). Merge onto I-40 and drive west for 22 miles (35 km). Take Exit 139, turn right and drive Route 66 west to Seligman (18 mi/29 km).

To continue to **Needles,** California, from Seligman, drive west on I-40 from Seligman for 133 miles (214 km), which takes about two hours.

DAY 9: Day Trip to the Grand Canyon

MORNING

❶ Enjoy a break from your car by taking the **Grand Canyon Railway** (800/843-8724, www.thetrain.com, $65-220 pp round-trip) from Williams to the Grand Canyon. Comedian-fiddlers often stroll through the cars, and on some trips there's even a mock train robbery complete with bandits on horseback with blazing six-shooters.

❷ It takes about 2.5 hours to get to the South Rim depot in **Grand Canyon National Park** (928/638-7888, www.nps.gov/grca, 24 hours daily, $35 per vehicle, $30 per motorcycle, $20 bicyclists and pedestrians).

AFTERNOON

❸ Take in the views from the **Rim Trail** (12.8 mi/20.6 km one-way, easy), the single best way to see all of the South Rim. Walk past historic buildings, famous lodges, and the most breathtaking views in the world. Perhaps the best thing about the Rim Trail is that

VIEW OF THE GRAND CANYON'S SOUTH RIM

you don't have to hike the whole 13 miles—far from it. There are at least 16 shuttle stops along the way, and you can hop on and off the trail at your leisure. Start the trail at Grand Canyon Village; an easy access point is behind the train station.

❹ Before taking the train back to Williams, get an appetizer or a drink at **El Tovar Dining Room** (928/638-2631, ext. 6432, www.grandcanyonlodges.com, 6:30am-10:30am, 11:15am-2pm, and 4:30pm-9:30pm daily, $17-35), a stylishly historical restaurant on the canyon's edge.

EVENING

❺ For dinner, indulge in a prime cut of meat from **Rod's Steak House** (301 E. Route 66, 928/635-2671, www.rods-steakhouse.com, 11am-9:30pm Mon.-Sat., $12-35), a Williams institution.

DAY 10: Williams to Los Angeles

440 miles/710 kilometers | 8 hours

ROUTE OVERVIEW: I-40 • I-15 • I-10

❶ After a good night's sleep, head out for the full-day journey to Los Angeles. This route starts off as a scenic drive through a pine tree-dotted landscape before becoming sparser. The most exciting part of the drive is crossing the Colorado River at the Arizona-California border into **Needles**. The **Giggling Cactus** (2411 W. Broadway, 760/326-2233, 5:30am-10pm Sun.-Thurs., 5:30am-10:30pm Fri.-Sat. summer, shorter hours in winter, $9-24) dishes out a diverse menu of breakfast, lunch, and dinner.

> *From Williams, follow I-40 W for 175 miles (282 km) to Needles.*

❷ From Needles, drive west to Barstow and then into the heart of Los Angeles. Be prepared to slow down when you hit traffic, which may extend your driving time exponentially. In downtown, stay at the **Ace Hotel** (929 S. Broadway, 213/623-3233, www.acehotel.com, $199-650), which has a theater that hosts major entertainment events and a rooftop bar that shows off the skyline.

> *Continue on I-40 W for 142 miles (229 km) to Barstow. Here, you'll pick up I-15 S, following it for 103 miles (166 km) to I-10 W. Take I-10 W into downtown Los Angeles.*

❸ Enjoy dinner at the hotel's restaurant, **Best Girl** (927 S. Broadway, 213/235-9660, www.bestgirldtla.com, 7am-11pm Sun.-Thurs., 7am-midnight Fri.-Sat., $16-33).

DAY 11: Los Angeles

40 miles/64 kilometers | 1.25 hours

MORNING

❶ Start your morning with coffee and avocado toast at **Verve Coffee** (883 Spring St., 213/455-5991, www.verve-coffee.com, 7am-7pm daily), a Santa Cruz-based chain that feels right at home in DTLA.

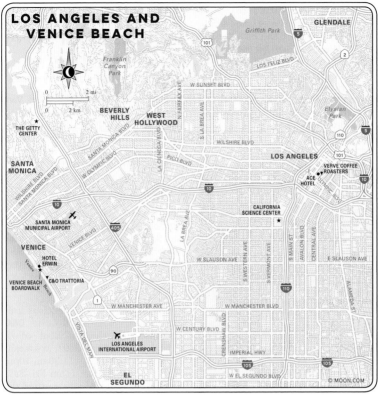

LOS ANGELES AND VENICE BEACH

© MOON.COM

❷ It's time to appreciate the achievements of civilization. See the Space Shuttle *Endeavour* at the **California Science Center** (700 Exposition Park Dr., 323/724-3623, www.california-sciencecenter.org, 10am-5pm daily, free, $10 parking), which is housed within Exposition Park. To see the shuttle exhibit, reserve a timed entry by calling (213/744-2019) or going online.

> *Merge onto Main St. from Spring St. Follow Main St. for 2 miles (3 km). Turn right onto W. Jefferson Blvd., then left onto Flower St. Turn right onto Exposition Blvd., then left onto Figueroa St. The entrance to Exposition Park is half a block down on the right.*

AFTERNOON AND EVENING

❸ Make your way into the hills to view the artistic masterpieces at **The Getty Center** (1200 Getty Center Dr., 310/440-7300, 10am-5:30pm Tues.-Fri. and Sun., 10am-9pm Sat., free, $5 audio tour, $20 parking). The art collections alone would make this sprawling museum worth a visit, but the soaring architecture, beautiful grounds, and remarkable city views seal the deal. Head back to the Ace Hotel in time to catch sunset from the rooftop bar.

THE GETTY CENTER

> *Take I-110 N to I-10 W. Follow I-10 W for 10 miles (16 km). Merge onto I-405 N. Continue for 4 miles (6 km), then take the exist for Moraga Dr. Turn left onto N. Sepulveda Blvd. After 1 mile (1.6 km), turn left onto Getty Center Dr. To get back to the Ace Hotel, take I-405 S to I-10 E. After 9 miles (14.5 km), take the exit for Grand Ave. Turn left onto S. Olive St., then right onto S. Broadway.*

▶ Playlist

BEST OF THE GOLDEN STATE

SONGS

- **"California Waiting" by Kings of Leon:** Solid drums, raspy vocals, and a fast guitar add up to a song ideal for a sunny road trip through the desert into Vegas.
- **"California" by Phantom Planet:** The Los Angeles-based band Phantom Planet sings endearingly about California in this happy indie pop song.
- **"Going to California" by Led Zeppelin:** One of the band's prettier songs, the light-as-a-feather guitar feels like fresh air through open car windows.

PODCASTS

- ***California Now:*** Hosted by Visit California, this is the be-all, end-all of travel podcasts. Episodes feature interviews with insiders—travel experts, chefs, guides, and notable Californians—who share their favorite must-sees and must-dos of the Golden State.

DAY 12: Los Angeles to Venice Beach

20 miles/32 kilometers | 1 hour

ROUTE OVERVIEW: I-10 • city streets

❶ Make your way to the lively **Venice Beach Boardwalk** (Ocean Front Walk at Venice Blvd., 310/396-6764, www.venicebeach.com), a paved coastal path in L.A.'s free-spirited Venice Beach, crowded with street performers, bodybuilders, and self-identified freaks.

> *Take I-10 W for 13 miles (21 km) and exit at 4th St. Turn left on 4th St., and right on Pico Blvd. Turn left on Neilson Way. After 1 mile (1.6 km), Neilson Way becomes Pacific Ave. Follow Pacific Ave. for another mile, then turn right onto Venice Boulevard, where you're just one block from the boardwalk.*

❷ For dinner, fill up on delicious Italian fare at longtime favorite **C&O Trattoria** (31 Washington Blvd., Marina del Rey, 310/823-9491, www.candorestaurants.com, 11:30am-10pm Sun.-Thurs., 11:30am-11pm Fri.-Sat., $13-23), less than a mile south of the boardwalk. Sit outside, enjoying the mild weather and the soft pastel frescoes on the exterior walls surrounding the courtyard.

❸ Sleep by the sea at the **Hotel Erwin** (1697 Pacific Ave., 800/786-7789, www.hotelerwin.com, $289-530), just feet from the boardwalk. Graffiti art adorns the exterior wall and some of its rooms; all have balconies and playful decor including lamps resembling the barbells used by the weightlifters at nearby Muscle Beach.

DAY 13: Venice Beach to San Luis Obispo

190 miles/315 kilometers | 4 hours

ROUTE OVERVIEW: CA-1 • US-101 • CA-154 • US-101

❶ The most difficult part of the trip along the **Pacific Coast Highway** (PCH) is deciding which of its many attractions deserve a stop. Experience fine living in **Santa Barbara,** with the regal

Mission Santa Barbara (2201 Laguna St., 805/682-4713, www.santabarbaramission.org, 9am-4:30pm daily, $9 adults, $4 children). Graceful architecture, serene surroundings, and an informative museum make this the "Queen of the Missions."

> Take CA-1 N (17 mi/27 km) through Malibu, then continue another 30 miles (48 km) to US-101 N. Take US-101 N for 39 miles (63 km) to the Mission St. exit for Santa Barbara.

2 You don't have to leave Santa Barbara to sample some of the region's award-winning wines. The city's **Urban Wine Trail** (http://urbanwinetrailsb.com) lists tons of tasting rooms that you can visit. After you've sipped your fill, grab authentic Mexican food at **La Super-Rica Taqueria** (622 N. Milpas St., 805/963-4940, 11am-9pm Sun.-Mon. and Thurs., 11am-9:30pm Fri.-Sat., $5). You'll have to wait in line with locals, commuters from Los Angeles, and even the occasional Hollywood celeb.

3 **San Luis Obispo** is around the midway point to San Francisco. Overrun with pink kitsch, the flamboyant **Madonna Inn** (100 Madonna Rd., 805/543-3000, www.madonnainn.com, $210-500) is a unique place to stop for the night.

> From Santa Barbara, get on CA-154 W. When it connects with US-101 N after 33 miles (53 km), follow it 57 miles (92 km) into San Luis Obispo.

DAY 14: San Luis Obispo to San Francisco

280 miles/450 kilometers | 6 hours

ROUTE OVERVIEW: CA-1 • CA-156 • US-101

1 Book an early tour of the opulent **Hearst Castle** (CA-1 and Hearst Castle Rd., 800/444-4445, www.hearstcastle.org, tours 9am-3:20pm daily) in **San Simeon.** Expect to walk for at least an hour on whichever tour you choose, and to climb up and down stairs.

> Follow CA-1 N for 42 miles (68 km) to San Simeon.

2 From San Simeon, head to **Julia Pfeiffer Burns State Park** (CA-1, 37 miles north of Ragged Point, 831/667-2315, www.parks.ca.gov, sunrise-sunset daily, $10), where you can walk to an overlook of the stunning **McWay Falls,** an 80-foot waterfall that cascades off a cliff and onto the beach of a remote cove.

> Continue north on CA-1 for 52 miles (84 km) to the state park.

3 Continue north through **Big Sur,** one of the most scenic drives in the world. This section of CA-1 passes redwood forests and crystal-clear streams and rivers while offering breathtaking, nearly constant views of the coast. As you make your way north, stop in **Carmel-By-The-Sea** for a late lunch.

MCWAY FALLS IN JULIA PFEIFFER BURNS STATE PARK

Best BIG SUR DAY HIKES

CONE PEAK TRAIL

The **Cone Peak Trail** (4 mi/6 km round-trip, strenuous) offers serious rewards for adventurous hikers willing to find its out-of-the-way trailhead. At 5,150 feet, Cone Peak is the second-highest peak in the Big Sur area. The ascent from the trailhead rises 1,355 feet without much shade, so bring water. At the summit of Cone Peak is a sensational 360-degree view. Look west, as the steep mountain range drops to sea level in less than three miles. To the east, you can see the Salinas Valley and, on clear days, the Sierra Nevada.

The trailhead is located on the unpaved **Cone Peak Road** (status 831/385-5434, closed Nov.-May). Drive 10 miles (16 km) north of Gorda on CA-1 until you reach **Nacimiento-Fergusson Road** on the right. Drive up the steep road for 7 miles (11 km) to its crest; there you will see dirt roads departing to your left and right. Take a left onto Cone Peak Road and follow it for almost 5.5 miles (9 km). Look for a trail sign and small area to park on the left.

EWOLDSEN TRAIL

The **Ewoldsen Trail** (4.5 mi/7 km round-trip, moderate-strenuous) in **Julia Pfeiffer Burns State Park** (CA-1, 37 mi/60 km north of Ragged Point, 831/667-2315, www.parks.ca.gov, sunrise-sunset daily, $10) takes you by a creek and lush greenery, along with some of Big Sur's finest redwoods. Part of the trail is perched on a ridgeline. Bring water, as this hike can take several hours.

RIDGE TRAIL AND PANORAMA TRAIL LOOP

For a coastal hike, take the **Ridge Trail and Panorama Trail Loop** (8 mi/13 km round-trip, moderate-strenuous) at **Andrew Molera State Park** (CA-1, 4.5 mi/7 km north of Pfeiffer Big Sur State Park, 831/667-2315, www.parks.ca.gov, sunrise-sunset daily, $10). Start at the parking lot on **Creamery Meadow Beach Trail,** then make a left onto the long and fairly steep **Ridge Trail.** Turn right onto **Panorama Trail,** which runs down to the coastal scrublands. From Panorama, you can take **Spring Trail,** a short spur, out to a secluded beach. Panorama Trail turns into **Bluffs Trail,** which takes you back to Creamery Meadow.

Get it to-go and have a picnic at **Carmel Beach** (Ocean Ave., 831/620-2000, http://ci.carmel.ca.us/carmel/), one of the Monterey Bay region's best beaches. It's another two hours or so from here to get back to **San Francisco.**

> Keep following CA-1 N for another 36 miles (58 km) through Big Sur to Carmel Beach. Continue on CA-1 N out of Monterey, linking up with CA-156 E. Follow this for 6 miles (10 km) to US-101 N, which will return you to San Francisco in 98 miles (158 km).

GETTING THERE

AIR

It's easy to fly into the San Francisco Bay Area. There are three major airports. Among them, you should be able to find a flight that fits your schedule. **San Francisco International Airport** (SFO, www.flysfo.com) is 15 miles (24 km) south of the city center. **Oakland Airport** (OAK, www.oaklandairport.com) is east of the city, and requires crossing the bay, either via the Bay Bridge or public transit. **Mineta San José Airport** (SJC, www.flysanjose.com) is the farthest away, roughly 50

CARMEL BEACH

miles (81 km) to the south. Some San Francisco hotels offer complimentary airport shuttles.

Several public transportation options can get you into San Francisco. **Bay Area Rapid Transit** (BART, www.bart.gov) connects directly with SFO's international terminal; an airport shuttle connects Oakland airport to the nearest station. **Caltrain** (www.caltrain.com, tickets $3.75-13.75) is a good option from San Jose; an airport shuttle connects to the train station. **Millbrae Station** is where the BART and Caltrain systems connect; it's designed to transfer from one line to the other.

TRAIN

Amtrak (www.amtrak.com) does not run directly into San Francisco, but you can ride to San Jose, Oakland, or Emeryville Stations, then take a connecting bus to San Francisco.

BUS

Greyhound (200 Folsom St., 415/495-1569, www.greyhound.com, 5:30am-1:30am daily) offers bus service to San Francisco from all over the country.

CAR

From the **San Francisco airport** to downtown San Francisco, it's 30-40 minutes (15 mi/24 km). Take US-101 N until the exit for downtown San Francisco.

From the **Oakland airport**, it's 45 minutes to an hour (19 mi/31 km). Take I-880 N, then follow signs for I-80 W and the Bay Bridge. Take any of the exits after you cross the bridge to reach downtown.

From the **San Jose airport**, it's 1-1.5 hours (50 mi/81 km). Take I-880 N, then I-80 W over the Bay Bridge. Take any of the exits after you cross the bridge to reach downtown.

CONNECT WITH

- At Los Angeles or Kingman: **Route 66** (PAGE 60)
- At San Francisco, Los Angeles, San Luis Obispo, Santa Barbara, or Big Sur: **Pacific Coast Highway: California** (PAGE 124)
- At Yosemite National Park: **Pacific Crest Trail: California** (PAGE 140)
- At San Francisco, Yosemite National Park, or Big Sur: **Northern California Loop** (PAGE 156)
- At Los Angeles: **Southern California and Route 66 Loop** (PAGE 178)

PACIFIC COAST HIGHWAY: CALIFORNIA

WHY GO: Whale-watching, charming beach towns, coastal drives, remote hikes, epic views, farm-to-table fare

TOTAL DISTANCE: 1,085 miles/ 1,745 kilometers

NUMBER OF DAYS: 11

SEASONS: Late spring through early fall

START: Crescent City, California

END: San Diego, California

▼ BIXBY CREEK BRIDGE ON PACIFIC COAST HIGHWAY

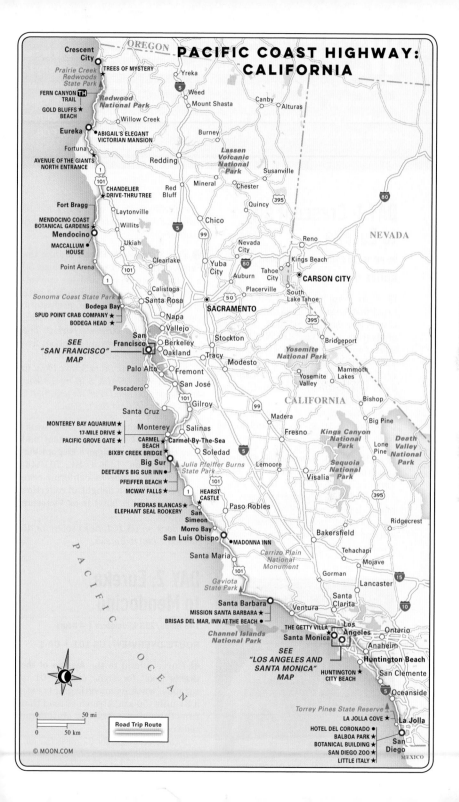

PACIFIC COAST HIGHWAY: CALIFORNIA

OREGON

Crescent City
TREES OF MYSTERY
Prairie Creek Redwoods State Park
FERN CANYON TRAIL **TH**
GOLD BLUFFS BEACH ★
Redwood National Park
Willow Creek
Eureka
ABIGAIL'S ELEGANT VICTORIAN MANSION ●
Fortuna
AVENUE OF THE GIANTS NORTH ENTRANCE
CHANDELIER DRIVE-THRU TREE ★
Fort Bragg
MENDOCINO COAST BOTANICAL GARDENS ★
Mendocino
MACCALLUM HOUSE ●
Point Arena

Yreka
Weed
Mount Shasta
Canby
Alturas
Burney
Redding
Lassen Volcanic National Park
Susanville
Red Bluff
Mineral
Chester
Quincy
Laytonville
Willits
Ukiah
Chico
Clearlake
Nevada City
Reno
Kings Beach
Yuba City
Auburn
Tahoe City
CARSON CITY
NEVADA

Calistoga
Santa Rosa
Sonoma Coast State Park
Bodega Bay
SPUD POINT CRAB COMPANY ★
BODEGA HEAD ★
Napa
Vallejo
SACRAMENTO
Placerville
South Lake Tahoe
San Francisco
Berkeley
Oakland
Stockton
Bridgeport
SEE "SAN FRANCISCO" MAP
Palo Alto
Fremont
Tracy
Modesto
Yosemite National Park
Pescadero
San José
Yosemite Valley
Mammoth Lakes
Santa Cruz
Gilroy
Madera
CALIFORNIA
Bishop
MONTEREY BAY AQUARIUM ★
17-MILE DRIVE ★
PACIFIC GROVE GATE ★
Monterey
Salinas
Fresno
Kings Canyon National Park
Big Pine
CARMEL BEACH
Carmel-By-The-Sea
Soledad
BIXBY CREEK BRIDGE ★
Big Sur
DEETJEN'S BIG SUR INN ●
Julia Pfeiffer Burns State Park
Lemoore
Sequoia National Park
Lone Pine
Death Valley National Park
PFEIFFER BEACH ★
MCWAY FALLS ★
Visalia
PIEDRAS BLANCAS ★
ELEPHANT SEAL ROOKERY
HEARST CASTLE
San Simeon
Paso Robles
Morro Bay
San Luis Obispo
MADONNA INN ●
Bakersfield
Ridgecrest
Santa Maria
Carrizo Plain National Monument
Tehachapi
Mojave
Gaviota State Park
Gorman
Lancaster
Santa Barbara
MISSION SANTA BARBARA ★
BRISAS DEL MAR, INN AT THE BEACH ★
Ventura
Santa Clarita
Channel Islands National Park
THE GETTY VILLA ★
Los Angeles
Santa Monica
Ontario
SEE "LOS ANGELES AND SANTA MONICA" MAP
Anaheim
Huntington Beach
HUNTINGTON CITY BEACH ★
San Clemente
Oceanside
Torrey Pines State Reserve
LA JOLLA COVE ★
La Jolla
HOTEL DEL CORONADO ●
BALBOA PARK ★
BOTANICAL BUILDING ★
SAN DIEGO ZOO ★
LITTLE ITALY ★
San Diego
MEXICO

PACIFIC OCEAN

0   50 mi
0   50 km
Road Trip Route

© MOON.COM

When you crave jaw dropping Pacific Ocean panoramas, there's only one place to go: California's Pacific Coast Highway. Craggy and wild in the north, wide and spacious in the south, this route from Crescent City to San Diego is the stuff of legend. Inspiring sightlines, windswept landscapes, and beautifully preserved parks greet you at every bend in the road. Enjoy delectable, gourmet cuisine at five-star restaurants, and find R&R at boutique lodges and high-end spas. You'll want for nothing when you travel the PCH.

DAY 1: Crescent City to Eureka

95 miles/153 kilometers | 3 hours

ROUTE OVERVIEW: US-101

1 Start your adventure with a late breakfast or early lunch in **Crescent City** before continuing on to the **Trees of Mystery** (15500 US-101 N., 707/482-2251, www.treesofmystery.net, 8am-7pm daily June-Aug., 9am-5pm daily Sept.-May, $15 adults, $8 children 6-12) to ride the gondola and browse Native American art.

> *Leave Crescent City via US-101 S. Continue for 16 miles (26 km) to the Trees of Mystery.*

2 At **Newton B. Drury Scenic Parkway,** explore **Prairie Creek Redwoods State Park** (127011 Newton B. Drury Pkwy., 707/488-2039, www.parks.ca.gov, 24 hours daily). You may be able to spot the resident herd of Roosevelt elk grazing in Elk Prairie from a viewing platform in the park.

> *Continue south on US-101 for 10 miles (16 km) to reach Newton B. Drury Scenic Pkwy.*

3 Visit **Gold Bluffs Beach** to hike the **Fern Canyon Trail** (1 mi/1.6 km loop, 30 minutes, easy, $8 per vehicle), marveling at the steep canyon dripping with green ferns—a vision of prehistoric times and one that Steven Spielberg used in his film *Jurassic Park 2.* The trailhead is at a parking lot about five miles off US-101 on Davison Road.

> *Use Newton B. Drury Scenic Pkwy. to reconnect with US-101 S (8 mi/13 km). At Davison Rd., head west for less than 5 miles (8 km) to Gold Bluffs Beach.*

4 Continue south to charming, walkable **Eureka.** Grab a good meal and stay the night at **Abigail's Elegant Victorian Mansion** (1406 C St., 707/444-3144, www.eureka-california.com, $135-145). With a delightful collection of antiques, this hotel is as Victorian as it gets.

> *Back on US-101, head south for 45 miles (72 km) to Eureka.*

DAY 2: Eureka to Mendocino

145 miles/233 kilometers | 4 hours

ROUTE OVERVIEW: US-101 • CA-1

1 Curve inland to the **Avenue of the Giants** (look for signs on US-101 to turnoffs, www.avenueofthegiants.net), a 31-mile (50-km) stretch of road that runs through magnificent, statuesque redwoods.

> *Drive US-101 S for 32 miles (52 km) to the northern entrance of Avenue of the Giants.*

PAUL BUNYAN STATUE AT TREES OF MYSTERY

Top 5 PACIFIC COAST HIGHWAY: CALIFORNIA

1. Hike the famous **Fern Canyon Trail** for a glimpse back to prehistoric times (PAGE 126).

2. Spot **gray whales** off the coast at **Bodega Head** (PAGE 128).

3. Live like a 1950s beatnik with a stay at San Francisco's **Hotel Boheme** (PAGE 129).

4. Witness the roaring McWay Falls at **Julia Pfeiffer Burns State Park** (PAGE 132).

5. Photograph Big Sur's **Bixby Creek Bridge,** one of the most visually stunning bridges in the country (PAGE 132).

HOTEL Boheme

MENDOCINO COAST

② Enjoy the admittedly cool tourist trap of **Chandelier Drive-Thru Tree** (67402 Drive-Thru Tree Rd., 707/925-6464, www.drivethrutree.com, 8:30am-dusk daily, $5 per car). It's a tree with an opening that's six feet wide and six feet high.

> Follow Avenue of the Giants south for 31 miles (50 km). Merge onto US-101 S and take it for 29 miles (47 km) to the Chandelier Drive-Thru Tree.

③ Drive south through **Fort Bragg**, stopping to explore the 47 acres of **Mendocino Coast Botanical Gardens** (18220 CA-1 N., 707/964-4352, www.gardenbythesea.org, 9am-5pm daily Mar.-Oct., 9am-4pm daily Nov.-Feb., $15 adults, $8 children 6-14). These gardens offer miles of walking and hiking through careful plantings and wild landscapes.

> Take CA-1 S for 45 miles (72 km) to Fort Bragg.

④ In **Mendocino,** spend the rest of the day strolling through art galleries and shops. Book a room at the charming **MacCallum House** (45020 Albion St., 800/609-0492, www.maccallumhouse.com, $150-350), where you can dine in the restaurant, enjoy a cocktail at the bar, or soak in a hot tub.

> Continue south on CA-1 for 8 miles (13 km) to Mendocino.

DAY 3: Mendocino to San Francisco

175 miles/280 kilometers | 5 hours

ROUTE OVERVIEW: CA-1 • US-101

① After breakfast in the garden at MacCallum House, simply enjoy the breathtaking stretch of coastline driving south, culminating with the rocky coves at **Sonoma Coast State Park** (707/875-3483, www.parks.ca.gov, day use $8 per vehicle).

> Drive south on CA-1 for 80 miles (129 km) to Sonoma Coast State Park, just south of Jenner.

② In **Bodega Head** (watch for the sign), you've arrived at the best spot for bird-watching and whale-watching, and home to **Spud Point Crab Company** (1910 Westshore Rd., 707/875-9472, www.spudpointcrab.com, 9am-5pm daily, $7-15). Grab fish sandwiches and clam chowder to go, then take

KEY RESERVATIONS

- To tour **Alcatraz,** book your tickets **two weeks** in advance.
- Even though admission is free to the **Getty Villa** in Pacific Palisades, reservations are required.

them to the Bodega Head trail to enjoy with panoramic views of the coast.

> *Continue on CA-1 S to Bodega Head (16 mi/26 km). To reach the Bodega Head trail from Spud Point, continue south along Westshore Rd. to its end.*

❸ Stop in the **Marin Headlands** (follow signs for Sausalito) to enjoy the view of the iconic **Golden Gate Bridge.** Park and walk to the **vista point** on Conzelman Road, which boasts arguably the best view of the bridge.

> *Continue on CA-1 S for 10 miles (16 km). Continue straight when you reach Valley Ford Rd. After 3 miles (5 km), turn left onto Roblar Rd. and follow it for 6.5 miles (10.5 km). Turn right onto Stony Point Rd. and drive for 3 miles (5 km) to US-101 S. Follow US-101 S for 36 miles (58 km) to the Alexander Ave. exit. Follow Bunker Rd. and McCullough Rd. to reach Conzelman Rd.*

❹ Cross over the bridge, but don't get distracted by the views! Check into the Beatnik throwback **Hotel Boheme** (444 Columbus Ave., 415/433-9111, www. hotelboheme.com, $235 and up). The hotel is in North Beach, San Francisco's Little Italy and the birthplace of the Beat Generation.

> *Take US-101 S for 5 miles (8 km), then city streets to reach Hotel Boheme.*

❺ Walk to nearby **Chinatown** (Grant Ave. and Stockton St.) for noodles, dumplings, and other traditional dishes. Established in 1848, it's the oldest Chinese district in the United States.

DAY 4: San Francisco

MORNING

❶ Start the morning by making your way to **Fisherman's Wharf.** From here, cross the bay to tour the famous island prison of **Alcatraz** (415/981-7625, www. alcatrazcruises.com, 8:45am-6:30pm daily, $37-90). A visit to Alcatraz involves a ferry ride to the island and an audio tour around the cell house. The tour lasts at least 2.5 hours. Buy your ticket at least two weeks in advance; they often sell out, especially on summer weekends. Ferries depart from Pier 33.

AFTERNOON

❷ After you get your land legs back, stroll the bayfront for lunch at the **Ferry Building** (1 Ferry Bldg., 415/983-8030, www.ferrybuildingmarketplace. com, 10am-7pm Mon.-Fri., 8am-6pm Sat., 11am-5pm Sun.). Inside the handsome structure, it's all about the food, from fresh produce and high-end wine to cheese and gourmet eateries. Sample from local favorites like Cowgirl Creamery, Acme Bread Company, and Blue Bottle Coffee.

❸ Grab a coffee to go and spend the rest of the afternoon at **Golden Gate Park** (main entrance at Stanyan St. at Fell St., 415/831-2700, www.goldengate-park.com). This huge urban park attracts millions of visitors annually with the amazing **de Young Museum** and **California Academy of Sciences,** gardens, and recreational fields.

THE GOLDEN GATE BRIDGE

SAN FRANCISCO

EVENING

❹ Top off the day with an excellent dinner in the **Mission District** (bounded by Market St., Church St., Cesar Chavez, and US-101), which is known for its street-style Mexican food.

DAY 5: San Francisco to Big Sur

170 miles/275 kilometers | 5 hours

ROUTE OVERVIEW: US-101 • I-280 • CA-1 • 17-Mile Drive • CA-1

❶ Move out early to head down CA-1, rounding Monterey Bay. Tour the famous **Monterey Bay Aquarium** (886 Cannery Row, 831/648-4800, www.montereybayaquarium.org, 9:30am-6pm daily Memorial Day weekend-Labor Day weekend, 10am-5pm daily rest of year, $50 adults, $30 children 3-12). The vast array of sealife and exhibits at this aquarium is astonishing.

> Take US-101 S for 3 miles (5 km) to I-280 S. I-280 connects to CA-1 S in 6 miles (10 km). Follow this for 108 miles (174 km) to Monterey and the aquarium.

❷ Hugging the coastline between Monterey and Pebble Beach, **17-Mile Drive** (Pacific Grove Gate, just past CA-68, $10 per vehicle, cash only, no motorcycles) offers an introduction to some of the most beautiful land- and

MONTEREY BAY AQUARIUM

Best VIEWS

NORTHERN CALIFORNIA

- **Bodega Head** (3 mi/4.8 km west of CA-1, Bodega Bay) offers rugged coastline views and occasional Pacific gray whales traveling their migration route.

- **Crescent Beach Overlook** (2 mi/3.2 km past Crescent Beach, Del Norte section) in Redwood National Park offers views of the seascape that are hard to beat.

- The **Marin Headlands** (Conzelman Rd., Sausalito) have the best views of the San Francisco skyline and the Golden Gate Bridge, while the city's **Baker Beach** (off Lincoln Blvd., San Francisco) offers the reverse view—bridge and headlands—from the opposite side.

CENTRAL CALIFORNIA

- At **Gaviota State Park** (US-101, 33 mi/53 km west of Santa Barbara, 805/968-1033, www.parks.ca.gov, 7am-sunset daily, $10 per vehicle), Gaviota Peak is at the end of a rugged three-mile trail that climaxes with stunning views of the Channel Islands.

- **Julia Pfeiffer Burns State Park** (CA-1, 37 mi/60 km south of Carmel, 12 mi/19 km south of Pfeiffer Big Sur State Park, 831/667-2315, www.parks. ca.gov, $10 per vehicle) is where you'll find the stunning view of McWay Falls cascading down the cliffside to a remote cove.

- **Pfeiffer Beach** (accessed via Sycamore Canyon Rd., about 0.25 mile south of Big Sur) showcases the best sunsets on the Big Sur coastline.

SOUTHERN CALIFORNIA

- **The Getty Center** (1200 Getty Center Dr., Los Angeles, 310/440-7300, 10am-5:30pm Tues.-Fri. and Sun., 10am-9pm Sat., free admission, $5 audio tour, $15 parking) is a hilltop museum with unmatched views of the L.A. skyline and coastline.

- **Cabrillo National Monument** (1800 Cabrillo Memorial Dr., San Diego, 619/557-5450, www.nps. gov/cabr, 9am-5pm daily, $10 per vehicle, $7 per motorcycle, $5 pedestrians) sits on the highest point in San Diego, looking down on the city, its namesake bay, Coronado, Mexico, and a vast expanse of ocean.

- **Point Dume State Beach** (Westward Beach Rd., Malibu, 310/457-8143, sunrise-sunset daily) has the best views of the Malibu coastline outside of a movie star's mega-mansion.

▼ VIEW FROM BAKER BEACH

▼ POINT DUME STATE BEACH

seascapes on the central coast. When you pay your fee at the **Pacific Grove gate,** you'll get a map of the sights that you will pass as you make your way along the winding coastal road. Continue south to **Carmel-By-The-Sea.** This adorable village offers pristine white sand at **Carmel Beach,** charming art galleries, and plenty of options for lunch.

> *Take David Ave. for 1 mile (1.6 km). Turn right on Forest Ave., then left on Sunset Dr., then left onto 17-Mile Dr. to reach the Pacific Grove gate. From 17-Mile Dr., turn right onto Carmel Way to reach Carmel-By-The-Sea.*

❸ The highway heading into **Big Sur** has some of the most scenic stretches in California. Be sure to snap some photographs, stopping or using pullouts only when it's safe. Enjoy breathtaking views at the **Bixby Creek Bridge** (CA-1, 11 mi/17.7 km north of Big Sur Village). This iconic landmark, perched alongside seaside cliffs, is one of the most photographed bridges in the world. Snap a photo from the north side of the bridge at the pull-off.

> *Take CA-1 S to reach Big Sur. Bixby Creek Bridge is 15 miles (24 km) south of Carmel Beach.*

❹ On the west side of CA-1, take Sycamore Canyon Road to **Pfeiffer Beach** (accessed via Sycamore Canyon Rd., about 0.25 mi/0.4 km south of Big Sur)

to see impressive rock formations like Keyhole Arch. Time your stop for sunset to get the most dramatic views.

> *Take CA-1 S for 14 miles (23 km). Turn right onto Sycamore Canyon Rd. and follow it for 2 miles (3 km) to reach the beach.*

❺ Retire to historic **Deetjens Big Sur Inn** (48865 CA-1, 831/667-2377, www.deetjens.com, $105-270), a rustic spot nestled in the redwoods.

> *Return to CA-1 via Sycamore Canyon Rd. and drive south for 2.5 miles (4 km) to reach the inn.*

DAY 6: Big Sur to San Luis Obispo

115 miles/185 kilometers | 3 hours

ROUTE OVERVIEW: CA-1

❶ Set out early, stopping at **Julia Pfeiffer Burns State Park** (47225 CA-1, 26 mi/42 km south of Carmel, 831/667-2315, www.parks.ca.gov, day-use $10) to hike the short trail to the scenic overlook of **McWay Falls.** Walk to the observation deck to view the waterfall, which cascades year-round off a cliff and onto the beach of a remote cove.

> *Drive south on CA-1 for 5 miles (8 km) to reach the parking area for the state park.*

❷ See the elephant seals at the **Piedras Blancas Elephant Seal Rookery** (4 mi/6.4 km north of Hearst Castle entrance on CA-1, 805/924-1628, www.elephantseal.org). Winter is the best

MCWAY FALLS IN JULIA PFEIFFER BURNS STATE PARK

time to view the males, females, and newborn pups. There is a large parking area, along with a boardwalk where a guide is available 10am-4pm to answer questions.

> *Continue south on CA-1 for 50 miles (81 km) to reach the rookery.*

❸ In **San Simeon,** stop for lunch before visiting the enchanting **Hearst Castle** (750 Hearst Castle Rd., 800/444-4445, www.hearstcastle.org, 9am-close daily, prices vary by tour). No visit to the California coast is complete without a tour of this grand mansion on a hill, conceived and built by publishing magnate William Randolph Hearst.

> *Drive another 4.5 miles south on CA-1 to reach San Simeon and Hearst Castle.*

❹ At **Morro Bay,** CA-1 moves inland. Continue toward **San Luis Obispo,** a lively little college town, where the kitschy and whimsical **Madonna Inn** (100 Madonna Rd., 805/543-3000, www.madonnainn.com, $210-500) is worth an overnight stay.

> *Continue south on CA-1 for 44 miles (71 km) to get to San Luis Obispo and the Madonna Inn.*

DAY 7: San Luis Obispo to Santa Barbara

110 miles/177 kilometers | 2.5 hours

ROUTE OVERVIEW: US-101 • city streets

❶ At **Gaviota State Park** (US-101, 33 mi/53 km west of Santa Barbara, 805/968-1033, www.parks.ca.gov, 7am-sunset daily, $10 per vehicle), you can hike to **Gaviota Peak** (6 mi/9.7 km round-trip, 2.5 hours, moderate) for stunning views of the Channel Islands.

> *Take US-101 S for 72 miles (116 km) to reach the state park.*

❷ Drive south to **Santa Barbara** to enjoy lunch and window-shopping on State Street. Spend the afternoon diving into Santa Barbara's history and culture, visiting **Old Mission Santa Barbara** (2201 Laguna St., 805/682-4713, www.santabarbaramission.org, 9am-5pm daily, self-guided tours $9 adults,

Playlist

PACIFIC COAST HIGHWAY: CALIFORNIA

SONGS

- **"Big Sur" by The Thrills:** This Irish band will elevate your trip with a jaunty tune about Big Sur.

- **"Midnight City" by M83:** This song has nothing to do with California or the Pacific Ocean, but as soon as you hear the swirling, anthemic, universe-busting sounds by French electronic group M83, you'll know it's big enough and grand enough to pair with the glorious natural environs laid out before you.

- **"Road to Nowhere" by The Talking Heads:** Even though you have a destination in mind, the endless expanse of ocean makes this punchy, cheery song by 1980s band The Talking Heads feel apt.

OLD MISSION SANTA BARBARA

$4 children 5-17). It's known as the "Queen of the Missions" for its beauty and lush setting.

> *Continue south on US-101 for 30 miles to reach Santa Barbara and the mission.*

③ Visit at least one of more than 30 tasting rooms on the **Santa Barbara Urban Wine Trail** (www.urbanwinetrailsb.com), then stroll along the beach for sunset before getting dinner downtown.

④ Get a room at the Spanish-style **Brisas del Mar** (223 Castillo St., 805/966-2219 or 800/468-1988, www.sbhotels.com, $200-320), just a short walk from the beach.

DAY 8: Santa Barbara to Santa Monica

90 miles/145 kilometers | 2.5 hours

ROUTE OVERVIEW: US-101 • CA-1 • city streets

① **Malibu** offers a fantastic coastal drive that passes by dreamy surf and million-dollar beach houses. Lovers of art and history should stop at the **Getty Villa** (17985 CA-1, Pacific Palisades, 310/440-7300, www.getty.edu, 10am-5pm Wed.-Mon., free but reservations required, $15 parking), a lush estate that houses 23 galleries of Etruscan, Greek, and Roman antiquities.

SANTA MONICA PIER

VENICE BEACH

> *Take US-101 S for 37 miles (60 km). Here, join CA-1 S and drive for 29 miles (47 km) into Malibu. Continue along this route for 14 miles (23 km) to the Getty Villa.*

② Once you reach **Santa Monica,** visit the **Santa Monica Pier** (Ocean Ave. at Colorado Ave., 310/458-8900, www.santamonicapier.org). Surrounded by a gorgeous beach and topped by a small amusement park, the pier is the center of attention here.

> *Drive 5 miles (8 km) south on CA-1 to Santa Monica and the pier.*

③ Head farther south to the funky 2.5-mile-long **Venice Beach Boardwalk** (Ocean Front Walk, spans Navy Ct. to S. Venice Blvd., www.venicebeach.com, free). Prepare yourself for people-watching of fantastic proportions. While a steady stream of bikers, skateboarders, and Rollerbladers cruise by, so, too, do hippies, oiled-up bodybuilders, yoga acrobats, buskers, tarot readers, breakdancing B-boys, roller disco mavens, street hustlers, and every shade of exhibitionist.

④ Head back to Santa Monica and stay the night at the beachfront art deco **Georgian Hotel** (1415 Ocean Ave., 310/395-9945 or 800/538-8147, www.georgianhotel.com, $200 and up).

Best BEACHES

NORTHERN CALIFORNIA

- **Black Sands Beach** (20 mi/32 km south of Ferndale along Mattole Rd.), composed of crumbly volcanic rock, is the most accessible sight on the remote Lost Coast.
- **Stinson Beach** (CA-1, Stinson Beach) is the favorite destination for San Franciscans seeking some surf and sunshine.

CENTRAL CALIFORNIA

- **Carmel Beach** (bottom of Ocean Ave., Carmel) features soft sand, blue water, and dogs roaming freely.
- **Moonstone Beach** (Moonstone Beach Dr., Cambria) is known for breathtaking views and surf-smoothed stones.
- **Pfeiffer Beach** (accessed via Sycamore Canyon Rd., about 0.25 mile south of Big Sur) is the best place to watch the sun set along the Big Sur coastline.

SOUTHERN CALIFORNIA

- **Black's Beach** (trailhead at Torrey Pines Gliderport, 2800 Torrey Pines Scenic Dr., La Jolla) requires a little hiking to get to, but the reward is a secluded beach backed by sandstone cliffs.
- **Coronado Beach** (along Ocean Blvd., San Diego) is a family-friendly beach considered among the world's best, especially in front of the famous Hotel del Coronado, where lounge chairs and cocktails are available.
- **Huntington City Beach** (103 CA-1 from Beach Blvd. to Seapoint St., Huntington Beach, 714/536-5281, www.surfcityusa.com, 5am-10pm daily), aka Surf City, USA, delivers waves, bikinis, volleyball nets, and a long bike path.
- **La Jolla Shores** (8300 Camino del Oro, La Jolla, 619/235-1169) is a beautiful stretch of sand great for families and beginning surfers.
- **Zuma Beach** (30000 CA-1, Malibu, http://beaches.lacounty.gov, $3-12.50), Malibu's classic beach party site, offers surfing, boogie boarding, and volleyball.

▲ HUNTINGTON CITY BEACH

DAY 9: Santa Monica to Los Angeles

40 miles/64 kilometers | 2.5 hours

ROUTE OVERVIEW: I-10 • I-405 • city streets • I-405 • US-101 • city streets

1 Wait for rush hour traffic to die down with a leisurely morning appreciating the art at **The Getty Center** (1200 Getty Center Dr., 310/440-7300, 10am-5:30pm Tues.-Fri. and Sun., 10am-9pm Sat., free, $15 parking). This fortress of travertine- and aluminum-clad pavilions was built to house the eclectic art collection of billionaire J. Paul Getty, which includes everything from Renaissance-era paintings to pop art.

> Take I-10 E for 3 miles (5 km) to merge onto I-405 N (5 mi/8 km). Take the exit for N. Sepulveda Blvd., then continue to The Getty Center.

2 It's time for a classic L.A. drive up **Sunset Boulevard** into **Hollywood.** See the **Walk of Fame** (Hollywood Blvd. from La Brea Ave. to Vine St., 323/469-8311, www.walkoffame.com). Since 1960, entertainment legends have wished for a spot on this sidewalk of the stars. Along the way, get an eyeful at the ornate **TCL Chinese Theatre** (6925 Hollywood Blvd., 323/461-3331, www.tclchinesetheatres.com). The hand- and footprints of silver screen stars here are what inspired the creation of the Walk of Fame.

> Head north on I-405 for 4 miles (6 km), following it to US-101 S toward Los Angeles (10 mi/16 km). Take the exit for Highland Ave./Hollywood Bowl. After 1 mile (1.6 km), turn right to reach the Walk of Fame. From here, it's less than a five-minute walk west on Hollywood Blvd. to the TCL Chinese Theatre.

3 Less than a half-block away, check in to your hotel at **The Hollywood Roosevelt** (7000 Hollywood Blvd., 323/856-1970, www.thehollywoodroosevelt.com, $262-345).

GRIFFITH OBSERVATORY

4 Enjoy some science along with city views from the popular **Griffith Observatory** (2800 E. Observatory Rd., 213/473-0800, noon-10pm Tues.-Fri., 10am-10pm Sat.-Sun., free), which resides within the 4,210-acre Griffith Park.

> Get onto Franklin Ave. and head east for 1.5 miles (2.5 km). Turn left onto N. Western Ave., which quickly becomes Los Feliz Blvd. Make a quick left onto Fern Dell Dr., which turns into Western Canyon Rd. after a while. Continue for 1.5 miles (2.5 km), then turn right onto W. Observatory Rd. This 5-mile (8-km) drive usually takes 20-25 minutes in traffic.

5 Take your pick of the city's exciting dining options before getting a taste of Hollywood nightlife on the **Sunset Strip** (Sunset Blvd. from Havenhurst Dr. to Sierra Dr.). Decades worth of up-and-coming rock acts first made their names on the Strip. Today, you'll still find many of the Strip's legendary rock clubs here.

> Retrace your steps to Franklin Ave. Go west on Franklin for 1.5 miles (2.5 km). Turn left onto Highland Ave., then make a quick right to get back on Franklin. Turn left onto La Brea Ave. after less than a mile, then right onto Hollywood Blvd. After 1 mile (1.6 km), turn left onto Laurel Ave. Turn right after two blocks to get onto Sunset Blvd. To return to The Hollywood Roosevelt, retrace your steps on Sunset and Hollywood Blvd.

DAY 10: Los Angeles to San Diego

145 miles/233 kilometers | 4.5 hours

ROUTE OVERVIEW: US-101 • I-5 • I-605 • I-405 • CA-1 • I-5 • CA-75

1 Head downtown first thing to visit **The Broad** (221 S. Grand Ave., 213/232-6200, www.thebroad.org, 11am-5pm Tues.-Wed., 11am-8pm Thurs.-Fri., 10am-8pm Sat., 10am-6pm Sun., free, touring exhibitions require tickets) to see why L.A. is the top contemporary art destination on the West Coast.

> From Hollywood, follow US-101 S for 6 miles (10 km). Take the exit for Temple St. to reach the museum.

2 Catch sun and waves in **Huntington Beach,** a surf mecca. **Huntington City Beach** (103 CA-1, from Beach Blvd. to Seapoint St., 714/536-5281, www.surfcityusa.com, 5am-10pm daily) constitutes 3.5 miles of good surf, volleyball courts, and a bike path. A pier in the center of the beach leads to Main Street, where you'll find a visitor information center, surf shops and rentals, restaurants, and bars.

> Take US-101 S and merge onto I-5 S after several miles. Follow I-5 for 9 miles (14 km), then pick up I-605 S for 11 miles (18 km). Merge onto I-405 S. Continue for less than 2 miles (3 km), then rejoin CA-1 S and follow it to Huntington Beach (9 mi/14 km).

3 Pass slowly through beautiful North County beach towns before reaching **Torrey Pines State Reserve** (12600 N. Torrey Pines Rd., 858/755-2063, www.torreypine.org, 9am-sunset daily, $15), one of the wildest stretches along the coastline north of **La Jolla.** The shortest walk here is the High Point Trail, only 100 yards up to views of the whole reserve, from the ocean to the lagoon to the forest and back.

> Continue on I-5 S for less than 5 miles (8 km) to Del Mar Heights Rd. Exit and turn right. Turn left on N. Torrey Pines Rd. to reach the reserve.

4 Drop into **La Jolla Cove** (northern tip of La Jolla village) for some kayaking or snorkeling. With its white sand and deep-blue water, this beach north of San Diego is a refuge from the road, and its sea caves are a refuge for diverse marinelife. Dine at one of the many incredible restaurants with a view in **La Jolla village.**

> Follow Torrey Pines Rd. south for about 7.5 miles (12 km) to reach La Jolla Cove.

LA JOLLA COVE

❺ Continue on to **San Diego** and check into the legendary **Hotel del Corona-do** (1500 Orange Ave., 619/435-6611 or 800/468-3533, www.hoteldel.com, $250 and up). This grand Victorian resort is famous for celebrity guests like Marilyn Monroe and its resident ghost.

> Take I-5 S for 12 miles (19 km), then follow the exit for CA-75. Take the Corona-do Bridge, then continue on CA-75 until Orange Ave. Turn left and follow Orange for 1 mile (1.6 km) until you see the ho-tel. Turn right onto R. H. Dana Pl. to reach the hotel.

DAY 11: San Diego

MORNING AND AFTERNOON

❶ Start your day by exploring **Balboa Park** (1549 El Prado, 619/239-0512, www.balboapark.org). This sprawl-ing urban park includes Spanish colo-nial architecture, lush gardens, multi-ple museums, and the grand **Botanical Building** (1549 El Prado, 619/239-0512, 10am-4pm Fri.-Wed., free).

BOTANICAL BUILDING IN BALBOA PARK

CRAFT BEER IN San Diego

Craft beer is a major tourist draw in San Diego, and most bars have a ter-rific tap list. But to taste the newest releases, you'll want to visit the brew-eries directly. To get a proper sam-pling, go explore **North Park**, a neigh-borhood that's home to more than a dozen high-quality microbreweries.

- San Diego's must-visit craft destinations include reputation-establishing originals **AleSmith** (9990 AleSmith Ct., 858/549-9888, www.alesmith.com, 11am-10pm Mon.-Thurs., 11am-11pm Fri.-Sat., 11am-9pm Sun.), about 20 minutes out of downtown in Miramar, and the more central **Stone Brewing** (2816 Historic Decatur Rd. #116, 619/269-2100, www.stonebrewing.com, 11:30am-9pm Mon.-Thurs., 11:30am-10pm Fri., 11am-10pm Sat., 11am-9pm Sun.), which has a restaurant and beer garden.

- The tops of the new breed are fresh IPA purists **Societe Brewing** (8262 Clairemont Mesa Blvd., 858/598-5409, www.societebrewing.com, noon-9pm Mon.-Wed., noon-10pm Thurs.-Sat., noon-8pm Sun.) and the quirky, creative **Modern Times** (3725 Greenwood St., 619/546-9694, www.moderntimesbeer.com, noon-10pm Sun.-Thurs., noon-midnight Fri.-Sat.).

- Visit the city's first craft brewpub downtown. Established in 1989, **Karl Strauss** (1157 Columbia St., 619/234-2739, www.karlstrauss.com, 11am-10pm Mon.-Thurs., 11am-11pm Fri.-Sat., 11:30am-10pm Sun.) has since grown to include a dozen brewpub locations throughout Southern California.

BALBOA PARK

② While you're in the park, spend time ogling pandas and polar bears at the world-famous **San Diego Zoo** (2920 Zoo Dr., 619/231-1515, 9am-5pm daily Nov.-Feb., 9am-6pm daily Mar.-May and Sept.-Oct., 9am-9pm daily June-Aug., $52 adults, $42 children).

EVENING

❸ Craft beer fans will find plenty of spots to sip in **Little Italy** (bounded by Pacific Hwy., W. Laurel St., I-5, and W. Ash St.). For dinner, stay in the neighborhood to sample the impressive restaurant and cocktail scene.

GETTING THERE

AIR

The major Northern California airport is **San Francisco International Airport** (SFO, 650/821-8211, www.flysfo.com), about 15 miles (24 km) south of the city center. **Del Norte County Regional Airport** (707/464-7288), also known as Jack McNamara Field, is 3 miles (5 km) northwest of Crescent City, in Del Norte County, with service provided by SkyWest Airlines to Eureka/Arcata, Sacramento, and San Francisco.

TRAIN

Amtrak (800/872-7245, www.amtrak.com) offers service on the **Coast Starlight** to Sacramento, Oakland, and Los Angeles. For travelers going long distances, Amtrak offers the USA Rail Pass, which is good for 15, 30, or 45 days.

BUS

Greyhound (800/231-2222, www.greyhound.com) offers routes along major highways and stops in numerous cities.

CAR

US-101 and **CA-1** (also known as Hwy. 1, Shoreline Highway, and Pacific Coast Highway) are the best north-south routes, providing a phenomenal scenic drive along most of California's Pacific coastline. CA-1 at times runs parallel to US-101. Its southern end is at I-5 near Dana Point and its northern end is at US-101 near Leggett.

To get to Crescent City from the **San Francisco airport**, it's a seven-hour drive north on US-101 (380 mi/612 km), traveling much of the route described in this trip. From the **Del Norte County airport**, it's a 10-minute drive (3 mi/5 km) south on surface streets to reach Crescent City.

GETTING BACK

To return to **Crescent City** from San Diego, the drive is 855 miles (1,376 km), which takes approximately 14 hours. In San Diego, hop on I-5 N. Follow it to CA-73 N, then take I-405 N. This will hook back up with I-5 N. Follow I-5 N until you reach I-580 W. Continue to US-101 N to reach Crescent City.

To return to **San Francisco** from San Diego, the drive is 508 miles (818 km), which takes approximately eight hours. Follow the directions for returning to Crescent City above; US-101 N routes through San Francisco.

CONNECT WITH

- At San Francisco or Los Angeles: **Best of the Golden State** (PAGE 108)

- At San Diego: **Pacific Crest Trail: California** (PAGE 140)

- At San Francisco, Big Sur, or Crescent City: **Northern California Loop** (PAGE 156)

- At Los Angeles or San Diego: **Southern California and Route 66 Loop** (PAGE 178)

- At Crescent City: **Pacific Coast Highway: Washington and Oregon** (PAGE 236)

PACIFIC CREST TRAIL: CALIFORNIA

WHY GO: Panoramic vistas, sparkling lakes, the best of California's hiking trails, camping, wildlife viewing

TOTAL DISTANCE: 1,585 miles/ 2,555 kilometers

NUMBER OF DAYS: 12

SEASONS: Spring through fall

START: San Diego, California

END: Ashland, Oregon

▼ TUOLUMNE MEADOWS IN YOSEMITE NATIONAL PARK

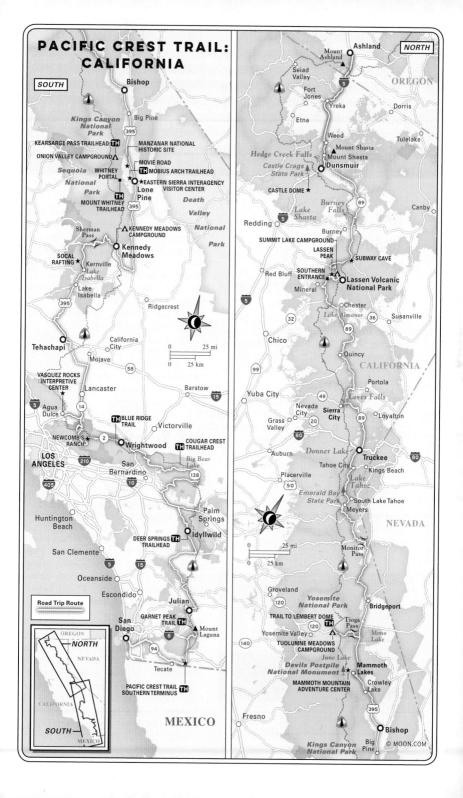

PACIFIC CREST TRAIL: CALIFORNIA

NORTH

SOUTH

SOUTH map (left panel):

Bishop

Kings Canyon National Park

Big Pine

395

Sequoia National Park

KEARSARGE PASS TRAILHEAD TH
ONION VALLEY CAMPGROUND

MANZANAR NATIONAL HISTORIC SITE

WHITNEY PORTAL
MOVIE ROAD
MOBIUS ARCH TRAILHEAD TH
EASTERN SIERRA INTERAGENCY VISITOR CENTER

Lone Pine

Death Valley National Park

MOUNT WHITNEY TRAILHEAD TH
395

Sherman Pass

KENNEDY MEADOWS CAMPGROUND

Kennedy Meadows

SOCAL RAFTING ★
Kernville
Lake Isabella

Lake Isabella

395

Ridgecrest

California City

Tehachapi

Mojave

58

VASQUEZ ROCKS INTERPRETIVE CENTER

Lancaster

Barstow

Agua Dulce
5
14

BLUE RIDGE TRAIL TH

Victorville
15

NEWCOMB'S RANCH ★
2

Wrightwood

COUGAR CREST TRAILHEAD TH

LOS ANGELES
210

San Bernardino

Big Bear Lake

138

405
10

Huntington Beach

Palm Springs

DEER SPRINGS TRAILHEAD TH

Idyllwild

San Clemente

Oceanside
5
15

Escondido

Road Trip Route

Julian

GARNET PEAK TRAIL TH

San Diego

Mount Laguna

94

8

Tecate

PACIFIC CREST TRAIL SOUTHERN TERMINUS TH

MEXICO

(Inset map, lower left): OREGON — NORTH — NEVADA — CALIFORNIA — SOUTH — MEXICO

NORTH map (right panel):

Mount Ashland
Ashland

NORTH

Seiad Valley
Fort Jones

OREGON

Yreka

Dorris

Etna

Weed

Tulelake

Mount Shasta

Hedge Creek Falls
Mount Shasta
Castle Crags State Park
Dunsmuir

Canby

CASTLE DOME ★

Burney Falls

Lake Shasta

Redding
5

Burney

89

SUMMIT LAKE CAMPGROUND

LASSEN PEAK

SUBWAY CAVE

Red Bluff

SOUTHERN ENTRANCE
Lassen Volcanic National Park

Mineral

Chester

Susanville

36

Lake Almanor

32

Chico

99

Quincy

CALIFORNIA

Portola

Yuba City

49

Loves Falls

Nevada City

Sierra City

Loyalton

Grass Valley
20
80

89

Auburn

Donner Lake

Truckee

80

Placerville

Tahoe City

Kings Beach

50

Lake Tahoe

Emerald Bay State Park

South Lake Tahoe

Meyers

NEVADA

Monitor Pass

Groveland
120

Yosemite National Park

Bridgeport

TRAIL TO LEMBERT DOME TH

Tioga Pass

Yosemite Valley
120

Mono Lake

TUOLUMNE MEADOWS CAMPGROUND

140

June Lake

Devils Postpile National Monument
Mammoth Lakes

MAMMOTH MOUNTAIN ADVENTURE CENTER

Crowley Lake

Fresno

395

Bishop

Kings Canyon National Park

Big Pine

© MOON.COM

0   25 mi
0   25 km

0   25 mi
0   25 km

t 2,653 miles (4,270 km) long, the Pacific Crest Trail stretches from the U.S.-Mexican border to the U.S.-Canadian border, passing through 25 national forests, seven national parks, and countless natural wonders like volcanoes, deep lakes, snowcapped mountain peaks, and granite cliffs. Though this is a route that's traditionally hiked for up to months at a time, it's possible to get a similar experience by taking an epic scenic drive along its length. Pull over whenever you can, lace up your hiking boots, and hit the trail. After, enjoy a hot meal and a cold craft beer in quaint trail towns.

DAY 1: San Diego to Julian

95 miles/153 kilometers | 2.5 hours

ROUTE OVERVIEW: CA-94 • Sunrise Hwy. • CA-79

❶ Hit the road out of San Diego. In the rural community of **Campo,** visit the **Pacific Crest Trail Southern Terminus Monument** on the U.S.-Mexico border.

> From San Diego, follow CA-94 E for 48 miles (77 km) to Campo.

❷ Head north on the **Sunrise Highway** to **Mount Laguna.** Stop at the **Pine House Café & Tavern** (9849 Sunrise Hwy., 619/473-8857, www.pinehouse-cafe.com, 5pm-7pm Thurs., noon-8pm Fri., 8am-8pm Sat., 8am-6pm Sun., $9-18) for a bowl of chili.

> Take Buckman Springs Rd. north. After 12 miles (19 km), the road becomes Old Hwy. 80. In 3.5 miles (5.5 km), turn onto Sunrise Hwy. and drive northeast for 9 miles (14.5 km) to Mount Laguna.

PACIFIC CREST TRAIL SOUTHERN TERMINUS MONUMENT

❸ Farther north, the **Garnet Peak Trail** (2.2 mi/3.5 km round-trip, 1.5 hours, easy/moderate) leads to a spectacular viewpoint overlooking Anza-Borrego Desert State Park. To get to the trailhead, look for the dirt parking area on the right side of the road (the eastern side) just north of mile marker 27. After the hike, continue north to Julian, where you'll spend the night.

> Continue north on the Sunrise Hwy. for 5 miles (8 km) to reach the trailhead. After the hike, go another 10 miles (16 km) on the Sunrise Hwy., and then turn onto CA-79 N. After 6 miles (10 km), the highway leads to Julian.

DAY 2: Julian to Idyllwild

80 miles/129 kilometers | 2 hours

ROUTE OVERVIEW: CA-79 • CA-371 • CA-74 • CA-243

❶ Wake up and grab breakfast—and some pie, for later—at **Mom's Pies** (2119 Main St., 760/765-2472, www.momspiesjulian.com, 7am-5pm Sun.-Fri., 7am-5:30pm Sat., $5-18) before heading north to **Idyllwild**.

❷ A hike on the **Deer Springs Trail** (10.6 mi/17.1 km one-way, 6 hours, strenuous) showcases the towering granite massifs of the San Jacinto Mountains. You can access the trailhead from CA-243, just before Cedar Glen Drive. The trail terminates at Humber Park, 3 miles (5 km) northeast of the Deer Springs trailhead. Arrange for a shuttle to meet you at

Top ⑤ PACIFIC CREST TRAIL: CALIFORNIA

① Ascend part of the trail leading to **Mount Whitney,** the highest peak in the Lower 48 (PAGE 147).

② Transport yourself to the Wild West in **Lone Pine** (PAGE 147).

③ Drive the 9,900-foot **Tioga Pass,** the highest highway pass in California (PAGE 150).

④ Hike to the top of a volcano at **Lassen Volcanic National Park** (PAGE 152).

⑤ Explore an underground lava tube at **Subway Cave** (PAGE 152).

DOWNTOWN IDYLLWILD

BIG BEAR LAKE FROM COUGAR CREST TRAIL

Humber Park to avoid the roadside walk back to your car.

> Head out on CA-79 N for 42 miles (68 km) to Aguanga, where you'll catch CA-371 E. In 21 miles (34 km) CA-371 dead-ends at CA-74. Turn left and take CA-74 W for 12 miles (19 km) to CA-243 N. Turn right on CA-243 and drive north for 5 miles (8 km) into Idyllwild and the trailhead.

❸ Catch live music at **Cafe Aroma** (54750 N. Circle Dr., 951/659-5212, www.cafearomaidyllwild.com, 11am-9pm Fri.-Tues., $12-29) during dinner before retreating to your cozy cottage or hotel room.

DAY 3: Idyllwild to Wrightwood

170 miles/275 kilometers | 5 hours

ROUTE OVERVIEW: CA-243 • I-10 • CA-38 • CA-18 • CA-138 • CA-2

❶ Get ready for a long day of driving on twisty scenic byways that traverse three unique mountain ranges and offer incredible views in every direction. Fuel up with coffee at **Higher Grounds** (54245 N. Circle Dr., 951/659-1379, www.highergroundscoffee.com, 6am-7pm Sun.-Thurs., 6am-9pm Fri.-Sat.) before making the two-hour trek to **Big Bear Lake.**

> Drive north on CA-243 for 25.5 miles (41 km) to I-10. Turn left and follow I-10 W to exit 79 (21 mi/34 km). Follow signs for CA-38. Turn right and take CA-38 E to Big Bear Lake (47 mi/76 km).

❷ Hike the **Cougar Crest Trail** (5.6 mi/9 km round-trip, 2.5 hours, moderate) to enjoy panoramic views of the lake and the San Bernardino Mountains. This trail is the easiest and most scenic way to access the PCT as it traverses the ridge on the north side of Big Bear Lake. The trailhead is just off CA-38, less than half a mile west of the Big Bear Discovery Center.

❸ Drive west to **Wrightwood.** Enjoy a frosty pint and a handcrafted sandwich at **Wrightwood Brew Co.** (1257 Apple Ave., 760/488-3163, www.wwbrewco.com, noon-8pm Mon.-Thurs., 11am-10pm Fri.-Sat., 11am-8pm Sun.). Bed down for the night in town.

> Take CA-38 W for 6 miles (10 km). Drive west on CA-18 for 23 miles (37 km) to Lake Gregory Dr. Turn right and continue for less than 5 miles (8 km) to Lake Dr. Turn left, then make a sharp right on Old Mill Rd. in less than a mile. Follow Old Mill Rd. for about a mile until it turns into CA-138. After 25 miles (40 km), turn left onto CA-2 and follow it to Wrightwood.

DAY 4: Wrightwood to Tehachapi

170 miles/275 kilometers | 3.5 hours

ROUTE OVERVIEW: CA-2 • I-210 • I-5 • CA-14 • surface streets

❶ Head west out of Wrightwood a few miles in the morning. Take a stroll on the PCT along the **Blue Ridge Trail** (4.5 mi/7.2 km round-trip, 2-2.5 hours, easy) to see the sun light up the San Gabriel Mountains. Your hike begins on the southern side of CA-2, just east of the parking area for Inspiration Point. The Blue Ridge Campground is a good turnaround point, but you can go farther along the PCT if you want a longer hike.

> Take CA-2 W for 3.5 miles (5.5 km) to reach the trailhead.

❷ Wind your way along CA-2, also known as the **Angeles Crest Scenic Byway.** This route affords you the chance to trace the path of the PCT through a remarkably rugged mountain range. Stop at **Newcomb's Ranch** (CA-2, 626/440-1001, www.newcombsranch. com, 9am-4pm Thurs.-Fri., 7am-4pm Sat.-Sun., $11-14) for lunch and admire the motorcycles and racecars parked in the lot.

> It's a 29-mile (47-km) drive west on CA-2 to the restaurant.

❸ In the tiny town of **Agua Dulce,** walk through **Vasquez Rocks** (3.5 mi/5.6 km round-trip, 1.5-2 hours, easy/moderate), a group of sculpted sandstone formations that have been the filming site of countless movies and TV shows. Stop at the **interpretive center** (10700 W. Escondido Canyon Rd., 661/268-0840, http://parks.lacounty.gov, 8am-5pm daily) to pick up a park map. Only some of the many trails in the park are labeled, so you'll want to carry a map or GPS with you. The parking area for the trailhead is 0.2 mile past the interpretive center, in a large dirt lot on the east side of the road.

WINERY IN AGUA DULCE

KEY RESERVATIONS

- Certain hikes along the PCT require taking a **shuttle** to and from the trailhead. Usually, you can arrange shuttle transportation on the day of, but for the **Deer Springs Trail** and **Devils Postpile National Monument,** it's best to call ahead to ensure service.

- Make advance reservations to guarantee site availability at **Tuolumne Meadows Campground** and **Summit Lake Campground.**

> Follow CA-2 W for 26 miles (42 km) to I-210. Follow I-210 W to I-5 N (19 mi/31 km). In less than 5 miles (8 km), take the exit for CA-14. Drive north on CA-14 for 15 miles (24 km), then turn left and follow Agua Dulce Canyon Rd. to reach the interpretive center.

❹ Continue northward to **Tehachapi.** Grab dinner at **Red House BBQ** (426 E. Tehachapi Blvd., 661/822-0772, 11am-8pm Wed.-Mon., $9-16) and get a comfy hotel room.

> Join CA-14 N and drive 43 miles (69 km) to exit 61 for Backus Rd. Turn left and follow Backus west for 8 miles (13 km) to Tehachapi Willow Springs Rd. Turn right and follow this road for 14 miles (23 km) to Highline Rd. Turn left and take Highline 3 miles (5 km) to Curry St., which leads into Tehachapi in 2 miles (3 km).

DAY 5: Tehachapi to Kennedy Meadows

145 miles/233 kilometers | 5 hours

ROUTE OVERVIEW: CA-58 • CA-178 • CA-155 • Mountain Hwy. 99 • Sherman Pass Rd.

❶ Take a scenic route through the Piute Mountains to the town of **Kernville.** Hop on a three-hour **whitewater rafting** trip on the Kern River with **SoCal Rafting** (11101 Kernville Rd., 888/537-6748, www.socalrafting.com, Mar.-July, $33-90).

TRUCKEE TO LONE PINE

4 days; 350 miles/565 kilometers

Fly into **Reno, Nevada,** in the morning, then make the short drive to **Truckee** to visit **Donner Lake.** Continue your day with the long drive south along **Lake Tahoe,** across the impressive **Tioga Pass,** and into **Yosemite National Park.** Spend the night at **Tuolumne Meadows Campground.**

Spend your **second day** exploring Yosemite. On your **third day,** drive south to **Lone Pine.** On your **last day,** hike part of the trail to **Mount Whitney.**

> Take CA-58 W for 28 miles (45 km) to Comanche Dr. Turn right and follow Comanche for 5 miles (8 km). At CA-178 E, turn right and drive for 31 miles (50 km) to CA-155 W. Follow CA-155 to Kernville (11 mi/18 km).

❷ Sip on a craft beer at **Kern River Brewing Company** (13415 Sierra Way, 760/376-2337, www.kernriverbrewing. com, 11am-9pm Sun.-Thurs., 11am-9:30pm Fri.-Sat., $10-13), owned by a former Olympic white-water kayaker.

❸ Stock up on water, food, and camping supplies in Kernville before making the drive on **Sherman Pass Road** (intersection with Mountain Hwy. 99, 16 mi/26 km north of Kernville, open late May/early June-Oct./early Nov.) to **Kennedy Meadows,** a remote community high on the Kern Plateau. On the way, stop at 9,200-foot **Sherman Pass** to gaze out over Sequoia National Forest and the South Sierra Wilderness.

> Take Sierra Way north out of Kernville. Sierra Way turns into Mountain Hwy. 99 in about a mile. Follow Mountain Hwy. 99 for 16 miles (26 km) to Sherman Pass Rd and turn right. Take Sherman Pass Rd. east to Kennedy Meadows (45 mi/72 km).

❹ Pitch your tent in **Kennedy Meadows Campground** (County Rd. J41, www.fs.usda.gov, $10), just steps from the PCT. Bring plenty of water for drinking, cooking, and washing—pit toilets and fire rings are the only amenities.

> Follow Sherman Pass Rd. to County Road J41, just east of the Kennedy Meadows General Store. Continue north on J41 for 3 miles (5 km) to the campground.

DAY 6: Kennedy Meadows to Lone Pine

105 miles/169 kilometers | 3 hours

ROUTE OVERVIEW: Sherman Pass Rd./Kennedy Meadows Rd. • US-395

❶ Let yourself get nice and hungry before visiting **Grumpy Bear's Retreat** (98887 Kennedy Meadow Rd., 559/850-2327, www.grumpybearsretreat.com, 8am-10pm daily Apr.-July,

VIEW FROM SHERMAN PASS

VIEW FROM EASTERN SIERRA INTERAGENCY VISITOR CENTER

8am-10pm Wed.-Sun. Aug.-Sept., 8am-10pm Fri.-Sun. Oct.-Mar., $7-12), where breakfast is served with unlimited 10-inch pancakes.

> *Retrace your path to return to Sherman Pass Rd./Kennedy Meadow Rd. Drive south for about 5 miles (8 km) to get to the restaurant.*

❷ Continue on to **Lone Pine.** Visit the **Eastern Sierra Interagency Visitor Center** (US-395 and CA-136, 760/876-6200, www.fs.usda.gov, 8am-5pm daily May-Oct., 8:30am-4:30pm daily Nov.-Apr.) at the south end of town to learn intriguing details about the region's natural wonders.

> *Drive south on Sherman Pass Rd./ Kennedy Meadow Rd. for 14 miles (23 km), when it turns into 9 Mile Canyon Rd. Continue for 10 miles (16 km) to US-395. Turn left and go north on US-395 to the southern end of Lone Pine (53 mi/85 km).*

❸ Follow **Whitney Portal Road** west out of Lone Pine to the eastern base of 14,505-foot **Mount Whitney** (www.nps.gov/seki), the highest peak in the lower 48 states. Hike to **Lone Pine Lake** via the **Mount Whitney Trail** (5.3 mi/8.5 km round-trip, 3 hours, moderate) to explore part of the route that climbs to the top of Whitney and showcases the landscape of the Eastern Sierra. The trailhead is on the north side of the parking lot at Whitney Portal.

> *Continue north on US-395 for 2 miles (3 km) to Whitney Portal Rd. Turn left and follow Whitney Portal Rd. west for 12 miles (19 km) to the trailhead.*

❹ Drive back to Lone Pine to visit the **Lone Pine Film History Museum** (701 S. Main St., 760/876-9909, www.museumofwesternfilmhistory.org, 10am-5pm Mon.-Sat., 10am-4pm Sun., $5 donation). Check out the exhibits on iconic actors including Gene Autry, Roy Rogers, and John Wayne.

> *Retrace your path to Lone Pine via Whitney Portal Rd., then turn right on US-395 S to reach the museum in less than a mile.*

❺ Eat dinner in town and grab a room at the historic **Dow Villa Motel** (310 S. Main St., 760/876-5521, www.dowvillamotel.com, $70-170), where many Western film stars have stayed over the years.

DAY 7: Lone Pine to Bishop

95 miles/153 kilometers | 2.5 hours

ROUTE OVERVIEW: US-395 • Onion Valley Rd. • US-395

❶ Get up early to beat the sun before exploring the **Alabama Hills** via **Movie Road** (2.8 mi/4.5 km west of Lone Pine), stopping for the brief hike to **Mobius Arch** (0.6 mi/1 km loop, 20 minutes, easy). Hundreds of movies and television shows (particularly Westerns) have been filmed in these hills.

> *Take Whitney Portal Rd. 3 miles (5 km) west to Movie Rd. Turn right and continue to Mobius Arch (2 mi/3 km).*

❷ Stop at **Manzanar National Historic Site** (5001 US-395, Independence, 760/878-2194, www.nps.gov/manz,

ALABAMA HILLS

HUNGRY HUNGRY *Hikers*

Trekking through the wilderness does wonders for the appetite. Here's a guide to the top restaurants for hungry hikers, with big portions, great deals, or impressive buffet spreads.

- **Idyllwild:** If you find yourself in town on a Tuesday, stop at **Los Gorditos** (26290 CA-243, 951/659-2842, www.gorditosidyllwild.com, 11am-8pm Tues. and Fri.-Sun., $8-20) for Taco Tuesday specials. With authentic street-style tacos for just $0.99 apiece, you can fill your belly for just a few bucks.

- **Big Bear:** After climbing 7,000 feet from the desert floor into the San Bernardino Mountains, PCT hikers flock to **Himalayan Restaurant** (672 Pine Knot Ave., 909/878-3068, www.himalayanbigbear.com, 11am-9pm Sun.-Thurs., 11am-10pm Fri.-Sat. $10-19) for lunch specials that include an entrée, *aaloo mattar,* lentils, rice, naan, and salad—all for $12 or less.

- **Kennedy Meadows:** The hiker breakfast at **Grumpy Bear's Retreat** (98887 Kennedy Meadow Rd., 559/850-2327, www.grumpybearsretreat.com, 8am-10pm daily Apr.-July, 8am-10pm Wed.-Sun. Aug.-Sept., 8am-10pm Fri.-Sun. Oct.-Mar., $7-12) includes eggs, bacon, potatoes, and all-you-can-eat 10-inch pancakes. For lunch, try The General: a double bacon cheeseburger, stacked high with lettuce, tomato, and pickles between two toasted buns, served with fries.

- **Bishop:** The dining room may be casual at **Back Alley Bowling Alley and Grill** (649 N. Main St., 760/873-5777, www.thebackalleybowlandgrill.com, 4pm-10pm Mon., 11am-10pm Tues.-Sat., 11am-9:30pm Sun., $8-20)—it's a bowling alley, after all—but it's the best spot in the Owens Valley for fresh and tasty surf-and-turf. Try the steak and shrimp entrée for $20, or visit Thursday-Sunday for prime rib.

- **Etna:** The beef for the $8 burgers at **Dotty's** (404 CA-3, 530/476-3303, www.dottysburger.com, 11am-8pm daily, $7-9) is raised just two miles away at the owners' family farm. Served with red onion marmalade between two buns from Grain Street Bakery (handcrafted by Erik Ryberg, Etna's mayor), a burger this good—not to mention this stylish—would easily sell for twice as much in one of the West Coast's trendy food cities.

- **Seiad Valley:** Find out if you have what it takes to win the pancake challenge at **Seiad Café** (44721 CA-96, 530/496-3360, 7am-2pm daily, $8-12) by digging into a stack of five 13-inch pancakes. If you can finish them all in less than two hours, your meal is on the house. According to the café owners, only 10 people have ever succeeded.

9am-4:30pm daily, free) for a glimpse into a chilling era in U.S. history during World War II. It was here that more than 10,000 Japanese Americans were detained for several years. Walk through life-size models of the camp's barracks and look around to imagine what daily life was like for the American citizens held prisoner here inside a square mile of barbed wire.

> *Follow Whitney Portal Rd. back to Lone Pine, then take US-395 N for 9 miles (14 km) to Manzanar National Historic Site.*

❸ The curvy **Onion Valley Road** winds and bends to **Onion Valley Campground.** Here, make the trek to 11,700-foot **Kearsarge Pass** (9 mi/14.5 km round-trip, 6 hours, strenuous) for a photo-worthy view of Kings Canyon National Park and the path of the PCT through what John Muir called the "Range of Light." Pick up the trailhead at the western terminus of Onion Valley Road.

> *Continue on US-395 N to Independence (5.5 mi/9 km). Here, turn left onto Market St., which turns into Onion Valley*

Rd. Drive Onion Valley Rd. for 13 miles (21 km) to the Kearsarge Pass trailhead.

❹ In **Bishop,** satisfy your hiker hunger (and thirst) at **Mountain Rambler Brewery** (186 S. Main St., 760/258-1348, www.mountainramblerbrewery.com, 11:30am-10:30pm Sun.-Thurs., 11:30am-11:30pm Fri.-Sat., $9-16) for artisan pizza and craft beer before retreating to your hotel room in town.

> Double back to US-395, then continue north for 42 miles (68 km) to Bishop.

DAY 8: Bishop to Yosemite National Park

100 miles/161 kilometers | 2.5 hours

ROUTE OVERVIEW: US-395 • CA-203 • US-395 • CA-158 • US-395 • CA-120

❶ Stock up on pastries and lunch sundries at **Erick Schat's Bakkery** (763 N. Main St., 760/873-7156, www.schatsbakery.com, 6am-6pm Sat.-Thurs., 6am-7pm Fri., $4-12) before heading north to **Mammoth Lakes.**

> Take US-395 N to CA-203 (36 mi/58 km). Follow CA-203 west to Mammoth Lakes (3 mi/5 km).

❷ Take the shuttle to **Devils Postpile National Monument** (Minaret Vista Rd., 760/934-2289, www.nps.gov/depo, 24 hours daily mid-June-mid-Oct., ranger station 9am-5pm daily late June-Labor Day, $8 adults, $4 children ages 3-15), where the Pacific Crest Trail passes beneath a dramatic formation of columnar basalt. Walk south along the San Joaquin River to **Rainbow Falls** (5 mi/8 km round-trip, 3 hours, easy). You'll pass the columnar rock formation known as Devils Postpile about a half mile in. The shuttle (7:15am-4:30pm daily July-early Sept.) picks up passengers at the Mammoth Mountain Adventure Center every 30-45 minutes.

> From the center of town, head up Mammoth Mountain via Minaret Rd./CA-203 to reach the shuttle pickup point.

❸ Once you're back at your car, head north to **June Lake,** a town set on a scenic loop (CA-158) that passes four sparkling lakes below craggy Sierra

---

▶ Playlist

PACIFIC CREST TRAIL: CALIFORNIA

SONGS

● **"Ends of the Earth" by Lord Huron:** When you crest a mountain ridge and see the valleys spill forth below, this song should be playing. This Los Angeles-based band spins riveting stories through captivating lyrics and uplifting melodies.

● **"Tuolumne" by Eddie Vedder:** An instrumental piece from the bittersweet film *Into the Wild.* This tune evokes all of the magic of the Pacific Crest Trail—its natural beauty, its wild lands, its coveted isolation.

PODCASTS

● ***Dear Sugars:*** This cult favorite podcast is helmed by Steve Almond and Cheryl Strayed, the acclaimed author of *Wild,* an autobiographical account of Strayed's solo thru-hike of the Pacific Crest Trail. Although the podcast isn't about her PCT journey, it's still an engaging, hilarious, and inspiring listen.

---

peaks. Stop at **June Lake Brewing** (131 S. Crawford Ave., 858/668-6340, www.junelakebrewing.com, noon-8pm Sun.-Thurs., noon-9pm Fri.-Sat., $5-10) for a creative brew, then grab Hawaiian soul food from **Ohanas 395** (www.ohanas395.com, noon-5pm daily, $6-14), the food truck parked outside.

JUNE LAKE

> *From Minaret Rd., turn left onto the Mammoth Scenic Loop and drive for 6 mi (10 km). Turn left onto US-395 N. In 9 miles (14 km), turn left onto CA-158. Continue for 2.5 miles (4 km) to June Lake.*

④ End the day with a scenic evening drive on **Tioga Pass Road**, which travels over the 9,900-foot **Tioga Pass** into **Yosemite National Park** (209/372-0200, www.nps.gov/yose, $35 per vehicle, $30 motorcycles, $20 pedestrians and bicycles).

> *To complete the June Lakes Loop, continue west and north along CA-158 for 13 miles until the highway rejoins CA-395. Continue north on CA-395 for 4 miles (6 km) until CA-120/Tioga Pass Rd. Turn left and drive 3.5 miles (5.5 km) west on CA-120 to Tioga Pass.*

⑤ Make sure you've got a reservation for a campsite at the popular **Tuolumne Meadows Campground** (Tioga Pass Rd. at Tuolumne Meadows, 877/444-6777, www.recreation.gov,

reservations advised, July-mid-Sept., $26). This is the park's largest campground, with more than 300 sites.

> *Continue west on CA-120/Tioga Pass Rd. for 16 miles (26 km) to the campground.*

DAY 9: Yosemite to Truckee

185 miles/300 kilometers | 4.5 hours

ROUTE OVERVIEW: CA-120 • US-395 • CA-89 • I-80

① Grab breakfast to go and hike to the top of **Lembert Dome** (2.8 mi/4.5 km round-trip, 2-3 hours, moderate), where you'll find a lovely vantage of **Tuolumne Meadows** and the surrounding granite massifs. To start the hike, find the Dog Lake trailhead, which is along Tuolumne Meadows Lodge Road.

② In **Bridgeport**, stop for lunch at **High Sierra Bakery** (172 Main St., 760/914-4002, www.highsierrabakery.com, 6am-3pm daily, $3-10). It's a two-hour drive over **Monitor Pass** and through the town of **Meyers** to the western shore of sparkling **Lake Tahoe**, the second-deepest lake in the country.

> *Drive east on CA-120 back over Tioga Pass to US-395 (19 mi/31 km). Turn left and follow US-395 N for 26 miles (42 km) to Bridgeport.*

③ Stretch your legs during a peaceful walk through **Emerald Bay State Park** (CA-89, 10 mi/16 km north of South Lake Tahoe, 530/541-3030 or

PACIFIC COAST TRAIL THROUGH TUOLUMNE MEADOWS

DONNER LAKE

530/525-3345, www.parks.ca.gov, $10 per vehicle) before driving 45 minutes north to **Truckee** to partake in happy hour at one of the city's many urbane restaurants.

> Continue north on US-395 to CA-89 (40 mi/64 km). Turn left and follow CA-89 N for 20 miles (32 km) to Emerald Bay State Park. Continue north on CA-89 to Truckee (31 mi/50 km).

④ Relax into a waterfront hotel room at **Loch Leven Lodge** (13855 Donner Pass Rd., Donner Lake, 530/587-3773, www.lochlevenlodge.com, $130-200) on **Donner Lake.** The outdoor hot tub is a lovely place to catch the sunset after a long day.

> Take I-80 W to Donner Lake (4 mi/ 6 km).

DAY 10: Truckee to Lassen Volcanic National Park

215 miles/345 kilometers | 4.5 hours

ROUTE OVERVIEW: CA-89 • CA-49 • CA-89 • CA-36 • CA-89

① Fuel up for the day at the famous breakfast joint **Squeeze In** (10060 Donner Pass Rd., 530/587-9814, www. squeezein.com, 7am-3pm daily, $15-30). The gigantic menu is a bit overwhelming, but it's impossible to choose poorly.

② It's about an hour to **Sierra City,** where you can take a short walk on the PCT to **Loves Falls** (1 mi/1.6 km

round-trip, 30 minutes, easy). The trail crosses right over CA-49, just northeast of Sierra City.

> Drive CA-89 N for 28 miles (45 km) to CA-49 N. Follow this into Sierra City (18 mi/29 km).

③ Drive along the western shore of Lake Almanor to the town of **Chester** to enjoy a soft-serve or ice-cream shake at **Pine Shack Frosty** (321 Main St., 530/258-2593, 11am-7pm Sun.-Tues., 11am-8pm Fri.-Sat. May-Sept., $5-10) and pick up camping supplies at the supermarket.

> Take CA-49 N out of Sierra City (5 mi/8 km). Make a left on Gold Lake Hwy. and follow it for 16 miles (26 km) until it joins CA-89. Take CA-89 N for 69 miles (111 km) to CA-36/Volcanic Legacy Scenic Byway. Turn right and follow CA-36/Volcanic Legacy Scenic Byway northeast to Chester (2 mi/3 km).

LASSEN PEAK FROM HIGHWAY 89

4 It's a 30-minute drive into **Lassen Volcanic National Park** (www.nps.gov/lavo, 530/595-4480, 9am-5pm daily, visitors center 530/595-4480, 9am-5pm daily Apr.-Oct., 9am-5pm Wed.-Sun. Nov.-Mar.), where you can see bubbling mud pots, smell steaming fumaroles, and, if you're up for it, hike to the top of **Lassen Peak** (5 mi/8 km round-trip, 3-4 hours, strenuous). It's not a long hike, but the trail gains more than 2,000 vertical feet in only 2.5 miles on the way up.

> *Head west on CA-36/Volcanic Legacy Scenic Byway and continue for 25 miles (40 km). Turn right onto CA-89 N and follow it for 5 miles (8 km) to reach the southern entrance to the park.*

5 Set up camp at **Summit Lake Campground** (877/444-6777, www.recreation.gov, late June-late Sept., $22-24) in the national park. Reservations are recommended, but some sites are designated walk-up only. Note that the northern campground has flush toilets, while the southern has only pit toilets.

DAY 11: Lassen to Dunsmuir

120 miles/193 kilometers | 3 hours

ROUTE OVERVIEW: CA-89 • I-5

1 Keep your headlamp handy to explore **Subway Cave** (east of CA-89, www.fs.usda.gov, dawn-dusk daily Apr.-Oct.), a huge underground lava tube in Lassen National Forest. Continue north for a day of majestic waterfalls.

> *Follow CA-89 N to exit the park from the north. Continue on CA-89 until it joins with CA-44. Turn right onto CA-44/CA-89. After 14 miles (23 km), follow signs for the cave, which is a short distance north of the CA-44/CA-89 junction in Old Station.*

2 Near the town of **Burney,** check out **Burney Falls** at **McArthur-Burney Falls Memorial State Park** (24898 CA-89, 530/335-2777, www.parks.ca.gov, $10 per vehicle). Here, dozens of springs surge out of a 130-foot cliff next to the rushing cascade of Burney Creek and splash into a misty plunge pool. You don't even have to hike to reach the falls; they're right by the parking lot.

> *Continue north on CA-89 for 27 miles (43 km) to the waterfall.*

3 Near the town of **Mount Shasta,** enjoy the short, easy trail to **Hedge Creek Falls** (north side of Mott Rd.) The parking area is at Mott Road and Siskiyou Avenue. The walk along the trail to reach the falls only takes a few minutes.

> *Continue on CA-89 for 51 miles (82 km) to I-5. Take I-5 S for 5 miles (8 km), then exit at Siskiyou Ave. Turn right onto Siskiyou, then right again onto Mott Rd. to reach the falls.*

4 Stop in **Dunsmuir,** where post-hike beers and burgers await you at **Dunsmuir Brewery Works** (5701 Dunsmuir Ave., 530/235-1900, www.dunsmuir-breweryworks.com, 11am-10pm daily Apr.-Oct., 11am-9pm Tues.-Sat., 11am-8pm Sun. Nov.-Mar., $8-16).

> *Continue south on I-5 for 2.5 miles (4 km) to the town of Dunsmuir.*

5 Retire to a perfectly appointed refurbished caboose at **Railroad Park Resort** (100 Railroad Park Rd., 530/235-4440, www.rrpark.com, $155-210), which is at the southern end of town.

HEDGE CREEK FALLS

Best TRAIL TOWNS

Famous for their warm hospitality, natural beauty, and small-town charm, these are the towns that make lasting impressions on Pacific Crest Trail hikers.

- **Mount Laguna:** Nestled in a sparse pine forest atop a dramatic mountain ridge, the community of Mount Laguna defies Southern California stereotypes. Visit during the spring to walk through mountain meadows and marvel at the many different bird species that make Mount Laguna an annual stop during their migration.

- **Idyllwild:** Catch live music every night of the week in this artsy mountain town, which is also home to fantastic restaurants and great shops. Trails into Mount San Jacinto State Park depart from the edges of town, leading to the PCT and the top of Mount San Jacinto.

- **Lone Pine:** Find yourself transported to the Wild West in Lone Pine, where you can explore the filming locations of hundreds of movies and TV shows. Mount Whitney, the tallest peak in the Lower 48, dominates the western skyline.

- **Bridgeport:** Without the crowds of the more popular areas farther south, Bridgeport is a no-frills town in the Eastern Sierra with craft beer, views galore, and two beautiful natural hot springs. Hike on the PCT at nearby Sonora Pass.

- **Truckee:** Not far from Lake Tahoe, this sophisticated mountain town has fantastic restaurants, great shops, and plenty of opportunities for year-round outdoor recreation at nearby Donner Lake and Donner Summit.

- **Mount Shasta:** In 2018, Mount Shasta became the first official Pacific Crest Trail Town. Castle Crags State Park is nearby, and the town is surrounded by some of the most rugged terrain in Northern California. Mount Shasta itself, a 14,180-foot volcano, is visible from about 500 miles of the PCT.

▼ TRUCKEE

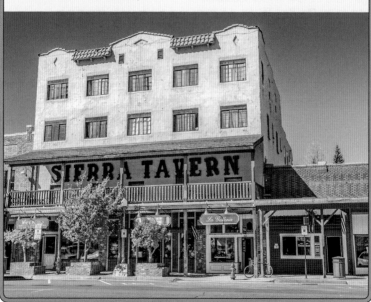

DAY 12: Dunsmuir to Ashland, Oregon

105 miles/169 kilometers | 3 hours

ROUTE OVERVIEW: I-5 • Mount Ashland Ski Rd. • I-5 • OR-99

❶ After breakfast in historic downtown Dunsmuir, drive a few minutes south to **Castle Crags State Park** (20022 Castle Creek Rd., Castella, 530/235-2684, www.parks.ca.gov, $10 per vehicle) for a hike to **Castle Dome** (5.7 mi/9.2 km round-trip, 3-3.5 hours, strenuous) and stellar views of snow-capped **Mount Shasta.**

> *Drive south on I-5 for 5 miles (8 km) to reach the state park.*

❷ After your hike, drive past the mighty volcano and into the state of Oregon. A pleasant drive on **Mount Ashland Ski Road** (Forest Rd. 20 and Siskiyou Summit Rd.) takes you to the top of **Mount Ashland,** paralleling the PCT most of the way. The 360-degree views from the top include snow-capped Mount Shasta, the city of Ashland, and an endless expanse of Cascade and Siskiyou peaks on every horizon.

> *Double back through Dunsmuir, taking I-5 N for 73 miles (117 km) into Oregon. Take the exit for Siskiyou/Summit, then follow Old Hwy. 99 for 4.5 miles*

CASTLE CRAGS

(7 km). Turn left onto Mount Ashland Ski Rd. and follow it for 4 miles (6 km) to the top of Mount Ashland.

❸ Cap off your trip with dinner at one of Ashland's world-class restaurants, such as **Amuse** (15 N. 1st St., 541/488-9000, www.amuserestaurant.com, 5:30pm-8pm Sun. and Wed.-Thurs., 5:30pm-9pm Fri.-Sat., $22-36), an elegant French restaurant with a menu that highlights organic, seasonal Pacific Northwest ingredients.

> *Retrace your path to I-5, then continue north on I-5 for 7 miles (11 km) to OR-99. Take OR-99 for 4 miles (6 km) north into Ashland.*

GETTING THERE

AIR

To start your trip near the beginning of the Pacific Crest Trail at the California-Mexico border, fly into **San Diego International Airport** (SAN, 619/400-2404, 3225 N. Harbor Dr., www.san.org). San Diego is the most convenient metropolis to the southernmost towns along the trail: Campo, Mount Laguna, and Julian.

Destinations farther north on the PCT, including the communities of Idyllwild, Big Bear, Wrightwood, and Tehachapi, are closer to the greater Los Angeles area and can be reached more quickly from airports in this region. **Los Angeles International Airport** (LAX, 1 World Way, 855/463-5252, www.flylax.com) is the biggest and busiest airport. Depending on when your flight arrives, you may find

MOUNT SHASTA

yourself fighting some of the nation's worst traffic just to get out of town and into the mountains.

Ontario International Airport (ONT, 2500-2900 E. Airport Dr., 909/544-5300, www.flyontario.com) is far less busy than LAX, and it's closer to the PCT. It's about a 90-minute drive from the airport to Idyllwild or Big Bear, and under an hour's drive to Wrightwood (depending on traffic, of course).

If the thought of sitting in freeway gridlock doesn't sound like the way to kick off your road trip into the wilderness, you can avoid the metro area altogether by flying into **Palm Springs International Airport** (PSP, 3400 E. Tahquitz Canyon Way, 760/318-3800, www.palmspringsca.gov). The airport is serviced by most international airlines and is about an hour's drive from the town of Idyllwild.

TRAIN

Amtrak (800/872-7245, www.amtrak.com) offers rail service to a number of stations within 50 miles of the Pacific Crest Trail: San Diego (Santa Fe Station, 1050 Kettner Blvd.), Los Angeles (Union Station, 800 N. Alameda St.), San Bernardino (1170 W. 3rd St.), Victorville (16858 D St.), and Palm Springs (Palm Springs Station Rd.). You'll need to rent a car or hop on a bus to access the PCT from any of these urban hubs.

BUS

Greyhound (800/231-2222, www.greyhound.com) offers bus service to San Diego (1313 National Ave., 619/515-1100) and Los Angeles (1716 E. 7th St., 213/629-8401).

BoltBus (877/265-8287, www.boltbus.com) also serves Los Angeles from select locations in California (Barstow, Fresno, Oakland, San Francisco, San Jose) and Nevada (Las Vegas).

You can take a **FlixBus** (855/626-8585, www.flixbus.com) to San Diego, San Bernardino, Anaheim, Los Angeles, or Bakersfield. Once arriving in one of these urban hubs, you'll need to rent a car to access the wilderness areas near the Pacific Crest Trail.

CAR

Most of the roads near the Pacific Crest Trail can be driven year-round. Rush hour traffic in the cities can be bad on weekdays, but less so in small, remote mountain communities where the trail is located. In winter, many roads close due to ice, rain, or snow. If driving to Mount Laguna, Idyllwild, Big Bear, or Wrightwood in the winter, check road conditions online with **CalTrans** (www.dot.ca.gov).

San Diego is the most convenient travel hub from which to start this drive. From downtown San Diego, **CA-94** heads 50 miles (81 km) east, becoming a rural, two-lane highway midway to **Campo.** This is the best way to reach the southern terminus of the PCT.

GETTING BACK

From **Ashland, Oregon,** to **San Diego, California,** it's a straight shot on I-5 S. The trip is 800 miles (1,290 km), and it takes approximately 12 hours, depending on traffic. Keep in mind that traffic can be heavy between Los Angeles and San Diego.

Another option is to fly into San Diego at the start of the road trip, then fly out of **Portland International Airport** (PDX, 7000 NE Airport Way, 503/460-4234, www.flypdx.com) at the trip's end. It's 290 miles (467 km) from Ashland to the Portland airport via I-5 N, a drive of about five hours.

CONNECT WITH

- At Yosemite National Park: **Best of the Golden State** (PAGE 108)

- At Ashland and Yosemite National Park: **Northern California Loop** (PAGE 156)

- At San Diego: **Pacific Coast Highway: California** (PAGE 124) and **Southern California and Route 66 Loop** (PAGE 178)

- At Ashland: **Pacific Crest Trail: Oregon and Washington** (PAGE 250)

NORTHERN CALIFORNIA LOOP

WHY GO: World-renowned wineries, giant redwoods, Yosemite hikes, stunning seascapes, side trip to Crater Lake

TOTAL DISTANCE: 1,965 miles/ 2,910 kilometers

NUMBER OF DAYS: 20

SEASONS: Summer through early fall

START/END: San Francisco, California

▼ LASSEN VOLCANIC NATIONAL PARK

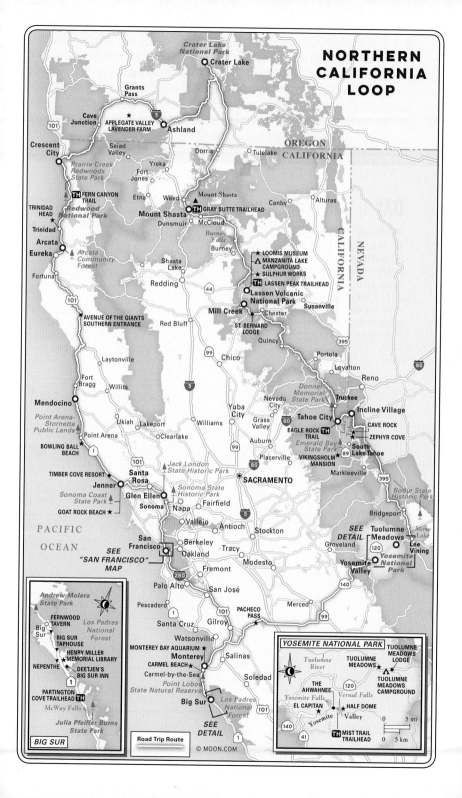

NORTHERN CALIFORNIA LOOP

Crater Lake
National Park
● **Crater Lake**

Grants
Pass
★ APPLEGATE VALLEY
LAVENDER FARM
Cave
Junction
Ashland

OREGON
CALIFORNIA

Crescent
City
Seiad
Valley
Dorris
Tulelake

Prairie Creek
Redwoods
State Park
Yreka
Fort
Jones

TH FERN CANYON
TRAIL
Etna   Weed   Mount Shasta

TRINIDAD
HEAD
Redwood
National Park
TH GRAY BUTTE TRAILHEAD
Mount Shasta
Canby
Alturas

Trinidad
Dunsmuir
McCloud

Arcata
Eureka
Arcata
Community
Forest
Shasta
Lake
Burney
Falls
Burney

Fortuna
CALIFORNIA   **NEVADA**

Redding
★ LOOMIS MUSEUM
△ MANZANITA LAKE
CAMPGROUND
★ SULPHUR WORKS
TH LASSEN PEAK TRAILHEAD

AVENUE OF THE GIANTS
SOUTHERN ENTRANCE
44
Lassen Volcanic
National Park
Susanville

Laytonville
Red Bluff
Mill Creek
Chester
ST. BERNARD
LODGE
Quincy

Fort
Bragg
99
Chico
Portola
395

Willits
5
Loyalton
80

Mendocino
Yuba
City
Nevada
City
Reno

Point Arena-
Stornetta
Public Lands
Ukiah   Lakeport
Williams
Grass
Valley
Donner
Memorial
State Park
Truckee

Point Arena
Clearlake
Tahoe City
Incline Village

BOWLING BALL
BEACH
99
Auburn
EAGLE ROCK
TRAIL
CAVE ROCK
ZEPHYR COVE

TIMBER COVE RESORT
Jack London
State Historic Park
Placerville
Emerald Bay
State Park
South
Lake Tahoe

Jenner
Santa
Rosa
80
VIKINGSHOLM
MANSION
89
Markleeville

Glen Ellen
Sonoma State
Historic Park
SACRAMENTO
395

GOAT ROCK BEACH ★
Sonoma
Fairfield
Bodie State
Historic Park

Sonoma Coast
State Park
Napa
Bridgeport

PACIFIC
Vallejo
Antioch
Stockton
SEE
DETAIL
Tuolumne
Meadows
Mono
Lake

OCEAN
SEE
"SAN FRANCISCO"
MAP
San
Francisco
Berkeley
Oakland
Tracy
Groveland
120
Lee
Vining

5
Fremont
Modesto
Yosemite
Valley
Yosemite
National
Park

Palo Alto
San José
Merced
140

Pescadero
101
PACHECO
PASS
99

1
Santa Cruz
Gilroy

Watsonville
MONTEREY BAY AQUARIUM ★
Monterey
Salinas

CARMEL BEACH ★
Carmel-by-the-Sea
Soledad

Point Lobos
State Natural Reserve
Big Sur
Los Padres
National
Forest

SEE
DETAIL
101

1

BIG SUR

Andrew Molera
State Park

FERNWOOD
TAVERN
Los Padres
National
Forest
Big
Sur
BIG SUR
TAPHOUSE
● HENRY MILLER
★ MEMORIAL LIBRARY
NEPENTHE ●
● DEETJEN'S
BIG SUR INN
1
PARTINGTON
COVE TRAILHEAD TH
McWay Falls
Julia Pfeiffer Burns
State Park

Road Trip Route
© MOON.COM

YOSEMITE NATIONAL PARK

TUOLUMNE
MEADOWS
LODGE
Tuolumne
River
TUOLUMNE
MEADOWS

THE
AHWAHNEE
120
△ TUOLUMNE
MEADOWS
CAMPGROUND

Yosemite Falls
EL CAPITAN ●
Vernal Falls
★ HALF DOME

Yosemite
140
Valley
0   5 mi

41
TH MIST TRAIL
TRAILHEAD
0   5 km

Bookended by urbane, culture-rich San Francisco, this road trip beckons travelers who adhere to the "go big or go home" adage. First, there are towering redwood trees, wondrous to behold. Then there's California's wine country, home to some of the best vintages in the world. There are also epic hikes in Yosemite, cliff-hugging coastal drives through Big Sur, ancient volcanoes, and underground lava tubes. Around every bend and over each mountain peak, another once-in-a-lifetime experience awaits.

DAY 1: San Francisco

MORNING AND AFTERNOON

❶ Start your day at the 1898 **Ferry Building** (1 Ferry Bldg., 415/983-8030, www.ferrybuildingmarketplace.com, 10am-7pm Mon.-Fri., 8am-6pm Sat., 11am-5pm Sun., individual business hours vary), which has been re-imagined as the foodie mecca of San Francisco.

❷ After you've had your fill of yummy eats, walk down the Embarcadero to the ferry that will transport you to **Alcatraz** (415/561-4900, www.nps.gov/alcatraz). Tour the infamous former maximum-security penitentiary situated in the middle of the bay.

EVENING

❸ For dinner, indulge in fresh seafood at **Tadich Grill** (240 California St., 415/391-1849, www.tadichgrill.com, 11am-9:30pm Mon.-Fri.,

© MOON.COM

Top **5** NORTHERN CALIFORNIA LOOP

1 Sip and sample some of the world's most impressive wines in the **Sonoma wine country** (PAGE 162).

2 Keep company with towering redwood trees—the tallest in the world—at **Redwood National Park** (PAGE 164).

3 Gaze into the crystalline blue depths of a geologic wonder on a side trip to **Crater Lake** (PAGE 165).

4 Get acquainted with sea creatures at **Monterey Bay Aquarium** (PAGE 173).

5 Snap some selfies in front of the iconic **Golden Gate Bridge** (PAGE 160).

KEY RESERVATIONS

- Book **Alcatraz** tours **two weeks** in advance.

- Secure camping reservations **at least a month** in advance for **Mazama Campground** in Crater Lake, **Tuolumne Meadows Campground** in Yosemite, and **Manzanita Lake Campground** in Lassen.

- Book a room **six months** in advance at **The Ahwahnee.**

11:30am-9:30pm Sat., $23-46), which has been open since 1849.

❹ Spend the night at the stylish, tech-savvy **Hotel Zetta** (55 5th St., 415/543-8555, 888/720-7004, www.viceroryhotelgroup.com, $299-1,214), a hot spot for creatives. Rooms come with Amazon Alexa, smart televisions, espresso machines, and plush robes.

DAY 2: San Francisco to Glen Ellen

60 miles/97 kilometers | 2 hours

ROUTE OVERVIEW: US-101 • CA-37 • CA-121 • CA-12

❶ Crossing the **Golden Gate Bridge,** head north out of San Francisco to charming Sonoma in the heart of wine country. Upon arrival, explore the historic buildings of **Sonoma State Historic Park** (707/938-9560, www.parks.ca.gov, 10am-5pm daily, adults $3,

JACK LONDON STATE HISTORIC PARK

children 6-17 $2), which includes Mexican-era barracks and the last mission built in California.

> Follow US-101 N for 22 miles (35 km) to CA-37. Drive east on CA-37 for 7 miles (11 km). At Sears Point, take CA-121 N and follow it for 8 miles (13 km). Turn left onto CA-12 W, then continue for 4 miles (6 km) into Sonoma.

❷ Walk through **Sonoma Plaza** before having lunch at **the girl & the fig** (110 W. Spain St., 707/938-3634, www.thegirlandthefig.com, 11:30am-10pm Mon.-Thurs., 11am-10pm Fri.-Sat., 10am-10pm Sun., $23-34), a favorite among fans of local, sustainable, and organic food.

❸ After lunch, drive north to the tiny hamlet of **Glen Ellen** and visit **Jack London State Historic Park** (2400 London Ranch Rd., 707/938-5216, www.jacklondonpark.com, 9am-5pm daily, $10 per vehicle), where there are a handful of worthwhile sites detailing the life of this literary legend. Stroll the easy mile-long hike to the Wolf House ruins.

> Continue on CA-12 W for 7 miles (11 km) to Glen Ellen. Take Arnold Dr. and London Ranch Rd. west for just over a mile to reach the park.

SONOMA VALLEY VINEYARDS

NAPA VALLEY

- **Grgich Hills Winery** (1829 St. Helena Hwy., Rutherford, 707/963-2784, www.grgich.com, 9:30am-4:30pm daily, from $40) put Napa Valley on the map with a win at the Paris Wine Tasting of 1976. It's still known for its chardonnay.

- **Mumm** (8445 Silverado Trl., Rutherford, 800/686-6272 Mon.-Fri., 707/967-7700 Sat.-Sun., http://mummnapa.com, 10am-6pm daily, $28-45) produces sparkling wines worth a taste.

- **Clos Pegase** (1060 Dunaweal Ln., Calistoga, 707/942-4981, www.clospegase.com, 10am-5pm daily, $30-45) showcases more than 100 artworks on the grounds, including sculptor Henry Moore's *Mother Earth* and a painting by Francis Bacon.

SONOMA VALLEY

- **Valley of the Moon Winery** (134 Church St., Sonoma, 707/939-4500, www.valleyofthemoonwinery.com, noon-6pm Mon.-Thurs., noon-8pm Fri.-Sun., $25-35) has been producing wine since the Civil War era.

- **Gundlach Bundschu** (2000 Denmark St., Sonoma, 707/938-5277, www.gunbun.com, 11am-5:30pm daily summer, 11am-4:30pm daily winter, $25-40) hosts big-time indie rock acts at its on-site amphitheater and inside its redwood barn.

ANDERSON VALLEY

- Both **Navarro Vineyards** (5601 CA-128, Philo, 707/895-3686 or 800/537-9463, www.navarrowine.com, 9am-6pm daily summer, 9am-5pm daily winter, free) and **Toulouse Vineyards** (8001 CA-128, Philo, 707/895-2828, http://toulousevineyards.com, 11am-5pm daily, $10) are known for gewürztraminer, an aromatic white wine.

CARMEL

- Head to **Caraccioli Cellars Tasting Room** (Dolores St. between Ocean Ave. and 7th Ave., 831/622-7722, www.caracciolicellars.com, 2pm-7pm Mon.-Thurs., 11am-10pm Fri.-Sat., 11am-7pm Sun., $25) for a high-end experience tasting their popular brut and brut rosé.

- Don't miss **Scheid Vineyards Carmel-By-The-Sea Tasting Room** (San Carlos St. and 7th Ave., 831/626-9463, www.scheidvineyards.com, noon-6pm Sun.-Thurs., noon-7pm Fri.-Sat., $10-20), where you can sip claret and cabernet sauvignon-syrah blends in a relaxed atmosphere.

- **Boekenoogen Vineyard & Winery** (24 W. Carmel Valley Rd., 831/659-4215, www.boekenoogenwines.com, 11am-5pm daily, $15-20), in inland Carmel Valley Village, has a garden patio where you can sample pinot noir, chardonnay, or syrah on sunny days.

- **I Brand & Family Winery** (19 E. Carmel Valley Rd., 831/298-7227, http://Ippwines.com, noon-6pm Wed.-Sun. and by appointment, $18) produces three different labels at three prices. Its owner was named 2018's Winemaker of the Year by the *San Francisco Chronicle*.

VINEYARD IN NAPA VALLEY

SAN FRANCISCO TO BIG SUR

4-5 days; 175 miles/282 kilometers

Spend **1-2 days** in **San Francisco.** Head south to **Monterey,** where you can spend **a day** eating local seafood, visiting the **Monterey Bay Aquarium,** and taking a boat tour. The **next day,** enjoy breakfast and a walk on the beach in **Carmel-By-The-Sea,** then indulge in superb wine-tasting in **Carmel Valley.** Take your **last day** to drive Highway 1 south to Big Sur, stopping often for photos and beach hikes.

SAN FRANCISCO TO MENDOCINO

4 days; 334 miles/538 kilometers

After taking **one day** to tour **San Francisco,** journey north to California's wine country. Spend your **second day** wine-tasting and checking out the area's incredible restaurants. On your **third day,** head west to the coast for ocean views at **Sonoma Coast State Park** and **Point Arena-Stornetta Public Lands.** Overnight in **Mendocino.** Spend your **last day** exploring the towering redwoods in **Humboldt Redwoods State Park.**

❹ Swap stories at the nearby **Valley of the Moon Winery** (777 Madrone Rd., 707/939-4500, www.valleyofthemoonwinery.com, 10am-5pm daily, $20-30), itself a historic site where wine has been made since the Civil War era.

> Take Arnold Dr. south for 2 miles (3 km), then turn left on Madrone Rd. to reach the winery.

❺ End the day with dinner in Glen Ellen and an overnight stay at the boutique inn **Gaige House + Ryokan** (13540 Arnold Dr., 800/234-1425, www.foursisters.com, $279-699), which blends Asian influences with wine country chic.

> Take CA-12 W for 2 miles (3 km) back to Glen Ellen to reach the inn.

DAY 3: Glen Ellen to Jenner

65 miles/105 kilometers | 2.5 hours

ROUTE OVERVIEW: Bennett Valley Rd. • CA-12 • CA-116 • CA-1

❶ Start the morning with a drive through the scenic wine region to **Santa Rosa.** Have lunch at **The Spinster Sisters** (401 S. A St., 707/528-7100, http://thespinstersisters.com, 8am-2:30pm Mon., 8am-2:30pm and 4pm-9pm Tues.-Fri., 9am-2:30pm and 5pm-9pm Sat., 9am-2:30pm Sun., $11-31), where you can savor the artsy eatery's local ingredients.

> Take Bennett Valley Rd. north out of Glen Ellen (10 mi/16 km). Turn right on Gordon Ln., then left on Maple Ave. Turn right on S. E St. In less than a mile, turn left onto 4th St. and continue into Santa Rosa.

❷ Walk to **Russian River Brewing Company** (725 4th St., 707/545-2337, http://russianriverbrewing.com, 11am-midnight daily, $9-28) to find out why beer connoisseurs are so drawn to the brewery's fabled Pliny the Elder.

❸ Follow the Russian River west to the coast. At **Goat Rock Beach** in **Sonoma Coast State Park** (707/875-3483, www.parks.ca.gov, sunrise-sunset daily, $8 per vehicle), take in the majesty of the Pacific Ocean.

> Take CA-12 W for 4 miles (6 km). Take the exit signed for Occidental Rd., making a right, then a quick left onto Occidental. Continue for 5 miles (8 km), then turn right to join CA-116 W. Continue on CA-116 for 23 miles (37 km). As you cross the river, CA-1 joins with CA-116. Turn right from CA-1 onto Goat Rock Rd. to reach the beach.

❹ End the day in nearby **Jenner** with a view of the Russian River and a fine, locally sourced meal at **River's End** (11048 CA-1, 707/865-2484, www.ilovesunsets.com, 11:30am-8:30pm Fri.-Tues., $20-55).

> Retrace your path back to CA-1, then cross over the river. Stay left and follow CA-1 for 2 miles (3 km) until you reach the restaurant.

5 Spend the night at the rugged yet chic **Timber Cove Resort** (21780 CA-1, 707/847-3231, www.timbercoveresort.com, $225-900).

> Take CA-1 N for 14 miles (23 km) to reach the resort.

DAY 4: Jenner to Mendocino

75 miles/121 kilometers | 2.5 hours

ROUTE OVERVIEW: CA-1

1 You'll want to leave early—the drive up the coast is winding and time consuming, although beautiful. If you hit **Bowling Ball Beach** (Schooner Gulch State Beach, Schooner Gulch Rd. and CA-1, 3 mi/4.8 km south of Point Arena, 707/937-5804, www.parks.ca.gov) at low tide, watch as the boulders set in neat rows are revealed on the rocky shore.

> Take CA-1 N for 34 miles (55 km) to reach the beach.

2 A little farther up the road in **Point Arena,** pick up baked goodies or lunch at the whimsical and welcoming **Franny's Cup & Saucer** (213 Main St., 707/882-2500, www.frannyscupandsaucer.com, 8am-4pm Wed.-Sat., $2-6, cash/check only).

> Continue north on CA-1 for 3 miles (5 km) to reach Point Arena.

3 Walk off your meal at the nearby **Point Arena-Stornetta Public Lands** of the **California Coastal National Monument** (Point Arena Cove north to Manchester State Park, 707/468-4000,

www.blm.gov, sunrise-sunset daily). See the greatest hits of the California coast: vertigo-inducing cliffs, far-ranging ocean views, sea arches, rocky points, and tidepools.

> Take CA-1 N for 2 miles (3 km), then turn left onto Lighthouse Rd. and continue for 1 mile (1.6 km) to reach the Point Arena-Stornetta Public Lands.

4 End the day in **Mendocino** with a pint and simple yet filling meal at the lively **Patterson's Pub** (10485 Lansing St., 707/937-4782, www.pattersonspub.com, 10am-midnight daily).

> Return to CA-1 and follow it north for 33 miles (53 km) to Mendocino.

5 Spoil yourself with a night at the upscale B&B **Brewery Gulch Inn** (9401 CA-1, 800/578-4454, www.brewerygulchinn.com, $385-545). Be sure to take advantage of the made-to-order hot breakfast in the morning.

DAY 5: Mendocino to Arcata

155 miles/250 kilometers | 4.5 hours

ROUTE OVERVIEW: CA-1 • US-101 • CA-254/Avenue of the Giants • US-101

1 After breakfast, take a scenic detour along the redwood-lined **Avenue of the Giants** (www.avenueofthegiants.net). The towering coast redwoods in **Humboldt Redwoods State Park** (CA-254, 707/946-2263, www.parks.ca.gov or www.humboldtredwoods.org, visitors center 9am-5pm daily Apr.-Sept., 10am-4pm daily Oct.-Mar., free) are a true must-see.

> Take CA-1 N until US-101 N (53 mi/85 km). Continue for 29 miles (47 km) to CA-254 and the southern entrance to Avenue of the Giants. Follow CA-254 N for another 16 miles (26 km) to reach the visitors center for Humboldt Redwoods State Park.

2 Head north to **Eureka** and stop to wander the city's Old Town and waterfront. Have lunch at the creative neighborhood Italian restaurant **Brick & Fire Bistro** (1630 F St., 707/268-8959, www.brickandfirebistro.com, 11:30am-9pm Wed.-Mon., $14-22).

POINT ARENA-STORNETTA PUBLIC LANDS

ARCATA PLAZA

> *Continue north on CA-254 for another 15 miles (24 km) until the northern terminus of Avenue of the Giants, near Pepperwood. Take US-101 N for 32 miles (52 km) to reach Eureka.*

❸ Continue north to charming **Arcata** for more redwoods at the **Arcata Community Forest** (east ends of 11th St., 14th St., and California St., 707/822-5951, www.cityofarcata.org, sunrise-sunset daily). This forest is an ideal place to stroll between the silent giants, many of which are cloaked in moss, and take lots of photos.

> *Continue north on US-101 for another 8 miles (13 km) to reach Arcata.*

❹ After dinner in Arcata Plaza, enjoy a pint of Imperial Golden Ale at **Redwood Curtain Brewing Company** (550 S. G St., 707-826-7222, www.redwoodcurtainbrewing.com, noon-11pm Sun.-Tues., noon-midnight Wed.-Sat.), then get a room at one of the lodging options downtown.

DAY 6: Arcata to Crescent City

95 miles/153 kilometers | 3.5 hours

ROUTE OVERVIEW: US-101 • Davison Rd. • US-101

❶ Fuel up with a tasty crepe from **Renata's Creperie and Espresso** (1030 G St., 707/825-8783, 8am-3pm Sun.-Thurs., 8am-9pm Fri.-Sat., $4-12) before hitting the road for your final day on the coast.

❷ North of Arcata, explore the coastal city of **Trinidad.** Have your camera handy for the views of beaches, the bay, and the town from **Trinidad Head** (end of Lighthouse Rd.). Stretch your legs on the mile-long loop trail atop the headlands, then head back down to admire the beach up close.

> *Take US-101 N for 15 miles (24 km) to Trinidad. From the highway, take Main St., Trinity St., Edwards St., and then Lighthouse Rd. to get to Trinidad Head.*

❸ If you're hungry, a lunch of creative comfort food awaits nearby at **The Lighthouse Grill** (Saunders Plaza, 355 Main St., 707/677-0077, http://trinidadlighthousegrill.com, 11am-8pm daily, $6-13).

❹ Follow up lunch with a visit to **Prairie Creek Redwoods State Park** (off US-101, 25 mi/40 km south of Crescent City, 707/488-2039, www.parks.ca.gov, sunrise-sunset daily, day use $8 per vehicle), part of **Redwood National Park** (www.nps.gov/redw). Hike the popular **Fern Canyon Trail** (1 mi/1.6 km round-trip, 30 minutes, easy), which passes through a steep canyon draped in bright green ferns. The trailhead is off Davison Road.

> *Take US-101 N for 23 miles (37 km). Turn left onto Davison Rd.; continue for 7 miles (11 km) until you reach the parking area at the trailhead.*

❺ Spend the evening in **Crescent City,** with a hearty meal and live music at **SeaQuake Brewing** (400 Front St., 707/465-4444, www.seaquakebrewing.com, 11am-9pm Tues.-Thurs., 11am-10pm Fri.-Sat., $10-19).

> *Retrace your path back along Davison Rd., returning to US-101. Take US-101 N for 39 miles (63 km) until Crescent City.*

DAY 7: Crescent City to Ashland, Oregon

175 miles/280 kilometers | 4.5 hours

ROUTE OVERVIEW: US-101 • US-199 • I-5 • OR-238 • OR-99

❶ Start early and cross into Oregon. Stop in the town of **Cave Junction** for a sweet deal on an unusually sliced

WILD RIVER BREWING AND PIZZA COMPANY

pizza at **Wild River Brewing and Pizza Company** (249 N. Redwood Hwy./US-199, 541/592-3556, www.wildriverbrewing.com, 10am-10pm daily, $6-33).

> Take US-101 N for 4 miles (6 km) to US-199 N. Continue for 48 miles (77 km) to Cave Junction.

❷ Continue north through evergreens and burled trees to **Grants Pass** and into **Medford.** Visit the famous **Harry & David Country Village** (1314 Center Dr., 541/864-2278, 9am-7pm Sun.-Thurs., 9am-8pm Fri.-Sat.) for samples, souvenirs, and a **factory tour** (877/322-8000, www.harryanddavid.com, tours 9:15am, 10:30am, 12:30pm, and 1:45pm Mon.-Fri., $5).

> Take US-199 N to Grants Pass (28 mi/45 km). In Grants Pass, get on I-5 S and continue for 25 miles (40 km) to Medford.

GRANTS PASS

❸ Next, detour over to the **Applegate Valley Lavender Farm** (15370 OR-238, 541/291-9229, www.applegatevalleylavenderfarm.com, hours vary in summer, closed in July) and make your own fragrant sachet, hand-picked from aromatic purple lavender fields.

> Follow OR-238 W for 20 miles (32 km) to the lavender farm.

❹ Make your way to **Ashland** for dinner. Order a glass of wine and lamb *sambousek* (a fried, stuffed pastry) at the **Brickroom** (35 N. Main St., 541/708-6030, www.brickroomashland.com, 8am-1am daily, $10-22).

> Take OR-238 E for 16 miles (26 km). Turn right on Cady Rd., then make a quick right onto Sterling Creek Rd. After a mile, turn left onto Poorman's Creek Rd., which becomes Griffin Creek Rd. after another mile. After 3 miles (5 km), turn right on Pioneer Rd. and continue for 5 miles (8 km) to Colver Rd. Turn right and follow Colver for 2 miles (3 km), then take OR-99 S for 6 miles (10 km) into Ashland.

❺ End the day with a sunset meander through **Lithia Park** (59 Winburn Way, 541/488-5340, www.ashland.or.us, dawn-11:30pm daily, free). This park, filled with bridges, gardens, domes, fountains, and sycamores, is also home to the famed Oregon Shakespeare Festival.

DAY 8: Ashland to Crater Lake National Park

145 miles/233 kilometers | 5 hours

ROUTE OVERVIEW: I-5 • OR-62 • Rim Drive

❶ In the morning, tuck into generous portions of fried eggs, country potatoes, and stacks of pancakes at **The Breadboard Restaurant** (744 N. Main St., 541/488-0295, www.breadboardashland.com, 7am-2pm daily, $8-13).

❷ Drive to **Crater Lake National Park** (www.nps.org/crla) and follow the spectacular **Rim Drive** (33 mi/53 km, usually open June-Oct.) around the lake for incredible views of this

CRATER LAKE

afternoon or early evening taking in the scenery before you bed down for the night. If you didn't nab a spot ahead of time, you'll need to drive to Medford to find a hotel.

DAY 9: Crater Lake to Mount Shasta, California

160 miles/260 kilometers | 4 hours

ROUTE OVERVIEW: OR-62 • US-97 • I-5

geologic wonder. Plan on devoting about 2-3 hours to the drive.

> *Take I-5 N for 11 miles (18 km) to OR-62 E. Continue for 71 miles (114 km), then turn left onto Munson Valley Rd., following signs for Crater Lake. This road leads to the park headquarters in 4 miles (6 km).*

❸ End at the **Rim Village Café** (Rim Village, 866/761-6668, www.travelcraterlake.com, 10am-6pm daily mid-May-early June and Oct.-early Nov., 9am-8pm daily June-early Sept., shorter hours in winter, $8-11), where you can have a light lunch.

❹ To secure a campsite at the park's **Mazama Campground** (Mazama Village, 866/761-6668, www.travelcraterlake.com, June-late Sept., $21 tents, $31-43 RVs), get here early. Once you're settled in, spend the late

❶ From the park, return to California, stopping in the town of **Weed** at the family-owned **Hi-Lo Café** (88 S. Weed Blvd., 530/938-2904, http://hi-lo-cafe.com, 6am-10pm daily, $10-18) for breakfast.

> *Take OR-62 E for 20 miles (32 km) to US-97 S. Follow this for 93 miles (150 km) to Weed.*

❷ Next up is the town of **Mount Shasta** for astonishing views of the eponymous snow-covered volcanic peak. If you want to hike Mount Shasta but don't have the time—or the level of training—to go all the way to the top, try a nice day hike to **Gray Butte** (3.4 mi/5.5 km round-trip, 1-3 hours, moderate), an intermediate peak on the south slope of the mountain. The trailhead is about 13 miles (21 km) east of town.

MOUNT SHASTA

SPRING

- **Big Sur International Marathon, Big Sur** (831/625-6226, www.bsim.org, $175-200, Apr.): Considered the most scenic marathon in the world, this event begins in Big Sur and ends north in Carmel.
- **Kool April Nites, Redding** (1666 E. Cypress Ave., 530/226-0844, http://koolaprilnites.com, Apr.): Restored classic cars cruise Redding's streets in a celebration of automotive nostalgia.
- **Kinetic Grand Championship, Humboldt County** (707/786-3443, www.kineticgrandchampionship.com, May): There's no better celebration of Humboldt County's eclectic individualism than this three-day event.

SUMMER

- **Broadway Under the Stars, Glen Ellen** (2400 London Ranch Rd., 707/938-5216, http://transcendencetheatre.org, summer): Every summer, this program produces four Broadway-inspired musicals in the stone ruins of a former winery.
- **Oregon Shakespeare Festival, Ashland** (800/219-8161, www.osfashland.org, Mar.-Oct., prices vary): This summer festival brings in some of the best actors and dramatists to re-create beloved works by William Shakespeare.

- **Mammoth Motocross, Mammoth Lakes** (Mammoth Mountain, 800/626-6684, www.mammothmotocross.com, June, $20): Watch the country's top dirt-bike riders race around a track filled with jumps, berms, and varying terrain.

FALL

- **Monterey Jazz Festival, Monterey** (Monterey County Fairgrounds, 2004 Fairground Rd., 831/373-3366, www.montereyjazzfestival.org, Sept.): Since 1958, the longest-running jazz festival in the world has hosted every major musician of the genre.
- **Hardly Strictly Bluegrass, San Francisco** (www.hardlystrictlybluegrass.com, late Sept./early Oct., free): Watch free performances by the best Americana musicians in Golden Gate Park.

WINTER

- **SnowGlobe Festival, South Lake Tahoe** (Lake Tahoe Community College, 1 College Dr., http://snowglobemusicfestival.com, 1:30pm-midnight Dec. 29-31, $139-400): This annual three-day electronic music festival caters to fans of Burning Man.

> Take I-5 S for 7 miles (11 km) to reach the town of Mount Shasta. From Mount Shasta Blvd., turn east onto Lake St. and follow the curve as it turns into Everett Memorial Hwy./County Rd. A10. Continue for 13 miles (21 km) to the trailhead.

3 Back in town, enjoy a reasonably priced meal at the original **Black Bear Diner** (401 W. Lake St., 530/926-4669, www.blackbeardiner.com, 6am-10pm daily, $13-18).

4 Cap off the evening with a cocktail at the **Gold Room** (903 S. Mt. Shasta Blvd., 530/926-4125, 11:30am-2am Mon.-Sat., 10am-2pm Sun., cash only), Mount Shasta's favorite bar with pool tables, darts, and vinyl-covered chairs.

5 Spend the night at the **Inn at Mount Shasta** (710 S. Mt. Shasta Blvd., 530/918-9292, http://innatmountshasta.com, $79-299). Built in 2000 and renovated in 2018, it's one of the newer facilities in the area.

DAY 10: Mount Shasta to Lassen Volcanic National Park

100 miles/161 kilometers | 2.5 hours

ROUTE OVERVIEW: CA-89

1 Take the **Volcanic Legacy Scenic Byway** (CA-89) southeast. Stop in the sleepy town of **McCloud** for a refreshing lavender iced tea at **Clearwater Coffee & Kitchen** (207 S. Quincy Ave., 530/316-4327, 8am-4pm daily).

> Follow CA-89/Volcanic Legacy Scenic Byway southeast for 9 miles (14 km) to reach McCloud.

2 Grab lunch at **Floyd's Frosty** (125 Broadway Ave., 530/964-9747, 11am-7pm daily late-May-early Sept., hours vary in winter, $6-12). Inside this old-school snack shack you'll find juicy burgers, crispy fries, and refreshing milkshakes.

3 After you've had your fill, take the scenic two-lane road that winds through mountainous terrain and past raging rivers. Stop to check out a roadside waterfall at **McArthur-Burney Falls Memorial State Park** (24898 CA-89, 530/335-2777, www.parks.ca.gov, sunrise-sunset daily, $10 per vehicle). No less a naturalist than Theodore Roosevelt declared **Burney Falls** one of the wonders of the world.

> Continue on CA-89 S for 40 miles (64 km) to the waterfall.

4 More natural wonders await at **Lassen Volcanic National Park** (530/595-4480, www.nps.gov/lavo, $25 per vehicle, $12 cyclists/pedestrians).

Check out the **Loomis Museum** (530/595-6140, 9am-5pm Fri.-Sun. mid-May-mid-June and Oct., 9am-5pm daily mid-June-early Oct., free) to learn about the history of Mount Lassen.

> Continue south on CA-89 for another 42 miles (68 km) to reach the park and museum.

5 Set up camp at nearby **Manzanita Lake** (179 sites, 877/444-6777, www.recreation.gov, campsites $26, cabins $72-97). This is the largest campground in the park, with both campsites and cabins and a full slate of amenities. Be sure to make your reservation in advance.

DAY 11: Lassen to Mill Creek

50 miles/81 kilometers | 1.5 hours

ROUTE OVERVIEW: CA-89 • CA-36

1 Start the day off right with an exhilarating hike on the **Lassen Peak Trail** (5 mi/8 km round-trip, 3 hours, difficult). The beauty and the views make the effort worthwhile.

> From the campground, drive south on CA-89 for 21 miles (34 km) to the trailhead.

2 Don't miss **Sulphur Works** (off CA-89, 1 mi/1.6 km north of the park's southwest entrance). It offers a peek at the geothermal features of Lassen. A boardwalk runs along the road, and a parking area is nearby, making it easy to get out of the car and examine the boiling mud pots and small steaming stream.

SULPHUR WORKS

> *Follow CA-89 S for another 6 miles (10 km) to reach the boardwalk.*

❸ Before exiting the park, pick up sundries, snacks, and souvenirs at **Lassen Café & Gift** (530/595-3555, 9am-5pm daily late May-mid-Oct., 11am-2pm Sat.-Sun. mid-Oct.-late May).

> *Continue south for another mile to reach the shop.*

❹ Head southeast to **Mill Creek** to arrive at **St. Bernard Lodge** (44801 CA-36, 530/258-3382, www.stbernardlodge.com, $102-110), where you'll be staying for the night. This bed-and-breakfast is in a cozy mansion rich in history.

> *Follow CA-89 S for 5 miles (8 km) to CA-36. Turn left onto CA-36 E and follow it for 15 miles (24 km) through Mill Creek and to the lodge.*

DAY 12: Mill Creek to Tahoe City

180 miles/290 kilometers | 3.5 hours

ROUTE OVERVIEW: CA-36 • US-395 • I-80 • CA-89

❶ Stop at **Cravings Cafe** (278 Main St., 530/258-2229, www.stoverlanding. com, 7am-2pm Thurs.-Mon., $8-11) in **Chester** for a latte and breakfast.

> *Drive east on CA-36 for 9 miles (14 km) to Chester.*

❷ Travel east to **Susanville,** where you can fill up on gas and grab a light lunch at **Lassen Ale Works at the Pioneer Saloon** (724 Main St., 530/257-7666, www.lassenaleworks.com, 4pm-10pm Mon., 11am-10pm Tues.-Thurs., 11am-11pm Fri.-Sat., $8-27). Housed in an old saloon, this spot serves upscale pub grub made from scratch.

> *Continue east on CA-36 for 35 miles (56 km) to Susanville.*

❸ Make the trek to **Truckee.** Along the way, the road swings through **Reno, Nevada,** before ducking back into California. Once you arrive in Truckee, visit **Donner Memorial State Park** (12915 Donner Pass Rd., off I-80, 530/582-7892, www.parks.ca.gov, sunrise-sunset daily, $5-10 per vehicle).

▶ *Playlist*

NORTHERN CALIFORNIA LOOP

SONGS

- **"I Left My Heart in San Francisco" by Tony Bennett:** A classic ode to the city, it's the perfect song to play at night's end when you're strolling the lamplit streets back to your hotel.

- **"Don't" by Zoe Kravitz:** The HBO miniseries *Big Little Lies* is set in Monterey, and the show's soundtrack dials in perfectly to the town's sleepy vibe. Kravitz's moody interpretation of this Elvis Presley song should accompany a coastal drive.

PODCASTS

- ***Sparkletack:*** This riveting podcast regales listeners with the rich history of San Francisco. Tune in before your trip so that as you tour the city, you can spot the landmarks you've just learned about.

> *Take US-395 S for 80 miles (129 km) to Reno. In Reno, catch I-80 W to Truckee (35 mi/56 km).*

❹ Drive south to **Tahoe City** and spend the night at the **Pepper Tree Inn** (645 N. Lake Blvd., 530/583-3711, www.peppertreetahoe.com, $120-180). Across from **Lake Tahoe** and close to restaurants, it's an ideal base.

> *Follow CA-89 S for 14 miles (23 km) to Tahoe City.*

DAY 13: Tahoe City to Incline Village, Nevada

60 miles/97 kilometers | 2.5 hours

ROUTE OVERVIEW: CA-89 • US-50 • NV-28

❶ It takes a little over two hours to drive the circumference of Lake Tahoe, but you'll want to make a full day of it. Head southwest and take a quick hike up **Eagle Rock** (1.5 mi/2.4 km round-trip, 20 minutes, easy-moderate), where you can soak up panoramic views of the lake. The trailhead is at a dirt pullout on CA-89, 1.6 miles (2.6 km) north of Homewood Mountain Resort.

> *Follow CA-89 S for 5 miles (8 km) to reach the trailhead.*

❷ Continue south to **Emerald Bay State Park** and tour the historic castle-like **Vikingsholm Mansion** (CA-89, 530/525-7232, http://vikingsholm.com or www.parks.ca.gov, tours 10:30am-3:30pm daily late May-Sept., grounds free, tours $10 adults, $8 ages 7-17).

> *Continue south on CA-89 for 14 miles (23 km) to reach the park.*

❸ Drive through **South Lake Tahoe** to **Zephyr Cove**. Here you can enjoy mountain vistas from the water with **Lake Tahoe Cruises** (760 US-50, 800/238-2463 or 775/589-4906, www.laketahoecruises.com or www.zephyrcove.com). Climb aboard the **MS *Dixie II*** (2.5-hr. tours, $55 adults, $33 children ages 3-11), a replica of a rear paddle wheeler imported from the Mississippi River.

> *Take CA-89 S for another 9 miles (14.5 km) to South Lake Tahoe. Turn left to get onto US-50, then continue for 9 miles (14.5 km) to the marina at Zephyr Cove.*

❹ Drive north along the East Shore through **Cave Rock** and into **Incline Village, Nevada**. Have dinner at **Crosby's Tavern & Gaming** (868 Tahoe Blvd., 775/833-1030, www.crosbyspub.com, 8am-11pm daily, $10-29), a locals' favorite thanks to its *Cheers*-like atmosphere and delicious food.

> *Go north on US-50 for 8 miles (13 km), then turn left to get on NV-28. Continue north for 10 miles (16 km) to reach Incline Village.*

❺ Stay the night at one of the top hotels in the world. The **Hyatt Regency Lake Tahoe** (111 Country Club Dr., 775/832-1234, www.laketahoe.regency.hyatt.com, $162-565) is a destination in itself.

DAY 14: Incline Village to Tuolumne Meadows

170 miles/275 kilometers | 4-5 hours

ROUTE OVERVIEW: NV-28 • US-50 • US-395 • CA-270 • US-395 • CA-120

❶ On this daylong drive to Yosemite, pull over in **Bridgeport** for a meal at the historic **Bridgeport Inn** (205 Main St., 760/932-7380, www.thebridgeportinn.com, 7am-9pm daily mid-Mar.-mid-Nov., $9-30), where you'll enjoy friendly service and excellent food.

> *Take NV-28 E for 10 miles (16 km) to US-50 E. Continue 10 miles (16 km) to US-395. Follow US-395 S for 78 miles (126 km) to Bridgeport.*

❷ If you have time, detour to **Bodie State Historic Park** (Hwy. 270, 760/647-6445, www.parks.ca.gov, 9am-6pm daily Apr.-Oct., 9am-4pm daily Nov.-Mar., $8 adults, $5 children 4-17, cash only). A state of "arrested decay" has preserved this 1877 gold-mining ghost town. Tours of the abandoned mine offer background on the settlement's sordid history.

EMERALD BAY STATE PARK

MONO LAKE TUFA STATE NATURAL RESERVE

> *Continue south on US-395 for 7 miles (11 km) to CA-270. Take CA-270 W for 13 miles (21 km) to the park.*

❸ At **Mono Lake,** gawk at the free-standing calcite towers, knobs, and spires that dot this alien landscape. A boardwalk in the **Mono Lake Tufa State Natural Reserve** (US-395, north of Lee Vining, 760/647-6331, www.parks. ca.gov, 24 hours daily, free) provides access to the North Tufa area, where you can wander through the different chunks of this preserve, which line the shore around the lake.

> *Follow the same route back to US-395, then continue south for 17 miles (27 km) to Mono Lake.*

❹ In nearby Lee Vining, buy camping supplies and firewood at the **Tioga Gas Mart** (CA-120 and US-395, 760/647-1088, www.whoanelliedeli.com). Inside the mart is the **Whoa Nellie Deli** (6:30am-9pm daily late Apr.-Oct., $8-23), where you can get a hearty meal of tacos, meatloaf, or pizza—this isn't your average gas station fare.

> *Continue south on US-395 for 2.5 miles (4 km) to CA-120/Tioga Pass Rd. Turn right and follow this less than a mile to Tioga Gas Mart.*

❺ Crossing **Tioga Pass** (CA-120, summer only) leads to **Yosemite National Park** (209/372-0200, www.nps.gove/yose, 24 hours daily year-round, $35 per vehicle, $30 motorcycles, $20 pedestrians/bicycles). If you nabbed a reservation, set up camp at **Tuolumne Meadows Campground** (Tioga Pass Rd. at Tuolumne Meadows, 209/372-4025 or 877/444-6777, www.recreation.gov,

304 sites, July-late Sept., reservations strongly advised, tents and RVs $26). Otherwise, stay in one of the rustic cabins at **Tuolumne Meadows Lodge** (888/413-8869, www.travelyosemite. com, early June-mid-Sept., $144).

> *Continue west on CA-120/Tioga Pass Rd. for 12 miles (19 km) to the Tioga Pass entrance of Yosemite. It's another 7 miles (11 km) on CA-120 W to Tuolumne Meadows.*

DAY 15: Tuolumne Meadows to Yosemite Valley

55 miles/89 kilometers | 2 hours

ROUTE OVERVIEW: CA-120 • Big Oak Flat Rd.

❶ Before you head out for the day, snap some pics of **Tuolumne Meadows,** a rare alpine meadow where numerous hiking trails thread through Yosemite's backcountry.

YOSEMITE VALLEY

HALF DOME

② Once you've driven into **Yosemite Valley,** park your car and use the **Yosemite Valley shuttle** (209/372-0200, 7am-10pm daily year-round, runs every 10-20 min., free) to see **Half Dome, El Capitan,** and **Yosemite Falls.**

> *Take CA-120 W for 39 miles (63 km) to Big Oak Flat Rd. Turn left and follow Big Oak Flat for 9.5 miles (15 km) to El Portal Rd. Turn left. In less than a mile, El Portal turns into Southside Dr. Follow this for 5 miles (8 km) to Sentinel Dr. Turn left, then head to Northside Dr. Turn left again and in less than a mile, arrive in Yosemite Valley.*

③ Looking for some exercise? Hike to **Vernal Fall** (2.4 mi/3.9 km round-trip, 3 hours, strenuous) on the **Mist Trail** (shuttle stop 16), with its steep, slick granite and 600-some stairs. For more ambitious hikers, there are options to extend the hike.

THE AHWAHNEE

④ Spend the night at the elegant **Ahwahnee** (888/413-8869, outside U.S. 602/278-8888, www.travelyosemite.com, $482-1,178), where historic luxury is the running theme in the rooms, cottages, and grand dining room with soaring ceilings.

DAY 16: Yosemite Valley to Monterey

200 miles/320 kilometers | 5-6 hours

ROUTE OVERVIEW: CA-140 • CA-49 • CA-140 • CA-152 • CA-156 • CA-1

① Say goodbye to Yosemite and settle in for a long drive. Stop for lunch and a much-needed leg-stretch past Pacheco Pass at **Casa de Fruta** (10021 CA-152, Hollister, 408/842-7282, www.casadefruta.com, 7am-8pm Mon. and Thurs., 7am-7pm Tues.-Wed., 7am-9pm Fri.-Sun.), a fruit stand from the 1940s that has since blossomed into a roadside attraction.

> *Take CA-140 W out of the park. Follow CA-140 for 30 miles (48 km) to CA-49 N. Turn right and drive less than 5 miles (8 km) to Mt. Bullion Cutoff Rd. In 3 miles (5 km), Mt. Bullion turns into CA-140. Continue west on CA-140 for 21 miles (34 km), then turn left on Plainsburg Rd. In 8 miles (13 km), Plainsburg becomes Sandy Mush Rd. In another 3 miles (5 km), turn left onto Bliss Rd. After 4 miles (6 km), Bliss becomes Hemlock Rd. In 3 miles (5 km) turn right to get onto CA-152 W. Continue for 60 miles (97 km) to reach Casa de Fruta.*

GREAT TIDE POOL AT MONTEREY BAY AQUARIUM

2 Reach **Monterey** in time to watch the sun set over the harbor while noshing on calamari and linguine at the Sicilian seafood restaurant **Paluca Trattoria** (6D Old Fishermans Wharf, 831/373-5559, http://palucatrattoria.com, 11:30am-9pm Sun.-Thurs., 11:30am-9:30pm Fri.-Sat., $17-28). If the outdoor dining area that overlooks the marina seems familiar, it's because the restaurant was one of the filming locations for the popular HBO television series *Big Little Lies*.

> Take CA-156 W for 34 miles (55 km) to reach CA-1. Take CA-1 S for 13 miles (21 km) to reach Monterey.

3 Spend the night downtown at the **Portola Hotel & Spa** (2 Portola Plaza, 800/342-4295, reservations 888/222-5851, www.portolahotel.com, $229-600). The comfortable rooms have patios or balconies—perfect for soaking up views of the harbor.

DAY 17: Monterey

MORNING

1 Spend the morning exploring **Monterey Bay** before the winds come up. **Adventures by the Sea** (299 Cannery Row, 831/372-1807, www. adventuresbythesea.com, 9am-sunset daily, kayak rentals $35/day, SUP rentals $50/day) rents kayaks and stand-up paddleboards and lets you choose your own route around the bay's kelp forest.

AFTERNOON

2 Further enrich your knowledge of the bay and its unique organisms at the **Monterey Bay Aquarium** (886 Cannery Row, 831/648-4800, www.montereybayaquarium.org, 9:30am-6pm daily, adults $50, children 3-12 $30). This mammoth aquarium astonishes with a vast array of sealife and exhibits on the local ecosystem.

EVENING

3 Relax with a beer at the downtown **Alvarado Street Brewery & Grill** (426 Alvarado St., 831/655-2337, www.alvaradostreetbrewery.com, 11:30am-10pm Sun.-Thurs., 11:30am-11pm Fri.-Sat.). Try to get a table out front on the sidewalk patio or in the beer garden in back.

4 End the day with dinner at the lovely **Montrio Bistro** (414 Calle Principal, 831/648-8880, www.montrio.com, 4:30pm-close daily, $19-46).

DAY 18: Monterey to Big Sur

40 miles/64 kilometers | 1.5 hours

ROUTE OVERVIEW: CA-1

❶ Your day begins with beautiful **Carmel-By-The-Sea.** Check out the superb breakfast offerings at the unassuming **Carmel Belle** (Doud Craft Studios, Ocean Ave. and San Carlos St., 831/624-1600, www.carmelbelle.com, 8am-6pm daily, $6-15). After, take a walk on the dog-friendly **Carmel Beach** (west end of Ocean Ave.).

> Follow CA-1 S for 4 miles (6 km) to Carmel-By-The-Sea.

❷ Make your way to the crown jewel of California's impressive state park system: **Point Lobos State Natural Reserve** (CA-1, 831/624-4909, www.parks.ca.gov or www.pointlobos.org, 8am-7pm daily spring-fall, 8am-sunset daily winter, $10 per vehicle). The pocket coves, tidepools, forests of Monterey cypress, and diverse marine and terrestrial wildlife are said to the be the inspiration behind the setting of Robert Louis Stevenson's *Treasure Island.*

> Continue south on CA-1 for 3.5 miles (5.5 km) to reach the reserve.

❸ Head south along **Big Sur Coast Highway** (CA-1), one of the most picturesque roads in the country. Go slowly and make time to stop at pull-outs so as to better experience the breathtaking views. If you're in the mood for a hike, visit **Andrew Molera State Park** (CA-1, 831/667-1112, www.parks.ca.gov, 30 minutes before sunrise-30 minutes after sunset daily, $10 per vehicle), where trails dip to the beach and climb into the forest.

> Follow CA-1 S for 19 miles (31 km) to reach the state park.

POINT LOBOS STATE NATURAL RESERVE

Best HIKES

EASY

- **Point Arena Lighthouse** (0.8 mi/1.3 km loop): This hike begins with views of Point Arena Cove from the bluffs above and levels out to a walk along the sea. Located in **California Coastal National Monument** (Point Arena Cove north to Manchester State Park, 707/468-4000, www.blm. gov, sunrise-sunset daily).

- **Fern Canyon Trail** (1 mi/1.6 km round-trip): Walk into a creek-carved canyon lush with bright green ferns dripping from the surrounding walls. Located in **Prairie Creek Redwoods State Park** (Newton B. Drury Scenic Pkwy., 707/488-2039, www. parks.ca.gov, sunrise-sunset daily, $8 per vehicle).

- **Kortum Trail** (4.6 mi/7.4 km round-trip): This blufftop trail parallels the Pacific Ocean, offering opportunities to access the park's beaches and coves. Located in **Sonoma Coast State Park** (707/875-3483, www.parks. ca.gov, sunrise-sunset daily, $8 per vehicle).

MODERATE

- **Glen Aulin Trail** (11 mi/18 km round-trip): This hike through the Tuolumne Meadows weaves past cascading waterfalls, lush valleys, and granite outcroppings. Located in **Yosemite National Park** (209/372-0200, www.nps.gov/ yose, $20-35).

- **Lundy Canyon Trail** (5.5 mi/8.9 km round-trip): Hike to a lake in the Eastern Sierra and see several waterfalls along the way. Located in **Hoover Wilderness** (Inyo National Forest, Bridgeport Ranger District, 760/932-7070, www.fs.usda.gov).

STRENUOUS

- **Lake Aloha** (12.5 mi/20 km round-trip): This long hike follows the Pacific Crest Trail to a series of alpine lakes. Located in **Desolation Wilderness** (visitors center: CA-89, 3 mi/4.8 km north of South Lake Tahoe, 530/543-2674, www.fs.usda.gov, hours vary, late May-Oct.).

- **Ridge Trail and Panorama Trail Loop** (8 mi/13 km round-trip): Take in the beauty of Big Sur on this loop trail that includes a detour down to a driftwood-covered beach. Located in **Andrew Molera State Park** (CA-1, 831/667-1112, www. parks.ca.gov, 30 minutes before sunrise-30 minutes after sunset daily, $10).

- **Sacramento River Trail** (up to 38 mi/61 km one-way): This scenic trail starts at the Sundial Bridge and continues all the way to the Shasta Dam. Eastern terminus located in **Redding** (844 Sundial Bridge Dr., www.cityofredding. com).

▼ KORTUM TRAIL, SONOMA COAST STATE PARK

❹ Dine early at the popular **Nepenthe** (48510 CA-1, 29 mi/47 km south of Carmel, 831/667-2345, www.nepenthebigsur.com, 11:30am-10pm daily, $18-50), where ocean views meet delicious cuisine.

> Take CA-1 S for another 9 miles (14.5 km) to reach the restaurant.

❺ Spend the night at **Deetjen's Big Sur Inn** (48865 CA-1, 831/667-2378, www.deetjens.com, $105-270), a rustic spot nestled in the redwoods. Be sure to get breakfast here the following morning. The restaurant (8am-noon and 6pm-9pm daily, $10-42) is known for its homey atmosphere and eggs Benedict.

> Drive less than a mile south on CA-1 to reach the inn.

DAY 19: Big Sur

20 miles/32 kilometers | 50 minutes

ROUTE OVERVIEW: CA-1

❶ Make the short drive south to **Julia Pfeiffer Burns State Park** (CA-1, 831/667-1112, www.parks.ca.gov, sunrise-sunset daily, $10 per vehicle). Hike the **Partington Cove Trail** (1 mi/1.6 km round-trip, 1 hour, easy) for a journey down to a tunnel cut through rock that leads to **McWay Falls**, a cascade that spills into a small and scenic rocky cove. This is as far south as you'll be driving on CA-1 for this trip.

> Take CA-1 S for 5 miles (8 km) to reach the state park.

BIG SUR

❷ Drive back north to **Henry Miller Memorial Library** (48603 CA-1, 831/667-2574, www.henrymiller.org, 11am-5pm Wed.-Sun.), a great bookstore and cultural arts hub. Buy a paperback and sip coffee on the shaded deck.

> Take CA-1 N for 5 miles (8 km) to reach the bookstore.

❸ Fill up on bar fare at the **Big Sur Taphouse** (47250 CA-1, 831/667-2197, www.bigsurtaphouse.com, noon-10pm daily). The cozy interior has wood tables, a fireplace, board games, and 10 rotating beers on tap.

> Continue north on CA-1 for 1.5 miles (2.5 km) to reach Big Sur Taphouse.

❹ Keep the night going with a visit to **Fernwood Tavern** (Fernwood Resort, 47200 CA-1, 831/667-2422, www.fernwoodbigsur.com, 11am-11pm Sun.-Thurs., 11am-1am Fri.-Sat.) for live music and a nightcap. Return to your room at Deetjen's once you're tuckered out.

> Take CA-1 N for another 2.5 miles (4 km) to reach the tavern. Deetjen's is 4.5 miles (7 km) south on CA-1.

DAY 20: Big Sur to San Francisco

160 miles/260 kilometers | 4 hours

ROUTE OVERVIEW: CA-1 • CA-156 • US-101 • I-80 • city streets

❶ Make your way north, past Monterey and back to San Francisco. At the legendary **Golden Gate Park** (Stanyan St. at Fell St., 415/831-2700, www.golden-gate-park.com), relax on the lawn and watch the city's hustle and bustle come to life.

> Take CA-1 N for 48 miles (77 km) to CA-156. Take CA-156 E for 6 miles (10 km) to US-101. Merge onto US-101 N and follow it for 98 miles (158 km) until you reach San Francisco. To get to the park, continue on US-101 N, following signs for Octavia Blvd. Turn left onto Fell St., following it for 1.5 miles (2.5 km) to the park.

❷ In the park, you can also visit the **Japanese Tea Garden** (75 Hagiwara Tea Garden Dr., 415/752-4227, http://japaneseteagardensf.com, 9am-6pm daily Mar.-Oct., 9am-4:45pm daily Nov.-Feb., adults $9, seniors and youth 12-17 $6, children 5-11 $2, children under 5 free).

❸ Spend the afternoon at the **San Francisco Museum of Modern Art** (151 3rd St., 415/357-4000, www.sfmoma. org, 10am-5pm Fri.-Tues., 10am-9pm Thurs., adults $25, free for children). SFMOMA showcases some of modern art's greatest hits, including a space dedicated to photography.

> Take Oak St. east for 2 miles (3 km), then turn right onto Octavia Blvd. and get on US-101 S. Merge onto I-80 E. In less than a mile, take the exit for 4th St. Turn left onto 3rd St., then continue four blocks to the museum.

❹ Have dinner at the museum's touted restaurant **In Situ** (151 3rd St., 415/941-6050, http://insitu.sfmoma. org, 11am-3:30pm Mon., 11am-3:30pm and 5pm-9pm Thurs.-Sat., 11am-3:30pm and 5pm-8pm Sun., $12-28) before tucking in for a good night's sleep.

GETTING THERE

AIR

It's easy to fly into the San Francisco Bay Area. There are three major airports. **San Francisco International Airport** (SFO, www.flysfo.com) is 15 miles (24 km) south of the city. Some San Francisco hotels offer complimentary airport shuttles.

Oakland Airport (OAK, www.oaklandairport.com) is 20 miles (32 km) east of the city but requires crossing the bay, via either the Bay Bridge or public transit. **Mineta San José Airport** (SJC, www.flysanjose.com) is the farthest away, roughly 50 miles (81 km) to the south.

TRAIN

Several public and private transportation options can get you into San Francisco. **Bay Area Rapid Transit** (BART, www.bart.gov) connects directly with SFO's international terminal; an airport shuttle connects Oakland airport to the nearest station.

Caltrain (www.caltrain.com, tickets $3.75-13.75) is a good option from

San Jose; an airport shuttle connects to the train station. Millbrae Station is where the BART and Caltrain systems connect; it's designed to transfer from one line to the other.

Amtrak (www.amtrak.com) does not run directly into San Francisco, but you can ride to the San Jose, Oakland, or Emeryville stations, then take a connecting bus to San Francisco.

BUS

Greyhound (200 Folsom St., 415/495-1569, www.greyhound.com, 5:15am-1am daily) offers bus service to San Francisco from all over the country.

CAR

From the **San Francisco airport** to downtown San Francisco, it's 30-40 minutes (15 mi/24 km). Take US-101 N until the exit for downtown San Francisco.

From the **Oakland airport,** it's 30-45 minutes (20 mi/32 km). Take I-880 N, then follow signs for I-80 W and the Bay Bridge. Take any of the exits after you cross the bridge to reach downtown.

From the **San Jose airport,** it's 1-1.5 hours (50 mi/81 km). Take I-880 N, then I-80 W over the Bay Bridge. Take any of the exits after you cross the bridge to reach downtown.

CONNECT WITH

- At San Francisco, Yosemite National Park, or Big Sur: **Best of the Golden State** (PAGE 108)

- At San Francisco, Big Sur, or Crescent City: **Pacific Coast Highway: California** (PAGE 124)

- At Yosemite National Park and Ashland: **Pacific Crest Trail: California** (PAGE 140)

- At Ashland: **Pacific Crest Trail: Oregon and Washington** (PAGE 250)

SOUTHERN CALIFORNIA AND ROUTE 66 LOOP

WHY GO: Beach fun, desert hikes, Hollywood glamour, Disneyland, family-friendly adventures

TOTAL DISTANCE: 865 miles/ 1,390 kilometers

NUMBER OF DAYS: 11

SEASONS: Spring through fall

START/END: Los Angeles, California

▼ SANTA MONICA BEACH

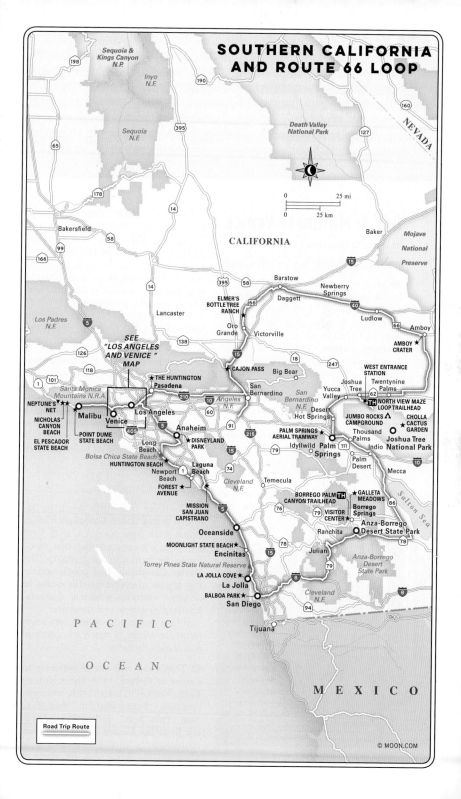

SOUTHERN CALIFORNIA AND ROUTE 66 LOOP

NEVADA

Sequoia & Kings Canyon N.P.

Inyo N.F.

Sequoia N.F.

Death Valley National Park

CALIFORNIA

Baker

Mojave National Preserve

Bakersfield

Barstow

Newberry Springs

Daggett

ELMER'S BOTTLE TREE RANCH

Ludlow

Amboy

Lancaster

Oro Grande

Victorville

AMBOY CRATER ★

Los Padres N.F.

SEE "LOS ANGELES AND VENICE" MAP

CAJON PASS ★

Big Bear

WEST ENTRANCE STATION

Twentynine Palms

★ THE HUNTINGTON
Pasadena

San Bernardino

San Bernardino N.F.

Joshua Tree

Yucca Valley

NORTH VIEW MAZE LOOP TRAILHEAD

NEPTUNE'S NET ★★★
NICHOLAS CANYON BEACH
EL PESCADOR STATE BEACH
POINT DUME STATE BEACH

Malibu

Venice

Los Angeles

Angeles N.F.

Desert Hot Springs

JUMBO ROCKS CAMPGROUND

CHOLLA CACTUS GARDEN

Anaheim

★ DISNEYLAND PARK

PALM SPRINGS AERIAL TRAMWAY ★

Thousand Palms

Joshua Tree National Park

Long Beach

Bolsa Chica State Beach

HUNTINGTON BEACH

Newport Beach

FOREST AVENUE ★

Laguna Beach

Cleveland N.F.

Idyllwild

Palm Springs

Indio

Mecca

Palm Desert

MISSION SAN JUAN CAPISTRANO

Temecula

BORREGO PALM CANYON TRAILHEAD

GALLETA MEADOWS

Salton Sea

Oceanside

MOONLIGHT STATE BEACH ★

Encinitas

Torrey Pines State Natural Reserve

LA JOLLA COVE ★

La Jolla

BALBOA PARK ★

San Diego

VISITOR CENTER ★

Borrego Springs

Anza-Borrego Desert State Park

Ranchita

Julian

Anza-Borrego Desert State Park

Cleveland N.F.

Tijuana

PACIFIC OCEAN

MEXICO

Road Trip Route

© MOON.COM

0 — 25 mi
0 — 25 km

This journey checks off every item on a road trip wish list: natural wonders, small towns, big cities, gourmet restaurants, family fun, deserts, beaches, history, and even roadside kitsch. Starting in Malibu at the Pacific Ocean, this trek winds south along the coast, dipping inland for visits to Hollywood and Disneyland, then curves back to the sea before beelining east to the craggy California desert. The best part? Your return trip home takes you along Route 66, the famed and historic Mother Road, with its Instagram-worthy neon signs and snapshots of Americana.

DAY 1: Malibu to Venice

45 miles/72 kilometers | 1.5 hours

ROUTE OVERVIEW: CA-1 • city streets

1 Start your drive in the "27 miles of scenic beauty" better known as **Malibu.** Choose from any of Malibu's gorgeous and remote **beaches** to spend time sunning and surfing. Some of the best are **Nicholas Canyon** (33850 CA-1, http://beaches.lacounty.gov, dawn-dusk daily, $3-10 parking), **El Pescador** (32860 CA-1, 310/457-1324, 8am-sunset daily), and **Point Dume State Beach** (Westward Beach Rd., 310/457-8143, www.parks.ca.gov, sunrise-sunset daily).

> Drive north on CA-1/Pacific Coast Hwy. to reach Point Dume (3.5 mi/5.5 km), El Pescador (7 mi/11 km), and Nicholas Canyon (8.5 mi/13.5 km).

2 Grab some casual seafood at the regional classic, **Neptune's Net**

VENICE BEACH BOARDWALK

(42505 CA-1, 310/457-3095, www.neptunesnet.com, 10:30am-8pm Mon.-Thurs., 10:30am-9pm Fri., 10am-8:30pm Sat.-Sun., $8-18). Sate your appetite with fresh seafood alongside Malibu surfers at this cliffside spot. Keep an eye out for dolphins and whales breaching offshore.

> From Nicholas Canyon, continue north on CA-1 for 3 miles (5 km) to the restaurant.

3 Drive south on CA-1 to **Santa Monica Pier** (Ocean Ave. at Colorado Ave., 310/458-8900, www.santamonicapier.org), surrounded by a gorgeous beach and crowned by a small amusement park. Ride the carousel and the Ferris wheel or rent a bike and cruise the bike path until you spot a nice patch of beach to call your own.

> Drive south on CA-1 for 29 miles (47 km) to Santa Monica Pier.

4 Continue two miles south to the famed **Venice Beach Boardwalk** (Ocean Front Walk from Navy Ct. to S. Venice Blvd., www.venicebeach.com, free). From the freaky to the fantastic, the Venice Boardwalk has people-watching of epic proportions. It's home to artists, weirdos, athletes, buskers, hustlers, gawkers, and hawkers.

> Take Ocean Ave./Neilson Way south for about a mile to reach the northern end of the boardwalk.

5 This stroll will segue perfectly to dinner at **Gjelina** (1429 Abbot Kinney Blvd., Venice, 310/450-1429, www.gjelina.com, 8am-midnight Mon.-Sat., 8am-11pm Sun., under $25). A far cry from the Venice Boardwalk, this contemporary dining destination is all about the flavor. Ask for seats at

Top ⑤ SOUTHERN CALIFORNIA AND ROUTE 66 LOOP

① **Surf** the Pacific Ocean in dreamy **Malibu** (PAGE 180).

② Meet Mickey and Minnie at **Disneyland Park** (PAGE 183).

③ **Snorkel** in San Diego's **La Jolla Cove** (PAGE 185).

④ See **bighorn sheep** in **Borrego Palm Canyon** (PAGE 186).

⑤ Drive a segment of one of the most iconic roads: **Route 66** (PAGE 189).

the community table, where you may wind up swapping stories with fellow travelers.

> *Take Windward Ave. northeast to Cabrillo Ave. Turn right, then make a quick left onto Andalusia Ave. Turn right onto Abbot Kinney Blvd. to reach the restaurant.*

DAY 2: Venice to Los Angeles

50 miles/81 kilometers | 2.5 hours

ROUTE OVERVIEW: I-10 • city streets • I-5 • US-101 • city streets

① Once you're up and at 'em, take the iconic L.A. drive up Sunset Boulevard into **Hollywood.** Wander the **Hollywood Walk of Fame** (Hollywood Blvd. from La Brea Ave. to Vine St., 323/469-8311, www.walkoffame.com). Since 1960, entertainment legends have wished for a spot on this iconic sidewalk of the stars.

> *Take I-10 E for 6 miles (9 km), exiting at La Cienega Blvd. Follow La Cienega for 4 miles (6 km), then turn right onto Fountain Ave. Continue for a mile, then turn left onto N. Fairfax Ave. Turn right onto Hollywood Blvd. to reach the Walk of Fame.*

② Get an eyeful at the ornate **TCL Chinese Theatre** (6925 Hollywood Blvd., 323/461-3331, www.tclchinesetheatres.com), famous for the celebrity handprints pressed into the concrete sidewalk out front. It's less than a 5-minute walk west on Hollywood Boulevard to reach the TCL Chinese Theatre.

HOLLYWOOD WALK OF FAME

GRIFFITH OBSERVATORY

③ Enjoy some science along with views of the city from the **Griffith Observatory** (2800 E. Observatory Rd., 213/473-0800, www.griffithobservatory.org, noon-10pm Tues.-Fri., 10am-10pm Sat.-Sun., free, parking $6-10), the most popular attraction at Griffith Park.

> *Take Hollywood Blvd. east to Bronson Ave. Turn left and follow this north to Franklin Ave. Turn right on Franklin and continue for 1.5 miles (2.5 km). Turn left onto N. Western Ave., which quickly becomes Los Feliz Blvd. Make a quick left onto Fern Dell Dr., which turns into Western Canyon Rd. after a while. Continue for 1.5 miles (2.5 km), then turn right onto W. Observatory Rd. This 5-mile (8-km) drive usually takes 20-25 minutes in traffic.*

④ Head downtown to visit **The Broad** (221 S. Grand Ave., 213/232-6200, www.thebroad.org, 11am-5pm Tues.-Wed., 11am-8pm Thurs.-Fri., 10am-8pm Sat., 10am-6pm Sun., free, touring exhibitions require tickets). This is L.A.'s top museum, featuring a who's who of modern art, plus touring exhibits by contemporary masters.

> *Take E. Observatory Rd. to N. Vermont Canyon Rd. Make a slight left on Hillhurst Ave., then turn left on Los Feliz Blvd. Follow this for a mile to Riverside Dr. Turn right, then merge onto I-5 S. Take I-5 S for 2 miles (3 km) to CA-110 S and continue for 1.5 miles (2.5 km). Exit at S. Grand Ave. to the museum.*

⑤ Take your pick of the city's exciting dining options before getting a taste of Hollywood nightlife on the **Sunset Strip** (Sunset Blvd. from Havenhurst Dr. to Sierra Dr., www.thesunsetstrip.com), home to many legendary rock clubs. At night, especially on weekends, no one is alone on the Strip. Spend the night nearby.

> Get on US-101 N and follow it north for 6 miles (10 km). Take exit 9B toward Hollywood Bowl. Turn right on Odin St., then left onto N. Highland Ave. Follow this to Franklin Ave. Turn right, then turn left on El Cerrito Pl. Turn right on Hollywood Blvd., then left on Laurel Ave. Turn right on Sunset Blvd. to reach the Sunset Strip.

DAY 3: Los Angeles to Anaheim

35 miles/56 kilometers | 1.5 hours

ROUTE OVERVIEW: city streets • US-101

1 Have breakfast at **Sqirl** (720 N. Virgil Ave., 323/284-8147, www.sqirlla. com, 6:30am-4pm Mon.-Fri., 8am-4pm Sat.-Sun., $12-18). You might have to wait in line, but the food at this small, cult-favorite Silver Lake bistro is worth every minute.

> Jog south from Sunset Blvd. to Melrose Ave. Take Melrose east for 4.5 mi (7 km) to reach the restaurant.

2 It's only an hour drive from Hollywood to **Anaheim.** Scoot south for a full day at **Disneyland Park** (1313 S. Disneyland Dr., Anaheim, 714/781-4565, www.disneyland.disney.go.com, 8am-11pm Tues.-Thurs., 8am-midnight Fri.-Mon., one-day ticket $104-149 ages 10 and up, $95-115 ages 3-9), the "Happiest Place on Earth." With popular rides like Pirates of the Caribbean, Mr. Toad's Wild Ride, and Indiana Jones Adventure Park, Disneyland is a thrill for visitors of all ages.

> Take US-101 S for 6 miles (10 km), then merge onto I-5. Continue south for 22 miles (35 km). Take exit 110B for Disneyland Dr.

3 You don't need reservations to spend time at **Star Wars: Galaxy's Edge,** a section of the park that brings a galaxy far, far away to life like never before. However, there is a capacity limit. Do this part of the park first so you won't miss out on your chance to pilot the *Millennium Falcon.*

KEY RESERVATIONS

- You don't need to buy your tickets to **Disneyland Park** in advance, but it's best to book your **lodging** ahead of time as hotels and motels fill up quickly. To dine at specific **restaurants** at the park, like Blue Bayou Restaurant, you'll need to book **several weeks** ahead of time.

- Tickets to the annual **Coachella Valley Music and Arts Festival** in Indio usually begin to go on sale about **10 months** out. Buy your tickets as soon as they go on sale, and book your **accommodations** at the same time.

- At **Joshua Tree National Park,** you should make reservations for the popular **Jumbo Rocks Campground.** Reservations can be made **up to six months** in advance.

4 Disneyland stays open late and the park lights up after dark. To maximize your fun, and minimize the drive, book a room near the park at the **Disneyland Hotel** (1150 Magic Way, 714/778-6600, http://disneyland.disney.go.com, $500-625). If you did it right, you'll be exhausted after a day of nostalgic characters and thrilling rides. The monorail stops inside the hotel, offering guests the easiest way into and out of the park without having to deal with parking.

DAY 4: Anaheim to Oceanside

85 miles/137 kilometers | 2.5 hours

ROUTE OVERVIEW: I-5 • CA-22 • CA-1 • CA-133 • CA-73 • I-5

1 A wealth of gorgeous Orange County beach cities lie ahead. Hit some waves in Surf City, USA, **Huntington Beach.** The best spot for beginners is **Bolsa Chica State Beach** (17851 Pacific Coast Hwy., 714/846-3460, www.parks. ca.gov, 6am-10pm daily), which has manageable and uncrowded waves.

> *Leave Anaheim via I-5 S. After 14 miles (23 km), take exit 107B to merge onto CA-22 W. Use exit 5 and turn left. Drive south for 4 miles (6 km) on Bolsa Chica Rd. Turn right on Warner Ave. and follow this to CA-1. Turn left and follow CA-1 about a mile to the beach.*

❷ Settle into a world of upscale shopping in **Laguna Beach.** For a taste of glamour, browse the boutiques, fine art galleries, and surf shops along tree-lined **Forest Avenue** (CA-1 to 3rd St.), across the highway from Main Beach.

> *Continue south on CA-1 for 19 miles (31 km) to reach Laguna Beach.*

❸ South of Laguna Beach, detour inland for a bit of local history at the **Mission San Juan Capistrano** (26801 Ortega Hwy., 949/234-1300, http://missionsjc.com, 9am-5pm daily, $10 adults, $7 children). This lovely historic mission is one of the oldest buildings in California and is home to an annual migration of swallows. Head south to **Oceanside,** where you can bed down for the night in a hotel by the water.

> *Take CA-133 N for 4 miles (6 km) to CA-73 S. Take CA-73 S for 5 miles (8 km) to I-5 S, then continue 3 miles (5 km) to Mission San Juan Capistrano. Continue south for 28 miles (45 km) on I-5 to Oceanside.*

DAY 5: Oceanside to La Jolla

30 miles/48 kilometers | 1.5 hours

ROUTE OVERVIEW: I-5 • city streets

❶ Stop in the pretty burb of **Encinitas** to nab quality beach time at breathtaking **Moonlight State Beach** (400 B St., 760/633-2740, www.parks.ca.gov, 5am-10pm daily). Expect to see surfers riding the mild waves. Parking is free here.

> *Follow I-5 S for 14 miles (23 km) to Encinitas.*

❷ You'll pass through several beach towns before reaching **Torrey Pines State Natural Reserve** (12600 N. Torrey Pines Rd., 858/755-2063, www.parks.ca.gov, 7:15am-sunset daily),

WITH LESS TIME

LOS ANGELES AND ROUTE 66

4 days

You'll need a car to explore **Los Angeles,** so while a visit to the City of Angels doesn't qualify as a road trip per se, you'll get plenty of driving in. Spend **one day** sightseeing in **Hollywood.** Check out **Griffith Observatory** for **one day** and the **Sunset Strip** on **another day,** enjoying the city's international **food and drink scene** all the while. Use the **last day** of your trip to get out of town and drive some of **Route 66.**

ANAHEIM TO SAN DIEGO

3-7 days; 105 miles/169 kilometers

Depending on how many days you spend at **Disneyland,** this shorter trip can range from **three days** to a **week.** From **Anaheim,** drive south to **Orange County** for **a day** in the sun and sand at **Huntington Beach, Laguna Beach,** and **Bolsa Chica State Beach.** Find a hotel by the sea in **Oceanside.**

The **next day,** continue south to **Moonlight State Beach** before reaching **San Diego,** where seafood, breweries, and more beaches will fill the rest of your **last day.**

PALM SPRINGS TO JOSHUA TREE

5 days; 38 miles/61 kilometers

You'll want at least **two days** to tour **Palm Springs.** Make time for **golfing** the city's renowned greens, riding the **tramway,** and soaking up the **mid-century vibe** at **tiki bars.**

It's a short drive to **Joshua Tree National Park** from Palm Springs. Spend **three days** hiking, camping, and **stargazing.**

one of the wildest stretches along the coast. It's easiest to park in the lot near the beach.

> *Continue on I-5 S for 4.5 miles (7 km) to Del Mar Heights Rd. Exit and turn right. Turn left on Torrey Pines Rd. to reach the reserve.*

Family road trips usually go more smoothly when architectural tours and historical sites are broken up by fun activities.

DISNEYLAND PARK

- Kids of all ages love **Disneyland Park** (1313 S. Disneyland Dr., Anaheim, 714/781-4565, www.disneyland. disney.go.com, 8am-11pm Tues.-Thurs., 8am-midnight Fri.-Mon., one-day ticket $104-154 ages 10 and up, $98-117 ages 3-9).

- With the addition of the park's **Star Wars: Galaxy's Edge,** everyone is bound to love it a whole lot more.

- Hotels within the park and its **Downtown Disney District** make it easy to for families to manage a visit to both Disneyland and **California Adventure Park** (8am-10pm daily, one-day ticket $104-154 ages 10 and up, $98-117 ages 3-9).

NEWPORT BEACH

- With wide beaches, a protected bay, and a **Fun Zone** (600 E. Bay Ave., Balboa Village, 949/903-2825, ww.balboaferriswheel.com, 11am-6pm Mon.-Thurs., 11am-9pm Fri., 11am-10pm Sat.) with amusement park rides, Newport Beach will satisfy kids who just want to play.

- Stay on or near **Balboa Peninsula** and ride its easy **bike path** or rent a **Duffy boat** (510 Edgewater Pl., 949/673-7200, www.boats4rent. com, 10am-6pm daily spring-fall, 10am-5pm daily winter, $85/hr) to scoot around the bay.

- Don't miss the local dessert specialty: chocolate- and nut-covered **frozen bananas.**

SAN DIEGO

- Between the shallow, waveless beaches of **Mission Bay,** the museums of **Balboa Park** (1549 El Prado, 619/239-0512, www. balboapark.org), and maritime exhibits on the waterfront, San Diego proves an exceptional family-friendly destination.

- Stay in **Mission Beach** or **Coronado** for easy access to beaches.

- You'll have no trouble packing in several days of activities at the **Fleet Science Center** (1875 El Prado, 619/238-1233, www.rhfleet. org, 10am-5pm Mon.-Thurs., 10am-8pm Fri., 10am-6pm Sat.-Sun., $20 adults, $17 children ages 3-12), the **Natural History Museum** (1788 El Prado, 877/946-7797, www.sdnhm. org, 10am-5pm daily, $19 adults, $12 children 3-17), the **Maritime Museum** (1492 N. Harbor Dr., 619/234-9153, www.sdmaritime. org, 9am-8pm daily, $18 adults, $8-13 children), and the **U.S.S.** *Midway* **Museum** (910 N. Harbor Dr., 619/544-9600, www.midway.org, 10am-5pm daily, $20 adults, $10 children 6-12).

❸ Drop down into **La Jolla Cove** (1100 Coast Blvd.) for some snorkeling, then dine at one of the incredible restaurants in **La Jolla,** every bit the Southern California jewel its name suggests.

> *Follow Torrey Pines Rd. south to Prospect Pl. Turn right. Follow Prospect Pl. as it curves into Prospect St. Prospect leads into La Jolla Cove. Continue on Prospect, then turn left on La Jolla Blvd. to reach La Jolla proper.*

LA JOLLA SHORE

DAY 6: La Jolla to San Diego

20 miles/32 kilometers | 1 hour

ROUTE OVERVIEW: I-5 • city streets • CA-163 • I-5 • city streets

① Once you get to **San Diego** proper, spend the afternoon exploring the museums, gardens, and architecture of **Balboa Park** (1549 El Prado, 619/239-0512, www.balboapark.org), the city's green space. This sprawling urban park includes Spanish colonial architecture, gorgeous gardens, multiple museums—and the San Diego Zoo.

> *Return to I-5 and drive south for 10 miles (16 km) to San Diego. Take the exit for Pershing Dr., following it east and north to Florida Dr. Take Florida north to reach the park.*

② To sample some world-class craft beer, head downtown to **Bottlecraft** (2252 India St., 619/487-9493, www.bottlecraftbeer.com, noon-10pm Mon.-Thurs., noon-midnight Fri.-Sat., 11am-10pm Sun.) in Little Italy.

> *Take Park Blvd. to CA-163 N, then merge onto I-5 N. Follow I-5 N for less than a mile. Exit at Hawthorn St., turn left, and then turn right on India St. to reach Bottlecraft.*

③ Afterward, head five blocks south to dine on seafood at **Ironside Fish**

BALBOA PARK

& Oyster (1654 India St., 619/269-3033, www.ironsidefishandoyster.com, 11:30am-midnight Sun.-Thurs., 11:30am-2am Fri.-Sat., $22-31), one of the city's top restaurants. Stunning interior design and amazing local seafood make this spot foodie- and photo-friendly.

④ Spend the night at the elegant **U.S. Grant Hotel** (326 Broadway, 619/232-3121, www.usgrant.com, from $220), built by the family of the 18th president of the United States, and named in his honor.

> *Take Kettner Blvd. south to A St. Follow A St. east, then turn right onto 3rd Ave, continuing three blocks to the hotel.*

DAY 7: San Diego to Anza-Borrego Desert State Park

110 miles/177 kilometers | 2.5 hours

ROUTE OVERVIEW: CA-94 • CA-125 • I-8 • CA-79 • CA-78

① Grab caffeine at the award-winning roastery **Bird Rock Coffee Roasters** (2295 Kettner Blvd., 619/272-0203, www.birdrockcoffee.com, 6am-6pm Mon.-Thurs., 6am-7pm Fri., 7am-7pm Sat., 7am-6pm Sun., $4-6).

② Drive over the mountains and into the low Colorado Desert, where you'll enter the ethereal **Anza-Borrego Desert State Park** (760/767-4205, www.parks.ca.gov, dawn-dusk daily, $10 per vehicle). Here, hiking trails pass through canyons en route to pictographs, rock formations, and sweeping views of the desert.

> *Take CA-94 E for 8 miles (13 km). Hop on CA-125 N for 2 miles (3 km) to I-8. Take I-8 E for 26 miles (42 km) to CA-79 N. Follow this for 23 miles (37 km) to Julian, where you'll turn right onto CA-78 E, then continue 18 miles (29 km) to Borrego Springs Rd. Turn left and stay on Borrego Springs, then turn left onto Palm Canyon Dr. Turn right and follow signs for Borrego Palm Canyon.*

③ Hike into the popular **Borrego Palm Canyon** (3 mi/5 km round-trip, 2 hours, easy-moderate). The canyon follows a

NIGHT SKY IN ANZA-BORREGO DESERT STATE PARK

stream 600 feet into a desert oasis; you may spot bighorn sheep along the way. The trailhead is at the west end of the Borrego Palm Canyon Campground.

④ Visit **Galleta Meadows** (Borrego Springs Rd. and Big Horn Rd., www.abdnha.org), home to one of the world's largest—and most whimsical—sculpture gardens. Giant metal sculptures of various animals are spread across the desert valley floor.

⑤ If there's a new moon, head to the roof of the **Anza-Borrego Desert State Park Visitors Center** (200 Palm Canyon Dr., 760/767-4205, 9am-5pm daily Oct.-May, daily 9am-5pm Sat.-Sun. June-Sept.) for some epic **stargazing.** Check with the visitors center ahead of time to verify event details. The tiny town of **Borrego Springs** just outside the park has a few restaurants and overnight options.

DAY 8: Anza-Borrego to Palm Springs

100 miles/161 kilometers | 2.5 hours

ROUTE OVERVIEW: CA-78 • CA-86 • I-10 • city streets

① Drive north out of Borrego and into the desert oasis of **Palm Springs,** where lounging poolside is second only to golf as the town's favorite recreation. If the desert heat gets to be too much, ride the **Palm Springs Aerial Tramway**

▶ **Playlist**

SOUTHERN CALIFORNIA AND ROUTE 66 LOOP

SONGS

- **"Surfin' USA" by The Beach Boys:** It's not a SoCal playlist without The Beach Boys. This fast and fun ditty about riding the waves is a classic.

- **"California Dreamin'" by The Mamas and the Papas:** Another oldie but goodie. You already know the lyrics to this '60s song hailing the virtues of Southern California, so sing it loud.

- **"L.A." by Murs:** A bouncy hip-hop song about living and loving in Los Angeles from L.A.-based rapper Murs.

PODCASTS

- **The Sweep Spot:** Insider info about Disneyland comes via this podcast, where former Disney cast members share behind-the-scenes stories, history, and the latest news about Disneyland.

(1 Tram Way, 760/325-1391, www.pstramway.com, 10am-8pm Mon.-Fri., 8am-8pm Sat.-Sun., $26) 6,000 feet up from the desert floor to the San Jacinto Mountains.

> *Take CA-78 E for 31 miles (50 km) to CA-86. Take CA-86 N for 34 miles (55 km), then merge onto I-10 W. After 18 miles (29 km), take the exit for Indian Canyon Dr. Follow Indian Canyon for 3 miles (5 km), then turn right onto W. San Rafael Dr. to reach the tramway.*

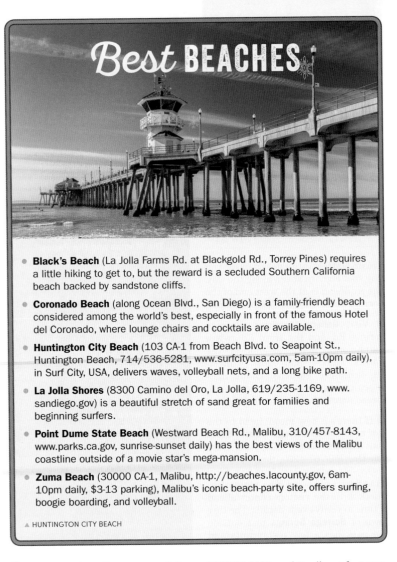

Best BEACHES

- **Black's Beach** (La Jolla Farms Rd. at Blackgold Rd., Torrey Pines) requires a little hiking to get to, but the reward is a secluded Southern California beach backed by sandstone cliffs.
- **Coronado Beach** (along Ocean Blvd., San Diego) is a family-friendly beach considered among the world's best, especially in front of the famous Hotel del Coronado, where lounge chairs and cocktails are available.
- **Huntington City Beach** (103 CA-1 from Beach Blvd. to Seapoint St., Huntington Beach, 714/536-5281, www.surfcityusa.com, 5am-10pm daily), in Surf City, USA, delivers waves, volleyball nets, and a long bike path.
- **La Jolla Shores** (8300 Camino del Oro, La Jolla, 619/235-1169, www.sandiego.gov) is a beautiful stretch of sand great for families and beginning surfers.
- **Point Dume State Beach** (Westward Beach Rd., Malibu, 310/457-8143, www.parks.ca.gov, sunrise-sunset daily) has the best views of the Malibu coastline outside of a movie star's mega-mansion.
- **Zuma Beach** (30000 CA-1, Malibu, http://beaches.lacounty.gov, 6am-10pm daily, $3-13 parking), Malibu's iconic beach-party site, offers surfing, boogie boarding, and volleyball.

▲ HUNTINGTON CITY BEACH

2 Head into town for an entertaining dinner at **Shanghai Red's Bar & Grill** (235 S. Indian Canyon Dr., 760/322-9293, www.fishermans.com, 5pm-10pm Mon.-Thurs., 5pm-11:30pm Fri.-Sat., bar opens at 4pm, $5-35). This favorite of the late Anthony Bourdain serves the best fish tacos in the desert.

> Take CA-111 or Indian Canyon Dr. south for about 3 miles (5 km) to get into Palm Springs proper.

3 Let yourself be fully transported to tiki times at the retro-chic **Tonga Hut** (254 N. Palm Canyon Dr., 760/322-4449, http://tongahut.com, 5pm-10pm Wed., 5pm-midnight Thurs., 4pm-2am Fri., noon-2am Sat., noon-10pm Sun.), where you'll enjoy drinks garnished with flair, atomic-era seating, low-lit lamps, and hand-carved island art.

4 Get a good night's rest at the **Orbit In** (562 W. Arenas Rd., 760/323-3585, www.orbitin.com, $209-269), a mid-century boutique hotel that overachieves with a sense of style, community, and funky one-of-a-kind rooms. Don't forget to pencil in some time to lounge by the saltwater pool.

DAY 9: Palm Springs to Joshua Tree National Park

85 miles/137 kilometers | 2.5 hours

ROUTE OVERVIEW: Indian Canyon Dr. • CA-62 • surface streets • Park Blvd.

1 Waking up in Palm Springs puts you about an hour's drive from the west entrance of **Joshua Tree National Park** (www.nps.gov/jotr, 24 hours daily year-round, $30 per vehicle, $25 per motorcycle, $15 bike or on foot), so rise early to take advantage of one of Southern California's most beloved natural settings.

> *Take N. Indian Canyon Dr. for 13 miles (21 km) to Twentynine Palms Highway/CA-62. Take CA-62 E for 14 miles (23 km), then turn right onto Sage Ave. Make a quick left onto Yucca Trail and continue for 3 miles (5 km), when it turns into Alta Loma Rd. Continue for another 3 miles (5 km), then turn right onto Quail Springs Rd. In 4 miles (6 km), you'll reach the West Entrance Station.*

2 In the Hidden Valley section of the park, hike the **North View Maze Loop** (6.4 mi/10 km round-trip, 3-4 hours, moderate) for fantastical boulder

CHOLLA CACTUS GARDEN

formations, Joshua tree forest, craggy viewpoints, desert wash, and even a window rock.

> *To get to the trailhead, drive Park Blvd. south for 1.5 miles (2.5 km).*

3 Admire cacti in the **Cholla Cactus Garden** (Park Blvd., 12 mi/19 km south of North Entrance), which offers a short boardwalk through the desert.

> *Continue south on Park Blvd. for 19 miles (31 km), then turn right to join Pinto Basin Rd. Continue for another 10 miles (16 km) to reach the cactus garden.*

4 Try for a campsite at **Jumbo Rocks Campground** (Park Blvd. east of Geology Tour Rd., www.nps.gov/jotr, $15). This popular campground starts to fill up on Thursday mornings for weekend outings. If you can't find a spot, head to the towns of **Joshua Tree** or **Twentynine Palms** on the northern border of the park; each offers a smattering of accommodations and dining options.

> *Retrace your path north back up Pinto Basin Rd. Turn left to get back onto Park Blvd. and continue for 3.5 miles (5.5 km) to reach the campground.*

DAY 10: Joshua Tree to Riverside

230 miles/370 kilometers | 5 hours

ROUTE OVERVIEW: Route 66 • I-15 • I-215 • CA-91

1 It's a long drive to the middle of nowhere, where the kitschy remains of **Route 66** icons beckon photo buffs and desert rats. First stop: **Amboy Crater** (760/326-7000, www.blm.gov, dawn-dusk daily, free), an extinct cinder cone rising from the desert floor. It's

JOSHUA TREE NATIONAL PARK

AMBOY CRATER

possible to hike the 1.7-mile (2.7-km) trail to the top of the crater, but don't attempt this in the summer or during windy conditions.

> Follow Amboy Rd. north for 42 miles (68 km). Turn left onto Route 66/National Trails Hwy. and continue for a mile to Amboy Crater.

② **Amboy** is the first of several ghost towns you'll see on Route 66. Snap a photo of the space-age sign outside **Roy's Motel & Café** (87520 National Trails Hwy., 760/733-1066, 7am-8pm daily). This abandoned motel in a remote ghost town remains an architectural treasure.

> Double back on Route 66 and follow it for 2 miles (3 km) to reach central Amboy.

③ Along this desolate, historic highway, stop for a hearty meal at the **Ludlow Café** (68315 National Trails Hwy., Ludlow, 760/733-4501, 6am-6pm daily, $6-12), a desert gem and classic roadside diner. Follow Route 66 west to **Barstow.**

> Take Route 66 west for 28 miles (45 km) to reach the diner. Continue for another 51 miles (82 km) to reach Barstow.

④ In **Oro Grande,** stretch your legs as you explore the eclectic **Elmer's Bottle Tree Ranch** (24266 National Trails Hwy., 760/684-2601, dawn-dusk daily, free). Folk artist Elmer Long created a veritable forest of glass and light in his front yard with 200 installations of "trees" comprising antique bottles and found-art objects.

> Continue west on Route 66 for 27 miles (43 km) to Oro Grande.

⑤ From here the Mother Road passes over the **Cajon Pass** before dipping south to resume its westward trajectory. Detour to **Riverside** to indulge in a relaxing stay at the historic **Mission Inn Hotel & Spa** (3649 Mission Inn Ave., Riverside, 951/784-0300, www.missioninn.com, from $199). Born during Southern California's citrus boom of the late 19th century, this opulent hotel is the largest Mission Revival structure in California.

> Stay on Route 66 for 11 miles (18 km) into Victorville, where you'll get on I-15 S. Follow this for 28 miles (45 km) to I-215. Take I-215 S toward Riverside (20 mi/32 km). Join with CA-91 W, then, after 1.5 miles (2.5 km), take exit 64 to reach the hotel.

ELMER'S BOTTLE TREE RANCH

DAY 11: Riverside to Los Angeles

75 miles/121 kilometers | 2.5 hours

ROUTE OVERVIEW: I-215 • CA-210 • I-210 • CA-110 • US-101

WIGWAM MOTEL

1 Today's your final stretch on Route 66. Head to **San Bernardino,** which parallels Route 66 west on its final run through the suburban sprawl of the Inland Empire. Pick up a kitschy Route 66 souvenir at the gift shop of the **Wigwam Motel** (2728 E. Foothill Blvd., Rialto, 909/875-3005, www.wigwammotel.com, 7am-8pm daily), then snap a photo in front of one of the 20-foot-tall tepees that serve as guest rooms.

> Take I-215 N for 10 miles (16 km) to San Bernardino. Take the exit for W. 5th St. Turn left and continue to the motel.

2 Stop in the pastoral city of **Pasadena.** Browse the downtown shops before exploring the extensive library and sprawling gardens of **The Huntington** (1151 Oxford Rd., San Marino, 626/405-2100, www.huntington.org, 10am-5pm Wed.-Mon., $25-29 adults, $13 children 4-11). It's no wonder why it's a popular filming location for movies and television shows.

> Go north on Pepper Ave. for 2 miles (3 km) to CA-210. After 28 miles (45 km), CA-210 W becomes I-210. Continue west for another 16 miles (26 km) into Pasadena. Take exit 27B, then turn left and follow Allen Ave. for 1.5 miles (2.5 km) to reach The Huntington.

3 For lunch, enjoy the best dim sum in the greater Los Angeles area at **Lunasia Dim Sum House** (239 E. Colorado

DESERT *Thrills*

For most of the year, the deserts of Southern California offer exactly what you expect: stark, high-contrast landscapes; scorched earth and sharp-needled cacti; and arid, sunny days blanketed by endless blue skies. But if you time it right, your desert adventures may include a smattering of special experiences that can make your excursion memorable.

MUSIC

- **Coachella Valley Music and Arts Festival** (www.coachella.com, Apr.): The most famous music and art gathering is Coachella, which takes place in Indio over two consecutive weekends in April. Hundreds of thousands of people attend the massive festival, which attracts the hottest names in the music industry. Hotel rates double (or triple) and rooms book up months in advance.

- **Pappy & Harriet's Pioneertown Palace** (53688 Pioneertown Rd., 760/365-5956, www. pappyandharriets.com): The week between Coachella is a fantastic time to head to Pioneertown, where headlining artists often perform intimate, last-minute sets.

- **Stagecoach Festival** (www. stagecoachfestival.com, end of Apr.): This massive outdoor country music festival is lesser-known than Coachella, but takes place on the same polo fields.

ART

- **Desert X** (mid-Feb.-mid-Apr.): This biennial art festival takes place during odd-numbered years (the next is in 2021) throughout hundreds of square miles of desert. Contemporary artists erect high-concept art installations, from massive sculptures to photography exhibits, many of which incorporate technology in new and interesting ways.

- **Bombay Beach Biennale** (Mar. or Apr.): Progressive artists gather on the shores of the shrinking Salton Sea for a weekend-long festival filled with oddball exhibitions, musical performances, and dystopian amusements.

NATURE

- **Spring Bloom:** Wildflowers blossom for a few weeks each spring, painting deserts bright with colorful flowers. In unusually wet winters, a high concentration of wildflowers erupts in a **superbloom** capable of covering hillsides in unforgettable kaleidoscopes of color. Large superbloom events take place in **Joshua Tree National Park** (www. nps.gov/jotr, 24 hours daily year-round) and **Anza-Borrego Desert State Park** (www.parks.ca.gov, dawn-dusk daily).

- **Stargazing:** When you look up at the night sky in a desert region, you will see millions of stars. **Anza-Borrego** is a designated **International Dark Sky Community.** Even the dimmest of stars become visible, as do broad swaths of nebulae and the Milky Way galaxy. Stargazing is at its best during a new moon.

ANZA-BORREGO DESERT STATE PARK

Blvd., 626/793-8822, www.lunasiad-imsum.com, 11am-9:30pm Mon.-Fri., 10am-9:30pm Sat.-Sun., $15-50). With a full stomach and the satisfaction of a road trip completed, continue the drive back to Los Angeles.

> *CA-110 W will take you about 8 miles (13 km) into Los Angeles. Take US-101 S to reach downtown L.A., or you can follow US-101 N to reach Hollywood.*

GETTING THERE

AIR

Several airports serve Los Angeles, but the largest by far is **Los Angeles International Airport** (LAX, 1 World Way, Los Angeles, 855/463-5252, www.flylax.com). It offers direct flights from around the world, but with constant traffic congestion and long lines from check-in to security, you must arrive two hours ahead of departure time—three for international or holiday flights. On the bright side, from each terminal convenient express buses zip back and forth from destinations including Hollywood and the downtown metro hub Union Station. Look for the signs **FlyAway Bus** (www.flylax.com, $8 Hollywood, $9.75 Union Station).

For a less crowded airport, seek flights to or from **Hollywood Burbank Airport** (BUR, 2627 N. Hollywood Way, Burbank, 818/840-8840, http://hollywoodburbankairport.com), which is much closer to Hollywood and downtown. **Long Beach Airport** (LGB, 4100 Donald Douglas Dr., Long Beach, 562/570-2600, www.lgb.org) is a half-hour drive or an hour metro ride from Los Angeles.

TRAIN

Amtrak (800/872-7245, www.amtrak.com) has an active rail hub in Los Angeles, with several lines passing through the metro center of **Union Station** (800 N. Alameda St.). The Pacific Surfliner route travels direct to Santa Barbara and San Luis Obispo and southbound to San Diego. The Coast Starlight route passes through the San Francisco Bay Area en route from Portland and Seattle. The San Joaquin route runs out to Sacramento via the Bay Area. The Sunset Limited route travels east-west from as far as New Orleans. The Southwest Chief route travels through six states on the way from Chicago.

From Union Station, you can access Los Angeles's commuter train line **Metrolink** (www.metrolinktrains.com), which operates trains to or from various spots in Southern California, including Ventura, Oceanside, and San Bernardino.

BUS

You can get to L.A. by bus from almost everywhere, but while some Greyhound buses stop at Union Station, most go to the main depot at **Los Angeles bus station** (1716 E. 7th St., 213/629-8401 or 800/231-2222, www.greyhound.com) near the Arts District, but also adjacent to Skid Row. To avoid that area, don't plan to walk between the Bus Station and Union Station. Take a car or ride the bus instead.

CAR

From **Los Angeles International Airport,** you can reach **Malibu** in 40-60 minutes via a 29-mile (47 km) route. Take CA-1 N to I-405 N. From I-405, take I-10 W to CA-1 N, and exit at Winding Way to Malibu. Alternatively, I-10 also leads west from downtown Los Angeles to meet the coast at **Santa Monica.** In 16 miles (26 km), I-10 merges onto CA-1 N, passing from Santa Monica into southern Malibu. Note that drive times will increase exponentially during rush hour traffic.

CONNECT WITH

- At Los Angeles: **Best of the Golden State** (PAGE 108) and **Pacific Coast Highway: California** (PAGE 124)

- At San Diego: **Pacific Coast Highway: California** (PAGE 124) and **Pacific Crest Trail: California** (PAGE 140)

- At Palm Springs or Joshua Tree National Park: **California Deserts** (PAGE 194)

- At Los Angeles: **Route 66** (PAGE 60)

CALIFORNIA DESERTS

WHY GO: Mid-century style, stark desert landscapes, date groves, quiet contemplation, Joshua trees

TOTAL DISTANCE: 335 miles/ 545 kilometers

NUMBER OF DAYS: 3

SEASON: Spring and fall

START: Palm Springs, California

END: Furnace Creek, California

▼ JOSHUA TREE NATIONAL PARK

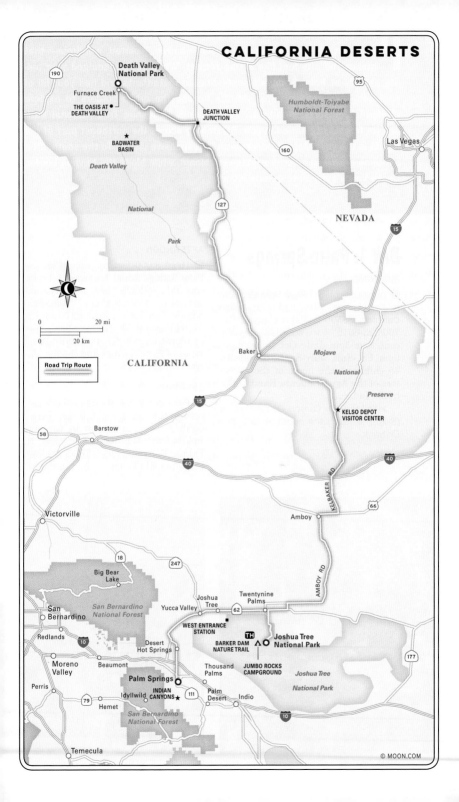

Palm Springs is beloved for its Old Hollywood glamour and mid-century vibe, but it's the surrounding desert—barren, isolated, wondrous—that makes the city feel like a true retreat. When you've indulged your palate aplenty at Palm Springs's sophisticated restaurants and had your fill of pool-side, palm-shaded naps, venture beyond the urban borders to explore California's deserts. Nearby to Palm Springs is Joshua Tree National Park and its forests of gnarled yucca. Stretching across the northeast part of the region is the vast Mojave Desert with its expansive vistas. To the south, lithe ocotillos grow and colorful wildflowers bloom, while along the Nevada border, Death Valley's desolate beauty looms.

DAY 1: Palm Springs

MORNING

❶ In candy-colored **Palm Springs**, take in the scenery with a hike at **Indian Canyons** (38500 S. Palm Canyon Dr., 760/323-6018, www.indian-canyons. com, 8am-5pm daily Oct.-June, 8am-5pm Fri.-Sun. July-Sept., $9 adults, $5 children), the home of the ancestors of the Agua Caliente Band of Cahuilla Indians.

> Follow Palm Canyon Dr. for 5 miles (8 km) to reach the entrance to Indian Canyons.

AFTERNOON

❷ Head 8,000 feet up, up, up on the **Palm Springs Aerial Tramway** (1 Tramway Rd., 760/325-1449, www.pstramway.com, 10am-9:45pm Mon.-Fri., 8am-9:45pm Sat.-Sun., $27 adults, $17 children 3-10). Nothing beats this exhilarating ride for its breathtaking views of Palm Springs and the San Jacinto Mountains.

EVENING

❸ For dinner, eat at one of the many restaurants on Palm Canyon Drive. Grab a drink and soak in the retro-kitsch at the **Tonga Hut** (254 N. Palm Canyon Dr., 760/322-4449, http://tongahut.com, 5pm-midnight

INDIAN CANYONS

VIEW FROM THE PALM SPRINGS AERIAL TRAMWAY

Top **3** CALIFORNIA DESERTS

1. Get a bird's-eye view of Palm Springs with a ride on the **Palm Springs Aerial Tramway** (PAGE 196).

2. Sleep under countless glittering stars at **Joshua Tree National Park** (PAGE 198).

3. Soak up the otherworldly landscape of the desert along the **Mojave National Preserve's** scenic drive (PAGE 199).

Tues.-Thurs., 5pm-2am Fri., 2pm-2am Sat., 2pm-midnight Sun.), an offshoot of the famed Hollywood tiki bar.

④ Settle in for the night at the mid-century modern **Orbit In** (562 W. Arenas Rd., 760/323-3585 or 877/996-7248, www.orbitin.com, $209-269).

DAY 2: Palm Springs to Joshua Tree National Park

60 miles/97 kilometers | 1.5 hours

ROUTE OVERVIEW: CA-62 • Park Blvd.

① In the morning, drive north to **Joshua Tree National Park** (760/367-5500, www.nps.gov/jotr, 24 hours daily, $30 per vehicle, $25 motorcyclists, $15 pedestrians or bicyclists) for nature both accessible and extreme. The northern half of the park sits in the high-altitude Mojave Desert.

> *Take N. Indian Canyon Dr. for 13 miles (21 km) to Twentynine Palms Highway/CA-62. Take CA-62 E for 14 miles (23 km), then turn right onto Sage Ave. Make a quick left onto Yucca Trail and continue for 3 miles (5 km), when it turns into Alta Loma Rd. Continue for another 3 miles (5 km), then turn right onto Quail Springs Rd. In 4 miles (6 km) you'll reach the West Entrance Station.*

KEY RESERVATIONS

- At **Joshua Tree National Park,** make advance reservations for a campsite at the park's popular **Jumbo Rocks Campground.** Reservations can be made up to **six months** in advance.

- For two weekends every April, the **Coachella Valley Music and Arts Festival** (www.coachella.com) takes over the region. Hundreds of thousands of people descend upon **Palm Springs and nearby cities,** booking up lodging, filling restaurants, and stalling traffic. Festival attendees usually reserve accommodations up to a year in advance. If you want to avoid the crowds, visit any other time of year; check the website for current dates.

② From the West Entrance Station, which is close to the town of Joshua Tree, drive Park Boulevard to the Hidden Valley area at the center of the park. Take the short hike to **Barker Dam** (1.3 mi/2.1 km loop, 30 minutes, easy), which passes a small pond amid boulders and Joshua trees.

> *Drive Park Blvd. south for 9 miles (14.5 km), then turn left and follow*

BARKER DAM IN JOSHUA TREE NATIONAL PARK

DETOUR FOR *Delicious Dates*

Before you head to Joshua Tree National Park, consider taking this detour to the south of Palm Springs. You'll have to backtrack through the city, but this tasty trip is worth it to visit the countless date groves, which provide most of the U.S. crop of this sweet fruit.

The **Oasis Date Gardens** (59-111 Grapefruit Blvd., Thermal, 800/827-8017, http://oasisdategardens.com, 9am-5pm daily) in the thriving metropolis of Thermal offer a store, café, and demonstration "arbor" of date palms. In the store, learn about the different varieties of dates and then sample almost all of them. You can buy whole dates and date candies. At the ice-cream counter, order the date shake—a super-sweet regional specialty that's perfect on both hot summer and mild winter days. In the orchard, you'll see how dates cluster and grow in the shade of thickly fronded palm trees.

Another famous date orchard open to the public is the **Shields Date Garden** (80-225 Hwy. 111, Indio, 800/414-2555, www.shieldsdategarden.com, 8:30am-4pm daily, $5). The café serves breakfast and lunch, and the oasis-like garden is a pleasant walk that threads through the 17-acre date farm.

Barker Dam Rd. for 1.5 miles (2.5 km) to reach the trailhead.

❸ To bed down under the dark desert sky, make a reservation for one of the 124 coveted sites at the park's **Jumbo Rocks Campground** (Park Blvd. east of Geology Tour Rd., reservation-only, www.nps.gov/jotr, $15), or opt for one of the unique lodging options in the town of Joshua Tree.

> Retrace your path back to Park Blvd. Continue south on Park Blvd. for 8.5 miles (13.5 km) to reach the campground.

DAY 3: Joshua Tree to Death Valley National Park

275 miles/445 kilometers | 6 hours

ROUTE OVERVIEW: CA-62 • Amboy Rd. • Route 66 • Kelbaker Rd. • CA-127 • CA-190 • Badwater Rd.

❶ Get breakfast in Joshua Tree before heading north to **Mojave National Preserve** (between I-15 and I-40, 760/928-2572, www.nps.gov/moja, free). The best introduction to this stark and seemingly endless region is the main visitors center, **Kelso Depot** (Kelso-Cima Rd. and Kelbaker Rd., Kelso, 760/252-6108, 10am-5pm Thurs.-Mon.). Originally a train station, this

renovated 1924 building offers exhibits, an art gallery, and a bookstore, as well as restrooms and water.

> Take Park Blvd. northeast for 8 miles (13 km) to exit the park via the town of Twentynine Palms. Take CA-62 E for 6 miles (10 km), then make a left onto Godwin Rd. Continue for 2 miles (3 km), then turn right onto Amboy Rd. Follow Amboy for 40 miles (64 km) to the town of Amboy. Get on Route 66/National Trails Hwy. heading east. In 6.5 miles (10.5 km), turn left and follow Kelbaker Rd. north for 34 miles (55 km) until you reach the visitors center.

❷ It's 1.5 hours from Mojave National Preserve to **Death Valley National Park** (760/786-3200, www.nps.gov/deva, 24 hours daily, $30 per vehicle, $25 motorcyclists, $15 pedestrians or

THE ROAD THROUGH DEATH VALLEY

DEATH VALLEY

bicyclists). You'll traverse the remote Mojave Desert to skirt the Nevada border before entering the park from the east at aptly named **Death Valley Junction.** Fill up on gas before entering the park, as services are limited.

> Continue north on Kelbaker Rd. for 35 miles (56 km) to exit the preserve via the town of Baker. Take CA-127 N for 83 miles (134 km) to Death Valley Junction.

❸ From CA-190 in the park hub of **Furnace Creek,** head south on Badwater Road to explore the parched valley's gorgeous sights. **Badwater Basin** (Badwater Rd., 18 mi/29 km south of Furnace Creek) is a dry lake bed situated at 282 feet below sea level, the lowest elevation in the Western Hemisphere.

> Take CA-190 W for 29 miles (47 km), then turn left onto Badwater Rd. Continue for 14 miles (22.5 km) to Badwater Basin.

❹ Spend the night at **The Oasis at Death Valley** (CA-190 at CA-178, Furnace Creek, 800/236-7916 or 760/786-2345, www.oasisatdeathvalley.com, $409-506), a lush resort offering casitas, suites, and even ranch-style accommodations.

> Retrace your path back north along Badwater Rd. for 14 miles to reach the resort.

GETTING THERE

AIR

The **Palm Springs International Airport** (PSP, 3400 E. Tahquitz Canyon Way, 760/318-3800, www.palmspringsairport.com) offers flights with most major carriers and a few minor airlines.

The largest airport serving Los Angeles is **Los Angeles International Airport** (LAX, 1 World Way, Los Angeles, 855/463-5252, www.flylax.com). It offers direct flights from around the world, but with constant traffic congestion and long lines from check-in to security, you must arrive two hours ahead of departure time—three for international or holiday flights.

For a less crowded airport, seek flights to or from **Ontario International Airport** (ONT, 2500 E. Airport Dr., Ontario, 909/544-5300, www.flyontario.com), which lies about 70 miles (115 km) west of Palm Springs. Airlines that serve this airport include Alaska, American, Delta, Southwest, and United.

TRAIN

Amtrak (800/872-7245, www.amtrak.com) serves Palm Springs via a barebones **station** (N. Indian Canyon Dr. and Palm Springs Station Rd., no phone) about 4 miles (6 km) north of town. Trains on the Sunset Limited (Los Angeles-New Orleans) and Texas Eagle (Los Angeles-Chicago) routes stop in Palm Springs several times a week.

BUS

Greyhound (800/231-2222, www.greyhound.com) has a **bus stop** (64200 20th Ave.) about 5 miles (8 km) north of town.

FlixBus (855/626-8585, www.flixbus.com) offers two stops in Palm Springs: **downtown** (N. Indian Canyon Dr. and E. Tachevah Dr.) and **north of**

town (6600 N. Indian Canyon Dr.) by about 5 miles (8 km).

CAR

The **Palm Springs airport** is just east of town. To get to Palm Canyon Drive from the airport, take Tahquitz Canyon Way west for 3 miles (5 km).

From the **Los Angeles-area airports,** I-10 is the most direct route east, running through Palm Springs and down through Indio, then east past the south entrance of Joshua Tree. Plan at least two hours for the 130-mile (209-km) drive from L.A.

GETTING BACK

It's 282 miles (454 km), a drive of 4-5 hours, from Furnace Creek back to **Palm Springs.** Drive CA-190 E to Death Valley Junction, where you'll link up with CA-127 S. Follow this to Baker. Here, take I-15 S until exit 183; take this exit for CA-247 S. Turn right onto CA-62 W and follow it to Palm Springs.

From Furnace Creek to **Los Angeles,** the journey is 268 miles (431 km) and 4-5 hours. Drive CA-190 W to Panamint Valley Road. Turn left. Panamint Valley becomes Trona Wildrose Road and then Trona Road. Follow this to Searles Station Cutoff. Turn right and drive to US-395 S. Take this to Garlock Road and turn right. From Garlock, merge onto Redrock Randsburg Road and follow this to CA-14 S. Drive CA-14 S to I-5 S to reach L.A.

The 142-mile (229-km) trip from Furnace Creek to **Las Vegas, Nevada,** runs about 2.5 hours. Drive CA-190 E to Death Valley Junction. Here, pick up CA-127 N. You'll cross into Nevada, where the route becomes NV-373 N. Stay on this to Amarosa Valley. Turn right onto US-95 S, which is a straight shot into Las Vegas.

CONNECT WITH

• At Palm Springs or Joshua Tree National Park: **Southern California and Route 66 Loop** (PAGE 178)

▶ **Playlist**

CALIFORNIA DESERTS

SONGS

• **"Strangest Thing" by The War on Drugs:** There's something about this Philly band's sound—perhaps it's the Bob Dylan-esque vocals or the spare instrumentation—that lends itself to desert road trips, where squinting into the shimmering, hot horizon inspires deep thoughts.

• **"I Wish I Was the Moon" by Neko Case:** Wait until the sun sets and the moon rises over the desert to cue up this melancholy song by this indie, country-noir singer-songwriter.

PODCASTS

• *Can't Feel the Heat:* This fascinating look at the Coachella Valley Music and Arts Festival, widely considered to be the greatest annual music event in the country, takes you behind the scenes of the music, artists, news, tech, and logistics of this culturally significant festival held every spring near Palm Springs.

GOLD COUNTRY RAMBLE

WHY GO: Wild and scenic beauty, wine-tasting, historical tours, white-water rafting

TOTAL DISTANCE: 210 miles/ 340 kilometers

NUMBER OF DAYS: 2

SEASONS: Year-round

START: Sacramento, California

END: Jamestown, California

▼ COLUMBIA STATE HISTORIC PARK

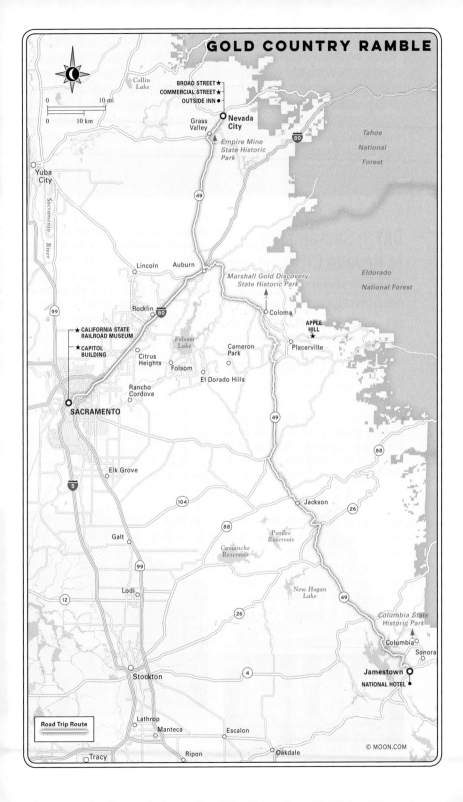

GOLD COUNTRY RAMBLE

Collin Lake

BROAD STREET ★
COMMERCIAL STREET ★
OUTSIDE INN ●

Nevada City

Grass Valley

Empire Mine State Historic Park

Tahoe National Forest

Yuba City

Sacramento River

Lincoln

Auburn

Marshall Gold Discovery State Historic Park

Eldorado National Forest

Rocklin

Coloma

APPLE HILL ★

Placerville

Folsom Lake

Cameron Park

★ CALIFORNIA STATE RAILROAD MUSEUM

★ CAPITOL BUILDING

Citrus Heights

Folsom

El Dorado Hills

Rancho Cordova

SACRAMENTO

Elk Grove

Jackson

Galt

Pardee Reservoir

Camanche Reservoir

Lodi

New Hogan Lake

Columbia State Historic Park

Columbia

Sonora

Stockton

Jamestown

NATIONAL HOTEL ●

Road Trip Route

Lathrop

Manteca

Escalon

Oakdale

Tracy

Ripon

© MOON.COM

0   10 mi
0   10 km

n California's Gold Country, you'll find a region rich in mining history, gold rush legends and lore, and small towns that welcome visitors with open arms. Gold was first discovered here in 1848, but the Old West still lives on today—in dusty saloons and pioneering spirits. The Gold Country criss-crosses the foothills of the Sierra Nevada, extending from Nevada City south to the Shenandoah Valley. See charming enclaves like Auburn, Grass Valley, Placerville, Coloma, and Jamestown. Sip wine and sample fresh produce from nearby farms. And if you dare, you can even challenge yourself to a white-water rafting adventure.

DAY 1: Sacramento to Nevada City

65 miles/105 kilometers | 1.5 hours

ROUTE OVERVIEW: I-80 • CA-49

① In **Sacramento,** start your day early with a tour of the **Capitol Building** (10th St. and L St., 916/324-0333, http://capitolmuseum.ca.gov, hourly, 7:30am-6pm Mon.-Fri., 9am-5pm Sat.-Sun., free) to see history-making in process.

② Walk over to the **California State Railroad Museum** (125 I St., 916/323-9280, www.parks.ca.gov, 10am-5pm daily, $12 adults, $6 children 6-17) in Old Sacramento, where the history of the gold rush and the golden era of the railroad come alive. Grab lunch at one of the many eateries downtown.

③ After lunch, head north toward **Grass Valley.** Stop at the **Empire Mine State Historic Park** (10791 E. Empire St., 530/273-8522, www.parks.ca.gov or www.empiremine.org, 10am-5pm daily, $7 adults, $3 children 6-16) and get a feel for the toil, hardship, dreams, and occasional wild luck that shaped the Gold Country.

> Take I-80 E for 33 miles (53 km) to Auburn. Take CA-49 N for 23 miles (37 km) to reach Grass Valley.

④ Head to nearby **Nevada City** and spend the evening strolling its picturesque streets. Most shops are on **Broad and Commercial Streets.** Have dinner

CAPITOL BUILDING, SACRAMENTO

EMPIRE MINE STATE HISTORIC PARK

Top **3** GOLD COUNTRY RAMBLE

1. Deepen your knowledge of **gold rush history** at the **California State Railroad Museum** (PAGE 204).

2. **Raft** the wild waters of the **American River** (PAGE 207).

3. Raise a toast to the Old West in the **saloon** at the 1850s-era **National Hotel** (PAGE 208).

KEY RESERVATIONS

- To join a **white-water rafting** excursion on the **American River**, you'll need to reserve your spot with an outfitter ideally **three weeks to a month** ahead of time.

GOLD PANNING

in town before spending the night in one of the unique, outdoor-themed guest rooms at **Outside Inn** (575 E. Broad St., 530/265-2233, www.outsideinn.com, $84-220).

> *Continue north on CA-49 for 4 miles (6 km) to reach Nevada City.*

DAY 2: Nevada City to Jamestown

145 miles/233 kilometers | 4 hours

ROUTE OVERVIEW: CA-49 • US-50 • surface streets • CA-49 • surface streets

❶ Fuel up with breakfast before heading south to the town of **Coloma.** At **Marshall Gold Discovery State Historic Park** (310 Back St., 530/622-3470, www.parks.ca.gov, 8am-8pm daily summer, 8am-5pm daily fall-spring,

$8 per vehicle), take the tour to see where James Marshall discovered gold in 1848.

> *Take CA-49 S for 45 miles (72 km) to reach Coloma.*

❷ Next, you have two choices. Thrill seekers can opt for a **white-water rafting tour** (see *Rafting the American River*) in Coloma. Vino fans can go **wine-tasting** at the wineries around **Apple Hill** (Apple Hill Dr./Carson Rd., near Camino, 530/644-7692, www.applehill.com), and sample Gold Country's best vintages. This 20-mile swath of grower heaven includes dozens of orchards, vineyards, and pit stops for lunch.

AUTUMN IN APPLE HILL

Coloma is the white-water capital of Gold Country. After you visit Marshall Gold Discovery State Historic Park (located just minutes from the outfitters listed here), get ready for a white-water adventure.

PLANNING YOUR TRIP

- Outfitters lead trips on all three forks of the American River, including the rugged **Class IV-V** rapids of the **North Fork** and the more moderate **Class III-IV** white water of the **Middle Fork.**

- Rafting trips are designed for **all experience levels.**

- **Overnight** and **multiday** excursions are available.

- The season runs **April-October,** but note that trips on the North Fork run April-May or June, depending on weather and water levels.

OUTFITTERS

- **All-Outdoors Whitewater Rafting** (800/247-2387, www.aorafting.com, $113-539) has a variety of options, including half- to multiday trips on the North, Middle, and South Forks of the American River and a few on the Stanislaus River in southern Gold Country. A less intense option is the full-day Tom Sawyer Float Trip along the rapids-free section of the South Fork.

- **American Whitewater Expeditions** (530/642-0804 or 800/825-3205, www.americanwhitewater.com, $74-399) specializes in the American River, offering the largest variety of half-day, full-day, and multiday trips to all three forks. Expeditions come with delicious meals, friendly guides, and jaw-dropping Sierra Nevada scenery.

- **Beyond Limits Adventures** (530/622-0553 or 800/234-7238, www.rivertrip.com, $89-300) offers half- and full-day excursions to the North, Middle, and South Forks. The kayak trips on the South Fork are great for kids and intermediate paddlers. The two-day trips on the South Fork include an overnight at a riverside resort.

- **O.A.R.S.** (209/736-4677 or 800/346-6277, www.oars.com, $110-320) guides are extremely knowledgeable and lead trips to all three forks of the American River. Choose from full-day trips to any of the forks, or go for a half-day or two-day adventure on the South Fork, meals included. One-day trips on the Stanislaus River in southern Gold Country are also available.

- **Whitewater Connection** (530/622-6446, www.whitewaterconnection.com, $129-249) offers half-, full-, and two-day trips to the North, Middle, and South Forks with great options for families. Half-day trips are on the calm "Chili Bar" section of the South Fork.

SOUTH FORK OF THE AMERICAN RIVER AT COLOMA, CALIFORNIA

▶ Playlist

GOLD COUNTRY RAMBLE

SONGS

- **"Folsom Prison Blues" by Johnny Cash:** Folsom isn't part of this road trip, but the town sits squarely in the middle of Gold Country and Cash's twangy guitar feels at home in this neck of the woods.

- **"California" by Dr. Dog:** More plucky guitar comes by way of this ode to the Golden State. Snappy and upbeat, this song shines as brightly as the California sun.

- **"Cosmia" by Joanna Newsom:** Let the strange-yet-beautiful harp and delicate-yet-powerful voice of Grass Valley-born Newsom overtake your car speakers as you drive through the Sierra Nevada foothills.

> To get to Apple Hill, take CA-49 S for 8 miles (13 km). In Placerville, follow US-50/El Dorado Fwy. for 1.5 miles (2.5 km), then take exit 48 for Schnell School Rd. Turn left and follow Schnell School and then Carson Rd. for several miles into Apple Hill.

❸ It's a winding drive to **Columbia**, where most of downtown is part of the **Columbia State Historic Park** (11255 Jackson St., 209/588-9128, www. parks.ca.gov, 10am-5pm daily, free). Stroll the perfectly preserved streets of this gold-rush boomtown to get a feel for what life was like when the mines operated.

> Return to CA-49 via the same route, following it for 73 miles (118 km). Turn left onto Springfield Rd. and follow that for 2 miles (3 km) to reach Columbia.

❹ **Jamestown** marks the southern end of Gold Country. Its historic downtown boasts gold rush-era buildings. Spend the evening unwinding at the saloon in the **National Hotel** (18183 Main St., 209/984-3446 or 800/894-3446, www. national-hotel.com, $140-160), which has been in operation since 1859.

> Take Springfield Rd. south for less than a mile, then continue onto Shaws Flat Rd. Follow that for 1 mile (1.6 km), then make a right onto Jamestown Rd. Continue for 4 miles (6 km). Once you cross over CA-49, the road becomes Main St. and you've reached Jamestown.

GOLD PANNING AT COLUMBIA STATE HISTORIC PARK

OLD SACRAMENTO

GETTING THERE

AIR

Sacramento International Airport
(SMF, 6900 Airport Blvd., 916/929-5411, www.sacramento.aero) is served
by several major airlines. To Midtown,
it's a 20-minute drive (13 mi/21 km)
from the airport. Take I-5 S to exit
519A for Q Street. Make a left on Q
Street, following it to 20th Street.
Make a left and you're in Midtown.

TRAIN

Amtrak (800/872-7245, www.amtrak.
com, $31-40 one-way) runs its Capitol
Corridor route between the **Sacramento train station** (401 I St.) and Oakland
and San Jose several times daily. The
trip takes 2-3 hours.

BUS

The **Greyhound bus station** (420 Richards Blvd., 800/231-2222, www.greyhound.com) is north of downtown with
service throughout the state.

CAR

Sacramento lies at the nexus of several freeways, notably I-80 (east-west),
I-5 (north-south), and U.S. 50 (east).

Gridlock traffic is legendary during
commuter times and on weekends.
Though it's only 90 miles north of San
Francisco on I-80, the drive can take
2-4 hours depending on traffic.

GETTING BACK

From Jamestown, the 100-mile (160-
km) drive back to **Sacramento** takes
two hours. Take CA-108 W to Obyrnes
Ferry Road. Turn right; go 12 miles
(19 km) and then continue onto Main
Street. Turn left onto CA-4 W and, after 35 miles (56 km), follow signs to
merge onto CA-99 N. In 44 miles (71
km), you'll reach Sacramento.

It's 128 miles (206 km) from Jamestown to **San Francisco.** Because of
heavy traffic, the drive takes about 2.5
hours. Take CA-108 W. Turn right onto
CA-120 W. Follow CA-120 W to I-205
W, I-580 W, and I-80 W to reach downtown San Francisco.

CONNECT WITH

● At Sacramento: **The Loneliest
Road** (PAGE 36)

PACIFIC NORTHWEST

In the Pacific Northwest, you'll discover a bit of everything: urban adventures in Seattle and Vancouver, epic hikes on Mount Rainier, craft beer and killer food in Portland, and the seaside-village charms of Victoria, British Columbia. Travel along the Columbia River Gorge for waterfalls and verdant views, then visit some of the best vineyards in the United States. For those who seek the solitude of rugged beaches and lush rainforests, look no further than the Pacific Coast Highway, the famed thoroughfare that parallels the Pacific Ocean along the coast of Washington and Oregon.

◄ OREGON COAST

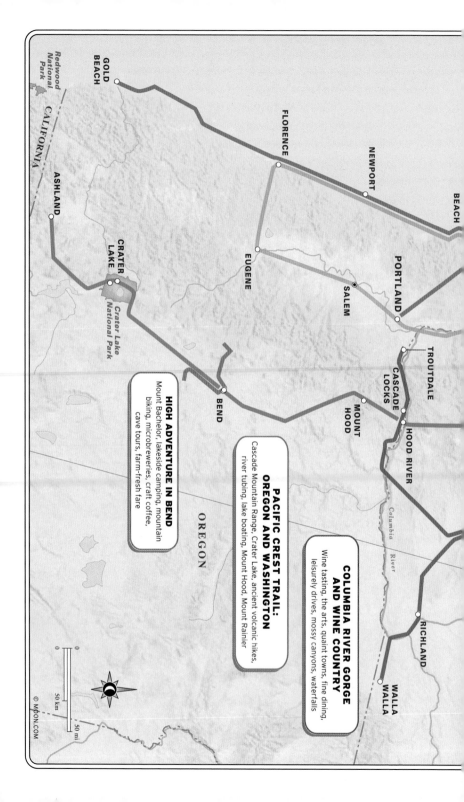

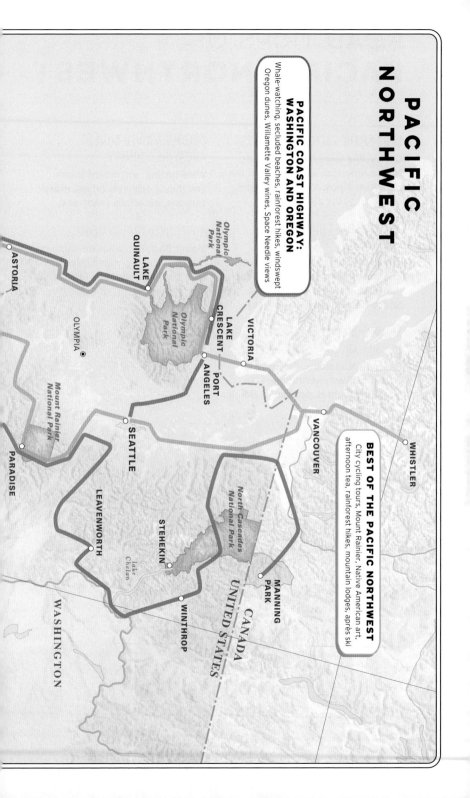

PACIFIC NORTHWEST

PACIFIC COAST HIGHWAY: WASHINGTON AND OREGON
Whale-watching, secluded beaches, rainforest hikes, windswept Oregon dunes, Willamette Valley wines, Space Needle views

BEST OF THE PACIFIC NORTHWEST
City cycling tours, Mount Rainier, Native American art, afternoon tea, rainforest hikes, mountain lodges, après ski

ASTORIA

LAKE QUINAULT

Olympic National Park

Olympic National Park

OLYMPIA

LAKE CRESCENT

PORT ANGELES

VICTORIA

Mount Rainier National Park

PARADISE

SEATTLE

VANCOUVER

WHISTLER

LEAVENWORTH

North Cascades National Park

STEHEKIN

Lake Chelen

MANNING PARK

WINTHROP

CANADA

UNITED STATES

WASHINGTON

ROAD TRIPS OF
PACIFIC NORTHWEST

BEST OF THE PACIFIC NORTHWEST

City cycling tours, Mount Rainier, Native American art, afternoon tea, rainforest hikes, mountain lodges, après ski (PAGE 216)

PACIFIC COAST HIGHWAY: WASHINGTON AND OREGON

Whale-watching, secluded beaches, rainforest hikes, windswept Oregon dunes, Willamette Valley wines, Space Needle views (PAGE 236)

PACIFIC CREST TRAIL: OREGON AND WASHINGTON

Cascade Mountains, Crater Lake, volcanic hikes, river tubing, lake boating, Mount Hood, Mount Rainier (PAGE 250)

COLUMBIA RIVER GORGE AND WINE COUNTRY

Wine-tasting, art, quaint towns, fine dining, leisurely drives, mossy canyons, waterfalls (PAGE 264)

HIGH ADVENTURE IN BEND

Mount Bachelor, lakeside camping, mountain biking, microbreweries, craft coffee, cave tours, farm-fresh fare (PAGE 274)

LEFT TO RIGHT: OREGON DUNES NATIONAL RECREATION AREA; SUNFLOWERS AND MOUNT HOOD; COLUMBIA RIVER GORGE

1. Nosh your way through the food stalls at the lively **Pike Place Market** in Seattle (PAGE 218).

2. Wander through acres of beautifully manicured flowers at **The Butchart Gardens** in Victoria (PAGE 223).

3. Hike the wild beauty of the **Quinault Rain Forest** in **Olympic National Park** (PAGE 242).

Pike Place Market

The Butchart Gardens in Victoria

Quinault Rain Forest

Deschutes River Trail

Crater Lake

4. Gaze into the abyss of **Crater Lake,** the deepest lake in the United States (PAGE 252).

5. In Bend, hike the scenic **Deschutes River Trail** (page 276).

BEST OF THE PACIFIC NORTHWEST

WHY GO: City cycling tours, Mount Rainier, Native American art, afternoon tea, rainforest hikes, mountain lodges, après ski

TOTAL DISTANCE: 1,405 miles/ 2,260 kilometers

NUMBER OF DAYS: 14

SEASONS: Spring through fall

START/END: Seattle, Washington

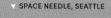
▼ SPACE NEEDLE, SEATTLE

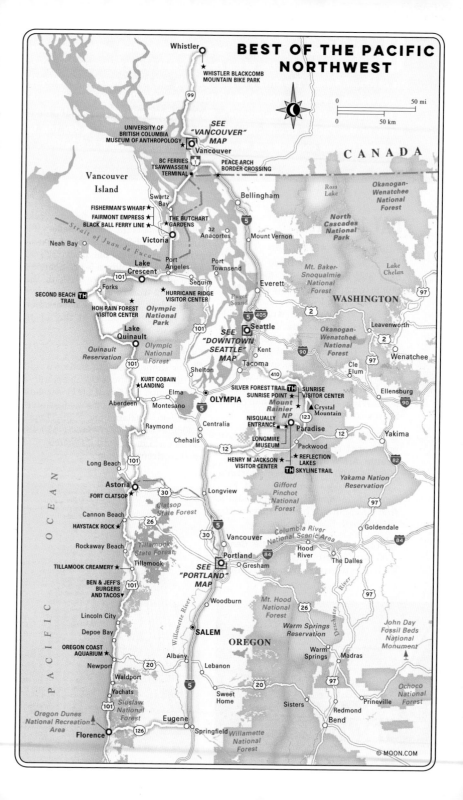

BEST OF THE PACIFIC NORTHWEST

Whistler

★ WHISTLER BLACKCOMB
MOUNTAIN BIKE PARK

99

CANADA

SEE "VANCOUVER" MAP

UNIVERSITY OF
BRITISH COLUMBIA
MUSEUM OF ANTHROPOLOGY
■ Vancouver

BC FERRIES
TSAWWASSEN
TERMINAL
1
PEACE ARCH
BORDER CROSSING

Vancouver Island

Bellingham

Ross Lake

Okanogan-Wenatchee National Forest

Swartz Bay

FISHERMAN'S WHARF ★
FAIRMONT EMPRESS ★
BLACK BALL FERRY LINE ★
THE BUTCHART
★ GARDENS
Victoria

32
Anacortes

Mount Vernon

5

North Cascades National Park

Mt. Baker-Snoqualmie National Forest

Lake Chelan

Neah Bay

Strait of Juan de Fuca

Port Angeles

Port Townsend

Lake Crescent

101

SECOND BEACH
TRAIL TH

Forks

Sequim

Everett

WASHINGTON

★ HURRICANE RIDGE
VISITOR CENTER

Puget Sound

2

Leavenworth

97

HOH RAIN FOREST
VISITOR CENTER ★

Olympic National Park

101

5 405

SEE "DOWNTOWN SEATTLE" MAP

■ ● Seattle

Okanogan-Wenatchee National Forest

2

Lake Quinault

Olympic National Forest

Kent

90

Wenatchee

Quinault Reservation

101

Shelton

Tacoma

Cle Elum

Ellensburg

90

KURT COBAIN
★ LANDING
Elma

410

SILVER FOREST TRAIL TH
SUNRISE POINT ●

SUNRISE
VISITOR CENTER

Aberdeen

Montesano

OLYMPIA

Mount Rainier NP

▲ Crystal Mountain

Yakima

Raymond

Centralia

5

NISQUALLY
ENTRANCE ■
123
■ ● Paradise

LONGMIRE
MUSEUM

Packwood

12

82

Chehalis

12

HENRY M JACKSON ★
VISITOR CENTER

★ REFLECTION
LAKES
TH SKYLINE TRAIL

Long Beach

101

Longview

Yakama Nation Reservation

97

Astoria ●
FORT CLATSOP ★

30

Clatsop State Forest

Gifford Pinchot National Forest

Goldendale

84

Cannon Beach

26

Columbia River National Scenic Area

HAYSTACK ROCK ★

5
Vancouver

Hood River

The Dalles

Rockaway Beach

30

Portland

84

97

TILLAMOOK CREAMERY ★

Tillamook State Forest

SEE "PORTLAND" MAP

■ ● Portland
Gresham

Mt. Hood National Forest

BEN & JEFF'S
BURGERS
AND TACOS▼

101

Tillamook

Woodburn

26

Warm Springs Reservation

John Day Fossil Beds National Monument

Lincoln City

Willamette River

SALEM

OREGON

Warm Springs

Madras

Depoe Bay

OREGON COAST
AQUARIUM ★

Newport

20

Albany

Lebanon

Deschutes River

97

Ochoco National Forest

Waldport

Yachats

Sweet Home

20

Sisters

Redmond
Bend

Prineville

Siuslaw National Forest

101

Oregon Dunes
National Recreation
Area

126

Florence ●

Eugene

Springfield

Willamette National Forest

PACIFIC OCEAN

0   50 mi
0   50 km

© MOON.COM

On this journey, you'll encounter the hippest cities in North America—Seattle, Vancouver, Portland—as well as astonishing wilderness areas, from the rugged beaches of the Oregon coast to the awe-inspiring volcano of Mount Rainier. The drive starts in Seattle and heads north to cosmopolitan Vancouver before turning to the British charms of Victoria. From Victoria, a ferry drops you off in Washington's Olympic Peninsula and a coastal drive leads to the Pacific Ocean and south through Oregon. After a day trip to Portland, the trip concludes at Mount Rainier before returning to Seattle.

DAY 1: Seattle

MORNING AND AFTERNOON

❶ Ditch the car for these first two days and get around on foot or via public transit. Explore **Pike Place Market** (Pike Pl. and Virginia St. between 1st Ave. and Western Ave., 206/682-7453, www.pikeplacemarket.org, 6am-1:30am daily), where fish are tossed through the air with the greatest of ease. Check out the rows upon rows of craft and food stands. But that's not this bustling farmers market's only famous seller—a little coffee shop called Starbucks started here in 1971.

❷ Walk to the *Hammering Man,* a permanent sculpture in front of the **Seattle Art Museum** (1300 1st Ave., 206/654-3100, www.seattleartmuseum.org, 10am-5pm Wed. and Fri.-Sun., 10am-9pm Thurs., $20 adults, free for children). Inside is one of the West Coast's best art collections.

❸ Take a cab to the **Seattle Center** (305 Harrison St., 206/684-7200, www.seattlecenter.com), which contains enough entertainment for a week. The pinnacle is the **Space Needle** (400 Broad St., 206/905-2100, www.spaceneedle.com, 10am-8pm daily, $33-38 adults, $25-29 children 5-12). Seattle's retro emblem may date back to the city's 1962 World's Fair, but the views are timeless. Travel to the **observation deck** (10am-8pm daily) at the top to experience them.

EVENING

❹ For dinner, head to Belltown and hit up one of the city's memorable restaurants: **Six Seven** (2411 Alaskan Way, 206/269-4575, www.edgewaterhotel.com, 6:30am-9pm Sun.-Thurs., 6:30am-9:30pm Fri.-Sat., $29-48) earns acclaim for both its seafood and its waterfront location.

PIKE PLACE MARKET

SEATTLE ART MUSEUM

Top **5** BEST OF THE PACIFIC NORTHWEST

1. Nosh your way through the food stalls at the lively **Pike Place Market** in Seattle (PAGE 218).

2. Wander acres of beautifully manicured flowers and arbors at **The Butchart Gardens** in Victoria (PAGE 223).

3. Pay tribute to the late, great frontman of Nirvana at **Kurt Cobain Landing** in Aberdeen (PAGE 227).

4. See where Lewis and Clark concluded their journey at **Fort Clatsop** (PAGE 228).

5. Climb the flank of **Mount Rainier** along the **Skyline Trail** (PAGE 234).

@MUNCHINGMINNIX

MAP: DOWNTOWN SEATTLE

❺ If you still have energy, return downtown for a symphony show at **Benaroya Hall** (200 University St., 206/215-4800, www.seattlesymphony.org/benaroya). Performances are most often under the direction of electric conductor Ludovic Morlot. A Dale Chihuly sculpture decorates the main hall, and giant windows open to a downtown vista.

DAY 2: Seattle

MORNING AND AFTERNOON

❶ Start the day with French toast and the breakfast toppings bar at **Portage Bay Cafe** (391 Terry Ave. N, 206/462-6400, www.portagebaycafe.com, 7:30am-2:30pm daily, $8.50-16) in South Lake Union.

❷ Head to Lake Union Park and the **Museum of History & Industry** (MOHAI, 860 Terry Ave. N, 206/324-1126, www.mohai.org, 10am-5pm Fri.-Wed., 10am-8pm Thurs. summer, 10am-5pm

daily winter, $20 adults, free for children). Ensconced in an old art deco armory building on Lake Union are artifacts like the city's favorite beer sign, a working periscope, and a flag made out of petticoats.

❸ Cross one of the city's many drawbridges to reach Ballard, a former fishing center. The **Hiram M. Chittenden Locks** (3015 54th St. NW,

MUSEUM OF HISTORY & INDUSTRY

206/783-7059, www.nws.usace.army. mil) are an engineering marvel; it's fun to watch the gates open and the locks fill as boats move in and out. There's also a fish ladder with underground viewing windows and a botanical garden.

EVENING

4 Before leaving Ballard, enjoy the neighborhood's fine dining. On Ballard Avenue, a must-try is the French fare at **Bastille Café & Bar** (5307 Ballard Ave. NW, 206/453-5014, www. bastilleseattle.com, 5:30pm-midnight Mon.-Thurs., 5:30pm-1am Fri.-Sat., 10am-3pm and 5:30pm-midnight Sun., $11-26).

5 Bars in Ballard are among the city's best. Take a tipple at **The Noble Fir** (5316 Ballard Ave. NW, 206/420-7425, www.thenoblefir.com, 4pm-midnight Tues.-Thurs., 4pm-1am Fri.-Sat., 1pm-9pm Sun.), a sleek establishment that gets more natural light than most firs in the forest. The beer menu shows evidence of fastidious selection, and one corner of the restaurant has a hiking- and travel-book reading nook. Make your way back downtown to your hotel.

DAY 3: Seattle to Vancouver, British Columbia

145 miles/233 kilometers | 3.5 hours

ROUTE OVERVIEW: I-5 • BC-99

1 As you head to **Vancouver**, British Columbia, leave plenty of time for delays at the **Peace Arch border crossing** between the United States and Canada; lanes back up on weekends and holidays. Once you're in Vancouver, grab a cup of coffee as you explore the **Gastown** neighborhood. Enjoy photo ops at the **Steam Clock** (Cambie St. and Water St.) and the **Gassy Jack Statue** (Alexander St. and Water St.).
> *Drive north on I-5 for 136 miles (219 km) to the Canadian border. Once you cross into Canada, continue on BC-99 N into Vancouver (6 mi/10 km).*

2 Wander through the (re-created) 15th century at **Dr. Sun Yat-Sen Classical Chinese Garden** (578 Carrall St., 604/662-3207, http://vancouverchine-segarden.com, 10am-6pm daily May-June 14 and Sept., 9:30am-7pm daily June 15-Aug., 10am-4:30pm daily Oct., 10am-4:30pm Tues.-Sun. Nov.-Apr., CAD$15 adults, CAD$12 children). More a historical manor house than a simple garden, this site is the jewel of Vancouver's Chinatown.

3 It's a 1.2-mile (2 km) walk west along Pacific Boulevard to **David Lam Park** (1300 Pacific Blvd., http://vancouver.ca, 10am-dusk daily). It's set right along the seawall that borders False Creek.

DR. SUN YAT-SEN CLASSICAL CHINESE GARDEN

④ Catch the tiny False Creek Ferry to **Granville Island.** Shop for food, flowers, soaps, jewelry, or just about anything else you can imagine among the endless stalls at the **Granville Island Public Market** (1661 Duranleau St., 604/666-6477, www.granvilleisland.com, 9am-7pm daily).

⑤ It might seem early for dinner, but you'll want to get to **Vij's** (3106 Cambie St., 604/736-6664, http://vijs-restaurant.ca, 5:30pm-10:30pm daily, CAD$24-35) early—the Indian eatery always has a line. Catch a cab, put your name on the list at the door, and then enjoy some free snacks while you wait.

DAY 4: Vancouver

MORNING AND AFTERNOON

① Rent a bike from **Spokes Bicycle Rental** (1798 W. Georgia St., 604/688-5141, www.spokesbicyclerentals.com, 8am-9pm daily summer, 9am-6:30pm

TOTEM POLES AT STANLEY PARK

daily winter, CAD$8.50-10.50 per hour) and cycle the 6-mile (10-km) **Seawall Promenade** at **Stanley Park** (604/257-8531, http://vancouver.ca), soaking in the great views along the periphery.

② From Stanley Park, follow Beach Avenue south to cross the Burrard Bridge. Head west on 4th Avenue to the **University of British Columbia Museum of Anthropology** (6393 NW Marine Dr., 604/822-5087, www.moa.ubc.ca, 10am-5pm Wed.-Mon., 10am-9pm

VIEW FROM VANCOUVER LOOKOUT

WHISTLER

Tues., CAD$18 adults, CAD$16 children). At this museum celebrating culture both at home and around the world, totem poles receive a regal, light-filled display.

EVENING

❸ You'll want to make it back downtown for dinner. Scoot over to Chinatown for Asian small plates at **Bao Bei** (163 Keefer St., 604/688-0876, www.bao-bei.ca, 5:30pm-midnight Tues.-Sat., 5:30pm-10pm Sun., CAD$14-25). Artisanal Asian plates are dished in this restaurant's narrow dining room.

❹ Conclude the day at the top of **Vancouver Lookout** (555 W Hastings St., 604/689-0421, www.vancouverlookout.com, 8:30am-10:30pm daily summer, 9am-9:30pm daily winter, CAD$18 adults, CAD$13 children 13-18, CAD$9.50 children 6-12), one of the tallest buildings in the city. You'll get a view of sparkling Vancouver from your spot right in the middle of it.

DAY 5: Day Trip to Whistler

150 miles/242 kilometers | 4 hours

ROUTE OVERVIEW: BC-99

❶ In **Whistler**, use the ski lifts for **hiking** in the summer, including a Peak 2 Peak ride. The **Whistler Mountain Bike Park** (866/218-9690, http://bike.whistlerblackcomb.com, from CAD$40 adults, from CAD$36 children 13-18, from CAD$24 children 5-12) is open May-October. The park uses some of the lifts and includes beginner, intermediate, and incredibly scary, gnarly, expert-only trails.

> Drive north on BC-99, also known as the Sea to Sky Highway, to Whistler (75 mi/121 km).

❷ Relax and recharge with an après-ski drink at **Garibaldi Lift Co. Bar & Grill** (4165 Springs Ln., 604/905-2220, www.whistlerblackcomb.com, 11am-1am daily, CAD$16-17). The lounge overlooks the slopes.

❸ The fare at **Rimrock Cafe** (2117 Whistler Rd., 604/932-5565, http://rimrockcafe.com, 5:30pm-9:30pm daily, CAD$35-52) is among the best in Whistler; especially delectable are the scallops and classic cocktails. Drive back to **Vancouver** and make sure you have your reservations set for the ferry ride tomorrow.

> Return the way you came, via BC-99 (75 mi/121 km).

DAY 6: Vancouver to Victoria

50 miles/81 kilometers | 4.5 hours, including ferry

ROUTE OVERVIEW: BC-99 • BC-17 • ferry • BC-17 • surface roads • BC-17

❶ At the **Tsawwassen ferry terminal,** board the **BC Ferry** (888/223-3779, www.bcferries.com, CAD$17.20 adults, CAD$8.60 children 5-12, CAD$57.50 vehicles, surcharges for fuel and large vehicles) to Victoria. After a 90-minute trip the boat arrives in **Swartz Bay**. Then it's a quick jaunt to Victoria, though traffic can build in the early morning.

> Drive BC-99 S for 14 miles (23 km) to BC-17. Go south on BC-17 for 8 miles (13 km) to the Tsawwassen ferry terminal.

❷ Along the way, stop at **The Butchart Gardens** (800 Benvenuto Ave., Brentwood Bay, 250/652-4422, www.butchartgardens.com, 9am-10pm daily June-Aug., shorter hours Sept.-May, CAD$35 adults, CAD$17.50 children

13-17, CAD$3 children 5-12). What started as an industrial limestone quarry is now a beautiful collection of manicured gardens. See the Sunken Garden, plus Italian, Japanese, Mediterranean, and rose gardens. Winter brings fewer blooms, but you can enjoy outdoor ice skating and holiday displays.

> *Take the ferry from Tsawwassen ferry terminal to Swartz Bay. From Swartz Bay, take BC-17 S for 7 miles (11 km) to Mt. Newton Cross Rd. Turn right and drive for 1 mile (1.6 km) to Wallace Dr. Turn left. Take Wallace to Benvenuto Ave. (3 mi/5.5 km). Turn right on Benvenuto to reach The Butchart Gardens.*

❸ Explore Victoria's **Inner Harbour.** Reserve an **afternoon tea** (www.teaattheempress.com, 11am-6pm daily, CAD$82) at the **Fairmont Empress** hotel (721 Government St., 800/441-1414, www.fairmont.com/empress-victoria), a tradition with a casually

FAIRMONT EMPRESS

elegant dress code. The tea served is a proprietary blend of leaves from Kenya, Tanzania, South India, Assam, Sri Lanka, and China—and the experience comes with a free sample to take home. Bites come on a multilevel tray filled with cucumber sandwiches, scones, and shortbread.

> *Take Benvenuto Ave. east for 3 miles (5 km) to BC-17A. Follow BC-17 S for 10 miles (16 km) to Victoria.*

❹ Take the Harbour Ferry to **Fisherman's Wharf** (Dallas Rd. and Erie St., 250/383-8326, www.fishermanswharfvictoria.com). The wharf's quaint floating homes provide a backdrop to waterfront food stands and great people- and wildlife-watching.

❺ End the day with an Italian meal at stately **Il Terrazzo** (555 Johnson St., 250/361-0028, www.ilterrazzo.com, 11:30am-3pm and 5pm-9pm Mon.-Fri., 5pm-9pm Sat.-Sun., CAD$16-42). Even if it isn't a special occasion, the brick fireplaces and delectable Italian food by candlelight makes the meal feel notable. Stroll the Inner Harbour again at night to see lights reflecting off the water.

WITH LESS TIME

SEATTLE TO VANCOUVER

4 days; 256 miles/412 kilometers

Hit the region's two biggest cities in a short road trip. Start in **Seattle** and spend **two days** exploring the downtown sights. On your third day, drive north to **Vancouver** and spend the rest of the day exploring the city. Spend your **last day** in the city, or take an outdoorsy side trip to the mountains north of the city or to **Whistler.**

PORTLAND LOOP

5 days; 362 miles/583 kilometers

An easy loop from Portland includes the best of city and nature. Spend **two days** discovering **Portland**'s neighborhood gems, then drive north into Washington. At **Longview,** jog west to **Astoria.** Spend **1-2 days** following US-101 south along the Oregon coast, with stops for whale-watching and beach strolls. Spend your last day driving east from **Newport** to **Corvallis** and **Albany,** then north to return to Portland.

CAPILANO SUSPENSION BRIDGE, NORTH VANCOUVER

Best ROADSIDE ATTRACTIONS

A drive across the Pacific Northwest is beautiful, but the best part of any trip is a surprising stop that breaks up a day on the road.

- **Taylor Shellfish Farms** (1521 Melrose Ave., Seattle, WA, 206/501-4321, www.taylorshellfishfarms.com, 11am-9pm Sun.-Thurs., 11am-11pm Fri.-Sat.): Oysters and clams are delightful regional delicacies, and this outpost of one of the region's biggest purveyors sits close to where they're harvested.

- **Chateau Ste. Michelle** (14111 NE 145th St., Woodinville, WA, 425/488-1133, www.ste-michelle.com, tastings and tours 10am-5pm daily, free): Woodinville's biggest winery is inside a French-style chateau surrounded by green lawns ripe for picnicking.

- **Deception Pass State Park** (WA-20 and Rosario Rd., Oak Harbor, WA, www.parks.wa.gov): Cross from Puget Sound's Whidbey Island to the mainland over a dramatic chasm, and then visit a tiny museum that celebrates the workers that built the classic park structures.

- **Capilano Suspension Bridge Park** (3735 Capilano Rd., North Vancouver, BC, 604/985-7474, www.capbridge.com, 8am-8pm daily mid-May-Sept., shorter hours Oct.-mid-May, CAD$54 adults, CAD$30 children 13-16, CAD$17 children 6-12): Dare to look down from the swinging wooden structure or tree houses at this park just outside Vancouver.

- **The Butchart Gardens** (800 Benvenuto Ave., Brentwood Bay, BC, 250/652-4422, www.butchartgardens.com, 9am-10pm daily June-Aug., shorter hours Sept.-May, CAD$35 adults, CAD$17.50 children 13-17, CAD$3 children 5-12): An old quarry has become a lush series of gardens, complete with a winter skating rink and boat tours.

- **Makah Museum** (1880 Bayview Ave., Neah Bay, WA, 360/645-2711, http://makahmuseum.com, 10am-5pm daily, $5 adults, $4 children): This cultural center celebrates the Makah, the Native American people who live in a remote corner of the Olympic Peninsula.

- **Olympia Farmers Market** (700 N. Capitol Way, Olympia, WA, 360/352-9096, www.olympiafarmersmarket.com, 10am-3pm Thurs.-Sun. Apr.-Oct., 10am-3pm Sat.-Sun. Nov.-Dec.): The capital city's food and craft market is on the waterfront, near lumberyards and marinas.

- **Sea Lion Caves** (91560 US-101, Florence, OR, 541/547-3111, www.sealioncaves.com, 9am-7pm daily, $14 adults, $8 children 5-12): Ride an elevator down to a cavern where barking sea lions live and play.

- **Edgefield** (2126 SW Halsey St., Troutdale, OR, 503/669-8610, www.mcmenamins.com/edgefield, $30 hostel, $50-115 shared bath, $155-175 private bath): This hotel property includes a brewery, movie theater, golf course, and music venues.

- **Northwest Trek Wildlife Park** (11610 Trek Dr. E., Eatonville, WA, 360/832-6117, www.nwtrek.org, 9:30am-6pm daily late June-early Sept., shorter hours early Sept.-late June, $25 adults, $17 children 5-12, $13 children 3-4): At this wildlife preserve, bison, elk, and bobcats are nursed back to health.

▶ Playlist

BEST OF THE PACIFIC NORTHWEST

SONGS

- **"Come as You Are" by Nirvana:** There is perhaps no band more associated with Seattle than Nirvana. Grunge rocker and lead singer Kurt Cobain achieved legend status when he was alive, but after he died in 1994, he became nothing short of a saint. Play this song as you drive to Cobain's memorial in his hometown of Aberdeen.

- **"Say Yes" by Elliott Smith:** A road trip playlist through Oregon must include a tune by Smith, one of the most important and influential singer-songwriters of the 1990s. The minimalist arrangement and melancholy lyrics of "Say Yes" complement long-drive brooding against a backdrop of crashing ocean waves.

- **"Love's Coming at Ya" by Blossom:** Trinidad and Tobago-born Keisha Chiddick—who has called Portland home since she was a child—sings neo-soul with a dash of 90s-influenced R&B and a sprinkling of reggae. This song offers up plenty of groove and funk for a chill bike ride through Portland.

PODCASTS

- ***Outside:*** A content sister of *Outside* magazine, this podcast features riveting storytelling about the outdoors. Portland-based Robbie Carver and Peter Frick-Wright keep listeners on the edge of their seats with topics such "The Wrong Way to Fight Off a Bear" and inspirational profiles of runners, hikers, climbers, and more.

DAY 7: Victoria to Lake Crescent, Washington

85 miles/137 kilometers | 4 hours, including ferry

ROUTE OVERVIEW: ferry • surface streets • Hurricane Ridge Rd. • US-101

❶ Take the **Black Ball Ferry Line** (Victoria Harbor, www.cohoferry.com, CAD$18.50 adults, CAD$9.25 children 5-11, CAD$64 for car and driver, CAD$11-16 reservation fee) across the Strait of Juan de Fuca, arriving in **Port Angeles,** Washington.

❷ Chow down at **Next Door Gastropub** (113 W. 1st St., Ste. A, 360/504-2613, www.nextdoorgastropub.com, 11am-11pm Mon.-Thurs., 11am-midnight Fri.-Sat., 10am-10pm Sun., $9-30). This friendly bar straddles the divide between neighborhood joint and sophisticated eatery.

❸ Explore **Olympic National Park** (www.nps.gov/olym, $30 per vehicle, $25 motorcycles, $15 for pedestrians and bicycles), starting at the **Hurricane Ridge Visitor Center** (360/565-3130, open daily in summer, shorter hours fall-spring). Hurricane Ridge is an alpine meadow overlooking the

HURRICANE RIDGE IN OLYMPIC NATIONAL PARK

LAKE CRESCENT IN OLYMPIC NATIONAL PARK

beaches on either side; the tides and crumbling coastline can be dangerous. Instead, return the way you came. Access the trailhead from a parking lot on La Push Road about 0.75 mile from where the road ends in La Push (past the Quileute tribal administration buildings).

> *Take US-101 W for 38 miles (61 km) to Forks. In Forks, follow WA-110 W/La Push Rd. west for 13 miles (21 km) to the trailhead.*

❷ More outdoor exploration comes via a visit to the southern sections of Olympic National Park. Enter at the **Hoh Rain Forest Visitor Center** (Upper Hoh Rd., 18 miles from U.S. 101, 360/374-6925, www.nps.gov/olym, daily June-Sept., Fri.-Tues. May-June, hours vary). More than 12 feet of rain fall on the park's stretch of old-growth forest, home to herds of Roosevelt elk.

> *Retrace your route the 13 miles (21 km) back to Forks along WA-110 W/La Push Rd. Turn right on US-101 S and drive it for 15 miles (24 km) to Upper Hoh Rd. Turn left to reach the visitors center (18 mi/29 km).*

❸ Continue on to **Lake Quinault** for nature walks and epic trees. Spend the night at **Lake Quinault Lodge** (345 S. Shore Rd., 360/288-2900 or 800/562-6672, www.olympicnationalparks.com, from $229). The original 1926 building has steep roofs and Catskill-resort charm, with Adirondack chairs dotting the lawn that slopes down to Lake Quinault.

> *Depart Hoh Rain Forest via the same route, joining US-101. Turn left on US-101 and go south for 53 miles (85 km) to Lake Quinault.*

peaks of the Olympic Mountains. Enjoy a short hike before driving back to Port Angeles.

> *Take E. 1st St. for 1 mile (1.6 km) to Race St. Turn right onto Race and head south for 1.5 miles (2.5 km) to Hurricane Ridge Rd. Follow Hurricane Ridge Rd. south for 17 miles (27 km) to the visitors center.*

❹ West of Port Angeles in Lake Crescent, spend the night at **Lake Crescent Lodge** (416 Lake Crescent Rd., 360/928-3211, www.olympicnational-parks.com, rooms $123-238, cottages $292-328). This old-fashioned lakeside hotel offers cozy individual cottages and boat rentals.

> *Leave the park via the same route to Port Angeles, then take US-101 W for 19 miles (31 km) to Lake Crescent Rd. Turn right and stay on Lake Crescent Rd. to the lodge.*

DAY 8: Lake Crescent to Lake Quinault

170 miles/275 kilometers | 6 hours

ROUTE OVERVIEW: US-101 • WA-110 • US-101 • Upper Hoh Rd. • US-101

❶ Pack a lunch, then make your way to the town of **La Push,** nestled along the Pacific coastline. Here, you can hike the **Second Beach Trail** (1.4 mi/2.3 km round-trip, 1 hour, easy), then enjoy lunch with views of the sea stacks. Don't try to cross the headlands to the

DAY 9: Lake Quinault to Astoria, Oregon

120 miles/193 kilometers | 3.5 hours

ROUTE OVERVIEW: US-101 • WA-4 • WA-401 • US-101

❶ On your way to Astoria, take a break in Aberdeen to stretch your legs. Visit **Kurt Cobain Landing** (E. 2nd St.), a hometown tribute to the late musician known as an icon in the

90s grunge music scene. There's little parking for the small site, but it's a pleasantly serene park in the middle of the industrial city.

> *Head south on US-101 for 38 miles (61 km) to reach Aberdeen.*

② Just south of Astoria is **Fort Clatsop** (92343 Fort Clatsop Rd., 503/861-2471, www.nps.gov/lewi, 8am-5pm daily Labor Day-mid-June, 8am-6pm daily mid-June-Labor Day, $5 peak season, $3 Labor Day-mid-June). Lewis and Clark finished their epic journey here. Today the spot includes a replica of the old fort and an exhibit hall. In the summer, ranger-led programs and costumed rangers bring the old Oregon to life on a daily basis.

> *Head south on US-101 for 55 miles (89 km) to WA-4. Turn left and drive WA-4 E for 5 miles (8 km). At WA-401 S, turn right and drive for 12 miles (19 km) until US-101. Turn left and take US-101 S into Astoria (4 mi/6 km). Turn left again and head south on US-101 BUS for 5 miles (8 km) to Fort Clatsop Rd.*

③ Grab a casual dinner in **Astoria,** then check into the **Cannery Pier Hotel & Spa** (10 Basin St., 503/325-4996, www.cannerypierhotel.com, $309-399) under the Astoria-Megler Bridge. Every room has a balcony with a river view and a fireplace, plus wine and lox are served each evening in the lobby.

> *Retrace your route via Fort Clatsop Rd. and US-101 BUS back to Astoria (6 mi/10 km).*

TILLAMOOK CREAMERY

DAY 10: Astoria to Florence

190 miles/305 kilometers | 5 hours

ROUTE OVERVIEW: US-101

① US-101 is your path to the beaches. No shore trip is complete without a stop to see **Haystack Rock** (near S. Hemlock St. and Pacific St.). This unofficial symbol of the Oregon coast is at **Cannon Beach,** where the photogenic rock also serves as a bird sanctuary.

> *Take US-101 S for 26 miles (42 km) to Cannon Beach.*

② Cheese-lovers shouldn't miss the **Tillamook Creamery** (4175 U.S. 101, Tillamook, 503/815-1300, www.tillamook.com, 8am-6pm daily Labor Day-mid-June, 8am-8pm daily mid-June-Labor Day, free). The warehouse gives guests a peek at its giant cheese-making and packaging floors, plus offers endless free samples.

> *Drive south on US-101 for 40 miles (64 km) to Tillamook.*

HAYSTACK ROCK AT CANNON BEACH

Best HIKES

VANCOUVER, BRITISH COLUMBIA

- **Grouse Grind** (1.8 mi/2.9 km one-way, 2 hours, strenuous; Skyride Terminal, 6400 Nancy Greene Way): The haul up Vancouver's city ski mountain is a challenge to the lungs and legs, but it comes with plenty of summit rewards.

OLYMPIC PENINSULA, WASHINGTON

- **Mount Storm King** (4.5 mi/7.2 km round-trip, 2.5 hours, moderate; Storm King Ranger Station): Brave some elevation gain through Olympic forest to reach Lake Crescent vistas.

- **Sol Duc Falls** (1.6 mi/2.7 km round-trip, 1 hour, easy; Sol Duc Hot Springs Rd.): One of the classic waterfalls of the famously lush Olympic Peninsula is just a short loop from the trailhead.

- **Hoh River Trail to Glacier Meadows** (up to 35 mi/56 km round-trip, 1 hour-multiple days, moderate; Hoh Rain Forest Visitor Center): Charge into the rainforest on a flat route along one of the Northwest's most picturesque rivers.

OREGON COAST

- **Devil's Churn** (2.2 mi/3.5 km round-trip, 1.5 hours, easy; Cape Perpetua Visitor Center, Yachats): The wild Pacific waves turn a section of Cape Perpetua into a frothing, active cauldron of seawater.

- **Hobbit Trail** (1 mi/1.6 km round-trip, 45 minutes, moderate; U.S. 101, near milepost 177): Reach the sands of the Oregon coastline through a magical, short hike that recalls a fantasy landscape.

MOUNT RAINIER, WASHINGTON

- **Skyline Trail** (4-5.5 mi/6.4-8.9 km round-trip, 2.5-4 hours, strenuous; Paradise Rd.): Take the first steps up Mount Rainier through alpine meadows, with views of the peak's giant glaciers.

- **Grove of the Patriarchs** (1.3 mi/2.1 km round-trip, 1 hour, easy; Stevens Canyon Rd.): A suspension bridge links sections of a flat and easy ramble through the Rainier area's biggest trees.

- **Eruption Trail** (0.5 mi/0.8 km round-trip, 30 minutes, easy; Johnston Ridge Observatory): The gaping crater of Mount St. Helens provides a backdrop to an educational walk through volcanic rock and wildflowers that thrive in the ashy dirt.

▼ SOL DUC WILDERNESS AT OLYMPIC NATIONAL PARK

❸ Those cheese samples will tide you over until lunch at **Ben & Jeff's Burgers and Tacos** (33260 Cape Kiwanda Dr., 503/483-1026, www.benandjeffs.com, 10am-5pm Mon. and Wed.-Fri., 9am-6pm Sat.-Sun., $8-19) in **Pacific City.** Grab a table inside or order food to go and stroll the beach.

> Drive 11 miles (18 km) south on US-101. Turn right onto Sandlake Rd. Follow this for 11 miles (18 km) until the road becomes Ferry Rd./McPhillips Dr. Continue for another 1.5 miles (2.5 km), at which point the road becomes Cape Kiwanda Dr. Follow this for another mile to reach Pacific City.

❹ In **Newport,** visit the massive **Oregon Coast Aquarium** (2820 SE Ferry Slip Rd., 541/867-3474, www.aquarium.org, 10am-6pm daily May-Sept., 10am-5pm daily Sept.-May, $23 adults, $20 children 13-17, $15 children 3-12). Local sealife is represented well with touch tanks and feeding shows. Don't miss seeing the Pacific octopus and puffins.

> Take US-101 S for 47 miles (76 km) to Newport.

❺ Follow US-101 south to **Florence,** where sunset is best spied from **Oregon Dunes National Recreation Area** (S. Jetty Rd. and US-101, www.fs.usda.gov). The sandy hills that guard Oregon's beaches also serve as an outdoor playground for dune buggies. End the day with a drink and a meal in Florence, before heading to bed at one of the hotels in town.

> Drive 49 miles (79 km) south on US-101 to Florence.

DAY 11: Florence to Portland

175 miles/280 kilometers | 3.5 hours

ROUTE OVERVIEW: OR-126 • I-5

❶ Depart early to drive to Portland, rolling into the city just after morning traffic. Start the day downtown. First, stow your luggage at one of the many hotels in the area, then stop at the **Portland Art Museum** (1219 SW Park Ave., 503/226-2811, www.portlandartmuseum.org, 10am-5pm Tues.-Wed.

PORTLAND ART MUSEUM

and Sat.-Sun., 10am-8pm Thurs.-Fri., $20 adults, free for children 17 and under). This expansive yet accessible art collection emphasizes Native American and Northwest art and houses striking sculptures.

> Take OR-126 E for 56 miles (90 km) to I-5 N. Take I-5 N to Portland (115 mi/185 km).

❷ At lunchtime, walk SW 9th Avenue to hit up the **food carts** near Alder Street. Work off your meal browsing the numerous aisles at **Powell's City of Books** (1005 W. Burnside St., 800/878-7323, www.powells.com, 11am-9pm daily). Portland's renowned bookstore fills a city block with more than a million volumes of new and used books.

❸ From Powell's, take TriMet bus no. 20 to **Forest Park** (NW 29th Ave. and Upshur St. to Newberry Rd., 503/223-5449, www.forestparkconservancy.org, 5am-10pm daily, free). More than 80 miles of trails await in one of the largest city forests in the country. Dozens of mammals and birds live among the Douglas firs and maples, including deer, bobcats, woodpeckers, coyotes, and even migratory elk.

❹ Take a taxi or ride-share to **Washington Park** (4001 SW Canyon Rd., 503/823-2525, http://explorewashingtonpark.org, free, parking $1.60/hour, $4/day Oct.-Mar., $6.40/day Apr.-Sept.), where the **International Rose Test Garden** (850 SW Rose Garden Way, 7:30am-9pm daily, free) offers a ramble through every color of petal imaginable. The acres of roses astound even those without green thumbs. The grassy amphitheater is an ideal resting spot after a busy day. Have dinner and catch a show in the Pearl District, then head back downtown to your hotel.

DAY 12: Portland

MORNING

❶ For breakfast, forget nutrition and brave the line at **Voodoo Doughnut** (22 SW 3rd Ave., 503/241-4704, www.voodoodoughnut.com, 24 hours daily, $1-12); don't worry, you're going to work off those carbs.

❷ Rent a bike from **Cycle Portland** (117 NW 2nd Ave., 844/739-2453, www.portlandbicycletours.com, 9am-6pm daily, rentals $5 per hour, $20-35 per day), where the rental fee includes a helmet, bike lock, and bicycle map. Cycle Portland welcomes walk-ins, so there's no need to make a rental reservation ahead of time.

AFTERNOON

❸ Use your bike lock to park your wheels at the **Oregon Museum of Science and Industry** (1945 SE Water Ave., 503/797-4000, www.omsi.edu, 9:30am-5:30pm daily, $15 adults, $10.50 children 3-13, parking $5). The

FOOD CARTS IN PORTLAND

indoor play space and outdoor submarine tour are so fun that you'll forget it's educational.

❹ For lunch, bike to SE Division and, if you have the patience, wait for a lunch table at **Pok Pok** (3226 SE Division St., 503/232-1387, https://pokpokdivision.com, 11:30am-10pm daily, $11-19) to indulge in bites you'd find at a Bangkok street cart. The spicy wings are the star, but the entire Southeast Asian menu bursts with flavor.

EVENING

❺ Bike across Hawthorne Bridge and stop at **Lucky Labrador Brew Pub** (915 SE Hawthorne Blvd., 503/236-3555, www.luckylab.com, 11am-midnight Mon.-Sat., noon-10pm Sun.) to enjoy a local pint and dinner on the patio. Beer is the signature quaff of Portland, perhaps the country's capital of craft brewing.

DAY 13: Portland to Mount Rainier National Park, Washington

155 miles/250 kilometers | 3.5 hours

ROUTE OVERVIEW: I-5 • US-12 • WA-7 • WA-706

❶ Leave Portland early (before rush-hour traffic) for the drive to the **Nisqually Entrance** of **Mount Rainier National Park** (360/569-2211, www.nps.gov/mora, $25 per vehicle). Once inside the park, you'll enjoy scenic drives, museums, and hiking trails, all within the grandeur of Mount Rainier—an active volcano with a prominence (13,210 feet/4,026 m) greater than that of K2, the world's second-tallest mountain.

> *Drive north on I-5 for 73 miles (118 km), then take US-12 E for 31 miles (50 km) to Morton. Drive WA-7 N for 16 miles (26 km) to WA-706. Turn right and follow WA-706 to the Nisqually Entrance of Mount Rainier National Park (14 mi/ 23 km).*

❷ Take the drive through the park to Longmire slowly, both to appreciate the thick forest and to maintain caution on the road's tight turns. In **Longmire,** pop into the **Longmire Museum** (360/569-6575, www.nps.gov/mora, 9am-4:30pm daily June-Sept.) to learn about the family that once settled here.

> *Once inside the park, drive 6 miles (10 km) along the park road to Longmire.*

❸ As you head to **Paradise,** Mount Rainier looms larger. Grab lunch at the deli inside the **Henry M. Jackson Visitor Center** (Paradise Rd. E., 360/569-6571, www.nps.gov/mora, 10am-7pm daily June-Sept., 10am-4:30pm Sat.-Sun. Oct.-May). There's a reason this part of Mount Rainier National Park is called Paradise—come for the mountain views, but stay for natural history exhibits and wildflower meadows that look like heaven.

> *Drive 11 miles (18 km) east on the park road to Paradise.*

HIKERS IN MOUNT RAINIER NATIONAL PARK

Best BREWPUBS AND TAPROOMS

SEATTLE, WASHINGTON

- **Rhein Haus** (912 12th Ave., 206/325-5409, www.rheinhausseattle.com, 3pm-2am Mon.-Fri., 10am-2am Sat.-Sun.): The bocce courts are always active and the beer steins always overflowing at this Bavarian-themed beer garden in Seattle.

▲ RHEIN HAUS BEER GARDEN

VANCOUVER, BRITISH COLUMBIA

- **Granville Island Brewing** (1441 Cartwright St., 604/687-2739, www.gib.ca, 11am-9pm daily): Tucked into Vancouver's waterfront arts and culture hub, this brewery crafts one of British Columbia's most popular brands of beer.

VICTORIA, BRITISH COLUMBIA

- **CANOE Brewpub** (450 Swift St., 250/361-1940, www.canoebrewpub.com, 11:30am-11pm Sun.-Wed., 11:30am-midnight Thurs., 11:30am-1am Fri.-Sat.): This Victoria brewer offers waterfront dining and welcomes children much of the day, all in a historic brick building downtown. The brewery also hosts live music.

OLYMPIC PENINSULA, WASHINGTON

- **Fish Tale Brewpub** (515 Jefferson St. SE, Olympia, 360/943-3650, www.fishbrewing.com, 11am-10pm Mon.-Thurs., 11am-midnight Fri., 9am-midnight Sat., 9am-10pm Sun.): In Olympia, a town once synonymous with a cheap, light beer, a new generation of brewers is creating organic ales and creative ciders, all served within their striking mural-covered building.

OREGON COAST

- **Fort George Brewery** (1483 Duane St., Astoria, 503/325-7468, www.fortgeorgebrewery.com, 11am-11pm Mon.-Thurs., 11am-midnight Fri.-Sat., noon-11pm Sun., $10-18): This brewer set up shop in an old service station and likes to bring a sense of humor to brewpub decor and beer names.

- **Pelican Pub & Brewery** (33180 Cape Kiwanda Dr., Pacific City, 503/965-7007, pelicanbrewing.com, 8am-10pm Sun.-Thurs., 8am-11pm Fri.-Sat., $12-24): Catch some salt air at this beachfront brewery in Pacific City, with a thorough menu of both pours and food options.

- **Rogue Ales Brewery** (2320 OSU Dr., Newport, 541/867-3664, www.rogue.com, 11am-9pm Sun.-Thurs., 11am-10pm Fri.-Sat.): One of Oregon's most popular beers is made here.

PORTLAND, OREGON

- **Hopworks Urban Brewery** (2944 SE Powell Blvd., 503/232-4677, www.hopworksbeer.com, 11am-11pm Sun.-Thurs., 11am-midnight Fri.-Sat.): Green practices and organic brewing give this bike-friendly beer spot an upbeat do-gooder vibe.

SKYLINE TRAIL

❹ Climb the **Skyline Trail** (4-5.5 mi/6.4-8.9 km round-trip, 2.5-4 hours, strenuous) along the flank of Mount Rainier. Starting from the Henry M. Jackson Visitor Center, this hike offers up-close views of the massive peak. It's a sweat-inducing climb, but it's also the best way to wander the Paradise meadows.

❺ Back at Paradise, check in to the **Paradise Inn** (98368 Paradise-Longmire Rd., 360/569-2275, www.mtrainierguestservices.com, May-Sept., $119-155 shared bath) and enjoy dinner in the lofty dining room. Curl up with a book in front of one of the lobby's cozy woodburning fireplaces before hitting the hay.

PARADISE INN

DAY 14: Mount Rainier National Park to Seattle

165 miles/265 kilometers | 3.5 hours

ROUTE OVERVIEW: surface roads • WA-410 • surface roads • WA-410 • WA-164 • WA-18 • I-5

❶ Fuel up on coffee and breakfast at the **Paradise Inn Dining Room** (7am-9:30am, noon-2pm, and 5:30pm-8pm daily May-Sept., $17-35).

❷ Make your way to **Sunrise Point,** on the northeast side of the park. On the way, stop for a picture at **Reflection Lakes.**
> Take the park road for 2 miles (3 km) to Stevens Canyon Rd. Turn left. Drive for 1 mile (1.6 km) to reach Reflection Lakes.

❸ At the **Sunrise Visitor Center** (Sunrise Rd., 360/663-2425, 10am-6pm daily July-Sept.), order a grilled sandwich from the café, then lace up your shoes for a hike on the **Silver Forest Trail** (2 mi/3.2 km round-trip, 1 hour, easy). The trek takes you to the Emmons Glacier Overlook. In late summer, the meadows explode with wildflowers, including purple lupine and Indian paintbrush. The trailhead is at the south end of the Sunrise parking lot.
> Drive 18 miles (29 km) on Stevens Canyon Rd. to WA-123. Turn left and continue north on WA-123 for 11 miles (18 km) as the road becomes WA-410 W. In 4 miles (6 km), turn left onto Sunrise Park Rd. Take Sunrise Park Rd. 15 miles (24 km) to Sunrise Visitor Center.

❹ At the ski resort of **Crystal Mountain** (33914 Crystal Mountain Blvd., 360/663-2265, www.crystalmountainresort.com), ride the resort's Mount Rainier Gondola ($8) up to a killer viewpoint.
> Return to WA-410 W via Sunrise Park Rd. Turn left on WA-410 West and exit the park in 4 miles (6 km). Turn right on Crystal Mountain Blvd. to access Crystal Mountain (8 mi/13 km).

❺ Grab dinner at the **Snorting Elk Cellar** (33818 Crystal Mountain Blvd., 888/754-6400, www.crystalhotels.com,

CRYSTAL MOUNTAIN

11am-10pm daily summer, 11am-10pm Sun.-Thurs., 11am-midnight Fri.-Sat. winter, $11-30). Low ceilings arch over a fireplace, and the bar offers warming libations like craft beers and hot toddies. Return to Seattle.

> To return to Seattle, drive back to WA-410. Follow WA-410 N for 33 miles (53 km) to Enumclaw, then continue west on WA-164 for 15 miles (24 km). Merge onto WA-18 W. Stay on WA-18 for 3 miles (5 km) to I-5. Follow I-5 N for 22 miles (35 km) to Seattle.

Getting There

AIR

The **Seattle-Tacoma International Airport** (SEA, 17801 International Blvd., 206/787-5388 or 800/544-1965, www.portseattle.org/sea-tac) is a busy facility that receives both domestic and international flights via nearly two dozen airlines. Parking ($3-4 per hour), car rentals (3150 S. 160th St.), and public transportation are available.

A taxi from the airport to the downtown core costs a flat rate of $40. The **Central Link light rail** (www.soundtransit.org, 5am-1am Mon.-Sat., 6am-midnight Sun., $3) traces a 40-minute ride through Seattle's southern neighborhoods before stopping in the downtown underground transit tunnel. The **Downtown Airporter** (425/981-7000, https://downtownairporter.hudsonltd.net) provides shuttle service from the airport to select hotels downtown.

TRAIN

Amtrak (800/872-7245, www.amtrak.com) trains arrive and depart daily from Seattle's **King Street Station** (303 S. Jackson St.), located near Pioneer Square just south of downtown. The Cascade Line travels from Vancouver, British Columbia, to Eugene, Oregon, with stops in Tacoma, Portland, and Salem; the Empire Builder route runs east all the way to Chicago; and the Coast Starlight travels south from Seattle with stops in Portland, Oregon, and throughout California.

BUS

Greyhound (503 S. Royal Brougham Way, Seattle, 800/231-2222, www.greyhound.com) offers special discounts to students and seniors, with routes and stops sticking to major highways and cities.

BoltBus (648 SW Salmon St., 877/265-8287, www.boltbus.com) is the cheapest way to travel south from Vancouver, British Columbia, with stops in Seattle, Portland, and Eugene.

CAR

From **Seattle-Tacoma International Airport,** it's 14 miles (23 km) to downtown Seattle, which takes 25-30 minutes via I-5 North.

CONNECT WITH

- At Portland: **Columbia River Gorge and Wine Country** (PAGE 264)
- At Seattle, Portland, and the Olympic Peninsula: **Pacific Coast Highway: Washington and Oregon** (PAGE 236)
- At Mount Rainier National Park: **Pacific Crest Trail: Oregon and Washington** (PAGE 250)

PACIFIC COAST HIGHWAY: WASHINGTON AND OREGON

WHY GO: Whale-watching, secluded beaches, rainforest hikes, windswept Oregon dunes, Willamette Valley wines, Space Needle views

TOTAL DISTANCE: 945 miles/ 1,535 kilometers

NUMBER OF DAYS: 7

SEASONS: Late spring through early fall

START: Seattle, Washington

END: Gold Beach, Oregon

▼ CANNON BEACH, OREGON

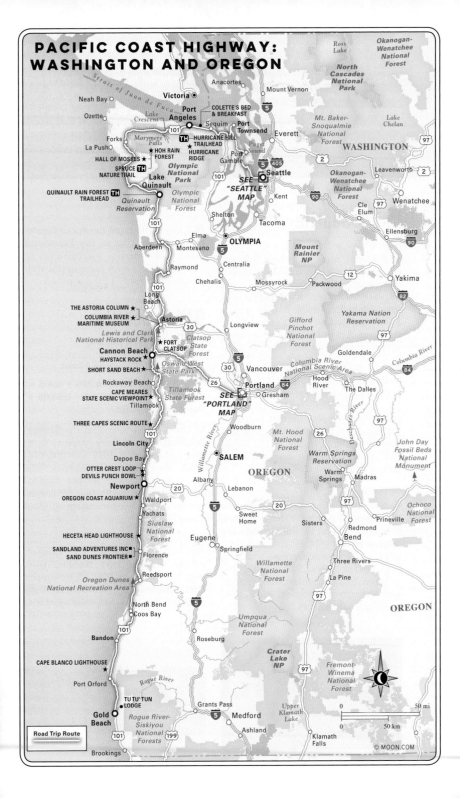

PACIFIC COAST HIGHWAY:
WASHINGTON AND OREGON

...om the tech hub of Seattle, Washington, this route crosses bridges, trac es peninsulas, carves through mountains, and hugs the coastline south to Oregon. Along the way, gritty port cities bump up against history-rich towns. Secluded beaches lead to hardy-yet-beautiful lighthouses that thrust out over the water. Scenic trails provide plenty of opportunities to stretch your legs, and a day trip to Portland affords the chance to eat and drink your way through the city. No matter what, have your camera or smartphone ready for some of the most iconic and photographed sights in the country.

DAY 1: Seattle

MORNING

1 Stunning mountain views from every direction are best spied from the top of the soaring **Space Needle** (400 Broad St., 206/905-2100, www.spaceneedle. com, 10am-8pm daily, $19-29 adults, $13-18 children 5-12). Built to celebrate the Space Age in 1962, the iconic tower is now synonymous with Seattle.

2 Ride the Monorail downtown, then walk a few blocks to **Pike Place Market** (Pike Pl. and Virginia St. between 1st Ave. and Western Ave., 206/682-7453, www.pikeplacemarket.org, 6am-1:30am daily) for lunch, shopping, and people-watching at one of the oldest continuously working markets in the United States.

AFTERNOON

3 Spend the afternoon exploring the city's past at historic **Pioneer Square,** the starting point for **Bill Speidel's Underground Tour** (614 1st Ave., 206/682-4646, www.undergroundtour.com, 8:30am-7pm daily, $22 adults, $10 children 7-12), an entertaining excursion through the original streets beneath the current city.

EVENING

4 Enjoy dinner and drinks in **Capitol Hill** before retiring to **The Paramount Hotel** (724 Pine St., 206/292-9500 or 800/426-0670, www.paramounthotel-seattle.com, from $199) downtown.

DAY 2: Seattle to Port Angeles

135 miles/236 kilometers | 4 hours

ROUTE OVERVIEW: WA-305 • WA-3 • WA-104 • WA-19 • WA-20 • US-101 • Hurricane Ridge Rd.

1 Cross Puget Sound on the **Seattle-Bainbridge Island Ferry** (departs from Pier 52, 888/808-7977 or 206/464-6400, www.wsdot.wa.gov/ferries, $18 per vehicle one-way, $8 per passenger, $4 children 6-18). Pier 52 is conveniently located just south of Pike Place Market.

2 Spend the first half of your day exploring cute waterside villages. Amble through **Port Gamble,** then stop for lunch in the Victorian-era **Port Townsend** at the **Fountain Cafe** (920 Washington St., 360/385-1364,

SEATTLE'S SKYLINE

PORT TOWNSEND

Top ③ PACIFIC COAST HIGHWAY: WASHINGTON AND OREGON

① Hike the wild beauty of the **Quinault Rain Forest** in **Olympic National Park** (PAGE 242).

② **Bicycle** along the banks of Oregon's gentle **Willamette River** (PAGE 245).

③ Glimpse sea lions below **Heceta Head,** one of the most photographed **lighthouses** in the country (PAGE 248).

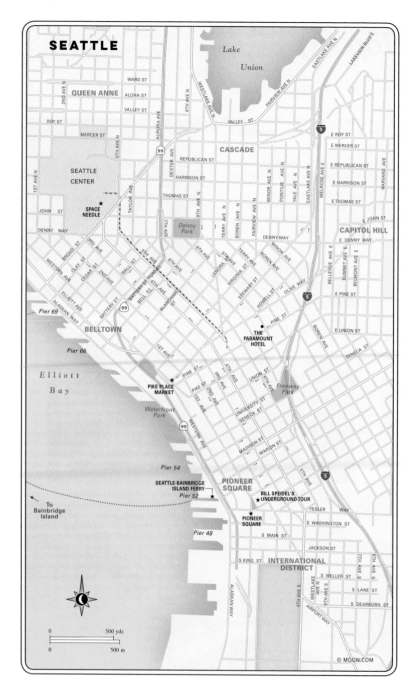

SEATTLE

11am-3pm and 5pm-9pm daily, $13-26), a funky eatery with eastern Mediterranean influences and art-lined walls.

> *From the ferry terminal on Bainbridge, take WA-305 N for 13 miles (21 km), then turn right to merge onto WA-3 N. Continue for 7 miles (11 km), then continue onto WA-104. In 1.5 miles (2.5 km), this will lead to Port Gamble. Back in the car, go west on WA-104, following it over the water, driving for a total of 8 miles (13 km) to WA-19. Turn right onto WA-19 N and continue for 14 miles (23 km) to WA-20, which leads into Port Townsend after 2 miles (3 km).*

❸ For the rest of the afternoon, enjoy spectacular panoramic views while hiking along **Hurricane Ridge** (Hurricane Ridge Rd.), the most popular spot in **Olympic National Park** (www.nps.gov/olym, $30 per vehicle, $25 motorcycles, $15 for pedestrians and bicycles. The easiest hike is the **Hurricane Hill Trail** (3.2 mi/5.2 km round-trip, 1.25 hours, easy), which begins at the parking lot at the end of Hurricane Ridge Road. The trail leads to the top of the hill and 360-degree views of mountain vistas, Port Angeles, and the Strait of Juan de Fuca.

> *Go south on WA-20 for 10 miles (16 km) to US-101. Turn right to join US-101 W, and continue for 33 miles (53 km) to Port Angeles. Turn left onto N. Race St., which becomes Hurricane Ridge Rd. in 1 mile (1.6 km). Continue south for 18 miles (29 km) to reach Hurricane Ridge.*

KEY RESERVATIONS

- **Seattle,** Washington, and **Portland,** Oregon, are both popular tourist destinations. While it's not necessary to make restaurant reservations or book tickets for attractions ahead of time, it's wise to book **lodging** in these two cities before your arrival.

❹ Conclude your day in **Port Angeles.** Enjoy a hearty dinner before spending the night at charming **Colette's Bed & Breakfast** (339 Finn Hall Rd., 360/457-9197, www.colettes.com, from $255).

> *Retrace your path by going north on Hurricane Ridge Rd. (18 mi/29 km) to return to Port Angeles.*

DAY 3: Port Angeles to Lake Quinault

170 miles/270 kilometers | 5.5-6 hours

ROUTE OVERVIEW: US-101 • Upper Hoh Rd. • US-101

❶ Your first stop today is **Lake Crescent** (www.nps.gov/olym) and its sapphire waters. With cold depths measured at more than 1,000 feet, this lake is a place of beauty and mystery—and the only place in the world to fish for Beardslee trout. From the southeastern side of the lake, hike to

HURRICANE RIDGE IN OLYMPIC NATIONAL PARK

KAYAKERS ON LAKE CRESCENT

Best BEACHES

WASHINGTON

- **Lake Crescent** (US-101, www.nps.gov/olym) offers easy swimming and access to boats and paddleboards.
- **Rialto Beach** (west end of Mora Rd., www.nps.gov/olym) boasts sea stacks, tidepools, and, best of all, solitude.

OREGON

- **Cannon Beach** (access along S. Hemlock St., www.cannonbeach.org) is where you'll find the ever-popular, photogenic Haystack Rock.
- **Oswald West State Park** (Arch Cape, 800/551-6949, http://oregonstateparks.org, daily year-round, free) is home to driftwood-laden and surfer-friendly Short Sands Beach.

▲ OREGON'S CANNON BEACH

Marymere Falls (1.8 mi/2.9 km round-trip, 45 minutes, easy), a spectacular 90-foot waterfall. The trail starts at the Storm King Ranger Station.

> Take US-101 W for 18 miles (29 km) to the Storm King Ranger Station at Lake Crescent.

TRAIL TO MARYMERE FALLS

❷ Plan on lunch in the old logging town of **Forks.** After lunch, set out to experience the highlight of your day: the **Hoh Rain Forest** (18 mi/29 km east along Upper Hoh Rd., www.nps.gov/olym), the idyllic western section of Olympic National Park. The **Hall of Mosses** (0.8 mi/1.3 km loop, 20 minutes, easy) and **Spruce Nature Trail** (1.25 mi/2 km loop, 30 minutes, easy) reveal a lush, canopied wonderland.

> Continue on US-101 W for 32 miles (51 km) to Forks, then drive on US-101 S for 13 miles (21 km) to Upper Hoh Rd. Turn left to reach Hoh Rain Forest Visitor Center (18 mi/29 km).

❸ Head south on US-101 to **Lake Quinault** and the **Quinault Rain Forest,** exploring some of the several trails in the area. Check in at historic

Lake Quinault Lodge (345 S. Shore Rd., 360/288-2900 or 800/562-6672, www.olympicnationalparks.com, from $229) for a relaxing evening. This regal lodge benefits from its magnificent setting on the lake.

> Follow Upper Hoh Rd. back to US-101, then turn left and take US-101 S for 52 miles (84 km) to Lake Quinault.

DAY 4: Lake Quinault to Cannon Beach

150 miles/241 kilometers | 4 hours

ROUTE OVERVIEW: US-101 • WA-4 • WA-401 • US-101 • US-101 BUS • US-101

❶ Get an early start, following US-101 along Willapa Bay before taking the Astoria-Megler Bridge across the Columbia River into Oregon. Stop in **Astoria** for lunch before climbing the 164-step spiral staircase to the top of the **Astoria Column** (1 Coxcomb Dr., 503/325-2963, sunrise-sunset daily, parking $2) for the perfect view of the river and coast.

> Follow US-101 S for 96 miles (154 km) to WA-4 E. Turn left and take WA-4 for 5 miles (8 km). At WA-401 S, turn right and drive for 12 miles (19 km) until US-101. Turn left, cross into Oregon, and take US-101 S for 4 miles (6 km) into Astoria.

❷ Check out the **Columbia River Maritime Museum** (1792 Marine Dr., 503/325-2323, 9:30am-5pm daily, $14 adults, $5 children 6-17), which displays some 30,000 artifacts of fishing, shipping, and military history. Docked behind the museum is the *Lightship Columbia;* it once served as a floating lighthouse.

FORT CLATSOP

❸ Explore **Fort Clatsop** (92343 Fort Clatsop Rd., 503/861-2471, www.nps.gov/lewi, 8am-5pm daily Labor Day-mid-June, 8am-6pm daily mid-June-Labor Day, $5 peak season, $3 Labor Day-mid-June). The centerpiece of sprawling **Lewis and Clark National Historical Park** is a reconstruction of the explorers' encampment during the grueling winter of 1805-1806.

> Head south from central Astoria until you reach Olney Ave. Turn right onto Olney, then make a left onto 5th St., which becomes US-101 BUS. Follow this across the Youngs River and Lewis and Clark River for 4 miles (6 km), then take a left onto Fort Clatsop Rd. and continue for less than a mile to reach the fort.

❹ Continue past the little towns of **Gearhart** and **Seaside** before arriving at artsy **Cannon Beach**—home to impressive **Haystack Rock** (beach access along S. Hemlock St.). This icon

COLUMBIA RIVER MARITIME MUSEUM

HAYSTACK ROCK AT CANNON BEACH

▶ Playlist

PACIFIC COAST HIGHWAY: WASHINGTON AND OREGON

SONGS

- **"Modern Girl" by Sleater-Kinney:** This all-female rock group hails from Washington, and is firmly ensconced in the Pacific Northwest music scene. Signed by legendary Seattle label Sub Pop Records, Sleater-Kinney rocks out so loud that you just have to scream along.

- **"Carry the Zero" by Built to Spill:** With his arrival in Seattle in 1989, lead singer and guitarist Doug Martsch led Built to Spill to become one of the Pacific Northwest's most influential alt-rock bands. This song builds and builds and builds, climbing to a musical and emotional crescendo that mirrors the dramatic escarpments that border the Pacific Ocean.

- **"Trailer Trash" by Modest Mouse:** The entirety of the 1997 album *The Lonesome Crowded West* by this Washington-bred, Portland-based band seems tailored to a road trip—wide-open, expansive, plaintive. But this song in particular feels like a richly woven narrative, full of twists and turns and a musical denouement fit for an air guitar moment.

of the Oregon coast attracts seabirds, marinelife, and photo-happy road-trippers. It's best approached while strolling south along the beach from town, but to grab a quick photo, follow a set of public stairs leading down from Hemlock Street at Arbor Lane.

> *Take Fort Clatsop Rd. back out to US-101 BUS and turn left. Follow this for 2 miles (3 km), then take US-101 S for 19 miles (31 km) to reach Cannon Beach.*

5 Check in at the enchanting **Stephanie Inn** (2740 S. Pacific St., 800/633-3466, http://stephanieinn.com, from $269), then finish the evening with a fine meal and local craft beer.

DAY 5: Cannon Beach to Portland

80 miles/129 kilometers | 2 hours

ROUTE OVERVIEW: US-101 • US-26

1 From Cannon Beach, head east to **Portland.** Once you're in the city, check into the well-appointed and historic **Sentinel** (614 SW 11th Ave., 503/224-3400, www.sentinelhotel.com, from $156). Leave your bags and your car here. Portland is easy to get around on foot, by bike, or by public transit.

> *Go north on US-101 for 4 miles (6 km). Take US-26 E for 78 miles (126 km) to reach Portland.*

2 Browse the famed **Powell's City of Books** (1005 W. Burnside St., 800/878-7323, www.powells.com, 11am-9pm

POWELL'S CITY OF BOOKS

daily), where more than 1.5 million new and used books take up residence in an entire city block.

❸ Enjoy a colorful, indulgent treat at the city's famous **Voodoo Doughnut** (22 SW 3rd Ave., 503/241-4704, www.voodoodoughnut.com, 24 hours daily).

GOODIES FROM VOODOO DOUGHNUT

❹ At sprawling **Washington Park** (4001 SW Canyon Rd., 503/823-2525, www.portlandonline.com, free, parking $1.60/hour, $4/day Oct.-Mar., $6.40/day Apr.-Sept.), you can sip tea in the **Portland Japanese Garden** (611 SW Kingston Ave., 503/223-1321, www.japanesegarden.com, noon-7pm Mon., 10am-7pm Tues.-Sun., $15 adults, $10.50 children 6-17). Arbors, pagodas, bridges, ponds, and stone walkways complement the meditative garden's landscape.

❺ Ride a bike along the banks of the **Willamette River** before winding up **downtown** for dinner at **Dan & Louis Oyster Bar** (208 SW Ankeny St., 503/227-5906, www.danandlouis.com, 11am-9pm Mon.-Thurs., 11am-10pm Fri.-Sat., noon-9pm Sun., $10-27), which has been slinging fresh oysters and seafood since 1907.

DAY 6: Portland to Newport

220 miles/355 kilometers | 6 hours

ROUTE OVERVIEW: US-26 • US-101 • OR-131 • Three Capes Scenic Route • US-101

1 Get up early for the 90-minute drive back to Cannon Beach. Once you arrive, head south to soak up memorable views along the coast. Wander in the shade of cedar and spruce and among ferns and salmonberry at **Oswald West State Park** (Arch Cape, 503/368-3575, http://oregonstateparks.org, daily year-round, free), then walk the half-mile trail beneath the highway to **Short Sand Beach,** a premier surfing destination.

> Take US-26 W for 74 miles (119 km) to US-101. Take US-101 S for 4 miles (6 km) to reach Cannon Beach. Continue south on US-101 for 6 miles (10 km) to reach the state park. Continue south for 4 miles (6 km) to Short Sand Beach.

2 Continue to the **Three Capes Scenic Route,** a well-marked stretch that strings together three captivating bluffs: **Cape Meares, Cape Lookout,** and **Cape Kiwanda.** Try to spot migrating whales from the **Cape Meares State Scenic Viewpoint** (Cape Meares Lighthouse Dr., 503/842-3182, http://oregonstateparks.org).

> Head south for 30 miles (48 km) on US-101 to Tillamook. Turn right into OR-131 and drive west for 2 miles (3 km). Turn right onto Bayocean Rd., following signs for the Three Capes Scenic Route. In about 6 miles (10 km), you'll reach Cape Meares. From here, continue south for 13 miles (21 km) on Bayshore Dr./Netarts Bay Dr./Cape Lookout Rd. to reach Cape Lookout. Next, head south on Cape Lookout Rd. for 3 miles (5 km), then turn right onto Sandlake Rd. Follow this for 6 miles (10 km) and continue onto Ferry Rd./McPhillips Dr. for 1 mile (1.6 km) to reach Cape Kiwanda.

3 Drive south to **Lincoln City,** a good stop for lunch. If you're here during June or October, head to the beach to watch colorful soaring kites. Keep heading south to check out **Devils Punchbowl** (west end of 1st St., http://oregonstateparks.gov), a wave-sculpted basin where sea and rock engage in a continuous battle.

> From Cape Kiwanda, head south on Cape Kiwanda Dr./McPhillips Dr. for 1 mile (1.6 km). Turn left onto Pacific Ave., then take a right onto Brooten Rd. and continue for 3 miles (5 km). Turn right to get onto US-101 S and continue for 19 miles (31 km) to reach Lincoln City. To reach Devils Punchbowl, head south on US-101 for another 17 miles (27 km).

BRIDGE NEAR NEWPORT

Best VIEWS

WASHINGTON

- The **Space Needle** (400 Broad St., 206/905-2100, www.spaceneedle. com, 8am-midnight daily, $19-29 adults, $13-18 children 5-12) in Seattle was built for panoramic views of Puget Sound and, on a clear day, Mount Rainier.

- The **Seattle Great Wheel** (1301 Alaskan Way, 206/623-8600, www.seattlegreatwheel.com, 10am-11pm Sun.-Thurs., 10am-midnight Fri.-Sat., $14 adults, $9 children 3-11) shows off the glittering city skyline.

- **Hurricane Ridge** (Hurricane Ridge Rd., www.nps.gov/olym) rises 5,757 feet from the Strait of Juan de Fuca, with views stretching from the Cascades to the Olympic Peninsula and beyond.

▲ SEATTLE GREAT WHEEL

OREGON

- **Ecola State Park** (84318 Ecola State Park Rd., 503/436-2844, www. oregonstateparks.org, dawn-dusk daily, $5 per vehicle) is where you'll find the most photographed view on the Oregon coast: the iconic Haystack Rock.

- **Cape Perpetua** (visitors center 2400 US-101, 541/547-3289, www. fs.usda.gov, 10am-4:30pm daily, $5 per vehicle) yields endless vistas of the coast from a rustic, WPA-built observation point.

▲ CAPE PERPETUA

4 In **Newport,** visit the renowned **Oregon Coast Aquarium** (2820 SE Ferry Slip Rd., 541/867-3474, www.aquarium.org, 10am-6pm daily May-Sept., 10am-5pm daily Oct.-Apr., $23 adults, $15-20 children). Once the home of the killer whale that played the title role in *Free Willy,* now the aquarium offers exhibits devoted to every kind of marine environment. See a giant Pacific octopus, a massive creature that can be quite shy, and don't miss the underwater tunnel that goes through a deepwater tank for a peek at the sharks.

> Keep heading south on US-101 for 7 miles (11 km) to reach Newport.

5 Head to Newport's quaint **Nye Beach** neighborhood for dinner. Stay at the literary-themed **Sylvia Beach Hotel** (267 NW Cliff St., 541/265-5428, www.sylviabeachhotel.com, from $135), which has rooms dedicated to authors like Jane Austen. It's the perfect place for curling up with a good book.

DAY 7: Newport to Gold Beach

190 miles/305 kilometers | 4.5-5 hours

ROUTE OVERVIEW: US-101

1 Fill up your tank for a forested drive between the mountains of the Coast Range and the Pacific Ocean. **Heceta Head Lighthouse** (92072 US-101, 541/547-3416, http://oregonstateparks.org, free, parking $5), one of the most photographed lighthouses in the

United States, is perched at the top of 1,000-foot-high **Heceta Head.**

> Take US-101 S for 38 miles (61 km), then go right onto Summer St. and follow it for less than a mile to reach the lighthouse.

2 Just past the lighthouse, spectacular windswept sand takes shape along the **Oregon Dunes National Recreation Area,** which stretches 47 miles from Florence in the north to North Bend in the south. The artistry of these crests of sand—some as high as 500 feet—inspired Frank Herbert's iconic sci-fi novel *Dune.* Put on a pair of goggles to ride the sand on a dune buggy tour with **Sandland Adventures** (85366 US-101 S., 541/997-8087, www.sandland.com, 9am-5pm daily summer, winter hours vary, $18 pp) or **Sand Dunes Frontier** (83960 US-101, 541/997-3544, www.sanddunesfrontier.com, 9am-6pm daily, $14 pp). Both outfitters are just south of the town of **Florence.**

> Continue south on US-101 for 14 miles (23 km) to reach Sandland Adventures. Sand Dunes Frontier is 3 miles (5 km) farther south on US-101.

3 Continue south, passing Lakeside, North Bend, and Coos Bay. Stop for photo ops in **Bandon,** with its dramatic views of boulders, sea stacks, and **Cape Blanco Lighthouse** (91100 Cape Blanco Rd., tours 10am-3:15pm Wed.-Mon. Apr.-Oct., $2 adults, free for children), the oldest lighthouse in Oregon.

> Take US-101 S for 68 miles (109 km) to reach Bandon. To reach the lighthouse, continue another 23 miles (37 km) south,

OREGON DUNES NATIONAL RECREATION AREA

BANDON, OREGON

then turn right onto Cape Blanco Rd. and follow it for 5 miles (8 km).

④ End your trip by spending a night at the luxurious and peaceful **Tu Tu' Tun Lodge** (96550 North Bank Rogue River Rd., 541/247-6664 or 800/864-6357, www.tututun.com, from $175), high above the Rogue River. To get there, you'll need to head inland, but the views are more than worth it. The lodge is northeast of **Gold Beach.**

> Get back onto US-101 S via Cape Blanco Rd. (5 mi/8 km). Go south on US-101 for 25 miles (40 km). Turn left at Edison Creek Rd. Follow this for 2.5 miles (4 km), then turn left onto North Bank Rogue River Rd. This will lead you to the lodge in 3 miles (5 km).

Getting There

AIR

The **Seattle-Tacoma International Airport** (SEA, 17801 International Blvd., 800/544-1965 or 206/787-5388, www.portseattle.org/sea-tac) is the usual point of entry and is served by about two dozen airlines. Another option is **Portland International** (PDX, 7000 NE Airport Way, 877/739-4636, www.pdx.com), which is only a three-hour drive from Seattle, over the Oregon border.

TRAIN

Amtrak (King Street Station, 303 S. Jackson St., Seattle, 800/872-7245, www.amtrak.com) provides transport service throughout the country to the Northwest. The Coast Starlight connects Seattle, Portland, Sacramento, Oakland, and Los Angeles. Amtrak also runs the Cascade Line, which runs between Eugene, Oregon, and Vancouver, British Columbia, with stops in Portland and Seattle.

BUS

Greyhound (503 S. Royal Brougham Way, Seattle, 800/231-2222, www.greyhound.com) offers special discounts to students and seniors, with routes and stops sticking to major highways and cities.

BoltBus (648 SW Salmon St., Portland, 877/265-8287, www.boltbus.com) is the cheapest way to travel south from Vancouver, British Columbia, with stops in Seattle, Portland, and Eugene.

CAR

From the **Seattle airport,** it's 14 miles (23 km) to downtown Seattle via WA-518 and I-5. With traffic, the drive is 30-45 minutes. Take exit 164A for Dearborn Street toward Madison Street to reach downtown. To get to Seattle from **Portland,** it's a three-hour drive of 170 miles (275 km) via I-5.

Getting Back

It's a nine-hour drive (465 mi/750 km) via US-101, OR-38, and I-5 to return to **Seattle** from Gold Beach. It's a 6.5-hour trip (315 mi/505 km) via US-101, OR-38, I-5, and I-84 to get to **Portland** from Gold Beach, a good option for travelers who don't want to drive all the way back to Seattle.

To continue on to **Crescent City** to drive the California section of the Pacific Coast Highway, continue south on US-101 for 54 miles (87 km), which will take about an hour.

📍 **CONNECT WITH**

● At Seattle and Portland: **Best of the Pacific Northwest** (PAGE 216)

● At Portland: **Oregon Trail** (PAGE 78)

● At Gold Beach: **Pacific Coast Highway: California** (PAGE 124)

PACIFIC CREST TRAIL: OREGON AND WASHINGTON

WHY GO: Cascade Mountains, Crater Lake, volcanic hikes, river tubing, lake boating, Mount Hood, Mount Rainier

TOTAL DISTANCE: 1,425 miles/ 2,300 kilometers

NUMBER OF DAYS: 9

SEASONS: Early summer through fall

START: Ashland, Oregon

END: Manning Park, British Columbia

▼ MOUNT HOOD

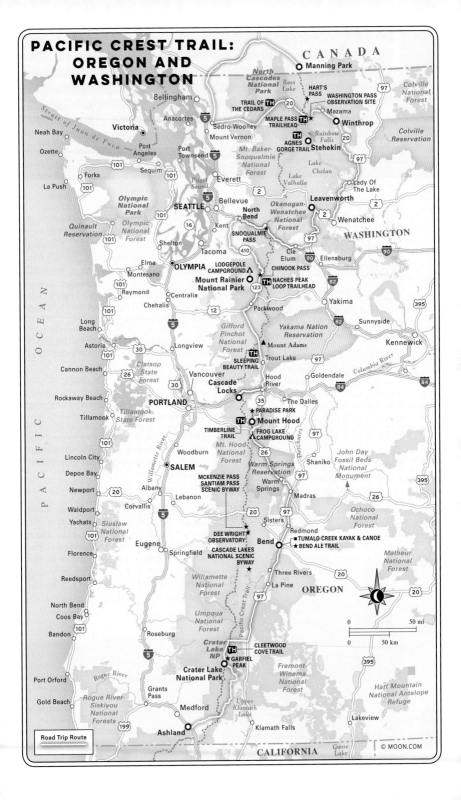

or travelers eager to explore the Pacific Northwest's astonishing natural beauty, this road trip offers it all—from hiking rocky mountain peaks to visiting a lakeside town accessible only by boat. The journey starts with epic Crater Lake, then heads north to the Deschutes River and the town of Bend before looping toward towering Mount Hood. The drive follows the Columbia River Gorge for a bit as it swings over the Cascade Locks and into Mount Rainier National Park, North Cascades National Park, and finally into Canada's Manning Park. It's here where the Pacific Crest Trail ends.

DAY 1: Ashland to Crater Lake National Park

75 miles/121 kilometers | 1.5-2 hours

ROUTE OVERVIEW: OR-66 • Dead Indian Memorial Rd. • OR-140 • Volcanic Legacy Scenic Byway

1 In **Ashland,** enjoy a decadent breakfast at **Morning Glory Cafe** (1149 Siskiyou Blvd., 541/488-8636, www.morningglorycafe.org, 8am-1:30pm daily, $10-15) before heading out of town. This place is famous for breakfast and brunch, so expect a line on weekends.

2 Drive 1.5 hours to **Crater Lake National Park** (541/594-3000, www.nps.gov/crla, hours vary by entrance, $25 per vehicle May-Oct., $10 per vehicle Nov.-Apr.). Here, walk along the edge of a giant caldera and stare into the abyss of the deepest lake in the nation.

> Head east out of Ashland via Main St. (3 mi/5 km). Use OR-66 to connect to Dead Indian Memorial Rd., following this for 36 miles (58 km). At OR-140, turn right and follow OR-140 E for 6 miles (10 km) to Volcanic Legacy Scenic Byway. Turn left and drive Volcanic Legacy Scenic Byway for 30 miles (48 km) to Crater Lake National Park.

3 In the park, hike down to the lake's lapping shore on the **Cleetwood Cove Trail** (2 mi/3.2 km round-trip, 1 hour, moderate). This is the only official path to the lakeshore. There are plenty of benches along the way offering places to rest.

4 There's no better way to experience the scale and magnitude of Crater Lake than by taking a **boat tour** (Cleetwood Cove, www.travelcraterlake.com, late June-early Sept., $32-57).

5 Retreat to historic **Crater Lake Lodge** (565 Rim Dr., 866/292-6720, www.travelcraterlake.com, late May-mid-Oct., $201-268) for an elegant Pacific Northwest-themed dinner in the dining room and a soft bed in a cozy guest room. The rooms here offer the best views in the park.

CRATER LAKE

KEY RESERVATIONS

- Book a **few months** in advance for a room at **Crater Lake Lodge** in **Crater Lake National Park** and for a campsite at **Lodgepole Campground** in **Okanogan-Wenatchee National Forest.**

Top ③ PACIFIC CREST TRAIL: OREGON AND WASHINGTON

① Gaze into the abyss of **Crater Lake National Park,** the deepest lake in the United States (PAGE 252).

② Rent a tube for a leisurely **float** down the **Deschutes River** (PAGE 254).

③ Hike the glacier-encrusted peaks of **North Cascades National Park** (PAGE 260).

DAY 2: Crater Lake to Bend

120 miles/193 kilometers | 3 hours

ROUTE OVERVIEW: OR-138 • US-97 • OR-58 • Cascade Lakes Scenic Byway

1 Hike from Crater Lake Lodge to the top of **Garfield Peak** (3.1 mi/5 km round-trip, 1.5 hours, moderate) to get a bird's-eye view of Crater Lake, Mount McLoughlin, Mount Thielsen, and the surrounding terrain.

2 As you drive north on the **Cascade Lakes National Scenic Byway** (www.oregon.gov/odot, May-Nov.), you'll venture into the heart of Central Oregon's mountains, where the Three Sisters, Broken Top, and Bachelor Butte tower over the road. Continue to the city of **Bend**.

> Depart Crater Lake National Park via OR-138 E (15 mi/24 km). From OR-138, turn left on US-97 N. Follow this for 18 miles (29 km) to OR-58 W. Drive OR-58 W to Cascade Lakes Scenic Byway (13 mi/21 km). At Cascade Lakes Scenic Byway, turn right and continue for 69 miles (111 km) into Bend.

3 Stop for lunch at woodsy **Brown Owl** (550 SW Industrial Way, 541/797-6581, www.brownowlbend.com, 11am-11pm daily, $9-13). Inside this lofted log cabin is a chandelier built into a canoe; outside on the patio are giant stumps for seating.

4 Rent a tube at **Tumalo Creek Kayak & Canoe** (Riverbend Park, 799 SW Columbia St., 541/317-9407, www.tumalocreek.com, 10am-3:30pm daily June-Sept., $15 for 2 hours, $30 for full day) to float the **Deschutes River** through the center of town.

5 Visit some of the craft breweries on the **Bend Ale Trail** (www.visitbend.com), passport in hand, to taste the beers that have made Bend's 20-plus microbreweries famous. No purchase is required to get a passport stamp; just show up with your printed passport or your app. Spend the night at a hotel in town.

DAY 3: Bend to Mount Hood

230 miles/370 kilometers | 5 hours

ROUTE OVERVIEW: US-20 • OR-242 • OR-126 • US-20 • OR-126 • US-97 • US-26

1 Start your day with a scenic drive on the 82-mile (132-km) **McKenzie Pass-Santiam Pass Scenic Byway** (from Sisters to McKenzie Pass, July-Oct.). Allow plenty of time to stop for photos during the wow-worthy drive through stark-black lava fields, pointy glacial peaks, and thundering waterfalls. The byway starts in the town of **Sisters**.

> Drive US-97 N for less than 5 miles (8 km) out of Bend. Merge onto US-20 W (19 mi/31 km) to Sisters.

2 Along the loop, stop at **Dee Wright Observatory** (OR-242, www.fs.usda.gov, May-Nov.). Climb the stairs to a little lava rock castle overlooking an otherworldly volcanic landscape at McKenzie Pass.

> In Sisters, pick up OR-242/McKenzie Pass-Santiam Pass Scenic Byway and take it west for 15 miles (24 km) to Dee Wright Observatory.

3 **Mount Hood** is Oregon's tallest volcano. Sleep in its towering shadow when you grab a campsite at **Frog Lake Campground** (US-26 and Frog Creek Rd., www.fs.usda.gov, May-Sept.), so named for the frogs that serenade you at night.

MCKENZIE PASS

DAY 4: Mount Hood to Cascade Locks

80 miles/129 kilometers | 2-2.5 hours

ROUTE OVERVIEW: US-26 • Timberline Hwy. • US-26 • OR-35 • US-30 • I-84

❶ Get up early to hit the road for your breakfast spot. After stuffing your belly to your heart's content at the gourmet buffet at the 1938-built **Timberline Lodge** (27500 E. Timberline Rd., 503/272-3311, www.timberlinelodge. com, 7:30am-10am and 11:30am-2pm Mon.-Fri., 7:30am-10:30am and 11:30am-3pm Sat.-Sun., $18-25), it's time to hit the trail.

> Go north on US-26 for 7 miles (11 km). Turn right to join Timberline Hwy. and continue for 6 miles (10 km) to reach the lodge.

❷ From the lodge, hike the **Timberline Trail** to **Paradise Park** (12.4 mi/20 km round-trip, 6-7 hours, strenuous). The meadows are colorful throughout hiking season—lush green grasses speckled with wildflowers in June and July, then ablaze with reds and yellows in the autumn—and always framed by the rocky outcroppings of Mount Hood's summit.

❸ Drive through **Hood River** and the **Columbia River Gorge** to the town of **Cascade Locks.** Soak up the view of the historic Bridge of the Gods from your perch at **Thunder Island Brewing**

VIEW OF MOUNT HOOD

> Continue west on OR-242 for 23 miles (37 km), then go north on OR-126 for 18 miles (29 km). Take US-20 E for 28 miles (45 km) to get back to Sisters. Take OR-126 E for 19 miles (31 km), then go north on US-97 for 26 miles (42 km). Go north on US-26 for 55 miles (89 km). Make a right onto Frog Creek Rd. to reach the campground.

❹ Head to **Mt. Hood Brewing Co.** (87304 Government Camp Loop, Government Camp, 503/272-3172, www. mthoodbrewing.com, 11am-9pm daily, $12-26) for dinner. Their ales are made with pure glacial water from the flanks of its namesake volcano.

> Go north on US-26 for 8 miles (13 km). Take a right onto Government Camp Loop to reach the brewpub. Retrace your path to return to your campsite for the night (8 mi/13 km).

COLUMBIA RIVER GORGE

GO *Wild*

Fans of Cheryl Strayed's book *Wild* and the movie starring Reese Witherspoon won't want to miss the chance to visit these filming locations.

- **Ashland, Oregon:** By the time Cheryl reached Ashland, she had hit her stride and was gaining confidence as a long-distance hiker. Scenes were filmed at shops and restaurants along **Main Street** and at **The Breadboard** (744 N. Main St., 541/488-0295, www.breadboardashland.com, 7am-2pm daily, $8-13), where Cheryl sinks her teeth into a juicy burger.

- **Crater Lake, Oregon:** It's easy to see why Cheryl felt such a baffling sense of disbelief upon her first glimpse of Crater Lake. The lake's deep-blue color (the result of ultraclear water that absorbs every shade of light except blue) is remarkable. Walk in her footsteps on the **Crater Lake Rim Trail** (6 mi/9.7 km one-way, 3 hours, moderate).

- **Cascade Locks, Oregon:** The finale of Cheryl's captivating story occurs at the northern end of the Oregon section of the Pacific Crest Trail. In Cascade Locks, the historic **Bridge of the Gods** (Wa Na Pa St., $1 pedestrian toll, $2 auto toll) stretches over a narrow section of the mighty Columbia River, offering passage from Oregon into Washington. You can cross the bridge by car or foot, or admire it from town or by walking through the **Cascade Locks Marine Park** (395 Portage Rd., 541/374-8619, www.portofcascadelocks.com).

BRIDGE OF THE GODS

(515 NW Portage Rd., 971/231-4599, www.thunderislandbrewing.com, 11am-9pm Sun.-Thurs., 11am-10pm Fri.-Sat., $10-15).

> Take Timberline Hwy. for 5 miles (8 km) to connect to US-26 E. Stay on this for 2 miles (3 km) to OR-35. Follow OR-35 N for 39 miles (63 km) to reach Hood River. Take US-30 west through Hood River (2 mi/3 km), then get onto I-84 and drive west for 17 miles (27 km). Take exit 44 to reach Cascade Locks.

④ Unwind in a comfy river-view room at the **Best Western Plus Columbia River Inn** (735 Wa Na Pa St., 541/374-8777, www.bestwestern.com, $130-250).

DAY 5: Cascade Locks to Mount Rainier National Park

180 miles/290 kilometers | 5-6 hours

ROUTE OVERVIEW: WA-14 • WA-141 • Forest Rd. 23 • WA-131 • US-12 • WA-123 • WA-410

① Cross the **Bridge of the Gods** ($2 auto toll) and drive for an hour to **Trout Lake,** where **Mount Adams** looms larger than life. Hike to the top of **Sleeping Beauty** (2.3 mi/3.7 km round-trip, 1.5 hours, moderate), an ancient volcanic basalt flow, to get expansive views of the southern Washington Cascade Range, including the spectacular sight of Mount Adams. To access the trailhead, turn right onto Forest Road 40, following signs for Sleeping Beauty Trail. The parking area is in 0.4 mile.

TROUT LAKE AND MOUNT ADAMS

APPROACHING CHINOOK PASS

> After crossing the Columbia River, head east on WA-14 for 22 miles (35 km) to WA-141. Turn left (north) and follow WA-141 for 23 miles (37 km) through Trout Lake. Turn right onto Trout Lake Creek Rd. and follow this for 5 miles (8 km). Veer right onto Forest Rd. 8810, continue for 6 miles (10 km), then turn right onto Forest Rd. 40 to reach the trailhead.

❷ Get a quick bite to eat back in Trout Lake, then make the twisty, three-hour drive to **Packwood,** where you can stock up on camping supplies and groceries. Enter **Mount Rainier National Park** (www.nps.gov/mora, $30 per vehicle) on WA-123 and drive to the top of **Chinook Pass,** where the PCT crosses WA-410.

> Retrace your path back down to Trout Lake via Forest Rd. 8810 (13 mi/21 km). Take Forest Rd. 23 for 51 miles (82 km), after which point the road becomes Cispus Rd. Continue for 2.5 miles (4 km), veer right onto WA-131, then turn right in 1 mile (1.6 km) onto US-12. Continue

for 16 miles (26 km) to reach Packwood. Take WA-123 north for 16 miles (26 km), then turn right onto WA-410 and continue for 4 miles (6 km) to cross Chinook Pass.

❸ The **Naches Peak Loop** (3.6 mi/5.8 km round-trip, 1.5-2 hours, easy) offers the chance to get up close and personal with the biggest volcano in the Cascade Range. It's an easy hike with incredible views. The trailhead is on the south side of WA-410 at Chinook Pass.

❹ Pitch a tent at **Lodgepole Campground** (WA-410, Naches, 509/653-1401, reservations 877/444-6777, www.recreation.gov, Memorial Day-Labor Day, $18), just east of the pass. Reservations are recommended. The campground is on the east side of the Cascade crest in the Okanogan-Wenatchee National Forest, and is likely to be sunnier and warmer than campgrounds inside the park.

> Follow WA-410 east for 8 miles (13 km) to reach the campground.

MOUNT RAINIER FROM THE NACHES PEAK LOOP TRAIL

▶ *Playlist*

PACIFIC CREST TRAIL: OREGON AND WASHINGTON

SONGS

- **"Let Go" by RAC:** Do you need a "I've been hiking for hours and I'm exhausted" turbocharged boost? This song—bouncy, poppy, and irresistibly upbeat—is it. It is produced by Portland-based Portuguese-American DJ/producer André Allen Anjos, who goes by his stage name RAC.

- **"Ripple" by Dusted and Eric D. Johnson:** When you reach the quiet conclusion of the Pacific Crest Trail, play this. The spare instrumentation and tender lyrics let the moment breathe. It's not surprising this song featured prominently in the PCT-hiking film *Wild,* based on Cheryl Strayed's book.

PODCASTS

- *Cascade Hiker:* Everything you ever wanted to know—from gear and nutrition tips to personal stories—about hiking and backpacking in Oregon, with a special focus on the Pacific Crest Trail and the Pacific Northwest National Scenic Trail.

MOUNT RAINIER

DAY 6: Mount Rainier National Park to Leavenworth

270 miles/435 kilometers | 6 hours

ROUTE OVERVIEW: WA-410 • WA-169 • WA-18 • I-90 • WA-970 • US-97 • US-2

❶ The steep terrain of the North Cascades makes for a circuitous two-hour drive to **North Bend.** Get food at **North Bend Bar & Grill** (145 E. North Bend Way, 425/888-1234, www.northbend-barandgrill.com, 8am-midnight daily, $13-24) before climbing over the mountains at **Snoqualmie Pass.**

> Follow WA-410 northwest for 51 miles (82 km) to WA-169 N. Use WA-169 to connect with WA-18. Drive WA-18 E for 8 miles (13 km) to I-90 E. Merge onto I-90 and drive it 5 miles (8 km) to North Bend. From here, take I-90 E for 24 miles (39 km) to Snoqualmie Pass.

❷ Circle the eastern edge of the craggy Cascade Range on your way to **Leavenworth,** an adorable Bavarian-themed village. If you have time, head about

LEAVENWORTH

30 miles (48 km) northwest of town for an evening hike on the PCT to **Lake Valhalla** (6.2 mi/10 km round-trip, 3 hours, moderate). This hike along the Pacific Crest Trail takes you to a shimmering alpine lake below Lichtenberg Mountain, a sharp granite peak.

> *Continue for 32 miles (51 km) on I-90 to WA-970. Stay on WA-970 for 10 miles (16 km) to US-97. Drive north for 40 miles (64 km) to Leavenworth. Take US-2 for 31 miles (50 km), then turn right onto Forest Rd. 6700, heading northwest for 2.7 miles (4.3 km) to the trailhead parking area. Look for signs for Smithbrook Trailhead.*

❸ Sip a craft brew and sink your teeth into a locally made wurst at **Munchen-Haus** (709 Front St., 509/548-1158, www.munchenhaus.com, 11am-10pm Sun.-Thurs., 11am-1am Fri.-Sat., $7-10) before settling into your hotel room.

> *Retrace your path along Forest Rd. 6700 and US-2 to return to Leavenworth (34 mi/55 km).*

DAY 7: Leavenworth to Stehekin

55 miles/89 kilometers | 1-1.5 hours

ROUTE OVERVIEW: US-2 • US-97 ALT

❶ You've got a boat to catch, so pack an overnight bag and scoot out of your hotel early to drive one hour to the **Lady of the Lake** (1418 W. Woodin Ave., Chelan, 509/682-4584, www.ladyofthelake.com, $40-61 round-trip). This is your shuttle across Lake Chelan to **Stehekin**, a remote town at the northern tip of the lake with no roads to the outside world.

> *Take US-2 E out of Leavenworth for 20 miles (32 km) to US-97 ALT. Turn left and go north on US-97 ALT for 35 miles (56 km) to Chelan, where you'll board the boat to Stehekin.*

❷ Ride the **red bus** to **Stehekin Pastry Company** (Stehekin Valley Rd., 509/682-7742, www.stehekinpastry. com, 7:30am-5pm daily mid-June-mid-Oct., 8am-3pm Wed.-Sun. May mid-June and late Oct., $5-9) for mouthwatering cinnamon rolls.

STEHEKIN PASTRY COMPANY

❸ At **Rainbow Falls,** a 300-foot cascade splashes into a vivid plunge pool before crashing over a series of smaller rocks and boulders. From Stehekin Valley Road, follow the short path to the lower viewpoint, where the waterfall is visible in its entirety. A higher viewpoint (left of the falls) offers a closer view of the white ribbon of water. The red shuttle bus makes a stop here, or you can walk or ride a bike to this trailhead.

❹ Hike the **Agnes Gorge Trail** (5 mi/8 km round-trip, 2 hours, easy) to catch a great glimpse of Agnes Peak and end at a dramatic turquoise waterfall. Take the red bus to High Bridge, the bus turnaround. Cross High Bridge, entering North Cascades National Park, then follow the dirt road for

RAINBOW FALLS

MAPLE PASS LOOP

0.25 mile past the PCT trailhead and up the hill to the well-signed Agnes Gorge Trail.

⑤ Dine and spend the night at the **North Cascades Lodge at Stehekin** (Stehekin Valley Rd., 509/682-4494, www.lodgeatstehekin.com, $145-250), which offers charming guest rooms and warm, cozy cabins; many offer views of the lakeshore, marina, and rugged peaks across the water.

DAY 8: Stehekin to Winthrop

125 miles/201 kilometers | 2.5 hours

ROUTE OVERVIEW: US-97 • WA-153 • WA-20

① Ride the boat back down the lake and hop into your car for the 1.5-hour drive to **Mazama**. Deli sandwiches at the **Mazama Store** (50 Lost River Rd., Mazama, 509/996-2855, www.themazamastore.com, 7am-6pm daily) are surprisingly gourmet considering the shop's remote location.

> *Drive north on US-97 ALT for 5 miles (8 km) to US-97. Follow this north to WA-153 (13 mi/21 km). Take WA-153 N to WA-20 W (31 mi/50 km). Drive WA-20 for 24 miles (39 km) to Mazama.*

② Stop at **Washington Pass Observation Site** for a breathtaking view of the North Cascades Scenic Byway as it meanders through impossibly steep and jagged peaks.

> *Continue on WA-20 W for 17 miles (27 km) to Washington Pass Observation Site.*

③ Hike into **North Cascades National Park** (360/854-7200, www.nps.gov/noca, free) on the **Maple Pass Loop** (6.7 mi/10.8 km round-trip, 3.5 hours, strenuous). Get a peek at glacier-encrusted peaks on this hike around a sparkling tarn. Reach the Maple Pass trailhead (also signed as Rainy Pass

MAZAMA STORE

VIEW FROM MAPLE PASS

Multiday treks through the wilderness do wonders for the appetites of thru-hikers. These are some of the best restaurants for hungry hikers, with big portions, great deals, or impressive buffet spreads.

- **Timberline Lodge, Oregon:** Watch in awe as ravenous backpackers fill their plates with mountains of food at the famous breakfast and lunch buffets at the **Cascade Dining Room** (27500 E. Timberline Rd., 503/272-3104, www.timberlinelodge.com, 7:30am-10am and 11:30am-2pm Mon.-Fri., 7:30am-10:30am and 11:30am-3pm Sat.-Sun., $18 breakfast, $25 lunch). With an elegant setting and a divine array of fresh, flavorful foods, this buffet attracts everyone from mud-crusted thru-hikers to polished luxury travelers.

- **Cascade Locks, Oregon:** If you're craving fresh veggies, the all-you-can-eat salad bar at **Bridgeside** (745 NW Wa Na Pa St., 541/374-8477, www.bridgesidedining. com, 6:30am-8pm daily, $9-18) satisfies your craving. Pile your plate as many times as you'd like with salad bar fixins—leafy greens, raw vegetables, cheeses, olives, dressings, nuts, and seeds—plus broccoli slaw, potato salad, and pasta salad.

- **Stehekin, Washington:** The giant cinnamon rolls at **Stehekin Pastry Company** (Stehekin Valley Rd., 509/682-7742, www. stehekinpastry.com, 7:30am-5pm daily mid-June-mid-Oct., 8am-3pm Wed.-Sun. May mid-June and late Oct., $5-9) beckon PCT hikers for days before their arrival in town. As this is the last stop in civilization for Canada-bound hikers, many take cinnamon rolls to go when they hit the trail. Ride the red bus or walk to the bakery to see (and taste) what makes these pastries famous.

and Lake Ann) via the large parking area located on the south side of WA-20.

> Go another 6 miles (10 km) west on WA-20 to reach the trailhead.

❹ Retreat to the luxurious, modern **Rolling Huts** (18381 WA-20, Winthrop, 509/996-4442, www.rollinghuts.com, $145) for the night. Equal parts tiny house, cabin, and luxury apartment, these unique "huts" are unlike anything else. You'll have to backtrack a bit on WA-20 to get here, so leave any gear you won't need for the day when you pass by on your way to the Maple Pass trailhead.

> Reach Rolling Huts via WA-20 E (26 mi/42 km).

DAY 9: Winthrop to Manning Park, British Columbia

290 miles/470 kilometers | 7 hours

ROUTE OVERVIEW: WA-20 • Lost River Rd. • WA-20 • WA-9 • BC-1 • BC-3

❶ To get a last glimpse of the Pacific Crest Trail in the United States, make the precarious drive to beautiful

DIABLO LAKE FROM THE DIABLO LAKE OVERLOOK

Hart's Pass (Forest Rd. 5400), a campground and hiking area at the end of Washington's highest road. Golden larches light up the steep mountainsides in early fall. North of this point, no more roads cross the PCT.

> *Head northwest for 4 miles (6 km) on WA-20 from Rolling Huts. Turn right on Lost River Rd., then make a left to stay on Lost River Rd. (6 mi/10 km). Continue onto Forest Rd. 5400 to reach Hart's Pass (11 mi/18 km).*

② Descend from the pass and drive west through North Cascades National Park, pausing for views at the **Ross Lake Overlook** (milepost 135, WA-20) and the **Diablo Lake Overlook** (milepost 132, WA-20).

> *Return to WA-20 via Lost River Rd. (17 mi/27 km). Take WA-20 west for 44 mi (71 km) to reach Ross Lake Overlook.*

Continue west for another 3 miles (5 km) to reach the Diablo Lake Overlook.

③ Stop in **Newhalem** and walk along the **Trail of the Cedars** (Main St., 0.3 mi/0.5 km), where a suspension bridge crosses the Skagit River.

> *Drive WA-20 W for another 15 miles (24 km) to reach Newhalem.*

④ From here, you'll continue north to Canada. The PCT ends in a quiet patch of forest in the town of **Manning Park, British Columbia**, just south of **Manning Park Resort** (7500 BC-3, 604/668-5922, www.manningpark.com).

> *Follow WA-20 W to WA-9 (55 mi/89 km). Turn right on WA-9 and take it north to Sumas (39 mi/63 km). Cross into Canada and drive BC-1 E for 48 miles (77 km) to BC-3 E. Follow BC-3 to Manning Park (42 mi/68 km).*

Getting There

AIR

Portland International Airport (PDX, 7000 NE Airport Way, 877/739-4636, www.pdx.com) is the major air hub in Oregon. The PCT in Cascade Locks is less than an hour's drive from this airport. If you're planning to start your trip in central or southern Oregon instead, fly into **Eugene Airport** (EUG, 28801 Douglas Dr., 541/682-5544, www.flyeug.com) and save 2-3 hours of driving to Ashland or Crater Lake. Rental cars are available at both airports.

Close to the city of Bend, **Redmond Municipal Airport** (RDM, 2522 SE Jesse Butler Circle, Redmond, 541/548-0646, www.flyrdm.com) offers daily direct flights from Denver, Los Angeles, Phoenix, Portland, Salt Lake City, San Francisco, and Seattle.

TRAIN

The Coast Starlight line on **Amtrak** (800/872-7245, www.amtrak.com) runs north-south along the I-5 corridor with stops in Portland, Oregon City, Salem, Albany, and Eugene. These cities offer access to the central and northern sections of the PCT including the Three Sisters, Mount Jefferson, Mount Hood, and the Columbia Gorge.

Amtrak also has stations in Chemult and Klamath Falls, which are convenient to the southern parts of the PCT, including Crater Lake and Mount McLoughlin. All train stations are within 50 miles of the PCT, but you'll need a car to get into the mountains.

BUS

Greyhound (800/231-2222, www.greyhound.com, $17-26) offers bus service along the I-5 corridor and has stations in Medford (near Ashland), Portland, and a few cities in between. **BoltBus** (877/265-8287, www.boltbus.com, $17-32) travels between Portland and Seattle with stops in Tacoma.

Both bus lines offer multiple departures daily, and buses have Wi-Fi. Advance tickets are recommended, but walk-up fares are sold on an availability basis.

CAR

From **Eugene,** the drive to Ashland is 180 miles (290 km) and takes about three hours. Use I-105 E to connect with I-5 S, then OR-99. Drive OR-99 into Ashland.

From **Portland** to Ashland, the drive is 285 miles (460 km) and takes five hours. Drive I-5 S to OR-99, then take OR-99 into Ashland.

I-5 enters Oregon near Ashland and continues north-south through Portland and into Washington. The Pacific Crest Trail is directly accessible off I-5, 12 miles (19.3 km) south of Ashland. From I-5, take exit 6 toward Mount Ashland. Continue south on OR-99 to meet the PCT where it crosses the road.

I-5 is easily accessible year-round. Routes through mountain passes, however, may be hazardous and can close in winter.

Getting Back

To return to **Ashland** from Manning Park, it's 660 miles (1,065 km) and takes 13 hours via BC-3 W, BC-1 W/ Trans-Canada Highway, BC-11 S (follow signs for the United States), WA-9 S, I-5 S, and OR-99.

If you choose to book a one-way flight home, **Vancouver International Airport** (YVR, 3211 Grant McConachie Way, Richmond, 604/207-7077, www.yvr.ca) is the closest major airport to Manning Park. It's a 2.5-hour drive (145 mi/230 km) from Manning Park to the Vancouver airport via BC-3 W, BC-1 W/Trans-Canada Highway, BC-17, BC-91 N, and BC-99 N.

CONNECT WITH

- At Cascade Locks: **Columbia River Gorge and Wine Country** (PAGE 264)
- At Bend: **High Adventure in Bend** (PAGE 274)
- At Ashland: **Pacific Crest Trail: California** (PAGE 140)
- At Hood River: **Oregon Trail** (PAGE 78)

COLUMBIA RIVER GORGE AND WINE COUNTRY

WHY GO: Wine-tasting, art, quaint towns, fine dining, leisurely drives, mossy canyons, waterfalls

TOTAL DISTANCE: 380 miles/ 610 kilometers

NUMBER OF DAYS: 4

SEASONS: Spring through fall

START: Portland, Oregon

END: Walla Walla, Washington

► COLUMBIA RIVER GORGE

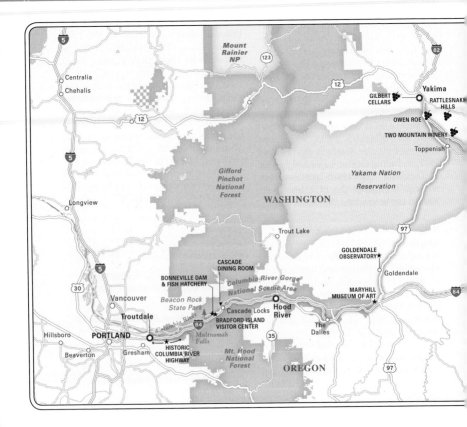

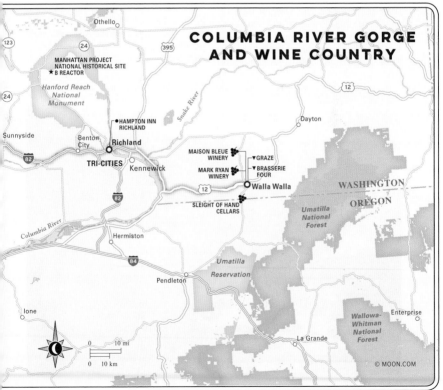

COLUMBIA RIVER GORGE AND WINE COUNTRY

© MOON.COM

Troutdale is the launching point for the Historic Columbia River Highway, your through-line for this low-key road trip. This excursion is what Sunday drives were made for. In fact, the highway was one of the first in the country designed for scenic touring. As it skirts along the Columbia River, the trip leads you through wildflowers, ferns, maple trees, and moss-covered canyons. Between Multnomah Falls and Yakima, you'll want to stop often to snap photos, stroll pathways to waterfalls, and check out the scenic viewpoints. From Yakima to Walla Walla, you'll want to stop often to visit art museums and taste the region's award-winning wines.

DAY 1: Troutdale to Hood River

85 miles/137 kilometers | 2.5-3 hours

ROUTE OVERVIEW: I-84/US-30 • Historic Columbia River Hwy. • US-30 • WA-14 • I-84 • US-30

① From Portland, it's a short drive to **Troutdale,** the official start of the **Historic Columbia River Highway.** Spend your morning on the Oregon side of the Columbia River, where the scenic journey takes you past many waterfalls. The crown jewel is **Multnomah Falls** (south of Multnomah Falls Lodge, 53000 E. Historic Columbia River Hwy., Corbett). At 635 feet tall, with an uninterrupted free fall of 542 feet, this is one of the tallest continually flowing falls in the United States. For most of the year the base of the falls is crowded with onlookers, and parking can be a trial. Options include the lot off of I-84 Multnomah Falls at exit 31, or the Columbia Gorge Highway lot directly in front of the Multnomah Falls Lodge.

> *Depart Portland via I-84/US-30 E to Troutdale (17 mi/27 km). From Troutdale, continue east on the Historic Columbia River Highway to Multnomah Falls (19 mi/31 km).*

COLUMBIA RIVER GORGE

Top ③ COLUMBIA RIVER GORGE AND WINE COUNTRY

① Experience the beauty and power of **Multnomah Falls,** one of the tallest continually flowing waterfalls in the nation (PAGE 266).

② Tour the remote **Maryhill Museum of Art,** deemed the "loneliest museum in the world" (PAGE 268).

③ Sample the terroir of Washington with **wine-tasting** in the **Rattlesnake Hills** (PAGE 269).

② Tour the Depression-era **Bonneville Dam** and its adjacent **fish hatchery**. At the dam's **Bradford Island Visitor Center** (Dam Rd., exit 40 off I-84, 541/374-8820, www.nwp.usace.army.mil/bonneville, 9am-5pm daily, free), visit historical exhibits and the fish ladder viewing area. On the guided tour, a ranger will give you a look at the generators, each of which is harnessing enough electricity to power a midsize town. Tours are conducted at 11am, 1pm, and 3pm on weekends throughout the year and daily June-August.

> *Continue east for 9 miles (14 km) along the Historic Columbia River Hwy./ US-30 to reach Bradford Island Visitors Center, just off Bonneville Way and Star Rte.*

③ Cross the river at **Cascade Locks,** then enjoy lunch on the Washington side at the Skamania Lodge's **Cascade Dining Room** (1131 SW Skamania Lodge Way, 509/314-4177, www.skamania.com, 7am-2pm and 5pm-9pm Mon.-Sat., 9am-2pm and 5pm-9pm Sun., $22-42). The food is good, but the atmosphere is better, with a wall of windows overlooking the Gorge.

> *Head northeast on Star Rte. for 1 mile (1.6 km) to Bonneville Way, which connects to US-30. Continue on US-30*

E *for 4 miles (6 km) to Cascade Locks. Cross the Bridge of the Gods and continue east on WA-14 for 5 miles (8 km) to Skamania Lodge.*

④ Spend a naturalist's dream afternoon at **Beacon Rock State Park** (34841 WA-14, 509/427-8265, http:// parks.state.wa.us, 8am-dusk daily, $10 parking). A short hiking trek up the switchback trail on the 848-foot-tall Beacon Rock yields spectacular views of the Gorge. Cross back over to the Oregon side for an evening in **Hood River**, a hip little resort town. Have dinner at one of Hood River's many brewpubs.

> *Drive southeast on Skamania Lodge Rd. At Rock Creek Dr., turn right, then make another right on WA-14 and follow this west for 7 miles (11 km). Cross back over the river and follow I-84 E to US-30 E to Hood River (26 mi/42 km).*

DAY 2: Hood River to Yakima, Washington

130 miles/209 kilometers | 3 hours

ROUTE OVERVIEW: I-84 • US-197/ US-30 • WA-14 • US-97 • I-82

① Back on the Washington side is one of the state's most remarkable cultural institutions, the **Maryhill Museum of Art** (35 Maryhill Museum of Art Dr., 509/773-3733, www.maryhillmuseum.org, 10am-5pm daily Mar. 15-Nov. 15, $9). It's as impressive as it is incongruous. Deemed "the loneliest museum in the world," this isolated gem has a wide-ranging collection that includes everything from Rodin

BEACON ROCK STATE PARK

MARYHILL MUSEUM OF ART

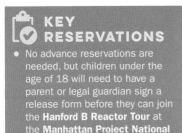

sculptures to miniature mannequins wearing French haute couture.

> *Drive east on I-84 to US-197 N/US-30 E (23 mi/37 km). At US-197 N/US-30 E, cross the river and drive for 4 miles (6 km) to WA-14 E. Take WA-14 for 15 miles (24 km) to Maryhill Museum of Art.*

② Head away from the river, making the 1.5-hour drive north to **Yakima,** your first stop in wine country. Along the way, visit **Goldendale Observatory** (1602 Observatory Dr., 509/773-3141, www.goldendaleobservatory.com, 10am-11:30pm Wed.-Sun. Apr.-Oct., 1pm-9pm Fri.-Sun. Nov.-Mar., free), home to some of the largest publicly accessible telescopes in the United States. The hilltop location provides lovely views of the surrounding region.

> *Take WA-14 E for 4 miles (6 km) to US-97. Take US-97 N for 10 miles (16 km) to Broadway St. Continue on Broadway to Columbus Ave., then to Observatory Dr. for a total of 2.5 miles (4 km) to reach the observatory.*

③ Once you reach Yakima, visit **Gilbert Cellars** (5 N. Front St., 509/249-9049, www.gilbertcellars.com, 1pm-7pm Mon.-Thurs., 1pm-9pm Fri.-Sat., 1pm-6pm Sun.). This tasting room is also the town's most stylish wine bar. Order a cheese plate to accompany the varied selection of wines. Spend the night at one of Yakima's plentiful chain hotels.

> *Take US-97 N for 63 miles (101 km), then merge onto I-82 W. Continue on I-82 for 5 miles (8 km), then take exit 33 onto Yakima Ave. to get into central Yakima.*

DAY 3: Yakima to Richland

95 miles/153 kilometers | 2.5-3 hours

ROUTE OVERVIEW: I-82 • Yakima Valley Hwy. • city streets • I-82 • I-182/US-12 • WA-240

① East of Yakima, the **Yakima Valley** is a hotbed for Washington's thriving wine industry. The most satisfying winery-touring area is the **Rattlesnake Hills,** where country roads northeast of I-82 take you to eclectic, friendly wineries. **Owen Roe** (309 Gangl Rd., 509/877-0454, www.owenroe.com, 11am-4pm daily, $10) is friendly and casual, but it's also deadly serious about the craft of making fine wine, with a primary focus on Bordeaux and Rhone varietals.

> *Drive I-82 E for 9 miles (14 km) to Thorp Rd. Turn left, then make a right on Gangl Rd. Continue straight onto Orchard Rd. to Owen Roe.*

② **Two Mountain Winery** (2151 Cheyne Rd., 509/829-3900, www.twomountainwinery.com, 10am-6pm daily) has the area's most fun tasting room,

TWO MOUNTAIN WINERY

With more than 120 wineries spread over five districts—Downtown, Southside, Westside, Airport, and Eastside—Walla Walla is home to a fine roundup of vineyards and tasting rooms worth exploring. To get out among the vines, your best bet is to visit the pastoral Southside. Here are a few top stops to put on your wine country list.

- **Northstar** (1736 J B George Rd., 509/525-6100, www.northstarwinery.com, 11am-5pm daily, $10): Northstar makes some of the best old-world merlot around.

- **Saviah Cellars** (1979 J B George Rd., 509/522-2181, www.saviahcellars.com, 10am-5pm daily, $10): The vineyards here are planted on the alluvial soils of the Walla Walla River bed, and yield syrah, mourvedre, malbec, and tempranillo.

- **Tertulia** (1564 Whiteley Rd., 509/525-5700, www.tertuliacellars.com,

11am-6pm Thurs.-Sat., 11am-5pm Sun.-Mon. Apr.-Dec., shorter hours Jan.-Mar., $15): Call ahead before visiting this laid-back tasting room, which offers delightful whites such as viognier and marsanne, as well as reds like merlot and cabernet franc.

- **Va Piano** (1793 J B George Rd., 509/529-0900, www.vapianovineyards.com, 11am-5pm daily, $15): In the Italian villa-style tasting room, sip cabernet sauvignon, syrah, merlot, cabernet franc, and petit verdot.

VINEYARD, WALLA WALLA

occupying a big barn. Sample everything from cab franc to lemberger.

> *Take Orchard Rd. back to Gangl Rd. Turn left and drive to Thorp Rd. Turn left and follow Thorp as it turns into Yakima Valley Hwy. Stay on Yakima Valley Hwy. for 11 miles (18 km) to Cheyne Rd. Turn left to reach Two Mountain Winery (1 mi/1.6 km).*

❸ Stop in the little town of **Toppenish,** also in the valley, where more than 80 historical murals adorn the streets. It's striking to walk around and take them in, but you can enrich the experience by picking up an annotated map explaining each picture's significance, available at the **Chamber of Commerce** (504 S. Elm St., 509/865-3262, www.visittoppenish.com).

> *Drive south on Cheyne Rd. for 2 miles (3 km) to 1st Ave. Turn right, then continue on N. Meyers Rd. for 2 miles (3 km) to Toppenish.*

❹ At the east end of the valley is the **Tri-Cities** area, which comprises Richland, Pasco, and Kennewick. The main business is dismantling the Hanford nuclear site, a remnant of the atomic

RICHLAND WATERFRONT

bombs that the United States dropped on Japan at the conclusion of World War II. The **Manhattan Project National Historic Park** (2000 Logston Blvd., www.nps.gov/mapr) is a sobering place to visit. On the four-hour **Hanford B Reactor Tour** (http://manhattanprojectbreactor.hanford.gov, spring-fall, free), you're taken by bus past 300 Area, where uranium fuel rods were fabricated, and 100 Area, where fuel rods were irradiated to produce nuclear weapons. You're then given a guided walking tour of B Reactor, the world's first full-scale plutonium production reactor.

> Take I-82 E out of Toppenish for 49 miles (79 km) to I-182 E/US-12 E. Stay on this for 5 miles (8 km). Take WA-240 W and continue for 5 miles (8 km). Take a right onto Logston Blvd. to reach the visitors center, the departure point for the tour.

❺ Spend the night in **Richland.** Among the dozens of mid-priced hotels in the Tri-Cities, the **Hampton Inn Richland** (486 Bradley Blvd., Richland, 509/943-4400, www.hamptoninn.com, $149-194) stands out for its attractive location overlooking the Columbia River. The free breakfast doesn't hurt either.

> Take WA-240 E for 1 mile (1.6 km), then continue onto Jadwin Ave. This will lead into central Richland in 3 miles (5 km).

DAY 4: Richland to Walla Walla

70 miles/113 kilometers | 2 hours

ROUTE OVERVIEW: US-12 • WA-125

❶ After breakfast, hit the road for **Walla Walla.** Hospitality culture thrives here, with appealing places to stay and a charming downtown where tasting rooms neighbor cute shops and great restaurants. Within a couple of blocks you can sample wine from a dozen different makers. In the heart

MAIN STREET, WALLA WALLA

of downtown, **Mark Ryan Winery** (26 E. Main St., 509/876-4577, www.markryanwinery.com, noon-4pm Sun.-Thurs., noon-6pm Fri.-Sat., $10) and **Maison Bleue** (20 N. 2nd Ave., 509/525-9084, www.mbwinery.com, 11am-6pm Wed.-Mon. summer, shorter hours fall-spring, $15) are among the most highly esteemed.

▶ Playlist

COLUMBIA RIVER GORGE AND WINE COUNTRY

SONGS

- **"Smoking Gun" by Robert Cray:** You might not associate blues with the Pacific Northwest, but Georgia-born Cray got his musical start in Eugene. With five Grammy awards under his belt, he's considered one of the foremost blues guitarists.

- **"Hang on Little Tomato" by Pink Martini:** With a retro, jazzy, old-soul sound that calls to mind slow drives on a leafy road in an old Caddy, this song keeps you motoring on for hours.

PODCASTS

- *Wine for Normal People:* While this podcast doesn't focus exclusively on Washington-area wines, its straightforward, laid-back approach to all things wine means you get a fun education in vino that's transferable to any region or AVA in which you find yourself.

> Take US-12 W out of Richland, driving southeast for 58 miles (93 km) to Walla Walla.

❷ Have lunch in town at **Graze** (5 S. Colville St., 509/522-9991, www.grazeevents.com, 10am-7:30pm Mon.-Sat., 10am-3:30pm Sun., $8-12), a delightful sandwich shop. Along with standards like pastrami and turkey with cheese, it offers banh mi sandwiches and pulled pork *tortas*.

❸ Head to the vineyards at the south of town. A prime example of the area's new generation of winemakers is **Sleight of Hand Cellars** (1959 J B George Rd., 509/525-3661, www.sofhcellars.com, 11am-5pm daily), which produces carefully crafted, sought-after bordeaux blends while maintaining a whimsical attitude evident on every label. Set the music mood for your tasting experience by browsing from—and playing—any of the thousands of records in the owner's collection.

> Take S. 9th Ave./WA-125 south out of town. Follow it for 4 miles (6 km), then turn left onto Old Milton Hwy. Make a quick left onto Peppers Bridge Rd. and drive south for 1.5 miles (2.5 km), then make another left onto J B George Rd. to reach the winery.

❹ Wrap up the day with dinner downtown at **Brasserie Four** (4 E. Main St., 509/529-2011, www.brasseriefour.com, noon-10pm Tues.-Sat., $15-30). What comes out of the kitchen is consistently delicious. Throw in a casually romantic dining room and polished service, and you have what's arguably Walla Walla's best restaurant.

> Take Peppers Bridge Rd., Old Milton Hwy., and WA-125 to get back into downtown Walla Walla (6 mi/10 km).

Getting There

AIR

Portland International Airport (PDX, 7000 NE Airport Way, 877/739-4636, www.pdx.com) is the major airport in Oregon. Another option is **Seattle-Tacoma International Airport** (SEA, 800/544-1965 or 206/787-5388, www.portseattle.org/seatac), which is Washington's busiest point of entry, served

A VINEYARD ON THE COLUMBIA RIVER GORGE

by about two dozen airlines. It's a 3.5-hour drive (180 mi/290 km) from Sea-Tac to Troutdale via I-5.

TRAIN

Amtrak (800/872-7245, www.amtrak.com) provides rail service throughout the country to the Northwest. The Coast Starlight connects Seattle, Portland, Sacramento, Oakland, and Los Angeles. Amtrak also operates the Cascade Line, which runs between Eugene, Oregon, and Vancouver, British Columbia, with stops in Portland and Seattle.

BUS

Greyhound (800/231-2222, www.greyhound.com) is the largest intercity bus service in the United States, connecting all major cities and many points in between. It offers discounts to students and seniors.

BoltBus (877/265-8287, www.boltbus.com) is the cheapest way to travel south from Vancouver, British Columbia, with stops in Seattle, Portland, and Eugene.

CAR

From **Portland International Airport**, hop on I-84/US-30 and drive east to Troutdale. The drive takes about 20-25 minutes.

If you fly into **Seattle-Tacoma International Airport**, the route to **Troutdale** takes 3.5 hours. Follow I-5 S to I-205, then merge onto I-84/US-30 E. Continue on I-84/US-30 to Troutdale.

Getting Back

It's a four-hour drive (245 mi/390 km) to return to **Portland** from Walla Walla. Take US-12 W to US-730 W, then merge onto I-82 E. Drive this to I-84 W and continue to the airport.

If you're headed to **Seattle,** buckle in for the 4.5-hour drive (280 mi/450 km), which will take you back through Yakima and over Snoqualmie Pass. From Walla Walla, take US-12 W to I-182/US-12 W. Take the exit for I-82 W, then merge onto I-90 W. Hop on I-405 S and take the exit for WA-518 W toward the airport.

CONNECT WITH

- At Portland: **Oregon Trail** (PAGE 78) and **Best of the Pacific Northwest** (PAGE 216)
- At Portland or Cascade Locks: **Pacific Crest Trail: Oregon and Washington** (PAGE 250)

HIGH ADVENTURE IN BEND

WHY GO: Mount Bachelor, lakeside camping, mountain biking, microbreweries, craft coffee, cave tours, farm-fresh fare

TOTAL DISTANCE: 290 miles/ 465 kilometers

NUMBER OF DAYS: 5

SEASONS: Spring through fall

START/END: Bend, Oregon

▼ MOUNT BACHELOR

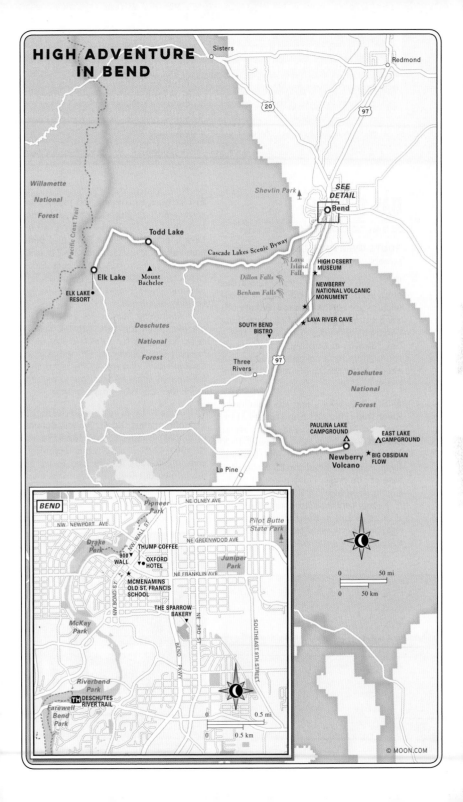

HIGH ADVENTURE IN BEND

Sisters

Redmond

Willamette
National
Forest

Pacific Crest Trail

Shevlin Park

SEE DETAIL

Bend

Todd Lake

Cascade Lakes Scenic Byway

Elk Lake

Mount Bachelor

ELK LAKE RESORT

Deschutes
National
Forest

Lava Island Falls

Dillon Falls

Benham Falls

HIGH DESERT MUSEUM

NEWBERRY NATIONAL VOLCANIC MONUMENT

LAVA RIVER CAVE

SOUTH BEND BISTRO

Three Rivers

Deschutes
National
Forest

PAULINA LAKE CAMPGROUND

EAST LAKE CAMPGROUND

Newberry Volcano

BIG OBSIDIAN FLOW

La Pine

0   50 mi
0   50 km

BEND

Pioneer Park

NE OLNEY AVE

NW NEWPORT AVE

Pilot Butte State Park

Drake Park

NW WALL ST

THUMP COFFEE

NE GREENWOOD AVE

900 WALL

OXFORD HOTEL

Juniper Park

NE FRANKLIN AVE

MCMENAMINS OLD ST. FRANCIS SCHOOL

NW BOND ST

THE SPARROW BAKERY

NE 3RD ST

McKay Park

BEND PKWY

SOUTHEAST 9TH STREET

Riverbend Park

TH DESCHUTES RIVER TRAIL

Farewell Bend Park

0   0.5 mi
0   0.5 km

© MOON.COM

In Central Oregon, the Deschutes River and craggy volcanic peaks cut through the high-desert town of Bend, a haven for hikers, skiers, mountain bikers, rafters, and kayakers. As a home base for high-adrenaline activities, Bend offers a lineup of craft breweries and solid restaurants at which to re-fuel, and cozy lodgings at which to rest up. Nature adventures are within an hour's drive, as are tamer—but no less interesting—outings, such as museum visits or dining on Oregon's fresh homegrown bounty.

DAY 1: Bend

20 miles/32 kilometers | 30-45 minutes

ROUTE OVERVIEW: US-97 • surface streets

1 Begin the day with a carda-mom-scented ocean roll (and a sand-wich to go) at **The Sparrow Bakery** (50 SE Scott St., 541/330-6321, www.thes-parrowbakery.net, 7am-2pm Mon.-Sat., 8am-2pm Sun.), a tiny gem sur-rounded by local artisans' studios and shops. If the weather's nice, sit on the patio.

2 Stroll or bike along the **Deschutes River Trail** (19 mi/31 km, Tumalo State Park to Meadow Picnic Area, www.bendparksandrec.org) in town. Pick up the trail in the **Old Mill District**, from Farewell Bend Park on the east side of the river. There's lots of park-ing on Reed Market Road.
> From central Bend, take US-97 S for 2 miles (3 km) to Reed Market Rd. Turn right and follow Reed Market Rd. west to the parking near the trailhead.

3 Get back in the car and follow the river south to hike a more outlying section of the Deschutes River Trail to **Lava Island Falls, Dillon Falls,** and **Ben-ham Falls** (7.2 mi/11.6 km, 2.5-3 hours, moderate). A Northwest Forest Pass (www.fs.usda.gov, $5) is required for parking along Forest Road 41 and in the day-use areas.
> Take Reed Market Rd. west across the river, then turn left onto SW Centu-ry Dr. Follow this for 5 miles (8 km), then turn left onto Dillon Falls Rd. Merge onto Conklin Rd./Forest Rd. 41. Take the first left and continue for less than a mile to reach the Lava Island day-use area.

4 Return to Bend and spend the night at **McMenamins Old St. Francis School** (700 NW Bond St., 541/382-5174 or 877/661-4228, www.mcmenamins.com, $205-300). It's in the heart of downtown but feels like it's in its own little world, enclosed by gardens with quiet sitting areas.

DESCHUTES RIVER TRAIL

BEND'S OLD MILL DISTRICT

Top ③ HIGH ADVENTURE IN BEND

① Ride a chairlift up the still-active volcano of **Mount Bachelor** for astonishing views of the Cascade peaks (PAGE 278).

② **Hike** along the scenic **Deschutes River Trail** (PAGE 276).

③ Traverse the caldera through the **Big Obsidian Flow** at **Newberry National Volcanic Monument** (PAGE 279).

TOURING BEND'S
Brewpubs

Bend's microbrewery scene is the fastest growing in the state. The best way to sip and sample the wares is along the **Bend Ale Trail.**

STAMP YOUR PASSPORT

Pick up a copy of the **Discovery Map of Central Oregon** (available at hotels and the Bend visitors center) and use the **Bend Ale Trail Map and Passport** to track down Bend breweries. The Ale Trail is also available as a **smartphone app.** Get your passport stamped at each stop. When you fill your passport, stop by the visitors center to receive a commemorative souvenir.

TAKE A TOUR

- The **Bend Brew Bus** (541/389-8359, www.bendbrewbus.com, $80) is operated by Wanderlust Tours, whose guides know both the outdoors and their way around a tasting room. You'll get to go behind the scenes at the breweries and, of course, do some tasting. There's also a **Local Pour tour** that visits Bend distillers, cideries, wineries, and kombucha makers. The bus picks you up at your hotel.

- For an active tour, board the **Cycle Pub** (541/678-5051, www.cyclepub.com, $185 for 4-6 people, $390 for 8-14 people). The multi-person bike, which looks more like a trolley, can be booked for pretty much any sort of tour you want to design. The two-hour tours begin at a local brewery where you can fill two growlers, so you can drink your beer as you go.

> Retrace your path back to SW Century Dr. (1 mi/1.6 km). Turn right onto SW Century and continue for 5 miles (8 km). At the second traffic circle veer right onto SW Colorado Ave. Follow this over the river for less than a mile to reach central Bend and your hotel.

DAY 2: Bend to Todd Lake

25 miles/40 kilometers | 30-45 minutes

ROUTE OVERVIEW: Cascade Lakes Scenic Byway

❶ Head to **Thump Coffee** (25 NW Minnesota Ave., 541/388-0226, www.thumpcoffee.com, 6am-5:30pm Mon.-Fri., 7am-5:30pm Sat., 7am-4:30pm Sun.) for small-batch-roasted coffee, good pastries, and friendly conversation.

❷ Head up **Cascade Lakes Scenic Byway** to explore the Pacific Northwest's largest ski area—and a still-active volcano. The ski resort **Mt. Bachelor** (541/382-1709, hours and snow report 541/382-7888, www.mtbachelor.com, $96 adults, $54 children 6-12) is situated at nearly 9,000 feet elevation, and has 12 lifts, trails that range from beginner to expert, and, in the off-season, **scenic chairlift rides** (541/382-1709, hours vary, $22 adults, $15 children 6-12) with tremendous views of Cascade lakes and peaks.

> Take SW Century Dr. to Cascade Lakes Scenic Byway (5 mi/8 km). Drive for 14 miles (23 km) on Cascade Lakes Scenic Byway to reach the resort.

❸ Set up camp at a hike-in site at **Todd Lake** (Forest Rd. 4600 370,

TODD LAKE

541/383-5300, www.fs.usda.gov, recreation pass required). Don't miss the captivating views of Broken Top to the north. There are plenty of nearby trails to check out. You'll also find good swimming and wading on the sandy shoal on the south end of the lake. There's no running water at the campground, but there are vault toilets. From the parking lot at the day-use area, it's about a 10-minute hike to reach the campground.

> Turn left onto Cascade Lakes Scenic Byway, following it 4 miles (6 km). Turn right onto Forest Rd. 4600 370 and continue for less than a mile to the day-use area for Todd Lake.

DAY 3: Todd Lake to Elk Lake

80 miles/129 kilometers | 2 hours

ROUTE OVERVIEW: Cascade Lakes Scenic Byway • surface streets • Cascade Lakes Scenic Byway

1 Pack up camp and head to the shores of **Elk Lake,** a favorite for windsurfing and sailing. Elk Lake makes a good base for exploring the trails, and during the winter it's open for cross-country skiers and snowmobilers.

> Drive Cascade Lakes Scenic Byway west and south for 8 miles (13 km) to Elk Lake. (Note: During winter, the Cascade Lakes Scenic Byway is closed beyond Mt. Bachelor. Contact the resort for transportation options.)

2 When you arrive, grab breakfast at the restaurant at **Elk Lake Resort** (60000 Century Dr., 541/480-7378, www.elklakeresort.net, 9am-11am Sat.-Sun., $12-15). This also where you'll be spending the night. Choose from small rustic cabins ($58), roomier cabins ($139-199), and modern homes ($399-459).

3 Just west of Bend, **Shevlin Park** (18920 NW Shevlin Park Rd., 541/388-5435, www.bendparksandrec.org, sunrise-sunset daily, free) lures hikers and mountain bikers with an easy 5-mile (8-km) loop through the pines along the Tumalo Creek Gorge. Several picnic areas offer quiet spots for lunch.

> Backtrack on Cascade Lakes Scenic Byway to Mt. Bachelor (11 mi/18 km). Continue east on Cascade Lakes Scenic Byway for another 19 miles (31 km). Take NW Mount Washington Dr. for 3 miles (5 km) to Shevlin Park Rd. Turn left and follow Shevlin Park Rd. to Shevlin Park (2 mi/3 km).

4 Enjoy dinner downtown at **900 Wall** (900 NW Wall St., 541/323-6295, www.900wall.com, 3pm-9pm Mon.-Fri., 3pm-10:30pm Sat.-Sun. summer, shorter hours in winter, $15-34). Try a wood-fired pizza (the prosciutto and arugula pizza drizzled with truffle oil is delicious) or high-class comfort food, such as duck confit or flat iron steak.

> Leave the park via Shevlin Park Rd., driving it to Newport Ave. (3 mi/5 km). Take Newport Ave. for 1.5 miles (2.5 km) to Wall St. Turn right to reach the restaurant. Take SW Century Dr. to Cascade Lakes Scenic Byway to return to Elk Lake Resort (30 mi/48 km).

DAY 4: Elk Lake to Newberry Volcano

125 miles/201 kilometers | 3 hours

ROUTE OVERVIEW: Cascade Lakes Scenic Byway • US-97 • Paulina Lake Rd. • US-97 • Paulina Lake Rd.

1 Start your day with a visit to **Newberry Volcano.** Head up to the caldera, where you can hike the trail through the **Big Obsidian Flow** at **Newberry National Volcanic Monument** (County Rd. 21, 541/593-2421, www.fs.usda.gov, recreation pass required). NASA sent astronauts to walk on this pumice-dusted surface in preparation for

NEWBERRY NATIONAL VOLCANIC MONUMENT

landing on the moon. A 0.9-mile trail crosses the obsidian flow. Find the trailhead on the road between Paulina Lake and East Lake.

> *Return to Bend via Cascade Lakes Scenic Byway and SW Century Dr. (33 mi/53 km). Pick up US-97 S and follow it for 23 miles (37 km). Turn left onto Paulina Lake Rd. and follow this for 14 miles*

HIGH ADVENTURE IN BEND

SONGS

- **"Kicks" by Paul Revere and the Raiders:** The raw, rockin' sound of this 1960s-era song energetically tees up a day of hiking. Fun fact: Paul Revere and the Raiders made music history when the Oregon band was the first rock act to sign to Columbia Records.

- **"Down by the Water" by The Decemberists:** This folk-rock band leans more rock than folk with a wild-abandon approach to making music that seems fitting for outdoor adventures.

PODCASTS

- *Offbeat Oregon History:* Each episode of this daily podcast is short, which means you can easily binge-listen to wild tales of shanghaied sailors, 19th-century serial killers, lost gold, heroes, baddies, con artists, and rascals—a perfect accompaniment to a mountain biking excursion or a volcano exploration.

(23 km) to the trailhead, which is on the southern side of the road.

❷ Set up camp at either **Paulina Lake** or **East Lake Campground** (off County Rd. 21, reservations 877/444-6777, www.recreation.gov, late May-mid-Oct., $18). These neighboring campgrounds have drinking water and are located at the top of Newberry Volcano.

> *To reach Paulina Lake Campground, backtrack 2.5 miles (4 km). To reach East Lake Campground, continue east from the trailhead for 2 miles (3 km). Both campgrounds are on the northern side of the road.*

❸ Head into **Sunriver** for dinner. You'll find the area's most interesting dining at **South Bend Bistro** (57080 Abbot Dr., 541/593-3991, www.southbend-bistro.com, 4pm-9pm daily, $19-33). The menu is influenced by the chef's years in Florence and his immersion into Oregon's bounty, with dishes like tuna niçoise and braised rabbit with prosciutto, roasted fennel, and provolone-stuffed risotto croquettes.

> *Retrace your path west along Paulina Lake Rd. to US-97 (14 mi/23 km). Go north on US-97 for 8 miles (13 km) and take exit 153. Follow Century Dr. west for 1.5 miles (2.5 km) to reach Sunriver. Reverse this route to get back to your campsite (25 mi/40 km).*

DAY 5: Newberry Volcano to Bend

40 miles/64 kilometers | 1-1.5 hours

ROUTE OVERVIEW: Paulina Lake Rd. • US-97

❶ After you break camp, head down the volcano and north on US-97. Stop to explore the **Lava River Cave** (541/593-2421, 10am-4pm Thurs.-Mon. May, 9am-4pm daily Memorial Day-Labor Day, 10am-4pm daily Sept., $5 per vehicle or NW Forest Pass). The cave is a cool 42°F year-round, so dress warmly and wear sturdy shoes—the walking surface is rocky and uneven. (To prevent the resident bats from acquiring white-nose syndrome, take care to wear clothing and shoes that you've never worn into another cave.)

KEY RESERVATIONS

- Make advance reservations for a tour of the **Lava River Cave,** as it's a popular destination. Make sure to dress warmly for this underground excursion.

- Reservations are required to camp at **Paulina Lake Campground** or **East Lake Campground;** both can fill early.

Parking is limited at this popular site; get here early.

> Take Paulina Lake Rd. west to US-97 (14 mi/23 km). Drive north on US-97 for 10 miles (16 km). Take exit 151 for Cottonwood Road to reach the Lava River Cave.

② Spend the afternoon at the **High Desert Museum** (59800 US-97 S., 541/382-4754, 9am-5pm daily May-Oct., 10am-4pm daily Nov.-Apr., $15 adults, $9 children 5-12). This indoor-outdoor museum has exhibits on contemporary Native American life, the development of the West, photography, and wildlife. Get a bite to eat at the on-site café before you go.

> Continue north on US-97 for 7 miles (11 km) to the High Desert Museum.

③ Splurge with a night at Bend's **Oxford Hotel** (10 NW Minnesota Ave., 541/382-8436 or 877/440-8436, www. oxfordhotelbend.com, $299-569), a stylish and eco-friendly boutique hotel in a great location. Relax in the steam room, sauna, or saline hot tub—perfect for decompressing from your outdoor adventures.

> Continue north for another 7 miles (11 km) on US-97 into Bend.

Getting There

AIR

With flights from Portland, Seattle, San Francisco, Denver, Los Angeles, Phoenix, and Salt Lake City, access to central Oregon is quite good from **Redmond Municipal Airport** (RDM, 2522 SE Jesse Butler Cir., Redmond, 541/548-0646, www.flyrdm.com), 16 miles (26 km) north of Bend and east

of US-97. Alamo, Avis, Budget, Hertz, National, and Enterprise have car rental offices in the terminal. Taxis, limos, and shuttle buses serve Bend at nominal cost. **Redmond Airport Shuttle** (541/382-1687 or 888/664-8449, www.redmondairportshuttle.net) offers door-to-door service to and from the airport.

TRAIN

The closest you can get to Bend via **Amtrak** (800/872-7245, www.amtrak.com) is Chemult, 60 miles (97 km) south on US-97. Amtrak can assist you in scheduling your transfer to Bend.

BUS

The **Central Oregon Breeze Shuttle** (541/389-7469 or 800/847-0157, www. cobreeze.com, $52 one-way, $95 round-trip) serves Bend to and from Portland International Airport and the Portland train station. **Pacific Crest Bus Lines** (541/923-1732, www.pacificcrest-buslines.com, $35) runs between Eugene and Bend and east as far as Ontario, Oregon.

Get to and from the airport or the Chemult Amtrak station on **High Desert Point** (541/382-4193, www.highdesert-point.com) buses, which also travel between Bend and Eugene.

CAR

US-97 and US-20 converge in Bend. **Portland** is 175 miles (282 km) via US-97 and US-26; **Salem** is 130 miles (209 km) via US-20 and OR-22; and **Eugene** is 121 miles (195 km) via US-20 and OR-126. **Crater Lake National Park** is 91 miles (146 km) south on US-97.

It's an easy 25-minute drive (17 mi/27 km) south on US-97 from **Redmond Municipal Airport** to Bend.

You can rent a car starting at around $40 per day from **Hertz** (2025 NE US-20, 541/388-1535; Redmond Municipal Airport, 541/923-1411) or **Budget** (519 SE 3rd St., 800/527-0700).

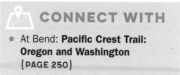

CONNECT WITH

- At Bend: **Pacific Crest Trail: Oregon and Washington** (PAGE 250)

THE SOUTHWEST *and* TEXAS

It's a mistake to define this region's wide-open spaces and untouched wilderness as a whole lot of nothing. Look closely at the surface of a granite outcropping in Mesa Verde and you'll see petroglyphs etched in stone. Beyond that grove of cottonwood trees? Yep. That's the Colorado River winding by. Between Arizona and Utah, the gaping mouth of the Grand Canyon—so deep it can be seen from space—suddenly appears out of a plateau. The arts-and-culture-rich cities of Santa Fe, Taos, Austin, Salt Lake City, and Phoenix match the region's wild beauty with urban sophistication.

◀ MONUMENT VALLEY NAVAJO TRIBAL PARK

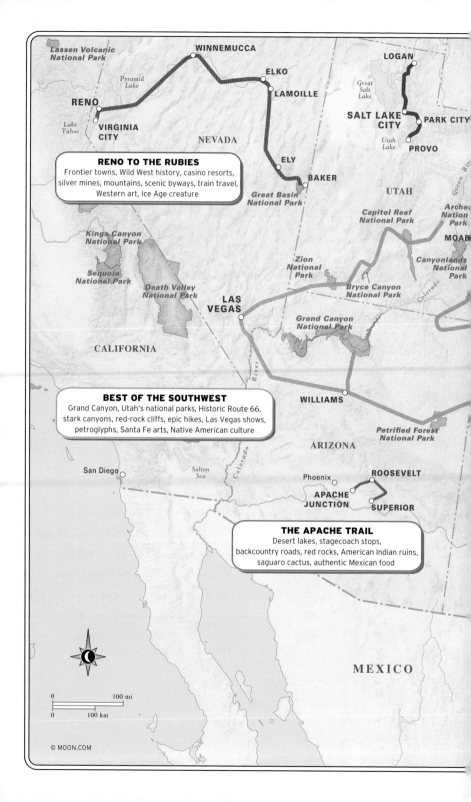

Lassen Volcanic National Park

WINNEMUCCA

ELKO

LAMOILLE

LOGAN

Pyramid Lake

Great Salt Lake

RENO

VIRGINIA CITY

Lake Tahoe

NEVADA

SALT LAKE CITY

PARK CITY

Utah Lake

PROVO

RENO TO THE RUBIES
Frontier towns, Wild West history, casino resorts, silver mines, mountains, scenic byways, train travel, Western art, Ice Age creature

ELY

BAKER

Great Basin National Park

UTAH

Green Ri...

Capitol Reef National Park

Arche... Nation Park

MOAB

Kings Canyon National Park

Zion National Park

Canyonlands National Park

Sequoia National Park

Death Valley National Park

LAS VEGAS

Bryce Canyon National Park

Colorado

Grand Canyon National Park

CALIFORNIA

River

Colorado

WILLIAMS

BEST OF THE SOUTHWEST
Grand Canyon, Utah's national parks, Historic Route 66, stark canyons, red-rock cliffs, epic hikes, Las Vegas shows, petroglyphs, Santa Fe arts, Native American culture

Petrified Forest National Park

ARIZONA

San Diego

Salton Sea

Colorado

Phoenix

ROOSEVELT

APACHE JUNCTION

SUPERIOR

THE APACHE TRAIL
Desert lakes, stagecoach stops, backcountry roads, red rocks, American Indian ruins, saguaro cactus, authentic Mexican food

MEXICO

0   100 mi
0   100 km

© MOON.COM

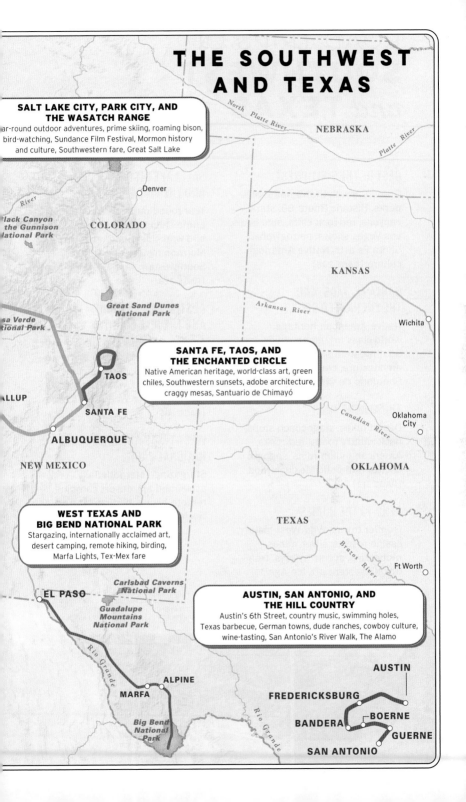

THE SOUTHWEST AND TEXAS

SALT LAKE CITY, PARK CITY, AND THE WASATCH RANGE
ar-round outdoor adventures, prime skiing, roaming bison, bird-watching, Sundance Film Festival, Mormon history and culture, Southwestern fare, Great Salt Lake

SANTA FE, TAOS, AND THE ENCHANTED CIRCLE
Native American heritage, world-class art, green chiles, Southwestern sunsets, adobe architecture, craggy mesas, Santuario de Chimayó

WEST TEXAS AND BIG BEND NATIONAL PARK
Stargazing, internationally acclaimed art, desert camping, remote hiking, birding, Marfa Lights, Tex-Mex fare

AUSTIN, SAN ANTONIO, AND THE HILL COUNTRY
Austin's 6th Street, country music, swimming holes, Texas barbecue, German towns, dude ranches, cowboy culture, wine-tasting, San Antonio's River Walk, The Alamo

NORTH PLATTE RIVER

NEBRASKA

Platte River

Denver

COLOROADO

KANSAS

Wichita

lack Canyon
the Gunnison
ational Park

Arkansas River

Great Sand Dunes
National Park

sa Verde
tional Park

TAOS

ALLUP

SANTA FE

ALBUQUERQUE

Canadian River

Oklahoma City

NEW MEXICO

OKLAHOMA

Carlsbad Caverns
National Park

EL PASO

Guadalupe
Mountains
National Park

TEXAS

Brazos River

Ft Worth

River

Rio Grande

ALPINE

MARFA

Big Bend
National
Park

Rio Grande

FREDERICKSBURG

BANDERA

AUSTIN

BOERNE

GUERNE

SAN ANTONIO

ROAD TRIPS OF
SOUTHWEST
and TEXAS

BEST OF THE SOUTHWEST

Grand Canyon, Utah's national parks, Historic Route 66, stark canyons, red-rock cliffs, epic hikes, Las Vegas shows, petroglyphs, Santa Fe arts, Native American culture (PAGE 288)

SANTA FE, TAOS, AND THE ENCHANTED CIRCLE

Native American heritage, world-class art, green chiles, Southwestern sunsets, adobe architecture, craggy mesas, Santuario de Chimayó (PAGE 304)

THE APACHE TRAIL

Desert lakes, stagecoach stops, backcountry roads, red rocks, American Indian ruins, saguaro cactus, authentic Mexican food (PAGE 312)

RENO TO THE RUBIES

Frontier towns, Wild West history, casino resorts, silver mines, mountains, scenic byways, train travel, Western art, Ice Age creatures (PAGE 318)

SALT LAKE CITY, PARK CITY, AND THE WASATCH RANGE

Year-round outdoor adventures, prime skiing, roaming bison, bird-watching, Sundance Resort, Mormon history and culture, Southwestern fare, Great Salt Lake (PAGE 328)

AUSTIN, SAN ANTONIO, AND THE HILL COUNTRY

Austin's 6th Street, country music, swimming holes, Texas barbecue, German towns, dude ranches, cowboy culture, wine-tasting, San Antonio's River Walk, The Alamo (PAGE 336)

WEST TEXAS AND BIG BEND NATIONAL PARK

Stargazing, internationally acclaimed art, desert camping, remote hiking, birding, Marfa Lights, Tex-Mex fare (PAGE 346)

LEFT TO RIGHT: ZION NATIONAL PARK; MARKETPLACE IN SANTA FE; THE ALAMO

1 Stay up all night in the 24-hour playground that is **Las Vegas** (PAGE 290).

2 Rumble into the **Grand Canyon** aboard the **Grand Canyon Railway** (PAGE 301).

3 Experience the reverence of a ceremonial dance at **Taos Pueblo** in New Mexico (PAGE 309).

4 Ski the snowy slopes of **Park City Mountain Resort** in Utah (PAGE 333).

Las Vegas

Grand Canyon Railway

Taos Pueblo

Marfa Lights

5 In West Texas, witness the mysterious **Marfa Lights,** multi-colored orbs that float just above the desert horizon come nightfall (PAGE 350).

skiing in Utah

BEST OF THE SOUTHWEST

WHY GO: Grand Canyon, Utah's national parks, Historic Route 66, stark canyons, red-rock cliffs, epic hikes, Las Vegas shows, petroglyphs, Santa Fe arts, Native American culture

TOTAL DISTANCE: 2,020 miles/ 3,255 kilometers

NUMBER OF DAYS: 13

SEASONS: Spring through early fall

START/END: Las Vegas, Nevada

▶ ROAD TO MONUMENT VALLEY

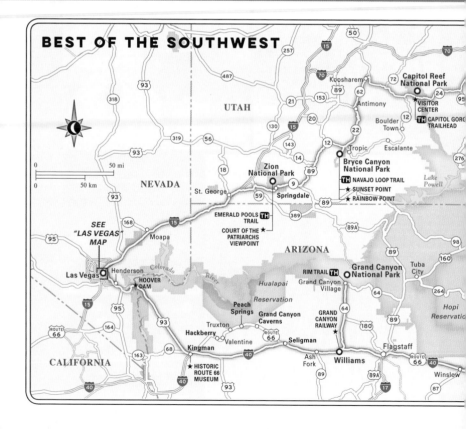

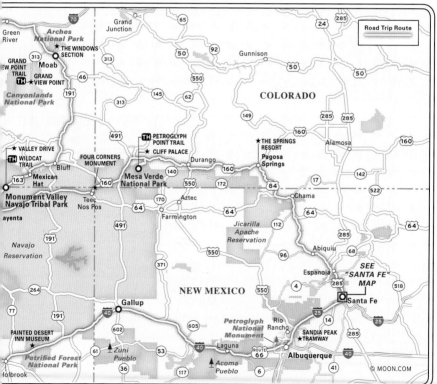

An expedition through the American Southwest yields life-altering experiences: Scramble over red-rock spires, hike through petrified forests, meet Navajo artists, and dine on *nopales* (cactus pads). There's no place on the planet where you'll see the stars twinkle as brightly or watch the sun sink so colorfully. Sometimes the road through the otherworldly beauty of the Southwest may seem desolate, with its uninterrupted sightlines for miles in every direction. But that's where the magic lies—in the open spaces and the quiet interludes between towns.

DAY 1: Las Vegas

MORNING AND AFTERNOON

❶ Walk the Strip and get acclimated to the lights, sounds, and thrills of Las Vegas, then luxuriate on a chaise lounge at one of the themed pools at **Caesars Palace** (3570 Las Vegas Blvd. S., 866/227-5938, www.caesars.com).

❷ Splurge on a room at the **Bellagio** (3600 Las Vegas Blvd. S., 702/693-7111

BELLAGIO

© MOON.COM

Top ⑤ BEST OF THE SOUTHWEST

① Stay up all night in the 24-hour playground that is **Las Vegas** (PAGE 290).

② See the dazzling green of the **Emerald Pools** set against the red cliffs of **Zion National Park** (PAGE 292).

③ Stand in four states at one time at the **Four Corners Monument** (PAGE 297).

④ Rumble into the **Grand Canyon** Old West-style aboard the **Grand Canyon Railway** (PAGE 301).

⑤ Drive the longest continuous stretch of **Historic Route 66** in the country (PAGE 302).

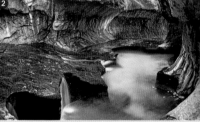

or 888/987-6667, www.bellagio.com, $199-349), where all the romance of Italy manifests through bubbling fountains, gondola rides, cozy bistros, and—in case the spirit moves you—a wedding chapel.

EVENING

③ Catch a showing of Cirque du Soleil's Beatles-themed *LOVE* (The Mirage, 3400 Las Vegas Blvd. S., 866/983-4279, www.cirquedusoleil.com/love, 7pm and 9:30pm Tues.-Sat., $86-196) in the evening. The show is a loose biography of the Beatles' creative journey, told by tumblers, roller skaters, acrobats, clowns, and the characters from John, Paul, George, and Ringo's songs—Eleanor Rigby, Lucy in the Sky, and Sgt. Pepper.

④ Grab a late-night meal at **Rose. Rabbit. Lie.** (The Cosmopolitan, 3708 Las Vegas Blvd. S., 702/698-7440, www.cosmopolitanlasvegas.com, 6pm-midnight Wed.-Sat., $70-125), equal parts supper club, nightclub, and jazz club. Order 6-8 small plates, and let the sultry torch singers and rousing dancers play on.

DAY 2: Las Vegas to Zion National Park

170 miles/275 kilometers | 3-4 hours

ROUTE OVERVIEW: I-15 • UT-9

① Grab coffee and breakfast from **The Egg & I** (4533 W. Sahara Ave., Ste. 5, 702/364-9686, http://theeggworks.com, 6am-3pm daily, $10-20) to keep you perky for the drive to Zion.

② Leave Las Vegas early to reach **Zion National Park** (435/772-3256, www.nps.gov/zion, $35 per vehicle, $30 motorcyclists, $20 pedestrians or bicyclists) with enough time to explore its natural wonders. The drive to the **Springdale entrance** takes about three hours; however, traffic, especially in summer and on weekends, can make it much longer.

> *Take I-15 N to UT-9 E (130 mi/209 km). Merge onto UT-9 and follow it east for 34 miles (55 km). At Floor of the Valley Rd./Zion Canyon Scenic Dr., turn left and drive 3 miles (5 km) to the Springdale entrance.*

ZION NATIONAL PARK

③ Take the Zion Canyon shuttle to the iconic **Court of the Patriarchs viewpoint** (Zion Canyon Scenic Dr.). The Patriarchs are emblematic of Zion's massive sandstone rocks. Spend a few moments trying to fit all three mountains into your camera's viewfinder. Although the official viewpoint is a beautiful place to relax and snap a few photos, you'll get an even better vantage point if you cross the road and head about 0.5 mile (0.8 km) up Sand Bench Trail.

④ Hike one of the trails to the **Emerald Pools** (0.6-1.4 mi/1-2.3 km one-way, 1-3 hours, easy-moderate). All three of these pools are indeed emerald green. The trails, of varying degrees of difficulty, are lined with wildflowers. The trailhead is across the footbridge from Zion Lodge; there's a shuttle stop at the lodge.

EMERALD POOLS

ZION LODGE

⑤ Make reservations ahead of time to spend the night in the comfort of the rustic **Zion Lodge** (435/772-7700 or 888/297-2757, www.zionlodge.com, $217-270). Plan to eat dinner here, too, as this is the only spot inside the park to get food.

DAY 3: Zion to Bryce Canyon National Park

110 miles/177 kilometers | 4-4.5 hours

ROUTE OVERVIEW: UT-9 • US-89 • UT-12 • UT-63

① Make the two-hour drive to **Bryce Canyon National Park** (435/834-5322, www.nps.gov/brca, $35 per vehicle, $30 motorcyclists, $20 pedestrians or bicyclists).

> *Follow UT-9 E to US-89 (23 mi/37 km). Turn left and drive US-89 N to UT-12 (43 mi/69 km). At UT-12, turn right and drive east for 14 miles (23 km) to UT-63. Turn right and go south on UT-63 to enter the park (3 mi/5 km).*

② Once you arrive, hike the **Navajo Loop Trail** (1.3 mi/2.1 km round-trip, 1.5 hours, moderate). The trail leads into a narrow canyon and then into deep, dark Wall Street—an even narrower canyon—before returning to the rim. The trailhead is at Sunset Point; the Bryce Canyon shuttle stops here.

③ Starting from the main road, do the 36-mile **scenic drive** through Bryce Canyon. At the end of the parkway, picnic at **Rainbow Point** (18 mi/29 km south of the park entrance), which shows off spectacular views

KEY RESERVATIONS

- Advance reservations are required at **Zion Lodge** in **Zion National Park,** and accommodations book up fast. Plan to reserve at least **two months** in advance. The same holds true for **The Lodge** at **Bryce Canyon National Park,** the only non-camping accommodations in the park.

- The popularity of the historic **La Fonda** hotel in **Santa Fe** means reservations—a **month** in advance—are a good idea.

- At **Monument Valley Navajo Tribal Park,** you'll need **permits** to hike **Rainbow Bridge, San Juan River,** and **Olijato.**

- As the only accommodations at **Mesa Verde National Park, Far View Lodge** fills quickly. Book **three weeks** in advance.

- While it's possible to snag same-day train tickets for the **Grand Canyon Railway,** it's not advised. Purchase advance tickets **two weeks** early.

of southern Utah. At an elevation of 9,115 feet (2,778 m), this is the highest area of the park.

> *Turn around and follow the road back to where you started (18 mi/29 km). Allow yourself around three hours to do the full drive.*

BRYCE CANYON NATIONAL PARK

❹ Make reservations in advance so you can stay the night at **The Lodge at Bryce Canyon** (435/834-8700 or 877/386-4383, https://brycecanyon-forever.com, Apr.-Oct., rooms $203-271, cabins $221), the only non-camping accommodations inside the park. Have dinner here; the menu includes a range of offerings, from vegetarian dishes to fresh fish.

DAY 4: Bryce Canyon to Capitol Reef National Park

150 miles/241 kilometers | 4-5 hours

ROUTE OVERVIEW: UT-63 • UT-12 • UT-24

❶ Aim for an early start for the trek to **Capitol Reef National Park** (435/425-3791, www.nps.gov/care, $20 per vehicle for travel on scenic drive, $10 cyclists and pedestrians), a scenic three-hour drive from Bryce Canyon. The overlooks along the route include pull-offs with parking, designed for travelers to stop and soak up the photo-worthy views.

> *Head north for 3 miles (5 km) on UT-63. At UT-12, turn right and continue on UT-12 for 110 miles (177 km) to UT-24. Turn left to reach Torrey in less than a mile.*

WITH LESS TIME

UTAH'S NATIONAL PARKS

6 days; 749 miles/1,205 kilometers

It's doable to tackle six national parks in just **6 days,** thanks to the proximity of Utah's southwestern parks to one another. From **Las Vegas,** make the 2.5-hour drive to **Zion National Park.** Spend the night here.

Visit **Bryce Canyon** on your **second day,** overnighting at the park. Your **third day** features **Capitol Reef National Park.** On your **fourth day,** drive on to **Moab** to visit **Arches** and **Canyonlands.**

Wrap up your parks tour with a visit to **Monument Valley** on your **fifth day.** Make the six-hour drive back to Las Vegas on your **final day.** For more details, see *Days 2-6.*

❷ Check in at the **Capitol Reef Inn & Cafe** (360 W. Main St., 435/425-3271, www.capitolreefinn.com, spring-fall, $72) in Torrey. You'll need to bring your own food and water into the park, so stock up while you're in town.

❸ From the visitors center, take the park's **scenic drive** (21 mi/34 km round-trip, 1.5 hours) to Capitol Gorge. The drive encompasses not

CAPITOL REEF NATIONAL PARK

only beautiful scenery and all its attendant geology, but also human history, pioneer sites, and even free fruit in season. Pick up a brochure at the visitors center for descriptions of geology along the road.

> Head east on UT-24, continuing for 11 miles (18 km) to the entrance to Capitol Reef National Park. Begin the scenic drive from the visitors center.

④ Leave your car in the parking area and hike into **Capitol Gorge** (2 mi/3.2 km round-trip, 1-2 hours, easy-moderate) to see petroglyphs, a pioneer registry carved into the canyon wall, and natural water tanks. From the turnoff to the water tanks, hikers can continue another 3 miles (4.8 km) downstream to Notom Road. Once you're done, head back to Torrey for the night.

DAY 5: Capitol Reef to Moab

220 miles/355 kilometers | 4-5 hours

ROUTE OVERVIEW: UT-24 • I-70 • US-191 • UT-313 • US-191

① You're hitting two national parks today, so get an early start. First stop: **Moab,** the gateway city to Arches and Canyonlands. Check into **The Gonzo Inn** (100 W. 200 S., 435/259-2515 or 800/791-4044, www.gonzoinn.com, $199-249), a brightly colored, Southwest-styled boutique hotel.

> Head east on UT-24 for 79 miles (127 km) to I-70. Turn right and merge onto I-70, following it east for 33 miles

ARCHES NATIONAL PARK

Capitol Reef was one of the last places in the West to be found by settlers. The region remained one of the most isolated in Utah until after World War II. Although its citizens have departed, the National Park Service maintains the orchards that evidence the area's long history. They are lovely in **late April,** when the trees are in bloom beneath the towering canyon walls.

Visitors are welcome to pick and carry away the **cherries, apricots, peaches, pears,** and **apples** during harvest seasons. Harvest begins in **late June-early July** and ends in **October.** You'll be charged about the same as in commercial u-pick orchards. You can also wander through any orchard and eat all you want on the spot for free before and during the designated picking season.

ORCHARD IN CAPITOL REEF NATIONAL PARK

(53 km). Take the exit for US-191 S. Follow US-191 for 31 miles (50 km) to Moab.

② After you drop off your bags and get a bite to eat in town, head to **Arches National Park** (435/719-2299, www.nps.gov/arch, $30 per vehicle, $25 motorcyclists, $15 bicyclists and pedestrians), which is 5 miles (8 km) away.

> Get back on US-191 and drive north for 5 miles (8 km) to the park entrance.

THE WINDOWS SECTION

❸ Drive to **The Windows Section** (2.5 mi/4 km past Balanced Rock) and stroll the easy paths that lead to four arches. Some of the park's largest arches are here—so are some of its largest crowds. Past the first arch, the crowds thin out.

❹ From Arches, it's a 40-minute drive to **Canyonlands National Park** (435/719-2313, www.nps.gov/cany, $30 per vehicle, $25 motorcyclists, $15 bicyclists and pedestrians). See how water, gravity, and time have shaped the mesas, buttes, spires, and canyons of this primitive wilderness area.

> Take US-191 N to UT-313 (7 mi/11 km). Turn left and follow UT-313 west to Grand View Point Road/Island in the Sky Rd. (15 mi/24 km). Continue for another 5 miles (8 km) to Canyonlands National Park.

❺ At the end of the main road in the park, in the Island in the Sky District, visit **Grand View Point** (12 mi/19.3 km south of the visitors center). This is perhaps the most spectacular panorama of the park. Monument Basin lies below; in the distance, you can see the Colorado River, The Needles, sharp canyons, and rugged mountains. Stretch your legs on the short **Grand View Trail** (1 mi/1.6 km, 1 hour, easy), a hike along slickrock cliffs that captures the essence of the Island in the Sky. Make the 45-minute drive back to Moab and grab some dinner in town.

> Follow UT-313 back to US-191, turn right, and drive south on US-191 back to Moab (30 mi/48 km).

DAY 6: Moab to Monument Valley

190 miles/305 kilometers | 4-5 hours

ROUTE OVERVIEW: US-191 • US-163

❶ It's an almost three-hour drive from Moab to **Monument Valley Navajo Tribal Park** (435/727-5874 or 435/727-5870, http://navajonationparks.org, 6am-8pm daily Apr.-Sept., 8am-5pm daily Oct.-Mar., $20 per vehicle, $10 motorcyclists, bicyclists, and pedestrians). It's a good idea to stop at one of the few gas stations in Mexican Hat, which is about 25 miles (40 km) northeast of the entrance to the park.

> Drive south on US-191 to US-163 (105 mi/69 km). Continue south on US-163 to Monument Valley Navajo Tribal Park (41 mi/66 km).

CANYONLANDS NATIONAL PARK

DRIVING THROUGH MONUMENT VALLEY

❷ Spend an hour or so doing the scenic 17-mile (27-km) **Valley Drive** (Monument Valley Rd.), stopping at the various pull-offs and viewpoints to admire the towering sandstone buttes and spires of the valley.

❸ Get a closer look at the park's huge natural sculptures along the red-dirt **Wildcat Trail** (3.2 mi/5.2 km loop, 2 hours, easy). The trail starts 0.4 mile (0.6 km) north of the visitors center. It's easy enough for kids, but there's no shade, and it can get windy out there. Take water with you.

❹ Stay the night in **Kayenta**, a 30-minute drive south of the park. The **Wetherill Inn** (US-163, 1000 Main St., 928/697-3231, www.wetherill-inn.com, $149) has comfortable rooms, an indoor pool, wireless Internet, a gift shop, and free breakfast.
> Drive south on US-163 for 23 miles (37 km).

DAY 7: Monument Valley to Mesa Verde National Park

150 miles/241 kilometers | 3.5-4 hours

ROUTE OVERVIEW: US-160

❶ At the **Four Corners Monument** (597 NM-597, Teec Nos Pos, 928/871-6647, 8am-5pm daily Sept.-May, 7am-8pm daily June-Aug., $5, cash only), stop for the requisite photo of yourself standing in four states (Arizona, New Mexico, Utah, and Colorado) at once,

DWELLINGS IN MESA VERDE NATIONAL PARK

the only place in the United States where you can do so. Peruse the beautiful creations of the Navajo vendors and artists that are set up here.
> Use US-163 S to connect with US-160 (1.5 mi/2.5 km). At US-160, drive east for 77 miles (124 km) to NM-597. Turn left and in less than a mile is the Four Corners Monument.

❷ Head to Colorado's **Mesa Verde National Park** (US-160, 970/529-4465, www.nps.gov/meve, $20-30 per vehicle, $15-25 motorcyclists, $10-15 bicyclists and pedestrians) to see the well-preserved Ancestral Puebloan cliff dwellings, ancient petroglyphs, and interesting archaeological sites.
> Take NM-597 for less than a mile to US-160. Turn left and drive east on US-160 for 49 miles (79 km) to Mesa Top Ruins Rd. Turn right and follow this into Mesa Verde National Park (20 mi/32 km).

❸ Tour **Cliff Palace** (tours every 30 minutes 9am-6pm daily late May-mid-Sept., call ahead for tour times mid-Sept.-Oct., $5), the park's largest cliff dwelling, with a knowledgeable ranger. Scramble up ladders (four of them, to be exact) and walk through the high plazas of an ancient stone city. Unless you're deathly afraid of heights, the climb is easy, fun, and definitely worth it.

❹ Hike **Petroglyph Point Trail** (2.8 mi/4.5 km round-trip, 2 hours, moderate-difficult), which takes you along the forested slopes of a canyon to a mysterious panel of symbols and figures, carved into the rocks by the native artists of Mesa Verde.

❺ Stay the night at the park's only hotel, the **Far View Lodge** (970/529-4422 or 800/449-2288, www.visitmesaverde.com, mid-Apr.-late Oct., $130-202).

FOUR CORNERS MONUMENT

Best VIEWS

LAS VEGAS

- The sleek, upscale **SkyBar** (3752 Las Vegas Blvd. S., 702/590-8888, www. waldorfastorialasvegas.com, 4pm-1am Sun.-Thurs., noon-2am Fri.-Sat.), on the 23rd floor of the Waldorf Astoria, has unforgettable views of the Strip.

- At **Stratosphere Tower** (2000 Las Vegas Blvd. S., 702/380-7777, www.stratospherehotel.com), the thrill rides on the **observation deck** (10am-1am Sun.-Thurs., 10am-2am Fri.-Sat., $20-25) are hair-raising, but head to the 107th floor and its namesake **107 Sky Lounge** (4pm-3am daily) for a tamer view—with cocktails.

ZION NATIONAL PARK

- **Court of the Patriarchs** (Zion Canyon Scenic Dr.) features three towering, jagged red-rock peaks with skirts of greenery, called Abraham, Isaac, and Jacob.

BRYCE CANYON NATIONAL PARK

- **Sunrise Point** (1 mi/1.6 km south of the visitors center) is the ideal place in Bryce to watch the sun climb over the great canyon's hoodoo forest.

CAPITOL REEF NATIONAL PARK

- It's said the area around **Panorama Point** (UT-24, 2.5 mi/4 km west of the visitors center) has some of the clearest skies in the United States, which enhances the sweeping view of Capitol Reef and the Henry Mountains.

- Watch a humble creek meander through the starkly beautiful canyon that it's been slowly carving for eons at **Goosenecks Overlook** (1 mi/1.6 km south of Panorama Point).

CANYONLANDS NATIONAL PARK

- At **Grand View Point** (12 mi/19 km south of the visitors center), you can see Canyonlands spread out before you.

- From the **Green River Overlook** (west of the junction with Upheaval Dome Rd.), you can watch the river snake its way across the plateau.

MONUMENT VALLEY

- Take in an otherworldly view from a high patio at **Monument Valley Navajo Tribal Park Visitor Center** (6am-8pm daily Apr.-Sept., 8am-5pm daily Oct.-Mar.).

MESA VERDE NATIONAL PARK

- Stop at the **Sun Point View overlook** (Mesa Top Loop Rd.) for a classic view of Balcony House, the largest cliff dwelling in North America.

SANTA FE

- For a perfect sunset drink, get to the **Bell Tower Bar** (100 E. San Francisco St., 505/982-5511, 11am-sunset daily May-Oct.) on the rooftop at La Fonda. It's usually packed with tourists, but the view is worth it.

GRAND CANYON NATIONAL PARK

- **Mather Point** is the most-visited viewpoint in the Grand Canyon for a reason: It offers a classic panorama that includes a quarter of the massive canyon below.

- Hanging off the Grand Canyon's South Rim, **Yavapai Observation Station and Geology Museum** (8am-8pm daily summer, 8am-6pm daily winter, free) puts your first glimpse of the canyon into context with interpretive exhibits.

DAY 8: Mesa Verde to Santa Fe

265 miles/430 kilometers | 5-6 hours

ROUTE OVERVIEW : US-160 • US-84

1 After a good night's sleep, launch for Santa Fe, stopping in **Pagosa Springs** to soak in one of the 18 pools at **The Springs Resort** (165 Hot Springs Blvd., 800/255-0934, www.pagosahotsprings. com, 7am-midnight daily Memorial Day-Labor Day, 7am-11pm daily Labor Day-Memorial Day, day passes $26-53 adults, $14-29 children under 13).

> *Take Mesa Top Ruins Rd. out of Mesa Verde National Park to US-160 (20 mi/32 km). Turn right and follow US-160 E to Pagosa Springs (94 mi/151 km).*

2 From Pagosa Springs, it's a three-hour drive to downtown Santa Fe. Check into the historic **La Fonda** (100 E. San Francisco St., 505/982-5511, www.lafondasantafe.com, $259 d). The Santa Fe Trail trade route ended on the doorstep of this hotel, which has harbored the city's assorted characters for centuries.

> *Follow US-84 E for 150 miles (241 km) to Santa Fe.*

3 Have dinner at **Cafe Pasqual's** (121 Don Gaspar St., 505/983-9340, http:// pasquals.com, 8am-3pm and 5:30pm-9:30pm daily, $29), a small, popular bistro in central Santa Fe that serves creative cuisine using organic ingredients.

DAY 9: Santa Fe

MORNING

1 Walk around the Santa Fe Plaza, shopping and chatting with the artists selling their wares on the sidewalks. Tour the **New Mexico Museum of Art** (107 W. Palace Ave., 505/476-5072, www.nmartmuseum.org, 10am-5pm daily May-Oct., 10am-5pm Tues.-Sun. Nov.-Apr., $12), which is famed as much for its Pueblo Revival architecture as for the New Mexican art it contains.

2 Check out the grandiose **Cathedral Basilica of St. Francis of Assisi** (131

CATHEDRAL BASILICA OF ST. FRANCIS OF ASSISI

Cathedral Pl., 505/982-5619, www.cbsfa.org, 9:30am-4:30pm Mon.-Sat., free). The inside is all Gothic-inspired light and space and glowing stained glass windows, with a gilt altar screen installed in 1987.

AFTERNOON AND EVENING

3 Have lunch at **Tia Sophia's** (210 W. San Francisco St., 505/983-9880, http://www.tiasophias.com, 7am-2pm Mon.-Sat., 8am-1pm Sun., $9). This authentic old favorite claims to have invented the breakfast burrito.

4 Head over to the **Canyon Road art galleries** (intersection of Paseo de Peralta and Canyon Rd.) to spend the afternoon in the heart of Santa Fe's art scene. There's a city parking lot at the east (upper) end of the road and public parking near the bottom, just north of Canyon Road on Delgado Street. Head

CANYON ROAD ART GALLERY

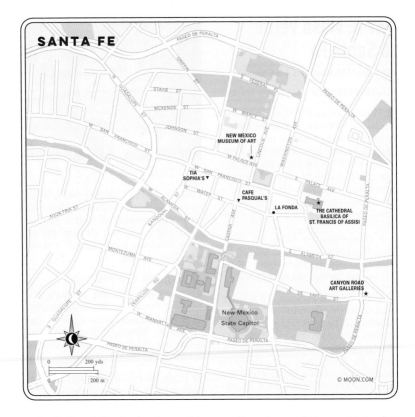

SANTA FE

(map labels)

PASEO DE PERALTA
GRIFFIN ST
STAAB ST
MCKENZIE ST
JOHNSON ST
W SAN FRANCISCO ST
S GUADALUPE ST
W SAN FRANCISCO ST
W PALACE AVE
W MARCY ST
S FEDERAL PL
LINCOLN AVE
WASHINGTON AVE
NEW MEXICO MUSEUM OF ART
TIA SOPHIA'S ▼
W SAN FRANCISCO ST
CAFE PASQUAL'S ▼
LA FONDA
E PALACE AVE
THE CATHEDRAL BASILICA OF ST. FRANCIS OF ASSISI ★
WATER ST
W ALAMEDA ST
ALAMEDA ST
SANDOVAL ST
GASPAR AVE
DON GASPAR AVE
AGUA FRIA ST
MONTEZUMA AVE
CERRILLOS RD
E ALAMEDA ST
CANYON ROAD ART GALLERIES ★
E DE VARGAS ST
W MANHATTAN AVE
New Mexico State Capitol
PASEO DE PERALTA
PASEO DE PERALTA
PASEO DE PERALTA
S GUADALUPE

0   200 yds
0   200 m

© MOON.COM

to the Railyard district for dinner. It's an easy walk from the plaza and has some of the better, quirkier dining options in town.

DAY 10: Santa Fe to Gallup

205 miles/330 kilometers | 3.5-4 hours

ROUTE OVERVIEW: I-25 • I-40/Route 66

❶ Depart Santa Fe to head south to **Albuquerque.** Once you arrive, check out **Petroglyph National Monument** (505/899-0205, www.nps.gov/petr, 8am-5pm daily). The city's West Mesa is covered with fine rock carvings made centuries ago by the ancestors of the local Pueblo people.

> Drive south on I-25 to Albuquerque (59 mi/95 km).

❷ Ride the **Sandia Peak Tramway** (30 Tramway Rd., 505/856-7325, www. sandiapeak.com, $25 round-trip, $15 one-way, $1 parking) to the crest of the mountain that looms over Albuquerque. At the top is a vertigo-inducing view.

❸ Head out of town in the afternoon and drive Historic Route 66 (also I-40) to **Gallup,** staying the night at the equally historic **El Rancho Hotel** (1000 E. Rte. 66, 505/863-9311, www. elranchohotel.com, $57-99). For sheer

SANDIA PEAK TRAMWAY

atmosphere, this is one of the best places in the state to get a taste of what tourism must've been like back when New Mexico really was the wild frontier.

> *Follow I-40 W/Route 66 for 136 miles (219 km) to Gallup.*

DAY 11: Gallup to Williams

240 miles/385 kilometers | 4.5-5 hours

ROUTE OVERVIEW: I-40 • Petrified Forest Rd. • US-180 • I-40

❶ The next morning, drive Historic Route 66/I-40 to **Petrified Forest National Park** (928/524-6228, www.nps.gov/pefo, 7am-7pm daily mid-Apr.-Aug., 7am-6pm daily Sept.-mid-Oct., 8am-5pm daily mid-Oct.-mid-Apr., $20 per vehicle, $15 motorcyclists, $10 bicyclists and pedestrians). Spend a few hours driving south along the park road, and make sure to stop at the **Painted Desert Inn Museum,** where you'll see one of the most dramatic petroglyphs in the state—a large, stylized mountain lion etched into a slab of rock.

> *Follow I-40 W from Gallup to Petrified Forest National Park (68 mi/109 km).*

❷ From the park road's southern terminus, drive west to **Winslow** and have lunch at La Posada's **Turquoise Room** (303 E. 2nd St., 928/289-2888, www.theturquoiseroom.net, $15-40), where the chef makes it a habit to incorporate native ingredients into nearly every dish. Insider tip: If you can't get a table in the dining room, opt for the

PETRIFIED FOREST NATIONAL PARK

lounge area. Next, head to the pine-forested mountain town of **Flagstaff** to wander its historic downtown, where breweries, coffee shops, boutiques, and bookstores line the sidewalks.

> *Take the 25-mile (40-km) drive through the park, then turn right to join US-180 W. Follow this for 18 miles (29 km), then merge onto I-40. Continue west for 29 miles (47 km) to reach Winslow. Continue west on I-40 for 53 miles (85 km) to reach Flagstaff.*

❸ Continue on to **Williams.** Check in to the 100-year-old **Red Garter Inn** (137 W. Railroad Ave., 800/328-1484, www.redgarter.com, $119-155) for the night, walk the town's Route 66-centric main strip, and have a dinner of excellent prime rib at **Miss Kitty's Steak House** (642 E. Rte. 66, 928/433-5889, 7am-10am and 5pm-9pm daily, $10-20).

> *Get back on I-40 and drive another 28 miles (45 km) west to reach Williams.*

DAY 12: Day Trip to Grand Canyon National Park

MORNING

❶ Get an early start for your visit to the **South Rim** of Grand Canyon National Park (928/638-7888, www.nps.gov/grca, 24 hours daily, $35 per vehicle, $30 motorcyclists, $20 bicyclists and pedestrians).

❷ Enjoy a break from your car by taking the **Grand Canyon Railway** (800/843-8724, www.thetrain.com, $65-220 round-trip) to the park from Williams. It takes about 2.5 hours to get to the South Rim depot. Comedian-fiddlers often stroll through the cars, and on some trips there's even a mock train robbery complete with bandits on horseback with blazing six-shooters.

AFTERNOON

❸ Take in the views from the **Rim Trail** (12.8 mi/20.6 km one-way, easy), the single best way to see all of the South Rim. Walk past historic buildings, famous lodges, and the most breathtaking views in the world. Perhaps

GRAND CANYON

the best thing about the Rim Trail is that you don't have to hike the whole 13 miles—far from it. There are at least 16 shuttle stops along the way, and you can hop on and off the trail at your pleasure. Get on the trail at Grand Canyon Village; an easy access point is behind the train station.

④ Before taking the train back to Williams, savor appetizers and drinks in the lounge at **El Tovar Dining Room** (928/638-2631, ext. 6432, www.grand-canyonlodges.com, 6:30am-11am, 11:30am-2pm, and 5pm-10pm daily, $17-35), a stylishly historical restaurant on the canyon's edge.

EVENING

⑤ For dinner, indulge in homemade comfort food—roast beef, pasta, pie—at **Pine Country Restaurant** (107 N. Grand Canyon Blvd., 928/635-9718, www.pinecountryrestaurant.com, 7am-9pm daily, $12-25).

DAY 13: Williams to Las Vegas

320 miles/515 kilometers | 6-7 hours

ROUTE OVERVIEW: I-40 • Route 66 • US-93 • I-11 • I-215 • I-15

① Have breakfast in Williams, then head west on I-40 for the 20-minute sprint to **Ash Fork,** the starting point for the longest continuous stretch of **Route 66.** In **Peach Springs,** take a

TAKING IN GRAND CANYON VIEWS

guided tour of **Grand Canyon Caverns** (Rte. 66, mile marker 115, 928/422-3223, www.gccaverns.com, 8am-6pm daily summer, 10am-4pm daily winter, $16-21), North America's largest dry cave, where crystals and other strange rock formations hide in the darkness.

> *Follow I-40 W from Williams to Ash Fork (15 mi/24 km). Continue onto Historic Route 66 to Grand Canyon Caverns (42 mi/68 km).*

❷ Next, browse the gift shops in **Seligman,** then grab snacks at the **Hackberry General Store** (11255 Rte. 66, Hackberry, 928/769-2605, www.hackberrygeneralstore.com, 9am-6pm daily).

> *Stay on Route 66 for 24 miles (39 km) to Seligman, then another 60 miles (97 km) to Hackberry.*

❸ Continue along Route 66 to **Kingman** and check out the life-size dioramas at the small-but-mighty **Historic Route 66 Museum** (Powerhouse Visitors Center, 120 W. Andy Devine Ave., 928/753-9889, www.route66museum. net, 9am-5pm daily, $4 adults, free for children under 13).

> *Continue west on Route 66 for 26 miles (42 km) to Kingman.*

❹ If you don't want to end your trip just yet, stop between Kingman and Las Vegas for a tour of **Hoover Dam** (702/494-2517, www.usbr.gov/lc/hooverdam, every 30 minutes, 9:30am-3:30pm daily, $30). The tour offers a guided exploration of the dam's power plant and walkways, and includes admission to the visitors center. A parking garage ($10) is convenient, but free parking is available at turnouts on both sides of the dam for those willing to walk.

> *Take US-93 N for 71 miles (114 km) to Hoover Dam.*

❺ Back in Las Vegas, check in to **The Cosmopolitan** (3708 Las Vegas Blvd. S., 702/698-7000, www.cosmopolitanlasvegas.com, $220-4,380) and take a well-deserved rest from the road and relax poolside.

> *Take I-11 to I-215 (20 mi/32 km). Drive west on I-215 to I-15 (11 mi/18 km), then go north on I-15 for 4 miles (6 km) to Las Vegas.*

Getting There

Las Vegas's **McCarran International Airport** (LAS, 5757 Wayne Newton Blvd., 702/261-5211, www.mccarran.com) is one of the busiest airports in the country. Terminal 1 hosts domestic flights, while Terminal 3 has domestic and international flights.

McCarran Airport provides easy transfers to the Las Vegas Strip using **shuttle vans, buses,** and **rental cars.** Limousines are available curbside for larger groups. A **taxi ride** from the airport to the Strip (15 minutes) or downtown (20 minutes) runs no more than $25. A $2 surcharge is assessed for pickups from the airport, and there is a $3 credit card processing fee.

If you rent your vehicle at the airport and drive to the Strip, the 5-mile (8 km) trip will take 10 minutes. Take I-15 N from the airport, and exit at Flamingo Road.

CONNECT WITH

- At Las Vegas: **Best of the Golden State** (PAGE 108)
- At Moab: **The Loneliest Road** (PAGE 36)
- At Santa Fe, Albuquerque, and Williams: **Route 66** (PAGE 60)
- At Santa Fe: **Santa Fe, Taos, and the Enchanted Circle** (PAGE 304)

SANTA FE, TAOS, AND THE ENCHANTED CIRCLE

WHY GO: Native American heritage, world-class art, green chiles, Southwestern sunsets, adobe architecture, craggy mesas, Santuario de Chimayó

TOTAL DISTANCE: 295 miles/ 475 kilometers

NUMBER OF DAYS: 4

SEASONS: Spring through early winter

START: Santa Fe, New Mexico

END: Taos, New Mexico

▼ TAOS PUEBLO

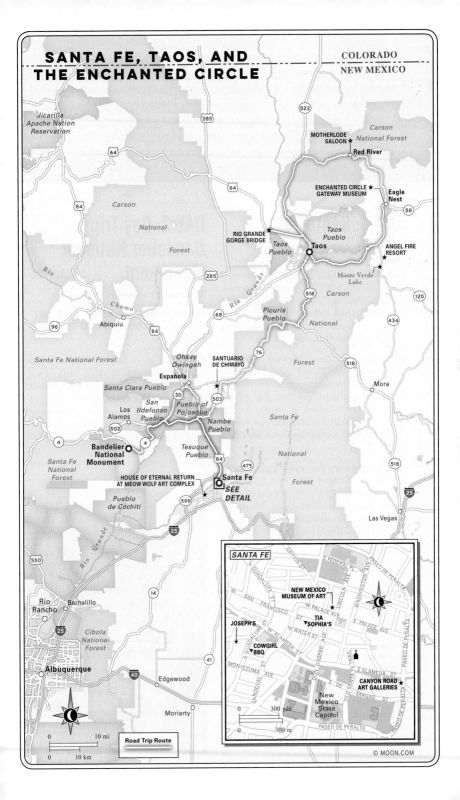

SANTA FE, TAOS, AND THE ENCHANTED CIRCLE

COLORADO
NEW MEXICO

Jicarilla
Apache Nation
Reservation

Carson

National

Forest

Carson
National Forest

MOTHERLODE
SALOON ★
● Red River

ENCHANTED CIRCLE ★
GATEWAY MUSEUM

Eagle
Nest

RIO GRANDE ★
GORGE BRIDGE

Taos
Pueblo

Taos
Pueblo

● Taos

ANGEL FIRE
RESORT ★

Monte Verde
Lake

Carson

Rio

Chama

Abiquiu

National

Forest

Picuris
Pueblo

Santa Fe National Forest

Ohkay
Owingeh

SANTUARIO
DE CHIMAYÓ ★

Española

Santa Clara Pueblo

San
Ildefonso
Pueblo

Los
Alamos

Pueblo of
Pojoaque

Santa Fe

National

Bandelier
National
Monument

Nambe
Pueblo

Tesuque
Pueblo

Santa Fe
National
Forest

HOUSE OF ETERNAL RETURN ★
AT MEOW WOLF ART COMPLEX

Santa Fe

SEE
DETAIL

Pueblo
de Cochiti

Las Vegas

Rio
Rancho

Bernalillo

Cibola
National
Forest

Albuquerque

Edgewood

Moriarty

0   10 mi

0   10 km

Road Trip Route

SANTA FE

NEW MEXICO
MUSEUM OF ART ★

TIA
SOPHIA'S ▼

JOSEPH'S

COWGIRL
BBQ

CANYON ROAD
ART GALLERIES ★

New
Mexico
State
Capitol

0   300 yds

0   300 m

© MOON.COM

Tucked in the Sangre de Cristo foothills, renowned for its arts scene, and swathed in adobe architecture, it would be tempting to spend a week in Santa Fe without venturing beyond the historic city's environs. But that would be a mistake. Because just beyond Santa Fe lies the enchanted beauty of Taos, the hidden canyons and cliffside homes of the Pueblo Indians, and family-run restaurants that serve authentic Southwestern food. With Santa Fe as your base, take a day trip to Bandelier National Monument, then head north to Taos for two nights, sandwiching in a day trip on the Enchanted Circle Byway.

DAY 1: Santa Fe

MORNING AND AFTERNOON

❶ Start with a breakfast burrito at **Tia Sophia's** (210 W. San Francisco St., 505/983-9880, www.tiasophias.com, 7am-2pm Mon.-Sat., 8am-1pm Sun., $9), then stroll around the plaza. Check in to one of the hotels close to the plaza and drop off your bags.

❷ Visit the **New Mexico Museum of Art** (107 W. Palace Ave., 505/476-5072, www.nmartmuseum.org, 10am-5pm daily, 10am-7pm first Fri. of the month, $12), famed as much for its Pueblo Revival architecture as for its collection of works by New Mexican artists.

❸ Pop in to see the winding staircase at **Loretto Chapel** (207 Old Santa Fe Tr., 505/982-0092, www.lorettochapel.com, 9am-5pm Mon.-Sat., 10:30am-5pm Sun., $3), the first Gothic structure west of the Mississippi.

EVENING

❹ Cruise the galleries on **Canyon Road** (Paseo de Peralta and Canyon Rd.). The heart of Santa Fe's art scene is a half-mile-long visual smorgasbord, packed with more than 80 galleries. On summer Fridays, most galleries have an open house or an exhibition opening, from around 5pm until 7pm or 8pm.

❺ Finish up with drinks and tapas, and maybe even dancing, at **El Farol** (808 Canyon Rd., 505/983-9912, www.elfarolsantafe.com, 11:30am-11pm daily, $7-36), one of the oldest restaurants in the country.

DAY 2: Day Trip to Bandelier National Monument

95 miles/153 kilometers | 2.5-3 hours

ROUTE OVERVIEW: US-84 • NM-502 • NM-4 • NM-502 • NM-30 • US-84/US-285

❶ Get an early start to **Bandelier National Monument** (505/672-3861, www.nps.gov/band, $25 per vehicle). Spend several hours exploring the once-hidden valley of Frijoles Canyon, where ancestors of today's Pueblo people constructed an elaborate city complex with cliffside cave homes. Summers get very busy, so you may need to hop on a shuttle.

BANDELIER NATIONAL MONUMENT

Top ③ SANTA FE, TAOS, AND THE ENCHANTED CIRCLE

① Answer the all-important question— red or green chile?—at famed eatery Tia Sophia's in **Santa Fe** (PAGE 306).

② See ancient Native American dwellings at **Taos Pueblo** (PAGE 309).

③ Drive the breathtaking 84-mile **Enchanted Circle** (PAGE 310).

Best OF SOUTHWEST CUISINE

Given the region's distinctive cuisine—from only-in-New Mexico hot chile to gourmet creativity—it would be easy to plan a vacation entirely around eating.

BEST TRADITIONAL NEW MEXICAN

"Red or green?" is the official state question, the dilemma diners face when they order anything that can be drowned in an earthy red-chile sauce or a chunky, vegetal green one (Hint: if you can't decide, choose "Christmas").

- **Tia Sophia's** (210 W. San Francisco St., Santa Fe, 505/983-9880, 7am-2pm Mon.-Sat., 8am-1pm Sun., $9): History was made in this old-school spot near the Santa Fe Plaza. It's allegedly where the breakfast burrito was invented.

- **Rancho de Chimayó** (County Rd. 98, Chimayó, 505/351-4444, www.ranchodechimayo.com, 11:30am-9pm daily May-Oct., 11:30am-8:30pm Tues.-Sun. Nov.-Apr., $12): An essential stop after visiting the nearby Santuario, this inviting inn has a menu full of immensely satisfying dishes such as *sopaipilla relleno*.

- **Orlando's** (1114 Don Juan Valdez Ln., Taos, 575/751-1450, 10:30am-2:30pm and 5pm-8:30pm Sun.-Thurs., 10:30am-2:30pm and 5pm-9pm Fri.-Sat.,

$7-14): The Taos favorite is known for its green-chile sauce, deceptively smooth and velvety, considering the heat it packs.

BEST GREEN-CHILE CHEESEBURGERS

This greasy treat is so genius, it has been immortalized in the official **New Mexico Green Chile Cheeseburger Trail** (www.newmexico.org). A few GCCB options:

- **Santa Fe Bite** (1616 St. Michael's Dr., Santa Fe, 505/428-0328, 7am-9pm Tues.-Sun., $13): This casual restaurant grinds its own meat and shapes the enormous patties by hand.

- **Bang Bite Filling Station** (411 Water St., Santa Fe, 505/469-2345): A food truck whose signature green-chile cheeseburger is worth the long lines and the wait.

- **Sugar's BBQ and Hamburgers** (1799 Hwy. 68, Embudo, 505/852-0604, 11am-6pm Thurs.-Sun., $6): If you're taking the low road to Taos, don't miss out on a juicy green-chile cheeseburger at this beloved institution.

> *Drive northwest on US-84 to NM-502 (15 mi/24 km). Turn left on NM-502 and continue west to NM-4 (12 mi/19 km). Follow NM-4 W to Bandelier National Monument (12 mi/19 km).*

❷ Have lunch in **Española** at **El Parasol** (603 Santa Cruz Rd., http://el-parasol.com/espanola, 505/753-8852, 7am-9pm Mon.-Thurs., 7am-9:30pm Fri.-Sat., 8am-8pm Sun., $5), a take-out stand serving cheap and delicious New Mexican classics.

> *Leave the monument via NM-4 E to NM-502 (12 mi/19 km). Take NM-502 for*

4 miles (6 km) to NM-30. Head north on NM-30 to Española (8 mi/13 km).

❸ In midafternoon, return to **Santa Fe** to explore the **House of Eternal Return** at the **Meow Wolf Art Complex** (1352 Rufina Circle, 505/395-6369, http://meowwolf.com, 10am-8pm Sun.-Thurs., 10am-10pm Fri.-Sat., $20). This immersive art experience is set in a massive space once occupied by a bowling alley.

> *Take US-84 E/US-285 for 22 miles (35 km) to return to Santa Fe.*

4 Enjoy the mellow patio scene during happy hour at **Cowgirl BBQ** (319 S. Guadalupe St., www.cowgirlsantafe. com, 505/982-2565, 11:30am-midnight Mon.-Thurs., 11am-1am Fri.-Sat., 11am-11:30pm Sun.) in the Railyard.

5 Settle in for a vegetable-centric dinner at the lovely, candlelit **Joseph's** (428 Agua Fria St., 505/982-1272, www.josephsofsantafe.com, 5:30pm-10pm Sun.-Thurs., 5:30pm-11pm Fri.-Sat., $16-44). Book ahead if you can, or try for a seat at the bar.

DAY 3: Santa Fe to Taos

105 miles/170 kilometers | 3-3.5 hours

ROUTE OVERVIEW: US-84 • NM-503 • NM-76 • NM-75 • NM-518 • NM-68 • Hwy. to Town of Taos • US-64

1 Drive to Taos via the low road, detouring to the pilgrimage site of **Santuario de Chimayó** (Juan Medina Rd. and Santuario Dr., 505/351-9961, www. holychimayo.us, 9am-6pm daily May-Sept., 9am-5pm daily Oct.-Apr.). Faith is palpable in this village church, known as "the Lourdes of America," thanks to the healing powers attributed to the holy dirt found here.

> Follow US-84 W to NM-503 (15 mi/24 km). Turn right onto NM-503 and drive 8 miles (13 km) to Juan Medina Rd. Turn left and follow Juan Medina Rd. for 2.5 miles (4 km) to Santuario de Chimayó.

2 Once you reach **Taos,** head straight to **Taos Pueblo** (120 Veterans Hwy., 575/758-1028, www.taospueblo.com, 8am-4:30pm Mon.-Sat., 8:30am-4:30pm Sun., $16 adults, free for children 10 and under). The stepped adobe buildings at New Mexico's most remarkable pueblo seem to rise organically from the earth. If you can time your visit for one of the ceremonial dances performed here (about eight times a year), you're in for an unforgettable day.

> Take Juan Medina Rd. for 1 mile (1.6 km) to NM-76. Drive north on NM-76 for 22 miles (35 km). At NM-75, turn right and drive 7 miles (11 km) east to NM-518. Turn left and continue north on NM-518 for 16 miles (26 km) to NM-68. Turn right and follow this for 4 miles (6 km) into Taos. Taos Pueblo is 3 miles (5 km) northeast of town via Hwy. to Town of Taos.

3 Admire the sunset at the **Rio Grande Gorge** (US-64, west of Hwy. 150 and Hwy. 522). Here, a pedestrian path along a delicate-looking bridge brings the depths below you into extremely sharp relief; viewing the gorge from here at sunset with the mountains looming in the backdrop can make for a stunning end to the day.

> Retrace your path south along Hwy. to Town of Taos, turning right after 1 mile (1.6 km) onto Hail Creek Rd. Follow this for less than a mile to US-64. Turn right and follow US-64 for 10 miles (16 km) to the bridge over the Rio Grande Gorge.

TAOS PUEBLO

RAFTING THE RIO GRANDE

❹ Drive back into town and stop at the **Adobe Bar** (125 Paseo del Pueblo Norte, 575/758-2233, 11am-10pm daily) at the **Taos Inn** for a margarita. You can plan on spending the night here; rooms run about $129-189 in the high season.

> *Take US-64 E for 12 miles (19 km) to get back to Taos proper.*

❺ Head up the road for dinner at the family-run **Orlando's** (1114 Don Juan Valdez Ln., 575/751-1450, 10:30am-2:30pm and 5pm-8:30pm Sun.-Thurs.,

Playlist

SANTA FE, TAOS, AND THE ENCHANTED CIRCLE

SONGS

- **"The Dance" by Robert Mirabel:** A Pueblo musician from Taos, Mirabel has won Grammy awards for his powerful music. Listen to this song as you drive the low road to Taos.

- **"Far From Any Road" by Handsome Family:** This Chicago alt-country band now calls Albuquerque home. This slow and moody tune (used as the *True Detective* opener) is best played after night falls on the open road.

- **"Santa Fe" by Samantha Crain:** A Choctaw Indian from Shawnee, Oklahoma, Crain sings this folksy, banjo-led tune about the blue skies and open roads of New Mexico in a soulful voice that'll stay in your head—and heart—for days.

10:30am-2:30pm and 5pm-9pm Fri.-Sat., $7-14). It's known for having the best chile in town.

DAY 4: Enchanted Circle Day Trip

95 miles/153 kilometers | 3 hours

ROUTE OVERVIEW: US-64 • Mountain View Blvd. • US-64 • NM-38 • NM-522 • US-64

❶ The **Enchanted Circle** is named for its breathtaking views of the Sangre de Cristo Mountains, including Wheeler Peak. First stop: **Angel Fire Resort** (10 Miller Ln., 800/633-7463, www.angelfireresort.com), a ski resort that, come summer, transforms itself with a full slate of warm-weather activities. The cool alpine waters of the resort's **Monte Verde Lake** are particularly appealing. Try your hand at stand-up paddleboarding ($20/hour) or fishing ($25 pp).

> *Take US-64 E for 21 miles (34 km). Turn right onto Mountain View Blvd./NM-434 and continue for 3 miles (5 km) to reach the resort.*

❷ In Angel Fire, fuel up with lunch at **The Bakery & Cafe** (3420 Mountain View Blvd., 575/377-3992, www.thebakeryatangelfire.com, 7am-2:30pm daily, $7-11). Enjoy generous portions of tasty *migas,* biscuits and gravy, and chicken-fried steak and eggs.

> *Head back to Mountain View Blvd. and drive for less than a mile to reach the café.*

❸ At the junction of US-64 and NM-38, **Eagle Nest** is a small strip of buildings, all that's left of what was a jumping gambling town in the 1920s and 1930s. The **Enchanted Circle Gateway Museum** (US-64, 575/377-5978, 9:30am-4pm Mon.-Sat., 11am-4pm Sun., donation), at the eastern edge of town, gives an overview of the good old days and often hosts events, such as a mountain-man rendezvous.

> *Go north on Mountain View Blvd. for 2.5 miles (4 km), then join US-64 E and drive for 10 miles (16 km) to reach Eagle Nest.*

4 Next up is **Red River,** a cluster of tidy rows of wooden buildings done up in Old West facades, complete with boardwalks and swinging saloon doors. This was once a community of wild prospectors, but when mining went bust, the town salvaged itself by renting out abandoned houses to vacationers escaping the summer heat.

> Take NM-38 northwest from Eagle Nest for 17 miles (27 km) to reach Red River.

5 Catch live music in Red River. At **Motherlode Saloon** (406 E. Main St., 575/754-6280, 6pm-2am daily), local rock and country acts take the stage and make it the most rollicking place in town. Head back to Taos to spend the night.

> Follow NM-38 W for 12 miles (19 km), then turn left onto NM-522. Follow this south for 20 miles (32 km) to US-64. Continue south on US-64 for 4 miles (6 km) to get back to Taos.

Getting There

AIR

Santa Fe Regional Airport (SAF, 121 Aviation Dr., 505/955-2900, www.santafenm.gov/airport), west of the city, receives direct flights from Dallas and Phoenix (seasonal) with American Airlines, and from Denver with United. Typically, fares are better to **Albuquerque International Sunport** (ABQ, 505/244-7700, www.cabq.gov/airport), an hour's drive away.

Sandia Shuttle Express (888/775-5696, www.sandiashuttle.com) does hourly pickups from the Albuquerque airport 4:45am-6:45pm and every 90 minutes 8pm-12:30am and will deliver to any hotel or B&B ($33 each way).

TRAIN

The **Rail Runner** (866/795-7245, www.riometro.org) goes from Albuquerque to downtown Santa Fe—the final stop is at the rail yard in the Guadalupe district (410 S. Guadalupe St.). The ride takes a little over 90 minutes and costs $10, or $11 for a day pass, and the last train back to Albuquerque leaves at 9pm weekdays, 10:14pm Saturday, and 8:10pm Sunday.

Amtrak (800/872-7245, www.amtrak.com) runs the Southwest Chief once a day through Lamy, 18 miles south of Santa Fe. It's a dramatic place to step off the train—with little visible civilization for miles around, it feels like entering a Wild West movie set. Trains arrive from Chicago and Los Angeles in the afternoon, and Amtrak provides a shuttle van to the city.

BUS

Santa Fe's **Greyhound bus station** (7 Colina Dr., 505/424-9265, www.greyhound.com) offers service between the city and destinations throughout the country.

CAR

From **Santa Fe Regional Airport** to downtown Santa Fe, it's 14 miles (23 km), which takes approximately 20 minutes. Follow NM-599 N to US-285 S. Use US-285 to connect with Guadalupe Street (make a left), which takes you into town.

From **Albuquerque** to Santa Fe, it's a straight shot north on I-25 for 65 miles (105 km); you'll reach Santa Fe in about an hour.

Getting Back

Driving back to **Santa Fe** from Taos, allow 1.5-2.5 hours, depending on whether you come on the low road (70 mi/113 km; on NM-68 and US-84/285, via Española), via Ojo Caliente (90 mi/145 km; mostly on US-285), or on the high road (75 mi/121 km; mostly on NM-76, via Truchas).

From Taos to **Albuquerque,** expect the 135-mile (217-km) drive to take 2.5-3.5 hours. Depart Taos via any of the above-mentioned routes and head into Santa Fe. Then continue south on I-25 for 65 miles (105 km) into Albuquerque.

CONNECT WITH

• At Santa Fe: **Route 66** (PAGE 60) and **Best of the Southwest** (PAGE 288)

THE APACHE TRAIL

WHY GO: Desert lakes, stagecoach stops, backcountry roads, red rocks, American Indian ruins, saguaro cactus, authentic Mexican food

TOTAL DISTANCE: 105 miles/ 170 kilometers

NUMBER OF DAYS: 2

SEASONS: Year-round

START: Apache Junction, Arizona

END: Superior, Arizona

▶ NEEDLE VISTA NEAR APACHE JUNCTION

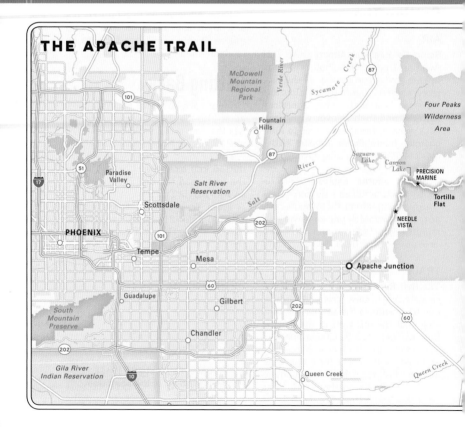

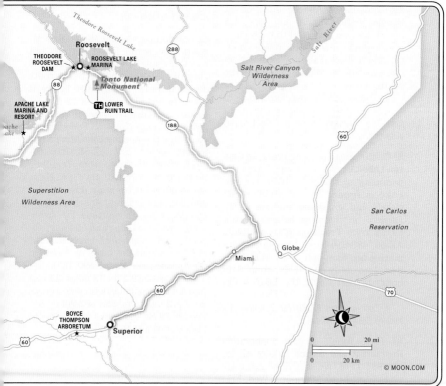

A dirt road bends through a pristine desert landscape, crystalline lakes dot the way, and a saloon pops up around a corner like a mirage. This is the Old West at its best, and it sits deep in the Superstition Mountains on the edge of Phoenix. When you embark on the Apache Trail (AZ-88), you're traveling back in time. The old stagecoach trail was named after the Apache people who used it to traverse the rugged wilderness of the Superstitions. Today, the trail is still wild and untamed, although lakeside resorts and marinas welcome road-trippers with modern amenities.

DAY 1: Apache Junction to Roosevelt

35 miles/56 kilometers | 1.5-2 hours

ROUTE OVERVIEW: AZ-88

1 Apache Junction, a small suburb east of Phoenix at the base of the Superstition Mountains, marks the beginning of the Apache Trail (AZ-88). The wild portion of the Apache Trail really gets started about 8 miles (13 km) outside of Apache Junction at **Needle Vista** (4 mi/6 km loop, 1.5 hours, easy), a loop trail that provides a sweeping view of the rough country and a good look at Weavers Needle, a distinctive rock formation to the south.

> Follow AZ-88 northeast out of Apache Junction to Needle Vista (8 mi/13 km). The trailhead is on the right (east) side of the road.

2 Continuing east, you'll come to **Canyon Lake.** A reservoir formed from the damming of the Salt River, Canyon Lake is framed by steep cliffs; look closely and you'll spot bighorn sheep perched on the rock ledges. Rent a kayak from **Precision Marine** (16802 AZ-88, 480/610-3300, http://precision-marine.biz, 8am-5pm daily Mar.-Nov., 9am-4pm daily Dec.-Feb., from $15/hour) to best enjoy the lake's calm waters.

> Continue on AZ-88 for 7 miles (11 km) to Canyon Lake.

3 Have lunch at the **Superstition Restaurant and Saloon** (20909 AZ-88, 480/984-1776, www.tortillaflataz.com/restaurant.html, 10am-5pm Wed.-Fri.,

9am-7pm Sat.-Sun. June-Sept., 10am-6pm Mon.-Fri., 9am-7pm Sat.-Sun. Oct.-May, $8-20) at **Tortilla Flat** (http://tortillaflataz.com), which was once a stage stop. The burgers, homemade chili, Mexican food, beers, and saddle-topped barstools are popular with Harley riders, who haunt the trail in large numbers on the weekends. This strange, charming little place, restored from the original but still romantically rustic, is named after a butte nearby that looks a bit like stacked tortillas.

> It's another 3 miles (5 km) east on AZ-88 to Tortilla Flat.

4 Continuing east on the trail, a saguaro and scrub forest spreads out on either side, and the Superstitions loom like giant jagged teeth. The route descends precipitously just before it turns to dirt. Then it's on to Apache Lake, a secluded reservoir in the middle of the Tonto National Forest. Here, you'll find the **Apache Lake Marina and Resort** (mile 229.5 AZ-88, 928/467-2511, www.apachelake.com, 7am-9pm Sun.-Thurs., 7am-10pm Fri.-Sat.), which offers boat rentals, a restaurant and bar, and lodging. Apache Lake is popular with Phoenicians for swimming, waterskiing, and fishing for small- and largemouth bass. Stay the night in one of the lakeside rooms at the **Apache Lake Motel** ($90-125).

> Follow AZ-88 E for 13 miles (21 km). Turn left and continue north onto Service Rd. 79 (2 mi/3 km). Stay straight on Service Rd. 79 for less than a mile to Apache Lake Marina and Resort.

Top ③ THE APACHE TRAIL

① Belly up to the bar at the restored **saloon** in **Tortilla Flat,** an old stagecoach stop (**PAGE 314**).

② Ply the waters on a **kayak** or a **motorboat** at **Apache Lake,** one of the four Salt River lakes (**PAGE 314**).

③ Explore the preserved ruins of the native Salado people at **Tonto National Monument** (**PAGE 316**).

DAY 2: Roosevelt to Superior

70 miles/113 kilometers | 2.5 hours

ROUTE OVERVIEW: AZ-88 • AZ-188 • US-60

① After breakfast at the lake's restaurant, it's time to hit the road. The dirt trail follows a narrow band of water. Then it climbs up, and the sheer rock wall of the **Theodore Roosevelt Dam** comes into sight. You can stop here and gaze at it from a promontory. Then the road passes the large **Roosevelt Dam Bridge** and the highway heading north to Payson and the Rim Country.

> Use Service Rd. 79 from Apache Lake Marina and Resort to return to AZ-88. Turn left onto AZ-88 and drive northeast for 11 miles (18 km) to Theodore Roosevelt Dam.

② The largest of the Salt River Lakes, **Roosevelt Lake**—128 miles of sandy shoreline and stunning red rocks that jut up all around—can be accessed through the **Roosevelt Lake Marina** (28085 N. AZ-188, 602/977-7170, www.rlmaz.com, 7am-7pm daily, $6 day use, $4 boat fee, campsites $10/night first come, first served). You can rent a boat, skid around on personal watercraft, or explore hidden coves and fishing spots.

> Continue on AZ-88 to AZ-188 (2 mi/3 km). Turn right to head south on AZ-188. In less than a mile, Roosevelt Lake Marina will be on the left.

③ Pass Roosevelt Lake and turn at the sign to get to **Tonto National Monument** (26260 N. AZ-188, Roosevelt, 928/467-2241, www.nps.gov/tont, 8am-5pm daily, $10 per person), a cliffside ruin inhabited by the Salado people from 1250 to 1450. It's so well preserved it appears—from far away, at least—as if people could still live here in the cool shade of a natural rock alcove high above the saguaro and cholla. The paved **Lower Ruin** trail is a 1-mile round-trip hike, most of it straight up. The visitors center showcases interesting artifacts of the Salado and has a good bit of information on this often-overlooked group. Tonto marks the western end of the Apache Trail.

> Continue south on AZ-188 to Tonto National Monument (2 mi/3 km).

④ For lunch, try **Guayo's on the Trail** (14249 AZ-188, Globe, 928/425-9969, www.guayosrestaurants.com, 10:30am-8:30pm Wed.-Sat., 10:30am-8pm Sun., $6.50-15), which serves outstanding traditional Mexican food based on old family recipes. This casual place has been around since 1938, and it's very popular with Apache Trail travelers, especially the motorcycle crowd.

> Follow AZ-188 S for 25 miles (40 km) to Guayo's on the Trail.

⑤ A stroll around the **Boyce Thompson Arboretum** (37615 US-60, 520/689-2811, http://ag.arizona.edu/bta, 6am-3pm daily May-Sept., 8am-5pm daily

▶ Playlist

THE APACHE TRAIL

SONGS

- **"Arizona" by Kings of Leon:** A slow, moody song that—when played late at night under the dark skies of the Grand Canyon State—eases you into an introspective frame of mind.

PODCASTS

- ***Thinking Sideways:*** Even though this podcast is now defunct, you can still find all of the episodes online, including one called "The Lost Dutchman's Mine." This episode delves into the mystery of a stash of gold supposedly hidden in the Superstition Mountains on the Apache Trail.

Oct.-Apr., $15 adults, $5 children 5-12) is the perfect capstone to an Apache Trail tour. Just three miles west of Superior along US-60, the arboretum invites you to walk to otherworldly cactus gardens, across a cottonwood-covered stream, along the shores of a desert lake, and even through an Australian eucalyptus forest, all surrounded by the huge, telltale boulder-mountains of the Central Arizona outback. This is not recommended in summer.

> Take AZ-188 for 1.5 miles (2.5 km) to US-60. Turn right and drive west on US-60 to Boyce Thompson Arboretum (24 mi/39 km).

Getting There

AIR

Phoenix Sky Harbor International Airport (PHX, 3400 E. Sky Harbor Blvd., 602/273-3300, www.skyharbor.com) is one of the Southwest's largest airports, with three terminals served by 18 domestic and international airlines offering flights to about 80 domestic and 22 international destinations.

Rent a vehicle from Sky Harbor's **Rental Car Center** (1805 Sky Harbor Cir., 602/683-3741, www.skyharbor.com, 24 hours daily). The center is a short shuttle ride from the airport's terminals. The shuttle picks up passengers every few minutes from the curb on the baggage claim levels of each terminal. Rental companies that service Phoenix Sky Harbor include Alamo, Avis, Budget, Dollar, Enterprise, Hertz, National, Silvercar, and Thrifty.

TRAIN

The **Amtrak Sunset Limited** (800/872-7245, www.amtrak.com), which runs along the southern route and through the Southwest three times a week from New Orleans, stops in Maricopa, Arizona, about 30 miles east of Phoenix. Note that transportation options from Maricopa to Phoenix are tough to come by and expensive.

BUS

Phoenix's **Greyhound bus station** (2115 E. Buckeye Rd., 602/389-4200, www.greyhound.com) is located near Sky Harbor International Airport. **Arizona**

KEY RESERVATIONS

- While it's not necessary to book a room at **Apache Lake Motel** ahead of time, accommodations fill up quickly on the weekends. Call **a few days** ahead to reserve a room.

Shuttle (800/888-2749, www.arizonashuttle.com, $48 pp, one-way) offers several daily trips between Flagstaff's Amtrak station and Sky Harbor International Airport.

CAR

From **Phoenix airport**, it's a 32-mile (52-km), 45-minute drive. Head east on AZ-202 Loop to AZ-101 Loop South. Follow AZ-101 Loop to US-60. Merge onto US-60, continuing east to exit 196 for AZ-88. Turn left onto AZ-88 and drive into Apache Junction.

I-10 passes through downtown Phoenix on its way to and from the California coast. Phoenix is 370 miles (600 km) east of Los Angeles, a straight five-hour shot on I-10. The Phoenix metro area is connected to the I-40 east-west corridor by I-17, which runs north 150 miles (241 km) from central Phoenix to Flagstaff, a two-hour drive.

Getting Back

It's 32 miles (52 km) to return to **Apache Junction** from Superior. Drive US-60 W to exit 199, turn right onto Goldfield Road, and then make a slight left onto Old West Highway. Follow Old West Highway northwest into Apache Junction.

Phoenix sits about 60 miles (97 km) west of Superior via US-60, a scenic hour-long stretch that skirts the edge of the Superstition Mountains and passes through Florence Junction and Gold Canyon. There's not much to look at along the route back to Phoenix save for awesome desert scenery. US-60 becomes the Superstition Freeway once you're back in the city.

RENO TO THE RUBIES

WHY GO: Frontier towns, Wild West history, casino resorts, silver mines, mountains, scenic byways, train travel, Western art, Ice Age creatures

TOTAL DISTANCE: 650 miles/ 1,050 kilometers

NUMBER OF DAYS: 7

SEASONS: Spring through fall

START: Reno, Nevada

END: Baker, Nevada

▶ GREAT BASIN NATIONAL PARK

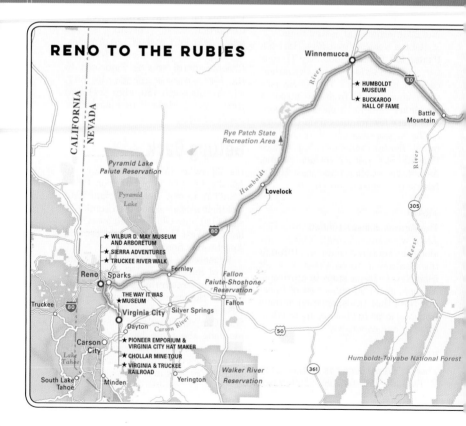

RENO TO THE RUBIES

Winnemucca

★ HUMBOLDT MUSEUM
★ BUCKAROO HALL OF FAME

Battle Mountain

Rye Patch State Recreation Area

CALIFORNIA / NEVADA

Pyramid Lake Paiute Reservation

Pyramid Lake

Humboldt

Lovelock

Reese River

★ WILBUR D. MAY MUSEUM AND ARBORETUM
★ SIERRA ADVENTURES
★ TRUCKEE RIVER WALK

Reno   Sparks

Fernley

Fallon Paiute-Shoshone Reservation

THE WAY IT WAS ★ MUSEUM

Virginia City   Silver Springs

Dayton   Carson River

Fallon

Truckee

Carson City

★ PIONEER EMPORIUM & VIRGINIA CITY HAT MAKER
★ CHOLLAR MINE TOUR
★ VIRGINIA & TRUCKEE RAILROAD

Lake Tahoe

South Lake Tahoe   Minden   Yerington

Walker River Reservation

Humboldt-Toiyabe National Forest

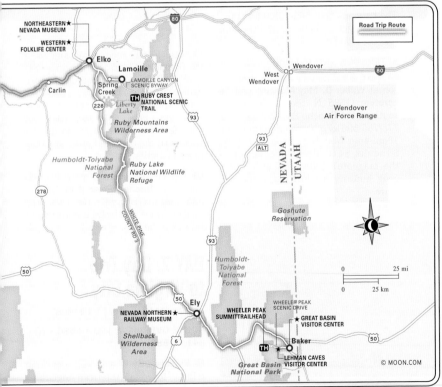

Reno is no Vegas. And for many, that's a plus. Nevada's original gambling town is laid-back, relaxed, and welcoming, and it serves as a bustling start to the stark high-desert journey that awaits you. As you travel through Nevada's northern frontier, you'll stop in Winnemucca and Elko, wind through the Ruby Mountains, and explore the dark skies and ancient bristlecone pines in Great Basin National Park. Most importantly, you'll encounter all sorts of Western treasures. See for yourself how the cliff-hugging mining towns, cowboy museums, tree-studded canyons, and alpine peaks have inspired artists, songwriters, poets, and photographers the world over.

DAY 1: Reno

MORNING

1 There's plenty to see before you drive across Nevada's northern frontier. For an experience unlike anything you've done before, call **Sierra Adventures** (775/323-8928 or 866/323-8928, www.wildsierra.com, from $330). This outfitter takes you on a three-hour hot-air balloon ride. The balloons take off as early as 6:30am in the summer. The balloons float 500-1,000 feet up—hovering gently between the treetops and the clouds.

AFTERNOON AND EVENING

2 Next, get a history and culture lesson at **Wilbur D. May Museum and Arboretum** (1595 N. Sierra St. at the south end of Rancho San Rafael Park, 775/785-5961, www.maycenter.com, 10am-4pm Wed.-Sat., noon-4pm Sun., $6 adults, $4 children), which displays the magnate's collections of Western gear, hunting trophies, Africana, and more.

TRUCKEE RIVER WALK

3 Lunch on enchiladas and beer at **Miguel's** (1415 S. Virginia St., 775/322-2722, www.miguelsmexicanrestaurantreno.com, 11am-9pm Tues.-Thurs., 11am-10pm Fri.-Sat., noon-8pm Sun., $10-15), then hit your favorite casino to spend quality time with the one-eyed jacks and one-armed bandits.

4 Top off the evening with a stroll along the **Truckee River Walk** (1st St. and Virginia St., www.renoriver.org), tasting wines and browsing art galleries along the way.

DAY 2: Day Trip to Virginia City

45 miles/72 kilometers | 1-1.5 hours

ROUTE OVERVIEW: I-80 • I-580 • NV-341 • I-580 • I-80

1 **Virginia City** is a living, breathing tribute to early American ingenuity, hard work, and, well, hedonism. Start

RENO AT NIGHT

Top **3** RENO TO THE RUBIES

1. Roll the dice and try your luck at **Eldorado Casino** in Reno (PAGE 323).

2. See the 13,000-year-old bones of a Columbian **mammoth** at **Humboldt Museum** (PAGE 324).

3. Tour the **Lehman Caves** at **Great Basin National Park** (PAGE 326).

Vertebrae of unidentified species, possibly camel

VINTAGE MINE CART IN VIRGINIA CITY

at **The Way It Was Museum** (113 N. C St., 775/847-0766, 10:30am-4:30pm daily, $4 adults, free for children under 12) to see how the silver went from mine to mill to amalgamation to bullion to mint. A short film puts the town in historical perspective.

> Take I-80 E for 1 mile (1.6 km) to I-580. Drive south on I-580 for 10 miles (16 km) to exit 57B. Continue onto S. Virginia St., then turn left onto NV-341 and travel east for 14 miles (23 km) to Virginia City.

❷ Before lunch, shop the mercantile goods—and perhaps order a custom Western hat—at **Pioneer Emporium & Virginia City Hat Maker** (144 S. C St., 775/847-9214, 10am-5pm daily). The handmade hats come in a variety of styles and combine traditional European hat-making techniques with modern American practices.

❸ If you're here in summer, escape the midday heat on a guided tour deep into **Chollar Mine** (615 S. F St., 775/847-0155, www.chollarminetours. com, 1pm-3:30pm Sat.-Thurs. May-Oct., $15 adults, $10 children 6-12). Rough timbers and old-time equipment will make you want to grab a pick and try your luck at finding a rich vein.

❹ Cap off your visit riding the rails of the **Virginia & Truckee Railroad** (165 F St., 775/847-0380, www.virginiatruckee.com, 10:30am-4pm daily late May-late Oct., $12-14 adults, $6-7 children 5-10) past mines, over trestle bridges, through tunnels, and back through time. Head back to **Reno** to bunk down for the night.

> Retrace your path to Reno: Go north on NV-341 for 14 miles (23 km), then continue north onto I-580 for 10 miles (16 km). Merge onto I-80 W, which will take you to downtown Reno in 2 miles (3 km).

DAY 3: Reno to Winnemucca

170 miles/275 kilometers | 3 hours

ROUTE OVERVIEW: I-80

❶ After breakfast, head northwest to **Lovelock.** If you're traveling with your significant other, stop and hang a padlock in **Lovers Lock Plaza** (400 Main St.) to symbolize your unbreakable love in the Chinese tradition. Throw away the key, of course. For lovers who decide to make their attachment more formal, the courthouse is next door.

> Take I-80 E to Lovelock (93 mi/ 150 km).

❷ Load up on picnic supplies, then continue to **Rye Patch State**

STOREFRONT IN VIRGINIA CITY

LOVERS LOCK PLAZA

5 MUST-VISIT *Reno Casinos*

The everything-under-one-roof nature of Reno's casinos means you could spend a week in just one and still experience a dream vacation. In addition to gaming, the city's casinos boast shops, restaurants, spas, variety shows, music concerts, and more. No matter your mood or interest, these sprawling indoor playgrounds offer something for everyone.

BEST RAT PACK VIBE

- In the heart of the casino district, **Eldorado** (345 N. Virginia St., 775/786-5700, www.eldoradoreno.com, $140-180) is rife with dark wood and glossy marble, showcasing an old-school opulence that Frank Sinatra and Dean Martin would feel right at home in.

MOST LUXURIOUS

- **Peppermill** (2707 S. Virginia St., 866/821-9996, www.peppermillreno.com, $89-170) separates its glitter-and-neon gambling den from its resort amenities. The property, decked out in marble and leather, might easily be mistaken for a luxury retreat in the Mediterranean.

BEST FOR HIGH ROLLERS

- The High Limit room at **Atlantis** (3800 S. Virginia St., 800/723-6500 or 775/825-4700, www.atlantiscasino.com, $180-260) offers private gaming tables, including baccarat, blackjack, video poker, and high-limit slots, plus exclusive amenities such as a private bar with complimentary food and drinks.

MOST FAMILY FRIENDLY

- Lively circus acts and a fun-filled midway welcome visitors of all ages to **Circus Circus** (500 N. Sierra St., 800/648-5010 or 775/329-0711, www.circusreno.com, $115-135). The world-class free circus shows please budget-minded families.

BEST ENTERTAINMENT

- **Grand Sierra** (2500 E. 2nd St., 775/789-2000 or 800/501-2651, www.grandsierraresort.com, $98-228) has the largest indoor stage in Nevada: the Grand Theatre, which hosts comedy, cover bands, and music headliners ranging from Kiss to Idina Menzel.

Recreation Area (2505 Rye Patch Reservoir Rd., 775/538-7321, http://parks.nv.gov, 24 hours daily, $5). Depending on the weather, go for a swim, watch the shore anglers, or hike into the western hills to search for ammonite fossils, agate, tourmaline, and other specimens.

> Drive east on I-80 to Rye Patch Dam (22 mi/35 km). Turn left on Rye Patch Rd., which turns into Rye Patch Reservoir Rd., and follow it for 1.5 miles (2.5 km) to Rye Patch State Recreation Area.

❸ Enjoy your picnic lunch, then continue to **Winnemucca** and a perusal of the **Buckaroo Hall of Fame** (30 W. Winnemucca Blvd., 775/623-5071, 8am-4pm Mon.-Sat., free), a tribute to the stylish wranglers who keep the area's ranches running.

> Take Rye Patch Reservoir Rd. back out to I-80. Turn left and continue northeast for 49 miles (79 km) on I-80 to Winnemucca.

❹ You're in for a real culinary treat at **The Martin Hotel** (94 W. Railroad St., 775/623-3197, http://themartinhotel.com, 11am-2pm and 4pm-9pm Mon.-Fri., 4pm-9pm Sat.-Sun., $25-40), one of the best authentic Basque restaurants in the country. Order the lamb and enjoy a full complement of side dishes: fries, beans, salad, soup, and more.

❺ The clean, quiet, quaint, no-frills rooms at the **Town House Motel** (375 Monroe St., 775/623-3620, http://townhouse-motel.com, $70-80) will provide the rest you'll need for tomorrow's leg of the journey.

DAY 4: Winnemucca to Elko

125 miles/201 kilometers | 2-2.5 hours

ROUTE OVERVIEW: I-80

DOWNTOWN ELKO

① Start the day at Winnemucca's fascinating **Humboldt Museum** (175 Museum Ave., 775/623-2912, http://humboldtmuseum.org, 9am-4pm Wed.-Fri., 10am-4pm Sat., free). Not only will you see items related to local history (period clothing, vintage cars, antique furniture), you'll also glimpse the skeletal remains of a mammoth found nearby.

② Get to **Elko** in time for a lunch of pot stickers and hot and sour soup at **Chef Cheng's Chinese Restaurant** (1309 Idaho St., 775/753-5788, 11am-9pm daily, $15-20), which is consistently ranked among the best Chinese restaurants in the country.

> Take I-80 E for 120 miles (193 km) to reach Elko.

③ Fill the afternoon by checking out the eclectic collection at the **Northeastern Nevada Museum** (1515 Idaho St., 775/738-3418, http://museumelko.org, 9am-5pm Tues.-Sat., 1pm-5pm Sun., adults $8). Two-million-year-old fossils are the highlight. Other exhibits include works by renowned Western artists Edward Borein, Will James, Ansel Adams, and Edward Weston.

④ A mile down Idaho Street is the top-notch **Western Folklife Center** (501 Railroad St., 775/738-7508, www.westernfolklife.org, 9am-5pm Tues.-Fri., $5 adults, $1 children 6-12), a museum, gallery, and performance venue that celebrates trail philosophy, cowboy sagacity, and ranch culture. Grab dinner in town, then get a good night's rest.

DAY 5: Elko to Lamoille

45 miles/72 kilometers | 2 hours

ROUTE OVERVIEW: NV-227 • Lamoille Canyon Scenic Byway/NF-660

① Welcome to the glacier-carved Ruby Mountains. The region's canyon, valley, and mountain beauty takes center

LAMOILLE CANYON IN THE RUBY MOUNTAINS

stage today. Just 20 minutes from Elko in the village of **Lamoille,** start with the **Lamoille Canyon Scenic Byway** (NF-660, 1 mi/1.6 km west of Lamoille), a winding 12-mile interpretive drive along Lamoille Creek. Stop to read the interpretive signs and gape at 11,249-foot Ruby Dome.

> *Head southeast on NV-227 for 20 miles (32 km) to Lamoille.*

Playlist

RENO TO THE RUBIES

SONGS

- **"The Promised Land" by Bruce Springsteen and the E Street Band:** This song appeared on Springsteen's 1978 album *Darkness on the Edge of Town,* widely considered to be one of the greatest rock albums of all time. Spare, sincere, and soulful, the album—and this song—was inspired by Springsteen's trip to Utah and Nevada.

- **"Reno Blues" by Woody Guthrie:** Acclaimed singer-songwriter Guthrie penned this song in 1937. It spins a tale of a character's efforts to steal another man's wife, and is based on Reno's divorce trade of the time.

- **"Virginia Avenue" by Tom Waits:** As part of his debut album, *Closing Time,* this song stands out for being a quieter, jazzier tune amid the folk sound of the rest of the album. It's said Waits wrote this about the closing of the 1930s-era Reno casino Harold's Club.

❷ Once you reach the southern end of the byway, park at the turnaround and pick up the **Ruby Crest National Scenic Trail** (southern end of NF-660). Hike the trail as far as stamina and daylight will allow, past Dollar and Lamoille Lakes and elevation changes from 8,780 to 10,893 feet. It's an 8-mile (13-km) round-trip to **Liberty Lake.**

> *To reach Liberty Lake, follow the Lamoille Canyon Scenic Byway/NF-660 from Lamoille (12 mi/19 km).*

❸ Head back to the village of Lamoille for a hearty dinner of steak or ribs at the **Pine Lodge Dinner House** (915 Lamoille Rd., 775/753-6363, 4pm-9pm Mon.-Sat., 4pm-8pm Sun., $30-40).

> *Retrace your path by heading north on NF-660 for 12 miles (19 km).*

❹ Right next door, at the budget-friendly **Hotel Lamoille** (925 Lamoille Hwy., 775/753-6871, $50-70), you can sit on the back porch and sip a sweet tea before retiring for the night.

DAY 6: Lamoille to Ely

170 miles/275 kilometers | 4 hours

ROUTE OVERVIEW: NV-227 • NV-228 • NF-113 • Ruby Valley Rd. • White Pine County Rd. 3 • US-50

❶ Pick up road food as you drive through **Spring Creek.** On your way out of the canyon, drive the auto tour at **Ruby Lake National Wildlife Refuge** (NV-228, 775/779-2237, www.fws.gov, sunrise-sunset daily), which encompasses a network of dikes that provide fine in-vehicle viewing of waterfowl and other wildlife.

> *Go west on NV-227 for 13 miles (21 km), passing through Spring Creek. Turn left onto NV-228 and drive south for 30 miles (48 km). Continue onto Harrison Pass Rd. for 3 miles (5 km). Then continue onto NF-113 for 4 miles (6 km), which turns into NF-357. After another mile, continue onto NF-113 for 6 miles (10 km). Turn right onto Ruby Valley Rd. and drive for 9 miles (14 km). Turn left on Brown Dike Rd. In less than a mile, turn left on Long Dike Rd., then make a quick right to reach the refuge.*

NEVADA NORTHERN RAILWAY MUSEUM

KEY RESERVATIONS

- If you plan to visit **Lehman Caves** during a **weekend,** it's best to buy tour tickets **a week or two** in advance.

DAY 7: Ely to Baker

95 miles/153 kilometers | 1.5-2 hours

ROUTE OVERVIEW: US-50 • NV-487 • NV-488 • Wheeler Peak Scenic Dr. • NV-488

❷ It's a rough trek on White Pine County Road 3 to US-50, and another luxurious-by-comparison ride to **Ely.** Head over to the **Nevada Northern Railway Museum** (1100 Ave. A, 775/289-2085, www.nevadanorthernrailway. net, 8am-5pm daily, $33 adults, $15 children 4-12) for a 90-minute steam excursion through tunnels, up steep grades, and into mining territory.

> *Retrace your path to Ruby Valley Rd., then continue south. After 4 miles (6 km), the road becomes White Pine County Rd. 3; follow it south for 58 miles (93 km) to US-50. Take US-50 E for 31 miles (50 km) to Ely.*

❸ In keeping with the railroad theme, walk the two blocks to **All Aboard Cafe & Inn** (220 E. 11th St. E., 775/289-3959, $11-16) for a lobster-roll meal. Book a night's stay in one of the inn's rooms ($120-150) while you're at it. Plan on taking advantage of the inn's included breakfast tomorrow morning.

❶ Spend the day at **Great Basin National Park,** an hour east of Ely. Take a tour of the **Lehman Caves** (every 2 hours 8:30am-4pm daily summer, fewer departures fall-spring, $8-10), the centerpiece of the park, to see stalagmites, stalactites, and other cool formations. It's a good idea to reserve in advance for weekends. Or take your chances and stop into the **Lehman Caves Visitor Center** (5500 W. NV-488, 775/234-7331, ext. 242, www.nps.gov/grba) to see if any walk-up spots are available.

> *Take US-50 E to NV-487 (57 mi/92 km). Turn right and take NV-487 for 5 miles (8 km) to NV-488. Turn right and stay on NV-488 to Great Basin National Park (5 mi/8 km).*

GREAT BASIN NATIONAL PARK

② From the visitors center, walk the short path to 100-year-old apricot trees. They ripen in mid-August; pluck one and enjoy! Next, check out the **Great Basin Visitor Center** (57 N. NV-487, Baker, 775/234-7331, www.nps.gov/grba, 11am-5pm daily Apr.-Oct.) and spend a quality hour with the orientation exhibits and videos there.

③ Drive the **Wheeler Peak Scenic Drive** (24 mi/39 km round-trip, June-Oct., weather permitting) along Lehman Creek, closer and closer to the looming peak. Hike the **Summit Trail** (4 mi/6.4 km one-way, 4 hours, strenuous); you'll gain 3,000 feet in elevation as you climb to the top of 13,063-foot Wheeler Peak. Start early to avoid getting caught in midafternoon thunderstorms, which can be treacherous. The parking lot for the trailhead is a mile before the Wheeler Peak Campground.

> From the park entrance at NV-488, take a right to get onto Wheeler Peak Scenic Dr. Continue for 12 miles (19 km) to the end of the drive, then retrace your path to return to the park entrance (12 mi/19 km).

④ Bunk at the boutique **Stargazer Inn** (115 Baker Ave., 775/234-7323, www.stargazernevada.com, $72-98) in **Baker**. Have dinner at the on-site restaurant, **Kerouac's** (7am-10am and 5pm-10pm Wed.-Mon. mid-Apr.-mid-Nov., $15-30).

> From the park entrance, go east on NV-488 for 5 miles (8 km) to get to Baker.

Getting There

AIR

Reno-Tahoe International Airport (RNO, 2001 E. Plumb Ln., 775/328-6400) offers an easy gateway to this section of the state. Alaska, Allegiant, American, Delta, JetBlue, Southwest, United, and Volaris transport passengers between Reno and West Coast and Midwest destinations, including nonstop flights to Chicago, Dallas, Denver, Las Vegas, Los Angeles, Phoenix, Salt Lake City, San Diego, San Francisco, and Seattle.

TRAIN

Amtrak (280 N. Center St., 800/872-7245, www.amtrak.com) runs cross-country rail service. Its California Zephyr route passes right through the middle of downtown Reno. The train stops in Reno once daily in each direction, heading west to Emeryville, in the San Francisco Bay Area, and east through Salt Lake City, Denver, and Omaha to Chicago. Nevada stops include Reno, Winnemucca, and Elko. Amtrak also operates several buses daily between Reno and Sacramento, to connect with other trains there. There is no direct service from Reno to Las Vegas.

BUS

Greyhound (www.greyhound.com) bus routes connect terminals in Las Vegas, Winnemucca, Wendover, Reno, Lovelock, Elko, and Battle Mountain. Buses arrive in **Reno** (155 Stevenson St.) every few hours from San Francisco, and there are two or three departures between Reno and Las Vegas each day.

CAR

The **Reno-Tahoe International Airport** is only a 10-minute (6 mi/10 km) drive from downtown, right off I-580.

Reno is 130 miles (210 km) from **Sacramento** via I-80 E. It's 440 miles (710 km) from **Las Vegas** via US-95 N.

Getting Back

From Baker, you can pick up US-93 S to **Las Vegas** (290 mi/470 km, 4.5 hours) or head back to **Reno** via US-50 (385 mi/620 km, 6 hours).

Another option is to book a one-way fare out of **Salt Lake City,** which is a 3.5-hour drive (229 mi/369 km) from Baker. Take US-50 E for 92 miles (148 km) to US-6 E. Follow US-6 to UT-132 E (16 mi/26 km). Continue east on UT-132 for 33 miles (53 km) to I-15. Go north on I-15 to Salt Lake City (79 mi/127 km).

CONNECT WITH

● At Virginia City and Baker: **The Loneliest Road** (PAGE 36)

SALT LAKE CITY, PARK CITY, AND THE WASATCH RANGE

WHY GO: Year-round outdoor adventures, prime skiing, roaming bison, bird-watching, Sundance Film Festival, Mormon history and culture, Southwestern fare, Great Salt Lake

TOTAL DISTANCE: 280 miles/ 500 kilometers

NUMBER OF DAYS: 4

SEASONS: Year-round

START: Salt Lake City, Utah

END: Provo, Utah

▼ ANTELOPE ISLAND STATE PARK

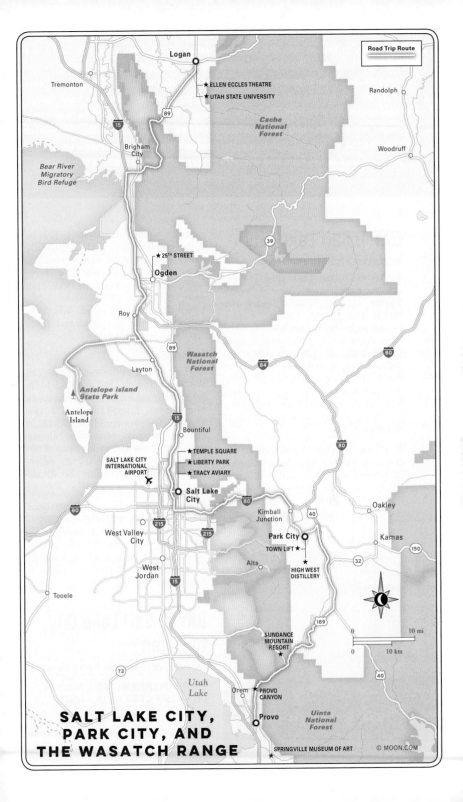

Road Trip Route

Logan
★ ELLEN ECCLES THEATRE
★ UTAH STATE UNIVERSITY

Tremonton

Randolph

Cache National Forest

Woodruff

Brigham City

Bear River Migratory Bird Refuge

39

★ 25TH STREET
Ogden

Roy

Wasatch National Forest

80

84

Layton

Antelope island State Park

Antelope Island

89

Bountiful

★ TEMPLE SQUARE
★ LIBERTY PARK
★ TRACY AVIARY

SALT LAKE CITY INTERNATIONAL AIRPORT

Salt Lake City

Oakley

Kimball Junction

40

West Valley City

215

215

Park City
TOWN LIFT ★
★ HIGH WEST DISTILLERY

Kamas

150

Alta

West Jordan

15

Tooele

32

189

SUNDANCE MOUNTAIN RESORT ★

0   10 mi
0   10 km

73

Utah Lake

Orem
PROVO CANYON

Provo

SPRINGVILLE MUSEUM OF ART

Uinta National Forest

40

SALT LAKE CITY, PARK CITY, AND THE WASATCH RANGE

© MOON.COM

This trip ventures north from Utah's cosmopolitan state capital, Salt Lake City, to the wildlife-rich Antelope Island State Park on Great Salt Lake and into the Wasatch Range, where you'll find the best skiing in the country. Opportunities for outdoor recreation abound, from hitting the slopes in winter to hiking and mountain biking in summer. Prefer to keep things adrenaline-free? Visit the region's renowned theaters, world-class museums, major universities, and Mormon historic sites. And film buffs shouldn't miss the chance to attend Sundance, an annual film festival created by Robert Redford that draws fans and industry professionals from across the globe.

DAY 1: Salt Lake City

MORNING AND AFTERNOON

① Arrive in **Salt Lake City.** Take in the Mormon historic sites at **Temple Square.** On the **Temple Square Historical Tour** (North Visitors' Center, www.templesquare.com, usually 9am-9pm daily, free), a guide will show you around this epicenter of Mormon faith—home to museums, public gardens, and eye-popping architecture. Whether you're a believer or not, you'll enjoy the spectacle. Tours depart every 10-15 minutes, and last about 45 minutes.

② Wander through the historic neighborhoods along South Temple Street, then head southeast of downtown to explore the large **Liberty Park** (bounded by 900 S, 1300 S, 500 E, and 700 E), a lovely park with walking and running paths, playgrounds, a lake with paddleboats, and beautifully manicured lawns. Be sure to visit the **Tracy Aviary** (589 E. 1300 S, 801/596-8500, www.tracyaviary.org, 9am-4pm daily, $10 adults, $6 children 3-12), which houses more than 400 individual birds of 135 species and offers shows with trained falcons.

EVENING

③ Have dinner at the **Red Iguana** (736 W. North Temple St., 801/322-1489, http://rediguana.com, 11am-10pm Mon.-Thurs., 11am-11pm Fri., 10am-11pm Sat., 10am-9pm Sun., $6-11), a favored Mexican restaurant among the city's locals and with plenty of national cred, too. Ask to try the different types of mole before you decide what to order.

④ Spend the night at **Hotel Monaco** (15 W. 200 S, 801/595-0000 or 877/294-9710, www.monaco-saltlakecity.com, $255-320), which occupies a grandly renovated historic office building in a convenient spot in the middle of downtown.

DAY 2: Salt Lake City to Logan

125 miles/201 kilometers | 3-3.5 hours

ROUTE OVERVIEW: I-15 • Antelope Dr. • I-15 • UT-53 • I-15 • US-89

① As you head north toward Ogden, take a short detour west to **Antelope Island State Park** (801/773-2941, http://stateparks.utah.gov, 6am-6pm

TEMPLE SQUARE

Top ③ SALT LAKE CITY, PARK CITY, AND THE WASATCH RANGE

① Spot Utah's largest free-roaming bison herd on a nature walk at **Antelope Island State Park** (PAGE 330).

② Visit **Sundance Mountain Resort,** home to the largest independent film festival in the country (PAGE 334).

③ Ski the snowy slopes of **Park City Mountain Resort** (PAGE 333).

☑ KEY RESERVATIONS

- Every January, the **Sundance Film Festival** in **Park City** draws crowds from around the world. Hotels book up, restaurants are packed, and traffic slows to a crawl. If you plan to attend the festival, or even just visit Park City during this time, it's best to coordinate your plans (festival tickets, lodging, dining) at least **six months** in advance.

daily, $10 per car, $3 bicycles and pedestrians). Here, dip your toes into the Great Salt Lake and look for wildlife, including the island's bison herd.

> Drive north on I-15 for 25 miles (40 km). Take the exit for Antelope Dr., which turns into W. 1700 and then Antelope Island Rd. Stay on this to Antelope Island State Park (15 mi/24 km).

❷ Continue to **Ogden.** Have lunch on historic **25th Street,** lined with historic storefronts now housing shops and cafés.

> Retrace your path to I-15 via Antelope Dr. (18 mi/29 km). Go north on I-15 for 10 miles (16 km). Exit onto UT-53 and follow this east into Ogden (2 mi/3 km).

❸ After lunch, go north to the verdant Cache Valley, where **Logan** is home to the **Utah Festival Opera and Musical**

Company (800/262-0074, www.ufoc. org). From mid-July to mid-August, the company takes over the beautifully restored **Ellen Eccles Theatre** (43 S. Main St.), a world-class performing arts center.

> Get back on I-15 N, driving for 18 miles (29 km) until US-89. Follow US-89 northeast into Logan (26 mi/42 km).

❹ Explore the campus of **Utah State University** (USU, www.usu.edu). While you're there, order a double scoop at the **Aggie Creamery** (750 N. 1200 E, 435/797-2112, http://aggieicecream. usu.edu, 9am-11pm Mon.-Fri., 10am-11pm Sat. May-Sept., shorter hours Oct.-Apr.), made by the university's dairy school.

❺ Spend the night at the **Best Western Plus Weston Inn** (250 N. Main St., 435/752-5700, www.bestwestern.com, $104-130), which has a great location in the center of downtown, plus an indoor heated pool and complimentary breakfast.

DAY 3: Logan to Park City

115 miles/185 kilometers | 2-2.5 hours

ROUTE OVERVIEW: US-89 • I-15 • I-80 • UT-224

❶ Head south to **Park City,** Utah's top ski resort and film festival center. The

MAIN STREET, PARK CITY

Utah's light, dry snow is beloved by skiers and snowboarders. If you're here in the winter, there are many ski areas and resorts to choose from, and they're all easy to get to from Salt Lake City. Reduce your carbon footprint by taking the city bus and shuttles to the resorts.

LITTLE COTTONWOOD CANYON

- **Alta Ski Area** (801/359-1078, snow report 801/572-3939, www.alta.com, lift tickets adults $96, children $50)

- **Snowbird Ski and Summer Resort** (801/933-2222 or 800/232-9542, www.snowbird.com, lift tickets adults $106, children $51)

BIG COTTONWOOD CANYON

- **Brighton Resort** (801/532-4731 or 855/201-7669, www.brightonresort.com, lift tickets adults $65-79, children $49)

- **Solitude Mountain Resort** (801/534-1400 or 800/748-4754, http://skisolitude.com, lift tickets adults $67-83, children $53)

PARK CITY

- **Deer Valley Resort** (435/649-1000 or 800/424-3337, www.deervalley.com, lift tickets adults $95-114, children $59-72)

- **Park City Mountain Resort** (435/658-9454 or 800/222-7275, www.parkcitymountain.com, lift tickets adults from $116, children from $74)

SUNDANCE

- **Sundance Resort** (801/223-4849, www.sundanceresort.com, lift tickets adults $60-70, children $39-43)

OGDEN

- **Nordic Valley** (801/745-3511, http://nordicvalley.com, lift tickets adults $30-50, children $22-35)

- **Snowbasin** (801/620-1000 or 888/437-5488, www.snowbasin.com, lift tickets adults $79-99, children $45-55)

SNOWBIRD SKI TRAM

Old Town area of Park City is a long and narrow street dating back to the town's beginnings as a mining camp. From downtown, ride the **Town Lift** (Main St., 10am-6pm daily, $25 adults, $21 children 5-12) for scenic mountain vistas, then wander along Main Street to shop the boutiques.

> Go south on US-89 to I-15 (26 mi/42 km). At I-15, turn left and drive south for 57 miles (92 km) to I-80. Turn left and follow I-80 east to UT-224 (22 mi/35 km). Head south on UT-224 for 6 miles (10 km) into Park City.

❷ For a fun dinner experience, head a block off Main to **High West Distillery and Saloon** (703 Park Ave., 435/649-8300, www.highwest.com, 11am-9pm, daily, $14-34), a whiskey distillery with good food and a Western vibe.

❸ Spend the night in style at **Marriott's Summit Watch Resort** (780 Main St., 435/647-4100, www.marriott.com, $349-522), a cluster of condominium hotels at the base of Main Street near the Town Lift.

DAY 4: Park City to Provo

70 miles/113 kilometers | 2 hours

ROUTE OVERVIEW: UT-248 • US-189 • UT-92 • US-189 • I-15 • US-89

① Drive from Park City to Provo through the very scenic **Provo Canyon.** Along the way, stop at Robert Redford's famed **Sundance Mountain Resort** (8841 N. Alpine Loop Rd., 866/259-7468, www.sundanceresort.com). The restaurants, shops, ski area, artist studios, and most other facilities are open to the public. Everything is tasteful, and to the extent possible, in accordance with nature.

> Go northeast on UT-248 out of Park City to connect with US-189 (3 mi/5 km). Take US-189 S for 15 miles (24 km), then turn right onto UT-92 W. In 2.5 miles (4 km), this will lead to the resort.

② A short drive south of **Provo** is the **Springville Museum of Art** (126 E. 400 S, Springville, 801/489-2727, www.smofa.org, 10am-5pm Tues. and Thurs.-Sat., 10am-9pm Wed., free). Both the building and its collection make this small-town museum worth visiting. Between late April and early July, the Spring Salon shows off the work of contemporary Utah artists.

> Take UT-92 E back to US-189 (2.5 mi/4 km). Follow US-189 S for 7 miles (11 km), then turn right onto E. 800 N and follow this for 4 miles (6 km). Merge onto I-15 S and drive for 11 miles (18 km). Take exit 260 for Springville, then merge onto W. 400 S. Continue on this road for 2 miles (3 km) to reach the museum.

③ For dinner, stop at Provo's **Black Sheep Cafe** (19 N. University Ave., 801/607-2485, http://blacksheepcafe.letseat.at, 11am-8pm Mon.-Thurs. and Sat., 11am-9pm Fri., noon-6pm Sun., $18-21). This spot serves creative takes on Native American dishes (Navajo tacos, for example), as well as Southwestern specialties such as posole. Dine in a tidy and modern space, where you can chat with a jeweler selling his beautiful silver-and-turquoise jewelry. Tuck in for the night at a hotel in town.

> Go north on US-89 for 5 miles (8 km) to reach Provo.

Getting There

AIR

Salt Lake City International Airport (SLC, 776 N. Terminal Dr., 801/575-2400, www.slcairport.com) is conveniently located less than 10 miles (16 km) west of downtown; take North Temple or I-80 to reach it. Most major U.S. carriers fly into Salt Lake City, and it is the western hub for Delta Air Lines, the region's air transportation leader.

SUNDANCE MOUNTAIN RESORT

The airport has three terminals; in each you'll find a ground-transportation information desk, food service, motel-hotel courtesy phones, and a ski-rental shop. Auto rentals (Hertz, Avis, National, Budget, and Dollar) are in the parking structure immediately across from the terminals. Just follow the signs.

By far the easiest way to get from the airport to downtown is via the **TRAX rail line** (6am-11pm Mon.-Sat., 9:45am-10pm Sun., $2.50 one-way), which runs between the SLC airport and the Salt Lake Central Station. The train stop is located at the south end of Terminal 1. Trains run every 15 minutes on weekdays, every 20 minutes on weekends.

TRAIN

Amtrak (information and reservations 800/872-7245, www.amtrak.com) trains stop at the **Salt Lake Central Station** (300 S. 600 W), which also serves as a terminus for local buses, light rail, and commuter trains. The only Amtrak route that passes through the city is the California Zephyr, which runs west to Reno and Oakland and east to Denver and Chicago once daily in each direction. Call for fares, as Amtrak prices tickets as airlines do, with advance-booking discounts, special seasonal prices, and other special rates available. Amtrak office hours, timed to meet the trains, are irregular, so call first.

BUS

Salt Lake City is at a crossroads of several major interstate highways and has good **Greyhound bus service** (300 S. 600 W, 801/355-9579 or 800/231-2222, www.greyhound.com). Generally speaking, buses go north and south along I-15 and east and west along I-80.

CAR

It's 8 miles (13 km) from the **airport** to downtown Salt Lake City. Leave the airport, drive east on I-80, and then take exit 121 to follow West 600 to Main Street.

▶ Playlist

SALT LAKE CITY, PARK CITY, AND THE WASATCH RANGE

SONGS

- **"Salt Lake City" by The Beach Boys:** The California singers apply their bright optimism to the biggest city in Utah.

- **"I Lost my Sugar in Salt Lake City" by Johnny Mercer:** Deep South crooner Mercer recorded this 1940s blues standard about a lost lover in SLC. The slow, sad, horn-centric song lingers long into the evening.

- **"Shot at the Night" by The Killers:** Even though this band formed in Nevada, lead singer Brandon Flowers grew up in Utah and the influence of the state's big landscapes is evident in this 2013 song, which is full of heart and bombast in the best ways.

- **"Used to Like" by Neon Trees:** Poppy and upbeat even when they're singing about heartbreak, Provo-formed Neon Trees can't record a tune that's not catchy. Try to resist the bubbly singability of this 2019 song.

Getting Back

To return to **Salt Lake City** from Provo, it's a quick 50-minute drive of 45 miles (72 km) north on I-15.

AUSTIN, SAN ANTONIO, AND THE HILL COUNTRY

WHY GO: Austin's 6th Street, country music, swimming holes, Texas barbecue, German towns, dude ranches, cowboy culture, wine-tasting, San Antonio's River Walk, The Alamo

TOTAL DISTANCE: 330 miles/ 530 kilometers

NUMBER OF DAYS: 6

SEASONS: Year-round

START: Austin, Texas

END: San Antonio, Texas

▼ HAMILTON POOL PRESERVE

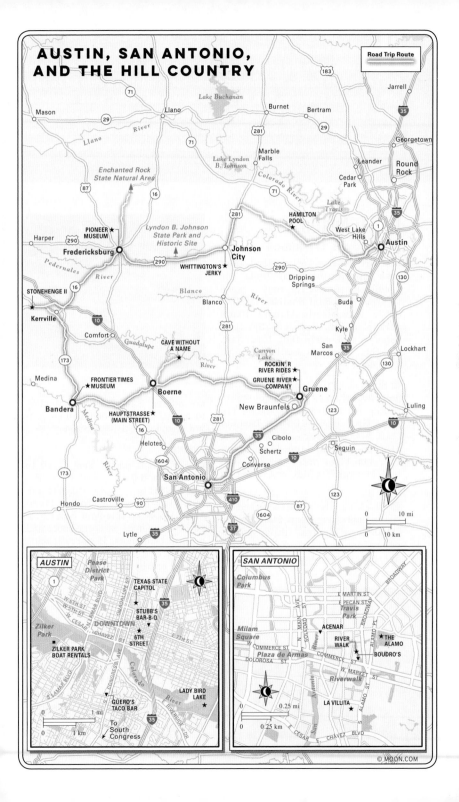

Not only do you venture through two of Texas's biggest cities—Austin and San Antonio—on this road trip, but the laid-back journey also gifts you with charming small towns and the friendly folk who inhabit them. This trip is both bucolic and cosmopolitan—not to mention a little bit country with a dash of European flair. As you go west from Austin, you'll encounter hidden swimming holes, German hamlets, live-music halls, cowboy towns, and plenty of good Texas barbecue. Then you'll head south and east through New Braunfels and Gruene before concluding in the history-rich city of San Antonio.

DAY 1: Austin

MORNING AND AFTERNOON

① Start the day early at **Lady Bird Lake** exploring its many trails. For a different perspective, rent a canoe at **Zilker Park Boat Rentals** (512/478-3852, www.zilkerboats.com, 10am-dark Mon.-Fri., 9am-dark Sat.-Sun. summer and early fall, 10am-dark Sat.-Sun. winter as weather permits, $18/hour).

② Stroll down the popular **South Congress Avenue,** lined with unique stores, boutiques, curiosity shops, and restaurants. Grab lunch at **Güero's Taco Bar** (1412 S. Congress Ave., 512/447-7688, http://gueros.com, 11am-11pm Mon.-Fri., 8am-11pm Sat.-Sun., $15), the best Mexican/Tex-Mex restaurant in Austin.

③ Check out the historically and visually impressive **Texas State Capitol** (1100 Congress Ave., http://tspb.texas.gov, 7am-10pm Mon.-Fri., 9am-8pm Sat.-Sun., free). Free guided tours

LADY BIRD LAKE

are offered 8:30am-4:30pm Monday through Friday, 9:30am-3:30pm Saturday, and noon-3:30pm Sunday.

EVENING

④ For dinner and a show, head to **Stubb's Bar-B-Q** (801 Red River St., 512/480-8341, www.stubbsaustin.com, 11am-10pm Mon.-Thurs., 11am-11pm Fri.-Sat., 2pm-9pm Sun., $13-26), known for its barbecue sauce and musical headliners. If you're looking for more of Austin's famous nightlife, explore nearby **6th Street**, where live music comes from every crack and crevice.

DAY 2: Austin to Fredericksburg

90 miles/145 kilometers | 2-2.5 hours

ROUTE OVERVIEW: TX-71 • Hamilton Pool Rd. • US-281 • TX-356 • US-290

① Head west from Austin to take in the stunning **Hamilton Pool Preserve** (Hamilton Pool Rd., FM 3238, Dripping Springs, 512/264-2740, http://

TEXAS STATE CAPITOL

Top ③ AUSTIN, SAN ANTONIO, AND THE HILL COUNTRY

① Indulge your inner cowboy or cowgirl with a stay at **Mayan Dude Ranch** in **Bandera** (PAGE 341).

② Tube down the **Guadalupe River** in **New Braunfels** (PAGE 342).

③ **Remember The Alamo** in San Antonio (PAGE 344).

KEY RESERVATIONS

- The only stop on this trip that requires advance reservations is **Hamilton Pool Preserve.** When you book, you'll be given the choice for a **morning or afternoon time slot.** Note that only one vehicle is allowed per reservation, with no more than eight people per reservation. Reservations must be made through the Travis County Hamilton Pool Preserve website.

parks.traviscountytx.gov, 9am-5:30pm daily, $11 fee plus $15 per vehicle, reservations required). It's considered the most beautiful natural swimming hole in Texas—a majestic 45-foot waterfall spills into a deep, grotto-like pool.

> Go south on TX-1 Loop to TX-71 (5 mi/8 km). Turn right onto TX-71 and follow it for 11 miles (18 km) to Hamilton Pool Rd. Turn left and continue on Hamilton Pool Rd. to Hamilton Pool Preserve (12 mi/19 km).

② Afterward, it's on to **Johnson City** to eat great Texas barbecue at **Ronnie's Ice House** (211 US-281, 830/868-7553, 6am-3pm daily, $10-20). Before leaving town, stop at **Whittington's Jerky** (602 US-281/US-290, 830/868-5500, www.whittingtonsjerky.com, 9am-5:30pm Mon.-Sat., 11am-6pm Sun.), because no Texas road trip is complete without some additional beef to gnaw on.

> Drive west on Hamilton Pool Rd. for 16 miles (26 km) to US-281. Hamilton Pool Rd. will turn into Farm Rd. 962. At US-281, turn left and drive south for 10 miles (16 km) to TX-356. Here, make a slight right and follow TX-356 into Johnson City (1 mi/1.6 km).

③ Head west toward Stonewall to **Lyndon B. Johnson State Park and Historic Site** (199 Park Rd. 52, off US-290 near Stonewall, 830/644-2252, www.nps.gov/lyjo, 8:30am-4pm daily, free). This ranch was President Lyndon B. Johnson's retreat from the world. While here, see the Texas White House and watch an old movie about the 36th president.

> Head west on US-290 to Lyndon B. Johnson State Park and Historic Site (14 mi/23 km).

HAMILTON POOL PRESERVE

④ A bit farther down the road, you'll come to the German hamlet of **Fredericksburg**. For dinner, opt for schnitzel, beer, and German polka music at **The Auslander** (323 E. Main St., 830/997-7714, http://theauslanderfredericksburg.com, 11am-9pm Thurs.-Tues., $13).

> *Continue west on US-290 to Fredericksburg (17 mi/27 km).*

⑤ If there's a jazz band playing at the **Hangar Hotel** (155 Airport Rd., 830/997-9990, www.hangarhotel.com, $149-189), head out to the airport for a swinging time. You can also stay at this World War II-era hangar for the night.

DAY 3: Fredericksburg to Bandera

105 miles/169 kilometers | 2.5-3 hours

ROUTE OVERVIEW: Ranch Rd. 965 • TX-16 • I-10 • TX-27 • TX-39 • TX-27 • TX-534 Loop • TX-173

① Walk Fredericksburg's charming Main Street, then visit the **Pioneer Museum** (325 W. Main St., 830/990-8441, www.pioneermuseum.net, 10am-5pm Mon.-Sat., $7.50 adults, $3 children 6-17). This well-put-together complex of historic buildings furnished with artifacts offers a rare glimpse into the day-to-day life of the pioneers of the Hill Country.

② Head north to one of the Hill Country's most precious natural wonders, **Enchanted Rock State Natural Area** (16710 RM 965, 830/685-3636, http://tpwd.texas.gov, 8am-10pm daily, $7 adults, free for children 12 and under). Take the time to hike the face of the enormous granite-domed rock to check out the view and ponder the myths and legends that were born here.

> *Take Ranch Rd. 965 north to Enchanted Rock State Natural Area (15 mi/24 km).*

③ Backtrack south to see **Stonehenge II** (Point Theatre Rd., Ingram, 830/367-5121, www.hcaf.com, dawn-dusk daily, free), a small version of the mysterious rock formation in Salisbury, England.

About two-thirds the size of the original, Stonehenge II is made from steel and concrete. Call ahead to make sure the site is open.

> *Follow Ranch Rd. 965 back south to Fredericksburg, then pick up TX-16. Drive south on TX-16 for 21 miles (34 km) to I-10. Merge onto I-10 W and follow it for 6 miles (10 km) to FM 1338/Goat Creek Rd. Head south on Goat Creek Rd. to TX-27 (2 mi/3 km). Turn right on TX-27 and drive 1 mile (1.6 km), then continue on TX-39. In less than a mile, you'll reach Stonehenge II.*

④ Continue east to **Kerrville,** then head south to your final destination, the Cowboy Capital of the World, **Bandera.** Have a meal at **O. S. T. Restaurant** (305 Main St., 830/796-3836, www.ostbandera.com, 6am-9pm Mon.-Sat., 7am-9pm Sun., $8). The food is down-home country cooking in the presence of John Wayne memorabilia.

> *Head east on TX-39 to TX-27. Continue onto TX-27, driving east to Kerrville (6 mi/10 km). From Kerrville, use TX-27 to connect with TX-534 Loop. Turn right on TX-534 Loop, then make a quick left on TX-173. Head south on TX-173 to Bandera (22 mi/35 km).*

⑤ You'll want to stay the night at one of the area's many dude ranches. Opt for **Mayan Dude Ranch** (Pecan St., 830/460-3036, www.mayanranch.com, $130-150 adults, $70-95 children under 18). In the morning, start the day with a cowboy-style breakfast at the dude ranch mess hall, followed by a horseback ride. A guide will take you into the backcountry on trails that have been trodden under hoof for centuries.

ENCHANTED ROCK STATE NATURAL AREA

DAY 4: Bandera to Boerne

25 miles/40 kilometers | 30-45 minutes

ROUTE OVERVIEW: TX-16 • TX-46

❶ After lunch at Mayan Dude Ranch—and a siesta—head downtown to check out the Western shops that line Bandera's dirt sidewalks. Then pay a visit to the **Frontier Times Museum** (510 13th St., 830/796-3864, www.frontiertimesmuseum.org, 10am-4:30pm Mon.-Sat., $6 adults, $2 children 6-17), the best small-town museum in Texas. Breathe in the scent of wood, peruse dusty artifacts, and soak up the Wild West's cowboy lore and Bandera's history.

❷ Next stop is the historic German pioneer town of **Boerne.** This lovely spot on Cibolo Creek is a great place to hunker down for the evening. The main activity is strolling Main Street, known to locals as **Hauptstrasse.** You'll find dozens of antiques shops, boutiques, and eateries, all in historic limestone buildings built by the German pioneers.
> *Drive east out of Bandera on TX-16 for 12 miles (19 km). At TX-46, turn left and follow TX-46 into Boerne (11 mi/18 km).*

❸ When you get hungry, cross the river, turn left, and walk down to **The Dodging Duck Brewhaus** (402 River Rd., 830/248-3825, 11am-9pm Sun.-Thurs., 11am-10pm Fri.-Sat., $11). Dinner with a beer on the outdoor patio is the only way to go. Stay overnight in a bed-and-breakfast, like most folks who come to Boerne do.

DAY 5: Boerne to Gruene

70 miles/113 kilometers | 2 hours

ROUTE OVERVIEW: FM 474 • Kreutzberg Rd. • FM 474 • TX-46 • city streets

❶ The first thing you'll want to do in the morning is drive north, where you'll explore the **Cave Without a Name**

GUADALUPE RIVER

(325 Kreutzberg Rd., 830/537-4212, www.cavewithoutaname.com, 9am-6pm daily summer, 10am-5pm daily winter, $20 adults, $10 children 6-12). The cave is full of intriguing rock formations, stalagmites, and stalactites.
> *Follow FM 474 N out of Boerne for 5 miles (8 km) to Kreutzberg Rd. Turn right and continue 4 miles (6 km) to Cave Without a Name.*

❷ Backtrack through Boerne and make your way to **New Braunfels** to go tubing down the **Guadalupe River.** In the summer you'll find thousands of people sunning, relaxing, and drinking as they bob down the river. For tube rentals there's **Rockin' R River Rides** (1405 Gruene Rd., 830/629-9999 or 800/553-5628, www.rockinr.com) and **Gruene River Company** (1404 Gruene Rd., 830/625-2800 or 888/705-2800, www.toobing.com).

TUBING ON THE GUADALUPE RIVER

Wineries have been cropping up throughout Texas, over 50 of which happen to be west of Austin in the beautiful Hill Country. These wineries have joined forces to create what is called the **Texas Hill Country Wineries Trail** (872/216-9463, www.texaswinetrail.com). Here are a few of the best wineries in this region.

- **Becker Vineyards** (464 Becker Farms Rd., Fredericksburg, 830/644-2681, www.beckervineyards.com)
- **Chisholm Trail Winery** (2367 Usener Rd., Fredericksburg, 830/990-2675, www.chisholmtrailwinery.com)
- **Driftwood Estate Winery** (4001 Elder Hill Rd., Driftwood, 512/858-9667, www.driftwoodwine.com)
- **Dry Comal Creek Vineyards & Winery** (1741 Herbelin Rd., New Braunfels, 830/885-4121, www.drycomalcreekvineyards.com)
- **Duchman Family Winery** (13308 FM 150 W., Driftwood, 512/858-1470, www.duchmanwinery.com)
- **Fall Creek Vineyards** (18059 FM 1826, Driftwood, 512/858-4050, www.fcv.com)
- **Fredericksburg Winery** (247 W. Main St., Fredericksburg, 830/990-8747, www.fbgwinery.com)

- **Grape Creek Vineyard** (10587 US-290, Fredericksburg, 830/644-2710, www.grapecreek.com)
- **Sister Creek Vineyards** (1142 Sisterdale Rd., Boerne, 830/324-6704, www.sistercreekvineyards.com)
- **Solaro Estate Winery** (13111 Silver Creek Rd., Dripping Springs, 832/660-8642, www.solaroestate.com)
- **Spicewood Vineyards** (1419 Co Rd 409, Spicewood, 830/693-5328, spicewoodvineyards.com)
- **Texas Hills Vineyard** (878 RR 2766, Johnson City, 830/868-2321, www.texashillsvineyard.com)
- **William Chris Vineyards** (10352 US-290, Johnson City, 830/998-7654, www.williamchriswines.com)

> *Return to Boerne via Kreutzberg Rd. and FM 474 (11 mi/18 km), then turn left onto TX-46. Drive east on TX-46 for 38 miles (61 km) to New Braunfels.*

❸ Jump across the river to explore the charming town of **Gruene** and its quaint buildings full of antiques and a few restaurants overlooking the beautiful Guadalupe River. Grab dinner at the **Gristmill River Restaurant & Bar** (1287 Gruene Rd., 830/625-0684, http://gristmillrestaurant.com, 11am-9pm Sun.-Thurs., 11am-10pm Fri.-Sat., $15), situated in the ruins of an old cotton gin.

> *Follow Gruene Rd. for less than a mile, crossing the river along the way, to reach Gruene.*

❹ A grand finale to your day should be a visit to the famous **Gruene Hall** (1281 Gruene Rd., 830/606-1281, www.gruenehall.com). This old structure with chicken-wire windows is Texas's oldest dance hall. Country music legends still fill this joint with great foot-stomping music. Spend the night at a hotel in Gruene.

GRUENE HALL

DAY 6: Gruene to San Antonio

40 miles/64 kilometers | 1 hour

ROUTE OVERVIEW: I-35 • I-37/ US-281

❶ Travel to San Antonio early in the day to see **The Alamo** (300 Alamo Plaza, 210/225-1391, www.thealamo.org, 9am-5:30pm daily winter, 9am-7pm daily summer, free) before the most venerated landmark in Texas gets crowded. Most visitors are surprised to see that The Alamo is small in size, and yet its history is so huge.

> Go south on I-35 for 33 miles (53 km) to exit 158B. Merge onto I-37 S/US-281 S. After 1.5 miles (2.5 km), take exit 141A to reach San Antonio.

❷ For lunch, dine on creative Mexican food at bold and colorful **Acenar** (146 E. Houston St., 210/222-2362, http://acenar.com, 11am-10pm Sun.-Thurs., 11am-11pm Fri.-Sat., $8-15). If it's not too hot, eat outside on the porch above the River Walk, where you're guaranteed to have one of those "life is good" moments.

❸ Walk down the old stone steps to the **River Walk** (www.thesanantonioriverwalk.com) to find shops, boats, and restaurants with umbrella tables, all lining the twisting **San Antonio River.** With arched bridges, stone stairways, and winding pathways at the edges of the calm, clear water, the walk is reminiscent of the canals of Venice.

SAN ANTONIO RIVER

❹ On the River Walk, you'll stumble on a historic yet touristy little spot called **La Villita** (418 Villita St., 210/207-8614, 10am-6pm daily, free). This is the original site of San Antonio's first neighborhood; today it houses art galleries, cafés, and funky shops.

❺ Wind down with a cocktail and dinner at a riverside table at the upscale **Boudro's** (421 E. Commerce St., 210/224-8484, www.boudros.com, 11am-11pm Sun.-Thurs., 11am-midnight Fri.-Sat., $14-42).

Getting There

AIR

The main airport that services the Austin metropolitan area is **Austin-Bergstrom International Airport** (300 Presidential Blvd., 512/530-2242), 10 miles southeast of downtown. There are several ways to get from the airport to town. The most economical way is **SuperShuttle** (512/258-3826 or 800/258-3826), which costs about $18 to take one person to downtown. Taking a cab to downtown costs about $30-40.

All the usual rental car companies are represented at Austin-Bergstrom International Airport. Car rental agencies include **Advantage** (800/777-5500, www.advantage.com), **Alamo** (800/462-5266, www.alamo.com), **Avis** (800/331-1212, www.avis.com), **Budget** (800/527-0700, www.budget.com), **Enterprise** (800/261-7331, www.enterprise.com), **Hertz** (800/654-3131, www.hertz.com), **National** (800/222-9058, www.nationalcar.com), and **Thrifty** (800/847-4389, http://beta.thrifty.com).

THE ALAMO

TRAIN

Traveling by train via **Amtrak** (800/872-7245, www.amtrak.com) is a great way to make your way to and from Austin. However, travel times can be much longer than via bus. Trains to Austin from San Antonio are available daily and leave at 7am. The travel time is about 2.5 hours and the standard fare is $17. The Amtrak **train station** (250 N. Lamar Blvd., 512/476-5684) is located right in the heart of downtown, near Lady Bird Lake.

BUS

The two bus lines available are **Greyhound** (800/231-2222, www.greyhound.com), which services just about anywhere in the contiguous United States, and **Kerrville Bus Company** (800/474-3352), which serves many of the smaller Texas towns, including several in the Hill Country. The **bus station** (916 E. Koenig Ln., 512/458-4463) is located far north of downtown. Capital Metro bus 15 (Red River) or 7 (Duval) going south can get you from the bus station in North Austin to downtown; the buses run approximately every 30 minutes and the fare is about $1.

CAR

The drive from **Austin-Bergstrom International Airport** to downtown is 10 miles (16 km). Exit the airport and take TX-71 W to I-35. Go north on I-35 into the city. The drive takes 20-40 minutes depending on traffic.

To get to Austin from **Houston,** the drive is 165 miles (265 km) and takes 2.5-3 hours via I-10 W and TX-71 W.

Getting Back

It's a 79-mile (127 km) trip to return to **Austin** from San Antonio, which takes about 90 minutes. Leave San Antonio via I-37 North. Follow I-37 to I-35. Drive I-35 North into Austin.

If you prefer to book one-way fares, there's **San Antonio International Airport** (SAT, 9800 Airport Blvd., 210/207-3411, www.sanantonio.gov), which is located 9 miles (14 km) from downtown San Antonio. Airlines serving SAT include Alaska, American, Delta,

▶ Playlist

AUSTIN, SAN ANTONIO, AND THE HILL COUNTRY

SONGS

- **"Mercedes Benz" by Janis Joplin:** Texas-born Joplin is known for her soulful growl that toes the line between blues, rock, and country. This a cappella song is pure poetry.

- **"Westfall" by Okkervil River:** This alt-country band hails from Austin, and their banjo-and-guitar songs sound best live in a crowded bar on 6th Street. But if you can't catch a performance, a good second choice is to play it as you roll through the hills west of Austin.

- **"Inside Out" by Spoon:** Austin-based Spoon embodies the spirit of the city—indie and upbeat, experimental but not *too* out there, rockin' but not *too* loud. In short, welcoming and solid. Their fast songs are fun to sing along to, but this tune is slow and steady and perfect for a drive through Texas's small towns.

Southwest, and United. To reach the airport, take I-37 North out of the city for less than 2 miles (3 km) to US-281. Drive north on US-281 for 7 miles (11 km) to the airport.

WEST TEXAS AND BIG BEND NATIONAL PARK

WHY GO: Stargazing, internationally acclaimed art, desert camping, remote hiking, birding, Marfa Lights, Tex-Mex fare

TOTAL DISTANCE: 440 miles/ 710 kilometers

NUMBER OF DAYS: 4

SEASONS: Fall through spring

START: El Paso, Texas

END: Big Bend National Park, Texas

▼ BIG BEND NATIONAL PARK

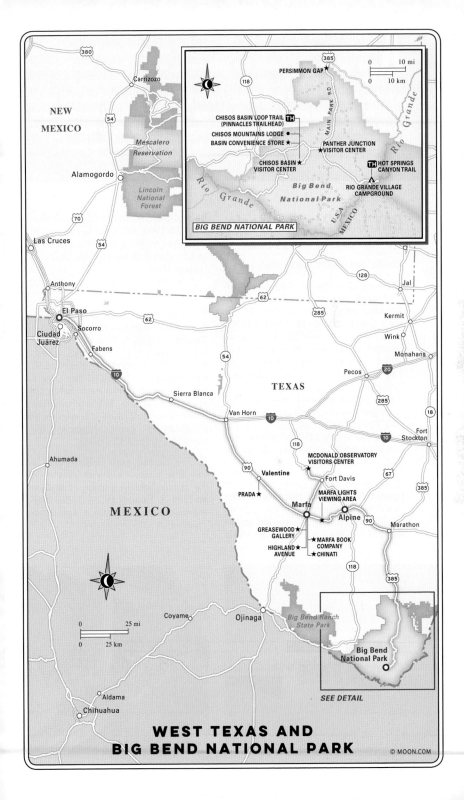

Inset: Big Bend National Park (detail)

PERSIMMON GAP

385

118

MAIN PARK RD

Rio Grande

0 ———— 10 mi
0 ———— 10 km

CHISOS BASIN LOOP TRAIL **TH**
(PINNACLES TRAILHEAD)
CHISOS MOUNTAINS LODGE ●
BASIN CONVENIENCE STORE ★

PANTHER JUNCTION
VISITOR CENTER

CHISOS BASIN ★
VISITOR CENTER

TH HOT SPRINGS
CANYON TRAIL

RIO GRANDE VILLAGE
CAMPGROUND

*Big Bend
National Park*

USA
MEXICO

BIG BEND NATIONAL PARK

Main Map

**NEW
MEXICO**

380

Carrizozo

54

*Mescalero
Reservation*

Alamogordo

*Lincoln
National
Forest*

70

Las Cruces

54

Anthony

128

Jal

62

285

Kermit

El Paso

Wink

62

Socorro

Monahans

20

*Ciudad
Juárez*

Fabens

54

Pecos

10

285

Sierra Blanca

TEXAS

18

Van Horn

10

Fort
Stockton

Ahumada

118

MCDONALD OBSERVATORY
VISITORS CENTER ★

10

385

90

Valentine

Fort Davis

67

PRADA ★

MARFA LIGHTS
VIEWING AREA

MEXICO

Marfa

★ Alpine

118

90

Marathon

GREASEWOOD ★
GALLERY

★ MARFA BOOK
COMPANY

HIGHLAND ★
AVENUE

★ CHINATI

118

385

0 ———— 25 mi
0 ———— 25 km

Coyame

Ojinaga

*Big Bend Ranch
State Park*

Aldama

**Big Bend
National Park**

Chihuahua

SEE DETAIL

WEST TEXAS AND
BIG BEND NATIONAL PARK

© MOON.COM

As soon as you exit busy I-10 to make the turn onto US-90, the vast expanse of West Texas spreads before you: dry, cracked earth, big cloudless skies, and a golden sun shimmering on a ribbon of blacktop that unspools ahead. Don't let the dusty terrain fool you. You're about to explore a region that's rich and welcoming. This trip leads you south to funky Marfa, with its renowned arts scene and glowing mystery lights; to friendly Alpine, cradled at the base of the Davis Mountains; and to Big Bend National Park, where 800,000 acres of wildland wedge between Texas and Mexico.

DAY 1: El Paso to Marfa

210 miles/340 kilometers | 3.5-4 hours

ROUTE OVERVIEW: I-10 • US-90

1 South of El Paso, US-90 doesn't afford much in the way of views, save for blue sky and scrub brush. But then this: **Prada Marfa** (14880 US-90), emerging like a mirage. This pop-art installation in the town of **Valentine** stands as both a stocked Prada store and a commentary on consumerism. The store remains locked, always; it's meant to be window-shopped and photographed by curious passersby.

> From El Paso, take I-10 E for 113 miles (182 km) to US-90. Turn right and follow US-90 E to Valentine (38 mi/61 km).

2 Shortly after Valentine, US-90 lands you in **Marfa. Highland Avenue** runs through the center of town. Stroll Highland, ducking into the **art galleries** that line the way. Don't miss **Marfa**

Book Company (105 S. Highland Ave., 432/729-3700, www.marfabookco.com, 9am-8pm daily), a bookstore, publisher, and performance space in the Saint George Hotel.

> Get back on US-90 E and continue to Marfa (35 mi/56 km).

3 Minimalist artist Donald Judd's large-scale architectural art museum **Chinati** (1 Cavalry Row, 432/729-4362, http://chinati.org, 9am-5pm Wed.-Sun., $25, reservations recommended), perched on a hill at the edge of Marfa, offers half-day tours led by the museum's docents. The internationally renowned collection is housed in 15 buildings on a giant campus and features the work of 12 artists.

4 For dinner, grab pulled pork tacos and queso (a Texas staple) in the string light-lit garden at **Al Campo** (200 S. Russell St., 432/729-2068, www.alcampomarfa.com, 4pm-10pm Thurs.-Sat., $15).

PRADA MARFA

MARFA BOOK COMPANY

① Witness the mysterious **Marfa Lights,** multicolored orbs that float just above the desert horizon come nightfall (PAGE 350).

② See the world-famous art collection at **Chinati** in Marfa (PAGE 348).

③ **Camp** along the **Rio Grande** at **Big Bend National Park** (PAGE 351).

▶ Playlist

WEST TEXAS AND BIG BEND NATIONAL PARK

SONGS

- **"On Hold" by The XX:** The band filmed the video to this 2016 song—electro dream-pop at its best—in Marfa. Some of the town's more notable landmarks feature prominently, along with Marfa locals. And even though The XX's native England is thousands of miles from West Texas, the band's feather-light sound fills the wide-open spaces of Big Bend like it's found home.

- **"West Texas Wind" by The Dixie Chicks:** The lyrics spin pure poetry. Try this on for size: "West Texas wind/ tell me why you try to hold me back/ tuggin' at my heart and pullin' on my sleeve/ you and this old guitar/ you're always up for pickin' just one more song/ and if I listen long enough to you/ I might never leave."

RADIO SERIES

- ***There's Something Out There:*** An aptly named documentary series from Marfa Public Radio about the strange, unexplainable, and completely true goings-on that happen in our everyday lives. You can download episodes from the station's website (http://marfapublicradio.org).

⑤ After dinner, head to the **Marfa Lights Viewing Area** (US-90, 10 mi/16 km east of Marfa, www.visitmarfa. com/marfa-lights, 24 hours daily) to witness the mysterious Marfa Lights, glowing orbs that dance on the horizon, bewildering people since the lights were first spotted in the 1880s. Are they ghosts, aliens, or merely headlights from far-off cars? Bring a chair and a blanket and see for yourself. Then spend the night at a hotel in town.

DAY 2: Marfa to Alpine

80 miles/129 kilometers | 2 hours

ROUTE OVERVIEW: TX-17 • TX-118

① Before you depart Marfa, visit Hotel Paisano's art collection at **Greasewood Gallery** (207 N. Highland Ave., 432/729-3669, http://hotelpaisano. com, 8am-8pm Mon.-Sat., 8am-6pm Sun., free). It features regional artists in varied media.

② Stop by **Marfa Burrito** (515 S. Highland Ave., 325/514-8675, 6am-2pm Mon.-Sat., cash only) for a breakfast burrito, quite possibly the best you'll ever eat. While you wait, watch chef-owner Ramona Tejada mix, knead, and toss the tortillas.

③ Then head to **McDonald Observatory** (3640 Dark Sky Dr., Fort Davis, 432/426-3640, www.mcdonaldobservatory.org, 10am-5:30pm daily, free), perched atop Mount Locke. Operated by the University of Texas at Austin, the observatory offers star parties and daily tours, and hosts StarDate Radio, the longest-airing science program in the country. Once you arrive, take advantage of the Solar Viewing ($4), an interesting lesson on the sun.

> *Take TX-17 N for 21 miles (34 km) to Fort Davis. Continue along TX-118 for 14 miles (23 km), then turn right and follow Dark Sky Dr. to the observatory.*

④ In **Alpine,** order chile relleno cheeseburgers from the food truck **Tri La Bite** (605 E. Holland Ave., 432/244-6060, http://trilabitefoodtruck.com, 5pm-9pm Mon.-Fri., $9-12).

> Retrace your path back along TX-118 into Fort Davis (15 mi/24 km), then continue southeast along TX-118 for another 24 miles (39 km) to reach Alpine.

⑤ Stay at **The Holland Hotel** (209 W. Holland Ave., 432/837-2800, www.thehollandhoteltexas.com, $155-250), built by a local rancher in 1928 and steeped in Old West elegance.

DAY 3: Alpine to Big Bend National Park

120 miles/193 kilometers | 2.5-3 hours

ROUTE OVERVIEW: US-90 • US-385 • Main Park Rd. • Park Rte. 12

① Eat a hearty breakfast at **Penny's Diner** (2407 US-90, 432/837-5711, 24 hours daily, $8-15), where the egg scrambles can't be beat. They've got strong, hot coffee, too, which you'll need for the drive to Big Bend National Park. It's not a long trip, but there's not much to see along the way.

② **Big Bend National Park** (432/477-2251, www.nps.gov/bibe, $30 per vehicle) is named after the bend in the Rio Grande, the body of water that borders Texas and Mexico for 1,000 miles; 118 of those miles form the park's southern boundary. Big Bend is one of the largest, most remote, and least-visited national parks in the country, making for wonderful crowd-free exploration. Enter the park at **Persimmon Gap.**

KEY RESERVATIONS

- Space is limited on guided tours of **Chinati**, Donald Judd's art museum in Marfa. Book your spot at least **three weeks** in advance.

- High season at **Big Bend National Park** is October-June. Make a reservation for a campsite at **Rio Grande Village Campground** or a room at **Chisos Mountain Lodge** at least **six months** in advance.

> Take US-90 E to US-385 (31 mi/50 km). At US-385, turn right and follow it to the Persimmon Gap entrance of the park (40 mi/64 km).

③ Drive first to **Panther Junction Visitor Center** (8:30am-5pm daily) to pick up maps and peruse the gift shop, then on to **Rio Grande Village Campground** (877/444-6777, www.recreation.gov, $14, reservations required), where you'll camp for the night. Set in a shady grove of cottonwoods, this campground neighbors the river, and offers toilets, running water, picnic tables, and access to hiking trails.

> Continue onto Main Park Rd. (26 mi/42 km) to reach Panther Junction Visitor Center. Take Park Rte. 12 southeast for 22 miles (35 km) to reach the campground.

RIO GRANDE, BIG BEND NATIONAL PARK

The Marfa mystique attracts creatives, artists, and thinkers from the world over, each seeking inspiration in the windswept plateaus of West Texas. There are nearly 50 galleries and studios in and around Marfa. Below are must-see stops. For a full overview, pick up a gallery guide at the **Marfa Visitor Center** (302 S. Highland Ave., 432/729-4772, www.visitmarfa.com, 8am-5pm Mon.-Fri., 10am-4pm Sat.-Sun.).

- **Ayn Foundation** (107-109 N. Highland Ave., 432/729-3315, www.aynfoundation.com, noon-5pm Thurs.-Sat. and by appointment) presents *Last Supper* by Andy Warhol.

- **Blackwell School Alliance** (501 S. Abbott St., www.theblackwellschool.org, 10am-4pm Sat.) is an art museum housed in a former segregated school for Mexican Americans from 1889 to 1965.

- **Brothers Fine Art Marfa** (208 W. Texas St., 432/729-4327, 10am-6pm Wed.-Sat.) presents contemporary works from international, national, and local artists.

- **Chinati Foundation** (1 Cavalry Row, 432/729-4362, www.chinati.org, 9am-5pm Wed.-Sun.) is an internationally renowned contemporary art museum founded by artist Donald Judd. It exhibits large-scale installations at Fort D. A. Russell and in buildings in Marfa.

- **Etherington Fine Art** (124 E. El Paso St., 508/221-1053, noon-3pm Thurs.-Sun. and by appointment) represents minimalist artists.

- **Exhibitions 2D** (400 S. Highland Ave., 432/729-1910, www.exhibitions2d.com, 11:30am-6pm Wed.-Sun. and by appointment) offers rotating exhibits of drawings and sculptures by artists from across the country.

- **Galleri Urbane: Marfa** (601 W. San Antonio St., 325/226-8015, www.galleriurbane.com, noon-5pm daily) represents emerging and established artists whose work spans media such as painting, sculpture, mixed media, and photography.

- **Garza Marfa** (103 N. Nevill St., 432/729-1946, www.garzamarfa.com, 1pm-5pm Fri.-Sat. and by appointment) features furniture and textiles.

- **Rule Gallery** (204 E. San Antonio St., 303/800-6776, www.rulegallery.com, 11am-5pm Wed.-Sat. and by appointment) exhibits contemporary and abstract works, including paintings, sculpture, and photography by established and emerging national artists.

④ Once you set up camp, lace up your boots for a hike. The **Hot Springs Canyon Trail** (6 mi/10 km round-trip, 2.5-3 hours, moderate) runs close to the river in some areas, while in others, it skirts the rim of Hot Springs Canyon. Be ready for stunning views of the Rio Grande, the Chisos Mountains, and the Del Carmen Mountains. Find the trailhead about a mile west of the campground, off of Daniel's Ranch Road. Return to your campsite. Once it's dark, spend some time gazing at the park's inky-black skies. Big Bend is considered one of the best **stargazing** spots in North America.

DAY 4: Big Bend National Park

30 miles/48 kilometers | 1 hour

ROUTE OVERVIEW: Park Rte. 12 • Basin Junction

① Pack up camp early. Tonight you'll stay at **Chisos Mountain Lodge** (1 Basin Rural Station, 432/477-2291, www.chisosmountainslodge.com, from $149), the only non-camping accommodations at the park. Choose one of the hotel rooms or stone cottages—all are tech-free (no televisions, phones,

CHISOS MOUNTAINS, BIG BEND NATIONAL PARK

Getting There

AIR

El Paso International Airport (ELP, 6701 Convair Rd., 915/212-0330, www.elpasointernationalairport.com) offers nonstop flights from Atlanta, Chicago, Dallas, Denver, Houston, Las Vegas, Los Angeles, Phoenix, San Diego, and Seattle. Airlines that serve ELP include Alaska, Allegiant, American, Delta, Frontier, Southwest, and United. You can rent a car from any of the major agencies (Avis, Budget, Dollar, Enterprise, Hertz, National) at the airport's on-site rental car center. When booking flights and planning travel, note that El Paso maintains Mountain Standard Time (MST), while the rest of Texas, including Marfa and Big Bend, are in Central Standard Time (CST).

TRAIN

Amtrak (800/872-7245, www.amtrak.com) offers train service to **Alpine** (102 W. Holland Ave.), which is 26 miles (42 km) from Marfa, and 72 miles (116 km) from Big Bend National Park.

BUS

There is no reliable bus service in West Texas, but several local outfitters offer shuttle service to and from Big Bend National Park. Contact **Big Bend National Park** (432/477-2251, www.nps.gov/bibe) for a full list of outfitters.

CAR

The **El Paso airport** is 8 miles (13 km) east of central El Paso, a 15- to 20-minute drive via US-62 and I-10.

Getting Back

It's a 287-mile (462-km) trip back to **El Paso** from Big Bend National Park. It takes approximately four hours. From the Persimmon Gap entrance of the park, drive US-385 N to US-90. Turn left on US-90 and follow it west to I-10. Drive I-10 W to El Paso.

or Wi-Fi)—set amid the forested, cooler clime of the **Chisos Mountains.**

> *Take Park Rte. 12 northwest for 20 miles (32 km). Turn left onto Basin Junction and continue for 6 miles (10 km) to the lodge.*

2 It's a short walk from the lodge to the **Chisos Basin Visitor Center** (8:30am-4pm daily) to pick up snacks and sundries from the **Basin Convenience Store,** then enjoy a picnic lunch.

3 Stretch your legs on the **Chisos Basin Loop Trail** (1.8 mi/2.9 km loop, 1 hour, moderate), a hike that climbs through stands of Mexican pine, juniper, and oak. Keep your eye out for jays chirping in the pine trees and hummingbirds flitting through the agaves. The trail is a loop, so no matter which way you go, you'll enjoy breathtaking views, but counterclockwise is easiest on the legs. The loop begins with Pinnacles Trail; find the trailhead by following the road southwest out of the Chisos Basin parking lot.

4 Dine at the **Chisos Mountain Lodge Restaurant** (1 Basin Rural Station, 432/477-2291, www.chisosmountainslodge.com, 5pm-8pm daily, $13-25), where you can order a Texas classic: chicken-fried steak and mashed potatoes.

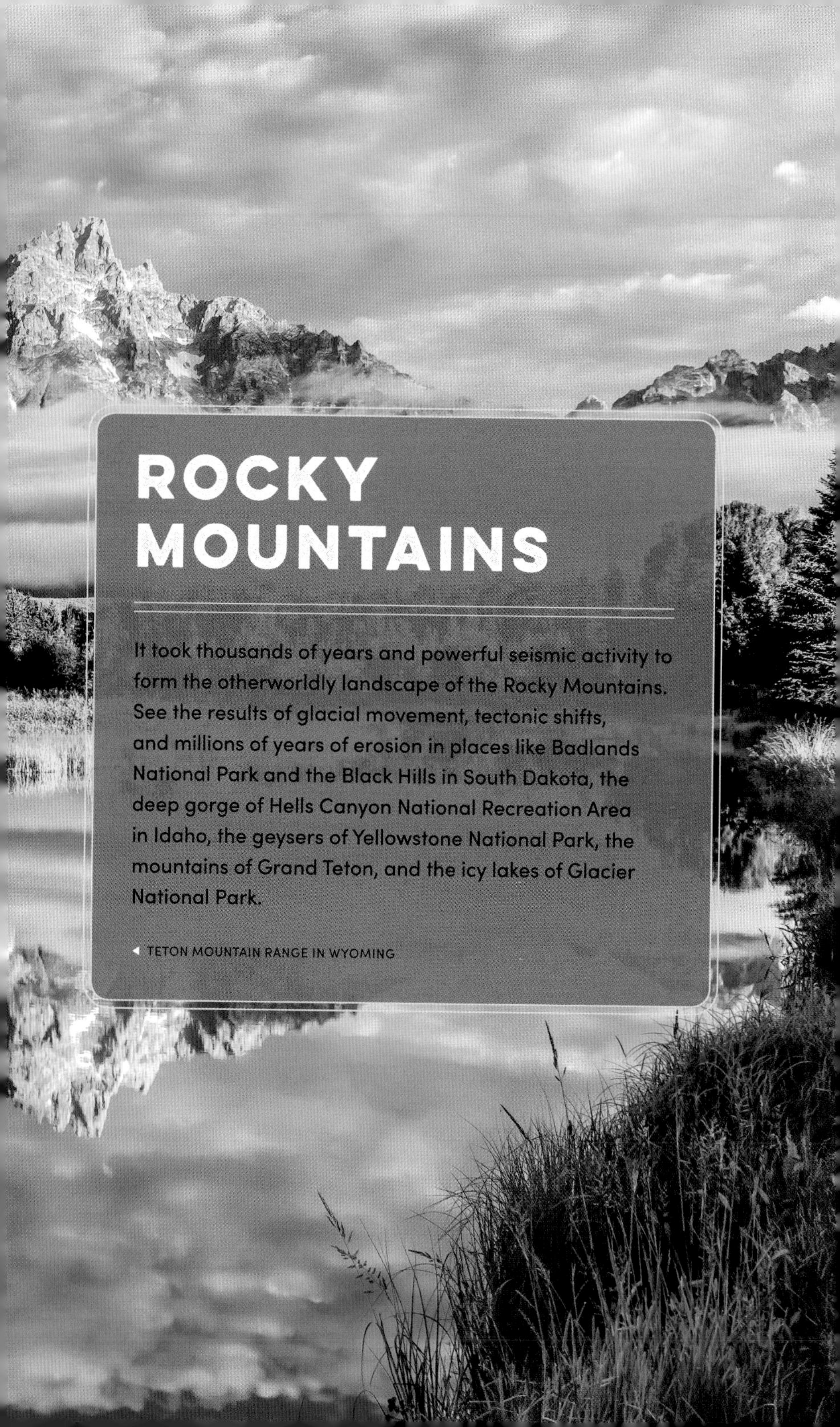

ROCKY MOUNTAINS

It took thousands of years and powerful seismic activity to form the otherworldly landscape of the Rocky Mountains. See the results of glacial movement, tectonic shifts, and millions of years of erosion in places like Badlands National Park and the Black Hills in South Dakota, the deep gorge of Hells Canyon National Recreation Area in Idaho, the geysers of Yellowstone National Park, the mountains of Grand Teton, and the icy lakes of Glacier National Park.

◄ TETON MOUNTAIN RANGE IN WYOMING

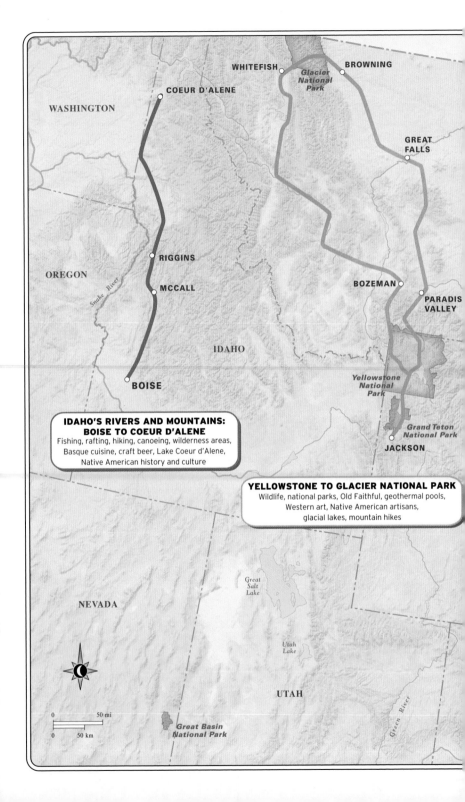

WHITEFISH

BROWNING

*Glacier
National
Park*

COEUR D'ALENE

WASHINGTON

GREAT
FALLS

RIGGINS

OREGON

Snake River

MCCALL

BOZEMAN

PARADIS
VALLEY

IDAHO

BOISE

*Yellowstone
National
Park*

**IDAHO'S RIVERS AND MOUNTAINS:
BOISE TO COEUR D'ALENE**
Fishing, rafting, hiking, canoeing, wilderness areas,
Basque cuisine, craft beer, Lake Coeur d'Alene,
Native American history and culture

*Grand Teton
National Park*

JACKSON

YELLOWSTONE TO GLACIER NATIONAL PARK
Wildlife, national parks, Old Faithful, geothermal pools,
Western art, Native American artisans,
glacial lakes, mountain hikes

NEVADA

*Great
Salt
Lake*

*Utah
Lake*

UTAH

0   50 mi

0   50 km

*Great Basin
National Park*

Green River

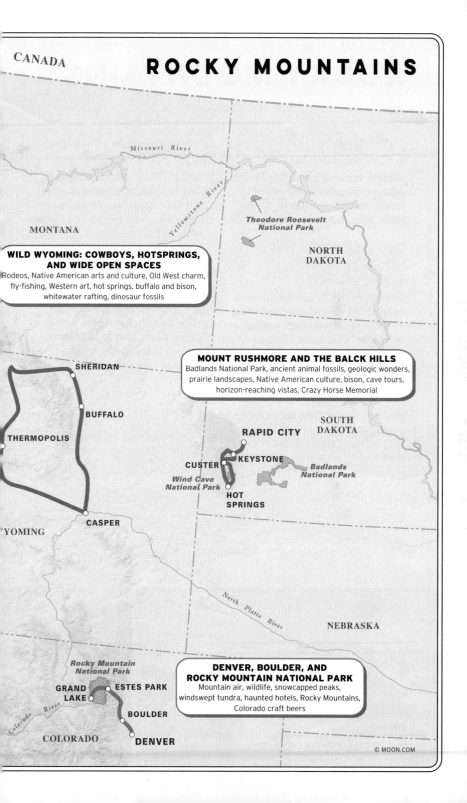

ROCKY MOUNTAINS

CANADA

MONTANA

Missouri River

Yellowstone River

Theodore Roosevelt
National Park

NORTH
DAKOTA

**WILD WYOMING: COWBOYS, HOTSPRINGS,
AND WIDE OPEN SPACES**
Rodeos, Native American arts and culture, Old West charm,
fly-fishing, Western art, hot springs, buffalo and bison,
whitewater rafting, dinosaur fossils

SHERIDAN

BUFFALO

THERMOPOLIS

MOUNT RUSHMORE AND THE BALCK HILLS
Badlands National Park, ancient animal fossils, geologic wonders,
prairie landscapes, Native American culture, bison, cave tours,
horizon-reaching vistas, Crazy Horse Memorial

SOUTH
DAKOTA

RAPID CITY

CUSTER   KEYSTONE

Wind Cave
National Park

Badlands
National Park

HOT
SPRINGS

CASPER

'YOMING

North Platte River

NEBRASKA

Rocky Mountain
National Park

GRAND   ESTES PARK
LAKE

Colorado River

BOULDER

COLORADO   DENVER

**DENVER, BOULDER, AND
ROCKY MOUNTAIN NATIONAL PARK**
Mountain air, wildlife, snowcapped peaks,
windswept tundra, haunted hotels, Rocky Mountains,
Colorado craft beers

© MOON.COM

ROAD TRIPS OF
ROCKY MOUNTAINS

YELLOWSTONE TO GLACIER NATIONAL PARK

Wildlife, national parks, Old Faithful, geothermal pools, Western art, Native American artisans, glacial lakes, mountain hikes (PAGE 360)

WILD WYOMING: COWBOYS, HOT SPRINGS, AND WIDE-OPEN SPACES

Rodeos, Native American arts and culture, Old West charm, fly-fishing, Western art, hot springs, buffalo and bison, whitewater rafting, dinosaur fossils (PAGE 378)

DENVER, BOULDER, AND ROCKY MOUNTAIN NATIONAL PARK

Mountain air, wildlife, snowcapped peaks, windswept tundra, haunted hotels, Rocky Mountains, Colorado craft beers (PAGE 388)

IDAHO'S RIVERS AND MOUNTAINS: BOISE TO COEUR D'ALENE

Fishing, rafting, hiking, canoeing, wilderness areas, Basque cuisine, craft beer, Lake Coeur d'Alene, Native American history and culture (PAGE 396)

MOUNT RUSHMORE AND THE BLACK HILLS

Badlands National Park, ancient animal fossils, geologic wonders, prairie landscapes, Native American culture, bison, cave tours, horizon-reaching vistas, Crazy Horse Memorial (PAGE 404)

LEFT TO RIGHT: MAMMOTH HOT SPRINGS IN YELLOWSTONE NATIONAL PARK; LAKE MCDONALD IN GLACIER NATIONAL PARK; BURROS IN CUSTER STATE PARK

1 Cross the Continental Divide along **Going-to-the-Sun Road** in Glacier National Park (PAGE 374).

2 Soak in soothing mineral hot springs at **Hot Springs State Park** in Thermopolis, Wyoming (PAGE 382).

3 Spend a haunted night at **The Stanley Hotel,** just outside Rocky Mountain National Park in Colorado (PAGE 394).

Going-to-the-Sun Road

Hot Springs State Park, Thermopolis

The Stanley Hotel

Badlands National Park

4 Raft the world-famous rapids of **Salmon River** in Riggins, Idaho (PAGE 401).

5 Hike through the striking pinnacles and spires of **Badlands National Park** in South Dakota (PAGE 411).

Salmon River, Idaho

YELLOWSTONE TO GLACIER NATIONAL PARK

WHY GO: Wildlife, national parks, Old Faithful, geothermal pools, Western art, Native American artisans, glacial lakes, mountain hikes

NUMBER OF DAYS: 14

SEASONS: Spring through fall

START/END: Bozeman, Montana

TOTAL DISTANCE: 1,375 miles/ 2,015 kilometers

▼ GRAND PRISMATIC SPRING IN YELLOWSTONE NATIONAL PARK

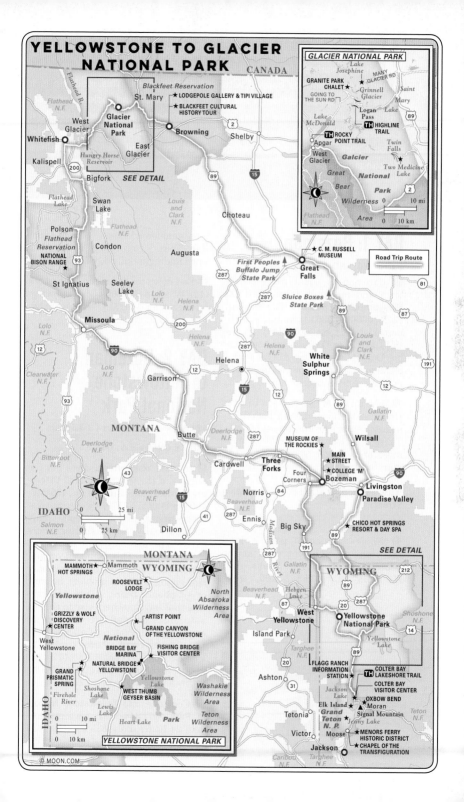

YELLOWSTONE TO GLACIER NATIONAL PARK

CANADA

GLACIER NATIONAL PARK

Blackfeet Reservation
St. Mary
★ LODGEPOLE GALLERY & TIPI VILLAGE
★ BLACKFEET CULTURAL HISTORY TOUR

Flathead N.F.

West Glacier
Glacier National Park
Whitefish
Kalispell
East Glacier
Browning
Hungry Horse Reservoir
Bigfork
Shelby

SEE DETAIL

Lake Josephine
MANY GLACIER RD
GRANITE PARK CHALET ★
Grinnell Glacier
GOING TO THE SUN RD
Logan Pass
TH HIGHLINE TRAIL
Lake McDonald
TH ROCKY POINT TRAIL
Apgar
West Glacier
Galcier
Twin Falls
Saint Mary
National
Two Medicine Lake
Great
Bear
Park
Wilderness
0   10 mi
Flathead N.F.
Area
0   10 km

Flathead Lake
Swan Lake
Condon
Louis and Clark N.F.
Choteau

Polson
Flathead Reservation
NATIONAL BISON RANGE
St Ignatius
Seeley Lake
Flathead N.F.
Augusta
First Peoples Buffalo Jump State Park
C. M. RUSSELL MUSEUM
Great Falls

Road Trip Route

Lolo N.F.
Helena N.F.
Sluice Boxes State Park

Missoula
Helena
Helena N.F.
Louis and Clark N.F.
White Sulphur Springs
Garrison

MONTANA
Butte
Deerlodge N.F.
Cardwell
MUSEUM OF THE ROCKIES ★
Three Forks
MAIN STREET ★
COLLEGE 'M' ★
Bozeman
Wilsall

Deerlodge N.F.
Bitterroot N.F.
Norris
Four Corners
Livingston
Paradise Valley
Beaverhead N.F.

IDAHO
0   25 mi
0   25 km
Ennis
Big Sky
CHICO HOT SPRINGS RESORT & DAY SPA ★
Dillon
Gallatin N.F.

Salmon N.F.
Beaverhead N.F.
Madison River

SEE DETAIL

MONTANA
WYOMING

MAMMOTH HOT SPRINGS ★ Mammoth
Yellowstone
ROOSEVELT LODGE ★
North Absaroka Wilderness Area
GRIZZLY & WOLF DISCOVERY CENTER ★
ARTIST POINT ★
GRAND CANYON OF THE YELLOWSTONE ★
West Yellowstone
National
BRIDGE BAY MARINA ★
NATURAL BRIDGE ★
YELLOWSTONE
FISHING BRIDGE VISITOR CENTER ★
GRAND PRISMATIC SPRING ★
Yellowstone Lake
Washakie Wilderness Area
Shoshone Lake
WEST THUMB GEYSER BASIN ★
IDAHO
Firehole River
Lewis Lake
0   10 mi
0   10 km
Heart Lake
Park
Teton Wilderness Area
YELLOWSTONE NATIONAL PARK

WYOMING

West Yellowstone
Yellowstone National Park
Shoshone N.F.
Island Park
Yellowstone Lake
Targhee N.F.
Ashton
FLAGG RANCH INFORMATION STATION
TH COLTER BAY LAKESHORE TRAIL
COLTER BAY VISITOR CENTER
OXBOW BEND ★
Jackson Lake
Elk Island
Moran
Signal Mountain ★
Grand Teton N.P.
Tetonia
Jenny Lake
Teton N.F.
Victor
Moose
MENORS FERRY HISTORIC DISTRICT ★
CHAPEL OF THE TRANSFIGURATION ★
Jackson
Caribou N.F.
Targhee N.F.

© MOON.COM

et ready to explore a terrain resplendent with lakes formed by slow-moving glaciers, canyons ribboned with waterfalls, and travertine bubbling with hot springs. Moose and bighorn sheep roam and hiking trails wind up and over mountains capped with 360-degree views. This road trip is a nature lover's dream, although the towns of Bozeman and Jackson offer sophisticated amenities, like luxury spas, renowned galleries, and chef-driven restaurants. Starting and ending in Bozeman, this loop drive hits up three national parks, several wildlife refuges, small towns, and even a hotel where you can sleep in a tipi.

DAY 1: Bozeman

MORNING AND AFTERNOON

① Bozeman is equal parts college town and mountain town. Visit the **Museum of the Rockies** (600 W. Kagy Blvd., 406/994-2251, www.museumoftherockies.org, 8am-6pm daily Memorial Day-Labor Day, shorter hours Labor Day-Memorial Day, $14.50 adults, $9.50 ages 5-17), renowned for its impressive dinosaur collection.

② Hike up the **M** (west side of Bridger Dr., across from Bozeman Fish Technology Center), just northeast of town. There is a steep route up (20-30 minutes) or a longer, gentler route (45 minutes-1 hour), making mix-and-match loops a possibility. Cool down with a shopping stroll on historic **Main Street.**

EVENING

③ Enjoy a game of pool, a local brew, and an excellent meal at the popular **Montana Ale Works** (611 E. Main St., 406/587-7700, www.

montanaaleworks.com, 4pm-10pm Sun.-Thurs., 4pm-11pm Fri.-Sat., bar until midnight daily, $10.50-24).

④ Bed down for the night at **The Lark** (122 W. Main St., 866/464-1000, www.larkbozeman.com, $187-349), a hip hotel with local art on every wall.

DAY 2: Bozeman to Yellowstone National Park

120 miles/193 kilometers | 3-3.5 hours

ROUTE OVERVIEW: US-191

① In **West Yellowstone,** check out the critters at the **Grizzly and Wolf Discovery Center** (201 S. Canyon St., 406/646-7001 or 800/257-2570, www.grizzlydiscoveryctr.org, 8:30am-8:30pm daily mid-May-early Sept., shorter hours early Sept.-mid-May, $13 adults, $8 children 5-12). This nonprofit organization acts something like an orphanage, giving homes to problem, injured, or abandoned bears, wolves, and raptors that have nowhere else to go. The naturalists on staff are excellent at engaging with visitors of all ages.

> Go west on US-191 for 7 miles (11 km). Turn left and continue south on US-191 for another 82 miles (132 km) to the Grizzly and Wolf Discovery Center.

② Continue into **Yellowstone National Park** (307/344-7381, www.nps.gov/yell, 24 hours daily, $35 vehicles, $30 motorcycles, $20 pedestrians and cyclists) via the West Yellowstone entrance. If it's a warm day, stop to swim

BOZEMAN

Top ⑤ YELLOWSTONE TO GLACIER NATIONAL PARK

① Watch Yellowstone's world-famous geyser **Old Faithful** erupt (PAGE 364).

② Peer over the edge of the dramatic **Grand Canyon of the Yellowstone** (PAGE 369).

③ Picnic at mirror-like **Jenny Lake** at **Grand Teton National Park** (PAGE 368).

④ Learn about Blackfeet Native American people on the **Blackfeet Cultural History Tour** (PAGE 371).

⑤ Cross the Continental Divide along the **Going-to-the-Sun Road** at **Glacier National Park** (PAGE 374).

HERD OF BISON ALONG THE FIREHOLE RIVER

in the geothermally heated water of the **Firehole River** (south end of Firehole Canyon Rd.). The popular swimming area is surrounded by high cliffs. Limited parking is available, as is a toilet. There are no lifeguards on duty.

> Take US-191/US-20 into the park via the West Yellowstone entrance. Continue for 14 miles (23 km), then turn right at the Madison junction to continue south on US-191. In less than a mile, turn right onto Firehole Canyon Rd. Follow this road to its southern end to reach the swimming area.

❸ Venture farther south on the park road and you'll be able to walk around **Midway Geyser Basin,** an area of massive hot springs and geysers. Among the most significant features is **Grand Prismatic Spring,** a photogenic spring that releases hundreds of gallons of water into the Firehole River every minute.

> Firehole Canyon Rd. links back up with US-191. Follow US-191 S for 8 miles (13 km) to reach Midway Geyser Basin.

❹ Make sure to see at least one eruption of the world-famous **Old Faithful,** which goes off every 45-90 minutes. The surrounding Upper Geyser Basin houses the largest concentration of geysers anywhere in the world, so it's worth spending an hour or more walking through the other marvelous thermal features of the area.

> Continue south on US-191 for 6 miles (10 km), following signs for Old Faithful.

❺ The classic **Old Faithful Inn** (early May-early Oct., from $160 shared bath, from $260 private bath) is the most popular lodging in the park for its historic log-and-stone architecture, not to mention its location just steps from the famous geyser. Enjoy a meal in the hotel's lovely dining room and settle in for the night. The inn is in the same complex with Old Faithful and its visitors center.

OLD FAITHFUL

OLD FAITHFUL INN

DAY 3: Yellowstone National Park to Jackson

120 miles/193 kilometers | 3.5-4 hours

ROUTE OVERVIEW: US-191

① After breakfast and perhaps one more eruption of Old Faithful, head toward **Yellowstone Lake,** stopping to explore the thermal features at **West Thumb Geyser Basin,** a collection of hot springs, geysers, mud pots, and fumaroles that dump a collective 3,100 gallons of hot water into the lake daily.

> Head east on US-191 for 18 miles (29 km). Turn left onto US-20 and continue for less than a mile to reach West Thumb Geyser Basin.

② Take your time, cruising south through Yellowstone and into **Grand Teton National Park** (307/739-3399, www.nps.gov/grte, 24 hours daily, $35 vehicles, $30 motorcycles, $20 pedestrians and cyclists). Dip your toes in the water, or just enjoy the scenery at various pullouts. There's no official entrance into the park from the north. Stop at the **Flagg Ranch Information Station** to pick up a park map.

> Continue south on US-191 for 44 miles (71 km) to reach Flagg Ranch.

③ Have lunch at Colter Bay and visit the **Colter Bay Visitor Center** (307/739-3594, 8am-7pm daily early June-Labor Day, 8am-5pm daily Labor Day-early Oct., free). This relatively

WITH LESS TIME

BOZEMAN TO JACKSON HOLE

5 days; 340 miles/547 kilometers

In just **five days,** you can explore both **Yellowstone** and **Grand Teton,** as well as the resort town of **Jackson,** Wyoming. On your **first day,** fly into Bozeman and drive into Yellowstone. See **Old Faithful** and spend the night in the park.

On your **second day,** drive through Yellowstone and Grand Teton and into Jackson to spend the night. Take **one day** to tour Jackson, **one day** to visit Grand Teton National Park, and a **final day** to catch any sights you missed in Yellowstone before returning to Bozeman.

unknown gem includes important Native American artifacts from tribes across the country. Native American artisans practice their crafts here intermittently through the summer.

> Keep heading south on US-191 for 16 miles (26 km). Turn right onto Colter Bay Village Rd. and continue for less than a mile to reach the visitors center.

④ While you're still at the visitors center, stretch your legs on the **Colter Bay Lakeshore Trail** (2 mi/3.2 km loop, 1.5 hours, easy), a hike with minimal hills and maximum scenery. Side trails reach beaches that yield views across Jackson Lake to the Teton Mountains.

WEST THUMB GEYSER BASIN

GRAND TETON NATIONAL PARK

⑤ In Jackson, settle in for three nights at **The Alpine House Lodge & Cottages** (285 N. Glenwood St., 307/739-1570, www.alpinehouse.com, $190-705). A cozy spot for outdoor adventure lovers, this downtown hotel is conveniently located, with superb amenities—from hearty breakfasts to an elegant little spa.

> Take US-191 S for 10 miles (16 km) to Moran. Turn right here to continue south on US-191 for 30 miles (48 km) to reach Jackson.

DAY 4: Jackson

MORNING

① Explore the **National Museum of Wildlife Art** (2820 Rungius Rd., 307/733-5771, www.wildlifeart.org, 9am-5pm daily May-Oct., shorter hours Nov.-Apr., $15 adults, $6 children). This collection is dedicated to all things wild, spanning George Catlin's bison to incredible works by Georgia O'Keeffe, Charlie Russell, and marvelous contemporary artists.

AFTERNOON

② Go on a **white-water rafting adventure on the Snake River,** which winds through the valley, giving floaters unparalleled access to the area's most stunning views. Here are just two of the more than two dozen outfitters to choose from: **Barker-Ewing** (800/448-4202, www.barker-ewing.com, $82-88 adults, $65-88 children) is a family-operated business that has been running trips for more than 50 years. **Dave Hansen Whitewater** (800/732-6295, www.davehansenwhitewater.com, $82-88

adults, $65-88 children) has been in the business since the late 1960s.

EVENING

③ Visit **Town Square** (bounded by US-191, E. Deloney Ave., Center St., and Broadway) to enjoy shopping, dining, and the **Jackson Hole Shootout** (6pm Mon.-Sat. late May-early Sept., free). Surrounded by archways constructed entirely from elk antlers, this is the heart of the community.

④ Save enough energy for an excellent meal at **Wild Sage** (175 N. Jackson St., 307/733-2000, www.rustyparrot. com, 5:30pm-9:30pm daily, $29-41), where dinner is a culinary adventure.

DAY 5: Grand Teton National Park

50 miles/81 kilometers | 2 hours

ROUTE OVERVIEW: US-191 • Teton Park Rd. • Moose Wilson Rd. • US-191

① The next morning, pick up a buttery French pastry and a picnic lunch at **Persephone Bakery** (145 E. Broadway, 307/200-6708, www.persephone-bakery.com, 7am-3pm daily summer, shorter winter hours, $9-14) and plan to spend the day in Grand Teton.

② In **Moose,** near the southern entrance of the park, visit the 1925-built **Chapel of the Transfiguration** (Menors Ferry Rd., 307/733-2603, services 8am and 10am Sun. Memorial Day-Sept.). This humble log cabin has the most spectacular mountain view framed in

RAFTING ON THE SNAKE RIVER

CHAPEL OF THE TRANSFIGURATION

The most obvious choice for prime wildlife-viewing is Yellowstone National Park, where animals have the right-of-way; just try telling a herd of rutting bison that you have to be somewhere. Grand Teton and Glacier National Parks are also great bets, although the restricted roads and dense forests can limit visibility. Still, this is the Wild West, and there are excellent opportunities to see wildlife almost anywhere.

YELLOWSTONE NATIONAL PARK

- The **Lamar Valley** is known as the Little Serengeti, and for good reason. Time it right and you could see bison, elk, coyotes, foxes, wolves, bears, and even the occasional moose in this grassy, wide-open valley.

- In summer, the **Hayden Valley** is the gorgeous green stomping ground for hundreds, maybe thousands of bison. Seeing such big herds is an unforgettable sight.

GRAND TETON NATIONAL PARK

- **Oxbow Bend,** between **Moran Junction** and **Jackson Lake Junction,** is an excellent place to look for moose, deer, birdlife, and the occasional bear. Dusk and dawn are the best times of day to see wildlife.

- Just outside **Jackson,** and south of the park, the **National Elk Refuge** (532 N. Cache St., 307/733-9212, reservations 307/733-0277 or 800/772-5386, www.fws.gov, tours 10am-4pm daily, $25 adults, $15 children 5-12, free for children under 5) is home to 6,000-7,000 elk or more throughout the winter months.

- In **Dubois,** the **National Bighorn Sheep Interpretive Center** (10 Bighorn Ln., 307/455-3429 or 888/209-2795, www.bighorn.org, 9am-6pm daily late May-early Sept., shorter hours early Sept.-late May, $6 adults, $3 children 8-17) offers winter tours of the nearby **Whiskey Mountain Habitat Area.** Self-guided tours take visitors into prime sheep country, where raptors and moose can often be seen.

GLACIER NATIONAL PARK

- The trails to **Avalanche Lake** (6.1 mi/9.8 km round-trip, 3 hours, moderate) and **Iceberg Lake** (10.4 mi/16.7 km round-trip, 5 hours, moderate) are among the best spots in Glacier to look for grizzly bears in May and June. Mountain goats can also be spotted.

- Hikers on the **Grinnell Glacier Trail** (11 mi/17.7 km round-trip, 6 hours, moderate-strenuous) often get a chance to see bighorn sheep, mountain goats, and the occasional moose.

BISON IN THE LAMAR VALLEY

the window behind the altar. Nearby are even more historic buildings at **Menors Ferry,** an 1890s homestead set on the banks of the Snake River.

> Take US-191 N for 12 miles (19 km). Turn left onto Teton Park Rd. and continue for 1 mile (1.6 km). Turn right onto Menors Ferry Rd. and continue for less than a mile to reach the chapel.

❸ Head to **Jenny Lake.** Resting like a mirror at the base of the Tetons, this alpine lake is a gem for hikers, boaters, and picnickers. Have a picnic, then hike to **Hidden Falls and Inspiration Point** (7.2 mi/11.6 km round-trip, 4 hours, moderate-strenuous). The glorious views along this popular trail are worth every step. If you take the boat shuttle from the west boat dock, the total distance of the hike is 2.4 miles (3.9 km).

> Head back to Teton Park Rd., then turn right and follow it for 7 miles (11 km) to Jenny Lake.

❹ Before you return to Jackson for another night on the town, visit the **Laurance S. Rockefeller Preserve** (off Moose Wilson Rd., 307/739-3654, 9am-5pm daily late May-late Sept.). Once the summer home of the Rockefeller family, the property today hosts miles of trails through forest, wetlands, and meadows.

> Retrace your path south on Teton Park Rd. (7 mi/11 km). Turn right onto Moose Wilson Rd. and continue for 4 miles (6 km) to the preserve. To get back to Jackson, retrace your path back up Moose Wilson Rd. (4 mi/6 km), then turn right onto Teton Park Rd. Follow this for less than a mile, then turn right into US-191 S. This will lead into Jackson in 12 miles (19 km).

DAY 6: Jackson to Yellowstone National Park

115 miles/185 kilometers | 3.5-4 hours

ROUTE OVERVIEW: US-191 • Teton Park Rd. • US-191 • US-20

❶ Head north to **Signal Mountain** (Signal Mountain Rd.), which offers one

VIEW FROM SIGNAL MOUNTAIN

of the greatest viewpoints in Grand Teton. Drive to the top for a magnificent view, or hike it if you want. Look for moose in the pond on the right as you start up the road. This drive is not suitable for RVs or vehicles with trailers.

> Take US-191 N for 12 miles (19 km), then turn left onto Teton Park Rd. Continue on this road for 17 miles (27 km). Turn left onto Signal Mountain Rd. and follow it for 4 miles (6 km) to the top of the mountain.

❷ Make a stop at **Oxbow Bend** to look for wildlife, including moose, beaver, otters, and a vast array of birds. One of the most photographed sites in the park, this area's slow-moving water perfectly reflects towering Mount Moran. Don't forget your binoculars and your camera.

> Follow Signal Mountain Rd. back down (4 mi/6 km). Turn right onto Teton Park Rd. and continue for 4 miles (6 km). Turn right again onto US-191 S and follow this for 1 mile (1.6 km) to reach Oxbow Bend.

OXBOW BEND

❸ For a real treat, take the three-hour **lunch cruise to Elk Island** (Colter Bay Marina, 307/543-2811, www.gtlc.com, 12:15pm Mon., Wed., and Fri.-Sat., $50 adults, $25 children 3-11). You'll have plenty of time to explore the island.

> Follow US-191 N for 7 miles (11 km). Turn left onto Colter Bay Village Rd. and continue for less than a mile to Colter Bay Marina.

❹ Keep heading north and back into **Yellowstone.** From the Bridge Bay Marina, hike to **Natural Bridge** (2.6 mi/4.2 km round-trip, 2 hours, easy), a 51-foot rock formation that has been eroded by water. Keep an eye open for grizzlies.

> Continue north on US-191 for 39 miles (63 km) to West Thumb. Turn right onto US-20 and continue for 17 miles (27 km) to reach Bridge Bay Marina.

❺ Settle in for the night at one of the cabins at **Lake Lodge** (459 Lake Village Rd., 307/344-3711, www.yellowstonenationalparklodges.com, mid-June-late Sept., from $158) and enjoy dinner in the dining room overlooking the lake.

> Take US-20 E for 2 miles (3 km), then turn right onto Lake Village Rd. Continue for less than a mile to reach the lodge.

DAY 7: Yellowstone to Paradise Valley

100 miles/161 kilometers | 3-3.5 hours

ROUTE OVERVIEW: US-20 • US-14/ US-20 • Grand Loop Rd. • US-89

❶ After breakfast, make your way to the **Fishing Bridge Visitor Center** (East Entrance Rd., 307/344-2450, 8am-7pm daily June-Aug., shorter hours late May and Sept.-mid-Oct.) for a great exhibit on Yellowstone Lake's geology. Take a picture of the old bridge itself, which used to be one of the best fishing spots in the park.

> Go north on US-20 for 1.5 miles (2.5 km), then turn right onto US-14/US-20. In less than a mile, you'll reach the visitors center.

❷ Keep driving to the **Grand Canyon of the Yellowstone** and take in the scenic views. The sheer cliffs and dramatic coloring of this canyon have inspired millions of visitors. From **Artist Point** (accessible from S. Rim Dr.), one of the largest and most inspiring lookouts, get a glorious view of the distant Lower Falls and the river as it snakes down the pinkish canyon.

> Take US-14/US-20 west for less than a mile, then turn right onto Grand Loop Rd. Follow this for 13 miles (21 km), then turn right onto S. Rim Dr. and continue for 1.5 miles (2.5 km) to reach the parking area for Artist Point.

❸ From there, plan on lunch at **Roosevelt Lodge** (866/439-7375, www.yellowstonenationalparklodges.com, 7am-9:30pm daily June-early Sept., $11-20). They serve barbecue beef, bison chili, and Wyoming cheesesteak.

> Take N. Rim Dr. west for 1.5 miles (2.5 km) to return to Grand Loop Rd. Follow this north for 18 miles (29 km) to reach the lodge.

❹ From Roosevelt, continue north to **Mammoth Hot Springs** (US-89, south of Albright Visitor Center) for a stroll around the boardwalks. The travertine terraces here look like an enormous cream-colored confection. Because the springs shift and change daily, a walk around the terraces is never the same experience twice.

MAMMOTH HOT SPRINGS

▶ *Playlist*

YELLOWSTONE TO GLACIER NATIONAL PARK

SONGS

- **"Out There Somewhere" by Little Jane and the Pistol Whips:** Sometimes this Montana-based band's songs showcase a fiddle or a strummy guitar; other times an accordion. But always the tunes feature the folksy talents of frontwoman Jane Holland. On this delicate song, she'll lead you down the sonic equivalent of a lonesome country road under a big, blue sky.

PODCASTS

- *Avalanche Basin:* In Glacier National Park, Avalanche Basin features Avalanche Lake and Avalanche Creek. Water drains from the basin's slopes to accumulate in the aquamarine creek, which then carves out the brilliant red walls of Avalanche Gorge. A series of podcasts tells the story—from geology to wildlife—of this basin, part of a project by the Crown of the Continent Research Learning Center and the University of Montana.

- *The Fine Line:* For armchair thrill seekers, there's this series. The episodes share real-life stories about risk and rescue in the backcountry of Jackson Hole.

> Head northwest on Grand Loop Rd. for 18 miles (29 km). Turn left onto US-89 and continue for less than a mile to the parking area.

5 When you exit the park, head for **Chico Hot Springs Resort** (163 Chico Rd., 23 mi/37 km south of Livingston, Pray, 406/333-4933, www.chicohotsprings.com, from $73) where you can soak, dine, and sleep to your heart's content.

> Take US-89 N out of the park. Drive 5 miles (8 km) to reach the town of Gardiner, then continue north for 31 miles (50 km). At the town of Emigrant, turn right onto Murphy Ln. Follow this for 1 mile (1.6 km), then turn left onto MT-540. Follow this for less than a mile, then turn right onto Chico Rd. Continue for 2 miles (3 km) to reach the resort.

DAY 8: Paradise Valley to Great Falls

200 miles/322 kilometers | 4 hours

ROUTE OVERVIEW: US-89 • I-90 • US-89 • US-87/US-89

1 After a big breakfast and a morning dip at Chico, drive north to the hip, artsy town of **Livingston,** where you can browse galleries and shop until you work up an appetite for lunch at **Gil's Goods** (207 W. Park St., 406/222-9463, www.gilsgoods.com, 7am-10pm daily, $10-17).

> Take Chico Rd. to MT-540 and turn right. Go north on MT-540 for 5 miles (8 km) to Mill Creek Rd. Turn left and use Mill Creek Rd. to connect to US-89. Turn right and drive north on US-89 to Livingston (17 mi/27 km).

2 Continue north through ranch country, including **Wilsall** and **White Sulphur Springs.** After you traverse Kings Hill Scenic Byway and the Little Belt Mountains, hike in the rugged beauty of **Sluice Boxes State Park** (38 Evans Riceville Rd., Belt, 406/454-5840, www.stateparks.mt.gov, sunrise-sunset daily, $6).

> Head east on I-90 for 6 miles (10 km) to US-89. Turn left and follow US-89 N through Wilsall (23 mi/37 km). Continue north for 43 miles (69 km) to White

GREAT FALLS

BROWNING

Sulphur Springs. From White Sulphur Springs, continue north on US-89 for 64 miles (103 km) to Sluice Boxes State Park.

3 Continue to **Great Falls.** Enjoy a local pie at **Howard's Pizza** (713 1st Ave. N., 406/453-1212, www.howardspizzamt.com, 4pm-midnight daily, $12-21), much beloved for its signature thin crust, famous sauce, and homemade ranch dressing.

> *Head north on US-89 for 10 miles (16 km), then turn left to continue west on US-87/US-89 for another 20 miles (32 km) to reach Great Falls.*

4 Get a room at the **O'Haire Motor Inn** (17 7th St. S., 406/454-2141 or 800/332-9819, http://ohairemotorinn.com, $90-150) and watch the nightly mermaid show at the inn's tiki bar, the Sip-N-Dip Lounge.

DAY 9: Great Falls to Browning

125 miles/201 kilometers | 2.5 hours

ROUTE OVERVIEW: I-15 • US-89/ MT-200 • US-89 • US-2/US-89

1 Spend the morning at the **C. M. Russell Museum** (400 13th St. N., 406/727-8787, www.cmrussell.org, 10am-5pm Tues.-Sun. mid-May-Oct., 10am-5pm Wed.-Sat. Nov.-mid-May, $9 adults, $4 children), one of the best and most intimate Western art museums in the country.

2 From Great Falls, make your way northwest past Freezeout Lake and Choteau. Arrive in **Browning** in time

for a **Blackfeet Cultural History Tour** (US-89, 2.5 mi/4 km west of Browning, www.blackfeetculturecamp.com, half-day tours from $100). These tours, led by Blackfeet tribe member, historian, and well-known artist Darryl Norman, offer a remarkable opportunity to explore the Blackfeet reservation and understand the history of the people here.

> *Go west on I-15 for 9 miles (15 km), then merge onto US-89/MT-200. Continue for 8 miles (13 km), then turn right to take US-89 northwest for the next 100 miles (161 km). Make a left onto US-2/ US-89 and follow this for 3 miles (5 km) to get into Browning.*

3 Settle in for a gourmet dinner and a tipi under the stars at the **Lodge Pole Gallery and Tipi Village** (US-89, 2 mi/3 km west of Browning, www.blackfeetculturecamp.com, tipis $70 pp, plus $16 for each additional person, $10 children under 12).

DAY 10: Browning to Glacier National Park

80 miles/129 kilometers | 2.5 hours

ROUTE OVERVIEW: US-2 • MT-49 • Two Medicine Rd. • MT-49 • US-89 • Rte. 3

1 Break camp and head to East Glacier for a big breakfast at **Two Medicine Grill** (314 US-2 E, 406/226-9227, www.seeglacier.com, 6:30am-9pm daily summer, 6:30am-8pm daily winter, $5-15), set on the grounds of the stately **Glacier Park Lodge.**

> *Take US-2 W to East Glacier (12 mi/19 km).*

Best HIKES

YELLOWSTONE NATIONAL PARK

- The **South Rim Trail to Point Sublime** (5.1 mi/8.2 km round-trip, 3 hours, moderate) offers overlooks of the Grand Canyon of the Yellowstone, including stunning vistas of both the Upper and Lower Falls. The trail winds through forest, down (and back up!) the strenuous Uncle Tom's Trail, and along an exposed section to Point Sublime.

- Overlooking the vast Lamar Valley, the hike up **Specimen Ridge** (3 mi/4.8 km round-trip, 3-4 hours, strenuous) leads hikers to one of the largest petrified forests in the world, with fossils dating back 50 million years. It's a steep climb, but the views of the valley from the top are well worth the effort, particularly when there are bison in residence.

GRAND TETON NATIONAL PARK

- The **Taggart Lake-Bradley Lake Loop** (5.9 mi/9.5 km round-trip, 4 hours, moderate) takes hikers to two glacially formed lakes at the base of the Tetons. This trail along water and through forest offers views of Nez Perce Peak, Middle and Grand Tetons, and Teewinot Mountain.

- **Hidden Falls Trail** (7.2 mi/11.6 km round-trip, 4 hours, moderate-strenuous) offers the best of the park—access to Jenny Lake, pristine conifer forests, rushing creeks, soaring alpine views, and a chance to encounter wildlife. The trail can be shortened to 2.4 miles (3.9 km) by taking the boat shuttle across Jenny Lake.

GLACIER NATIONAL PARK

- The **Highline Trail** (11.4 mi/18.4 km one-way, 5-6 hours, strenuous) is popular for good reason. Best in midsummer when the wildflowers explode with color, this hike offers outstanding scenery, including a stretch along the Garden Wall, a ledge that will delight thrill seekers.

- A short hike through alpine meadows, the **Hidden Lake Overlook Trail** (2.6 mi/4.2 km round-trip, 2 hours, easy), also known as the Hidden Lake Nature Trail, offers extraordinary views of Clements Mountain, the Garden Wall, and Mount Oberlin. The trail crosses the Continental Divide and is often snow-covered, even in midsummer.

▼ HIDDEN LAKE IN GLACIER NATIONAL PARK

> *Take MT-49 N for 4 miles (6 km), then turn left onto Two Medicine Rd. Continue for another 4 miles (6 km) to reach the Two Medicine entrance to the park. Keep going on Two Medicine Rd. for 3 miles (5 km) to reach the lake.*

❸ Stay at the storied **Many Glacier Hotel** (855/733-4522, www.glaciernationalparklodges.com, mid-June–mid-Sept., $207-476). Set on the idyllic shores of **Swiftcurrent Lake,** this Swiss-style chalet puts guests in the heart of the Many Glacier region with old-world accommodations and loads of activities.

> *Backtrack on Two Medicine Rd. for 7 miles (11 km), then turn left onto MT-49. Take this for 8 miles (13 km), then get onto US-89 and continue for 27 miles (43 km). Just south of Babb, turn left to get onto Rte. 3. Head west for 8 miles (13 km), at which point you'll reenter the park at the Many Glacier entrance. Continue for another 4 miles (6 km) to reach the hotel.*

❹ For dinner, feast on bison tenderloin or the wild mushroom stroganoff in Many Glacier Hotel's **Ptarmigan Dining Room** (855/733-4522, www.glaciernationalparklodges.com, 6:30am-10am, 11:30am-2:30pm, and 5pm-9:30pm daily mid-June–mid-Sept., $20-44).

TWO MEDICINE LAKE

❷ As you head toward the park, stop for some recreation in the isolated **Two Medicine Valley.** Take a 45-minute **cruise** with the **Glacier Park Boat Company** (406/257-2426, www.glacierparkboats.com, $17 adults, $8 children 4-12) on **Two Medicine Lake.** As part of the cruise, you can add a 2.5-hour guided hike to **Twin Falls** at no cost.

SWIFTCURRENT LAKE AT MANY GLACIER

DAY 11: Glacier National Park

MORNING AND AFTERNOON

① To see the famed **Grinnell Glacier,** take a boat across Lake Josephine with **Glacier Park Boat Company** (406/257-2426, www.glacierparkboats.com, $27.50 adults, $13.75 children 4-12) and hike the remainder of the trail (3.8 mi/6.1 km one-way) from the head of Lake Josephine. Scientists anticipate that the glaciers in the park could disappear entirely by 2030, which means seeing Grinnell Glacier may be a once-in-a-lifetime opportunity. If you time it right, the ranger-led version of this full-day outing is especially worthwhile.

② Hike the short version of the **Swiftcurrent Valley and Lookout Trail** (3.6 mi/5.8 km round-trip, 2 hours, easy). You'll wind through pine trees and aspen groves to reach Red Rock Lake and Falls.

EVENING

③ For dinner, grab pizza from **'Nell's** (855/733-4522, www.glaciernationalparklodges.com, 6:30am-10am and 11am-10pm daily mid-June-mid-Sept., $10-21), the casual eatery at the Swiftcurrent Motor Inn & Cabins. Spend another night at Many Glacier Hotel.

DAY 12: Glacier National Park

70 miles/113 kilometers | 3 hours

ROUTE OVERVIEW: Rte. 3 • US-89 • Going-to-the-Sun Road • US-2

① Head out of the park at Many Glacier and back in again at St. Mary to go up and over the magnificent **Going-to-the-Sun Road,** the drive you've been waiting for the entire trip—and maybe your whole life. Stretching just over 50 miles (81 km), this phenomenal feat of engineering gives viewers an extraordinary overview of Glacier as it crosses over the Continental Divide.

> *Take Rte. 3 back to US-89 (11 mi/18 km). Turn right and follow US-89 S to the park entrance at St. Mary (9 mi/14 km). Turn right onto Going-to-the-Sun Road.*

② Take the time to park at **Logan Pass** and take a hike. The **Highline Trail** (11.4 mi/18.4 km one-way, 5-6 hours, strenuous) is among the best-loved trails in the park. It climbs to the historic **Granite Park Chalet** and then drops back to Going-to-the-Sun Road. The views are staggering (skip it if you're afraid of heights). You'll need to board a park shuttle to get back to your car at Logan Pass. Bring plenty of water and food. The earlier you start, the better your chance of getting a parking spot.

GOING-TO-THE-SUN ROAD

LOGAN PASS, GLACIER NATIONAL PARK

> *Follow Going-to-the-Sun Road west for 18 miles (29 km) to reach Logan Pass.*

❸ Head down the pass for a refreshing dip at glacially carved **Lake Mc-Donald,** the park's largest lake and arguably one of the most beautiful.

> *Continue following Going-to-the-Sun Road for 24 miles (39 km) to reach Lake McDonald.*

❹ For dinner, a gourmet meal at **Belton Chalet** (12575 US-2 E., 406/888-5000 or 888/235-8665, www.belton-chalet.com, 5pm-9pm daily summer,

$22-41) will not disappoint. Set in a beautifully appointed 1910 railroad chalet, this upscale place serves innovative and gourmet cuisine including Montana Wagyu beef, lamb linguini, and wild salmon. Plan on spending the night in nearby **Apgar,** at an inn or in a campground.

> *Follow Going-to-the-Sun Road for 6 miles (10 km), then turn left to reach the western end of the road in 2 miles (3 km). Turn left onto US-2. This leads to Belton Chalet in less than a mile.*

DAY 13: Glacier National Park to Whitefish

35 miles/56 kilometers | 1-1.5 hours

ROUTE OVERVIEW: US-2 • MT-40 • US-93

❶ Take your time getting out of the park—you're going to miss this place. Take a morning hike to **Rocky Point** (1.6 mi/2.6 km round-trip, 1 hour, easy), along the north shore of Lake McDonald. Don't forget your camera: The view from Rocky Point looks up toward the Continental Divide and includes Mount Jackson and Mount Edwards to the south. If the lake is calm, photos can capture stunning reflections.

KAYAKING ON LAKE MCDONALD

> *Take Camas Rd. north for 1 mile (1.6 km), then turn right on Fish Creek Campground Rd. and continue for 1.5 miles (2.5 km) to reach the trailhead.*

❷ When you're ready, drive through **West Glacier** and on to **Whitefish,** where you can shop in downtown, which is filled with art galleries, spas, bars, and restaurants. A stop at **Kettle Care Organics** (3575 US-93, Whitefish, 888/556-2316, www.kettlecare. com, 9am-6pm Mon.-Fri., 10am-3pm Sat.) is well worth the visit. The ingredients for the shop's all-natural body care products come from its certified organic farm and are created, packaged, and labeled for sale on-site.

> *Retrace your path down Camas Rd. (2 mi/3 km), then turn right onto Going-to-the-Sun Road. Continue for 2 miles (3 km), then turn right onto US-2. Follow this for 19 miles (31 km), at which point the road becomes MT-40. Keep heading west for 5 miles (8 km), then turn right onto US-93 N. In 2 miles (3 km), this will take you into Whitefish.*

❸ Have dinner at **Latitude 48 Bistro** (147 Central Ave., 406/863-2323, www. latitude48bistro.com, 5pm-10pm daily, $7-32), an urban oasis with a phenomenal menu that offers small plates like seared beef tips and lamb sirloin, creative wood-fired pizzas, and substantial main courses in a fusion of traditional and contemporary trends.

❹ Settle in for the night at the charming, five-bedroom **Garden Wall Inn** (504 Spokane Ave., 406/862-3440 or 888/530-1700, www.gardenwallinn. com, $155-395).

DAY 14: Whitefish to Bozeman

360 miles/580 kilometers | 6-7 hours

ROUTE OVERVIEW: US-93 • MT-212 • MT-200 • US-93 • I-90

❶ The longest day of the trip by far, there is a lot of ground to cover between Whitefish and Bozeman. Whatever your plan, you'll want to fuel up with breakfast at **Loula's Café** (300 2nd St. E., 406/862-5614, www.

whitefishrestaurant.com, 7am-3pm Sun.-Mon., 7am-3pm and 5pm-9:30pm Tues.-Sat., $11-22).

❷ Drive through the beautiful **National Bison Range** (58355 Bison Range Rd., 406/644-2211, www.fws. gov, gate hours 6:30am-10pm daily summer, shorter hours fall-spring, $5 vehicles May-Oct.). On a low, rolling mountain near the Mission Mountains, some 400 bison wander on one of the country's oldest wildlife refuges. Stretch your legs on the refuge's riverside trail. You might also spot bighorn sheep, pronghorn, and elk while you're here. Stop into the visitors center for more information on the drives and hikes available.

> *Follow US-93 S for 86 miles (138 km). Take a right onto MT-212 and continue for 13 miles (21 km). Turn left onto Bison Range Rd. and continue for less than a mile to reach the visitors center.*

❸ Once you reach **Missoula,** grab lunch at **Caffé Dolce** (500 Brooks St., 406/830-3055, www.caffedolce.com, 8am-3pm Mon., 8am-9pm Tues.-Sat., 9am-2pm Sun., $15-29), which offers fresh, healthy, and utterly delicious fare.

> *Retrace your path back to MT-212 and continue south to MT-200 (5 mi/8 km). Turn left onto MT-200 and follow this for 6 miles (10 km). Turn right to join US-93 S. Follow this for 27 miles (43 km), then merge onto I-90 E. Drive southeast for 8 miles (13 km) to reach Missoula.*

❹ From here, it's all highway driving east through Butte and on to Bozeman. Stop near **Three Forks** for a hike

WHITEFISH

MADISON BUFFALO JUMP STATE PARK

AIR

Bozeman Yellowstone International Airport (BZN, 406/388-8321, www.bozemanairport.com) is 8 miles (12.9 km) northwest of downtown Bozeman in the nearby town of Belgrade. Delta, Alaska, American, Allegiant, Frontier, JetBlue, and United all offer daily nonstop service to and from major U.S. cities, including Salt Lake City, Minneapolis, Seattle, Atlanta, Chicago, and Denver. Seasonal nonstop flights serve Houston, Las Vegas, Los Angeles, New York, Phoenix, Portland, and San Francisco.

A number of car rental agencies are at the airport; the car rental center is located next to the baggage claim. Alamo, Avis, Budget, Enterprise, Dollar, Hertz, Thrifty, and National have on-site counters.

BUS

Greyhound travels to almost 40 towns and cities in Montana from the **bus depot** (1205 E. Main St., 612/499-3468, 10am-3pm daily).

CAR

Off I-90, Bozeman is easily accessible by car. It is 85 miles (137 km) east of **Butte** on I-90, about a 90-minute drive. From **Helena**, it's 100 miles (161 km) southeast on US-287 and I-90, a drive of about 1 hour and 40 minutes.

It's 10 miles (16 km) from the **Bozeman airport** to downtown Bozeman on I-90 E. The drive takes about 15 minutes.

There are a handful of places in Bozeman where RVs can be rented, including **Cruise America RV Rental** (80675b Gallatin Rd., 800/671-8042 or 406/624-0424, www.cruiseamerica.com), **Blacksford** (at the Bozeman Yellowstone Airport, 406/763-6395, www.blacksford.com), and **C&T Motorhome Rentals** (31908 E. Frontage Rd., 406/587-8610 or 406/587-0351, www.ctrvrentals.com).

at **Madison Buffalo Jump State Park** (6990 Buffalo Jump Rd., 7 mi/11.3 km south of Logan off I-90, 406/994-4042, www.stateparks.mt.gov, sunrise-sunset daily, $6 vehicles). A hike on this park's cliff is both a lesson in Native American history and an exercise in solitude.

> *Take I-90 E for 115 miles (185 km). Keep right as you approach Butte to stay on I-90, continuing for another 60 miles (97 km). Take exit 283 for Logan, then turn right onto Buffalo Jump Rd. Follow this for 7 miles (11 km) to reach the state park.*

⑤ By the time you roll into **Bozeman,** you'll be ready for a sensational meal at **Blackbird Kitchen** (140 E. Main St., 406/586-0010, www.blackbirdkitchen.com, 5pm-9pm Mon.-Thurs., 5pm-9:30pm Fri.-Sat., $12-30). This tiny little spot is usually standing room only. Go for the handmade pasta or the hearty lamb chop. If you leave without sampling the chocolate pudding sprinkled with sea salt and drizzled with olive oil, you've made a mistake.

> *Retrace your path back up to I-90 (7 mi/11 km). Take I-90 E for 23 miles (37 km) to exit 306. Turn right and follow 7th Ave. for less than a mile into downtown Bozeman.*

WILD WYOMING: COWBOYS, HOT SPRINGS, AND WIDE-OPEN SPACES

WHY GO: Rodeos, Native American arts and culture, Old West charm, fly-fishing, Western art, hot springs, buffalo and bison, whitewater rafting, dinosaur fossils

TOTAL DISTANCE: 565 miles/ 910 kilometers

NUMBER OF DAYS: 6

SEASONS: Spring through fall

START/END: Sheridan, Wyoming

▼ BIGHORN MOUNTAINS NEAR SHERIDAN

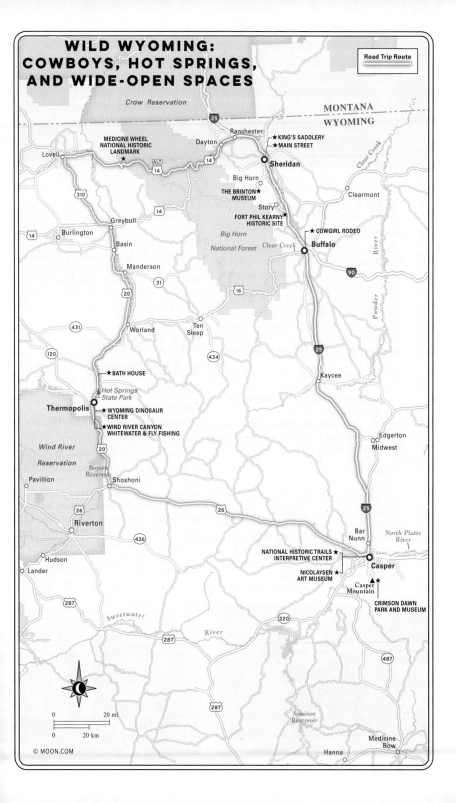

WILD WYOMING: COWBOYS, HOT SPRINGS, AND WIDE-OPEN SPACES

Road Trip Route

Crow Reservation

MONTANA
WYOMING

Ranchester

★ KING'S SADDLERY
★ MAIN STREET

Dayton

MEDICINE WHEEL
NATIONAL HISTORIC
LANDMARK ★

Lovell

Sheridan

Clear Creek

Big Horn

Clearmont

THE BRINTON ★
MUSEUM

Greybull

Story

FORT PHIL KEARNY ★
HISTORIC SITE

Burlington

Basin

★ COWGIRL RODEO

Manderson

Big Horn

National Forest Clear Creek

Buffalo

Powder River

Worland

Ten
Sleep

Bath House ★

BATH HOUSE

Kaycee

*Hot Springs
State Park*

Thermopolis

★ WYOMING DINOSAUR
CENTER

★ WIND RIVER CANYON
WHITEWATER & FLY FISHING

Edgerton
Midwest

Wind River

Reservation

*Boysen
Reservoir*

Shoshoni

Pavillion

Bar
Nunn

*North Platte
River*

NATIONAL HISTORIC TRAILS ★
INTERPRETIVE CENTER

Casper

Riverton

NICOLAYSEN ★
ART MUSEUM

Hudson

Lander

Casper
Mountain ▲ ★

CRIMSON DAWN
PARK AND MUSEUM

Sweetwater

River

N

0   20 mi

0   20 km

© MOON.COM

Medicine
Bow

Hanna

*Seminoe
Reservoir*

You'll start your Wyoming adventure in Sheridan, where the Old West meets the New West. Armed with your newly purchased Western hat, you'll follow the Bighorn Scenic Byway to ancient and sacred Native American sites, then on to healing hot springs and historic Western towns. The dramatic vistas open up before you and friendly locals—eager to teach you how to fly fish or to guide you on a white-water rafting trip—await around every small-town corner.

DAY 1: Sheridan

MORNING

❶ Browse the Western duds at the legendary **King's Saddlery** (184 N. Main St., 307/672-2702 or 800/443-8919, www.kingssaddlery.com, 8am-5pm Mon.-Sat.). Don't leave without a King Ropes baseball cap, which is de rigueur in the West. Wander around Sheridan, nosing into some of the shops and galleries along **Main Street.**

AFTERNOON

❷ Tuck into a hearty lunch of steak or baby back ribs at **Wyoming's Rib & Chop House** (847 N. Main St., 307/673-4700, www.ribandchophouse.com, 11am-9pm Sun.-Thurs., 11am-10pm Fri.-Sat., $14-45).

EVENING

❸ Stop for a drink at the most famous of all Sheridan's watering holes, the **Mint Bar** (151 N. Main St., 307/674-9696, www.mintbarwyo.com, 10am-2am Mon.-Sat.). It boasts hundreds of artifacts and mounts, as well as local cattle brands on the wall, and ambience that cannot be beat.

❹ Find a comfy bed at the historic **Sheridan Inn** (856 Broadway, 307/674-2178, www.sheridaninn.com, $179-349). Built in 1893 and reopened as a hotel in 2015, the property has long been a hub of the community. Buffalo Bill even auditioned performers for his Wild West Show on the rambling front porch.

DAY 2: Sheridan to Thermopolis

210 miles/340 kilometers | 4.5 hours

ROUTE OVERVIEW: I-90 • US-14 • US-14 ALT • US-310 • US-14/US-20 • WY-433 • US-20

❶ The beautiful route from Sheridan to Thermopolis takes you on the **Bighorn Scenic Byway.** This route climbs up and over the mountains past such sights as the **Medicine Wheel National Historic Landmark** (Forest Rd. 12, off US-14, 307/674-2600, www.fs.usda.gov, late June-mid-Sept.). High in the Bighorns on a narrow ridge is this Stonehenge-esque feature thought to

MINT BAR IN SHERIDAN

MEDICINE WHEEL NATIONAL HISTORIC LANDMARK

Top ③ WILD WYOMING: COWBOYS, HOT SPRINGS, AND WIDE-OPEN SPACES

① Shop for authentic Western wear at **King's Saddlery** in Sheridan (PAGE 380).

② Soak in soothing mineral hot springs at **Hot Springs State Park** in Thermopolis (PAGE 382).

③ Spend the night in the historic 1880s **Occidental Hotel** in Buffalo (PAGE 384).

SCENERY ALONG BIGHORN SCENIC BYWAY

be nearly 800 years old. Made of limestone slabs and boulders and forming a circle with 28 spokes, the Medicine Wheel is a sacred landmark with spiritual significance to many Native American groups. Driving directly to Medicine Wheel is restricted, so park at the lot and walk about 1.5 miles (2.4 km) on a gravel road to reach the site.

> *Head west on I-90 to US-14 (14 mi/23 km). Continue west on US-14 for 32 miles (52 km). Keep right to follow US-14 ALT and continue for 21 miles (34 km). At Forest Rd. 12, turn right and follow it 2 miles (3 km) to the parking lot for Medicine Wheel.*

❷ As you pull into **Thermopolis,** head to **Hot Springs State Park** (220 N. Park St., 307/864-2176, http://wyoparks.state.wy.us, 6am-10pm daily, free), where water from mineral hot springs flows over smooth limestone terraces. Take a therapeutic dip at the park's historic **State Bath House** (8am-5:30pm Mon.-Sat., noon-5:30pm Sun., free), then admire the Swinging Bridge, a suspension footbridge over the Bighorn River.

> *Retrace your path back to US-14 ALT (2 mi/3 km). Turn right to rejoin US-14 ALT and head west for 31 miles (50 km). Turn left to join US-310 E and drive south for 27 miles (43 km). Turn left again to get onto US-14 E/US-20 E. Follow this for 23*

miles (37 km), then turn right onto WY-433 S. Follow this for 19 miles (31 km), then turn right to continue south on US-20. Follow this for 32 miles (52 km) to reach Thermopolis.

❸ Check in to the **Best Western Plaza Hotel** (116 E. Park St., 307/864-2939, www.bestwesternwyoming.com, $103-249), a snazzy historic hotel right in Hot Springs State Park.

❹ For dinner, grab a burger at the **One Eyed Buffalo Brewing Company** (528 Broadway St., 307/864-3555, www.oneeyedbuffalobrewing.com, 4pm-9:30pm Mon., 11am-9:30pm Tues.-Sat., 11am-8pm Sun., $9-24), widely considered the best restaurant in town.

HOT SPRINGS STATE PARK

CASPER MOUNTAIN

DAY 3: Thermopolis to Casper

145 miles/235 kilometers | 2.5 hours

ROUTE OVERVIEW: US-20 • US-26/ US-20 • surface streets

❶ In Thermopolis, arrange for a tour of the **Wyoming Dinosaur Center and Dig Sites** (110 Carter Ranch Rd., 307/864-2997 or 800/455-3466, www. wyodino.org, 8am-6pm daily mid-May-mid-Sept., 10am-5pm daily mid-Sept.-mid-May, from $12 adults, $11 seniors and children 4-12), where you can learn about dinosaurs, see their remains up close, and even dig for fossils.

❷ Fill your belly with the biggest cinnamon roll you can imagine at the **Black Bear Café** (111 N. 5th St., 307/864-3221, 6:30am-3pm Mon.-Thurs., 6:30am-3pm and 5pm-8pm Fri., 7am-3pm and 5pm-8pm Sat., 7am-3pm Sun., $4-12).

❸ Go on a two-hour **white-water excursion** with **Wind River Canyon White-water and Fly Fishing** (210 US-20 S, 307/864-9343 or 888/246-9343, www. windrivercanyon.com, from $59 pp), the only outfitter licensed to operate on the Wind River Reservation. Keep your eyes peeled for bighorn sheep.

> Leave town via 6th St., joining up with US-20 E. Continue for 1.5 miles (2.5 km) to reach the outfitter.

❹ Make your way southeast to **Casper.** Settle in for two nights at the **Sunburst Lodge** (2700 Micro Rd., 307/235-9086, www.sunburst-lodge.com, $135-165)

on **Casper Mountain,** just 20 minutes from town. The lodge offers cozy accommodations and sumptuous meals.

> Continue on US-20 E for 30 miles (48 km). Turn left onto US-26 E/US-20 E and follow this for 98 miles (158 km) to reach Casper. To continue to Casper Mountain, go south on Poplar St. for 3 miles (5 km). Turn left onto WY-258/Wyoming Blvd. SW and follow it for less than a mile. Turn right onto WY-251/Casper Mountain Rd. and follow it for 6 miles (10 km). Keep right to follow Hogadon Rd. and drive for 1 mile (1.6 km). Turn left onto Micro Rd. and follow it for less than a mile to reach the lodge.

DAY 4: Casper

40 miles/64 kilometers | 1.5-2 hours

ROUTE OVERVIEW: WY-251/Casper Mountain Rd. • surface streets • WY-251/Casper Mountain Rd.

❶ Wake up in the wilderness on **Casper Mountain.** Recreational opportunities and fascinating local folklore abound here. For a change of pace, fish on the **North Platte River.** A good place to start for a license and regulations is **Wyoming Game and Fish** (3030 Energy Ln., Ste. 100, 307/473-3400, http://wgfd.wyo.gov, 8am-5pm Mon.-Fri.). Casper offers an abundance of fly shops and guides.

> From the mountain, retrace your path back into town via WY-251/Casper Mountain Rd. (7 mi/11 km). Turn left onto WY-258/Wyoming Blvd. SW and follow this for 3 miles (5 km). Turn left onto WY-220/CY Ave. and continue for less than a mile to Energy Ln. Turn right to reach the Game and Fish office.

❷ For a cultural experience, head to the **Nicolaysen Art Museum and Discovery Center** (400 E. Collins Dr., 307/235-5247, www.thenic.org, 10am-5pm Wed.-Sat., noon-4pm Sun., $5 adults, $3 children 3-17). With an impressive collection of more than 6,000 works by contemporary artists, The Nic is a phenomenal tribute to the current art scene in the West.

> Head east on WY-220/CY Ave. for 3 miles (5 km). Turn left onto S. Poplar St. and, in less than a mile, turn right onto

W. Collins Dr. Follow this for less than a mile to reach the museum.

❸ Have lunch at **The Cottage Café** (116 S. Lincoln St., 307/234-1157, www.cottagecafe.com, 11am-1:30pm Mon.-Fri., $11-13), a somewhat hidden but marvelous spot serving delicious homemade soups, panini, and pasta. It's walking distance from the museum.

❹ Visit the wonderful **National Historic Trails Interpretive Center** (1501 N. Poplar St., 307/261-7700, www.blm.gov, 8am-5pm Tues.-Sun. late May-early Sept., 9am-4:30pm Tues.-Sat. early Sept.-late May, free). Among the best museums in the state, this place gives visitors a sense of pioneer life on many of the historic trails that crisscross Wyoming.

> *From the museum, get onto Center St. and take it north for less than a mile. Turn left onto W. F St. and take the second right onto N. Poplar St. Follow this for 1 mile (1.6 km), then turn right onto Wilkins Way to reach the interpretive center.*

❺ Head back up the mountain. If the **Crimson Dawn Museum** (1620 Crimson Dawn Rd., 307/235-1303, 10am-7pm Sat.-Sun. June-Sept.) is open, stop in to drink in the lore of the mountain. The museum is the site of the former homestead of writer and artist Elizabeth "Neal" Forsling, a beloved local figure.

> *Take N. Poplar St. south for 3 miles (5 km), then turn left onto W. 17th St., then left again onto College Dr. Turn right onto WY-251/Casper Mountain Rd. and follow this up the mountain for 9 miles (15 km). To continue to the museum, take a left at Tower Loop and continue on Towerhill Campground Rd. for less than a mile. Continue onto East End Rd. for 1 mile (1.6 km), then turn right onto Crimson Dawn Rd. To return to the Sunburst Lodge from the museum, it's just a 5-mile (8-km) drive. Head back out to WY-251/Casper Mountain Rd. (2 mi/3 km). Turn right onto WY-251, then left onto Archery Range Rd./Lemers Rd. Turn right onto K2 Tower Rd., then left onto Hogadon Rd. Turn left again onto Micro Rd.*

DAY 5: Casper to Buffalo

125 miles/201 kilometers | 2 hours

ROUTE OVERVIEW: I-25

❶ The drive to **Buffalo** offers a glimpse of Wyoming's open landscapes. Once you arrive in town, step into the historic **Occidental Hotel** (10 N. Main St., 307/684-0451, www.occidentalwyoming.com, $110-285)—and step back in time. The building has been painstakingly restored to its 1880s splendor, which includes many of its original furnishings, light fixtures, tin ceilings, and stained glass. Even the bullet holes throughout the bar are mementos of rowdier days. Leave your bags in one of their cozy rooms.

> *Head back down Casper Mountain via WY-251 into Casper (7 mi/11 km). Turn left onto WY-258, then turn right onto Poplar St. Follow this for 4 miles (6 km), then merge onto I-25 N. Follow this for 109 miles (175 km), then take exit 298 for I-25 BUS. Turn left, and I-25 BUS will lead you into Buffalo in 1 mile (1.6 km).*

❷ For a little exercise, hit the 13-mile (21-km) **Clear Creek Trail System.** The well-marked trails can be accessed around town at various spots, including the historic shopping district on Main Street. Mountain bikes are

OCCIDENTAL HOTEL, BUFFALO

Small-Town Rodeos:
THE BIGGEST PARTIES IN THE WEST

With more than 100 annual events on the calendar between May and November, it's hard to drive through Wyoming without running into rodeo action somewhere. Sitting on a sunbaked wooden bench, cold beer in one hand and a bag of popcorn in the other, is a great window into these small towns.

- **Thermopolis Cowboy Rendezvous** (Hot Springs County Fairgrounds, Thermopolis, www.thermopoliscowboyrendezvous.com, 4th weekend in June, $15 adults, $10 children 6-12): From tailgate parties and a Western dance to a pancake breakfast and parade, this small-town rodeo in Thermopolis offers plenty of action and family fun.

- **Cody Stampede Rodeo** (Stampede Park, Cody, www.codystampederodeo.com, July 1-4, $20-25): With all the showmanship one would expect from a town named after Buffalo Bill Cody, this professional rodeo lets the town shine with all the classic events, including bareback riding, roping, steer wrestling, barrel racing, and saddle bronc and bull riding.

- **Ten Sleep Fourth of July Rodeo** (Ten Sleep Rodeo Grounds, Ten Sleep, July 4-5, $10): With a rodeo history that dates back to 1908 and includes some of the biggest names in the sport, Ten Sleep hosts an annual Fourth of July shindig that includes a Pony Express Ride, a parade, an old-fashioned rodeo, fireworks, and a wild horse race.

- **Sheridan WYO Rodeo** (Sheridan County Fairgrounds, Sheridan, www.sheridanwyorodeo.com, 2nd week in July, from $17): This is the biggest week of the year for Sheridan. There is a golf tournament, art show, rodeo royalty pageant, carnival, parade, and street dance on top of four nights of professional rodeo action.

RODEO IN CODY

▶ Playlist

WILD WYOMING: COWBOYS, HOT SPRINGS, AND WIDE-OPEN SPACES

SONGS

- **"I Can Still Make Cheyenne" by George Strait:** In this land of cowboys, wranglers, and ranchers, you need a little George Strait humming through your speakers. True, you can probably tune into any local radio station to get your country music fix, but this soulful song about coming home to Wyoming also does the trick.

PODCASTS

- *HumaNature:* Get ready for riveting storytelling with this podcast of real-life outdoor adventure stories as told by the people who lived them. You'll laugh, you'll cry, you'll gasp out loud. Episodes include one about a female bow hunter tracking elk and a snowmobiler who accidentally drank antifreeze in the middle of nowhere (he's fine).

- *Right to Roam:* Hosted by professional wildlife biologists, this podcast aims to inform and entertain listeners about issues involving living with wildlife in Wyoming—think topical subjects such as sheep ranching and grizzly bear management.

welcome on the trail, and maps are available at the Buffalo Chamber of Commerce (307/684-5544 or 800/227-5122, www.buffalowyo.com).

❸ If you're lucky, you'll be able to catch the weekly **Cowgirl Rodeo** (Johnson County Fairgrounds, http://johnsoncountycowgirls.com) on Tuesdays, June through August. Watch women, girls, and boys under 16 compete in events like roping, steer stopping, and goat tying.

DAY 6: Buffalo to Sheridan

45 miles/72 kilometers | 1 hour

ROUTE OVERVIEW: I-90/US-87 • US-87 • surface streets • WY-335 • WY-332 • city streets

❶ On your way to Sheridan, stop at **Fort Phil Kearny State Historic Site** (528 Wagon Box Rd., Banner, 307/684-7629, www.fortphilkearny.com, grounds dawn-dusk daily, $2-4 adults, free for children under 18), a commemoration of the fort that stood here 1866-1868. Take a self-guided tour of the grounds and several nearby battlefields.

> *Take N. Main St. north out of town for 2 miles (3 km) to get onto I-90 W/US-87 N. Follow this for 11 miles (18 km), then take exit 44 for Piney Creek Rd. Head northwest on US-87 N for 2 miles (3 km) to Kearny Ln. Turn left and follow signs for the fort.*

❷ Next, make your way to the tiny town of **Big Horn** to see the **Bradford Brinton Memorial and Museum** (239 Brinton Rd., 307/672-3173, www.thebrintonmuseum.org, 9:30am-5pm Wed.-Sun., $10 adults, free for children under 13). This exquisite museum is housed on the site of a former working ranch from the 1920s and '30s. It contains one of the most important collections of Native American and Western art in the Rocky Mountains.

> *Take US-87 N from the fort to Kruse Creek Rd. (12 mi/19 km). Turn left and stay on Kruse Creek for 2 miles (3 km), then continue onto Bird Farm Rd. for another 2 miles (3 km). Turn left onto WY-335 to reach Big Horn.*

FORT PHIL KEARNY STATE HISTORIC SITE

3 Enjoy a last meal—Wyoming gourmet—at **Frackelton's** (55 N. Main St., 307/675-6055, www.frackeltons.com, 10am-2pm and 4pm-10pm Mon.-Sat., 10am-2pm Sun., $12-34) in **Sheridan.** Local favorites include the penne pasta with gorgonzola sauce, pan-roasted beef tenderloin, and the house burger.

> Go north on WY-335. In 3 miles (5 km), turn left onto WY-332/Big Horn Ave. Drive WY-332 N for 5 miles (8 km). At Heald St., turn right, then make a left on Main St., staying on Main into Sheridan.

Getting There

AIR

The tiny **Sheridan County Airport** (SHR, 908 W. Brundage Ln., www. flysheridan.com) offers daily flights to and from Denver and Riverton on United Express's operator SkyWest Airlines. Car rentals are available at the airport through Avis, Budget, and Enterprise.

The nearest larger airport is a two-hour drive from Sheridan, in Billings, Montana. **Billings Logan International Airport** (BIL, 1901 Terminal Cir., 406/247-8609 or 406/657-8495, www. flybillings.com) is situated atop the rimrocks off I-90 at the 27th Street exit. Delta, United, Allegiant, Alaska Airlines, American, and Cape Air offer regular flights. Enterprise, Thrifty,

Dollar, Hertz, Alamo, Avis, Budget, and National have on-site car rental counters.

BUS

Bus service in the region is provided by **Jefferson Bus Lines** (307/674-6188 or 800/451-5333, www.jeffersonlines. com), which serves destinations in Arkansas, Idaho, Iowa, Kansas, Minnesota, Missouri, Montana, Nebraska, North Dakota, Oklahoma, South Dakota, Washington, Wisconsin, and Wyoming. The non-ticketing bus stop in Sheridan is at **Good 2 Go Food Store** (1229 Brundage Ln., 307/672-6802). The nearest ticketing stop is in Buffalo, Wyoming.

CAR

From the **Sheridan County Airport,** it's just a short drive of 2 miles (3 km) and less than 10 minutes to get into Sheridan proper via WY-332/Main Street.

From **Billings Logan International Airport** to Sheridan, it's a 130-mile (210-km) drive that takes about two hours via I-90.

CONNECT WITH

● At Casper: **Oregon Trail** (PAGE 78)

DENVER, BOULDER, AND ROCKY MOUNTAIN NATIONAL PARK

WHY GO: Mountain air, wildlife, snowcapped peaks, windswept tundra, haunted hotels, Rocky Mountains, Colorado craft beers

TOTAL DISTANCE: 155 miles/ 250 kilometers

NUMBER OF DAYS: 4

SEASONS: Spring through fall

START: Denver, Colorado

END: Grand Lake, Colorado

▼ MORAINE PARK, ROCKY MOUNTAIN NATIONAL PARK

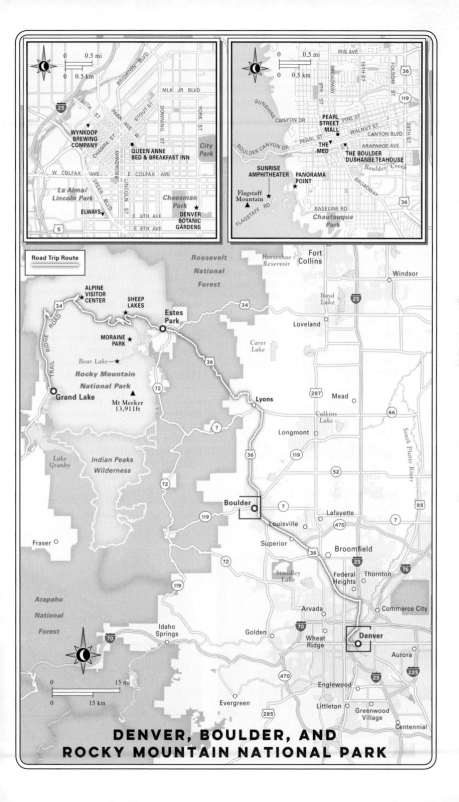

DENVER, BOULDER, AND
ROCKY MOUNTAIN NATIONAL PARK

I n mile-high Denver, you'll enjoy big-city sophistication with astonishing mountain views. Then you'll head to the college town of Boulder, where craft beer and outdoorsy adventures reign supreme. From Boulder, venture up to Estes Park, where elk roam the hillsides, cozy lodges and hotels welcome visitors, and the imposing Rocky Mountains surround it all. This trip takes you through, up, and over the Rockies, dropping you off in Grand Lake, so named after the largest natural body of water in Colorado.

DAY 1: Denver

MORNING

❶ Arrive at Denver International Airport and transfer to one of the Mile High City's cozy bed-and-breakfasts, the **Queen Anne Bed & Breakfast Inn** (2147 Tremont Place, 303/296-6666, www.queenannebnb.com, $175-250), on the eastern edge of downtown. Some rooms overlook the peaceful garden, where the owners grow more than 100 varieties of fruits, herbs, and vegetables.

❷ Stroll through the **Denver Botanic Gardens** (1007 York St., 720/865-3500, www.botanicgardens.org, 9am-8pm daily, $12.50), a lush urban oasis featuring the continent's largest collection of plants from cold, temperate climates. Its 45 gardens host 34,000 different plants and include the 1986 Xeriscape Demonstration Garden, a Japanese show garden, and a peaceful water garden.

AFTERNOON

❸ Shop in bustling **Larimer Square** (14th and 15th Sts. at Larimer St., www.larimersquare.com), the city's oldest block. This spirited district bustles with colorful art galleries, exclusive boutiques, lively bars, and hip restaurants, many of which are set in lovingly restored buildings that date to the 1880s.

❹ Enjoy a cold craft beer at **Wynkoop Brewing Company** (1634 18th St., 303/297-2700, www.wynkoop.com, 11am-midnight Sun.-Thurs., 11am-2am Fri.-Sat.), Colorado's first brewpub. Started in the 1980s, it's one of the state's largest breweries and still known for its innovative brews, which over the years have included some unusual ingredients like green chiles and gummy bears.

EVENING

❺ For dinner, order one of the juicy steaks at upscale **Elway's** (2500 E. 1st

DENVER BOTANIC GARDENS

LARIMER SQUARE

Top ③ DENVER, BOULDER, AND ROCKY MOUNTAIN NATIONAL PARK

1. Sip Persian tea in a traditional setting at the **Boulder Dushanbe Teahouse** (PAGE 392).

2. Spot **elk** roaming the meadows of **Rocky Mountain National Park** (PAGE 393).

3. Spend a haunted night at **The Stanley Hotel** in Estes Park (PAGE 394).

Ave., 303/399-5353, www.elways.com, 11am-9pm Mon.-Thurs., 11am-10pm Fri.-Sat., 10:30am-9pm Sun., $17-67), named after cofounder and former Denver Broncos quarterback John Elway. The beautifully appointed dining room feels relaxed yet upscale, with understated decor, muted lighting, and white tablecloths.

DAY 2: Denver to Boulder

35 miles/56 kilometers | 1 hour

ROUTE OVERVIEW: I-25 • US-36 • city streets

① Head north to Boulder and hike in gorgeous **Chautauqua Park** (900 Baseline Rd., http://bouldercolorado.gov), the jewel of the city's extensive open-space system. Set at the base of the Flatirons, this park is an idyllic spot to enjoy stunning views and stretch your legs. On weekdays, it's best to go early in the morning to find a parking spot. On summer weekends the city offers a **shuttle to Chautauqua** (http://bouldercolorado.gov, 8am-8pm Sat.-Sun. late May-early Sept., free) from downtown Boulder.

> Drive I-25 N to US-36 W (6 mi/10 km). Follow US-36 to Boulder (20 mi/32 km). Take the exit for Baseline Rd., turn left, and follow Baseline west as it turns into Flagstaff Rd. Stay on Flagstaff to Chautauqua Park (1.5 miles/2.5 km).

CHAUTAUQUA PARK

BOULDER DUSHANABE TEAHOUSE

② Drive up **Flagstaff Mountain** (Flagstaff Rd., http://bouldercolorado.gov) for gorgeous panoramic views. **Panorama Point,** the first parking area on the right, and the **Sunrise Amphitheater** at the summit offer incredible views of the city, including straight-as-an-arrow Baseline Road—so named because it follows the 40th parallel north.

> Take Flagstaff Rd. to reach Panorama Point in less than a mile. It's another 2 miles (3 km) to the summit.

③ Head back down the mountain and into town. Sip a cup of tea seated at a *topchan* at the **Boulder Dushanbe Teahouse** (1770 13th St., 303/442-4993, http://boulderteahouse.com, 8am-9pm daily, $14-24). The only Persian-style teahouse in the Western Hemisphere, the structure was handcrafted by more than 40 Tajik artisans using traditional Persian designs that feature gardens and water.

> Retrace your path back down the mountain to Baseline Rd. (3 mi/5 km). Turn left onto 9th St. and follow this for 1 mile (1.6 km) to Arapahoe Ave. Turn right; in less than a mile, turn left onto 13th St. to reach the teahouse.

④ Next, head a few blocks north. Go shopping and people-watching along the **Pearl Street Mall** (Pearl St.

PEARL STREET MALL

between 11th and 15th Sts., www.boulderdowntown.com). Boulder's heart lies in this four-block, brick-paved pedestrian mall, home to some of the best restaurants, bars, galleries, and shops in the state.

❺ Settle into a downtown hotel and dine at **The Med** (1002 Walnut St., 303/444-5335, www.themedboulder.com, 11am-10pm Mon.-Thurs., 11am-11pm Fri.-Sat., 11am-9pm Sun., $9-33), a local favorite for its large selection of tapas, excellent Mediterranean-inspired entrées, wood-fired pizzas, and one of Boulder's liveliest happy hours.

DAY 3: Boulder to Estes Park

70 miles/113 kilometers | 2.5-3 hours

ROUTE OVERVIEW: US-36 • US-34/ Fall River Rd. • US-36 • Bear Lake Rd. • US-36

❶ Drive through artsy **Lyons** en route to **Estes Park,** the gateway to **Rocky Mountain National Park** (970/586-1206, www.nps.gov/romo, 24 hours daily, $25-35 vehicles, $15 cyclists and pedestrians). Look for bighorn sheep at **Sheep Lakes** (2 mi/3 km west of Fall River Visitor Center), nestled in the large surrounding valley called Horseshoe Park. Although the movements of any wildlife are difficult to predict, the sheep are typically in this area between 9am and 3pm, and sightings can range from lone individuals to groups of up to 60.

> Take Broadway north for 4 miles (6 km) to US-36. Turn left and follow US-36 N to Lyons (12 mi/19 km). To continue to Estes Park, head northwest on US-36 (20 mi/32 km). Head into the park by taking US-34/Fall River Rd. for 3 miles (5 km) to the Fall River Entrance Station. Continue west for 2 miles (3 km) to Sheep Lakes.

❷ Continue to **Moraine Park** (Bear Lake Rd., southwest of Beaver Meadows Entrance Station). This is one of the best places in the park to spot elk; they typically graze in this meadow in the spring and again in fall, when they descend from the tundra to breed.

> Follow US-34 for another 2 miles (3 km). Turn left onto US-36 E and drive for 3 miles (5 km). Turn right onto Bear Lake Rd. for views of Moraine Park.

❸ At sparkling **Bear Lake** (off Bear Lake Rd.), stroll the undulating walking path (0.5 mi/0.8 km loop) that circles the lake, being sure to check out the stunning view of Longs Peak from the northern shore.

> Follow Bear Lake Rd. south for 8 miles (13 km). to reach the trailhead.

❹ Head back to Estes Park in the evening. Feast on one of the massive charcuterie boards served at **Bird & Jim** (915 Moraine Ave., 970/586-9832,

BEAR LAKE

▶ Playlist

DENVER, BOULDER, AND ROCKY MOUNTAIN NATIONAL PARK

SONGS

- **"Rocky Mountain High" by John Denver:** Too on the nose? Nah. Inspired by John Denver's love of Colorado, this folk song lyrically and emotionally connects you to the land through which you're traversing.

- **"How it Ends" by DeVotchKa:** This is perhaps the most famous song by the Denver-based, multi-instrumental band, made popular in the 2006 film *Little Miss Sunshine.* It's a slow build—quiet and dreamy in the beginning, atmospheric and symphonic by the end—almost like driving from Denver to the peak of the Rocky Mountains.

- **"In the Mood" by Glenn Miller:** Iowa-born Miller studied at the University of Colorado in Boulder in the 1920s, and this big-band song is undeniably his most popular. The 1939 recording was inducted into the Grammy Hall of Fame and the Library of Congress National Recording Registry. Its loose, jazzy vibe keeps you calm as you drive Colorado's twisty mountain roads.

www.birdandjim.com, 11am-close Mon.-Sat., 10:30am-close Sun., $16-38), an upscale restaurant named after two local legends, Isabella Bird and James "Rocky Mountain Jim" Nugent. Be sure to try one of their hand-crafted cocktails.

> Retrace your path along Bear Lake Rd. to US-36 (9 mi/15 km). Take US-36 E back into Estes Park (4 mi/6 km).

❺ Spend the night telling ghost stories at **The Stanley Hotel** (333 Wonderview Ave., 970/577-4040, www.stanleyhotel.com, $249-449), which served as the inspiration for the terrifying Overlook Hotel in Stephen King's best-seller *The Shining.* If you're brave enough, you can try to reserve one of the five haunted rooms, including Suite 217 where Stephen King stayed, as well as the *Ghost Hunters'* favorite room, 401 (only bookable by phone).

DAY 4: Estes Park to Grand Lake

50 miles/81 kilometers | 2 hours

ROUTE OVERVIEW: US-36 • Trail Ridge Rd./US-34

❶ Fuel up with organic, direct-trade coffee and a freshly baked muffin at **Notchtop Bakery & Cafe** (459 E. Wonderview Ave., 970/586-0272, www.thenotchtop.com, 7am-3pm daily, $6-12).

❷ Reenter the park to drive the winding hairpins along **Trail Ridge Road** (US-34, May-mid-Oct.), one of Colorado's most spectacular drives and the only road that crosses the park. The best views are from the section above

TRAIL RIDGE ROAD

ALPINE VISITOR CENTER

tree line, where you are surrounded by windswept tundra stretching in every direction toward snowcapped peaks, dramatic steep-walled cirques, and deep valleys. Along the way, stop at the vista points, trailheads, and **Alpine Visitor Center** (Trail Ridge Rd., 970/586-1222, www.nps.gov, 9am-5pm daily late May-mid-Oct.). The center's back windows and deck have one of the best views in Colorado, a panorama looking down Fall River Canyon toward Longs Peak and Estes Park far below.

> *Take US-36 W into the park, entering via Beaver Meadows (4 mi/6 km). Continue for another 3 miles (5 km) on US-36 to Trail Ridge Rd./US-34. Continue west on Trail Ridge Rd. for 17 miles (27 km). Turn right onto Old Fall River Rd. to reach Alpine Visitor Center.*

❸ Spend the night at the rustic **Grand Lake Lodge** (15500 US-34, 970/627-3967, http://highwaywestvacations.com, May-Sept., $160-205), perched high above **Grand Lake,** a year-round recreation hub on the park's west side. Have dinner in the historic dining room, then nab a seat in the lobby and cozy up near the massive circular fireplace.

> *Take Trail Ridge Rd./US-34 W for 21 miles (34 km). Turn left onto Grand Lake Lodge Rd. to reach the lodge.*

Getting There

AIR

About 25 miles (40 km) east of downtown Denver, **Denver International Airport** (DEN, 8500 Peña Blvd.,

303/342-2000, www.flydenver.com) is the city's primary commercial airport. Serviced by 20 airlines, including all major American airlines, the airport is a hub for United, Southwest, and Frontier Airlines. It is Colorado's primary location from which to connect to flights to other cities in Colorado, including the mountain resorts.

All of the major car rental companies have depots at or near the airport, including **Avis** (800/352-7900, www.avis.com), **Hertz** (800/654-3131, www.hertz.com), and **Thrifty** (800/847-4389, www.thrifty.com). Most require you to first visit their desk on Level 5, then ride a shuttle a short distance to the depot. Shuttles pick up and drop off from Level 5, Island 4, outside doors 505-513 on the east side and 504-512 on the west side.

TRAIN

Amtrak (800/872-7245, www.amtrak.com) offers daily service to Denver along the California Zephyr route, which runs between Chicago and San Francisco. Tickets are available online or in person at **Union Station** (1701 Wynkoop St.). In addition to stopping in Denver, the Zephyr route stops in Omaha and Salt Lake City.

BUS

Greyhound (www.greyhound.com) and the Colorado Department of Transportation's **Bustang** (800/900-3011, www.ridebustang.com) offer regional service between **Union Station** (1701 Wynkoop St.) and locations such as Colorado Springs, Chicago, Las Vegas, Phoenix, Albuquerque, Kansas City, Santa Fe, Vail, and Grand Junction.

CAR

To reach downtown Denver from **Denver International Airport,** it's a drive of 25 miles (40 km) that takes 45 minutes via Peña Boulevard, I-70, and I-25.

Getting Back

To get back to **Denver** from Grand Lake, it's 100 miles (161 km) and takes 2.5-3 hours via US-34, US-40, I-70, and US-6.

IDAHO'S RIVERS AND MOUNTAINS: BOISE TO COEUR D'ALENE

WHY GO: Fishing, rafting, hiking, canoeing, wilderness areas, Basque cuisine, craft beer, Lake Coeur d'Alene, Native American history and culture

TOTAL DISTANCE: 440 miles/ 710 kilometers

NUMBER OF DAYS: 7

SEASONS: Spring through fall

START: Boise, Idaho

END: Coeur d'Alene, Idaho

▼ KAYAKERS ON COEUR D'ALENE LAKE

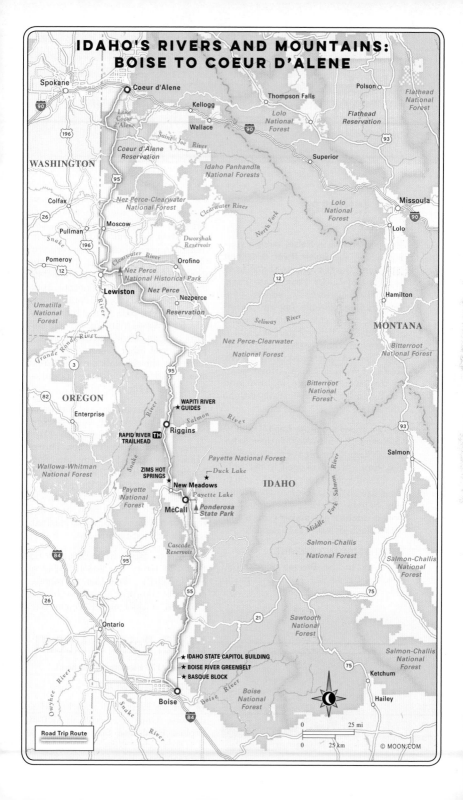

Prepare to be overwhelmed by the staggering natural beauty of Idaho. Mountains loom on either side of the road, and forests cover most of the state. Icy rivers snake through the carved landscape, tempting anglers and rafters alike. The craggy wilderness provides a stunning backdrop for your road-trip adventure. From exploring Boise's Basque community to soaking in hot springs to sipping locally roasted coffee in Coeur d'Alene, you'll be taken with all there is to do and see in the Gem State.

DAY 1: Boise

MORNING

❶ Upon arrival in **Boise,** stretch your legs along the **Boise River Greenbelt** (spanning Garden City to the Discovery Unit of Lucky Peak State Park, www.cityofboise.org, sunrise-sunset daily), a 25-mile (40-km) series of paved trails connecting parks and wetlands. You'll see waterfowl, and if you are lucky, bald eagles, blue herons, great horned owls, muskrats, beavers, foxes, or even a cougar. Head down to the river anywhere in town and you'll find the Greenbelt trails with no difficulty.

❷ Visit the **Idaho State Capitol** (700 W. Jefferson St., http://legislature.idaho. gov, 6:30am-7pm Mon.-Fri., 9am-5pm Sat.-Sun.), which is open to the public for self-guided tours. On the fourth floor are the entrances to the House and Senate galleries, where you can watch Idaho's lawmakers in action when the legislature is in session.

AFTERNOON AND EVENING

❸ Walk to the **Basque Block** (600 block of Grove St.). Boise is home to the largest Basque population in the United States, and the group has its own enclave in downtown Boise, with a cultural center, museum, and Basque eateries. On the corner of Grove and 6th Streets is the **Basque Center** (601 W. Grove St., 208/342-9983, www.basquecenter.com, 3pm-9pm Tues.-Wed., 3pm-10pm Thurs., 2pm-1am Fri.-Sat., 2pm-11pm Sun.), which serves as a hub for Basque culture, hosting music and dance performances and other events. The center has a bar; the sidewalk patio is a great spot to soak in the culture while enjoying a glass of rioja.

❹ Dine on Basque fare at **Bar Gernika** (202 S. Capitol Blvd., 208/344-2175, www.bargernika.com, 11am-11pm Mon., 11am-midnight Tues.-Thurs., 11am-1am Fri., 11:30am-1am Sat., $5-10), a tiny place that borrows its name from a city in the Basque region of Spain. Try the croquettes (crunchy fritters made with chicken stock and roux) or a *solomo* sandwich (marinated pork loin with pimentos).

❺ Call it a night at the **Modern Hotel** (1314 Grove St., 208/424-8244 or 866/780-6012, www.themodernhotel. com, $99-200), but not before having a cocktail in the hotel's Euro-chic bar.

DAY 2: Boise to McCall

110 miles/177 kilometers | 2.5 hours

ROUTE OVERVIEW: ID-55

❶ Get up early and grab breakfast in Boise. Once you arrive in **McCall,** explore **Ponderosa State Park** (1920 N. Davis Ave., 208/634-2164, http:// parksandrecreation.idaho.gov, $5 per

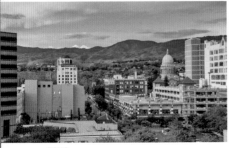

BOISE

Top 3 IDAHO'S RIVERS AND MOUNTAINS: BOISE TO COEUR D'ALENE

1. Explore the **Basque Block** in **Boise,** a vibrant part of town that's home to the largest Basque community in the United States (PAGE 398).
2. **Raft** the world-famous rapids of the **Salmon River** in Riggins (PAGE 401).
3. Relax on the picturesque shores of **Lake Coeur d'Alene** in the city named after it (PAGE 401).

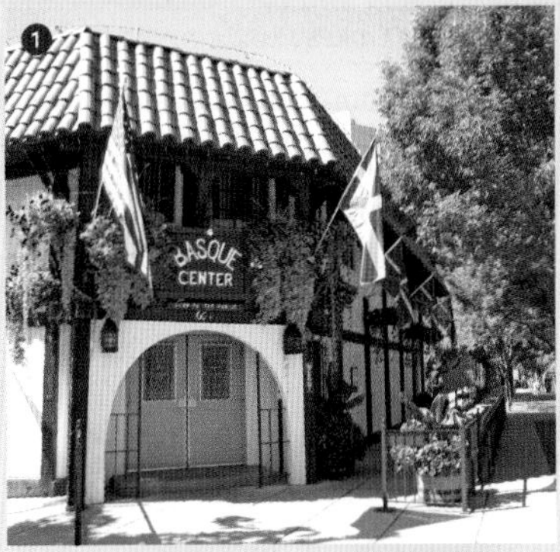

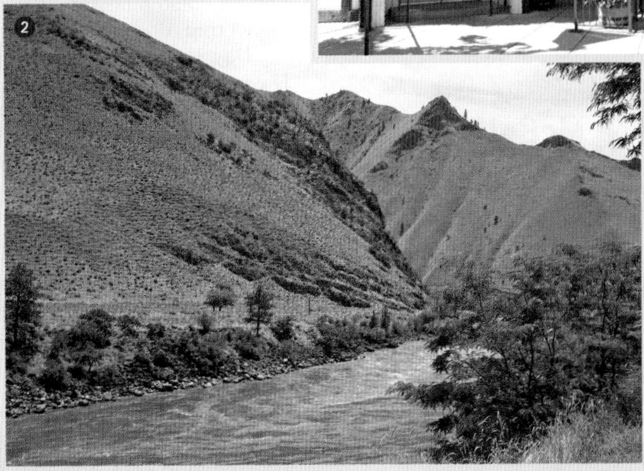

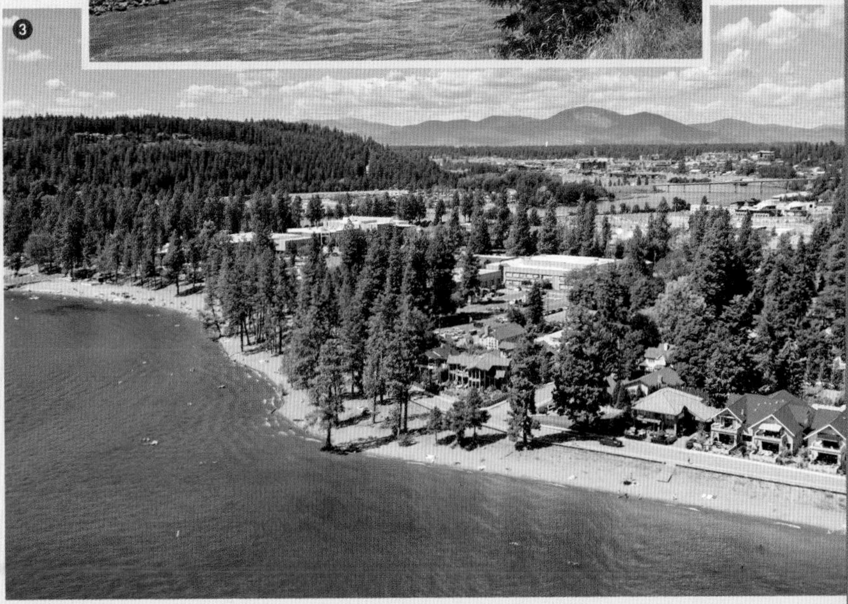

vehicle). The crown jewel of Idaho's park system is 1,000 acres of forested wonderland near Payette Lake—ideal for outdoor fun. Spend the rest of the day hiking, biking, and fishing around the wooded park.

> Take State St. northwest to ID-55 (8 mi/13 km). Turn right onto ID-55 and drive for 100 miles (161 km) to McCall.

❷ Get a room at the beautiful **Hotel McCall** (1101 N. 3rd St., 208/634-8105 or 866/800-1183, www.hotelmccall.com, $135-150, suites from $300 d), which has been in operation since 1904.

❸ You won't have to go far once you're ready for dinner: **Rupert's** (1101 N. 3rd St., 208/634-8108, www.rupertsathotelmccall.com, 5pm-9pm Thurs.-Mon., $19-32), one of the finest restaurants in town, is right in your hotel.

DAY 3: McCall

45 miles/72 kilometers | 2.5-3 hours

ROUTE OVERVIEW: Lick Creek Rd.

❶ After breakfast, drive an hour into the mountains just beyond town. Hike to **Duck Lake** (2 mi/3.2 km round-trip, 45 minutes, easy), where an overlook at the summit provides panoramic views of the glacier-carved landscape. Find the trailhead on Lick Creek Road (Forest Rd. 48).

> Take Lake St. east to where it turns into 3rd Street. Make a quick left on Railroad Ave., which becomes Pine St. From Pine, merge onto Lenora St., then turn left on Davis Ave. In less than a mile, turn right onto Lick Creek Rd. and follow it for 19 miles (31 km) to Duck Lake.

❷ Return to town and **rent a canoe** from **Mile High Marina** (1300 E. Lake St., 208/634-8605) for a mellow paddle around the mountain-ringed **Payette Lake.** Spend time hanging out on the beach.

> Retrace your path down Lick Creek Rd. to get back into town (22 mi/35 km).

❸ Stop by **Salmon River Brewery** (411 Railroad Ave., 208/634-4772, www.salmonriverbrewery.com, 11am-11pm daily, $8-13) for dinner and handcrafted beers.

PAYETTE LAKE IN MCCALL

DAY 4: McCall to Riggins

55 miles/89 kilometers | 1.5-2 hours

ROUTE OVERVIEW: ID-55 • US-95

❶ Get up early and drive to **New Meadows,** then north to **Zim's Hot Springs** (2995 Zims Rd., 208/347-2686, 9am-11pm daily Memorial Day-Labor Day, 10am-10pm Tues.-Sun. Labor Day-Memorial Day, $7 adults, $6 children 3-17) for a morning soak in the heated pools.

> Drive north on ID-55 to New Meadows (11 mi/18 km). Turn right onto US-95 N and drive for 4 miles (6 km). Turn left onto Circle C Ln. and follow it for less than a mile to the hot springs.

❷ Head north and into the wilderness for a hike along the **Rapid River Trail** (8.6 mi/13.8 km round-trip, 3.5-4 hours, moderate). The out-and-back trail takes you along the Rapid River, rolling up and down as it goes, transitioning from dry and dusty at the beginning to lush and cool as you progress into the river canyon. The trailhead is at the end of Rapid River Road, past the hatchery.

> Take US-95 N for 26 miles (42 km), then turn left onto Rapid River Rd. Follow this for 3 miles (5 km) to reach the trailhead.

A BRIDGE LEADING INTO RIGGINS

📋✓ KEY
RESERVATIONS

- For a rafting trip with the outfitter **Wapiti River Guides** in Riggins, you'll want to reserve your spot ahead of time, at least **4-6 weeks.**

- Make your reservation a **week** ahead of time at **Angelo's Ristorante** in Coeur d'Alene.

③ Drive onward to **Riggins,** a little hamlet where the Salmon and Little Salmon Rivers come together in a wild exhibition of rapids. Check in to the **Salmon Rapids Lodge** (1010 S. Main St., 208/628-2743, from $90) for two nights. The lodge enjoys prime real estate at the confluence of the Salmon and Little Salmon Rivers.

> Retrace your path along Rapid River Rd. to US-95 (3 mi/5 km). Go north on US-95 for 4 miles (6 km) to reach Riggins.

DAY 5: Riggins

MORNING AND AFTERNOON

① Order one of the delicious omelets at **River Rock Cafe** (1149 S. Main St., 208/628-3434, 6am-9pm Sun.-Thurs., 6am-10pm Fri.-Sat., $12-24) to fuel up for the day ahead.

② The **Salmon River** in Riggins is world-famous for its wild rapids. Several guide services offer float trips on either the main Salmon run above town or the Salmon River Gorge stretch downstream from Riggins. One recommended company is **Wapiti River Guides** (208/628-3523, www.doryfun.com, $59 half day, $97 full day). Expect to get a little wet along the

way, but the guides are good at keeping the rafts upright. Be sure to reserve your spot ahead of time.

EVENING

③ After shooting the tube all day, head to the **Back Eddy Grill & Alehouse** (533 N. Main St., 208/628-9233, 11am-10pm Sun.-Thurs., 11am-11pm Fri.-Sat., $8-10) for an elk burger and a few microbrews. Here you can swap tall river tales with fellow rafters on the patio.

DAY 6: Riggins to Coeur d'Alene

230 miles/370 kilometers | 4-4.5 hours

ROUTE OVERVIEW: US-95

① After breakfast, make your way to the **Clearwater River** near Lewiston. Here you'll find the visitors center for the **Nez Perce National Historic Park** (39063 US-95, Lapwai, 208/843-7001, www.nps.gov/nepe, 9am-5pm daily Memorial Day-Labor Day, shorter hours Labor Day-Memorial Day, free), adjacent to the Spalding Mission site. This is an excellent spot for a picnic and to learn about Idaho's Native American history. Lewis and Clark's Corps of Discovery famously traveled through this area on their way to and from the Pacific Ocean in the early 19th century.

> Follow US-95 N to the visitors center (105 miles/169 km).

② Continue heading north until you reach **Coeur d'Alene** and the shores of its namesake lake. Check in to the **Flamingo Motel** (718 Sherman Ave., 208/664-2159, www.flamingomotelidaho.com, from $90 d), just a few blocks from the lake.

> Continue north on US-95 for 121 miles (195 km) to Coeur d'Alene.

③ Make a reservation at **Angelo's Ristorante** (846 N. 4th St., 208/765-2850, www.angelosristorante.net, 5pm-10pm daily, $16-28) for fine Italian dining. Here you'll find an elegant space and upscale preparations of antipasto, pasta, risotto, scampi, steaks, and rack of lamb.

WHITE-WATER FUN IN RIGGINS

THE QUEST FOR
Perfect Powder

In the winter, the Gem State boasts some of the best skiing in the country. Skiers and snowboarders love Idaho for its killer powder and relatively short lift lines. Here's a look at some ski resorts worth checking out.

- Just north of Boise is **Bogus Basin Ski Resort** (2600 Bogus Basin Rd., 208/332-5100 or 800/367-4397, snow report 208/342-2100, www.bogusbasin. org, lifts 10am-10pm Mon.-Fri., 9am-10pm Sat.-Sun., full-day lift tickets $25, 4pm-10pm lift tickets $20), which has 2,600 acres of skiable runs and a vertical drop of 1,800 feet. The resort can get crowded at times, but the views of Boise from the top are spectacular.

- For remarkable powder and great views of Payette Lake, head to **Brundage Mountain** (208/634-4151, snow report 208/634-7669, www.brundage.com, lifts 9:30am-4:30pm daily, full-day lift tickets $60 adults, $37 children 12-17, $23 children 7-11) just outside McCall. This small resort, which can be somewhat empty if you come midweek, has a vertical drop of 1,800 feet and 1,500 skiable acres.

- **Tamarack Resort** (311 Village Dr., Tamarack, 208/325-1000, www.tamarackidaho.com, 9am-4pm daily Dec.-Mar., full-day pass $52 adults, $43 children 13-17, $25 children 7-12), nestled in the West-Central Mountains near Donnelly, is an up-and-coming all-season resort with panoramic views of Lake Cascade. It has a vertical drop of 2,800 feet and around 1,000 acres of lift-accessed runs.

DAY 7: Coeur d'Alene

MORNING

❶ Sip the best coffee in town at **Evans Brothers Coffee Roasters** (504 E. Sherman Ave., 208/930-4065, www.evans-brotherscoffee.com, 7am-5pm Mon.-Fri., 8am-4pm Sat., 8am-2pm Sun.). All beans are roasted in-house, and the café features a slow bar for single-cup brewing. Ask for a Roaster's Reserve coffee, which rotates frequently.

❷ Spend some time frolicking in the lake—with its more than 130 miles of shoreline—and relaxing on a beach chair at **City Beach** (adjacent to City Park, 415 Fort Ground Dr., www. cdaid.org, 5am-11pm daily).

AFTERNOON AND EVENING

❸ Peruse the multitude of cool shops and art galleries on **Sherman Avenue.** Go to dinner at **Beverly's** (115 S. 2nd St., 208/765-4000, https://beverlyscda. com, 11am-2:30pm Mon.-Sat., 5pm-9pm Sun.-Thurs., 5pm-10pm Sat.-Sun., $18-47), an elegant contemporary restaurant that sources lots of local foodstuffs.

❹ After dinner, head to beautiful **Tubbs Hill** (210 S. 3rd St., www.cdaid. org, 24 hours daily, free), a wooded preserve that juts into the lake. Climb to the top of the hill and watch the fiery sunset.

Getting There

AIR

The **Boise Airport** (BOI, 3201 Airport Way, 208/383-3110, www.iflyboise.com) is on the southeast edge of town at I-84 exit 53 (Vista Ave.). Airlines serving the city include Delta/SkyWest, which offers daily flights (through its Salt Lake City hub) to Minneapolis, Los Angeles, and Salt Lake City; Southwest, offering direct daily flights between Boise and Denver, Las Vegas, Phoenix, Oakland, and Spokane; and United, with direct daily flights to and from San Francisco, Chicago, Houston, Denver, and Los Angeles. Alaska Airlines/Horizon Air offers nonstop daily flights between Boise and Portland, Sacramento, San Diego, San Jose, Seattle, and Lewiston.

Car rental companies with offices in the airport include **Avis** (208/383-3350 or 800/331-1212), **Budget** (208/383-3090 or 800/527-0700), **Enterprise** (208/381-0650 or 800/736-8222), **Hertz** (208/383-3100 or 800/654-3131), and **National** (208/383-3210 or 800/227-7368).

BUS

Downtown, you'll find an old, scuffed-up **Greyhound terminal** (1212 W. Bannock St., 208/343-3681, www.greyhound.com), where three buses daily connect Boise with Portland as well as Salt Lake City. Sharing the Greyhound terminal is **Northwestern Trailways** (509/838-4029, www.northwesterntrailways.com), which offers one bus daily to McCall, Grangeville, Lewiston, Coeur d'Alene, and Spokane (with onward connections to Seattle).

CAR

I-84 runs east-west across southern Idaho, connecting **Portland** (430 mi/690 km), about a seven-hour drive, to the west and **Salt Lake City** (345 mi/560 km), about a five-hour drive, to the southeast.

The **Boise airport** is 10 minutes (4 mi/6 km) from downtown Boise via Vista Avenue and Capitol Boulevard.

Getting Back

To return to **Boise** from Coeur d'Alene is a seven-hour trip of 308 miles (610 km) via US-95 and ID-55.

If you opt to fly out of **Spokane, Washington,** just over the border from Coeur d'Alene, **Spokane International Airport** (GEG, 9000 W. Airport Dr., 509/455-6455, http://spokaneairports.net) offers service via the major airlines (American, Delta, Southwest, United) to destinations around the country, such as Chicago, Atlanta, Los Angeles, Seattle, Dallas, Houston, Las Vegas, and Phoenix. The airport is 39 miles (63 km) from Coeur d'Alene; drive west on I-90.

 *Playlist*

IDAHO'S RIVERS AND MOUNTAINS: BOISE TO COEUR D'ALENE

SONGS

- **"Idaho" by Josh Ritter:** Idaho-born singer-songwriter Ritter crafts soulful narratives steeped in Americana out of each of his songs. In this one, he sings of a man at sea who longs for his landlocked home of Idaho.

- **"Else" by Built to Spill:** This Boise band's messy, sometimes playful, sometimes feisty garage-rock sound has cultivated a loyal following since the band came onto the scene in the 1990s. This song keeps things breezy and subdued in a way that suits a rambling road trip.

- **"Private Idaho" by The B-52's:** Debuting in 1980, this song references what Georgia-based songwriter Fred Schneider referred to as the unknowable, mysterious quality of Idaho. The percussive-heavy, surf guitar-driven song inspired film director Gus Van Sant to title his 1991 movie *My Own Private Idaho.*

CONNECT WITH

- At Boise: **Oregon Trail** (PAGE 78)

MOUNT RUSHMORE AND THE BLACK HILLS

WHY GO: Badlands National Park, ancient animal fossils, geologic wonders, prairie landscapes, Native American culture, bison, cave tours, horizon-reaching vistas, Crazy Horse Memorial

TOTAL DISTANCE: 390 miles/ 630 kilometers

NUMBER OF DAYS: 7

SEASONS: Spring through fall

START/END: Rapid City, South Dakota

▼ MOUNT RUSHMORE

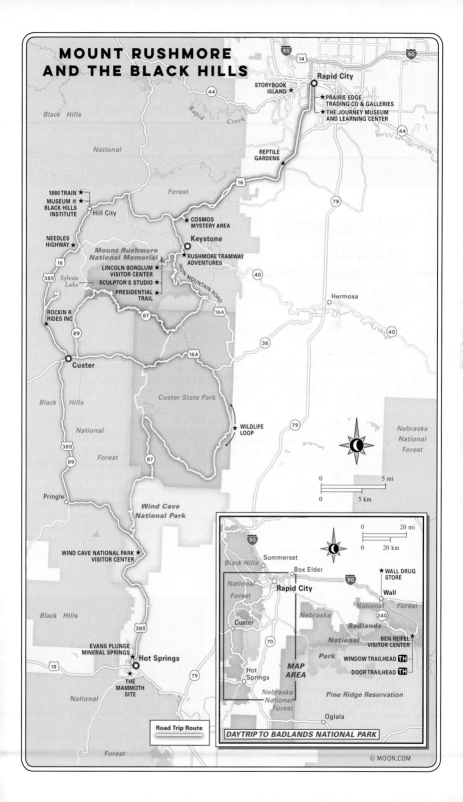

MOUNT RUSHMORE AND THE BLACK HILLS

Black Hills

National

Forest

Rapid Creek

Rapid City

STORYBOOK ISLAND ★

★ PRAIRIE EDGE TRADING CO & GALLERIES
★ THE JOURNEY MUSEUM AND LEARNING CENTER

REPTILE GARDENS ★

1880 TRAIN ★
MUSEUM @ ★ BLACK HILLS INSTITUTE

Hill City

NEEDLES HIGHWAY ★

Mount Rushmore National Memorial

COSMOS MYSTERY AREA ★

Keystone

RUSHMORE TRAMWAY ADVENTURES ★

LINCOLN BORGLUM ★ VISITOR CENTER
SCULPTOR'S STUDIO ★
PRESIDENTIAL ★ TRAIL

Sylvan Lake

ROCKIN R RIDES INC ★

IRON MOUNTAIN ROAD

Hermosa

Custer

Black Hills

National

Forest

Custer State Park

WILDLIFE LOOP ★

Nebraska National Forest

0   5 mi
0   5 km

Pringle

Wind Cave National Park

WIND CAVE NATIONAL PARK ★ VISITOR CENTER

Black Hills

National

EVANS PLUNGE MINERAL SPRINGS ★

Hot Springs

THE MAMMOTH SITE ★

National

Forest

Road Trip Route

DAYTRIP TO BADLANDS NATIONAL PARK

Black Hills

National

Forest

Summerset

Box Elder

Rapid City

Custer

Hot Springs

MAP AREA

Nebraska National Forest

Oglala

0   20 mi
0   20 km

WALL DRUG STORE ★

Wall

Nebraska

National

Forest

Badlands

National

Park

BEN REIFEL ★ VISITOR CENTER

WINDOW TRAILHEAD 🆃🅷

DOOR TRAILHEAD 🆃🅷

Pine Ridge Reservation

© MOON.COM

On this road trip, you'll dip up and over rolling prairielands, curve around mountains, and tour Mount Rushmore, one of the country's most iconic national monuments. You'll see bison, eagles, and deer, and you'll encounter the otherworldly beauty of Badlands National Park—a place so vast, you might not see another person while you're there. The route also takes you to Custer State Park and the Crazy Horse Memorial, as well as the bustling little enclave of Rapid City. GPS and Wi-Fi are spotty in this region, so shelve your digital devices and let the big skies of South Dakota be your guide.

DAY 1: Rapid City to Keystone

30 miles/48 kilometers | 45 minutes

ROUTE OVERVIEW: US-16 • US-16A • SD-244 • US-16A

❶ Along US-16, also known as Mount Rushmore Road, spend a few hours at **Reptile Gardens** (8955 S. US-16, 605/342-5873 or 800/335-0275, www.reptilegardens.com, 8am-6pm daily Memorial Day-Labor Day, 9am-4pm daily Mar.-Memorial Day and Labor Day-Oct., 9am-3pm daily Nov., $10-18 adults, $7-12 children 5-12), an attraction where you'll meet crocodiles, snakes, and raptors. Best of all are the free-roaming giant tortoises.

> Head south on US-16 to Reptile Gardens (7 mi/11 km).

❷ Continue on to **Mount Rushmore National Memorial** (13000 SD-244, 605/574-2523, www.nps.gov/moru, 8am-10pm daily June-mid-Aug., 8am-9pm daily mid-Aug.-Sept., 8am-5pm daily Oct.-May, free admission, parking $10). First, visit the **Lincoln Borglum Visitor Center,** the park's main visitors center. Next, check out the **Sculptor's Studio** (8am-7pm daily June-Aug., 9am-5pm daily Sept.). Everything you'd ever want to know about the process of carving Mount Rushmore, including the time line, the people who worked on the mountain, and the tools they used, can be found here. Finally, hike the **Presidential Trail** (0.5 mi/0.8 km loop) to the base of the mountain.

> Continue southwest on US-16 to US-16A/Iron Mountain Rd. (11 mi/18 km). Drive south on US-16A to SD-244 (4 mi/6 km). Continue straight onto SD-244 to Mount Rushmore.

❸ Head to **Keystone** and stop at **Rushmore Tramway Adventures** (203 Cemetery Rd., 605/666-4478, www.rushmoretramwayadventures.com, 11am-5pm Sat.-Sun. May and Sept., 10am-6pm daily mid-June and Aug., 10am-7pm daily July, prices vary by activity). Take a ride on the ski lift and zoom down the Alpine Slide or climb the ladders and platforms amid a forest at the Aerial Adventure Park.

> Follow SD-244 back to US-16A/Iron Mountain Rd. (2 mi/3 km). Once on US-16A, in 1 mile (1.6 km), turn right on Reed St. to drive into Keystone.

❹ Be sure to sample the saltwater taffy at **Rushmore Mountain Taffy Shop** (203 Winter St., 605/666-4430, www.rushmoremountaintaffy.com, 8am-9pm daily May-Sept., 8am-5pm daily off-season). The most popular flavors include cinnamon and huckleberry, but you could also try strawberry cheesecake, chocolate cherry, or even jalapeño.

RUSHMORE TRAMWAY ADVENTURES

1. See the astonishing stone carvings of George Washington, Thomas Jefferson, Theodore Roosevelt, and Abraham Lincoln at **Mount Rushmore** (PAGE 406).

2. Tour the fifth-longest cave in the world by candlelight at **Wind Cave National Park** (PAGE 409).

3. Hike through the striking pinnacles and spires of **Badlands National Park** (PAGE 411).

⑤ Spend the night at the **Powder House Lodge** (24125 US-16A, 605/666-4646 or 800/321-0692, www.powderhouselodge.com, mid-May-mid-Oct., $90-130). Get dinner at the lodge's cozy wood-paneled restaurant.

DAY 2: Keystone to Custer

35 miles/56 kilometers | 1.5-2 hours

ROUTE OVERVIEW: US-16A • CR-753 • US-87 • US-89

① After breakfast, follow **Iron Mountain Road,** a twisting, turning, tunnel-filled scenic drive. County Road 753 (Black Hills Playhouse Rd.) enters **Custer State Park** and joins up with the **Needles Highway,** one of the most scenic byways in the state. Head north on Needles Highway to **Sylvan Lake.** Hike around the lake and or take a ride on a paddleboat.

> *Get on US-16A/Iron Mountain Rd. and drive for 11 miles (18 km); do not head toward Mount Rushmore on SD-244. Take CR-753 to connect with US-87 (4 mi/6 km). Drive north on US-87 to Sylvan Lake (11 mi/18 km).*

② Treat yourself to lunch in the dining room of **Sylvan Lake Lodge** (24572 US-87, 605/574-2561, www.custerresorts.com, 7am-8pm daily late Apr.-mid-May, 7am-9pm daily mid-May-Sept., 7am-11am and 4pm-8pm daily Oct., $15-36). Harney Peak sits in view from every spot in the restaurant.

IRON MOUNTAIN ROAD

SYLVAN LAKE

③ Take US-89 South to **Custer.** Spend the night at the **Shady Rest Motel** (238 Gordon St., 605/673-4478, www.shady-rest-motel.com, May-Sept., $80-140), a collection of charming cabins that date back to the 1930s. Views from the cabins extend to the Cathedral Spires of Custer State Park, and the backyard is national forest.

> *Drive US-89 S to Custer (6 mi/10 km).*

④ Look for dessert at the hard-to-miss **Bobkat's Purple Pie Place** (19 Mt. Rushmore Rd., 605/673-4070, www.purplepieplace.com, 11am-9pm daily mid-Apr.-Oct.). The local favorite bumbleberry pie is made from rhubarb, apples, strawberries, blueberries, and raspberries.

DAY 3: Custer to Hot Springs

65 miles/105 kilometers | 3 hours

ROUTE OVERVIEW: US-16A • Wildlife Loop • SD-87 • US-385

① Get an early start at **Baker's Bakery** (541 Mt. Rushmore Rd., 605/673-2253, www.bakersbakerycafe.com, 6:30am-3pm Wed.-Mon. spring, 6:30am-4pm daily summer and fall, $9-12). The small but choice breakfast menu includes omelets, pancakes, biscuits and gravy, and egg dishes; the specialties of the house include homemade bread, great coffee, pastries, and caramel rolls.

② Head into **Custer State Park** (13329 US-16A, 605/255-4515, www.custerstatepark.com, $20 vehicles, $10 motorcycles), one of the largest state

WIND CAVE NATIONAL PARK

KEY RESERVATIONS

- To embark on the **candlelight tour** at **Wind Cave National Park**, reservations are recommended.

- Near Crazy Horse Memorial, make reservations **two days** in advance for a **horseback adventure** at **Rockin' R Rides**.

- In **Rapid City,** make reservations **a day** ahead of time for dinner at **Delmonico Grill.**

parks in the United States. It offers much in the way of scenic diversity and outdoor activities. Drive the **Wildlife Loop** (east of State Game Lodge of US-16A), an 18-mile (29-km) road where you might spot bison, pronghorn, prairie dogs, mule deer, white-tailed deer, and wild turkeys grazing placidly, undisturbed by their many admirers. Traveling this road is most rewarding early in the day. Stop to feed the wild burros (bring carrots!).

> Head east on US-16A for 14 miles (23 km) to reach the Custer State Park Visitor Center, which marks the beginning of the Wildlife Loop. Follow the road, which heads south for about 10 miles (16 km) before looping back north again and intersecting with SD-87.

❸ At the end of the loop, drive south on SD-87 to **Wind Cave National Park** (26611 US-385, 605/745-4600, www. nps.gov/wica, 24 hours daily, free) and stop at the **visitors center** to join a tour of the fifth-longest cave in the world. There are different tour options offered year-round, including a candlelight tour.

> Go south on SD-87 to US-385 (13 mi/21 km). Turn left on US-385 and in less than a mile, turn right on Wind Cave Rd. and follow it to Wind Cave National Park.

❹ Continue on to **Hot Springs** and stop at **Evans Plunge Indoor Pool and Mineral Spa** (1145 N. River St., 605/745-5165, www.evansplunge.com, 6am-8pm Mon.-Fri., 10am-8pm Sat.-Sun. Memorial Day-Oct., 6am-8pm daily Nov.-May, $14 adults, $10 children). You'll enjoy the spring-fed pool; kids will love the waterslide.

> Take US-385 S for another 11 miles (18 km) into Hot Springs.

❺ Stay at the **Budget Host Hills Inn** (640 S. 6th St., 605/745-3130 or 800/283-4678, www.hotspringshillsinn.com, mid-Apr.-mid-Oct. $84-94, spring and early fall $59-75) and play mini golf at **Putt-4-Fun** next door; it's free to guests of the inn.

DAY 4: Hot Springs to Custer

45 miles/72 kilometers | 1.5 hours

ROUTE OVERVIEW: US-385

❶ Start the day at the southern edge of town with a visit to **Mammoth Site** (1800 Hwy. 18, 605/745-6017, www. mammothsite.com, 8am-8pm daily mid-May-mid-Aug., shorter hours mid-Aug.-mid-May, $11 adults, $8 children 4-12), where the skeletal remains of 58 mammoths, a short-faced bear, and other Pleistocene-era animals are displayed.

MAMMOTH SITE

NATIVE AMERICANS PERFORMING AT CRAZY HORSE MEMORIAL

DAY 5: Custer to Rapid City

45 miles/72 kilometers | 1 hour

ROUTE OVERVIEW: US-385 • US-16/ US-385 • surface streets

❷ In **Custer,** have lunch at **Black Hills Burger & Bun** (441 Mt. Rushmore Rd., 605/673-3411, www.blackhills-burgerandbun.com, 11am-2pm and 5pm-7:30pm Wed.-Sat., $9).

> Follow US-385 N for 30 miles (48 km) to Custer.

❸ Enjoy riding horses with **Rockin' R Rides** (24853 Village Ave., 605/673-2999, www.rockingrtrailrides.com, 8am-5pm daily Memorial Day-Sept., from $39 adults, from $36 children). Vistas of the Crazy Horse Memorial, just a mile or so away, are available intermittently along the ride.

> Continue north on US-385 for 3 miles (5 km) to Rockin' R Rides.

❹ Just a couple of miles up the highway, **Crazy Horse Memorial** (12151 Avenue of the Chiefs, Crazy Horse, 605/673-4681, www.crazyhorsememorial.org, 7am-dark daily summer, 8am-5pm daily winter, $12 pp or $30 per vehicle, $7 pp on motorcycle or bicycle) is the most ambitious mountain carving project in the world, in progress since 1948. When completed, the carving of Crazy Horse (Tasunke Witco) will depict the great Lakota leader astride a horse, pointing to the Black Hills, his homeland. It will be 641 feet long by 563 feet high. Make sure to watch the video at the visitors center and take a piece of the rock that was blasted off the mountain home for a souvenir.

> Take US-385 N for 1.5 miles (2.5 km). Turn right onto Ave. of the Chiefs and continue for less than a mile to reach the memorial.

❺ Spend the night in **Custer** at the **Bavarian Inn** (855 N. 5th St./US-385, 605/673-2802 or 800/657-4312, www.bavarianinnsd.com, $159-179), a beautiful chalet-style property.

> Return to Custer by driving south on US-385 (5 mi/8 km).

❶ It's train time! Drive up to **Hill City** in the morning and take a round-trip ride on the **1880 Train** (103 Winter St., 605/574-2222, www.1880train.com, mid-May-mid-Oct., round-trip $29 adults, $14 children ages 3-12) to Keystone and back. There's plenty of time to relax and enjoy the scenery as the steam train huffs up the hills and through the canyons.

> Go north on US-385 for 14 miles (23 km) to Hill City.

❷ After the ride, it's a short walk to visit the **Museum at Black Hills Institute** (117 Main St., 605/574-3919, www.bhigr.com/museum, 9:30am-6:30pm Mon.-Sat., 10am-5pm Sun. Memorial Day-Labor Day, 9:30am-5pm Mon.-Sat. Labor Day-Memorial Day, $7.50 adults, $4 children 6-15) to view its great dinosaur collection. The most complete *T. rex,* Stan, is on display at the museum. Other displays include ammonites, minerals, and fossil remains of many other dinosaurs, including duck-billed dinosaurs and triceratops.

❸ Head back in the general direction of Rapid City. Stop at the **Cosmos Mystery Area** (24040 Cosmos Rd., 605/343-9802, www.cosmosmysteryarea.com, 8am-8pm daily June-July, 9am-7pm

1880 TRAIN

MUSEUM AT BLACK HILLS INSTITUTE

mid-Apr.-May, 7am-7pm daily June-Aug., 8am-5pm daily Sept.-Oct., 8am-4pm daily Nov.-mid-Apr.) to learn about everything in Badlands National Park—with an award-winning video, exhibits, lots of books, maps, and knowledgeable rangers.

> Travel east on SD-44 for 73 miles (117 km) to the town of Interior. Here, turn left (north) on SD-377 and follow it for 2 miles (3 km) to the park entrance and the visitors center.

❷ Hike the **Door Trail** (0.75 mi/1.2 km round-trip, 30 minutes, easy). The first 150 yards are on a boardwalk that is wheelchair accessible. Once the boardwalk ends, the trail slopes upward and travels through a "door" in the Badlands Wall to give great views of the grasslands and the outer wall of the Badlands. Find the trailhead northeast of the visitors center, at the north end of the Door & Window parking lot.

> Head northeast for 2 miles (3 km) on SD-240 to reach the trailhead.

❸ You're right next to the **Window Trail** (0.25 mi/0.4 km round-trip, 20 minutes, easy), so there's no reason not to hit the trail again. This boardwalk path leads to a window in the Badlands Wall where views of the grasslands, an erosion-carved canyon, and the spires of the Wall are visible. The trailhead is in the center of the Door & Window parking lot.

❹ Continue driving the Badlands Loop Road. Head out of the park into the town of **Wall** and visit **Wall Drug** (510 Main St., 605/279-2175, www.walldrug.com, 7am-9pm daily June-Aug., 7am-5:30pm daily Sept.-May). A sign advertising free ice water led to the creation of this massive roadside attraction that's like a world of its own. Take pictures of the jackalope, do a little gold panning, and indulge in ice cream. Drive back to **Rapid City** on I-90.

> Follow SD-240 back toward the visitors center, then continue for a total of 32 miles (52 km). You'll exit the park on the north side at the town of Wall. From here, hop on I-90 W and follow it for 53 miles (85 km). Take the exit for I-190, heading south for 1.5 miles (2.5 km) to SD-44. Turn left and drive into Rapid City.

daily Aug., 9am-4:30pm daily late Apr.-May and Sept.-Oct., $11 adults, $6 children 5-11), a quick but fun roadside attraction where the rules of physics are challenged.

> Head east on US-16/US-385, keeping right to stay on US-16. It's 10 miles (16 km) to Cosmos Mystery Area.

❹ Continue your journey back to **Rapid City** and spend the night on the shores of Canyon Lake, staying at the **Canyon Lake Resort** (2720 Chapel Ln., 605/343-0234, www.canyonlakeresorts.com, Memorial Day-Labor Day $109, shoulder and winter $59-79), where the kids can enjoy the heated outdoor pool, paddleboats, or a walk on the path along the lakeshore.

> Continue east on US-16 to Rapid City (17 mi/27 km). To reach the resort from Rapid City, follow Main St. for less than a mile to Jackson Blvd. Turn left and drive to Chapel Ln. (3 mi/5 km). Turn left onto Chapel, then make a quick left on Shore Dr. and continue to the resort.

DAY 6: Day Trip to Badlands National Park

170 miles/275 kilometers | 3.5-4 hours

ROUTE OVERVIEW: SD-44 • SD-377 • SD-240/Badlands Loop Rd. • I-90 • I-190 • SD-44

❶ Enjoy the scenic drive along SD-44 to **Badlands National Park** (605/433-5361, www.nps.gov/badl, 24 hours daily, $25 vehicles, $15 motorcycles and cyclists, $12 pedestrians). Stop at the **Ben Reifel Visitor Center** (25216 Ben Reifel Rd./SD-240, 8am-5pm daily

The Black Hills offers inspiring experiences for both the wildly adventuresome and the quietly contemplative. Here are some of the best:

- **Go underground at Wind Cave National Park:** The **Wild Cave Tour** (605/745-4600, www.nps.gov/wica) will have you crawling through narrow passages as you learn the basics of safe caving and see the deeper sections of one of the longest caves in the world.

- **Climb a rock at Custer State Park:** Have the adventure of your life with **Sylvan Rocks Climbing School & Guide Service** (605/484-7585, www.sylvanrocks.com). Learn to climb in the Needles or take the best routes with the most knowledgeable climbers in the hills.

- **Backpack the Sage Creek Wilderness Area:** Bring plenty of water and sunscreen and spend a few days in the remote and otherworldly **Badlands National Park** (605/433-5361, www.nps.gov/badl, 24 hours daily, $25 vehicles, $15 motorcycles and cyclists, $12 pedestrians). Camping is free, but facilities are primitive.

- **Hike a long-distance trail:** The 111-mile **Centennial Trail** (www.fs.usda.gov) highlights the diversity of the Black Hills and runs from Bear Butte in the north through Wind Cave in the south. Many sections of the trail are bike accessible.

- **Challenge your balance:** Visit **Rushmore Tramway Adventures** (203 Cemetery Rd., Keystone, 605/666-4478, www.rushmoretramwayadventures.com, 11am-5pm Sat.-Sun. May and Sept., 10am-6pm daily mid-June and Aug., 10am-7pm daily July) and take to the trees. Think suspended bridges, log ladders, walking on cables, and flying on zip lines.

- **Balloon the Black Hills:** Drift over Custer State Park in the open-air basket of a colorful balloon with **Black Hills Balloons** (605/673-2520, www.blackhillsballoons.com, May-Oct., other months by arrangement, $295 adults, $245 children 12 and under). Bring a new perspective to your sightseeing as you get a bird's-eye view of herds of bison and pronghorn roaming the park.

- **Golf:** Play the **Southern Hills Municipal Golf Course** (W. US-18, Hot Springs, 605/745-6400, www.hotspringssdgolf.com, $26 for 9 holes, $40 for 18 holes). There are stunning views from every tee of the award-winning front nine.

DAY 7: Rapid City

MORNING

❶ Visit the **Journey Museum & Learning Center** (222 New York St., 605/394-6923, www.journeymuseum.org, 9am-6pm Mon.-Sat., 11am-5pm Sun. May-Sept., 10am-5pm Mon.-Sat., 1pm-5pm Sun. Oct.-Apr., $10 adults, $7 children 6-17). This definitive museum of the Black Hills has great interactive exhibits on Lakota culture, pioneer history, archaeology, geology, and local ecology.

AFTERNOON

❷ Visit **Storybook Island** (1301 Sheridan Lake Rd., 605/342-6357, www.storybookisland.org, 9am-7pm daily Memorial Day-Labor Day, free), a theme park where fairy tales and nursery rhymes come to life. Children can meet the Three Little Pigs, the Cat in the Hat, Winnie the Pooh, and over 100 other characters.

❸ Spend some time at **Prairie Edge Trading Company and Galleries** (606 Main St., 605/342-3086 or 800/541-2388, www.prairieedge.com, 9am-9pm Mon.-Sat., 10am-5pm Sun. summer,

9am-7pm Mon.-Sat., 10am-5pm Sun. spring and fall, 10am-6pm Mon.-Sat., 11am-5pm Sun. winter). Experience the best in contemporary and historic Native American arts, including exquisite beadwork, star quilts, powwow regalia, and music.

EVENING

④ Treat yourself to a nice dinner at **Delmonico Grill** (609 Main St., 605/791-1664, www.delmonicogrill.com, 11am-2pm and 5pm-10pm Mon.-Fri., 5pm-10pm Sat., 5pm-9pm Sun., $33-40), a beautiful fine-dining establishment. Choose from a variety of steak cuts either dry or wet aged, plus handmade pasta, seafood, and pork. Reservations are recommended.

Getting There

AIR

The **Rapid City Regional Airport** (4550 Terminal Rd., 605/393-9924, flight information 605/393-2850, www.rcgov.org/airport) is about 11 miles from downtown, off SD-44 headed east. Shuttle service between the airport and downtown is provided by **Airport Express Shuttle** (605/399-9999 or 800/357-9998, $25 for one person, $35 for two, and $15 each for three or more).

Car rental companies at the airport include **Alamo/National** (605/393-2664), **Hertz** (605/393-0160), **Avis** (605/393-0740), **Budget** (605/393-0488), and **Enterprise** (605/393-4311).

BUS

Rapid City has limited city-to-city bus service. **Jefferson Lines** (605/348-3300 or 800/451-5333, www.jeffersonlines.com) has one departure headed east and one departure headed west daily. The line is the contract carrier in the Midwest for Greyhound and covers the route between Minneapolis and Billings, Montana.

Greyhound (800/231-2222, www.greyhound.com) can get you to Rapid City, but travel times are exceedingly long. There is one bus a day from the Denver area to Rapid City, for instance, and travel time is over 13 hours. The distance from Denver to Rapid City is a little over 350 miles and can be driven in about 6.5 hours. The bus arrives and departs from the **Milo Barber Transportation Center** (333 6th St., 605/348-3300).

CAR

From **Rapid City Regional Airport** to Rapid City proper, it's 11 miles (18 km), which takes about 20 minutes via SD-44.

MOUNT RUSHMORE AND THE BLACK HILLS

SONGS

• **"Rapid City, South Dakota"** by Dwight Yoakam: Kentucky-born Yoakam, a country music star who elevated the genre in the 1980s and '90s, weaves a character-driven story throughout this twangy song about Rapid City.

• **"The Black Hills of Dakota" by Doris Day:** Written for the 1953 film *Calamity Jane,* this song captures the love of, and longing for, the beauty of the Black Hills.

PODCASTS

• *America's National Parks:* Cue up the episodes about **Badlands National Park** and **Mount Rushmore** to shed greater insights into these two incredible national parks.

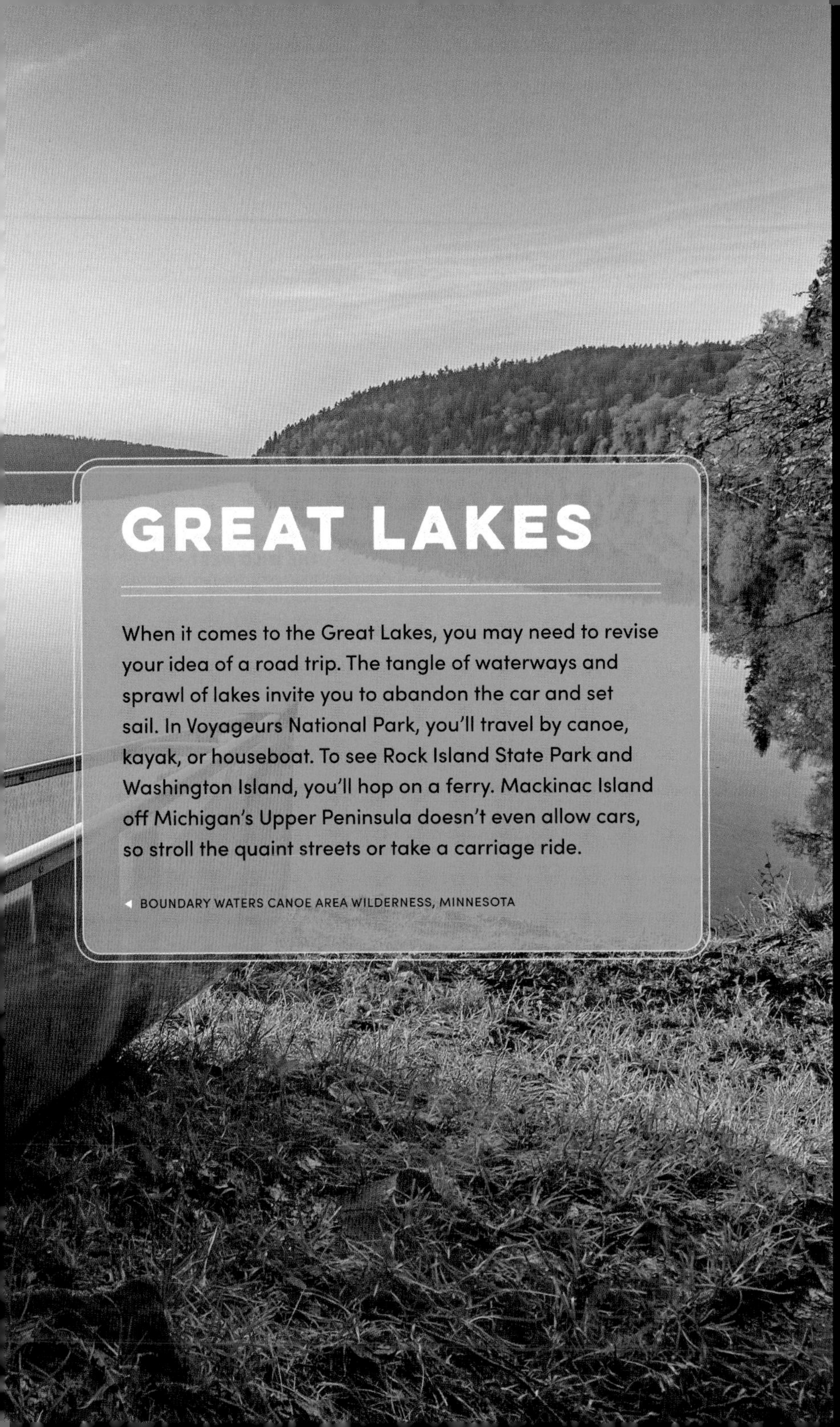

GREAT LAKES

When it comes to the Great Lakes, you may need to revise your idea of a road trip. The tangle of waterways and sprawl of lakes invite you to abandon the car and set sail. In Voyageurs National Park, you'll travel by canoe, kayak, or houseboat. To see Rock Island State Park and Washington Island, you'll hop on a ferry. Mackinac Island off Michigan's Upper Peninsula doesn't even allow cars, so stroll the quaint streets or take a carriage ride.

◄ BOUNDARY WATERS CANOE AREA WILDERNESS, MINNESOTA

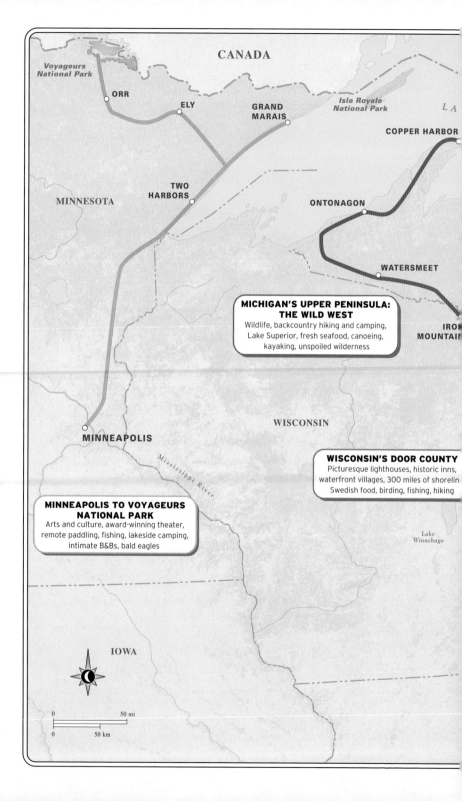

CANADA

Voyageurs National Park

ORR

ELY

GRAND MARAIS

Isle Royale National Park

L A

COPPER HARBOR

MINNESOTA

TWO HARBORS

ONTONAGON

WATERSMEET

MICHIGAN'S UPPER PENINSULA: THE WILD WEST
Wildlife, backcountry hiking and camping, Lake Superior, fresh seafood, canoeing, kayaking, unspoiled wilderness

IRON MOUNTAIN

WISCONSIN

MINNEAPOLIS

Mississippi River

WISCONSIN'S DOOR COUNTY
Picturesque lighthouses, historic inns, waterfront villages, 300 miles of shorelin Swedish food, birding, fishing, hiking

MINNEAPOLIS TO VOYAGEURS NATIONAL PARK
Arts and culture, award-winning theater, remote paddling, fishing, lakeside camping, intimate B&Bs, bald eagles

Lake Winnebago

IOWA

0   50 mi
0   50 km

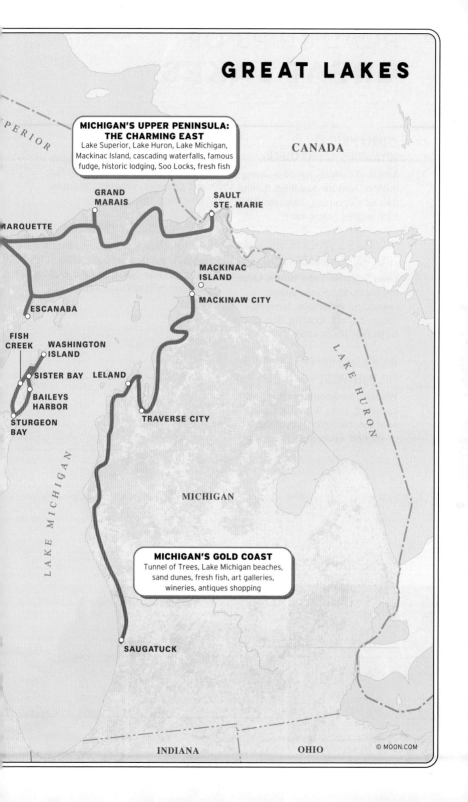

GREAT LAKES

**MICHIGAN'S UPPER PENINSULA:
THE CHARMING EAST**
Lake Superior, Lake Huron, Lake Michigan,
Mackinac Island, cascading waterfalls, famous
fudge, historic lodging, Soo Locks, fresh fish

SUPERIOR

CANADA

GRAND
MARAIS

SAULT
STE. MARIE

MARQUETTE

MACKINAC
ISLAND

MACKINAW CITY

ESCANABA

FISH
CREEK

WASHINGTON
ISLAND

SISTER BAY   LELAND

BAILEYS
HARBOR

STURGEON
BAY

TRAVERSE CITY

LAKE HURON

LAKE MICHIGAN

MICHIGAN

MICHIGAN'S GOLD COAST
Tunnel of Trees, Lake Michigan beaches,
sand dunes, fresh fish, art galleries,
wineries, antiques shopping

SAUGATUCK

INDIANA   OHIO   © MOON.COM

ROAD TRIPS OF
GREAT LAKES

MINNEAPOLIS TO VOYAGEURS NATIONAL PARK

Arts and culture, award-winning theater, remote paddling, fishing, lakeside camping, intimate B&Bs, bald eagles (PAGE 420)

MICHIGAN'S UPPER PENINSULA: THE CHARMING EAST

Lake Superior, Lake Huron, Lake Michigan, Mackinac Island, cascading waterfalls, famous fudge, historic lodging, Soo Locks, fresh fish (PAGE 430)

MICHIGAN'S UPPER PENINSULA: THE WILD WEST

Wildlife, backcountry hiking and camping, Lake Superior, fresh seafood, canoeing, kayaking, unspoiled wilderness (PAGE 440)

MICHIGAN'S GOLD COAST

Tunnel of Trees, Lake Michigan beaches, sand dunes, fresh fish, art galleries, wineries, antiques shopping (PAGE 450)

WISCONSIN'S DOOR COUNTY

Picturesque lighthouses, historic inns, waterfront villages, 300 miles of shoreline, Swedish food, birding, fishing, hiking (PAGE 460)

LEFT TO RIGHT: GOOSEBERRY FALLS STATE PARK; COPPER HARBOR; WHITEFISH DUNES STATE PARK

1 See a Tony award-winning show at the **Guthrie Theater** in Minneapolis (PAGE 422).

2 Spot the **northern lights** and the Milky Way in the dark skies of Minnesota's **Voyageurs National Park** (PAGE 427).

3 Walk the quaint, car-free streets of **Mackinac Island** on Michigan's Upper Peninsula (PAGE 432).

4 See sparkling Lake Michigan from the shores of **Sleeping Bear Dunes National Lakeshore** (PAGE 454).

Guthrie Theater

northern lights in Minnesota

Mackinac Island

Sleeping Bear Dunes National Lakeshore

Swedish panckakes at Al Johnson's

5 Eat authentic Swedish fare at **Al Johnson's Swedish Restaurant** in Sister Bay, Wisconsin (PAGE 466).

MINNEAPOLIS TO VOYAGEURS NATIONAL PARK

WHY GO: Arts and culture, award-winning theater, remote paddling, fishing, lakeside camping, intimate B&Bs, bald eagles

TOTAL DISTANCE: 535 miles/ 865 kilometers

NUMBER OF DAYS: 6

SEASONS: Spring through fall

START: Minneapolis, Minnesota

END: Orr, Minnesota

▼ BOUNDARY WATERS CANOE AREA WILDERNESS

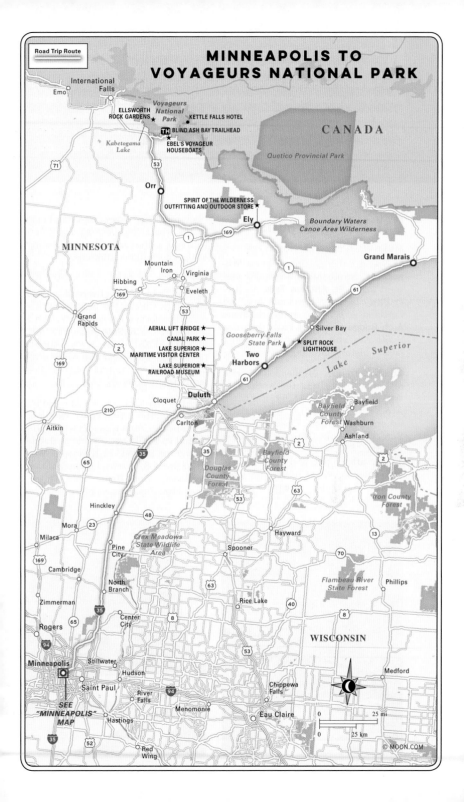

MINNEAPOLIS TO VOYAGEURS NATIONAL PARK

Road Trip Route

CANADA

Quetico Provincial Park

International Falls

Emo

Voyageurs National Park

ELLSWORTH ROCK GARDENS ★
KETTLE FALLS HOTEL ●
TH BLIND ASH BAY TRAILHEAD

Kabetogama Lake

★ EBEL'S VOYAGEUR HOUSEBOATS

71

53

Orr

SPIRIT OF THE WILDERNESS OUTFITTING AND OUTDOOR STORE ★

Boundary Waters Canoe Area Wilderness

1   169   Ely

MINNESOTA

Grand Marais

Mountain Iron   Virginia

Hibbing

169   Eveleth

1

61

Grand Rapids

53

2

AERIAL LIFT BRIDGE ★
CANAL PARK ★
LAKE SUPERIOR MARITIME VISITOR CENTER ★
LAKE SUPERIOR RAILROAD MUSEUM ★

Gooseberry Falls State Park ▲

Silver Bay ●
★ SPLIT ROCK LIGHTHOUSE

Lake Superior

169

Two Harbors

Duluth

61

Cloquet

Bayfield County Forest   Bayfield

Aitkin

210

Carlton

Washburn

35

35

Ashland

2

2

65

Douglas County Forest

Bayfield County Forest

63

Iron County Forest

Hinckley

53

Mora   23

Milaca

48

Crex Meadows State Wildlife Area

Hayward

13

Pine City

169

Spooner

70

Cambridge

Flambeau River State Forest

Phillips

Zimmerman

North Branch

63

Rice Lake

40

8

Rogers   65

35

Center City

8

Minneapolis

94

Stillwater

53

WISCONSIN

SEE "MINNEAPOLIS" MAP

Hudson

Saint Paul

River Falls

94

Menomonie

Chippewa Falls

Medford

Hastings

Eau Claire

0   25 mi
0   25 km

35   52

Red Wing

© MOON.COM

Renowned for its groundbreaking art, theater, and music, the urban haven of Minneapolis is the starting point for this trip. The route leaves the big city to curve north toward Duluth, where giant ships navigate the waters and maritime museums beckon. Follow the western shore of Lake Superior north to the quaint village of Grand Marais, then inland to Ely and the astonishing beauty of the Boundary Waters Canoe Area Wilderness. More boating adventures await in Voyageurs National Park, where you'll leave the car behind to explore miles of untouched shoreline at Minnesota's only national park.

DAY 1: Minneapolis

MORNING AND AFTERNOON

➊ Spend a day getting to know **Minneapolis.** Stroll the Mississippi riverfront to see **St. Anthony Falls** (W. River Pkwy. between Hennepin Ave. and Portland Ave.), the landmark **Stone Arch Bridge** (W. River Pkwy. between S. 5th Ave. and Portland Ave.), and a host of historic buildings.

➋ Experience Minneapolis's rich art scene by visiting the world-class **Walker Art Center** (1750 Hennepin Ave., 612/375-7600, www.walkerart.org, 11am-5pm Tues.-Wed. and Sun., 11am-9pm Thurs., 11am-6pm Fri.-Sat., $15 adults, free admission Thurs. after 5pm and first Sat. of each month), which focuses on modern art. The center's **sculpture garden** (6am-midnight daily, free) is home to the iconic *Spoonbridge and Cherry,* along with many other interesting sculptures and installations.

EVENING

➌ The Twin Cities is second only to New York City in the number of theatrical performances per capita. Catch a show at the **Guthrie Theater** (818 S. 2nd St., 612/377-2224, www.guthrietheater.org), known far and wide for its innovative presentations of both classic and contemporary plays.

➍ After the show, grab a late dinner at one of the city's many excellent restaurants. For a feast of meaty dishes and cocktails, get a table at **Butcher and the Boar** (1121 Hennepin Ave., 612/238-8888, www.butcherandtheboar.com, 5pm-10pm Sun.-Thurs., 5pm-11pm Fri.-Sat., $13-69).

MINNEAPOLIS RIVERFRONT

WALKER ART CENTER

Top ③ MINNEAPOLIS TO VOYAGEURS NATIONAL PARK

① See a Tony award-winning show at the **Guthrie Theater** in Minneapolis (PAGE 422).

② **Canoe** the wild and scenic **Boundary Waters Canoe Area Wilderness** (PAGE 426).

③ Spot the **northern lights** and the Milky Way in the dark skies of **Voyageurs National Park** (PAGE 427).

MINNEAPOLIS

DAY 2: Minneapolis to Two Harbors

185 miles/300 kilometers | 3-3.5 hours

ROUTE OVERVIEW: I-35W • I-35 • MN-61

① Drive three hours north to **Duluth** to watch massive ships slip under the **Aerial Lift Bridge** (601 S. Lake Ave. at the pier), a feat of engineering constructed from 1901 to 1905. Tip: Bring earplugs! The ship captains and bridge operators greet each other with a series of loud horn blasts.

> Go north on I-35W for 23 miles (37 km) until it becomes I-35. Continue north on I-35 for 129 miles (208 km). Take exit 256B for Lake Ave. to reach downtown Duluth.

② Visit some of the many museums in and around the city's reclaimed warehouse district, **Canal Park**. The **Lake Superior Maritime Visitor Center** (600 Canal Park Dr., 217/720-5260, www. lsmma.com, 10am-5pm daily, free) houses an excellent collection of local shipping-related exhibits, including a giant steam engine. Telescopes let you examine ships out on the lake waiting for their dock to free up.

③ The **Lake Superior Railroad Museum** (506 W. Michigan St., 218/727-8025, www.lsrm.org, Memorial Day-Labor

DULUTH AERIAL LIFT BRIDGE

Day 9am-6pm daily, Labor Day-Memorial Day 9am-5pm daily, $14 adults, $6 children 3-13) is a top draw in downtown Duluth. The outstanding collection of classic rolling stock includes an 1861 woodburning steam engine, a railway post office, and a rotary snowplow.

❹ Have dinner in the city before driving north to **Two Harbors.** Spend the night in the **Lighthouse Bed & Breakfast** (1 Lighthouse Point Dr., 888/832-5606, www.lighthousebb.org, $160-175) in the restored Two Harbors Lighthouse. There are only three guest rooms, so make your reservations well in advance.

> *Take I-35 N for 3 miles (5 km). Merge onto MN-61 and continue for 25 miles (40 km) to Two Harbors.*

DAY 3: Two Harbors to Grand Marais

85 miles/137 kilometers | 2 hours

ROUTE OVERVIEW: MN-61

❶ Today's drive hugs the north shore of Lake Superior, passing state parks each more impressive than the last. At **Gooseberry Falls State Park** (3206 MN-61, 218/595-7100, http://dnr.state.mn.us, 8am-10pm daily), the swift Gooseberry River shoots around a narrow bend, drops over Upper Falls and into a rocky gorge, blankets the 100-foot-wide rock wall forming Middle Falls, and plunges over the split

🔲 KEY RESERVATIONS

- In Two Harbors, the three guest rooms at **Lighthouse Bed & Breakfast** book up fast, so reserve **a month or two** in advance.

- Reservations are highly recommended for **dinner** at **Burntside Lodge** in Ely. Book a **few weeks** before your arrival and note that there is a dress code of resort casual.

- **Blue Heron Bed & Breakfast** in Ely requires reservations and a two-night minimum.

- Make your reservation at **Ebel's Voyageur Houseboats** at Voyageurs National Park **several months** in advance.

Lower Falls before marching on to Lake Superior. The whole 90-foot drop sits just a short stroll down a wheelchair-accessible trail.

> *Follow MN-61 N to the state park (13 mi/21 km).*

❷ Located at the park bearing its name, **Split Rock Lighthouse** (3755 Split Rock Lighthouse Rd., 218/595-7625, http://dnr.state.mn.us, 8am-10pm daily) is a Minnesota icon. Beginning operations in 1910, this 370,000-candlepower beacon steered ships away from the treacherous shore for 59 years before onboard navigational equipment made it obsolete.

GOOSEBERRY FALLS STATE PARK

SPLIT ROCK LIGHTHOUSE

This is one of the best spots on the North Shore to explore by kayak, and there are put-ins near both ends of the park's 6.25-mile shoreline.

> Continue on MN-61 N for 7 miles (11 km) to the lighthouse.

❸ Have dinner in charming **Grand Marais** at the beloved **Angry Trout Cafe** (416 Hwy. 61 W., 218/387-1265, www.angrytroutcafe.com, 11am-7:30pm Sun.-Thurs., 11am-8:30pm. Fri.-Sat. May-Nov., $9-22), which serves fresh and smoked fish right out of Lake Superior. Spend the night at a waterfront lodging.

> Follow MN-61 N for another 63 miles (101 km) to Grand Marais.

DAY 4: Grand Marais to Ely

115 miles/185 kilometers | 2.5-3 hours

ROUTE OVERVIEW: MN-61 • MN-1 • MN-169

❶ Head to **Ely,** gateway to the **Boundary Waters Canoe Area Wilderness,** and enjoy paddling one of the world's most beautiful and wildlife-rich wildernesses. But first, fuel up on breakfast at **Insula Restaurant** (145 E. Sheridan St., www.insularestaurant.com, 218/365-4855, 7am-11am Mon.-Sat., 7am-noon Sun., $9-15), a wonderful little joint where everything is locally, ethically, and responsibly sourced.

> Head south on MN-61 for 44 miles (71 km) to Little Marais Rd. Turn right and follow Little Marais Rd. for 7 miles (11 km) to MN-1. Drive MN-1 W into Ely (55 mi/89 km).

❷ It's time to get out on the water. **Spirit of the Wilderness Outfitting and Outdoor Store** (2030 E. Sheridan St., 218/365-3149, http://elycanoetrips.com) offers myriad options to assist your exploration, including canoe and kayak rentals, camping gear, single- and multiday outfitting packages, plus permits and transportation to Boundary Waters entry points.

❸ Reward yourself with an elegant post-paddle dinner at **Burntside Lodge** (2755 Burntside Lodge Rd., 218/365-3894, www.burntsidelodge.com, 5:30pm-close Wed.-Mon., $16-36), which got its start as a hunting camp in the early 1900s. The National Park Service has since added the lodge to the National Register of Historic Places. Dress code is resort casual.

❹ Spend the night at **Blue Heron Bed & Breakfast** (827 Kawishiwi Trail, 218/365-3223, www.blueheronbnb.com, $148-178), where the

BOUNDARY WATERS CANOE AREA WILDERNESS

CANOE ON THE BOUNDARY WATERS

north-facing lake views are phenomenal. The five inviting guest rooms, each with private bath, require a two-night minimum stay in the summer and fall. Don't miss the wood-fired sauna.

> Go east on MN-169, following it for 2 miles (3 km). Turn right onto Kawishiwi Trail and continue for 6 miles (10 km) to the B&B.

DAY 5: Ely to Voyageurs National Park

110 miles/177 kilometers | 2-2.5 hours

ROUTE OVERVIEW: MN-169 • Old Hwy. 77 • County Rd. 115 • US-53

① Before heading to Voyageurs National Park, stock up on groceries in **Orr** for tonight's dinner and tomorrow's breakfast. Drive north to the **Ash River Visitor Center** (9899 Mead Wood Rd., 218/374-3221, 10am-4pm Thurs.-Sun. mid-May-mid-Sept.) at **Voyageurs National Park** (218/283-6600, www.nps.gov/voya, free). At Minnesota's only national park, you'll be able to choose your adventure on 500-plus islands, 655 miles of shoreline, and 218,000 acres of land and water.

> Head west into Ely via Kawishiwi Trail for 6 miles (10 km), then turn left onto MN-169. Follow this southwest for 29 miles (47 km), then turn right onto Angus Rd. and head north. In 4 miles (6 km), the road becomes Old Hwy. 77. Follow this for 2 miles (3 km), then continue as the road becomes County Rd. 115. Follow this for another 15 miles (24 km). Here, the road becomes US-53 N. Follow this for 16 miles (26 km) into Orr. To reach the visitors center, continue north on US-53 for 26 miles (42 km). Turn right onto Ash River Trail/Ness Rd. After 8 miles (13 km), turn left onto Mead Wood Rd. and drive for another 3 miles (5 km) to reach the visitors center.

VOYAGEURS NATIONAL PARK

▶ Playlist

MINNEAPOLIS TO VOYAGEURS NATIONAL PARK

SONGS

- **"Uptown" by Prince:** Prince was born in Minneapolis, and his decades-long music career yielded some of the most influential songs in pop history. It's impossible to pick just one for a playlist. But if you have to choose, opt for this funk-driven 1980 song about a Minneapolis neighborhood that Prince frequented.

- **"I Will Dare" by The Replacements:** One of the most notable musicians to come out of Minneapolis is Paul Westerberg, lead singer for '80s garage-rock band The Replacements. Their 1984 album *Let It Be* is considered one of the greatest rock albums of all time, even though it leans more post-punk than rock.

- **"Keep It Up" by Soul Asylum:** The '90s-era grunge band Soul Asylum is yet another great band to come out of the rich Minneapolis music scene. This song features heavy drums, fuzzy guitars, and gravelly voiced lyrics.

RADIO SHOWS/PODCASTS

- *Live from Here:* Airing live from the Fitzgerald Theater in St. Paul, this variety show hosted by Chris Thile is known for its musical guests and tongue-in-cheek radio dramas. Formerly known as *A Prairie Home Companion* and hosted by Garrison Keillor, the show changed hosts and titles in 2016. The best way to listen is to stream past episodes from the website (www.livefromhere.org).

② Since most points of interest are only accessible by boat, rent a houseboat from **Ebel's Voyageur Houseboats** (10326 Ash River Trail, 888/883-2357, www.ebels.com, $345-710 per day), which operates out of the Ash River Visitor Center. This popular option for exploring Voyageurs lets you enjoy the wilderness with all the comforts of home. No experience (or license) is needed, and the rental company will set you up with everything you need, from linens and dishes to maps.

③ Cruise west from Ash River to **Kabetogama Lake.** Find a spot to drop anchor for the night and enjoy Voyageurs' famed dark skies. Soak up unforgettable views of the constellations, the Milky Way, meteors—and maybe the northern lights.

DAY 6: Voyageurs National Park to Orr

40 miles/64 kilometers | 1 hour

ROUTE OVERVIEW: Mead Wood Rd. • Ash River Trail • US-53 • Old Hwy. 53

① Eat an early breakfast, then trundle to **Ellsworth Rock Gardens** (free) on the north shore of Kabetogama Lake. It features more than 50 terraced flower beds, 13,000 lilies and other flower varieties, and over 150 geometric and animal-themed sculptures assembled out of the local granite.

TOUR BOAT IN VOYAGEURS NATIONAL PARK

❷ Return to the Ash River Visitor Center, drop off your houseboat, and then join the two-hour **Kettle Falls Hotel Cruise** (218/283-6600, www.nps.gov/voya, 10am-3pm Mon.-Tues. and Fri. summer, 10am-3:30pm Sun., Tues., and Thurs. fall, $40 adults, $30 children) to the 1913 **Kettle Falls Hotel.** You'll have time to disembark and explore the historic grounds. Eat lunch at the hotel.

❸ Once back at Ash River, regain your land legs with a quick but invigorating hike on the **Blind Ash Bay Trail** (2.5 mi/4 km loop, 1 hour, moderate), arguably Voyageurs' most beautiful short mainland trail. The hilly path follows a rocky ridge—there are great views of Kabetogama Lake from the top—and looks out over the narrow namesake bay. Find the trailhead at the Kabetogama Lake Overlook.

> *From the Ash River Visitor Center, follow Mead Wood Rd. south for less than a mile to the Kabetogama Lake Overlook.*

❹ Leave the park and spend the night in Orr at **Hundred Acre Woods** (5048 Old Hwy. 53, 218/757-0070, www.voyageurcountry.com, from $129), a modern home with two Northwoods-themed guest rooms; one has a sauna and the other has a whirlpool tub.

> *Take Mead Wood Rd. south for 3 miles (5 km) and then turn right onto Ash River Trail. Follow this for 8 miles (13 km), then turn left onto US-53 S. Continue for 23 miles (37 km), then turn left onto Old Hwy. 53. Continue for less than a mile to reach the B&B.*

Getting There

AIR

Minneapolis-St. Paul International Airport (MSP, 612/726-5555, www.mspairport.com), conveniently located right on the edge of the Twin Cities, is one of the Midwest's largest hubs. Seventeen airlines serve MSP, including American, Delta, JetBlue, Southwest, and United. On-site car rental companies are at both terminals.

TRAIN

The Empire Builder route run by **Amtrak** (800/872-7245, www.amtrak.

com), between Chicago and Seattle/Portland, passes through Minnesota once a day in each direction with stops in Winona, Red Wing, St. Paul, St. Cloud, Staples, Detroit Lakes, and Fargo, North Dakota.

BUS

Getting to Minnesota by bus is easy. **Greyhound** (800/231-2222, www.greyhound.com) has routes from Minneapolis north through Duluth (from $25 one-way), east through Chicago (from $23 one-way), and west to Fargo ($37 one-way). The most extensive service in Minnesota is with **Jefferson Lines** (888/864-2832, www.jeffersonlines.com), which connects Minneapolis to far more outstate towns.

Megabus (877/462-6342, www.megabus.com), a low-cost express carrier, connects Minneapolis to many Midwestern cities through Chicago.

CAR

It's a 25-minute drive of 14 miles (23 km) from the airport to downtown Minneapolis via MN-5, MN-55, MN-62, and I-35.

Getting Back

It's a 280-mile (450-km) drive of five hours to return to **Minneapolis** from Voyageurs National Park via US-53, MN-33, and I-35.

Falls International Airport (INL, 3214 2nd Ave. E., International Falls, 218/283-4461, www.internationalfallsairport.com), in the town of International Falls, is about 40 miles (64 km) northwest of the Ash River Visitor Center in Voyageurs National Park via US-53, a drive that takes 45 minutes to an hour. The airport offers service by Delta.

Another option for returning home is **Duluth International Airport** (DLH, 4701 Grinden Dr., www.duluthairport.com). It's 150 miles (240 km) southeast of the Ash River Visitor Center in Voyageurs National Park via US-53, a drive of 2.5-3 hours. The airport offers Delta-operated flights to the Twin Cities and Detroit, and you'll find most major rental car companies here.

MICHIGAN'S UPPER PENINSULA: THE CHARMING EAST

WHY GO: Lake Superior, Lake Huron, Lake Michigan, Mackinac Island, cascading waterfalls, famous fudge, historic lodging, Soo Locks, fresh fish

TOTAL DISTANCE: 465 miles/ 750 kilometers

NUMBER OF DAYS: 6

SEASONS: Late spring through fall

START: Mackinaw City, Michigan

END: Sault Ste. Marie, Michigan

▶ MACKINAC ISLAND

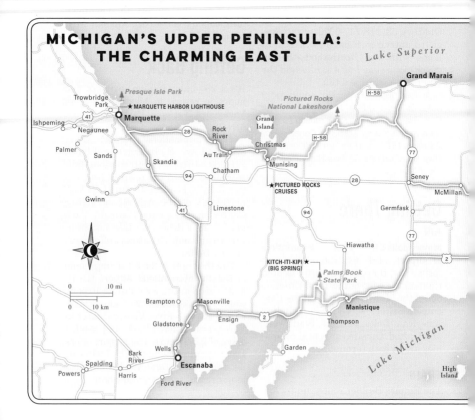

MICHIGAN'S UPPER PENINSULA: THE CHARMING EAST

S haped by glacial movement 10,000 years ago, Lake Superior is the world's largest body of freshwater. This trip along the eastern edge of Michigan's Upper Peninsula takes you deep into the coastal villages, waterfalls, and dense forests of the region, affording you many glimpses of Lake Superior and the equally impressive Lakes Huron and Michigan. You'll journey north from Mackinaw City over the five-mile-long Mackinac Bridge and into the wonderful wilderness that is the eastern U.P. From the wind- and water-shaped shorelines and the dramatic beauty of Pictured Rocks to the craft brews and historical architecture of urban Marquette, this retreat invites thoughtful exploration.

DAY 1: Mackinaw City

MORNING AND AFTERNOON

❶ Once you arrive in **Mackinaw City**, check into **Brigadoon Bed & Breakfast** (207 Langlade St., 231/436-8882, www.mackinawbrigadoon.com, May-early Nov., $95-170). Its 10 rooms blend modern amenities with a taste of the Old World.

❷ Dine at the renovated **Dixie Saloon** (401 E. Central Ave., 231/436-5449, www.dixiesaloon.com, 11am-11pm daily, bar until 2am, $10-25), a Mackinaw City mainstay from the 1890s, before taking time to wander the sights downtown.

EVENING

❸ For sunset views, your best bet is **McGulpin Point Lighthouse** (500 Headlands Rd., 231/436-5860, www.mcgulpinpoint.org, 9am-8pm daily June-Sept., limited hours May and Oct., by donation). Not only has this late 19th-century lighthouse been painstakingly restored, it's also a museum, and a perfect spot for panoramic vistas.

DAY 2: Day Trip to Mackinac Island

MORNING

❶ You won't need the car today. Catch an early ferry to **Mackinac Island** on **Shepler's Mackinac Island Ferry** (231/436-5023, www.sheplersferry.com, round-trip $25 adults, $13 ages 5-12) or the **Star Line** (800/638-9892, www.mackinawferry.com, $26 adults, $14 ages 5-12). The vehicle-free Mackinac Island sits smack-dab in the middle of Lake Huron, between Michigan's peninsulas.

❷ **Fort Mackinac** (Huron Rd., 231/436-4100, www.mackinacparks.com, 9:30am-6pm daily June-late Aug., shorter hours May and late Aug.-mid-Oct., $13.50 adults, $8 children 5-17) is worth a visit for the views of downtown, the marina, and Lake Huron alone. At this military outpost, which the British and Americans haggled over for nearly 40 years, you can visit more than a dozen buildings and watch reenactments with costumed guides.

MCGULPIN POINT LIGHTHOUSE

Top ③ MICHIGAN'S UPPER PENINSULA: THE CHARMING EAST

① Walk the quaint, car-free streets of **Mackinac Island,** where each step takes you further back in time (PAGE 432).

② Propel across **Big Spring** via raft at **Palms Book State Park** (PAGE 435).

③ See the colorful, carved rock escarpments at **Pictured Rocks National Lakeshore** on a boat tour (PAGE 436).

FORT MACKINAC

AFTERNOON

❸ Take a personalized carriage tour with the island's largest livery, **Mackinac Island Carriage Tours** (7396 Market St., 906/847-3307, www.mict.com, $110-189 per hour), operating since 1869. Tours begin on Market Street, near the Father Marquette statue.

❹ Admire the opulence of the iconic 1887 **Grand Hotel** (286 Grand Ave., 800/334-7263, www.grandhotel.com). You don't have to be a guest to wander the stately grounds, but there is a $10 admission fee, which includes "veranda privileges." What's that, you ask? It's a chance to relax in a rocking chair on the longest porch in the world (660 feet) and soak up the views of the Mackinac Bridge.

EVENING

❺ Pick up a wedge or two of world-famous Mackinac Island fudge at either **Murdick's Fudge** (7363 Main St., 906/847-3530, www.murdicksfudge-mackinacisland.com, 9am-10pm daily) or **Ryba's** (7245 Main St., 906/847-3347, www.ryba.com, 9am-10pm daily). Enjoy dinner on the island before returning to your lodgings on the mainland.

KEY RESERVATIONS

- The **ferries** from **Mackinaw City to Mackinac Island** shut down in late fall and don't run again until the spring, so if a visit to the island is on your must-do list, plan your travel during spring, summer, or early fall.

DAY 3: Mackinaw City to Escanaba

160 miles/260 kilometers | 3-3.5 hours

ROUTE OVERVIEW: I-75 • US-2 • surface streets • US-2/US-41

❶ You have some driving to do today, so rise and shine early for a hearty breakfast at **Darrow's Family Restaurant** (301 Louvigney St., 231/436-5514, www.darrowsrestaurant.com, 7:30am-8:30pm Sun.-Thurs., 7:30am-9pm Fri.-Sat., $8-18).

❷ Cross the massive **Mackinac Bridge** and make a photo stop at **Straits State Park** (on Church St., south of US-2, 906/643-8620, www.michigan.gov/dnr, 8am-10pm daily Memorial Day-mid-Sept., $9). The park's viewing platform is the ideal spot at which to snap pics of the bridge and the boats traveling the Straits of Mackinac.

> Take I-75 N across Mackinac Bridge to the state park (7 mi/11 km).

❸ On your way to **Manistique,** stop at one of the many turnouts that offer a pleasing panorama of the Lake Michigan shore, with St. Helena Island in

MACKINAC ISLAND

MACKINAC BRIDGE

PALMS BOOK STATE PARK

the distance. In town, you'll want to grab lunch at **Clyde's Drive-In No. 2** (201 Chippewa Ave., 906/341-6021, 9am-7pm Mon.-Thurs., 9am-8pm Fri.-Sat., 11am-7pm Sun. Memorial Day-Labor Day, $9-12) for a big burger and a malt.

> Follow US-2 W for 88 miles (142 km) to Manistique.

④ After lunch, head to **Palms Book State Park** (M-149, 906/341-2355, www.michigan.gov/dnr, 8am-10pm daily, $9) to see **Kitch-Iti-Kipi,** better known as **Big Spring.** Here, water bubbles out of the earth at a staggering 10,000 to 16,000 gallons per minute. The park maintains a convenient raft that allows you to propel yourself across the spring with the help of a hand-powered cable tethered to either shore.

> Head east on Deer St. for 1 mile (1.6 km) to County Hwy. 442. Continue on County Hwy. 442 for 4 miles (6 km) to M-149 N. Drive for 1 mile (1.6 km) to County Rd. 455. Turn right and drive for 4 miles (6 km) to reconnect with M-149. Turn right and continue for less than a mile to reach Big Spring.

⑤ End your day's sojourn in **Escanaba.** Have dinner and stay the night at the historic **House of Ludington** (223 Ludington St., 906/786-6300, www. houseofludington.net, $65-105). It's old and quirky, but it's a memorable place to stay, enhanced by wonderful water views.

> Follow M-149 S for 5 miles (8 km). Turn right onto Forest Hwy. 13 and continue east then south for 6 miles (10 km). Turn right again to join US-2 W. Continue on this for 39 miles (63 km); eventually the road joins up with US-41 and runs directly into Escanaba.

DAY 4: Escanaba to Marquette

75 miles/121 kilometers | 1.5-2 hours

ROUTE OVERVIEW: US-41 • surface streets

① When you sit down for a home-cooked breakfast at the **Swedish Pantry** (819 Ludington St., 906/786-9606, www.swedishpantry.com, 8am-6pm daily, $10-22), you have an important decision to make: Swedish pancakes with meatballs, potato pancakes with applesauce and sour cream, or Swedish fries and eggs?

MARQUETTE HARBOR LIGHTHOUSE

2 Head to **Marquette,** the Upper Peninsula's largest and most cosmopolitan city. A waterfront stroll invigorates after time behind the wheel. Don't miss the **Marquette Harbor Lighthouse** (300 Lakeshore Blvd., 906/226-2006, http://mqtmaritimemuseum.com, 11am-4pm daily late May-Oct., $7 adults, $3 children under 13), a photogenic lighthouse that's also open for guided tours.

> *Take US-41 N to Marquette (64 mi/103 km).*

3 Grab lunch and spend the rest of the afternoon at **Presque Isle Park** (Peter White Dr., no phone, http://

PRESQUE ISLE PARK

marquettemi.gov, 7am-11pm daily summer, 7am-8pm daily winter). The park offers a microcosm of the area's natural beauty: rocky red bluffs, tall pines, and Lake Superior vistas. You can drive through the 323-acre park, but you'd do better to get out and walk among the many trails.

> *Head north on 3rd St. to Fair Ave. Turn right, then make a left on Pine St. Follow Pine to Lake Shore Blvd. Turn left and drive Lake Shore to Peter White Dr. (2 mi/3 km). Continue onto Peter White Dr., turning left to stay on it until you get to Presque Isle Park in less than a mile.*

4 For dinner, eat at the century-old **Vierling Restaurant and Marquette Harbor Brewery** (119 S. Front St., 906/228-3533, http://thevierling.com, 11am-10pm Mon.-Sat., $18-39). For the best sightline of the docks, sit near the large windows in back. Downstairs is a microbrewery featuring British-style ales.

> *Retrace your path along Peter White Dr., Lake Shore Blvd., Pine St., Fair Ave., and 3rd St. to return to Marquette (4 mi/6 km).*

DAY 5: Marquette to Grand Marais

95 miles/153 kilometers | 3 hours

ROUTE OVERVIEW: US-41 • M-28 • H-58

1 Give yourself plenty of time to check out **Pictured Rocks National Lakeshore** (906/387-3700, www.nps.gov/piro). The colorful rocks can only be seen from the water, so book a three-hour boat tour with **Pictured Rocks Cruises** (100 City Park Dr., 906/387-2379, www.picturedrocks.com, Memorial Day-mid Oct., $38 adults, $10 children 6-12, $1 children under 6), which sails out of the town of **Munising.**

> *Take US-41 S out of Marquette for 2 miles (3 km) to link up with M-28. Drive east on M-28 for 37 miles (60 km) to Munising.*

2 Back on land again, make the scenic drive through Pictured Rocks National Lakeshore to **Grand Marais.** Toast the day's journey with a craft

PICTURED ROCKS NATIONAL LAKESHORE

beer at **Lake Superior Brewing Company** (14283 Lake Ave., 906/494-2337, noon-2am daily, $10-15), where they do the microbrewery tradition proud. Pair the Sandstone Pale Ale or the Granite Brown with a fresh sandwich or a delicious and cheesy pizza.

> Take Munising Ave. east out of town for 3 miles (5 km). Continue onto Adams Trail/H-58 and keep going for another 46 miles (74 km) to complete the scenic drive to Grand Marais.

❸ Rent a fully stocked cabin at **Hilltop Cabins** (14176 Ellen St., 906/494-2331, www.hilltopcabinsmi.com, $85-195). Located right in town and offering Lake Superior views, these accommodations feel like a cozy home away from home.

DAY 6: Grand Marais to Sault Ste. Marie

135 miles/217 kilometers | 3.5 hours

ROUTE OVERVIEW: H-58 • County Rd. 407 • M-123 • Lake Superior Shoreline Rd./Lakeshore Dr. • surface streets

❶ Hit the road for **Tahquamenon Falls State Park** (41382 M-123, 906/492-3415, www.michigan.gov/dnr, 8am-10pm daily, $9). These spectacular waterfalls comprise one of Michigan's most photographed and widely loved landmarks. You can see the Upper Falls from the observation deck, which is only a short walk from the parking area.

Scattered around the U.P. are no less than 300 waterfalls that punctuate its vast network of rivers and streams. Be sure not to miss these beauties:

- **Tahquamenon Falls** (41382 M-123, Paradise, 906/492-3415, www.michigan.gov/dnr)
- **Bond Falls** (3 mi/5 km east on Bond Falls Rd. from Paulding, 906/353-6558, www.michigan.gov/dnr)
- **Presque Isle Falls** (Porcupine Mountains Wilderness State Park, 906/885-5275, www.michigan.gov/dnr)

BOND FALLS IN SPRING

TAHQUAMENON FALLS

▶ Playlist

MICHIGAN'S UPPER PENINSULA: THE CHARMING EAST

SONGS

- **"The Wreck of the Edmund Fitzgerald" by Gordon Lightfoot:** Perhaps not the happiest song, but singer-songwriter Lightfoot's ode to the true story of the 1975 sinking of an American freighter in Lake Superior pairs history with a solid melody.

- **"Pretty Girl from Michigan" by The Avett Brothers:** These southern rockers sing a heartfelt ditty about love and loss in Michigan. The electric guitars and upbeat vibe belie sad lyrics—and also make it easier to blast the song from your car's speakers at top volume.

- **"The Upper Peninsula" by Sufjan Stevens:** Soft-voiced singer Stevens was born in Detroit, and in 2003 he recorded an entire album dedicated to, and inspired by, his home state: *Michigan.* The concept album references places, events, and people from the state. This delicate song—best played at sunset—features a folksy guitar.

TAHQUAMENON FALLS

> *Follow H-58 east for 12 miles (19 km), then turn left onto County Rd. 407/ Deer Park Rd. Follow this for 29 miles (47 km), then turn left onto M-123. Continue for 22 miles (35 km), then make a right turn to enter the park. Continue for less than a mile to reach the parking lot.*

❷ Once in **Sault Ste. Marie,** sail through the **Soo Locks** (800/432-6301, www.soolocks.com, early May-mid-Oct., $31 adults, $12 ages 5-12) with **Soo Locks Boat Tours.** You'll marvel at how gargantuan ships transit the locks with just inches to spare. Boats depart from two docks on Portage Avenue.

> *Retrace your path back to M-123. Head east for 10 miles (16 km) to the town of Paradise. Turn right to head south on M-123 and drive another 11 miles (18 km). Turn left onto Lake Superior Shoreline Rd. and continue for 9 miles (15 km). Here, the road becomes Lakeshore Dr. Continue east for another 23 miles (37 km), at which point the road becomes 6 Mile Rd. Follow this for another 9 miles (15 km), then turn left onto S. Mackinac Trail. In 3 miles (5 km), follow signs for I-75 Business Spur at the traffic circle. This will lead into Sault Ste. Marie in another 3 miles (5 km).*

❸ Check into your room at the historic **Ramada Plaza by Wyndham Sault Ste. Marie Ojibway** (240 W. Portage Ave., 906/632-4100 or 800/654-2929, www.ojibwayhotel.com, $149-225), an elegant 1927 building restored to its old-world charm.

④ Cap off your road trip with dinner at the hotel's on-site restaurant, **Freighters** (240 Portage Ave., 906/632-4211, www.ojibwayhotel.com, 8am-10pm Mon., Wed., and Fri.-Sat., 8am-9pm Tues. and Sun., $14-29), where a wall of windows overlooks the locks. The menu boasts a selection of steaks and seafood, with an emphasis on local fish.

Getting There

AIR

Detroit Metropolitan Airport (DTW, 800/642-1978) is the area hub for **Delta Airlines** (888/750-3284, www.delta.com), allowing you fly to Detroit from anywhere in the United States and overseas. Connections are available to several of the Upper Peninsula's commercial airports, including Escanaba, Marquette, Pellston/Mackinac Island, and Sault Ste. Marie. Flights from Detroit to the Upper Peninsula are limited, with only one or two arrivals and departures per day at regional airports.

Delta Airlines has several flights daily to **Pellston Regional Airport** (PLN, US-31, Pellston, 231/539-8441, www.pellstonairport.com), about 15 miles south of Mackinaw City. Shuttle transportation is available from **Wolverine Stages** (800/825-1450, www.wolverinestages.com, reservations preferred) and **Mackinaw Shuttle** (231/539-7005, www.mackinawshuttle.com).

The other airports for U.P. destinations are **Chippewa County International Airport** (CIU, 119 Airport Dr., Kincheloe, 906/495-2522, www.airciu.com) and **Delta County Airport** (ESC, 3300 Airport Rd., Escanaba, 906/786-4902, http://flyesc.com).

TRAIN

There's no direct **Amtrak** (800/872-7245, www.amtrak.com) service to St. Ignace, but the company partners with Greyhound to provide bus transportation from several major cities in southwest Michigan.

BUS

Indian Trails (800/292-3831, www.indiantrails.com), a Michigan-based company, runs regularly scheduled bus routes throughout Michigan, including the Upper Peninsula. Main routes go between Calumet and Milwaukee via Marquette and to St. Ignace and Ironwood via Escanaba. St. Ignace buses stop at the **St. Ignace Transportation Center** (700 W. US-2). **Greyhound** (800/231-2222, www.greyhound.com) provides service from points across the country. Buses also stop at the St. Ignace Transportation Center.

CAR

The 300-mile (480-km) drive from **Detroit Metropolitan Airport** to Mackinaw City takes approximately four hours via I-94, US-23, I-75, and I-17. From **Pellston Regional Airport**, it's 15 miles (24 km) to Mackinaw City. The drive takes less than 30 minutes via US-3.

Chippewa County International Airport is 45 miles (72 km) north of Mackinaw City, a one-hour drive via I-75. **Delta County Airport** is 150 miles (240 km) west of Mackinaw City, a 2.5-hour drive via US-2.

Getting Back

To return to **Mackinaw City** from Sault St. Marie, it's a 60-mile (97-km) drive of a little over an hour. Take I-75 and US-23 to reach Mackinaw City.

Another option is to fly back home from **Chippewa County International Airport** (CIU, 119 Airport Dr., Kincheloe, 906/495-2522, www.airciu.com). It's a 20-mile (32-km) drive south from Sault Ste. Marie, which takes 30 minutes via I-75.

CONNECT WITH

● At Mackinaw City: **Michigan's Gold Coast** (PAGE 450)

● At Escanaba: **Michigan's Upper Peninsula: The Wild West** (PAGE 440)

MICHIGAN'S UPPER PENINSULA: THE WILD WEST

WHY GO: Wildlife, backcountry hiking and camping, Lake Superior, fresh seafood, canoeing, kayaking, unspoiled wilderness

TOTAL DISTANCE: 300 miles/ 475 kilometers

NUMBER OF DAYS: 6

SEASONS: Late spring through fall

START: Iron Mountain, Michigan

END: Copper Harbor, Michigan

▼ COPPER HARBOR

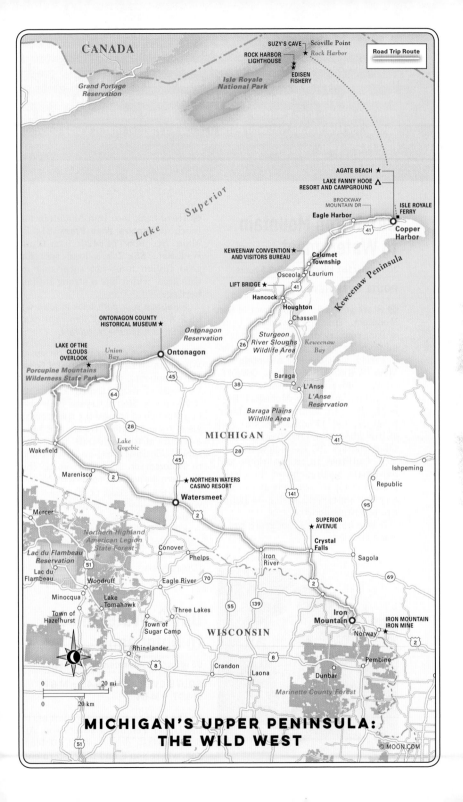

CANADA

Grand Portage
Reservation

SUZY'S CAVE ★   Scoville Point
ROCK HARBOR ★   Rock Harbor
LIGHTHOUSE
Isle Royale   ★
National Park   EDISEN
                  FISHERY

AGATE BEACH ★
LAKE FANNY HOOE
RESORT AND CAMPGROUND   △

Lake   Superior
                           BROCKWAY
                           MOUNTAIN DR   ISLE ROYALE
                           Eagle Harbor   FERRY
                                      41   Copper
                                            Harbor

KEEWEENAW CONVENTION ★   Calumet
AND VISITORS BUREAU   Township

                    Osceola Laurium

LIFT BRIDGE ★   41
            Hancock
                    Houghton   Keeweenaw Peninsula
                    Chassell

ONTONAGON COUNTY
HISTORICAL MUSEUM ★
                Ontonagon
                Reservation   Sturgeon
                               River Sloughs   Keeweenaw
LAKE OF THE   Union   Wildlife Area   Bay
CLOUDS   Bay   26
OVERLOOK ★ Ontonagon
Porcupine Mountains
Wilderness State Park   45
                         38   Baraga
          64   L'Anse
                                   L'Anse
                    Baraga Plains Reservation
                    Wildlife Area
          28
        Lake   45   28   41
        Gogebic MICHIGAN
Wakefield
                                                        Ishpeming
  Marenisco   2   ★ NORTHERN WATERS   141   Republic
                      CASINO RESORT
Mercer   Watersmeet   95
            Northern Highland 2
            American Legion   SUPERIOR
Lac du   State Forest   ★ AVENUE
Flambeau   51   Conover Phelps
Reservation   Iron   Crystal
Lac du   Eagle River 70 River   Falls   Sagola
Flambeau   Woodruff
                                              2   69
Minocqua   Iron Mountain
        Lake   Three Lakes   55   139   Iron Mine ★
Town of Tomahawk   Iron   Norway   2
Hazelhurst   Town of   Mountain
          Rhinelander Sugar Camp WISCONSIN   Pembine
                                    8
0   20 mi   Crandon Laona   Dunbar
0   20 km   Marinette County Forest
51

MICHIGAN'S UPPER PENINSULA:
THE WILD WEST

Road Trip Route

© MOON.COM

This is a wild part of the world where bald eagles soar, wolves roam, and moose meander. *Remote* doesn't even begin to describe this journey, which includes the least visited national park in the country. Start in the mining town of Iron Mountain, then head north, skirting the edge of Lake Superior. A stop in Porcupine Mountains Wilderness State Park, a 65,000-acre old-growth forest dotted with hiking trails and waterfalls, is just an appetizer for Isle Royale National Park, a place so rugged that it's only open for part of the year.

DAY 1: Iron Mountain to Watersmeet

100 miles/161 kilometers | 2-2.5 hours

ROUTE OVERVIEW: US-2

① Start your trip in the town of **Iron Mountain.** This area was the heart of iron country during the heyday of mining. To learn about this historic period, visit the **Iron Mountain Iron Mine** (W4852 US-2, Vulcan, 906/563-8077, www.ironmountainironmine. com, 9am-5pm daily Memorial Day-Sept. 30, $15 adults, $10 children 6-12), located 11 miles (18 km) east of Iron Mountain. The 40-minute tour takes visitors 400 feet below the surface. Outfitted in rain slickers and hard hats, visitors board an underground train to learn about the history and process of mining, including equipment demonstrations.

> Take US-2 E for 11 miles (18 km) to reach the mine.

IRON MOUNTAIN

② Head back into Iron Mountain for lunch at **Bimbo's Wine Press** (314 E. Main St., 906/774-8420, 9am-10pm Wed.-Sat., $8). It's a local spot for good Italian fare—not surprising in this area, which has a strong Italian heritage.

> Retrace your path back to town via US-2 W (11 mi/18 km). Turn right onto Main St. to reach the restaurant.

③ Take a brief detour into a corner of Wisconsin on the way to **Crystal Falls.** You're entering the Superior Upland, the area of rough beauty known as iron country. Stop in Crystal Falls just long enough to admire the spectacular view along **Superior Avenue** and take a picture of the highlands in the distance. Continue west until you come to **Watersmeet.** Book a room at the **Northern Waters Casino Resort** (N5384 US-45, 906/358-4226 or 800/583-3599, www.lvdcasino.com, from $96) for a well-deserved rest.

> Take US-2 W for 28 miles (45 km) into Crystal Falls. The road turns into 5th St., which intersects with Superior Ave. Continue west on US-2 for another 45 miles (72 km) to reach Watersmeet.

DAY 2: Watersmeet to Ontonagon

95 miles/153 kilometers | 2-2.5 hours

ROUTE OVERVIEW: US-45 • M-64 • M-107 • M-64

① The most picturesque wilderness of the Upper Peninsula awaits you. After breakfast, drive north to **Ontonagon,** where you'll find the eastern end

Top 3 MICHIGAN'S UPPER PENINSULA: THE WILD WEST

1. Venture 400 feet below the surface during a **mine tour** at **Iron Mountain Iron Mine** (PAGE 442).

2. Travel to the **Keweenaw Peninsula,** the **northernmost point** of mainland Michigan (PAGE 444).

3. Explore **Isle Royale National Park,** which is only accessible by boat (PAGE 445).

of **Porcupine Mountains Wilderness State Park** (906/885-5275, www.michigan.gov/dnr, 8am-6pm daily mid-May-mid-Oct., $9).

> Go north on US-45 for 33 miles (53 km). Turn left to stay on US-45 and continue for 14 miles (23 km) to reach Ontonagon.

❷ Pick up picnic supplies in Ontonagon before taking M-107 up the large hill to **Lake of the Clouds Overlook** (west end of M-107). Park your car and make the very short hike up to the top of the cliff to take in the breathtaking view. Double back on M-107. After exiting the park near **Union Bay** you'll find a series of scenic turnouts along the Lake Superior shore. Most have tables, so stop here to enjoy your picnic lunch and chat with fellow travelers.

> Head west on M-64 for 13 miles (21 km). Continue straight when the road becomes M-107. Follow the road for 10 miles (16 km) to the overlook. Retrace your path on M-107 back to Union Bay (10 mi/16 km).

❸ After lunch, head back to Ontonagon to take in the **Ontonagon County Historical Museum** (422 River St., 906/884-6165, www.ontonagonmuseum.org, 10am-4pm Tues.-Sat. May-Oct., 10am-4pm Thurs.-Sat. Nov.-Apr., $5), which offers a fascinating look at the community's past, with an emphasis on the logging and mining industries. The historical society also offers tours of the Ontonagon Lighthouse, an 1853 structure gradually being restored.

> Continue east on M-64 for 13 miles (21 km) to return to Ontonagon.

❹ Grab dinner at **Syl's Cafe** (713 River St., 906/884-2522, 7am-9pm daily, $7-12), a classic small-town café with some of the best pasties around. Stay in one of the motels scattered along M-64.

DAY 3: Ontonagon to Copper Harbor

100 miles/161 kilometers | 3 hours

ROUTE OVERVIEW: M-38 • M-26 • US-41 • M-26 • Brockway Mountain Dr. • M-26 • US-41

❶ Today you'll be heading to the **Keweenaw Peninsula,** as north as you can go and still be in mainland Michigan. As you progress, you'll see more pine and spruce trees mixed with the maples and elms. When you come to **Houghton,** a college town that's home to Michigan Technological University, stop and take a leisurely break at **Cyberia Café** (800 Sharon Ave., 906/482-2233, 7am-11pm Mon.-Fri., 9am-11pm

LAKE OF THE CLOUDS OVERLOOK

VIEW FROM BROCKWAY MOUNTAIN DRIVE

Sat.-Sun.). Enjoy the cushy couches, board games, excellent coffee, and the best cinnamon rolls around.

> *Drive southeast on M-38 to M-26 (14 mi/23 km). Follow M-26 N for 37 miles (60 km) to Houghton.*

❷ Check out the unusual **lift bridge** linking the city to **Hancock** across the Keweenaw Waterway. Continue north until you come to **Calumet,** considered by some to be the capital of the once-dominant copper industry. Look around at the magnificent if somewhat neglected architecture flanked by abandoned mines. The **Keweenaw Convention and Visitors Bureau** (56638 Calumet Ave., 906/337-4579 or 800/338-7982, www.keweenaw.info, 9am-5pm Mon.-Fri.) offers a walking tour.

> *Follow US-41 N for 13 miles (21 km) to Calumet.*

❸ Drive north to **Eagle Harbor,** where you'll pick up **Brockway Mountain Drive** (Eagle Harbor to Copper Harbor), one of the most beautiful roads in the state. This 9-mile (13-km) route traces the spine of a 735-foot-high ridge between Copper Harbor and Eagle Harbor. A parking area midway allows you to stop and soak in the panorama of Lake Superior and the rolling forests of the Keweenaw. Watch for ravens, bald eagles, and peregrine falcons.

> *Continue on US-41 N for 14 miles (23 km). Turn left onto Eagle Harbor Cutoff Rd. and follow it for 2.5 miles (4 km). Turn right onto M-26 and follow it for 4*

miles (6 km). Continue straight onto Brockway Mountain Dr. from here.

❹ Once you arrive in **Copper Harbor,** check into one of the cabins at the **Keweenaw Mountain Lodge** (906/289-4403 or 888/685-6343, www.atthelodge.com, $150-220). Reservations can be difficult to obtain, so plan ahead.

> *Follow Brockway Mountain Dr. to its eastern end. Make a slight right onto M-26, which will lead to Copper Harbor in less than a mile. To continue to the lodge, turn right onto US-41 and follow it south for 1 mile (1.6 km). Turn left onto Golf Course Rd. to reach the lodge.*

DAY 4: Copper Harbor to Isle Royale National Park

MORNING

❶ Shift into nautical mode and board the **Isle Royale Queen IV** (14 Waterfront Landing, 906/289-4437, www.isleroyale.com, mid-May-Sept., round-trip $124-136 adults, $94-100 children under 12) for the 3.5-hour trip to **Isle Royale National Park** (906/482-0984, www.nps.gov/isro, mid-Apr.-Oct., $7 pp), the least-visited property in the National Park system. No motorized vehicles are allowed on the island, so be prepared to enjoy a true dip into nature. You can leave your vehicle at the ferry landing ($10 per night).

ISLE ROYALE NATIONAL PARK

> *It's a short 2-mile (3-km) drive from Keweenaw Mountain Lodge to the Isle Royale ferry departure. Take US-41 N to 6th St. Make a left onto 5th St. to the ferry landing.*

AFTERNOON AND EVENING

❷ Although the park is very rugged and most visitors choose to camp, indoor accommodations are available at the **Rock Harbor Lodge** (906/337-4993, www.rockharborlodge.com, $234-379) at the far eastern tip. The lodge has rooms with private baths and views of Lake Superior, as well as cottages, plus an on-site dining room, snack bar, gift shop, dockside store, and marina where you can rent motorboats, kayaks, and canoes.

ROCK HARBOR

❸ Once on the island, spend some time hiking, fishing, boating, or simply observing wildlife. Don't miss the hike to **Scoville Point** (4.2 mi/6.8 km loop, 1.5 hours, moderate), which features interpretive signs as it traces a rocky finger of land east of Rock Harbor. Even if you're camping, have dinner at the lodge. After a day of wilderness adventure, a hot meal will feel like a gourmet feast.

DAY 5: Isle Royale National Park

MORNING

❶ Strap those hiking boots on again. A popular short hike is the trail to **Suzy's Cave** (3.8 mi/6.1 km loop, 1.5 hours, moderate). This cave was formed by the wave action of a once much-deeper Lake Superior. Start on the Rock Harbor Trail and turn inland to follow the sign leading to the cave. Find the trailhead at the Rock Harbor Campground.

AFTERNOON AND EVENING

❷ Take a guided **boat tour** on the National Park Service's 25-passenger **MV Sandy** (906/482-0984, www.nps.gov/isro, times and rates vary). There are several options to choose from. An especially interesting trip is to **Edisen Fishery.** The historic fishery of Peter and Laura Edisen has been restored to show what life was like at the commercial fisheries that once thrived on the island. From Edisen Fishery, it's a short walk to the stout and simple **Rock Harbor Lighthouse,** a white edifice built in 1855 to guide ships to Isle

Best HIKES

What better way to experience the abundance of natural beauty in the UP than with a hike? Here are a few winners:

PORCUPINE MOUNTAINS WILDERNESS STATE PARK

- The **Escarpment Trail** (8.8 mi/14.2 km round-trip, 3.5 hours) is a wonderfully scenic hike. The relatively high elevation offers a view of the Lake of the Clouds to the south, where summer greenery resembles a vast, lush carpet. Lake Superior is visible to the north.

PICTURED ROCKS NATIONAL LAKESHORE

- A delightful option for those unable to undertake a longer trek, **Miner Falls Trail** (2.4 mi/3.9 km round-trip, 1 hour) is an easy, flat, and well-maintained walk through sparse maple forest. Its low density allows for excellent viewing of deer and an occasional moose. The big payoff, however, comes at the end—the roaring, majestic Miners Falls.

TAHQUAMENON FALLS STATE PARK

- The great **Tahquamenon River Trail** (8 mi/12.9 km round-trip, 3 hours) hugs the shore of the Tahquamenon River between the Upper and Lower Falls—you're never more than about 20 feet from the roaring river. This is an especially nice walk in the springtime, when the current is strongest due to the melting of the winter snow and ice.

ISLE ROYALE NATIONAL PARK

- Intended for the serious hiker/backpacker, the **Greenstone Trail** (42.2 mi/68 km one-way) is perhaps the least ventured trail in the least visited park in the National Park system. Talk about experiencing nature in solitude. This four-day, three-night adventure will take you along the spine of the main island of the park. Seeing moose is not uncommon; if you're lucky, you may even see a gray wolf.

KEWEENAW PENINSULA

- The challenging **Keweenaw State Trail** (51.7 mi/83.2 km one-way) makes for an interesting backpacking trip. The trail follows U.S. 41 at widely varying elevations, with portions consisting of old railroad beds that pierce through both pine and hardwood forests. It's especially enjoyable during the fall for leaf-peepers.

▼ ESCARPMENT TRAIL, PORCUPINE MOUNTAINS WILDERNESS STATE PARK

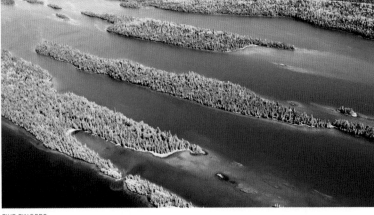

FIVE FINGERS

Royale's then-busy copper ports. Boat tour tickets are available from Rock Harbor Lodge.

3 Once you return to Rock Harbor, **rent a kayak** or **canoe** (Rock Harbor Marina, 906/337-4993, www.rockharborlodge.com, from $23) to pilot your own vessel through the area's waters. First-time visitors should paddle the **Five Fingers,** the collection of fjord-like harbors and rocky promontories on the east end of the island. Of these, be sure to explore **Tobin Harbor.** Pack lunches and take them with you.

DAY 6: Isle Royale National Park to Copper Harbor

MORNING AND AFTERNOON

1 Spend the morning taking one last hike, or getting out on the water again. Make sure you're back at the ferry dock by 2:45pm for the ride back to **Copper Harbor.** You'll get into town

AGATE BEACH NEAR COPPER HARBOR

around 6pm. Once you arrive back on the mainland in Copper Harbor, everything is within walking distance. Take a walk along **Agate Beach** (eastern end of Harbor Coast Ln.), on the Lake Superior side of Copper Harbor. This is a good spot to look for the eponymous banded rocks.

EVENING

2 Head to **Harbor Haus** (77 Brockway Ave., 906/289-4502, www.harborhaus.com, 4pm-8:30pm daily, $22-42) for dinner. This restaurant offers top-notch dining overlooking the water.

3 Near the western tip of Lake Fanny Hooe, **Lake Fanny Hooe Resort and Campground** (505 2nd St., 906/289-4451, www.fannyhooe.com, from $105) offers a variety of accommodations, including a lakefront motel, cottages, and a chalet.

Getting There

AIR

There are a few nearby options for flying to Iron Mountain. **Ford Airport** (IMT, 500 Riverhills Rd., Kingsford, 906/774-4870, www.fordairport.org) in Kingsford has flights on Delta Airlines from Minneapolis and Detroit. Car rentals are offered by Avis.

Delta County Airport (ESC, 3300 Airport Rd., Escanaba, 906/786-4902, http://flyesc.com), a small airport just southwest of Escanaba, has flights from Detroit on Delta Airlines. You can rent a car from Alamo.

Sawyer International Airport (MQT, 125 G Ave., Gwinn, 906/346-3308, www.sawyerairport.com) has daily flights from Chicago, Detroit, and Minneapolis on American Airlines and Delta. You'll find major car rental agencies, including Alamo, Avis, Budget, Dollar, Hertz, National, and Thrifty. Sawyer is just south of Marquette and about two hours' drive from Iron Mountain, but with more regular flights, it can be the easier option.

BUS

Iron Mountain is served by **Indian Trails** (800/292-3831, www.indiantrails.com), a Michigan-based bus company. It offers regularly scheduled bus routes throughout Michigan, including the Upper Peninsula.

CAR

Iron Mountain is located on Michigan's border with Wisconsin, at the intersection of two major highways. Driving into town from the east, take US-2, which is US-2 and US-141 when you come from the west. North from Wisconsin or south from other parts of the U.P., US-141 leads into town. Take US-2/141 north to Crystal Falls, US-2 east to Norway, and US-2 west to Iron River.

It's 4 miles (6 km) from **Ford Airport** to Iron Mountain, a 10-minute drive via Woodard Avenue. It's 55 miles (89 km) from **Delta County Airport** to Iron Mountain, which is about a one-hour drive. From the airport, follow US-2 to Ludington Street into town.

From **Sawyer International Airport** to Iron Mountain, it's 90 miles (145 km), which takes about two hours via M-95.

Getting Back

The 160-mile (260-km) drive from Copper Harbor back to **Iron Mountain** takes a little over three hours. Go south on US-41, then take US-141 S into town. Note that US-141 is also US-2. To fly home from **Sawyer International Airport,** it's a 155-mile (250-km) drive of about three hours. To get to the airport, take US-41 and M-553.

Playlist

MICHIGAN'S UPPER PENINSULA: THE WILD WEST

SONGS

- **"America" by Simon and Garfunkel:** Inspired by a road trip he took with his girlfriend, Paul Simon penned this 1960s song about a search for America, both literally and figuratively. Its moody melody is sure to lead you down your own introspective path. That's what road trips are all about, right?

- **"Road to Nowhere" by Talking Heads:** Lead singer David Byrne describes this song as a "joyful look at doom," but it's on this playlist more for its literal meaning. As this trip takes you north to the edge of the mainland, it can feel as if you're on a road to nowhere—in the best, most liberating sense.

- **"Band on the Run" by Wings:** The 1973 song by Paul McCartney's post-Beatles band, Wings, is wonderfully lighthearted. The medley of three different musical passages sonically mirrors the shifting landscape of your drive.

CONNECT WITH

- At Iron Mountain: **Michigan's Upper Peninsula: The Charming East** (PAGE 430)

MICHIGAN'S GOLD COAST

WHY GO: Tunnel of Trees, Lake Michigan beaches, sand dunes, fresh fish, art galleries, wineries, antiques shopping

TOTAL DISTANCE: 425 miles/ 685 kilometers

NUMBER OF DAYS: 5

SEASONS: Summer and fall

START: Saugatuck and Douglas, Michigan

END: Mackinaw City, Michigan

▼ SLEEPING BEAR DUNES NATIONAL LAKESHORE

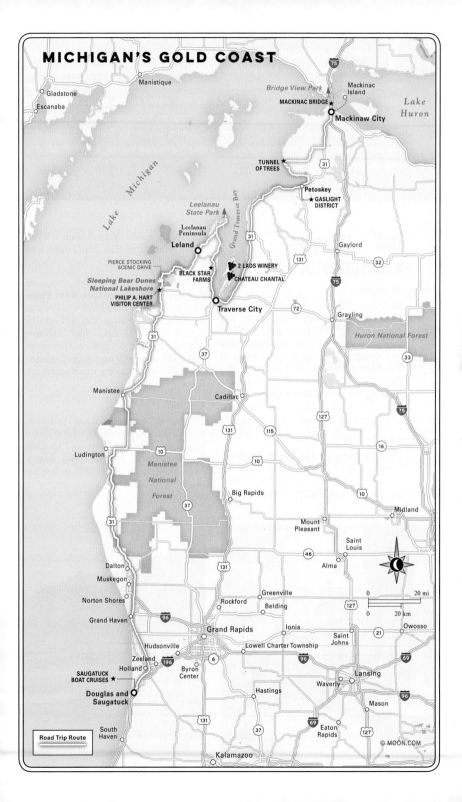

You're never far from water views when you drive along Michigan's Gold Coast, where nearly 300 miles of coastline stretch before you. But charming inns, cozy bed-and-breakfasts, freshwater seafood restaurants, wineries, art galleries, and forested drives tempt you inland. Don't fight temptation; just go with it. You'll be back to the water in no time. Starting in the picturesque towns of Saugatuck and Douglas, this trip follows the coast north, explores the Leelanau Peninsula, ducks inland to Traverse City, and then continues north to Mackinaw City and Mackinac Island, a delightful day trip accessible only by boat.

DAY 1: Douglas and Saugatuck

MORNING

❶ You won't need the car today. Explore the **Art Coast,** a cluster of art galleries in and around the adjacent coastal villages of **Saugatuck** and **Douglas.** A good place to start is the **Button Gallery** (33-35 Center St., Douglas, 269/857-2175, www.buttonartgallery.com, hours vary), which offers an array of paintings, ceramics, sculptures, glasswork, and prints.

AFTERNOON

❷ Grab a spot on the patio or pick up sandwiches or a charcuterie board for a picnic at **Pumpernickels** (202 Butler St., Saugatuck, 269/857-1196, www. pumpernickelssaugatuck.com, 9am-10pm Mon. and Wed.-Sat., 9am-3pm Sun., $6-26).

❸ Spend the rest of the afternoon on the water with **Saugatuck Boat Cruises** (716 Water St., 269/857-4261, www.saugatuckboatcruises.com, $27 adults, $15 children 3-12). The two-level sternwheeler docked on the riverfront, the *Star of Saugatuck II,* passes beautiful homes along the Kalamazoo River.

EVENING

❹ Stay at one of the many bed-and-breakfasts in the area. The 1860 Victorian-style **Twin Oaks Inn** (227 Griffith St., Saugatuck, 269/857-1600, http://twinoaksbb.com, $110-150) is among the friendliest.

DOWNTOWN SAUGATUCK

STAR OF SAUGATUCK II

Top **3** MICHIGAN'S GOLD COAST

1 See sparkling Lake Michigan from the shores of **Sleeping Bear Dunes National Lakeshore** (PAGE 454).

2 At **Black Star Farms,** sample wines, spirits, and other locally grown goodies (PAGE 455).

3 Drive through the twisty, scenic, otherworldly **Tunnel of Trees** near Mackinaw City (PAGE 458).

DAY 2: Saugatuck to Leland

210 miles/340 kilometers | 4-4.5 hours

ROUTE OVERVIEW: US-31 • M-22 • M-109/S. Dune Hwy. • Pierce Stocking Scenic Dr. • M-109 • M-22

① Fuel up for a long day by grabbing coffee at **Uncommon Coffee Roasters** (127 Hoffman St., Saugatuck, 269/857-3333, www.uncommoncoffeeroasters.com, 7am-7pm Sun.-Thurs., 7am-8pm Fri.-Sat., $3-12), an ecologically sensitive coffee importer that takes pride in working with small growers and cooperatives.

② Head north to the incredible **Sleeping Bear Dunes National Lakeshore** (www.nps.gov/slbe, 24 hours daily, $25 vehicles, $20 motorcycles, $15 pedestrians), a marvelous 35-mile stretch of beaches, dunes, and lakes that lies alongside Lake Michigan. Stop into the **Philip A. Hart Visitor Center** (9922 Front St., Empire, 231/326-4700, 8am-6pm daily Memorial Day-mid-Oct., 8:30am-4pm daily mid-Oct.-Memorial Day) for park information and maps.

> Drive north on I-196/US-31 for 5 miles (8 km), then take US-31 N for 92 miles (148 km). Turn right onto US-10 and follow it east for 5 miles (8 km), then turn left to rejoin US-31. Continue north for another 58 miles (93 km). At Indian Hill Rd., turn left and drive for 6 miles (10 km) to Fowler Rd. Turn left, then turn right on M-22. Go north on M-22 for 5 miles (8 km), then turn left onto Front St. to reach the visitors center.

③ To sample the national lakeshore, take the short **Pierce Stocking Scenic Drive** (off of S. Dune Hwy., 7.4 mi/11.9 km). This popular paved loop provides easy access to the scenic overlooks of Glen Lake, the dunes, and Lake Michigan.

> Continue north on M-22 for 2 miles (3 km). Turn left onto M-109/S. Dune Hwy. and continue for 1 mile (1.6 km). Take a left onto Pierce Stocking Scenic Dr. and follow the loop counterclockwise.

④ It's a short drive north to **Leland**, where a stay at **The Riverside Inn** (302 River St., 231/256-9971, www.theriverside-inn.com, $168-225) affords you a tranquil retreat along the Leland River. The inn offers four guest rooms, each tastefully appointed, and free Wi-Fi. There are no televisions though, so get your entertainment by sipping a cocktail on the expansive deck.

> From M-109/S. Dune Hwy., continue north for 4 miles (6 km). Turn right to stay on M-109 and continue for 2 miles (3 km). Continue on M-22 N for another 19 miles (31 km) to reach Leland.

SLEEPING BEAR DUNES NATIONAL LAKESHORE

LEELANAU STATE PARK

DAY 3: Leelanau Peninsula to Traverse City

60 miles/97 kilometers | 1.5-2 hours

ROUTE OVERVIEW: M-22 • surface streets • M-22

❶ Head to **Leelanau State Park** (15310 N. Lighthouse Point Rd., Northport, 231/386-5422 summer, 231/922-5270 winter, www.michigandnr.com, 8am-10pm daily, $9). It's split into two units: the popular northern unit, with its lighthouse and campground, and the less visited southern portion, where you can have lovely beaches and trails to yourself.

> *Take M-22 N for 11 miles (18 km) to Northport. Here, pick up Mill St., driving it north for 2 miles (3 km) until it turns into Woolsey Lake Rd. Stay on Woolsey Lake Rd. for 4 miles (6 km) to Lighthouse Rd. Go left on Lighthouse for 2.5 miles (4 km) to the state park.*

❷ On your way south, stop by **Black Star Farms** (10844 E. Revold Rd., 231/944-1270, www.blackstar-farms.com, 10am-6pm Mon.-Thurs., 10am-8pm Fri.-Sat., noon-5pm Sun. May-Nov., $220-425). This fascinating winery, distillery, creamery, and farmers market also offers a welcoming tasting room and a luxurious bed-and-breakfast.

> *Retrace your path to Northport (10 mi/16 km). Hop on M-22 and follow it south for 14 miles (23 km). Turn right onto Revold Rd. to reach Black Star Farms.*

❸ Head down to **Traverse City** and experience the booming craft beer scene at one of the many breweries in town. Grab a pint and dinner at **North Peak Brewing Company** (400 W. Front St., 231/941-7325, www.northpeak.net, 11am-11pm Mon.-Thurs., 11am-midnight Fri.-Sat., noon-10pm Sun., $12-25).

> *Continue south on M-22 into Traverse City (13 mi/21 km).*

❹ Spend the night at **Park Place Hotel** (300 E. State St., 231/946-5000, www.park-place-hotel.com, $155-289), an 1870s downtown landmark fully restored to its original opulence.

DAY 4: Traverse City

35 miles/56 kilometers | 1 hour

ROUTE OVERVIEW: M-37

❶ Drive to the northern tip of the Old Mission Peninsula to explore some of Michigan's many wineries. Check out **2 Lads Winery** (16985 Smokey Hollow

CHATEAU CHANTAL

Rd., 231/223-7722, www.2lwinery. com, 11am-6pm Mon.-Sat., 11am-5pm Sun. May-Oct., 11am-5pm Mon.-Sat., 11am-4pm Sun. Nov.-Apr., $12), which offers a sleek, modern tasting room to sample their northern sparkling varieties.

> *Take M-37 N for 11 miles (18 km). At Smokey Hollow Rd., turn right and drive 2 miles (3 km) to reach the winery.*

❷ For more wine country, visit **Chateau Chantal** (15900 Rue de Vin, 231/223-4110 or 800/969-4009, www. chateauchantal.com, 11am-8pm Mon.-Sat., 11am-6pm Sun. Memorial Day-Labor Day, shorter hours Labor Day-Memorial Day, $7-9), a French château-inspired winery where you can enjoy a stunning view of Grand Traverse Bay.

> *Double back on Smokey Hollow Rd., and in less than a mile, turn right onto Ladd Rd. Turn left onto M-37, then left again onto Rue de Vin to reach Chateau Chantal, which is 2.5 miles (4 km) from 2 Lads.*

❸ Head back to Traverse City and wind down for the evening with dinner at **Mission Table at Bowers Harbor Inn** (13512 Peninsula Dr., 231/223-4222, www.missiontable.net, 5pm-9pm daily, $18-27), which offers elegant dining in an 1880s mansion, complete with a resident ghost.

> *Get back on M-37 and head south to return to Traverse City (14 mi/23 km).*

DAY 5: Traverse City to Mackinaw City

120 miles/193 kilometers | 3-3.5 hours

ROUTE OVERVIEW: US-31 • M-119 • W. Levering Rd. • US-31 • Mackinaw Hwy.

❶ Head north to **Petoskey,** where you'll find a charming downtown perfect for strolling. The **Gaslight District** (Lake St. and Howard St.) mixes upscale boutiques with bookstores, art

PETOSKEY'S QUAINT GASLIGHT DISTRICT

No trip to Michigan would be complete with a visit to **Mackinac Island,** a charming vacation spot that has long banned automobiles in favor of bikes and horse-drawn carriages. Rife with Victorian mansions, this nostalgic island offers a true step back in time.

GETTING THERE

From Mackinaw City, take the short **ferry ride** to the island with **Shepler's Mackinac Island Ferry** (231/436-5023, 906/643-9440, or 800/828-6157, www.sheplersferry.com, late Apr.-Oct., round-trip $25 adults, $14 children 5-12, $10 bikes) or **Star Line** (800/638-9892, www.mackinacferry.com, late Apr.-Oct., round-trip $25 adults, $14 children 5-12, $12 bikes).

MORNING

Start with a horse-drawn tour of the island with **Mackinac Island Carriage Tours** (906/847-3307, www.mict.com, 9am-5pm daily mid-June-Labor Day, shorter hours May-mid-June and Labor Day-Oct., $30.50 adults, $11 children 5-12).

LUNCH

Head up to the **Fort Mackinac Tea Room** (906/847-3328, www.grandhotel.com, 11am-3pm daily June-Sept., $10-15), where you can enjoy delicious soups, salads, and sandwiches from a picturesque terrace with a stunning view of the waterfront.

AFTERNOON

The **Grand Hotel** (286 Grand Ave., 906/847-3331 or 800/334-7263, www.grandhotel.com) has become practically synonymous with Mackinac Island, a graceful edifice built on a truly grand scale. Opened in 1887, it boasts the world's longest porch and a guest list that's included at least five U.S. presidents.

Next, head to the bustling downtown area, along **Main and Market Streets,** where you can browse shops, sample fudge, and visit historic homes.

DINNER

The **Yankee Rebel Tavern** (1493 Astor St., 906/847-6249, www.yankeerebel-tavern.com, 10:30am-midnight daily, $14-37) is a nice choice for dinner, with its fireplace seating, ample wine and beer selection, and a variety of winning dishes, from slow-roasted ribs to pistachio-crusted whitefish.

GRAND HOTEL, MACKINAC ISLAND

TUNNEL OF TREES

galleries, antiques haunts, and restaurants. The eight-block area of well-preserved Victorian brick storefronts has drawn shoppers since the early 1900s.

> *Follow US-31 N to Petoskey (65 mi/105 km).*

2 Enjoy lunch at the centrally located and historic **City Park Grill** (432 E. Lake St., 231/347-0101, www.cityparkgrill.com, 11:30am-9pm Sun.-Thurs., 11:30am-10pm Fri.-Sat., bar closes later, $10-35).

3 Continue north toward the **Tunnel of Trees** (M-119, from Harbor Springs to Cross Village), where you'll enjoy one of the most scenic drives in America. The narrow lane twists and turns as it follows Lake Michigan from high atop a bluff, yet it's the trees that take top billing, arching overhead to form a sun-dappled tunnel.

> *Continue north on US-31 for 3 miles (5 km), then turn left to join M-119 N. Follow this for 7 miles (11 km) to reach the Tunnel of Trees.*

4 Make your way to **Mackinaw City.** Be sure to check out the iconic **Mackinac Bridge** (I-75, one-way toll $4), the third-longest suspension bridge in the world. Once you've crossed the bridge, make a quick stop at lovely **Bridge View Park** (off Boulevard Dr., St. Ignace), where you can snap pictures of this modern engineering marvel.

> *Continue north on M-119 for 11 miles (18 km). Turn right onto State St., then make the second left onto W. Levering Rd. Take this east for 13 miles (21 km), then turn left to join US-31 N. Follow this for 8 miles (13 km), then turn left to get onto Mackinaw Hwy. This will lead to Mackinaw City in 3 miles (5 km).*

5 Dinner is at **Darrow's Family Restaurant** (301 Louvigney St., 231/436-5514, www.darrowsrestaurant.com, 7:30am-8:30pm Sun.-Thurs., 7:30am-9pm Fri.-Sat., $8-18). Order the fresh, locally caught whitefish and choose from four preparation styles: deep-fried, broiled, Cajun, or parmesan-crusted.

Getting There

AIR

There are three major airports near Saugatuck and Douglas: **Kalamazoo/Battle Creek International Airport** (AZO, 5235 Portage Rd., Kalamazoo, 269/388-3668, www.azoairport.com), **Gerald R. Ford International Airport** (GRR, 5500 44th St. SE, Grand Rapids, 616/233-6000, www.grr.org), and **Muskegon County Airport** (MKG, 99 Sinclair Dr., Muskegon, 231/798-4596, www.muskegonairport.com). All offer rental car services, so reaching the Art Coast is easy.

Detroit Metropolitan Airport (DTW, 800/642-1978) is the area hub, allowing you fly to Detroit from anywhere in the United States and overseas, connecting to several regional airports.

CAR

It's 60 miles (98 km) from **Kalamazoo/Battle Creek International Airport** to Saugatuck, a drive of a little over an hour via I-94, US-131, M-222 and M-89. The adjacent town of Douglas lies about a mile south of Saugatuck on County Road A2, just across Kalamazoo Lake.

The 45-mile (72 km) drive from **Gerald R. Ford International Airport** to

Saugatuck takes about 45 minutes via M-6 and I-196. From **Muskegon County Airport** to Saugatuck, the route is 40 miles (64 km) and takes approximately an hour. Get there via US-31 and I-196.

It'll take approximately three hours to complete the 190-mile (305-km) drive from **Detroit Metropolitan Airport** to Saugatuck. Get there by taking I-275, I-96, M-6, and I-196. To get to Saugatuck from **Chicago**, it's a 140-mile (225-km) drive that takes 2.5-3 hours. Get there via I-90, I-94, and I-196. En route from Chicago, parts of I-90 and I-94 serve as the Indiana Toll Road.

TRAIN

Kalamazoo has an **Amtrak train station** (459 N. Burdick St., Kalamazoo, 800/872-7245, www.amtrak.com). To get to Saugatuck from there, take US-131, M-89, and County Road A2 (Blue Star Hwy.); in light traffic, the 50-mile (81-km) trip should take little more than an hour. Grand Rapids also has an **Amtrak train station** (431 Wealthy St. SW, Grand Rapids, 800/872-7245, www.amtrak.com). From there, follow I-196 west to County Road A2 (Blue Star Hwy.) to reach Saugatuck, a 40-mile (64-km) trip that usually takes 40 minutes.

Getting Back

To return to **Saugatuck and Douglas** from Mackinaw City, it's 275 miles (440 km), which takes a little over four hours via I-75, US-127, M-55, US-131, and I-196.

If you opt to fly out of an airport near Mackinaw City, your best options are **Pellston Regional Airport** (PLN, US-31, Pellston, 231/539-8441, www.pellstonairport.com), which offers daily flights on Delta Airlines, and **Chippewa County International Airport** (CIU, 119 Airport Dr., Kincheloe, 906/495-2522, www.airciu.com). From Pellston, it's 15 miles (24 km) to Mackinaw City via US-31, which takes 20-30 minutes. From Chippewa County International Airport to Mackinaw City, it takes 45 minutes to drive the 40-mile (64-km) route on I-75.

▶ *Playlist*

MICHIGAN'S GOLD COAST

SONGS

- **"Do Right Woman, Do Right Man" by Aretha Franklin:** Few cities have birthed the quantity and quality of musical talent as Detroit, Michigan. From Motown, blues, and rap to gospel, rock, and pop, Detroit has sown the seeds of some of the most influential musicians and singers in the world, Aretha Franklin among them. This soulful song is perfect for quiet moments overlooking the vast expanse of Lake Michigan.

- **"Give Me Just a Little More Time" by Chairmen of the Board:** This 1970s Detroit-based soul group hit it big with this song, their debut single, an upbeat ditty about taking things slow in love.

- **"Like a Prayer" by Madonna:** There are endless options for including a Madonna song on your road trip playlist, but for this particular journey through her home state, you need something soaring, swelling, and sweeping—music to match the limitless horizon of Lake Michigan.

CONNECT WITH

- At Mackinaw City: **Michigan's Upper Peninsula: The Charming East** (PAGE 430)

WISCONSIN'S DOOR COUNTY

WHY GO: Picturesque lighthouses, historic inns, waterfront villages, 300 miles of shoreline, Swedish food, birding, fishing, hiking

TOTAL DISTANCE: 130 miles/ 210 kilometers

NUMBER OF DAYS: 7

SEASONS: Late spring through late fall

START/END: Sturgeon Bay, Wisconsin

▼ WHITEFISH DUNES STATE PARK

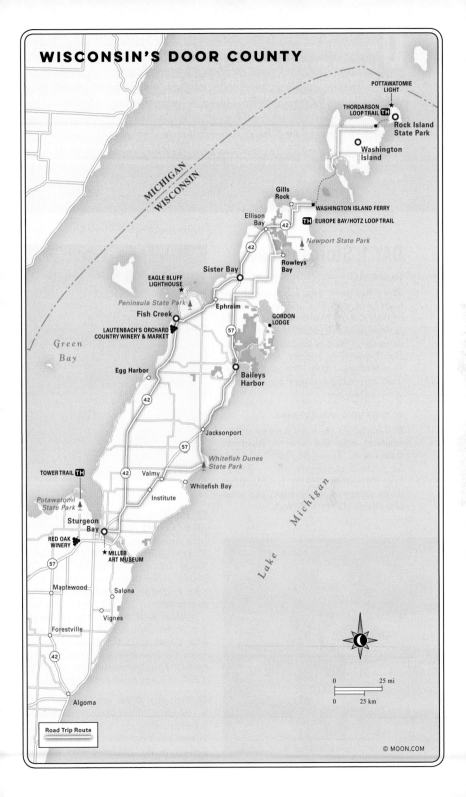

WISCONSIN'S DOOR COUNTY

POTTAWATOMIE
LIGHT

THORDARSON
LOOP TRAIL **TH**
Rock Island
State Park

Washington
Island

MICHIGAN
WISCONSIN

Gills
Rock
WASHINGTON ISLAND FERRY
Ellison
Bay   **TH** EUROPE BAY/HOTZ LOOP TRAIL
          42
                    Newport State Park

Sister Bay
                    Rowleys
                    Bay
EAGLE BLUFF
LIGHTHOUSE
          Peninsula State Park
Fish Creek   Ephraim
                          GORDON
                          LODGE
LAUTENBACH'S ORCHARD   57
COUNTRY WINERY & MARKET

Green
Bay   Egg Harbor   Baileys
                          Harbor
          42

          57   Jacksonport

                    Whitefish Dunes
                    State Park
TOWER TRAIL **TH**   42   Valmy
Potawatomi   Institute   Whitefish Bay
State Park

Sturgeon
Bay
RED OAK
WINERY   Lake Michigan
          ★ MILLER
          57   ART MUSEUM

Maplewood   Salona

          Vignes

Forestville

          42

          Algoma

0   25 mi
0   25 km

Road Trip Route

© MOON.COM

Door County stretches across a peninsula that juts into Lake Michigan. Dozens of lighthouses—the highest concentration in any U.S. county, in fact—dot the rocky shoreline. Ferries connect the mainland to islands such as Washington Island and the remote and isolated Rock Island State Park. Outdoorsy travelers will delight in the untouched beauty of the area's sublime state parks, and history buffs will marvel at inns, restaurants, and pubs that are more than a century old. Orchards, wineries, maritime museums, charming waterfront towns, and family-run restaurants cooking up fine Swedish fare can all be discovered in this tucked-away region where time seems to stand still.

DAY 1: Sturgeon Bay

MORNING

① In **Sturgeon Bay,** learn about the history of shipping and shipbuilding at **Door County Maritime Museum** (120 N. Madison Ave., 920/743-5958, www.dcmm.org, 9am-5pm daily Memorial Day-Labor Day, shorter hours Labor Day-Memorial Day, $10 adults). The vast, sparkling complex has splendid views of the bay.

AFTERNOON AND EVENING

② Lunch is a short walk away at the casually chic and eclectic **Bluefront Café** (86 W. Maple St., 920/743-9218, http://thebluefrontcafe.com, 11am-3pm Tues.-Sun., $8-18). It's Sturgeon Bay's eatery of choice when you need something cheery and fresh.

POTAWATOMI STATE PARK

STURGEON BAY

③ Head for **Potawatomi State Park** (3740 County Rd. PD, 920/746-2890, http://dnr.wi.gov, 6am-11pm daily, $8-11 per vehicle) and hike the popular **Tower Trail** (3.6 mi/5.8 km loop, 1.5 hours, moderate), which runs up and over ridges to a 75-foot-tall observation tower.

> Head west on Maple St. to Duluth Ave. In less than a mile, turn right and take Duluth to County C. Turn left and follow the road for 1.5 miles (2.5 km) to Park Dr. Turn right on Park and take it for 1 mile (1.6 km) to reach the state park.

④ Visit the **Miller Art Museum** (107 S. 4th Ave., 920/746-0707, www.millerartmuseum.org, 10am-8pm Mon., 10am-5pm Tues.-Sat., free), a fine-art gallery in the Sturgeon Bay library. The top floor houses the permanent

Top **3** WISCONSIN'S DOOR COUNTY

① Spend the night at **White Gull Inn,** the longest-running inn in Door County (PAGE 464).

② Eat authentic Swedish fare at **Al Johnson's Swedish Restaurant** in Sister Bay (PAGE 466).

③ Duck into caves and walk over dunes at **Whitefish Dunes State Park** (PAGE 468).

WILD TOMATO IN FISH CREEK

collection, with an emphasis on 20th-century Wisconsin artists. Overnight at one of the charming beachfront hotels and B&Bs.

> *Retrace your path on Park Dr., County C, N. Duluth, and Maple St. to return to Sturgeon Bay proper (4 mi/6 km).*

DAY 2: Sturgeon Bay to Fish Creek

24 miles/39 kilometers | 45 minutes-1 hour

ROUTE OVERVIEW: WI-42

❶ Head north toward Fish Creek. Though it takes less than an hour to reach Fish Creek, you'll want to devote the entire morning to the trip up the bay. Along the way, you'll drive through picturesque **Egg Harbor,** where you can stop for a late breakfast or lunch at **Macready Artisan Bread** (7836 WI-42, 920/868-2233, http://macreadyartisanbread.com, 9am-4pm Thurs.-Mon., from $5). The house-made bread is heavenly and the proprietors are two of the nicest folks you will meet.

> *Take WI-42 N for 16 miles (26 km) to reach Egg Harbor.*

❷ As you approach Fish Creek, stop for a wine or cider tasting at **Lautenbach's Orchard Country Winery & Market** (Hwy. 42 S., 866/946-3263, www.orchardcountry.com, 9am-5:30pm Sun.-Thurs., 9am-6pm Fri.-Sat.), perhaps the most accessible winery in Door County. During summer, they also offer an hour-long tour (1-2 times daily, $5) of their orchards, vineyards, and production area, which also includes a private tasting.

> *Continue north on WI-42 for 5 miles (8 km) to reach the winery.*

❸ In **Fish Creek,** unpack at a historic inn such as the **White Gull Inn** (4255 Main St., 920/868-3517, www.whitegullinn.com, from $200). A proud old guesthouse since 1897, it's truly the grande dame of Door County, the longest-running inn in the county.

> *Go north on WI-42 for less than a mile, then turn left onto Main St. to reach the inn.*

❹ Unwind with pizza at **Wild Tomato** (4023 Hwy. 42, 920/868-3095, http://wildtomatopizza.com, 11am-10pm daily summer, shorter hours fall-spring, $10-21) and a stroll through the historic downtown.

DAY 3: Fish Creek to Sister Bay

15 miles/24 kilometers | 45 minutes-1 hour

ROUTE OVERVIEW: WI-42 • Shore Rd. • WI-42

❶ Spend the bulk of the day exploring **Peninsula State Park** (9462 Shore Rd., 920/868-3258, http://dnr.wi.gov, 6am-11pm daily, $8-11 per vehicle). A

EAGLE BLUFF LIGHTHOUSE IN PENINSULA STATE PARK

must-see here is the **Eagle Bluff Lighthouse** (920/421-3636). Built during the Civil War, it stands atop the bluff and can be seen for 15 miles; the views from the top stretch even farther.

> To reach the lighthouse from Fish Creek, go north on WI-42 for less than a mile. Enter the park and follow Shore Rd. for 4 miles (6 km).

② Continue up the coast, appreciating the vistas on the short drive to perfectly preserved **Ephraim**. Once there, make a stop in the heart of the village at **Wilson's** (9990 Water St., 920/854-2041, from 11am daily May-Oct.), an old-fashioned ice cream parlor with cones as big as bullhorns.

> Follow Shore Rd. south for less than a mile, then turn left at the sign for the White Cedar Nature Center. Continue on this road for 3 miles (5 km), until you leave the eastern part of the park. Turn left onto Water St. S./WI-42 and continue for 1 mile (1.6 km) into Ephraim.

③ Head to nearby **Sister Bay** and walk the quaint waterfront park before staying the night at **Country House Resort** (2468 Sunnyside Rd., 920/854-4551 or 800/424-0041, www.countryhouseresort.com, $140-360). The grounds cover 16 heavily wooded acres with private nature trails and a 1,000-foot shoreline. Plus, it's dog friendly, a bonus for road-trippers with four-legged companions.

> Follow WI-42 N for 4 miles (6 km) to reach Sister Bay.

PENINSULA STATE PARK

One of the best views of Door County is of the shoreline. Get out on the water to see lighthouses, cliffs, caves, and islands.

STURGEON BAY

- **Door County Fireboat Cruises** (120 N. Madison Ave., 920/495-6454, www.ridethefireboat.com, $25 pp) uses a retired Chicago fireboat to chug along for two-hour cruises on Lake Michigan or Sturgeon Bay.

FISH CREEK

- A sunset cruise with **Fish Creek Scenic Boat Tours** (9448 Spruce St., 920/421-4442, http://doorcountyboats.com, $40) is the easiest way to take in the views of Chambers Island.

- **Friendly Charters** (920/256-9042, www.friendlycharters.com, from $45 pp) offers quiet tours of Fish Creek on their sailboat.

GILLS ROCK

- **Gills Rock Charters & Cruises** (920/421-0922, http://shorelinecharters.net, $42 pp) has narrated boat tours of Death's Door as well as popular sunset cruises.

BAILEYS HARBOR

- **Lakeshore Adventures** (8113 Hwy. 57, 920/839-2055, http://lakeshore-adventures.com, $59 pp) offers guided tours of the local bays in a clear-bottomed kayak.

DOOR COUNTY SHORELINE

DAY 4: Sister Bay to Washington Island

20 miles/32 kilometers | 1.5 hours, including ferry ride

ROUTE OVERVIEW: WI-42 • WI-42 Trunk • ferry • surface streets

❶ Grab breakfast at **Al Johnson's Swedish Restaurant** (10698 N. Bay Shore Dr., 920/854-2626, http://aljohnsons.com, 6am-9pm daily summer, shorter hours fall-spring, $8-18), the most famous eatery in the county. Atop the building's sod roof are live goats munching away.

❷ Take the awe-inspiring drive up and over the bluffs to the fishing village of **Gills Rock,** then hop a ferry to rustic **Washington Island** (Washington Island Ferry, 215 WI-42, Ellison Bay, 920/847-2546 or 800/223-2094, www.wisferry.com, round-trip $26 per vehicle, $13.50 passengers).

WASHINGTON ISLAND

> *Follow WI-42 N for 10 miles (16 km) to reach Gills Rock. Turn right onto WI-42 Trunk and continue for 2 miles (3 km) to reach the ferry departure point.*

❸ The nicest place on the island is **Jackson Harbor Inn** (920/847-2454, http://jacksonharborinn.com, Easter weekend-Oct., $60-120). Its guest rooms and cottage are meticulously kept by very friendly owners.

> *To reach the inn from the ferry landing, follow Lobdell Point Rd. north for 1.5 miles (2.5 km). Turn left onto Main Rd. and continue for 3 miles (5 km). Turn right onto Jackson Harbor Rd. and follow this for 4 miles (6 km) to the inn.*

DAY 5: Day Trip to Rock Island State Park

MORNING AND AFTERNOON

❶ Come morning, board the passenger-only ferry **Karfi** (920/847-2252, daily late May-mid-October, $11 round-trip) to the most isolated state park in Wisconsin, **Rock Island State Park** (920/847-2235, http://dnr.wi.gov, 6am-11pm daily). Note that drinking water is available on the island, but that's all; you have to bring everything you'll need and pack it out when you leave.

❷ You can cover Rock Island's perimeter on the **Thordarson Loop Trail** (5.2 mi/8.4 km loop, 2.5 hours, moderate). On the hike, you'll see one of the original lighthouses in Wisconsin, **Pottawatomie Light,** which was built in

1836. The trail's northeast section offers a magnificent view—on a clear day you can see all the way to Michigan's Upper Peninsula.

EVENING

❸ Take the ferry back to Washington Island. Grab dinner at **Nelsen's Hall Bitters Pub & Restaurant** (1201 Main Rd., 920/847-2496, from 11:30am daily, $18-25), set in a century-old structure in the center of the island. You'll hear quite a bit about the potent bitters—a traditional Scandinavian beverage. If you can stomach a shot, you'll be an official member of the Bitters Club, initiated in 1899.

> *Take Jackson Harbor Rd. to County Rd. W. Turn left and stay on County Rd. W as it travels west, then turns left to head south to Nelsen's Hall for a total of 5 miles (8 km).*

ROCK ISLAND STATE PARK

DAY 6: Washington Island to Baileys Harbor

35 miles/56 kilometers | 1.5 hours, including ferry ride

ROUTE OVERVIEW: Ferry • WI-42 Trunk • surface streets • WI-42 • surface streets

1 Take the earliest ferry back to the mainland and delve into the wilderness of **Newport State Park** (475 County Hwy. NP, 920/854-2500, http://dnr.wi.gov, 6am-11pm daily, $8-11 per vehicle). A popular trail is the **Europe Bay/Hotz Loop** (7 mi/11.3 km round-trip, 3 hours, moderate) to Europe Lake, one of the largest of the county's inland lakes and a pristine sandy gem uncluttered by development. The trail runs through sandy forests to rocky beaches with great views.

> Disembark the ferry at Gills Rock, then drive WI-42 Trunk for 2 miles (3 km) to Timberline Rd. Turn left and head to County Rd. NP (3 mi/5 km). Turn left, then make a right onto Newport Ln., following it to the state park.

2 Stop for a sweet treat in **Rowleys Bay** at **Grandma's Swedish Bakery** (1041 County Rd. ZZ, 920/854-2385, 7am-3pm daily May-Oct.). The specialties are the Swedish pastries—*limpa* and *skorpa* (thinly sliced pecan rolls sprinkled with cinnamon sugar and dried in the oven).

NEWPORT STATE PARK

> Retrace your path back to County Rd. NP and follow it west to WI-42 (3 mi/5 km). Turn left and take WI-42 S for 2 miles (3 km), then turn left onto Mink River Rd. Follow this for 3 miles (5 km), then turn left onto County Rd. ZZ to reach the bakery.

3 **Baileys Harbor** makes an unassuming retreat. Stay the night at what may be the most enviably sited lodging in all of Door County, **Gordon Lodge** (1420 Pine Dr., 920/839-2331, www.gordonlodge.com, $245-425). Spread across the tip of a promontory jutting into Lake Michigan's North Bay, the lodge offers lake views and rustic charm.

> Follow County Rd. ZZ for 5 miles (8 km) to Old Stage Rd. Turn left and drive 2.5 miles (4 km) to Woodcrest Rd. Turn left, then make another left at the first cross street onto County Q. Take County Q for 4 miles (6 km) to Gordon Lodge. Gordon Lodge is 6 miles (10 km) northeast of Baileys Harbor.

DAY 7: Baileys Harbor to Sturgeon Bay

35 miles/56 kilometers | 45 minutes-1 hour

ROUTE OVERVIEW: WI-57 • WI-42

1 Start your day with breakfast at **Harbor Fish Market and Grille** (8080 Hwy. 57, 920/839-9999, http://harborfishmarket-grille.com, from 7:30am daily Apr.-Oct., shorter hours Oct.-Dec., $10-16), a casual fine-dining place in a 120-year-old building.

2 Take a lazy drive down the lakeside to another happy place, **Whitefish Dunes State Park** (3275 Clark Lake Rd., 920/823-2400, http://dnr.wi.gov, 6am-8pm daily, $8-11 per vehicle). The buttermilk-colored dunes were formed by rough waves. Hike to the water, wander the beech forests, and explore the wetlands. Afterward, take the 2.5-mile (4 km) trail to explore Cave Point County Park's namesake caves.

> Take County Q for 5 miles (8 km) from Gordon Lodge to WI-57. On WI-57, drive south for 1 mile (1.6 km) to Baileys Harbor. From here, continue south on WI-57 to Cave Point Rd. (8 mi/13 km). Turn

WHITEFISH DUNES STATE PARK

left and follow Cave Point Rd. to the state park (3 mi/5 km).

❸ End your trip back in Sturgeon Bay at **Red Oak Winery** (3017 Enterprise Rd., 920/743-7729, www.redoakvineyard.com, 10:30am-5:30pm Sun.-Thurs., 9:30am-6pm Fri.-Sat., tasting $6). At this downtown tasting room, you can sample wines made from California grapes and one local cherry wine.

> Leaving the state park, drive southwest on Clarks Lake Rd. to access WI-57 (4 mi/6 km). Turn left and travel south on WI-57 to WI-42 (6 mi/10 km). Turn left and take WI-42 for 7 miles (11 km) to Red Oak Winery in Sturgeon Bay.

Getting There

There are no buses, no trains, and no ferries to Sturgeon Bay from points south. Auto traffic on a peak weekend here is intense, so be prepared and pack your patience.

AIR

The most direct option is to fly into Green Bay's **Austin Straubel International Airport** (GRB, 2077 Airport Dr., 920/498-4800, http://flygrb.com), which has daily flights from Chicago, Detroit, Minneapolis, Denver, Orlando, and Atlanta. There are car rentals available at the airport.

Milwaukee's **General Mitchell International Airport** (MKE, 5300 S. Howell Ave., 414/747-5300, www.mitchellairport.com) is the only international airport in the state and has the most direct flights around the country.

CAR

From **Austin Straubel International Airport** in Green Bay, it's 55 miles (89 km), which takes about an hour via WI-172, I-43, and WI-57.

To reach Sturgeon Bay from Milwaukee's **General Mitchell International Airport** requires a three-hour drive of 160 miles (255 km). Get there via I-43, WI-32, and WI-57.

WISCONSIN'S DOOR COUNTY

SONGS

● **"The World Is Waiting for the Sunrise" by Les Paul:** Self-taught jazz, blues, and country guitarist Les Paul is so legendary that his virtuoso techniques inspired the Gibson Les Paul guitar. He's also from Wisconsin. You can't go wrong with any Les Paul tune, but this 1950 song, recorded by Paul with Mary Ford, shows off his nimble-fingered talent.

● **"Skinny Love" by Bon Iver:** Wisconsin musician Justin Vernon heads up the folk-indie band Bon Iver, making music that's atmospheric and moody. This song, with its gentle guitar strums and Vernon's dreamy voice, was recorded in an isolated northern Wisconsin cabin.

● **"Blister in the Sun" by Violent Femmes:** This '80s-era rock-punk band hails from Milwaukee. Sing along to the fast drums and live-wire energy of this song after an invigorating hike at Potawatomi State Park.

NEW ENGLAND, NEW YORK, and PENNSYLVANIA

New England is a many-faceted region, home to bustling Boston, lighthouse-dotted Maine, New Hampshire's tall mountains, and the pretty villages of Vermont. In the Hudson River Valley, you'll cross paths with opulent estates and restaurants helmed by esteemed chefs. From there, you can venture into the wild landscapes of the Adirondacks and the Catskills. Bookended by Philadelphia and Pittsburgh, Pennsylvania Dutch Country rolls with gentle hills, home to Amish people and some of the nation's most historic sites.

◄ COVERED BRIDGE IN THE WHITE MOUNTAINS

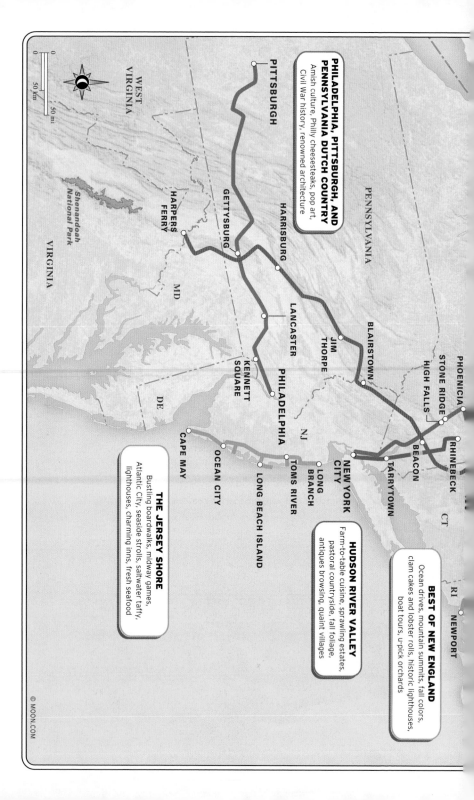

PHILADELPHIA, PITTSBURGH, AND PENNSYLVANIA DUTCH COUNTRY
Amish culture, Philly cheesesteaks, pop art, Civil War history, renowned architecture

HUDSON RIVER VALLEY
Farm-to-table cuisine, sprawling estates, pastoral countryside, fall foliage, antiques browsing, quaint villages

BEST OF NEW ENGLAND
Ocean drives, mountain summits, fall colors, clam cakes and lobster rolls, historic lighthouses, boat tours, u-pick orchards

THE JERSEY SHORE
Bustling boardwalks, midway games, Atlantic City, seaside strolls, saltwater taffy, lighthouses, charming inns, fresh seafood

PITTSBURGH

WEST VIRGINIA

VIRGINIA

Shenandoah National Park

HARPERS FERRY

GETTYSBURG

HARRISBURG

MD

DE

LANCASTER

JIM THORPE

KENNETT SQUARE

PHILADELPHIA

NJ

PENNSYLVANIA

BLAIRSTOWN

STONE RIDGE

HIGH FALLS

PHOENICIA

RHINEBECK

BEACON

TARRYTOWN

NEW YORK CITY

LONG BRANCH

TOMS RIVER

LONG BEACH ISLAND

OCEAN CITY

CAPE MAY

CT

RI

NEWPORT

0   50 km
0   50 mi

© MOON.COM

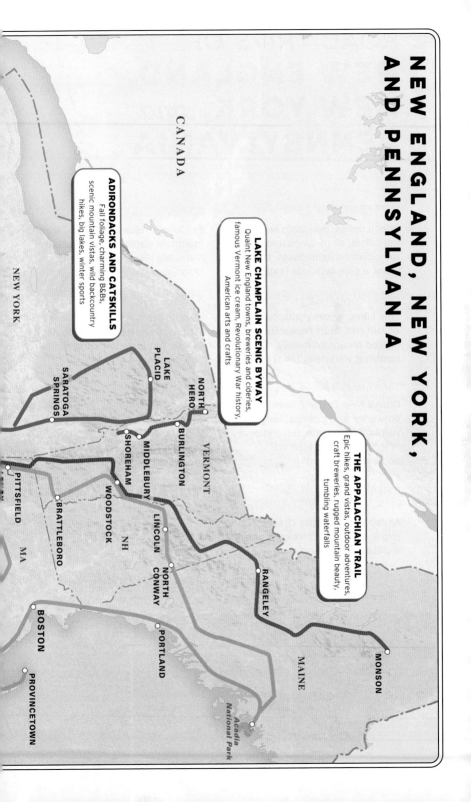

NEW ENGLAND, NEW YORK, AND PENNSYLVANIA

CANADA

ADIRONDACKS AND CATSKILLS
Fall foliage, charming B&Bs, scenic mountain vistas, wild backcountry hikes, big lakes, winter sports

LAKE CHAMPLAIN SCENIC BYWAY
Quaint New England towns, breweries and cideries, famous Vermont ice cream, Revolutionary War history, American arts and crafts

THE APPALACHIAN TRAIL
Epic hikes, grand vistas, outdoor adventures, craft breweries, rugged mountain beauty, tumbling waterfalls

NEW YORK

LAKE PLACID

SARATOGA SPRINGS

NORTH HERO

BURLINGTON

SHOREHAM

MIDDLEBURY

VERMONT

PITTSFIELD

BRATTLEBORO

WOODSTOCK

NH

LINCOLN

NORTH CONWAY

RANGELEY

MONSON

MA

BOSTON

PORTLAND

MAINE

PROVINCETOWN

Acadia National Park

ROAD TRIPS OF
NEW ENGLAND,
NEW YORK, *and*
PENNSYLVANIA

BEST OF NEW ENGLAND

Ocean drives, mountain summits, fall colors, clam cakes and lobster rolls, historic lighthouses, boat tours, u-pick orchards (PAGE 476)

THE APPALACHIAN TRAIL

Epic hikes, grand vistas, outdoor adventures, craft breweries, rugged mountain beauty, tumbling waterfalls (PAGE 494)

LAKE CHAMPLAIN SCENIC BYWAY

Quaint New England towns, breweries and cideries, famous Vermont ice cream, Revolutionary War history, American arts and crafts (PAGE 510)

PHILADELPHIA, PITTSBURGH, AND PENNSYLVANIA DUTCH COUNTRY

Amish culture, Philly cheesesteaks, pop art, Civil War history, renowned architecture (PAGE 518)

ADIRONDACKS AND CATSKILLS

Fall foliage, charming B&Bs, scenic mountain vistas, wild backcountry hikes, big lakes, winter sports (PAGE 530)

HUDSON RIVER VALLEY

Farm-to-table cuisine, sprawling estates, pastoral countryside, fall foliage, antiques browsing, quaint villages (PAGE 540)

THE JERSEY SHORE

Bustling boardwalks, midway games, Atlantic City, seaside strolls, saltwater taffy, lighthouses, charming inns, fresh seafood (PAGE 548)

LEFT TO RIGHT: WOODSTOCK, VERMONT; MOUNT WASHINGTON, NEW HAMPSHIRE; GETTYSBURG NATIONAL MILITARY PARK

1 Watch the sun crest over the Atlantic Ocean at **Acadia National Park** in Maine (PAGE 483).

2 Imagine what it's like to be a thru-hiker at the symbolic **midpoint of the Appalachian Trail** in **Harpers Ferry,** Maryland (PAGE 496).

3 Order a **Philly cheesesteak** like a local: "whiz wit" or "prov witout" (PAGE 520).

Acadia National Park

Harpers Ferry

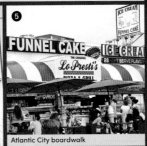

Philly cheesesteak

Brooklyn Bridge

Atlantic City boardwalk

4 Walk across the **Brooklyn Bridge,** stopping for Instagram-worthy photos along the way (PAGE 538).

5 Stroll **Atlantic City's** famous boardwalk (PAGE 552).

BEST OF
NEW ENGLAND

WHY GO: Ocean drives, mountain summits, fall colors, clam cakes and lobster rolls, historic lighthouses, boat tours, u-pick orchards

TOTAL DISTANCE: 1,340 miles/ 2,160 kilometers

NUMBER OF DAYS: 14

SEASONS: Late spring through autumn

START/END: Boston, Massachusetts

▼ ACADIA NATIONAL PARK

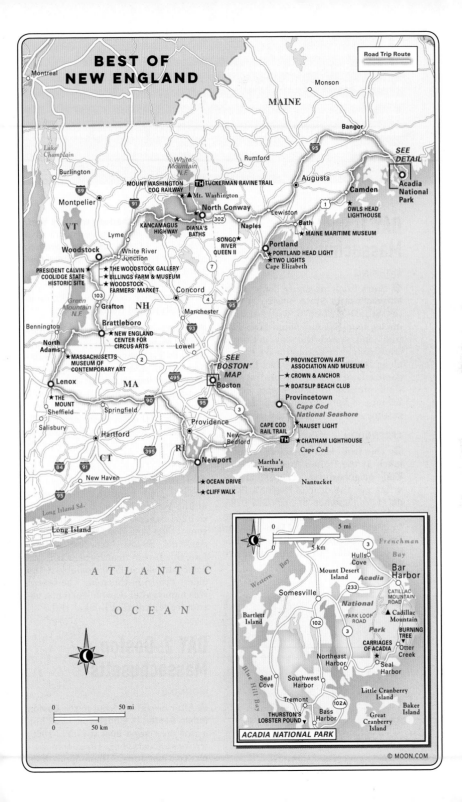

BEST OF NEW ENGLAND

Road Trip Route

MAINE

Montreal

Monson

Bangor

95

SEE DETAIL

Augusta

Rumford

Camden

Lake Champlain

Burlington

White Mountain N.F.

Acadia National Park

MOUNT WASHINGTON COG RAILWAY

TUCKERMAN RAVINE TRAIL

1

OWLS HEAD LIGHTHOUSE

89

Montpelier

91

▲ Mt. Washington

North Conway

Lewiston

Bath

VT

KANCAMAGUS HIGHWAY

302

Naples

★ MAINE MARITIME MUSEUM

Lyme

DIANA'S BATHS

SONGO RIVER QUEEN II

Portland

White River Junction

Woodstock

7

★ PORTLAND HEAD LIGHT

★ TWO LIGHTS

Cape Elizabeth

PRESIDENT CALVIN COOLIDGE STATE HISTORIC SITE

★ THE WOODSTOCK GALLERY

★ BILLINGS FARM & MUSEUM

★ WOODSTOCK FARMERS' MARKET

Concord

103

Grafton

NH

4

Green Mountain N.F.

Manchester

Bennington

Brattleboro

93

★ NEW ENGLAND CENTER FOR CIRCUS ARTS

North Adams

Lowell

★ MASSACHUSETTS MUSEUM OF CONTEMPORARY ART

2

495

Lenox

SEE "BOSTON" MAP

★ THE MOUNT

Boston

★ PROVINCETOWN ART ASSOCIATION AND MUSEUM

Sheffield

Springfield

MA

90

★ CROWN & ANCHOR

★ BOATSLIP BEACH CLUB

Salisbury

Hartford

Provincetown

Cape Cod National Seashore

95

★ NAUSET LIGHT

CT

84

91

New Haven

395

RI

Providence

3

New Bedford

CAPE COD RAIL TRAIL

TH

★ CHATHAM LIGHTHOUSE

Cape Cod

95

Newport

Martha's Vineyard

Nantucket

★ OCEAN DRIVE

★ CLIFF WALK

Long Island Sd.

Long Island

ATLANTIC

OCEAN

ACADIA NATIONAL PARK

0   5 mi

0   5 km

Frenchman Bay

3

Hulls Cove

Bar Harbor

Western Bay

Mount Desert Island

Acadia

233

CATILLAC MOUNTAIN ROAD

Somesville

National

▲ Cadillac Mountain

Bartlett Island

102

PARK LOOP ROAD

BURNING TREE

Park

3

Otter Creek

CARRIAGES OF ACADIA

★

Blue Hill Bay

Northeast Harbor

Seal Harbor

Little Cranberry Island

Seal Cove

Southwest Harbor

Baker Island

Tremont

102A

Bass Harbor

Great Cranberry Island

THURSTON'S LOBSTER POUND ▼

© MOON.COM

Boston is this trip's origination point, tempting you to stay awhile with its Revolutionary War history, convivial gathering spots, and belly-filling food. Once you depart the bustling city, you're in for a coastal-drive treat: a winding road trip dotted with charming seaside towns, shacks serving incredible seafood, and sunrises over the Atlantic Ocean. Be prepared to stop often. Whether it's to join a sailing excursion, take pictures of autumn foliage, trundle up a mountain on a train, or explore a funky arts scene, this road trip urges you to slow down and soak up the New England flavor.

DAY 1: Boston, Massachusetts

MORNING

❶ Start from the shiny dome of the **Massachusetts State House** (24 Beacon St., 617/727-3676, www.sec.state.ma.us, tours 10am-3:30pm Mon.-Fri., free) and spend the day getting a crash course in Revolutionary history along the **Freedom Trail** (www.thefreedomtrail.org). A red line on the sidewalk connects 16 historic sites on this 2.5-mile (4-km) walking trail ideal for getting your bearings in the city.

AFTERNOON

❷ The trail isn't complete without lunch at the Italian American North End neighborhood. There's always a line out the door of **Regina's Pizzeria** (11½ Thatcher St., 617/227-0765, www.reginapizzeria.com, 11am-11:30pm Sun.-Thurs., 11am-12:30am Fri.-Sat., $8-16), but joining the line is part of the fun at this landmark destination.

MASSACHUSETTS STATE HOUSE

❸ Stop by the **Charlestown Navy Yard**, where every 30 minutes sailors give free tours of the **USS Constitution,** aka "Old Ironsides." The **visitors center** (Charlestown Navy Yard, Building 5, 617/242-5601, www.nps.gov/bost, 9am-6pm daily, free) gives background on the ships and the naval yard.

❹ The Freedom Trail ends at the **Bunker Hill Monument** (Monument Square, 617/242-5641, www.nps.gov/bost, 9am-5pm daily mid-Mar.-Nov., 1pm-5pm Mon.-Fri., 9am-5pm Sat.-Sun. Dec.-mid-Mar., free). This 221-foot granite obelisk commemorates the first major battle of the Revolutionary War. To learn more, head across the street to the museum.

EVENING

❺ Unwind with a colonial-inspired cocktail and hand-shucked oysters at **The Warren Tavern** (2 Pleasant St., 617/241-8142, www.warrentavern.com, 11am-1am Mon.-Fri., 10am-1am Sat.-Sun., $8-25). According to local lore, this tavern near Bunker Hill has been here since 1780, making it the oldest tavern in the state. The tavern was named after Joseph Warren, a patriot leader killed at Bunker Hill.

DAY 2: Boston, Massachusetts

MORNING

❶ After breakfast, head to the **Boston Public Garden** (4 Charles St.) and hop a ride on a **swan boat** (617/522-1966, www.swanboats.com, 10am-4pm daily Apr.-mid-June, 10am-5pm daily

Top **5** BEST OF NEW ENGLAND

1. Travel back in time on Boston's historic 2.5-mile **Freedom Trail** (PAGE 478).

2. Watch the sun crest over the Atlantic Ocean at dawn at **Acadia National Park** (PAGE 483).

3. Summit **Mount Washington,** the highest peak in the northeastern United States (PAGE 485).

4. Journey to the "end of the world" at the far tip of **Cape Cod** (PAGE 490).

5. Eat Maine lobster rolls overlooking the iconic twin lighthouses, **Two Lights** (PAGE 481).

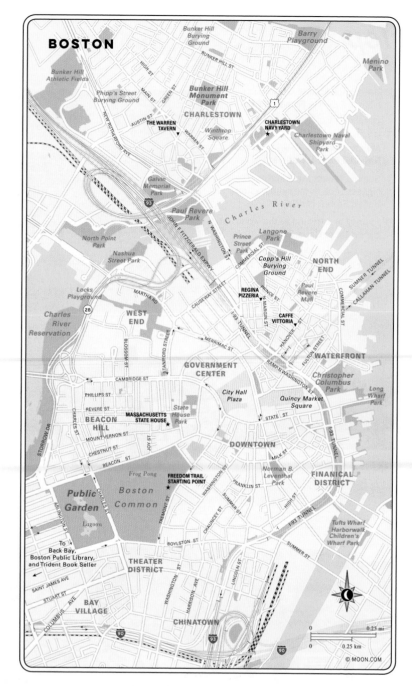

BOSTON

Bunker Hill
Burying
Ground

Barry
Playground

Menino
Park

Bunker Hill
Athletic Fields

HIGH ST
BUNKER HILL ST

Bunker Hill
Monument
Park

Phipp's Street
Burying Ground

MAIN ST
GREEN ST

CHARLESTOWN

NEW RUTHERFORD AVE

AUSTIN ST

THE WARREN
TAVERN

WARREN ST

Winthrop
Square

CHARLESTOWN
NAVY YARD

Charlestown Naval
Shipyard
Park

Galvin
Memorial
Park

93

Paul Revere
Park

Charles River

JOHN F FITZGERALD EXPWY

North Point
Park

N WASHINGTON ST

Prince
Street
Park

Langone
Park

COMMERCIAL ST

Nashua
Street Park

Copp's Hill
Burying
Ground

NORTH
END

SUMNER TUNNEL

CALLAHAN TUNNEL

Locks
Playground

MARTHA RD

28

CAUSEWAY STREET

REGINA
PIZZERIA

PRINCE ST

MARGIN ST

Paul
Revere
Mall

COMMERCIAL ST

Charles
River
Reservation

WEST
END

STANIFORD STREET

BLOSSOM ST

I-93 TUNNEL

MERRIMAC ST

CAFFE
VITTORIA

HANOVER ST

FULTON STREET

WATERFRONT

CAMBRIDGE ST

GOVERNMENT
CENTER

HAMPDEN ST

N WASHINGTON ST

Christopher
Columbus
Park

Long
Wharf
Park

PHILLIPS ST

CHARLES ST

REVERE ST

BEACON
HILL

MASSACHUSETTS
STATE HOUSE

State
House
Park

City Hall
Plaza

Quincy Market
Square

STORROW DR

MOUNT VERNON ST

JOY ST

STATE ST

CHESTNUT ST

DOWNTOWN

BEACON ST

MILK ST

I-93 TUNNEL

Frog Pong

FREEDOM TRAIL
STARTING POINT

Norman B.
Leventhal
Park

FINANICAL
DISTRICT

Public
Garden

Boston
Common

CHARLES ST

TREMONT ST

WASHINGTON ST

FRANKLIN ST

SUMMER ST

HIGH ST

ARLINGTON ST

Lagoon

CHAUNCEY ST

I-93 TUNNEL

To
Back Bay,
Boston Public Library,
and Trident Book Seller

BOYLSTON ST

SUMMER ST

Tufts Wharf
Harborwalk
Children's
Wharf Park

SAINT JAMES AVE

THEATER
DISTRICT

WASHINGTON ST

STUART ST

HARRISON AVE

LINCOLN ST

BAY
VILLAGE

COLUMBUS AVE

90

CHINATOWN

93

90

0   0.23 mi

0   0.25 km

© MOON.COM

AUTUMN IN BOSTON PUBLIC GARDEN

DAY 3: Boston to Portland, Maine

130 miles/209 kilometers | 2.5-3 hours

ROUTE OVERVIEW: I-93 • I-95 • US-1/Main St. • ME-77

❶ Stop by **Caffe Vittoria** (290 Hanover St., 617/227-7606, www.caffevittoria. com, 7am-midnight Sun.-Thurs., 7am-12:30am Fri.-Sat., $3-9) in the North End for an old-world cappuccino before heading to Portland, an easy, two-hour drive up the interstate.

❷ Just before you reach Portland, make a short detour to **Cape Elizabeth** to try a classic lobster roll at **The Lobster Shack** (225 Cape Lights Rd., 207/799-1677, www.lobstershack-twolights.com, 11am-8pm daily Mar.-Oct., $12-18). The restaurant perches above the crashing surf and overlooks **Two Lights,** famous twin lighthouses built in 1828. Although not open to the public, the eastern light is still an active light station, visible 17 miles at sea, while the western light stopped operating in 1924.

> Head north for 11 miles (18 km) on I-93, then merge onto I-95 N. Follow I-95 N for 95 miles (153 km) to US-1 S/Main St. Turn right on US-1 S/Main St. to Pleasant Hill Rd. Turn left, taking Pleasant Hill Rd. to ME-77. Turn left and drive 4 miles (6 km) to Two Lights Rd., following the road to The Lobster Shack.

❸ A short jog up the road is the most iconic among Portland's lighthouses, **Portland Head Light** (12 Captain Strout

mid-June-early Sept., shorter hours Apr.-mid-June and early Sept.-mid-Sept., $3.50 adults, $2 children 2-15). Take in the lagoon as you trace lazy circles—note the fairy-tale bridge, the surrounding willow trees trailing their branch tips in the water, and the tiny island in the center of the lagoon, which is used by ducks that pad up out of the water on an adorable, ducks-only ramp.

❷ Explore the most fashionable neighborhood in Boston, **Back Bay.** Duck into the **Boston Public Library** (700 Boylston St., 617/536-5400, www. bpl.org, 9am-9pm Mon.-Thurs., 9am-5pm Fri.-Sat., 1pm-5pm Sun.) and soak up the scholarly atmosphere and exquisite architecture.

AFTERNOON AND EVENING

❸ Keep with the literary vibe and swing by **Trident Booksellers and Café** (338 Newbury St., 617/267-8688, www. tridentbookscafe.com, 8am-midnight daily). Tucked inside a bookstore packed with wall-to-wall shelves of books and magazines, you'll find a bistro that serves breakfast and lunch, plus an espresso and tea bar.

❹ Spend the rest of the afternoon at the **Museum of Fine Arts** (465 Huntington Ave., 617/267-9300, www. mfa.org, 10am-5pm Sat.-Tues., 10am-10pm Wed.-Fri., $25 adults, $17 children under 18) and discover Impressionist treasures and artifacts from around the world. Grab dinner at one of Boston's many fabulous restaurants and stay the night in the city.

PORTLAND HEAD LIGHT

Cir., www.portlandheadlight.com, museum and gift shop 10am-4pm daily, park sunrise-sunset daily). Take in its slender proportions and red-roofed keeper's house, perfectly offset by jagged outcroppings and crashing waves.

> *Get back on ME-77 N and follow it for 2 miles (3 km) north to Shore Rd. Turn right and take Shore Rd. to Captain Strout Circle toward Portland Head Light.*

❹ Once in **Portland,** get a taste of the city's maritime life on a boat tour of Casco Bay with **Portland Schooner Co.** (Maine State Pier, 56 Commercial St., 207/766-2500, www.portlandschooner. com, $46 adults, $31 children 3-13). Take a turn hoisting the gaff-rigged sails—or let someone else do the work—on a two-hour cruise aboard the *Bagheera* or *Wendameen,* the company's 72- and 88-foot schooners.

> *Continue on Shore Rd. until you reach Broadway. Make a left and continue on to ME-77 N for 1.5 miles (2.5 km) into Portland.*

❺ Kick off the evening by exploring the city's evolving microbrewery scene. **Bunker Brewing Company** (17 Westfield St., 207/613-9471, www.bunkerbrewingco.com, noon-9pm Mon.-Thurs., noon-10pm Fri., 11am-10pm Sat., 11am-9pm Sun.) offers the mainstay Machine Czech Pilz, but also constantly turns out funky one-offs and collaborations like the Long Island Potato Stout.

DAY 4: Portland to Acadia National Park, Maine

170 miles/275 kilometers | 4-5 hours

ROUTE OVERVIEW: I-295 • US-1 • ME-73 • surface streets • ME-73 • US-1 • ME-3

❶ Make an essential breakfast stop at Portland's **Holy Donut** (7 Exchange St., 207/775-7776, www.theholydonut. com, 7:30am-4pm Mon.-Thurs., 8am-5pm Fri.-Sun., $2-5), a pilgrimage place for doughnut lovers. Arrive early for the best selection.

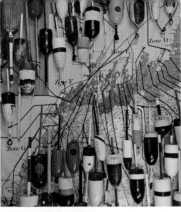

MAINE MARITIME MUSEUM

❷ Hit the road for a day of lighthouse-hopping and harbor-strolling. Drive up to **Bath** and work your way through the **Maine Maritime Museum** (243 Washington St., 207/443-1316, www.mainemaritimemuseum. org, 9:30am-5pm daily, $15.50 adults, $10 children 6-12), located in the Percy & Small shipyard. The yard is dominated by a soaring metal skeleton that evokes the *Wyoming,* the largest schooner ever made.

> *Take I-295 N for 22 miles (35 km) to US-1. Follow US-1 N for 9 miles (15 km) into Bath.*

❸ On your way up the coast, make a brief detour to the short and pert **Owls Head Lighthouse** (Lighthouse Rd., Owls Head, free). It commands beautiful views of the rocky coastline, and is accessible via a short, gentle walk through coastal forest.

⏱ WITH LESS TIME

PORTLAND TO ACADIA NATIONAL PARK

3 days; 210 miles/338 kilometers

In **three days,** you can savor the charms of **Portland** and nearby attractions in **one day,** such as the Maine Maritime Museum and Owls Head Lighthouse, before heading to **Acadia National Park.** This coastal park, sitting snugly on Mount Desert Island, warrants **two days** for hiking, camping, wildlife-watching, and exploration of **Bar Harbor** and other quaint seaside towns.

PICTURESQUE CAMDEN

DAY 5: Acadia National Park, Maine

40 miles/64 kilometers | 1.5 hours

ROUTE OVERVIEW: ME-3 • ME-102 • ME-3

1 Start the day early to catch **sunrise on Cadillac Mountain,** a pilgrimage place where you can see the first sunlight hit the U.S. coast. The 3.5-mile (5.6-km) **Cadillac Mountain Road,** off the Park Loop Road, winds up the mountain, which is how most visitors arrive in the early-morning hours, though there are also several walking trails to the summit.

2 Enjoy a low-key lunch with the local crowd at **Burning Tree Restaurant** (69 Otter Creek Dr., 207/288-9331, 5am-10pm Wed.-Mon., $25-36), located just outside of the park. Think scallops, mussels, just-caught halibut, and freshly grown veggies and herbs.

> *From the park entrance, drive 4 miles (6 km) on ME-3 E to the restaurant.*

3 Enjoy the rest of the day car-free in the national park. Rent a bike and cruise the extensive network of carriage trails that link great stone bridges, viewpoints, and rolling mountains. To really immerse yourself, take an actual carriage ride with **Carriages of Acadia** (Wildwood Stables, Park Loop Rd., 207/276-3622, tours from $20 adults, $12 children 6-12, $7 children 4-5).

> *To return to the park, head north then west on ME-3 (4 mi/6 km).*

> *Leave Bath on US-1 N, driving for 41 miles (66 km) to Buttermilk Ln. Turn right on Buttermilk and take it to ME-73. Turn left. Drive ME-73 N to Shore Dr.; turn right, and go then left on Main St. Next, turn left on Lighthouse Rd. to Owls Head Lighthouse.*

4 About a half-hour further is picturesque **Camden.** Stop for a stroll around the nautical boutiques. For lunch, grab nautical sandwiches from **Camden Deli** (37 Main St., 207/236-8343, www.camdendeli.com, 7am-10pm daily, $7-10) to take around the corner to the small park where benches face the water. Schooners and sleek yachts stand to attention at mooring buoys and floating docks.

> *Leave Owls Head via Lighthouse Rd. and Shore Dr. When you get to ME-73, turn right and continue on ME-73 N for 2 miles (3 km) until it turns into Main St. Stay on Main heading north as it becomes US-1 N. Drive this for 8 miles (13 km) to Camden.*

5 Make the final push to **Acadia National Park** (www.nps.gov/acad, $25 vehicles, $20 motorcycles, $12 cyclists and pedestrians) on **Mount Desert Island.** Settle in for the night at one of the park's campgrounds, or find a room at one of several inns that are just outside the park. Once you've bought your park pass, leave it displayed on your dashboard, as you'll be passing in and out of park lands while you're on Mount Desert Island.

> *Stay on US-1 N for 56 miles (90 km) until you get to Ellsworth. In Ellsworth, take ME-3 E for 16 miles (26 km) to Acadia National Park.*

SUNRISE VIEW FROM CADILLAC MOUNTAIN

KEY RESERVATIONS

- You'll need advance reservations to embark on the **Dive-In Theater Boat Cruise** at **Acadia National Park.**

- Book ahead for **train tickets** on the **Mount Washington Cog Railway** in New Hampshire.

DIANA'S BATHS

4 End the day with a real Maine lobster dinner at **Thurston's Lobster Pound** (9 Thurston Rd., Bernard, 207/244-7600, www.thurstonforlobster.com, 11am-9pm daily, $7-30), located at the edge of a scenic harbor.

> *Leave the park via ME-3, connecting to ME-102 N and continuing for 12 miles (19 km) to Thurston's Lobster Pound. Use the same route back to the park if you're camping there overnight.*

DAY 6: Acadia National Park to North Conway, New Hampshire

220 miles/355 kilometers | 5 hours

ROUTE OVERVIEW: ME-3 • US-1A • I-95 • ME-122 • ME-11 • ME-35 • US-302

1 The route to the White Mountains traverses the dark, deep forests of inland Maine, ticking off a series of towns that recall the state's immigrant heritage: Naples, Sweden, and Denmark. A worthy stop is **Naples**, where you can board the **Songo River Queen II** (841 Roosevelt Tr., 207/693-6861, www.songoriverqueen.net, $18-28 adults, $9-14 children 4-12). The double-decker Mississippi River-style paddle wheeler offers narrated cruises of Long Lake and unparalleled views of the White Mountains. Pick from one- or two-hour cruises, and enjoy snacks and drinks on board.

> *Leave Acadia via ME-3 N, driving for 16 miles (26 km) to Ellsworth. In Ellsworth, hop on US-1A W, following it for 13 miles (21 km). Get on I-95 S. Follow it for 105 miles (169 km). Take the exit for ME-122 W and continue for 10 miles (16 km). Turn left on ME-11 S. Follow it for 10 miles (16 km) until ME-35 N. Turn right to arrive in Naples.*

2 Stretch your legs on the walk to **Diana's Baths** (0.6 mi/1 km one-way, 45 minutes, easy), a series of small waterfalls perfect for an early-evening dip (if there's enough water). The trailhead is off West Side Road, northwest of North Conway. A parking lot is on the left with a self-service, cash-only fee station ($3).

> *Drive ME-35 S to US-302 (2 mi/3 km). Take US-302 W for 32 miles (51 km), then turn left on River Rd./West Side Rd. for 2.5 miles (4 km) to reach the parking lot for Diana's Baths.*

3 Head back south to **North Conway.** Fortify yourself with dinner and a beer at **May Kelly's Cottage** (3002 US-302, 603/356-7005, www.maykellys.com, 4pm-9pm Tues.-Thurs., noon-10pm Fri.-Sat., noon-8pm Sun., $9-22), which serves hearty Irish classics and American pub fare in a relaxed, old-world setting. With fabulous mountain views, the outdoor patio is perfect for an evening meal.

> *Retrace your path back to US-302 (2.5 mi/4 km). Turn left and head north on US-302 for less than a mile to reach May Kelly's Cottage.*

- **Boston Tea Party Ships and Museum, Boston** (306 Congress St., 617/338-1773, www.bostonteapartyship.com, 10am-5pm daily, $30 adults, $22 children): Get a taste of Revolutionary history at a hands-on museum with costumed actors and interactive exhibits.

- **Dive-In Theater Boat Cruise, Acadia National Park** (105 Eden St., Bar Harbor, 207/288-3483, www.divered.com, $42 adults, $32 children 6-11, $16 children under 6): See what's beneath the surface in this splashy, kid-focused nature outing from Bar Harbor with Diver Ed, who brings up touchable critters like sea stars, lobsters, and sea cucumbers.

- **Mount Washington Cog Railway, New Hampshire's White Mountains** (Base Rd., off Rte. 302, Bretton Woods, 603/278-5404, www.thecog.com, $72-87 adults, $41 children 4-12): Aspiring engineers and mountaineers will love the slow-moving, scenic trip on this 150-year-old mountain railway.

- **Scott Farm Orchard, Southern Vermont** (707 Kipling Rd., Dummerston, 802/254-6868, www.scottfarmvermont.com, 9am-5pm daily July-Nov.): Pick apples in a scenic orchard by Rudyard Kipling's Vermont home.

- **Cape Cod Baseball League, Cape Cod** (www.capecodbaseball.org): The free outdoor games held up and down the Cape are family-friendly ways to enjoy our national pastime without the crowds or hype—and you may just spot a future baseball great.

BOSTON TEA PARTY SHIPS AND MUSEUM

DAY 7: Day Trip to Mount Washington, New Hampshire

75 miles/121 kilometers | 2 hours

ROUTE OVERVIEW: US-302

❶ To take in the mountain peaks and rugged scenery of the White Mountains, chug to the top of **Mount Washington**—the highest peak in the northeastern United States—in colorful carriages on the 150-year-old **cog railway** (Base Station Rd., Bretton Woods, 603/278-5404, www.thecog.com, $69-75 adults, $39 children 4-12). When going to the summit, it's worth bringing more clothing than seems necessary, as temperatures can be frigid even when the valley is balmy.

> *Leave North Conway on US-302 W and go 31 miles (50 km). At Base Station Rd., turn right. Follow Base Station for 6 miles (10 km) to Mount Washington Cog Railway.*

❷ If the weather is clear at the summit of Mount Washington, consider hiking the **Tuckerman Ravine Trail** (4.2 mi/6.8 km one-way, 3 hours, strenuous) back instead of taking the railway down. Make sure to bring

THE COG RAILWAY ON MOUNT WASHINGTON

sturdy hiking shoes, plenty of water and snacks, and wear layered clothing. Temperatures at the summit can be bone-chillingly cold.

❸ Back in town, spend the night at the cozy **Red Elephant Inn Bed & Breakfast** (28 Locust Ln., 603/356-3548, www.redelephantinn.com, $129-209), where you'll find modern comforts and gourmet treats.

> *Retrace your path to North Conway via Base Station Rd. (6 mi/10 km) and US-302 E (31 mi/50 km).*

WOODSTOCK, VERMONT

DAY 8: North Conway to Woodstock, Vermont

120 miles/193 kilometers | 3-3.5 hours

ROUTE OVERVIEW: US-302 • NH-112 • NH-116 • NH-10 • River Rd. • NH-25 • VT-25 • I-91 • I-89 • US-4

❶ Take the **Kancamagus Highway** (35 mi/56 km) from Conway to Lincoln for a swooping, scenic drive through the mountains. This cross section of the White Mountains' rugged terrain has fabulous views, especially when autumn turns the surrounding forest into a riot of color. There are plenty of places to stop along the way on the Kancamagus Highway—look for clusters of cars along the side of the road, which often signals a favorite local swimming spot.

> *Take US-302 E out of Conway to NH-112 W (5 mi/8 km). Turn right and drive for 35 miles (56 km) to Lincoln.*

❷ Make your way across the border into Vermont and reach **Woodstock.** Wander the downtown area and visit the town's vibrant art galleries; they are in a compact central cluster on Elm and Central Streets and easily managed on foot. Start on Elm at **The Woodstock Gallery** (6 Elm St., 802/457-2012, www.woodstockgalleryvt.com, 10am-5pm Mon.-Sat., noon-4:30pm Sun.), where fine and folk artists offer their takes on the New England landscape.

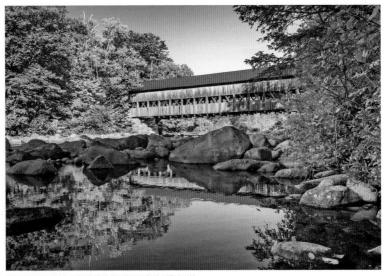

COVERED BRIDGE ALONG THE KANCAMAGUS HIGHWAY

> Continue on NH-112 W for 13 miles (21 km) to NH-116. Take NH-116 W for 10 miles (16 km) to NH-10. Follow NH-10 S for 6 miles (10 km) to River Rd. Turn right. Take River Rd. 4 miles (6 km) to NH-25 W, following it into Vermont. Continue on VT-25 N to I-91. Take I-91 S for 27 miles (43 km). Use I-89 N to access US-4. Stay on US-4 W for 10 miles (16 km) into Woodstock.

❸ After lunch, experience Vermont's agricultural heritage with wagon rides, award-winning cheddar, and a picture-perfect herd of Jersey cows at the **Billings Farm & Museum** (53 Elm St., 802/457-2355, www.billingsfarm. org, 10am-5pm daily May-Oct., shorter hours Nov.-Feb., $14 adults, $8 children 5-15, $4 children 3-4).

❹ Wind down for the evening with dinner at the relaxed and convivial **Worthy Kitchen** (442 E. Woodstock Rd., 802/457-7281, www.worthyvermont. com, 4pm-10pm Mon.-Fri., 11am-10pm Sat., 10am-9pm Sun., $8-15), a "farm diner" that has a hearty selection of pub food with flair, from fried chicken to poutine. Stay the night in town.

DAY 9: Woodstock to Brattleboro, Vermont

75 miles/121 kilometers | 2-2.5 hours

ROUTE OVERVIEW: US-4 • VT-100A • VT-100 • VT-103 • VT-35

❶ Before starting the day's scenic drive to Brattleboro, pick up some picnic supplies at the **Woodstock Farmers' Market** (979 W. Woodstock Rd., 802/457-3658, www.woodstockfarmersmarket.com, 7:30am-7pm Tues.-Sat., 8am-6pm Sun.), a specialty food shop that stocks locally made treats, cheese, beer, and wine.

❷ Hit the road and make your way to the **President Calvin Coolidge State Historic Site** (3780 VT-100A, 802/672-3773, www.vtstateparks.com, 9:30am-5pm daily late May-mid-Oct., $9 adults, $2 children 6-14) to see the 30th president's family homestead. This is one of the best presidential historic sites in the country. Outdoor tables have an idyllic view of Silent Cal's childhood home and make for an ideal lunch spot.

> Drive 8 miles (13 km) via US-4 W, then turn left on VT-100A S. Take this for 6 miles (10 km) to the President Calvin Coolidge State Historic Site.

▶ **Playlist**

BEST OF NEW ENGLAND

SONGS

● **"More Than a Feeling" by Boston:** This is a great road trip song on its own merit—propulsive, fist-pumping, sing-along-worthy—but it's apt because this 1970s-era band hails from Beantown. Let this be your launch song.

● **"Mrs. Robinson" by The Lemonheads:** Boston-bred band The Lemonheads—of 1990s, not-quite-grunge fame—retooled this Simon and Garfunkel classic into something faster and edgier. It's an ideal accompaniment for a drive along the rocky New England cliffs of the Atlantic Ocean.

● **"Moonlight in Vermont" by Ella Fitzgerald and Louis Armstrong:** Ms. Fitzgerald and Mr. Armstrong play this song slow and moody and jazzy. If you're driving through the Green Mountain State when the weather is cool, listen to this as you pull your sweater tighter and wrap your fingers around a mug of warm cocoa.

GRAFTON, VERMONT

3 Continue south, winding through pretty villages. Be sure to stop at picture-perfect **Grafton** to taste some of Vermont's finest cheddar at the **Grafton Village Cheese Company** (56 Townshend Rd., 802/843-1062, www.graftonvillagecheese.com, 10am-5pm daily).

> Continue on VT-100A S to VT-100 S. Turn left and drive for 9 miles (15 km). Make a left onto VT-103 S, following it for 15 miles (24 km). In Chester, pick up VT-35 S, driving it for 7 miles (11 km) to Grafton.

4 Once in **Brattleboro,** catch a performance at the town's **New England Center for Circus Arts** (209 Austine Dr., www.necenterforcircusarts.org, $10-20) and have dinner at one of the town's many farm-to-table restaurants.

> Leave Grafton on VT-35 S, taking it to VT-30 S (4 mi/6 km). Stay on VT-30 S for 17 miles (27 km) to Brattleboro.

DAY 10: Brattleboro to Lenox, Massachusetts

75 miles/121 kilometers | 2-2.5 hours

ROUTE OVERVIEW: VT-9 • VT-8 • MA-8 • Merrill Rd. • US-7

1 After breakfast, make your way south into Massachusetts, watching as the mountains taper into gentle hills. Spend the morning with cutting-edge modern art in **North Adams**

at the **Massachusetts Museum of Contemporary Art** (1040 MASS MoCA Way, 413/662-2111, www.massmoca.org, 11am-5pm Wed.-Mon. late June-Sept., 10am-6pm Sun.-Wed., 10am-7pm Thurs.-Sat. Oct.-late June, $18 adults, $8 children 6-16). Composed of 27 redbrick former factory buildings and connected by an interlocking network of bridges, walkways, and courtyards, Mass MoCA, as it's known, has vast gallery spaces that allow for artwork of an unusually epic scale.

> Drive VT-9 W for 26 miles (42 km) out of Brattleboro. In Searsburg, turn left on VT-8 S. Take this for 13 miles (21 km) into Massachusetts, where it becomes MA-8. Stay on MA-8 S for 4 miles (6 km) into North Adams.

2 Just down the street is **Public Eat + Drink** (34 Holden St., 413/664-4444, www.publiceatanddrink.com, from 4pm Mon.-Thurs., from 11:30am Fri.-Sun., $10-20), where industrial cool meets farm-to-table.

3 After lunch, continue south to **Lenox** to visit the elegant home of Edith Wharton. Tour **The Mount** (2 Plunkett St., 413/551-5100, www.edithwharton.org, 10am-5pm daily mid-May-Oct., $18 adults, free for children under 18) and see where the famous author hosted a who's who of intellectuals and artists.

> Leave North Adams via MA-8 S, driving it for 18 miles (29 km) to Merrill Rd. Follow Merrill Rd. for 6 miles (10 km) to US-7, then drive 9 miles (14 km) on US-7 S to Lenox.

THE MOUNT, HOME OF EDITH WHARTON

④ Enjoy a quiet evening at **Brava** (27 Housatonic St., 413/637-9171, www.bravalenox.com, 5pm-1am daily, $14-22), a wine bar where you can mingle with musicians from nearby Tanglewood. Spend the night in town.

DAY 11: Lenox to Newport, Rhode Island

170 miles/275 kilometers | 3.5-4 hours

ROUTE OVERVIEW: I-90 • MA-146 • RI-146 • I-295 • I-95 • RI-4 • RI-138 • Ocean Dr.

① Head for the coast to wind up in the pretty port city of **Newport,** Rhode Island. Start your exploration with the waterside **Cliff Walk** (175 Memorial Blvd., signed entrance at the western edge of Easton's Beach, www.cliffwalk.com), making your way from Easton's Beach towards Baily's Beach. Along the way, gawk at some of the grandest Gilded Age estates in New England.

> Get on I-90 E and follow it for 150 miles (241 km). Take the exit for MA-146 and drive MA-146 S for 25 miles (40 km), crossing into Rhode Island, where it turns into RI-146 S. Then take I-295 S, driving it 19 miles (31 km) until it merges with I-95 S, staying on it for 3 miles (5 km), and then jumping on RI-4 S for 11 miles (18 km). Take RI-138 E for 9 miles (14 km) into Newport.

② At the end of the walk, reward yourself with great piles of clam cakes, lobster rolls, and stuffed quahogs at **Flo's Clam Shack** (4 Wave Ave., Middletown, 401/847-8141, www.flosclamshacks.com, 11am-9pm daily, $5-22), before heading to the beach to while away the day in the sand.

③ When the sun begins to slip, hop on **Ocean Drive** (10 mi/16 km) to trace the southern tip of Aquidneck Island on a scenic drive past a historic fort, elegant inns, and Rhode Island's finest kite-flying. There's no better way to catch the sunset. While Ocean Drive follows various roads, it's clearly signposted at every turn.

> Join Ocean Dr. by going south on Bellevue Ave. to Ruggles Ave. Go west on Ruggles for less than a mile, then turn left onto Carroll Ave. This leads to Ocean Dr. in less than a mile.

④ On Ocean Drive, stop at **Castle Hill Inn** (590 Ocean Dr., 401/849-3800, www.castlehillinn.com, 11:30am-7pm

CASTLE HILL INN, NEWPORT, RHODE ISLAND

daily) for sundowners on The Lawn, one of the loveliest stretches of grass in Newport. Stay the night downtown; there's an inn on every corner.

> To reach Castle Hill Inn, head to the westernmost point of Ocean Dr. To return downtown, follow Ridge Rd./Harrison Ave. east to Ruggles Ave. (3 mi/5 km).

DAY 12: Newport to Provincetown, Massachusetts

120 miles/193 kilometers | 3 hours

ROUTE OVERVIEW: RI-24 • MA-24 • I-195 • MA-25 • US-6

NAUSET LIGHT

① Drive all the way to "the end of the world"—that's colorful, creative **Provincetown** to you—to spend your last days exploring **Cape Cod**. Make a beeline for the **Cape Cod National Seashore** (Salt Pond Visitor Center, Rte. 6 at Nauset Rd., Eastham, 508/255-3421, www.nps.gov/caco, 9am-5pm daily late May-mid-Oct., shorter hours mid-Oct.-late May) when you arrive, where you'll find the finest beaches in New England. Spend a day wandering the miles of sandy beaches with nothing but waves between you and Portugal.

> Depart Newport on W. Main Rd. for 7 miles (11 km), then take RI-24 N for 8 miles (13 km). As it enters Massachusetts, RI-24 N turns into MA-24 N. Follow it to I-195 E, driving this route for 26 miles (42 km). Then take MA-25 E for 10 miles (16 km) to US-6 E for 35 miles (56 km). At the traffic circle, continue north on US-6 for another 3 miles (5 km) to reach the Salt Pond Visitor Center.

② For a scenic walk, it's hard to beat a stroll down Coast Guard Beach to **Nauset Light.** The 1.5-mile (2.5-km) stretch of sand is among the finest in the Northeast. The stairs to Nauset Light often get washed away in winter storms and may not be accessible early in the season. Keep your eyes peeled for seals and whales; this is a particularly good place to watch wildlife from the shore.

> Go north on School House Rd. for 1 mile (1.6 km). Turn left onto Nauset Rd., then right onto Cable Rd. Follow this for less than a mile to the beach.

CAPE COD NATIONAL SEASHORE

Coastal CHARM

New England's got beaches for days. Here are some of the best ones.

- **Popham Beach, Coastal Maine** (10 Perkins Farm Ln., Phippsburg, 207/389-1335, $8 adults, $1 children 5-11): This stretch of shoreline offers the best of Maine: a sandy beach at the end of a scenic peninsula and a little rocky island to explore at low tide.

- **Bar Island, Acadia National Park** (follow Bridge St. from downtown Bar Harbor): The path from Bar Harbor to this forested islet only becomes a beach at low tide, which makes it the perfect place to find stranded sea creatures and tidepools.

- **Sachuest Beach, Newport** (aka Second Beach, 474 Sachuest Point Rd., 401/847-1993, parking $20 weekends, $10 weekdays): Catch an

easygoing summer swell at Sachuest Beach, a favorite surf spot just outside of downtown Newport.

- **Coast Guard Beach, Cape Cod** (Cape Cod National Seashore, www.nps.gov/caco): Endless sand lined with wild roses, dramatic cliffs, and windswept lighthouses make this one of the best beaches in the East, and it's a favorite place for watching whales without leaving dry land.

- **Race Point Beach, Cape Cod** (Race Point Beach, Rte. 6, 508/487-9930, www.racepointlighthouse.org): The far tip of Cape Cod is nothing but beach, rolling dunes, and hidden shacks—for the ultimate "end of the world" experience, sleep at the remote Race Point Light.

SACHUEST BEACH, NEWPORT

❸ Stay the night in Provincetown at the secluded **Land's End Inn** (22 Commercial St., 508/487-0706, www.landsendinn.com, $405-680) and watch the sun rise—and set—from a glassed-in tower. A breakfast buffet, afternoon wine bar, and 24-hour tea and coffee make this a soothing place to watch the tide come in.

> *Retrace your path to US-6 (2 mi/3 km), then continue north for 19 miles (31 km) to reach Provincetown.*

DAY 13: Provincetown, Massachusetts

MORNING AND AFTERNOON

❶ Get a taste of Provincetown's artistic heritage by strolling the downtown galleries. The majority are on **Commercial Street** between Montello Street and Howland Street. If you only make one stop for art here, the **Provincetown Art Association and Museum** (460 Commercial St., 508/487-1750, www.paam.org, 11am-8pm Tues.-Fri.,

11am-5pm Sat.-Mon. June-Sept., shorter hours Oct.-May, $10) is a treasure trove of local artwork.

❷ Stop for lunch at **Canteen** (225 Commercial St., 508/487-3800, www.thecanteenptown.com, 10am-8pm daily summer, shorter hours fall-spring, $7-19), a tourist joint that's also a local favorite. The nautical theme of this casual lunch spot is bright and hip, and the lack of elbow room at large communal tables means it's easy to make friends.

❸ Join **Art's Dune Tours** (4 Standish St., 508/487-1950, www.artsdunetours.com, Apr.-Nov., $29 adults, $18 children 6-11) for a tour of the rustic artists' shacks scattered amid the rolling sand dunes.

EVENING

❹ Start your evening early at the Tea Dance at the **Boatslip Beach Club** (161 Commercial St., 508/487-1669, www.boatslipresort.com, 4pm-7pm daily summer, 4pm-7pm Sat.-Sun. spring and fall), where revelers sip a dangerously powerful planter's punch that sloughs both inhibitions and clothing.

❺ Spend a night on the town in true P-town style with tickets to a drag show. The surreal Dina Martina is a fixture of the scene, with regular appearances at the **Crown & Anchor** (247 Commercial St., 508/487-1430, www.onlyatthecrown.com, $28). Dina's offbeat monologues and comically bad singing make her a local favorite.

DAY 14: Provincetown to Boston, Massachusetts

145 miles/233 kilometers | 3-4 hours

ROUTE OVERVIEW: US-6 • surface streets • MA-28 • US-6 • MA-3

❶ Start your last day of New England adventures with fried-dough *malasadas,* lightly caramelized egg tarts, and cream-filled *bolas de berlim* from Provincetown's **Portuguese Bakery** (299 Commercial St., 508/487-1803, 8am-5pm daily Apr.-Nov., $2-8).

❷ If traffic is hopelessly snarled on the Cape's one highway, take a break and explore the **Cape Cod Rail Trail,** a mostly flat 22-mile (35-km) bicycle path. Swap your car for a bike at **Dennis Cycle Center** (249 Great Western Rd., South Dennis, 508/398-0011, www.denniscyclecenter.com, rentals from $14).

COMMERCIAL STREET, PROVINCETOWN

CHATHAM LIGHTHOUSE

> *To get to the rental shop, go south on US-6 for 34 miles (55 km). The rail trail is directly behind the shop.*

❸ Break up the return drive to Boston with a stop to see the pretty **Chatham Lighthouse** (37 Main St., tours 1pm-3:30pm Wed. May-Oct., free). Continue to Boston and wave goodbye to New England on your flight home.

> *From the bike rental shop, head east on Great Western Rd. for 2.5 miles (4 km). Once it turns into Main St., follow it for another mile, then take a right onto Chatham Rd. and continue for 1.5 miles (2.5 km). Turn left onto MA-28 S and continue for 5 miles (8 km). Continue along Main St. for 1 mile (1.6 km) to reach the lighthouse. To return to Boston, retrace your path to US-6 (7 mi/11 km). Follow US-6 W for 30 miles (48 km), then continue north on MA-3 for 52 miles (84 km). Take exit 23 for Government Center to reach central Boston.*

Getting There

AIR

Flights to Boston's **Logan International Airport** (BOS, www.massport.com/logan) are available from almost all major cities. From Logan, ground transportation can be arranged from the information desk at baggage claim. The most efficient way to get into the city is via taxi, though expect to pay a minimum of $25 for downtown locations, or shared van service to downtown and Back Bay for $20-25 per person.

Far cheaper (and almost as quick) is the MBTA Silver Line bus (www.mbta.com); inbound rides on SL1 from Logan Airport to Boston's South Station are free, and leave from stops directly in front of each terminal. Buses leave several times an hour 5am-1am, and reach South Station in 15-25 minutes. If you're continuing to downtown stops or Cambridge, request a free transfer for the MBTA Red Line subway route.

TRAIN

From most destinations, **Amtrak** (South Station, Summer St. and Atlantic Ave., 800/872-7245, www.amtrak.com) runs service to both the South Station and Back Bay Station. (Amtrak trains from all destinations in Maine run to the North Station.) The **Massachusetts Bay Transportation Authority** (617/222-5000, www.mbta.com) also runs commuter rail service from locations in Greater Boston for fares of up to $6.

BUS

Buses arrive at the **South Station** (Summer St. and Atlantic Ave.). Most U.S. destinations are served by **Greyhound** (800/231-2222, www.greyhound.com). However, smaller bus companies also run from various locations around the region, such as the **BoltBus** (877/265-8287, www.boltbus.com), **Megabus** (www.megabus.com), and **Peter Pan Bus** (800/343-9999, www.peterpanbus.com).

CAR

It's less than 5 miles (8 km) from Logan International Airport to Boston's city center, but heavy traffic turns the trip into a nearly 20-minute drive. From the airport, take MA-1A South directly into town.

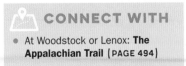

CONNECT WITH

● At Woodstock or Lenox: **The Appalachian Trail** (PAGE 494)

THE APPALACHIAN TRAIL

WHY GO: Epic hikes, grand vistas, outdoor adventures, craft breweries, rugged mountain beauty, tumbling waterfalls

TOTAL DISTANCE: 1,185 miles/ 1,910 kilometers

NUMBER OF DAYS: 11

SEASONS: Spring through fall

START: Harpers Ferry, West Virginia

END: Baxter State Park, Maine

▼ BAXTER STATE PARK, MAINE

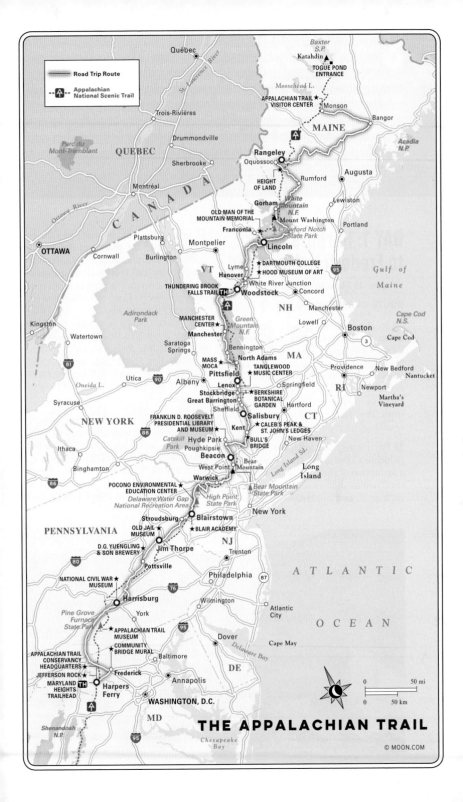

THE APPALACHIAN TRAIL

Starting in Harpers Ferry, West Virginia, this trip follows the northern sections of the epic Appalachian Trail—the world's longest continuously marked hiking trail. The journey heads north into nine states: Maryland, Pennsylvania, New Jersey, New York, Connecticut, Massachusetts, Vermont, New Hampshire, and Maine. Travelers will enjoy plenty of spots to hike portions of the historic Appalachian Trail, including summit hikes that reward hard work with panoramic views. Mountain vistas line the drive, and pleasant strolls that end in crashing waterfalls make this a worthy road trip for non-hikers, too.

DAY 1: Harpers Ferry to Frederick, Maryland

30 miles/48 kilometers | 1 hour

ROUTE OVERVIEW: US-340 • I-70

❶ In **Harpers Ferry**, visit the **Appalachian Trail Conservancy Headquarters** (799 Washington St., 304/535-6331, www.appalachiantrail.org, 9am-5pm daily), the symbolic midpoint of the Appalachian Trail for thru-hikers. Pick up maps or AT-themed books from the shop, or just absorb the wealth of trail history.

❷ Pay respects at **Jefferson Rock** (Appalachian Trail south from Church St.), a formation of Harpers shale named after Thomas Jefferson. (Don't climb or sit it on it, as it's extremely unstable.)

❸ Hop in the car; it's not very far to the trailhead for **Maryland Heights** (3 mi/5 km round-trip, 2 hours, moderate). Where the trail ends is an overlook that provides a premium view of Harpers Ferry. Find the trailhead on Harpers Ferry Road.

> Follow US-340 N/William L. Wilson Fwy. for 3 miles (5 km). Take the exit for Keep Tryst Rd., then turn right on Sandy Hook Rd. Follow this for 1.5 miles (2.5 km), after which it becomes Harpers Ferry Rd. to reach Maryland Heights Trailhead.

❹ Continue on to **Frederick,** where you'll spend the night; be sure to walk downtown and glimpse the **Community Bridge Mural** (S. Carroll St. between E. Patrick and E. All Saints Sts.). Here, a concrete bridge has been painted to look like an old stone bridge and

VIEW OF HARPERS FERRY FROM MARYLAND HEIGHTS

Top ⑤ THE APPALACHIAN TRAIL

① Imagine what it's like to be a thru-hiker at the symbolic **midpoint of the Appalachian Trail** (PAGE 496).

② Tour the **Yuengling Brewery,** where the East Coast-favored beer is made (PAGE 499).

③ Glimpse the Hudson River from the top of **Bear Mountain** (PAGE 502).

④ Enjoy an outdoor performance at **Tanglewood Music Center,** summer home of the Boston Symphony Orchestra (PAGE 504).

⑤ Hike to the jaw-dropping **Arethusa Falls** in **White Mountain National Forest** (PAGE 506).

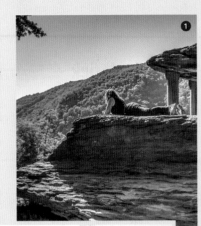

incorporates 180 unique images, some of which look like they were "carved" into the fake stone.

> Follow Sandy Hook Rd. back to the freeway and join US-340 E (2 mi/3 km). Follow US-340 E to I-70 E for 17 miles (27 km). Exit for South East St. Turn left and drive into Frederick.

DAY 2: Frederick to Harrisburg, Pennsylvania

100 miles/161 kilometers | 2.5 hours

ROUTE OVERVIEW: US-15 • PA-394 • Old Carlisle Rd. • PA-34 • I-81 • US-22 • surface streets

❶ Grab breakfast in Frederick, then drive to **Pine Grove Furnace State Park** (1100 Pine Grove Rd., Gardners, 717/486-7174, www.dcnr.pa.gov, 8am-9pm daily, free) to see the true halfway point of the trail at the **Appalachian Trail Museum** (1120 Pine Grove Rd., Gardners, 717/486-8126, www.atmuseum.org, Apr.-Oct., free). It celebrates the experience of the trail, highlighting the stories of thru-hikers and trail pioneers like Grandma Gatewood, Gene Espy, and Ed Garvey.

> Join US-15 N, driving it for 38 miles (61 km). Take the PA-394 exit. Turn left to follow PA-394 for 3 miles (5 km) to Old Carlisle Rd. Take a slight right onto Old Carlisle and follow it north for 7 miles (11 km), when the road becomes PA-34. Continue north for 4 miles (6 km). Turn left onto Pine Grove Rd. and follow it for 4 miles (6 km) to reach the state park.

❷ Get to **Harrisburg,** Pennsylvania, in time to visit the **National Civil War Museum** (1 Lincoln Cir. at Reservoir Park, 717/260-1861, www.nationalcivilwarmuseum.org, 10am-5pm Mon.-Tues. and Thurs.-Sat., 10am-8pm Wed., noon-5pm Sun., $13 adults, $11 children 6-17). You'll find uniforms, weapons, and tools used by soldiers more than 150 years ago.

> Retrace your path back to PA-34 (4 mi/6 km), turning left at Green Mountain Rd. to rejoin PA-34. Continue north for 8 miles (13 km). Merge onto I-81 N and continue for 20 miles (32 km). Take the exit for US-22 E; follow this for 1 mile (1.6 km) until it becomes Arsenal Blvd. Follow Arsenal for another mile; it will lead you to central Harrisburg and the museum.

❸ Spend the evening walking Harrisburg's historic streets and enjoying a nice dinner at **Home 231** (231 North St., 717/232-4663, www.home231.com, 11am-2pm and 5pm-10pm Mon.-Fri., 5pm-10pm Sat., 9am-2pm Sun., $29-35).

PINE GROVE FURNACE STATE PARK

DAY 3: Harrisburg to Jim Thorpe, Pennsylvania

85 miles/137 kilometers | 2-2.5 hours

ROUTE OVERVIEW: US-22 • I-81 • PA-125 • US-209 • PA-309 • PA-54 • US-209

❶ After breakfast in Harrisburg, drive through the towns of Pennsylvania coal country. Stop to stretch your legs in the old mining city of **Pottsville.** Here, you can take a tour of **D.G. Yuengling & Son Brewery** (Mahantongo St. and S. 5th St., 570/628-4890, www.yuengling.com, 9am-4pm Mon.-Fri., 10am-3pm Sat., free), which people know—and love—today as simply Yuengling. Closed-toe shoes are required for the tour.

> Take US-22 W to I-81 N (2 mi/3 km). Follow I-81 N for 35 miles (56 km). Take exit 104 toward PA-125. Follow PA-125 N for 4 miles (6 km) to US-209 N, driving for 11 miles (18 km) to Pottsville. Turn right onto 6th St. and left on Mahantongo St. to reach the brewery.

❷ Just a few blocks away, get sustenance at **Ruby's Kitchen** (212 S. 2nd St., 570/581-8772, 10am-4pm Mon.-Fri., under $15), a lunch counter for the midday crowd serving up mouthwatering fare like chicken salad croissants and cheesesteaks.

❸ Continue to the town of **Jim Thorpe,** where you can visit the 27 cells of the

D.G. YUENGLING & SON BREWERY, POTTSVILLE, PENNSYLVANIA

Old Jail Museum (128 W. Broadway, 570/325-5259, www.theoldjailmuseum.com, tours noon-4:15pm Thurs.-Tues. summer, noon-4:15pm Sat.-Sun. Sept.-Oct., $5-7).

> From Pottsville, get on US-209 N and drive for 15 miles (24 km). In Tamaqua, turn left onto Mauch Chunk St., then left again onto PA-309 N/Pine St. Follow this for 1 mile (1.6 km), then turn right onto PA-54. Follow this for 8 miles (13 km), then continue on US-209 N for 4 miles (6 km). Turn left onto North St./PA-903 and cross the Lehigh River into Jim Thorpe.

❹ Savor a delightful feast at **Moya** (24 Race St., 570/325-8530, www.jimthorpemoya.com, 5pm-9pm Mon.-Tues. and Thurs., 5pm-10pm Fri.-Sat., 5pm-8pm Sun., $13-19). The menu features bold twists on traditional dishes, such as lamb shank or beef short ribs.

JIM THORPE, PENNSYLVANIA

DAY 4: Jim Thorpe to Blairstown, New Jersey

95 miles/153 kilometers | 2.5-3 hours

ROUTE OVERVIEW: PA-903 • I-80 • US-209/PA-447 • surface streets • US-206 • surface streets • NJ-94

① Hit the road for **Stroudsburg** bright and early. Eat breakfast at **The Cure Café** (517 Main St., 570/664-2888, 7:30am-2:30pm Wed.-Mon., $9-12), which specializes in frittatas and build-your-own omelets.

> Head north on PA-903 for 19 miles (31 km) to meet I-80 E. After 23 miles (37 km), take exit 307 for Stroudsburg.

② Next, visit **Delaware Water Gap National Recreation Area** (1978 River Rd., Bushkill, 570/426-2452) and hike the **Tumbling Waters Trail** (3 mi/4.8 km loop, 1.5-2 hours, easy). This trail provides vistas, a solid ascent and descent, and of course, a fantastic waterfall. Find the trailhead at the **Pocono Environmental Education Center** (538 Emery Rd., Dingmans Ferry).

> Follow I-80 E for 2 miles (3 km), then take the exit for US-209/PA-447. Continue on US-209 N/PA-447 N for 11 miles (18 km). Turn left onto Bushkill Falls Rd. and drive for 1.5 miles (2.5 km). Turn right onto Milford Rd.; follow this for 6 miles (10 km). Turn right onto Brisco Mountain

DELAWARE WATER GAP NATIONAL RECREATION AREA

Rd. and continue for 1 mile (1.6 km). Turn left onto Emery Rd. to reach the trailhead.

③ Make your way to **Blairstown,** New Jersey. Dine at the 1950s **Blairstown Diner** (53 NJ-94, 908/362-6070, www.blairstowndiner.com, 6am-7pm Mon.-Fri., 7am-3pm Sat.-Sun., $6-16) of horror movie *Friday the 13th* fame.

> Follow Emery Rd. north for 2.5 miles (4 km). This turns into Chestnut Ridge Rd., then Wilson Hill Rd. Continue for 2 miles (3 km), then turn left onto US-209

DELAWARE WATER GAP NATIONAL RECREATION AREA

Best BREWERIES

An exhilarating hike begs to be celebrated with a cold beer. Good thing you have your pick of top-notch breweries from Pennsylvania to New Hampshire.

- **Zeroday Brewing Co.,** Harrisburg, PA (250 Reily St., 717/745-6218, www.zerodaybrewing.com, 4pm-11pm Tues.-Thurs., 4pm-midnight Fri., noon-midnight Sat., noon-8pm Sun.): Named for that very important rest day for thru-hikers the world over, this hangout has big Belgians and a great sense of humor. Hit it up after hiking to Hawk Rock Overlook across the Susquehanna River in Duncannon.

- **Hudson Valley Brewery,** Beacon, NY (2 Churchill St., 845/218-9156, 5pm-10pm Thurs.-Fri., 2pm-10pm Sat.-Sun.): A short hike from Breakneck Ridge, this innovative brewery is a bit off the trail but completely worth it.

- **Long Trail Brewing Company,** Bridgewater Corners, VT (5520 US-4, 802/672-5011, www.longtrail.com, 10am-7pm daily): After taking on Killington Peak, book it to this brewing mecca and spend some time at its family-friendly taproom.

- **Moat Mountain Smokehouse & Brewing Co.,** North Conway, NH (3378 NH-16, 603/356-6381, www.moatmountain.com, 11:30am-11:45pm daily): Chow down on a burger or some barbecue while downing a pint or two after hiking Mount Washington. You've earned it.

▼ LONG TRAIL BREWING COMPANY, BRIDGEWATER CORNERS, VERMONT

N/Federal Rd. Turn right onto PA-739/Dingmans Turnpike and follow this across the Delaware River into New Jersey. The road becomes Tuttles Corner Dingmans Rd.; continue on this for 2.5 miles (4 km), then turn left to stay on it and continue for another 2 miles (3 km). Turn right to join US-206 S and continue for 2.5 miles (4 km). Turn right onto Owassa Turnpike and drive south for 17 miles (27 km); along the way the road changes names several times, ending at Stillwater Rd. Turn right onto NJ-94 in Blairstown to reach the diner.

❹ With your camera ready, walk downtown to see the impressive Richardson Romanesque buildings of **Blair Academy** (2 Park St., 908/362-6121, www.blair.edu).

DAY 5: Blairstown to Beacon, New York

95 miles/153 kilometers | 2.5-3 hours

ROUTE OVERVIEW: NJ-94 • US-206 • surface streets • NJ-23 • surface streets • NY-17/US-6 • US-202 • NY-9D

① Point the car north. You'll want to stop to view the scenic beauty of the Hudson Valley on this trek. Find an excellent vantage point during a hike on the **High Point Trail** (4 mi/6.4 km round-trip, 2-2.5 hours, moderate) in **High Point State Park** (1840 NJ-23, Sussex, 973/875-4800, www.state. nj.us, 8am-8pm daily, $10-20 per vehicle). At 1,803 feet (550 m), the highest point in New Jersey is an obelisk with an observation deck that provides sweeping views. The trailhead is at the Appalachian Trail parking lot off NJ-23.

> *Take NJ-94 N for 13 miles (21 km). In the town of Newton, the road becomes US-206/Water St. Follow this for 5 miles (8 km), at which point the road becomes County Rd. 565/Ross Corner Sussex Rd. Continue for another 7 miles (11 km), to where the road becomes Loomis Ave. Follow this for 1 mile (1.6 km), then turn left onto Mill St. and continue onto Bank St. This road becomes NJ-23 N/Clove Ave. Follow this for 8 miles (13 km) to reach the trailhead parking lot.*

② Continue to **Warwick,** New York, for lunch at **Fetch** (48 Main St., 845/987-8200, http://fetchbarandgrill.com,

VIEW FROM BEAR MOUNTAIN

11am-10pm Sun.-Thurs., 11am-11pm Fri.-Sat., $7-15). A partnership with the local pet shelter makes Fetch the go-to for dog lovers, with photos of adoption-ready dogs on the walls. The food, elevated pub grub, is worthy of a tail wag.

> *Head east on NJ-23 for less than a mile; turn left onto Greenville Rd. and follow this for 1.5 miles (2.5 km). Turn right onto Mt. Salem Rd. and continue for 4 miles (6 km). Turn left onto County Rd. 36/Unionville Rd., then follow this as it becomes Main St. Turn right to continue on NY-284, then make a left onto State Line Rd. In 3 miles (5 km), turn left onto Liberty Corners Rd. Follow it for 2 miles (3 km) as the road becomes Pine Island Turnpike. Continue for 6 miles (10 km), then turn left onto West St., which leads into Warwick.*

③ Save room for the next-level ice cream at **Bellvale Farms Creamery** (1390 NY-17A, 845/988-1818, www. bellvalefarms.com, noon-8pm Mon.-Wed., noon-9pm Thurs.-Sun.). Lines are typically long, but you can enjoy your ice cream on benches overlooking the vast Warwick Valley.

④ End the day on another high note with a sunset hike to the top of **Bear Mountain** (5 mi/8 km round-trip, 4 hours, moderate), at the eponymous **Bear Mountain State Park** (3006 Seven Lakes Dr., Bear Mountain, 845/786-2701, http://parks.ny.gov, 8am-sunset daily, $10 per vehicle). The first Appalachian Trail markers were posted on this quintessential New York peak overlooking the mighty Hudson River. Find the trailhead at Major Welch Trail at Hessian Lake. Spend the night in **Beacon.**

> *Take Colonial Ave. east out of Warwick. This becomes County Rd. 13/Kings Hwy. Follow this for 8 miles (13 km), then turn right onto NY-17M/Brookside Ave. In 1 mile (1.6 km), join NY-17 E/US-6 E. Follow this for 16 miles (26 km), then take the exit for US-202 W. Turn right onto Seven Lakes Dr. to reach the trailhead. To continue to Beacon, join US-202 E. In 1 mile (1.6 km), turn left onto NY-9D and go north for 15 miles (24 km). NY-9D will take you directly through Beacon.*

DAY 6: Beacon to Salisbury, Connecticut

85 miles/137 kilometers | 2.5-3 hours

ROUTE OVERVIEW: NY-9 • surface streets • NY-115 • US-44 • NY-82 • NY-343 • NY-22 • NY-55 • US-7 • CT-341 • surface streets • CT-41 • US-44

❶ Head north to **Hyde Park.** Visit the **Franklin D. Roosevelt Presidential Library and Museum** (4079 Albany Post Rd./NY-9, 845/486-7770, www.fdrlibrary.marist.edu, adults $18, free for children under 16). Roosevelt set in motion the tradition of presidential libraries and museums with this complex on his family property overlooking the Hudson River.

> Go north on NY-9D for 8 miles (13 km). Turn left onto NY-9 N and continue for 13 miles (21 km) to Hyde Park.

❷ Head toward Connecticut and stop in **Kent** to see **Bull's Bridge** (Bulls Bridge Rd. and US-7), one of only two operational covered bridges in Connecticut.

> Take NY-9 S to St. Andrew Rd. Turn left, then go left on Violet Ave. to Creek Rd. Turn right and stay on Creek Rd. for 1 mile (1.6 km) to E. Dorsey Ln. Make a left, then a quick right to stay on E. Dorsey. Drive for 1 mile (1.6 km) to reach NY-115. Follow NY-115 N to W Rd. Go right and take W Rd. to US-44. Stay on US-44 E for 6 miles (10 km) to NY-82 S. Take this for 4 miles (6 km) to NY-343. Continue on NY-343 E for 8 miles (13 km) to NY-22 S. Drive for 5 miles (8 km) to Cricket Hill Rd. Turn left onto NY-55. Follow this east for 1 mile (1.6 km), then turn left on Dog Tail Corners Rd. Stay on Dog Tail Corners Rd. for 4 miles (6 km) until it turns into Bull's Bridge Rd., which leads to the bridge.

❸ **Caleb's Peak & St. John's Ledges** (4 mi/6.4 km one-way, 2.5-3 hours, moderate) makes a great half-day hike. St. John's Ledges offers an ideal photo op overlooking the Housatonic River. Soak up more views at Caleb's Peak, which also has a larger area for picnicking. The trailhead is on River Road.

> Take US-7 N for 4 miles (6 km). Turn left onto CT-341 W and cross the Housatonic River. Turn right onto Skiff Mountain Rd./River Rd. Follow this for about 2 miles (3 km) to reach the trailhead.

❹ Spend the evening in **Salisbury.** Dine at the quintessentially New England **White Hart Restaurant & Inn** (15 Under Mountain Rd., 860/435-0030, 11am-3pm and 5pm-8:30pm Sun., 5pm-9pm Mon. and Wed.-Thurs., 5pm-9:30pm Fri.-Sat., $16-34), then tuck in for the night at one of the inn's 16 guest rooms ($250-450).

> Retrace your path to CT-341 (2 mi/3 km). Turn right onto CT-341 and continue for 2.5 miles (4 km). The road then becomes Bog Hollow Rd.; continue for 3 miles (5 km). The road then becomes Kent Rd. Follow this for less than a mile, then turn right onto S. Amenia Rd. Continue on Amenia for 2 miles (3 km), then turn right onto CT-41. Continue for another 11 miles (18 km), then turn right onto US-44 and drive for 2 miles (3 km) to reach Salisbury.

DAY 7: Salisbury to Pittsfield, Massachusetts

55 miles/89 kilometers | 2-2.5 hours

ROUTE OVERVIEW: US-44 • surface streets • NY-22 • NY-344 • surface streets • MA-41 • US-7 • MA-102 • MA-183 • US-20

❶ Spend a leisurely day in Massachusetts, starting with a light hike on the **Bash Bish Falls Trail** (1 mi/1.6 km round-trip, 30 minutes, easy/

BULL'S BRIDGE IN KENT, CONNECTICUT

BASH BISH FALLS

moderate). A hike made for waterfall tourists who want to feel adventurous, this romp down to the base of the falls and back up is slightly taxing but manageable for just about every skill level. The trailhead is at the upper falls parking lot for Bash Bish Falls.

> *Take US-44 W for 2 miles (3 km) out of Salisbury. Turn right on Belgo Rd. and follow it into New York (2 mi/3 km), where it turns into Shagroy Rd. In less than a mile, turn right onto Rudd Pond Rd. and drive north for 2 miles (3 km) to NY-22. Turn right and follow NY-22 N for 9 miles (15 km) to NY-344. Turn right and stay on NY-344 E as it takes you back into Massachusetts for 2 miles (3 km) to reach the trailhead.*

2 Visit **Great Barrington** for a late breakfast at the industrial-chic **Fuel Coffee Shop** (293 Main St., 413/528-5505, www.fuelgreatbarrington.com, 7am-6pm Mon.-Tues., 7am-10pm Wed.-Sat., 8am-6pm Sun., $8-11).

> *Head southeast on Falls Rd. for 1.5 miles (2.5 km) to West St. Turn left and follow West St. for 1.5 miles (2.5 km). At East St., turn left and follow it north. In less than a mile, it turns into Mt. Washington Rd. Drive for 5 miles (8 km) to MA-41. Take MA-41 N for 4 miles (6 km) into Great Barrington.*

3 Now that your body is refueled and your legs refreshed, embark on a hike of **Monument Mountain** (3.8 mi/6.1 km round-trip, 3 hours, moderate). The best views are at a distinctive rock outcrop that shows off the region's rolling hills and dipping valleys. The trailhead is on US-7, several miles north of Great Barrington. There's a $5 parking fee at the trailhead lot.

> *Take US-7 N for 4 miles (6 km) to the trailhead.*

4 Have lunch in **Stockbridge** before visiting the **Berkshire Botanical Garden** (5 W. Stockbridge Rd., 413/298-3926, www.berkshirebotanical.org, 9am-5pm daily summer, $12-15), which occupies more than 15 acres and houses thousands of native floral species.

> *Take US-7 N for 3 miles (5 km), then turn left onto MA-102 W and continue for less than a mile into Stockbridge. Continue heading northwest on MA-102 to reach the botanical garden.*

5 Spend a few hours in **Lenox,** maybe enjoying a show at **Tanglewood Music Center** (297 West St., 413/637-5180, www.bso.org). The summer home of the Boston Symphony Orchestra is also one of the finest outdoor amphitheaters for music under the stars. Stay overnight in **Pittsfield.**

> *Take MA-183 N for 5 miles (8 km) to reach Tanglewood and Lenox. Go north on MA-7A for 1 mile (1.6 km) to join US-20, heading north for 6 miles (10 km) to reach Pittsfield.*

DAY 8: Pittsfield to Woodstock, Vermont

130 miles/209 kilometers | 3.5-4 hours

ROUTE OVERVIEW: MA-8 • surface streets • US-7 • surface streets • US-4

1 Stop in **North Adams** to visit **MASS MoCA** (1040 Mass MoCA Way, 413/662-2111, http://massmoca.org, 10am-6pm Sun.-Wed., 10am-7pm Thurs.-Sat. summer, 11am-5pm Wed.-Mon. fall-spring, $20 adults, $8 children 6-16). Comprising more than two dozen brick warehouses, this mecca for contemporary art provides a full day of fun.

> *Take MA-8 N for 21 miles (34 km) to reach MASS MoCA.*

MASS MOCA, NORTH ADAMS, MASSACHUSETTS

THUNDERING BROOK FALLS

DAY 9: Woodstock to Lincoln, New Hampshire

140 miles/225 kilometers | 3-3.5 hours

ROUTE OVERVIEW: US-4 • I-89 • I-91 • US-5 • NH-10 • NH-116 • I-93 • US-3 • US-302 • US-3 • I-93

1 In **Hanover,** check out **Dartmouth College** (603/646-1110, www.dartmouth.edu) and the **Hood Museum of Art** (6 E. Wheelock St., 603/646-2808, www.hoodmuseum.dartmouth.edu, 10am-5pm Tues. and Thurs.-Sat., 10am-9pm Wed., noon-5pm Sun., free). See everything from 9th-century stone reliefs to modern works by Georgia O'Keeffe at this acclaimed exhibit space.

> Drive US-4 E for 10 miles (16 km) to I-89. After 3 miles (5 km), join I-91 N, following it for 6 miles (10 km) to Hanover.

2 Stop in **Franconia** and **White Mountain National Forest** (71 White Mountain Dr., Campton, 603/536-6100) to visit the **Old Man of the Mountain Memorial** (Tramway Dr. at US-3, Franconia), an ode to a collapsed rock formation that resembled the profile of a man's face.

> Follow US-5 N for 30 miles (48 km) to Newbury Crossing Rd. Turn right, taking Newbury Crossing to NH-10. Follow NH-10 N for 4 miles (6 km) to NH-116. Drive NH-116 E for 11 miles (18 km) to NH-116 N. Take NH-116 N for 11 miles (18 km) to Franconia.

2 **Manchester Center,** a community within the town of **Manchester,** has plenty of lunch options, but *the* place at which to enjoy a sweet treat is **Mrs. Murphy's Donuts** (374 Depot St., Manchester Center, 802/362-1874, 5am-6pm Mon.-Fri., 5am-4pm Sat., 5am-2pm Sun.).

> Drive Massachusetts Ave. west for 3 miles (5 km) to N. Hoosac Rd., following this for 2 miles (3 km) to Bridges Rd. At US-7, turn right and follow US-7 for 35 miles (56 km) north to Manchester.

3 For a quick post-meal hike, **Thundering Brook Falls** (1 mi/1.6 km round-trip, 30 minutes, easy), a wheelchair-accessible boardwalk trail, gets the blood moving. The trailhead is on River Road north of Thundering Brook Road.

> Take US-7 for 30 miles (48 km) north to Clarendon. Here, turn right on N. Shrewsbury Rd., then left on Cold River Rd., which turns into Stratton Rd. Follow this for a total of 5 miles (8 km) to US-4. Stay on US-4 E for 12 miles (19 km) to River Rd. Turn left and take River Rd. to the trailhead.

4 Before you reach Woodstock, stop at the creek-side pub and brewery **Long Trail Brewing Company** (5520 US-4, Bridgewater Corners, 802/672-5011, www.longtrail.com, 10am-7pm daily, $13-15). Order your beers inside, then find a sunny spot on the patio or near the water. Stay the night in **Woodstock.**

> Continue on US-4 E for 10 miles (16 km) to the brewery. From Long Trail, it's 8 miles (13 km) southeast on US-4 into Woodstock.

TRAIL IN WHITE MOUNTAIN NATIONAL FOREST

③ Hike **Arethusa Falls** (4.2 mi/6.6 km loop, 3 hours, moderate). Within **Crawford Notch State Park** (1464 US-302, Harts Location, 603/374-2272, www.nhstateparks.org, dawn-dusk daily), which is inside White Mountain National Forest, Arethusa Falls is a brilliant waterfall dropping 140 feet from a granite cliff. Find the trailhead at US-302 at Arethusa Falls Road.

> Get on I-93 S, following it to US-3. Stay on US-3 N for 9 miles (15 km) to US-302. Drive US-302 E for 12 miles (19 km) to the state park.

④ Settle in for dinner in **Lincoln** at **Black Mtn. Burger Co.** (264 Main St., Lincoln, 603/745-3444, www.blackmtnburger.com, 11:30am-9pm Thurs.-Tues., $8-16).

> Retrace your path back to I-93 via US-302 and US-3 (22 mi/35 km), then drive I-93 S 12.5 miles (20 km) to Lincoln.

DAY 10: Lincoln to Rangeley, Maine

170 miles/275 kilometers | 4.5-5 hours

ROUTE OVERVIEW: I-93 • US-3 • NH-115 • US-2 • NH-16 • Mount Washington Auto Rd. • NH-16 • US-2 • surface streets • ME-17 • ME-4

① Start the day by driving through **Gorham** and up the **Mount Washington Auto Road** (1 Mount Washington Auto Rd., off NH-16, hours vary May-Oct., $31 vehicle and driver, $17 motorcycles, $9 adults, $7 children 5-12) to the summit of **Mount Washington,** the tallest mountain in the White Mountain National Forest—and all of the Northeast. Keep your eye out for wildlife, including moose.

> Leave Lincoln via I-93 N. Drive for 12 miles (19 km) to US-3. Continue on US-3 N for 12 miles (19 km) to NH-115. Stay on NH-115 N for 10 miles (16 km). At US-2 E, turn right and drive for 13 miles (21 km) to Gorham. From Gorham, take NH-16 S to join Mount Washington Auto Rd. It's 7 miles (11 km) to the summit.

② Head east on US-2 to **Gorham** and grab pub fare at **Mr. Pizza** (160 Main St., 603/466-5573, www.mrpizzanh.com, 11am-11pm Sun.-Thurs.,

HEIGHT OF LAND NEAR RANGELEY, MAINE

11am-midnight Fri.-Sat., $10-22), a friendly restaurant with outdoor seating.

> Retrace your path back down the mountain to NH-16 (7 mi/11 km). Follow NH-16 N back to Gorham (8 mi/13 km).

③ Take US-2 to ME-17 and enjoy the wild drive north toward Rangeley. Be sure to stop at **Height of Land** (ME-17 and Appalachian Trail, Roxbury), maybe the finest scenic overlook in America.

> Follow US-2 E for 43 miles (69 km). In Rumford, turn left onto Franklin St., then continue onto Rumford Ave. Follow Rumford as it turns into Hancock St. and continue for 3 miles (5 km), then turn right onto Black Bridge Rd. Turn left to follow ME-17 and drive north for 22 miles (35 km) to Height of Land.

④ As you continue toward Rangeley, hike **Bald Mountain** (2.5 mi/4 km round-trip, 1.5 hours, moderate), which is a sufficient challenge without

---

⏱ WITH LESS TIME

PITTSFIELD, MASSACHUSETTS TO RANGELEY, MAINE

3 days; 415 miles/669 kilometers

In **three days,** you can get in plenty of great Appalachian Trail hikes, including the biggie of **Mount Washington** in New Hampshire. Plus, you'll enjoy your share of New England's best **craft breweries,** as well as impressive art at **MASS MoCA** in North Adams, Massachusetts, and at **Hood Museum of Art** in Hanover, New Hampshire. (See Days 8–10 for more details.)

Best VIEWS

These are some of the coolest places to check out fall colors, cityscapes, and long sunsets.

- **The Pinnacle, PA** (trailhead at 400 Reservoir Rd., Hamburg) offers an impressive view of central Pennsylvania valleys, but only after a tough five-hour hike through Rocksylvania terrain.

- **High Point, NJ** (High Point State Park, 1840 NJ-23, Sussex, 973/875-4800, www.state. nj.us, 8am-8pm daily) is not only a monument at the high point of New Jersey, it's also a slightly terrifying walk up a staircase with grand views.

- **Bear Mountain, NY** (Bear Mountain State Park, 3006 Seven Lakes Dr., Bear Mountain, 845/786-2701, http://parks. ny.gov, 8am-sunset daily) is a worthy peak capped by an impressive rock pile. Sit atop and enjoy the fresh air.

- **Mount Greylock, MA** (Mount Greylock State Reservation, Rockwell Rd., Lanesborough, 413/499-4262, www.mass. gov, dawn-dusk daily) stands at 3,491 feet (1,064 m), providing sightlines of the Berkshires and the towns below.

- **Mount Moosilauke, NH** (trailhead at Beaver Brook, NH-112, North Woodstock) is a challenging summit, but at the top you'll gaze upon the White Mountains and Adirondacks.

- **Height of Land, ME** (ME-17 and Appalachian Trail, Roxbury) sits atop Spruce Mountain, offering an unbelievable view of wild Maine forests, lakes, and mountains.

▼ HEIGHT OF LAND IN MAINE

becoming an all-day affair. Find the trailhead at Bald Mountain Road less than a mile south of ME-4.

> Head north on ME-17 for 11 miles (18 km). Turn left onto ME-4 and continue for 1 mile (1.6 km). Turn left onto Bald Mountain Rd. and continue for less than a mile to reach the trailhead.

5 Stay the night in **Rangeley** and dine at **The Shed** (2647 Main St., 207/864-2219, www.getshedfaced. com, noon-9pm Mon.-Sat., $9-24). This quintessential Maine hideout offers true-blue 'cue in the form of ribs, pulled pork dinners, and beef brisket.

> To continue to Rangeley, follow Bald Mountain Rd. back to ME-4. Continue east on ME-4 for 8 miles (13 km) to get into town.

▶ **Playlist**

THE APPALACHIAN TRAIL

SONGS

- **"Into the Wild" by LP:** When you're getting ready to summit Bear Mountain or Mount Washington, you need a song that matches the powerful beauty of nature spread before you. The swelling chorus of this tune does the trick.

- **"Wagon Wheel" by Old Crow Medicine Show:** Appalachian Trail thru-hikers swear by this jaunty, folksy, joyful song. It doesn't matter your age or musical taste; everyone knows the words and joins in for a sing-along. Add this to your playlist to become an official member of the "AT Club."

PODCASTS

- **Stories from the Trail:** A biweekly chat that covers all things long-distance backpacking, including interviews with thru-hiking authors, documentarians, and aspiring thru-hikers.

DAY 11: Rangeley to Baxter State Park, Maine

200 miles/322 kilometers | 4.5-5 hours

ROUTE OVERVIEW: ME-4 • ME-145 • ME-234 • US-201A • US-201 • ME-16 • ME-6 • ME-150 • ME-6 • ME-11

❶ On this final day, you have your drive cut out for you. Start off with a slight detour west to **Oquossoc** for a hearty breakfast of eggs Benedict at **The Gingerbread House Restaurant** (55 Carry Rd., 207/864-3602, www.gingerbreadhouserestaurant.net, 7am-3pm daily, $6-15).

> Go west on ME-4 N for 7 miles (11 km) to reach Oquossoc.

❷ In **Monson,** visit the **Appalachian Trail Visitor Center** (ME-6 and Water St., 207/573-0163, 8am-11am and 1pm-5pm June-Oct.), which is inside the Monson Historical Society building.

> Head east on ME-4 S for 29 miles (47 km) to ME-145. Turn left on ME-145 and continue north to Strong, then make a sharp right onto ME-234. Drive ME-234 E for 19 miles (31 km). At US-201A, turn left and drive north for 8 miles (13 km). Then turn left on US-201 N, taking that route for 8 miles (13 km). Turn right on ME-16. Stay on ME-16 E for 25 miles (40 km). In Abbot, turn left on ME-6 W, driving it 8 miles (13 km) to Monson.

❸ Eat lunch in town at **Spring Creek Bar-B-Q** (26 Greenville Rd., 207/997-7025, www.springcreekbar-b-qmaine.com, 11am-7pm Thurs., 11am-8pm Fri.-Sat., 11am-5pm Sun., $5-10), a fun joint where owners Mike and Kim keep a positive vibe while serving up pretty darn good 'cue.

❹ Continue on ME-6, then ME-11, past the 100-Mile Wilderness to **Millinocket** and **Baxter State Park** (Baxter Park Rd., Millinocket, 207/723-5140, http://baxterstatepark.org, dawn-dusk daily, $15 per vehicle May-Oct.). Enter the park via its southern entrance, **Togue Pond.** Enjoy the views of **Katahdin,** the northern end of the Appalachian Trail and the highest peak in Maine.

KATAHDIN

> *Follow N. Guilford Rd. and ME-150 S to rejoin ME-6 (10 mi/16 km). Drive ME-6 E for 21 miles (34 km) to ME-11. Turn left and stay on ME-11 N for 39 miles (63 km) to Millinocket. Take Bates St./Millinocket Rd. northwest out of town for 8 miles (13 km). Continue to follow Baxter Park Rd. to reach the entrance (8 mi/13 km).*

Getting There

AIR

The nearest airport to Harpers Ferry is **Dulles International Airport** (IAD, 703/572-2700, http://flydulles.com) near **Washington DC**. Major airlines that fly into Dulles include Allegiant, American Airlines, Delta, Southwest, and United. The rental car center at Dulles offers vehicle rentals via Alamo, Enterprise, and Hertz. Major airlines also fly into **Ronald Reagan Washington National Airport** (DCA, 703/417-8000 www.flyreagan.com) or **Baltimore/Washington International Thurgood Marshall Airport** (BWI, 410/859-7111, www.bwiairport.com), both near Washington DC.

CAR

The drive from **Washington DC**—where the Dulles and Ronald Reagan airports are located—to Harpers Ferry is 70 miles (115 km) and takes about 1.5 hours via I-495, I-270, I-70, and US-340.

To get to Harpers Ferry from the **Baltimore airport,** it's a 70-mile (115-km) drive that takes a little over an hour via I-70 and US-340.

BUS

Harpers Ferry is a train ride away from Washington DC with **Amtrak** (Potomac and Shenandoah Sts., 800/872-7245, www.amtrak.com). Harpers Ferry is on the Capitol Limited Line, which runs from Washington DC to Chicago. A train heading west daily from Washington stops in Harpers Ferry at 5:16pm, while a train heading east daily from Chicago stops there at 11:31am.

You can also get to Harpers Ferry on **MARC** (www.mta.maryland.gov/marctrain). The commuter-friendly Brunswick Line runs through the town. The eastbound trains toward Washington DC stop in Harpers Ferry three times per day Monday-Friday (5:25am-6:50am), while the westbound trains toward Martinsburg stop five times per day Monday-Friday (after 5pm).

You can drive into Harpers Ferry and park at the train station's public lot, but once spots are taken there's really nowhere else to go, as there's no parking allowed on the streets in the Lower Town. The better bet, especially on weekends and really anytime in the summer or fall, is to park at the main parking lot at the **visitors center** (171 Shoreline Dr.) and step onto a shuttle bus (free) that gets to the Lower Town within 10 minutes. Shuttle buses run every 10 minutes from the visitors center.

Getting Back

It's a long drive back to the Washington DC area from Millinocket, so a better option is to book a one-way flight home out of **Bangor**. Bangor is 70 miles (115 km) and just over an hour south of Millinocket via US-95. For a slightly more scenic route to Bangor, you can take ME-157 to US-2 and drive that south along the Penobscot River. You'll add about 15 miles (24 km) and 45 minutes with this detour.

Bangor International Airport (BGR, 287 Godfrey Blvd., 207/992-4600, www.flybangor.com) serves New York City, Philadelphia, Washington DC, Charlotte, Chicago, and cities in Florida through American Airlines, Allegiant, Delta, and United. Most Appalachian Trail shuttle services pick up and take hikers from and to Bangor.

Concord Coach Lines (www.concordcoachlines.com) services Bangor at the **Bangor Transportation Center** (1039 Union St., 800/639-3317, 6:30am-6:30pm daily) and connects passengers to Logan International Airport in Boston.

CONNECT WITH

- At Woodstock: **Best of New England** (PAGE 476)
- At Beacon: **Hudson River Valley** (PAGE 540)

LAKE CHAMPLAIN SCENIC BYWAY

WHY GO: Quaint New England towns, breweries and cideries, famous Vermont ice cream, Revolutionary War history, American arts and crafts

TOTAL DISTANCE: 95 miles/ 150 kilometers

NUMBER OF DAYS: 3

SEASONS: Late spring through late fall

START: Shoreham, Vermont

END: North Hero, Vermont

▼ SHELBURNE MUSEUM

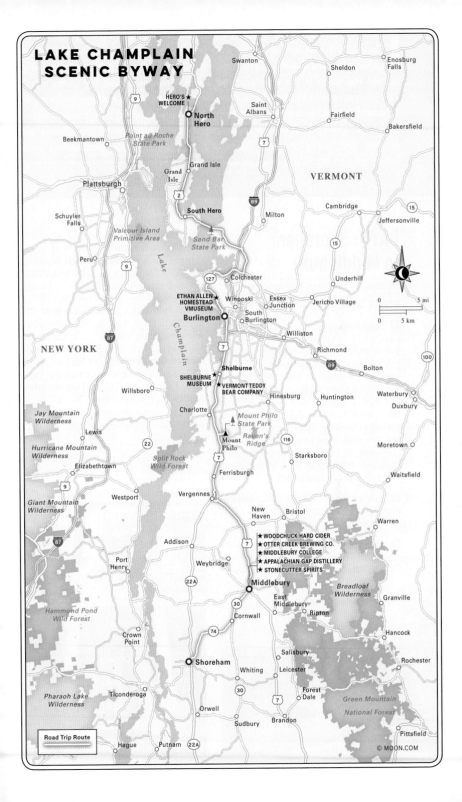

ake Champlain is the country's sixth-largest lake, stretching 107 miles long (172 km) and plunging 400 feet deep (122 m). Vermont's famed scenic byway travels north along the lake with the Adirondacks rising across the water in the west and the Green Mountains towering to the east. The journey starts in Shoreham, then wends north to the college enclaves of Middlebury and Burlington. Dairy farms dot the way, along with historic sites, orchards, vineyards, and art museums. Once it crosses to the Champlain Islands, the byway carves a pastoral path through untouched beauty with lake views as far as the eye can see.

DAY 1: Shoreham to Middlebury

15 miles/24 kilometers | 30 minutes

ROUTE OVERVIEW: VT-74 • VT-30

❶ **Shoreham** is at the southern tip of the Lake Champlain Scenic Byway. As you head north, drive slowly to soak up the rambling countryside and historic farmhouses. In lively **Middlebury**, tour **Middlebury College** (visitor parking at Mahaney Arts Center, 72 Porter Field Rd., 802/443-3168, www.middlebury.edu) and make time to browse the downtown shops and boutiques.

> Take VT-74 E for 8 miles (13 km), then turn left onto VT-30. Continue for 4 miles (6 km) into Middlebury.

❷ Check in to your room at the **Middlebury Inn** (16 Court Sq., 802/388-4961, www.middleburyinn.com, $169-250).

❸ Head out to explore the breweries, distilleries, and cideries on the **Middlebury Tasting Trail** (www.middtastingtrail.com), many of which are within walking distance of each other. Check out **Otter Creek Brewing Co.** (793 Exchange St., 802/388-0727, www.ottercreekbrewing.com, 11am-6pm Sun.-Thurs., 11am-8pm Fri., 11am-7pm Sat.), **Woodchuck Hard Cider** (1321 Exchange St., 802/388-0700, www.woodchuck.com, 11am-6pm Wed.-Fri., 11am-5pm Sat.-Sun.), **Appalachian Gap Distillery** (88 Mainelli Rd., 802/989-7362, www.appalachiangap.com, 1pm-5pm daily), and **Stonecutter Spirits** (1197 Exchange St., 802/388-3000, www.stonecutterspirits.com, 4pm-8pm Fri., noon-8pm Sat.).

❹ Steeped in memorabilia and named after a poem by Robert Frost, a Middlebury local, **Fire & Ice Restaurant**

MIDDLEBURY INN

MIDDLEBURY

Top ③ LAKE CHAMPLAIN SCENIC BYWAY

① Sample the state's best brews and spirits on the **Middlebury Tasting Trail** (PAGE 512).

② Experience breathtaking views from the peak of Vermont's **Mount Philo** (PAGE 514).

③ Explore **Burlington,** including the **Ethan Allen Homestead** (PAGE 515).

(25 Seymour St., 800/367-7166, www.fireandicerestaurant.com, 5pm-9pm Mon.-Thurs., noon-9pm Fri.-Sun., $12-35) is a perfect spot to wind down. Ask for a cozily lit booth in the pub area, which serves the restaurant's full menu of seafood, steaks, burgers, and salads.

DAY 2: Middlebury to Burlington

40 miles/64 kilometers | 1.5 hours

ROUTE OVERVIEW: US-7

❶ You have a big day ahead of you—not in distance, but in things to see and do. At times, the byway strays inland, offering only glimpses of Lake Champlain. However, at **Mount Philo State Park** (5425 Mt. Philo Rd., Charlotte, 802/425-2390, http://vtstateparks.com, 8am-sunset daily Memorial Day-late Oct., $4 adults, $2 children), Vermont's first state park, you're afforded unrivaled lake views. To reach the top of **Mount Philo** (1.2 mi/1.9 km round-trip, 30 minutes, moderate), take the shaded, albeit steep, paved road. It's also possible to drive and park in the lot at the top.

> Take US-7 N for 20 miles (32 km), then turn right onto State Park Rd. Continue for 2 miles (3 km) to reach the entrance to the state park.

❷ As you travel north to Burlington, stop in **Shelburne** at the **Vermont Teddy Bear Company** (6655 Shelburne Rd., 800/829-2327, www.vermontteddybear.com, 9am-6pm daily summer, shorter hours fall-spring, tours $4 adults, free for children 12 and under),

VERMONT TEDDY BEAR COMPANY

one of the largest producers of teddy bears in the world. Factory tours run every hour, on the hour, from 10am to 3pm.

> Head back to US-7 (2 mi/3 km). Take US-7 N for 6 miles (10 km), then turn right onto S. Park Rd. to reach the Vermont Teddy Bear Company.

❸ Just up the road is the **Shelburne Museum** (6000 Shelburne Rd., 802/985-3346, www.shelburnemuseum.org, 10am-5pm daily, $25 adults, $14 children 13-17, $12 children 5-12), a wonderland of Americana arts, crafts, and architecture. See more than 150,000 works exhibited in 39 buildings, 25 of which are historic and were relocated to the museum grounds.

> Go 1 mile (1.6 km) north on US-7 to reach the museum.

VIEW OF THE ADIRONDACKS FROM MOUNT PHILO STATE PARK

Foodie ADVENTURES

When touring the small towns and lakeside communities of the Lake Champlain Scenic Byway, it's best to come hungry. The region's farms, dairies, orchards, and maple houses offer endless ways to savor local flavor.

- **Champlain Orchards & Cidery** (3597 VT-74, Shoreham, 802/897-2777, www.champlainorchards.com, 9am-5pm daily): Pick your own fruit, including apples, cherries, peaches, plums and raspberries; tour the orchards; or browse the homegrown goods—including hard ciders—at the market.

- **Ledge Haven Farms** (145 Mt. Independence Rd., Orwell, 888/534-4286, www.vtmaple.net, by appointment): The maple syrup at this family-run dairy and sugarhouse is out of this world. Owner Tom Audet taps the trees in the woods surrounding the property. To tour the sugarhouse or purchase maple syrup, phone ahead to schedule an appointment.

- **Goodies Snack Bar** (6035 VT-17, Addison, 802/759-2276, 4pm-9pm Fri., noon-9pm Sat., noon-8pm Sun.): Vermont's dairy industry produces some of the world's best cheeses, milks, and ice cream. Get a chocolate or vanilla "creemee" (don't call it soft serve in these parts!) at this roadside snack shop.

- **Shelburne Farms** (1611 Harbor Rd., Shelburne, 802/985-8686, http://shelburnefarms.org, 10am-5pm daily, $8 adults, $5 children): Learn about the farm's sustainable practices on a farm tour, then sample farmstead cheese, organic fruits and veggies, and pasture-raised beef and poultry.

- **Champlain Islands Farmers Market** (http://champlainislandsfarmersmarket.org, times vary by location): Sample the best of Vermont's local bounty in several locations on the islands. Choose from jams, jellies, pies, maple syrup, wines, ciders, pickles, eggs, free-range poultry, grass-fed beef, artisan bread, heirloom tomatoes, honey, and more.

GOODIES SNACK BAR

SHELBURNE MUSEUM

4 End the day in the bustling port city of **Burlington,** home of the University of Vermont. No matter where you enjoy dinner, save room for dessert at **Ben & Jerry's Scoop Shop** (36 Church St., 802/862-9620, www.benjerry.com, 11am-10pm daily); the famous ice cream company was founded here.

> *Take US-7 N for 7 miles (11 km) to reach Burlington.*

5 Spend the night at **Willard Street Inn** (349 S. Willard St., 800/577-8712, www.willardstreetinn.com, $155-305), a sprawling country mansion turned B&B.

DAY 3: Burlington to North Hero

40 miles/64 kilometers | 1.5 hours

ROUTE OVERVIEW: VT-127 • surface streets • US-2

① Revolutionary War hero and statesman Ethan Allen was instrumental in helping Vermont secure statehood during the nation's early days. Visit Allen's historic 1787 home on your way out of town. The **Ethan Allen Homestead Museum** (1 Ethan Allen Homestead, 802/865-4556, www.ethanallenhomestead.org, 10am-4pm daily, $10 adults, $6 children 5-17) invites visitors to walk the trails, explore the exhibits, and see what 18th-century life was like for Vermont's founder.

> Take VT-127 N out of Burlington for 1 mile (1.6 km). Take the exit for North Ave./Beaches, then turn right onto Ethan Allen Homestead and continue for less than a mile.

② Before you leave the mainland for the Champlain Islands, check out **Sand Bar State Park** (1215 US-2, Milton, 802/893-2825, http://vtstateparks.com, 10am-8pm daily, $4 adults, $2 children). Stroll the beach, spot wildlife, or rent a kayak to venture out on the water.

> Take VT-127 N for 6 miles (10 km). Turn left onto Lakeshore Dr. and follow this for 1.5 miles (2.5 km). Here, the road becomes Bay Rd. Follow this for 1.5 miles (2.5 km), then turn left to join US-2. Follow this for 8 miles (13 km) to reach the state park.

③ On **South Hero Island,** indulge in a lobster roll at **Blue Paddle Bistro** (316 US-2, 802/372-4814, http://blue-paddlebistro.com, 5pm-8pm Mon., 11:30am-2pm and 5pm-8pm Tues.-Sat., 10am-2pm and 5pm-8pm Sun., $15-30).

> Continue on US-2 W for 4 miles (6 km), crossing Lake Champlain to reach South Hero Island and the restaurant.

▶ Playlist

LAKE CHAMPLAIN SCENIC BYWAY

SONGS

- **"The Divided Sky" by Phish:** Vermont jam band Phish has a cult following, not unlike The Grateful Dead, with fans touring the country to see the band live. Play this song as you drive the roads that likely inspired the band.

- **"Forsythia" by Cricket Blue:** Duo Laura Heaberlin and Taylor Smith met at Middlebury College, and their introspective folk songs encourage contemplation as you gaze out the car window at Lake Champlain.

RADIO STATIONS

- **102.7 WEQX:** Go old school and tune into local radio. Broadcasting from Manchester, Vermont, this excellent station plays a solid lineup of indie pop and alt rock, as well as keeps you informed of local festivals and concerts.

SOUTH HERO ISLAND

4 The byway gently winds through the wild regions of the Champlain Islands, with each bend in the road more scenic than the last. Ditch the car and see the sights on two wheels. **Hero's Welcome** (3537 US-2, North Hero, 802/372-4161, http://heroswelcome.com, 6:30am-6pm Mon.-Fri., 7am-6pm Sat., 8am-5pm Sun.) rents bicycles ($15 per hour) and offers tips for navigating the **Lake Champlain Bikeways Network** (www.champlainbikeways.org).

> Continue another 13 miles (21 km) north on US-2 to reach the rental shop.

5 At **Shore Acres Inn & Restaurant** (237 Shore Acres Dr., North Hero, 802/372-8722, www.shoreacres.com, $139-260 hotel, $12-40 restaurant), not only can you dine on fresh fish with uninterrupted views of Lake Champlain, you can also spend the night. After dinner, order a nightcap and take it outside on the grassy lawn to watch the sunset from your very own Adirondack chair. This is New England living at its best.

> Retrace your path south on US-2 for less than a mile, then turn left onto Shore Acres Dr. to reach the inn.

Getting There

AIR

Albany International Airport (ALB, 518/242-2200, www.albanyairport.com) is the best option for accessing the Lake Champlain Scenic Byway. Among the airlines flying into Albany are American Airlines, Delta, Southwest, and United. Albany Airport has a full-service rental car center with Alamo, Budget, Enterprise, and Hertz on site.

Burlington International Airport (BTV, 802/863-2874, www.btv.aero) is located along the Lake Champlain Scenic Byway, making it the most direct option; however, it's situated in the middle of the byway, so no matter in which direction you travel, you'll inevitably be backtracking a section of the route. It's also a smaller airport, so airfare can be pricey. American Airlines, Delta, and United all fly into Burlington. Burlington Airport offers car rentals from Alamo, Budget, and Enterprise.

TRAIN

This region is accessible by **Amtrak** (800/872-7245, www.amtrak.com). The company's Vermonter train departs Washington DC and New York City, and includes a stop in Essex Junction/Burlington. Amtrak's Adirondack service departs New York City and stops in Albany and Ticonderoga, which is an easily accessible point on the New York side of Lake Champlain. Both the Vermonter and Adirondack trains offer one northbound and one southbound trip daily.

CAR

Albany International Airport is located 95 miles (150 km) south of Shoreham, the southern origin of Lake Champlain Scenic Byway. The drive takes two hours. To get to Shoreham, take I-87, US-9, and NY-9N to the town of Ticonderoga. In Ticonderoga, pick up NY-74, driving it for less than 2 miles (3 km) to the **Fort Ticonderoga Ferry** (802/897-7999, www.forttiferry.com, 7am-7pm daily early July-Labor Day, shorter hours Memorial Day-early July and Labor Day-Oct., $12 one-way, $18 round-trip). The ferry is based in Shoreham, Vermont, and shuttles passengers across Lake Champlain between Ticonderoga and Shoreham.

Getting Back

From North Hero, it's 195 miles (315 km) back to **Albany International Airport,** a drive of 3.5 hours. Take US-2, crossing Lake Champlain into New York. Here, pick up NY-9B and follow it to US-9. Take NY-191 to I-87, which leads to the airport.

If you choose to fly out of **Burlington International Airport,** it's 35 miles (60 km) from North Hero, a drive of less than an hour. Follow US-2 to I-89, then merge back onto US-2. Continue on US-2 to the airport.

CONNECT WITH

- At Shoreham: **Adirondacks and Catskills** (PAGE 530)

PHILADELPHIA, PITTSBURGH, AND PENNSYLVANIA DUTCH COUNTRY

WHY GO: Amish culture, Philly cheesesteaks, pop art, Civil War history, renowned architecture

TOTAL DISTANCE: 370 miles/ 595 kilometers

NUMBER OF DAYS: 7

SEASONS: Spring through fall

START: Philadelphia, Pennsylvania

END: Pittsburgh, Pennsylvania

▶ PHILADELPHIA

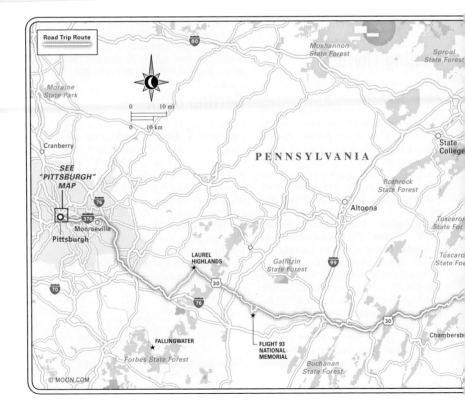

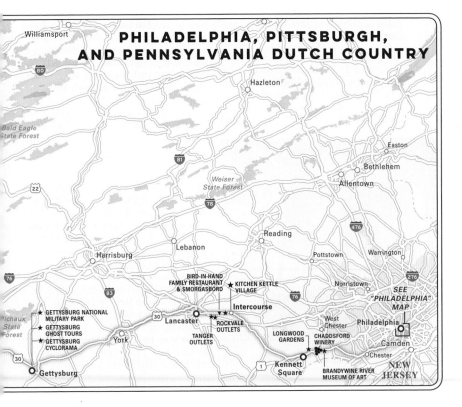

PHILADELPHIA, PITTSBURGH, AND PENNSYLVANIA DUTCH COUNTRY

Williamsport

Hazleton

Bald Eagle State Forest

Easton

Bethlehem

Weiser State Forest

Allentown

Reading

Harrisburg

Lebanon

Pottstown

Warrington

Norristown

SEE "PHILADELPHIA" MAP

★ GETTYSBURG NATIONAL MILITARY PARK
★ GETTYSBURG GHOST TOURS
★ GETTYSBURG CYCLORAMA

BIRD-IN-HAND FAMILY RESTAURANT & SMORGASBORD
★ KITCHEN KETTLE VILLAGE

Intercourse

Lancaster
★ ROCKVALE OUTLETS

West Chester

Philadelphia

Michaux State Forest

York

TANGER OUTLETS

LONGWOOD GARDENS
CHADDSFORD WINERY

Camden

Chester

Gettysburg

Kennett Square

BRANDYWINE RIVER MUSEUM OF ART

NEW JERSEY

This journey starts at the place of origin for the United States: Philadelphia. Soak up all that the City of Brotherly Love has to offer, from its historic roots to the burgeoning food scene, before heading west into the heart of Amish country. Slow down and take in the rolling landscape dotted with farm-fresh markets and little shops filled with Amish-made goods. The route continues west to Gettysburg, an important place in our country's complicated history. Then it's on to your final destination in Pittsburgh, where acclaimed art galleries, museums, and botanical gardens await.

DAY 1: Philadelphia

MORNING

❶ Begin where our country did: Philadelphia, the nation's birthplace. Pick up a timed ticket to **Independence Hall** (Chestnut St. between 5th and 6th Sts., 215/965-2305, www.nps.gov/inde, 9am-5pm daily, free tours, timed ticket required Mar.-Dec.) at the Independence Visitor Center, loading up on maps and brochures while you're at it. It's here that the Founding Fathers debated and drafted the Declaration of Independence and later the Constitution.

❷ Before your Independence Hall tour, stroll down the oldest residential street in the country, **Elfreth's Alley** (off 2nd St., between Arch and Race Sts., www.elfrethsalley.org). The 30-some houses that line it were built between the 1720s and 1830s and have been so meticulously restored that the block feels like a movie set.

AFTERNOON

❸ Make your way to the **Liberty Bell** (Market St. between 5th and 6th Sts., 215/965-2305, www.nps.gov/inde, hours vary by season, generally 9am-5pm daily, free) for a photo of the iconic bell against the backdrop of Independence Hall.

❹ Try a Supreme Court robe on for size at the **National Constitution Center** (525 Arch St., 215/409-6600, www.constitutioncenter.org, 9:30am-5pm Mon.-Sat., noon-5pm Sun., $14.50 adults, $11 children 6-18). An hour or two is enough to hit the highlights, including Signers' Hall, featuring selfie-worthy life-size bronze statues of the 39 men who signed the Constitution—and the 3 dissenters who did not.

EVENING

❺ Dinner is at the neon-lit intersection of 9th Street and Passyunk Avenue in South Philly, home to rival cheesesteakeries **Pat's King of Steaks** (1237 E. Passyunk Ave., 215/468-1546, www.patskingofsteaks.com, 24 hours daily) and **Geno's Steaks** (1219 S. 9th St., 215/389-0659, www.genosteaks.com, 24 hours daily). Insider tip: When it comes time to order, it's best to know what you're doing. Don't order a "Philly cheesesteak." Instead, say "whiz wit" for Cheez Whiz with fried onions, and "prov witout" for provolone cheese without fried onions.

LIBERTY BELL

Top 5 PHILADELPHIA, PITTSBURGH, AND PENNSYLVANIA DUTCH COUNTRY

1. Walk down the oldest residential street in the country, **Elfreth's Alley** in Philadelphia (PAGE 520).

2. Order a **Philly cheesesteak** like a local: "whiz wit" or "prov witout" (PAGE 520).

3. Ride an **Amish buggy** through the countryside (PAGE 524).

4. Tour **Gettysburg National Military Park,** site of the Civil War's bloodiest battle (PAGE 525).

5. Visit Pittsburgh's **Andy Warhol Museum,** the largest U.S. museum dedicated to a single artist (PAGE 526).

PHILADELPHIA

© MOON.COM

DAY 2: Philadelphia

MORNING

❶ "Do time" at **Eastern State Penitentiary** (2027 Fairmount Ave., 215/236-3300, www.easternstate.org, 10am-5pm daily, $16 adults, $12 children). Opened in 1829, this sprawling prison served as a model for hundreds around the world, horrified Charles Dickens, and hosted Al "Scarface" Capone. It closed in 1971 but hasn't lost its eerie edge.

❷ Sprint up the so-called **Rocky steps** and wander the rooms of the stunning **Philadelphia Museum of Art** (2600 Benjamin Franklin Pkwy., 215/763-8100, www.philamuseum.org, 10am-5pm Tues., Thurs., and Sat.-Sun., 10am-8:45pm Wed. and Fri., $20 adults, $14 children 13-18). The nation's third-largest art museum is home to more than 240,000 objects.

AFTERNOON

❸ Walk along the picturesque Benjamin Franklin Parkway and visit the **Barnes Foundation** (2025 Benjamin Franklin Pkwy., 215/278-7000, www.barnesfoundation.org, 10am-5pm Wed.-Mon., $25 adults, $10 children 6-18). This renowned art collection encompasses works by Renoir, Cézanne, van Gogh, and other Impressionist and Postimpressionist masters.

PHILADELPHIA MUSEUM OF ART

EVENING

④ Treat your culturally enriched self to a show on the **Avenue of the Arts** (S. Broad St.). The most striking venue is the **Kimmel Center for the Performing Arts** (Broad and Spruce Sts., 215/893-1999, www.kimmelcenter.org). Described by architect Rafael Viñoly as "two jewels inside a glass box," the building consists of two freestanding performance halls beneath a vaulted glass ceiling.

⑤ Finish the night with dinner at **Vedge** (1221 Locust St., 215/320-7500, www.vedgerestaurant.com, 5pm-10pm Mon.-Thurs., 5pm-11pm Fri.-Sat., $12-18), a vegan spot where carnivores won't miss a thing.

DAY 3: Philadelphia to Kennett Square

40 miles/64 kilometers | 1.5 hours

ROUTE OVERVIEW: I-95 • US-322 • US-1

① The **Brandywine River Museum of Art** (1 Hoffman's Mill Rd., Chadds Ford, 610/388-2700, www.brandywinemuseum.org, 9:30am-5pm daily, $18 adults, $6 children) opened in 1971 in a converted Civil War-era gristmill. The museum is home to an unparalleled collection of works by three generations of Wyeths.

> *Get on I-95 S, driving it for 9 miles (15 km) to US-322. Continue on US-322 W for 7 miles (11 km). Turn left on US-1 S and follow it to the museum.*

② Nearby, check out **Chaddsford Winery** (632 Baltimore Pike, Chadds Ford, 610/388-6221, www.chaddsford.com, 10am-6pm Tues.-Fri. and Sun., 11am-7pm Sat., tasting fee $10), one of Pennsylvania's largest makers of grown-up grape juice.

> *Drive 5 miles (8 km) on US-1 S to the winery.*

③ The beautiful **Longwood Gardens** (1001 Longwood Rd., Kennett Square, 610/388-1000, www.longwoodgardens.org, 9am-6pm daily winter, 9am-6pm Sun.-Wed., 9am-10pm Thurs.-Sat. summer, $23-30 adults, $12-16

Eating Well ON PASSYUNK AVENUE

There's no need to stray far from tourist attractions to eat well in Philadelphia, but if you have extra time, visiting **East Passyunk Avenue** in South Philly is worth a detour. Restaurants line this diagonal avenue from Broad Street to 10th Street. It's known for being one of the best foodie streets in the country.

- At French-American **Laurel** (1617 E. Passyunk Ave., 215/271-8299, www.restaurantlaurel.com, 5:30pm-9:15pm Tues.-Sat., reservations recommended, $85-125), opt for a seasonal six- or nine-course tasting menu, expertly crafted by *Top Chef*-winning maestro Nick Elmi.

- Try the meat pie and mashed potatoes at British pie shop **Stargazy** (1838 E. Passyunk Ave., 215/309-2761, 11am-7pm Tues.-Fri., 11am-8pm Sat., 11am-2pm Sun., $7-11).

- Order the seitan fajitas and join the raucous crowd fueled by frozen margaritas at **Cantina Los Caballitos** (1651 E. Passyunk Ave., 215/755-3550, www.cantinaloscaballitos.com, 11am-2am daily, kitchen open until 1am, $8-20).

- For classic Italian-American dishes, **Marra's** (1734 E. Passyunk Ave., 215/463-9249, www.marrasone.com, 11:30am-10pm Tues.-Thurs., 11:30am-11pm Fri., noon-11pm Sat., 1pm-9pm Sun., $7-20) is an old-school charmer.

- At the small, colorful **Bing Bing Dim Sum** (1648 E. Passyunk Ave., 215/279-7702, www.bingbingdimsum.com, 5pm-10pm Mon.-Thurs., noon-11pm Fri.-Sat., noon-10pm Sun., $13-16), you'll find Asian-inspired food that puts a unique spin on traditional dishes.

LONGWOOD GARDENS

children 5-18) deserves a full afternoon. Illuminated jets of water shoot 175 feet in the air during the popular **Illuminated Fountain Performances** (Thurs.-Sat. May-Oct.). Buy a timed ticket ahead of your visit, whether you're coming during the day or in the evening. Spend the night in nearby **Kennett Square.**

> Continue on US-1 S for 3 miles (5 km) to Longwood Gardens. Follow US-1 S for 2 more miles (3 km) to reach Kennett Square.

DAY 4: Kennett Square to Lancaster

45 miles/72 kilometers | 1.5-2 hours

ROUTE OVERVIEW: US-1 • PA-41 • US-30 • PA-772/PA-340 • PA-896 • US-30 • PA-896 • PA-340 • PA-23

❶ The town of **Intercourse** (go ahead and laugh) is one of several Lancaster County burgs with an eyebrow-raising name. Taste your way through **Kitchen Kettle Village** (3529 Old Philadelphia Pike, Intercourse, 717/768-8261, www.kitchenkettle.com, 9am-6pm Mon.-Sat. May-Oct., 9am-5pm Mon.-Sat. Nov.-Dec. and Mar.-Apr., hours vary by shop Jan.-Feb.), a collection of 40 specialty shops that started as a canning kitchen. Note that because the kitchen is staffed by Amish women, photos aren't permitted.

> Take US-1 S for 8 miles (13 km). Turn right on PA-41. Follow this north for 16 miles (26 km) until it becomes US-30 E. After less than a mile, turn right on PA-772 W/PA-340 W and continue for 5 miles (8 km) to Intercourse.

KEY RESERVATIONS

• You'll need advance reservations for the **Illuminated Fountain Performances** at **Longwood Gardens** in Kennett Square.

• Book ahead to tour Frank Lloyd Wright's **Fallingwater** in Mill Run.

❷ Just down the road sits **Plain & Fancy Farm** (3121 Old Philadelphia Pike, Bird-in-Hand, 717/768-4400, www.plainandfancyfarm.com), where you can learn all about Amish life and take a **buggy ride** (Aaron and Jessica's Buggy Rides, 717/768-8828, www.amishbuggyrides.com, 9am-6pm daily Apr.-Oct., 9am-4:30pm daily Nov.-Mar., from $10 adults, from $6 children 3-12) through the countryside.

> Head west on PA-772/PA-340 for 2 miles (3 km) to reach Plain & Fancy.

❸ Shop your heart out at the **Rockvale Outlets** (35 S. Willowdale Dr., Lancaster, 717/293-9292, www.rockvaleoutletslancaster.com, 9:30am-9pm Mon.-Sat., 11am-5pm Sun.) and **Tanger Outlets** (311 Stanley K. Tanger Blvd., Lancaster, 717/392-7260, www.tangeroutlet.com, 9am-9pm Mon.-Sat., 10am-7pm Sun.).

> Follow PA-340 W for 3 miles (5 km) to PA-896 S. Turn left and drive PA-896 for 1 mile (1.6 km) to US-30 W. Turn right; the outlets are on the south side of US-30.

❹ Eateries close early in these parts, so come dinnertime hustle to a smorgasbord restaurant like **Bird-in-Hand Family Restaurant & Smorgasbord** (2760 Old Philadelphia Pike,

PARKING LOT AT BIRD-IN-HAND RESTAURANT

Bird-in-Hand, 717/768-1500, www.bird-in-hand.com, 6am-8pm Mon.-Sat., $9-21, age-based pricing for children 4-12), a from-scratch, farm-fresh restaurant that serves Pennsylvania Dutch fare, such as chicken pot pie, roast turkey and gravy, pork and sauerkraut, and baked lima beans.

> *Retrace your path back up to PA-340 via PA-896 (1.5 mi/2.5 km), then turn right onto PA-340 and head east for 1 mile (1.6 km) to reach the restaurant.*

❺ Bed down in **Lancaster** proper at the **Lancaster Arts Hotel** (300 Harrisburg Ave., 717/299-3000, www.lancasterartshotel.com, $179-369), an elegant boutique hotel that boasts more than 200 works by 36 Pennsylvania artists. Enjoy the hotel's complimentary breakfast the next morning before heading out for the day.

> *Take PA-340 W for 5 miles (8 km) to downtown Lancaster.*

DAY 5: Lancaster to Gettysburg

60 miles/97 kilometers | 2 hours

ROUTE OVERVIEW: US-30 • PA-234 • US-15 • PA-97 • surface streets

❶ Your first stop should be **Gettysburg National Military Park** (717/334-1124, www.nps.gov/gett, 6am-10pm daily Apr.-Oct., 6am-7pm daily Nov.-Mar., free), site of the Civil War's bloodiest battle. This national park is heaven for history buffs. Take your pick of battlefield tours—horseback and Segway are two ways to go—and don't leave without seeing the **Gettysburg Cyclorama** ($15 adults, $10 children 6-12) in the visitors center. It's the largest painting in the country, measuring 42 feet high and 377 feet in circumference. It's easy to make a full day out of a visit here, if you have extra time.

> *Take US-30 W for 32 miles (51 km) to Big Mount Rd. Turn right and follow this for 1.5 miles (2.5 km) to PA-234 W. Turn left and drive 12 miles (19 km) to US-15. Merge onto US-15 S. Take this for 11 miles (18 km) to the exit for PA-97 toward Baltimore St. Exit and turn right on Baltimore St., taking it to Gettysburg National Military Park.*

❷ For an early dinner, indulge in colonial-style chow in Gettysburg's oldest building at the 1776-built **Dobbin House Tavern** (89 Steinwehr Ave., 717/334-2100, www.dobbinhouse.com). Choose between casual dining in the Springhouse Tavern (from 11:30am daily, $8-25) or fine dining in the candlelit Alexander Dobbin Dining Rooms (5pm-close daily, $24-43).

> *Follow Baltimore St. north for 1.5 miles (2.5 km) to reach central Gettysburg.*

❸ Check in to **The Gaslight Inn Bed & Breakfast** (33 E. Middle St., 717/337-9100, www.thegaslightinn.com, $128-145), a charming and historic inn built in 1872. Tastefully appointed guest rooms each offer private bathrooms and large, cozy beds.

❹ Conclude the evening with an adventure that's equal parts history and paranormal activity. **Gettysburg Ghost Tours** (47 Steinwehr Ave., 717/338-1818, http://gettysburgghosttours.com, 10am-10:30pm Sun.-Thurs.,

GETTYSBURG NATIONAL MILITARY PARK

DOBBIN HOUSE TAVERN

9am-11pm Fri.-Sat., $10 adults, $5 children 6-12) offers one-hour themed walking tours, from haunted cemetery strolls to craft beer walkabouts.

DAY 6: Gettysburg to Pittsburgh

225 miles/360 kilometers | 5 hours

ROUTE OVERVIEW: US-30 • PA-281 • PA-653 • PA-381 • I-76/PA Turnpike • I-376/US-22

❶ Get an early start, as you have several hours of driving ahead today. On your way, pay your respects to some of the victims of the tragic 9/11 attacks at the **Flight 93 National Memorial** (6424 Lincoln Hwy., Stoystown, 814/893-6322, www.nps.gov/flni, visitors center 9am-5pm daily, grounds sunrise-sunset daily, free). It's a powerful tribute to the men and women who thwarted a planned attack on the nation's capital. A tall white wall is composed of 40 marble panels, each inscribed with the name of a passenger or crew member. The Wall of Names is aligned with the plane's flight path. A boulder marks the impact point.

> From Gettysburg, join US-30 W and drive for 103 miles (166 km) to reach the memorial.

❷ Once you reach the **Laurel Highlands,** head to Frank Lloyd Wright's **Fallingwater** (1491 Mill Run Rd., Mill Run, 724/329-8501, www.fallingwater.org, Thurs.-Tues., tours from $30 adults, from $18 children 6-12, children under 6 not permitted). Wright designed the house in 1935 and positioned it directly over a 30-foot waterfall, creating an enchanting illusion that the house springs from nature. Be sure to reserve your ticket in advance.

> Continue on US-30 W to PA-281 (4 mi/6 km). Turn left and drive PA-281 S for 21 miles (34 km) to New Centerville. Get on PA-653 W and take it for 11 miles (18 km) to Kooser Rd. Follow this for 4 miles (6 km), then turn left onto PA-381. Continue south for another 4 miles (6 km), then turn right onto Fallingwater Rd.

❸ From Fallingwater, head to **Pittsburgh,** where you'll spend the night at the **Kimpton Hotel Monaco Pittsburgh** (620 William Penn Pl., 412/471-1170, www.monaco-pittsburgh.com, $260-350). This 1903 beaux arts building once housed an electric company and a law firm. Enjoy the excellent on-site restaurant, then take in the Pittsburgh skyline at the rooftop bar.

> From Fallingwater Rd., get back on PA-381 and drive north for 7 miles (11 km). Turn right to continue on PA-381/PA-711 for 6 miles (10 km). Turn left onto Melcroft Rd., which becomes Hellein School Rd. in 3 miles (5 km). Continue on this for another 1.5 miles (2.5 km). Turn right onto PA-31, then make the first left to get onto I-76/PA Turnpike. Follow the turnpike for 34 miles (55 km), then take exit 57 for I-376/US-22 W. Continue on I-376 for 14 miles (23 km) to reach downtown Pittsburgh.

DAY 7: Pittsburgh

MORNING

❶ Start your day in Pittsburgh with a visit to **The Andy Warhol Museum** (117 Sandusky St., 412/237-8300, www.warhol.org, 10am-5pm Tues.-Thurs. and Sat.-Sun., 10am-10pm Fri., $20 adults, $10 children 3-18). It's the largest U.S. museum dedicated to a single artist. The collection includes about 900 paintings and 2,000 drawings, along with sculptures, prints, photographs, films, videos, books, and even wallpaper designed by the artist.

FALLINGWATER

PHIPPS CONSERVATORY AND BOTANICAL GARDENS

② Head to the **Mattress Factory** (500 Sampsonia Way, 412/231-3169, www.mattress.org, 10am-5pm Tues.-Sat., 1pm-5pm Sun., $20 adults, $15 children 6-17) for more jaw-dropping art in the form of installations created on-site. Its permanent pieces include work by James Turrell, Bill Woodrow, and Yayoi Kusama.

AFTERNOON AND EVENING

③ Spend the afternoon in the Oakland neighborhood, where you can wander through the **Phipps Conservatory and Botanical Gardens** (1 Schenley Park, 412/622-6914, www.phipps.conservatory.org, 9:30am-5pm daily and until 10pm Fri., $18 adults, $12

PITTSBURGH

© MOON.COM

VIEW OF DOWNTOWN PITTSBURGH FROM THE DUQUESNE INCLINE

children 2-18) in Schenley Park. The floral displays in Pittsburgh's "crystal palace" will make you forget you're anywhere near a bustling city.

❹ After dinner head straight to the **South Side** to ascend Mount Washington via a 19th-century cable car on the **Duquesne Incline** (lower station 1197 W. Carson St., 412/381-1665, www.duquesneincline.org, 5:30am-12:30am Mon.-Sat., 7am-12:30am Sun., one-way fare $2.50 adults, $1.25 children 6-11) for spectacular nighttime views.

Getting There

AIR

Philadelphia International Airport (PHL, 215/937-6937, www.phl.org) boasts seven terminals, four runways, and daily departures to more than 120 cities. It's served by about a dozen airlines, including budget carriers JetBlue, Spirit, and Frontier. Located seven miles southwest of Center City, the airport offers the usual array of ground transportation options, including rental cars, taxis, and shared-ride vans. The airport website has a directory of ground transportation providers. Call 215/937-6958 to chat with a ground transportation specialist.

SEPTA (215/580-7800, www.septa.org) offers rail service from the airport. Trains depart every 30 minutes from shortly after 5am to shortly after midnight.

TRAIN

30th Street Station (2955 Market St.), located just across the Schuylkill River from Center City, is one of the nation's busiest intercity passenger rail stations. It's a stop along several **Amtrak** (800/872-7245, www.amtrak.com) routes, including the Northeast Regional, which connects Boston, New York, Baltimore, and Washington DC, among other cities; the Pennsylvanian, which runs between New York and Pittsburgh; and the Cardinal, running between New York and Chicago.

New Jersey's public transportation system, **NJ Transit** (973/275-5555, www.njtransit.com), has a commuter rail line between Atlantic City, New Jersey, and 30th Street Station. Its bus route network also extends into Philly.

The Southeastern Pennsylvania Transportation Authority, or **SEPTA** (215/580-7800, www.septa.org), provides service to Philadelphia from countless suburban towns, Philadelphia International Airport, New

30TH STREET STATION IN PHILADELPHIA

Jersey's capital of Trenton, and Wilmington, Delaware.

BUS

Traveling to Philly can be dirt cheap. **Greyhound** (800/231-2222, www.greyhound.com) buses collect Philly-bound travelers from all over the country and deposit them at Filbert and 10th Streets in Center City.

Megabus (877/462-6342, www.megabus.com) offers service to Philadelphia from about a dozen cities, including Pittsburgh, Boston, New York, Baltimore, Washington DC, and Toronto. Its main stop in Philadelphia is on JFK Boulevard near North 30th Street, a stone's throw from 30th Street Station. **BoltBus** (877/265-8287, www.boltbus.com) leaves from almost the same location—3131 JFK Boulevard—and travels to Boston, New York, and Newark, New Jersey.

FERRY

Philadelphia is a port city, and arriving by boat is possible in the warmer months. The **RiverLink Ferry** (215/925-5465, www.riverlinkferry.org, service daily Memorial Day-Labor Day and weekends in May and Sept., $9 adults, $7 children) shuttles between Philly and its New Jersey neighbor, Camden.

CAR

Philadelphia is a straightforward drive from several major cities: about 95 miles (155 km) southwest of **New York** via I-95, 105 miles (170 km) northeast of **Baltimore** via I-95, and 300 miles (485 km) east of **Pittsburgh** via the Pennsylvania Turnpike.

It's about 10 miles (16 km) from **Philadelphia International Airport** to downtown, but thanks to traffic, it'll take about 25 minutes. Hop on I-95 North, taking it to the exit for US-30 East/Independence Hall. Exit, merging onto Callowhill Street, then turn left on North 6th Street. Follow this to Market Street.

Getting Back

It's a 5.5-hour trip of 310 miles (500 km) back to **Philadelphia** from downtown Pittsburgh. Follow I-376 to I-76,

 Playlist

PHILADELPHIA, PITTSBURGH, AND PENNSYLVANIA DUTCH COUNTRY

SONGS

- **"You Make My Dreams" by Hall & Oates:** There's no shame in bopping around to this 1980 classic by pop duo Daryl Hall and John Oates, especially given that the legendary pair launched their career in Philadelphia.

- **"Gonna Fly Now" by Bill Conti:** One of the songs most associated with Philadelphia, the swelling sounds of this inspirational hit from *Rocky* are a must-play as you drive into town.

- **"Positively Lost Me" by The Rave-Ups:** This 1980s punk group formed in Pittsburgh, then made it big in Los Angeles, mainly due to this drum-forward song featured in the John Hughes mega-hit *Pretty in Pink,* starring Molly Ringwald.

then merge onto I-476. From there, take I-95 to the airport.

You can also book a one-way fare home from Pittsburgh. A 20-mile (32-km) drive that's 30 minutes from downtown, **Pittsburgh International Airport** (PIT, 412/472-3525, www.flypittsburgh.com) is served by about a dozen carriers, including budget airlines JetBlue, Frontier, and Spirit. Take I-376 all the way to the airport from downtown Pittsburgh.

ADIRONDACKS AND CATSKILLS

WHY GO: Fall foliage, charming B&Bs, scenic mountain vistas, wild backcountry hikes, big lakes, winter sports

TOTAL DISTANCE: 545 miles/ 875 kilometers

NUMBER OF DAYS: 6

SEASONS: Summer, fall, and winter

START: Saratoga Springs, New York

END: New York City, New York

▼ LAKE PLACID

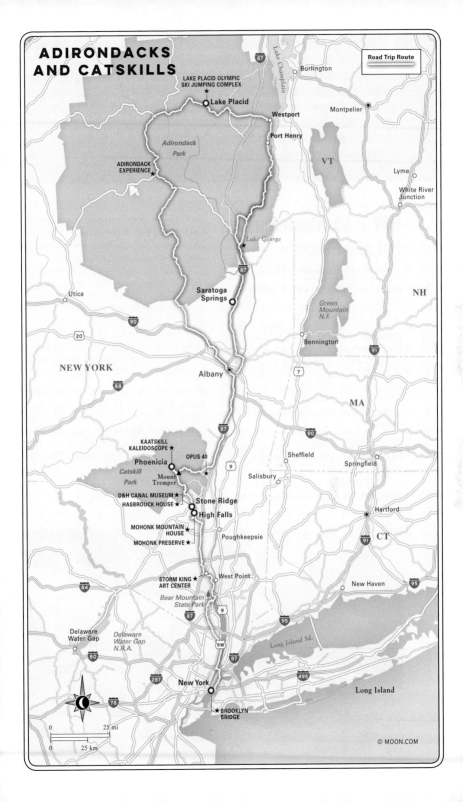

The Adirondacks are one of the largest protected natural areas in the country, and between this mountainous region and the Catskills just to the south, you're primed to experience thousands of acres of wildland, nearly 100 peaks, lakes and waterways, and farm-fresh cuisine. Launching from the thoroughbred horse racing hub of Saratoga Springs, you'll set out north, traveling along Lake George and Lake Champlain before ducking inland to Lake Placid. You'll journey through the Adirondacks, head south to the Catskills, and end up in New York City.

DAY 1: Saratoga Springs to Lake Placid

125 miles/201 kilometers | 3 hours

ROUTE OVERVIEW: I-87 • NY-9N • NY-73

❶ Before hitting the road out of **Saratoga Springs,** grab breakfast at **Mrs. London's Bakery** (464 Broadway, 518/581-1652, www.mrslondonsbakery.com, 7am-6pm Mon.-Thurs., 7am-9pm Fri.-Sat., 7am-6pm Sun.), which offers a mouthwatering selection of desserts, baked goods, and gourmet coffees.

❷ Drive north along the shores of **Lake George** and **Lake Champlain.** Take in the sights of the picturesque lakeside villages, such as **Port Henry** and **Westport,** on your way to **Lake Placid.**

Once there, grab lunch at the popular **Lake Placid Pub & Brewery** (813 Mirror Lake Dr., 518/523-3813, www.ubuale.com, lunch and dinner daily, $13).

> Take I-87 N for 24 miles (39 km), then continue north onto NY-9N for another 37 miles (60 km) to reach Port Henry. It's another 10 miles (16 km) north on NY-9N to reach Westport. From here, follow NY-9N inland for 21 miles (34 km). Make a left to continue onto NY-73 and head west for 14 miles (23 km) to reach Lake Placid.

❸ Get a room or suite at the posh **Mirror Lake Inn** (77 Mirror Lake Dr., 518/523-2544, www.mirrorlakeinn.com, rooms $240-350, suites $420-660), and plan on relaxing for the rest of the day at this resort. Two on-site restaurants, a spa, and a private beach are more than enough of a reason to take it easy today.

PASTRIES AT MRS. LONDON'S BAKERY, SARATOGA SPRINGS

Top ③ ADIRONDACKS AND CATSKILLS

① Gaze at the thrilling high jumps from the sky deck at the **Olympic Ski Jumping Complex** (PAGE 534).

② Hike the Adirondacks peaks, using **Adirondak Loj** as your basecamp for access to the trailheads (PAGE 534).

③ Walk across the **Brooklyn Bridge**, stopping for Instagram-worthy photos along the way (PAGE 538).

LAKE PLACID

DAY 2: Lake Placid

20 miles/32 kilometers | 30-45 minutes

ROUTE OVERVIEW: NY-73

❶ Start the day with a tasty scone at **Bluesberry Bakery** (2436 Main St., 518/523-4539, www.lakeplacidbakery.com, 7:30am-5pm Thurs.-Tues.).

❷ Head to the **Olympic Ski Jumping Complex** (5486 Cascade Rd., 518/523-2202, www.whiteface.com, 9am-4pm daily, $8-16) and see the gasp-worthy view of the 90- and 120-meter high jumps from an elevator-accessible sky deck.

> *Drive south on NY-73 E for 1 mile (1.6 km) to the Olympic Ski Jumping Complex.*

❸ Make the short drive south to the shores of Heart Lake to **Adirondak Loj** (1002 Adirondak Loj Rd., 518/523-3441, www.adk.org). The lodge is the trailhead for many stunning trails that ascend the region's incomparable peaks. The helpful staff at the information center will advise you in selecting the right trail before sending you on your way. Once you've tired yourself out, head back to the Mirror Lake Inn for a good night's sleep.

OLYMPIC SKI JUMPING COMPLEX

> *Take NY-73 E for 1.5 miles (2.5 km), then turn right onto Adirondack Loj Rd. Follow this for 5 miles (8 km) to reach the lodge. To return to Lake Placid, follow Adirondack Loj Rd. back to NY-73 (5 mi/8 km). Take NY-73 W for 3 miles (5 km) to return to town.*

DAY 3: Lake Placid to Phoenicia

250 miles/400 kilometers | 5-6 hours

ROUTE OVERVIEW: NY-86 • NY-3 • NY-30 • NY-28N/NY-30 • I-90 • I-87 • NY-212

❶ Scenic NY-30 runs through the heart of the Adirondacks. Budget several hours for driving to the Catskills. Along the way, you can stop at the **Adirondack Experience** (9097 NY-30, 518/352-7311, www.adkmuseum.org, 10am-5pm daily late May-mid-Oct., $20 adults, $12 children 6-17). By far the most important museum in the region, the 22-building complex has exhibits on local history, natural science, culture, and art.

> *Head west out of Lake Placid, taking NY-86 for 6 miles (10 km). Turn left onto River St., then continue onto NY-3 W for 20 miles (32 km) to the town of Tupper Lake. From here, continue south on NY-30 for 22 miles (35 km), then turn right to follow NY-30 as it joins with NY-28N. Follow this for another 10 miles (16 km) to reach the museum.*

MAIN STREET, PHOENICIA

❷ Once you reach **Phoenicia**, have dinner at **Brio's** (68 Main St., 845/688-5370, www.brios.net, 7am-11pm daily summer, shorter hours fall-spring, $12), a dependable pizzeria.

> *Go south on NY-28/NY-30 for 11 miles (18 km), then turn right to continue south on NY-30 for another 76 miles (122 km) to the town of Amsterdam. Here, you'll jump on I-90 E. Follow this for 25 miles (40 km) to I-87. Take I-87 S for 47 miles (76 km) to NY-212 W. After 20 miles (32 km), turn right and follow Mt. Tremper-Phoenicia Rd. for 4 miles (6 km) into Phoenicia.*

❸ Overnight at **The Graham & Co.** (80 NY-214, 845/688-7871, www.thegrahamandco.com, $125-390), a hip boutique hotel.

DAY 4: Phoenicia to Stone Ridge

40 miles/64 kilometers | 1.5 hours

ROUTE OVERVIEW: NY-28 • NY-212 • Glasco Turnpike • US-9W • US-209

❶ With over a dozen types of pancakes on the menu, **Sweet Sue's** (49 Main St., 845/688-7852, 8am-3pm Thurs.-Mon., $12) is the perfect place to fuel up for the day.

❷ Want to see the world's largest kaleidoscope? Then stop in **Mount Tremper** at **Kaatskill Kaleidoscope** (5340 NY-28, 877/688-2828, 10am-5pm Mon.-Thurs., 10am-6pm Fri.-Sun., $5 adults, free for children under 11). Housed in a former grain silo, the 56-foot-tall kaleidoscope lets you stare straight up into myriad colorful images multiplied by 254 facets and covering about 45 feet.

> *Follow NY-28 E for 3 miles (5 km) to Kaatskill Kaleidoscope.*

❸ Just before Saugerties, stop at **Opus 40** (50 Fite Rd., 845/246-3400, www.opus40.org, 11am-5:30pm Thurs.-Sun. June-Oct., $10 adults, $3 children 6-12), an earthwork sculpture park and museum created by artist Harvey Fite over a period of 37 years. Its pools, fountains, sculptures,

OPUS 40

and walkways all center on a towering blue-gray monolith reminiscent of Stonehenge.

> *Take NY-212 E for 8 miles (13 km), then turn left onto Glasco Turnpike. Follow this for 7 miles (11 km), then turn left onto Fite Rd. to reach Opus 40.*

④ Bed down for the night in the town of **Stone Ridge. Hasbrouck House** (3805 US-209, 845/687-0736, www.hasbrouckhouseny.com, $195-425) is an elegant 18th-century colonial mansion with a decidedly modern vibe. It offers 25 guest rooms, a farm-to-table restaurant, 50 acres of gardens and woods, and a lake.

> *Head back out to Glasco Turnpike and drive east for 4 miles (6 km). Turn right onto US-9W and drive south for 4 miles (6 km). Merge onto US-209 and continue south for 13 miles (21 km) to reach Stone Ridge.*

DAY 5: Stone Ridge to High Falls

10 miles/16 kilometers | 30 minutes

ROUTE OVERVIEW: NY-213 • Mohonk Rd.

① After breakfast, it's a quick drive to the tiny canal town of **High Falls,** where the **D&H Canal Museum** (23 Mohonk Rd., 845/687-9311, www.

MOHONK MOUNTAIN HOUSE

canalmuseum.org, 11am-5pm Mon. and Thurs.-Sat., 1pm-5pm Sun. June-Sept., hours vary Oct.-May, $5 adults, $3 children) tells the story of the Delaware and Hudson Canal.

> *From Stone Ridge, take NY-213 southeast for 2 miles (3 km) to reach High Falls.*

❷ Check in at the nearby **Mohonk Mountain House** (1000 Mountain Rest Rd., 855/883-3798, www.mohonk.com, $200-500). The Victorian mountaintop castle is more than 140 years old and the region's loveliest resort.

> *Go south on Mohonk Rd. for 5 miles (8 km) to reach Mohonk Mountain House.*

❸ Purchase a day pass and head into the adjacent **Mohonk Preserve** (845/255-0919, www.mohonkpreserve. org, dawn-dusk daily, $12 adults, free for children under 12) to enjoy miles of hiking trails dotted with hand-hewn wooden gazebos for rest stops and plenty of wildlife and nature viewing. If visiting in winter, take a hot cocoa break by the massive stone ice-skating pavilion's bonfire.

DAY 6: High Falls to New York City

100 miles/161 kilometers | 3 hours

ROUTE OVERVIEW: NY-299 • I-87 • NY-300 • NY-32 • US-9W • US-202 • US-6 • Palisades Pkwy. • I-95 • surface streets

❶ Head south to **Storm King Art Center** (Old Pleasant Hill Rd., 845/534-3115, www.stormking.org, 10am-5pm Wed.-Sun. early Apr.-late Nov., $18 adults, $8 children over 5), a breathtakingly beautiful sculpture park built on a hilltop. About 120 permanent works and many more temporary ones are scattered over green lawns and wheat-blond fields. In the distance are the dusky-blue Shawangunks.

> *Take Mohonk Rd. to Mt. Rest Rd. Follow this for 3 miles (5 km) to NY-299. Turn left onto NY-299 E and drive 2 miles (3 km) to I-87. In 16 miles (26 km), take exit 17 for NY-300. Drive NY-300 S for 5 miles (8 km) to NY-32 S. Drive this for 1.5 miles*

▶ *Playlist*

ADIRONDACKS AND CATSKILLS

SONGS

● **"Fall in Love" by Phantogram:** Electronic rock duo Phantogram got their start in Saratoga Springs. The driving sound pushing this song from start to finish makes you crank it louder and louder. Keep the car windows open for this one.

● **"I Know This Bar" by Ani Difranco:** Singer, songwriter, poet, and activist Difranco hails from Buffalo. This road trip doesn't stray that far west, but you should still add this reflective and lyrically detailed song to your playlist.

● **"Brooklyn Baby" by Lana Del Rey:** Before you set foot on the Brooklyn Bridge, cue up this dreamy song from the ever-ethereal singer-songwriter Del Rey, who grew up in Lake Placid.

(2.5 km) to Orrs Mills Rd. Turn right and follow this to Storm King Art Center.

❷ In **Cornwall**, order a bowl of French onion soup at **Storm King Café** (18 Ridge Rd., 845/458-5655, www.stormkingtavern.com, 11:30am-7pm Mon.-Tues., 11:30am-9pm Wed.-Thurs., 11:30am-10pm Fri.-Sat., $14), a welcoming tavern with panoramic views located at the historic Storm King Golf Club.

> *Get back onto NY-32 S, then turn left and head east on Quaker Ave. for less than a mile to reach Cornwall.*

The Adirondacks and Catskills are well known for their wild places. Here's a list of some of the best spots to explore.

- Nearest to New York City, find excellent hiking at **Bear Mountain State Park** (Palisades Pkwy., 845/786-2701, www.nysparks.com, 8am-dusk daily, $10 vehicles) and **Harriman State Park** (Palisades Pkwy., 845/786-2701, www. nysparks.com, hours vary by section of park, $6-10 vehicles).

- In Ulster County, the ancient **Shawangunk Mountains** are a mecca for rock-climbing enthusiasts. One local rock-climbing guide service and school is **HighXposure Adventures** (800/777-2546, www. high-xposure.com). **Minnewaska State Park** (5281 US-44/NY-55, 845/255-0752, www.nysparks.com, hours vary seasonally, $8 vehicles) holds two stunning glacial lakes, accessible by foot only.

- **Adirondack Park** is a six-million-acre refuge with an unusual mixture of public and private lands. The **Adirondack Park Visitor Interpretive Center** (5922 NY-28N, 518/582-2000, www.esf.edu/aic, 10am-4pm Tues.-Sat., free) offers a thorough introduction to the park.

- Skiing and other winter sports make the **Lake Placid** area a four-season option for nature lovers. The excellent **Olympic Cross-Country Biathlon Center** (www.whiteface. com) on Mount Van Hoevenberg offers a 31-mile (50-km) system of ski trails.

- If you're short on time, a visit to **The Wild Center** (45 Museum Dr., 518/359-7800, www.wildcenter.org, hours vary by season, $17 adults, $10 children 5-17) in **Tupper Lake** will give you a sense of the area's natural wonders.

ADIRONDACK PARK

❸ Make your way to **Bear Mountain State Park** (Palisades Pkwy., 845/786-2701, www.nysparks.com, daily 8am-dusk, $10 vehicles), where you can take a short hike or drive to the top of Bear Mountain. If it's a clear day, you'll be able to see the NYC skyline.

> Head south on US-9W for 10 miles (16 km), then join US-202 heading south to get to the state park in less than a mile.

❹ Head to **New York City.** Check into your hotel, then take a walk across the **Brooklyn Bridge.** End your trip with a

BROOKLYN BRIDGE

toast to the Empire State at one of the city's many craft cocktail bars.

> Take US-6 W for 2.5 miles (4 km). Continue onto Palisades Pkwy. for 34 miles (55 km). Follow signs to get onto I-95 and cross the George Washington Bridge. Turn right and take Harlem River Dr. south for 4 miles (6 km) until the road becomes FDR Dr. This will lead all the way south to Lower Manhattan and the base of the Brooklyn Bridge.

Getting There

AIR

Albany International Airport (ALB, Albany Shaker Rd., Colonie, 518/242-2200, www.albanyairport.com) is the closest major airport to Saratoga Springs. It's served by American Airlines, Delta, Southwest, and United.

It's also possible to fly into the Hudson Valley via **Stewart International Airport** (SWF, 1180 1st St., New Windsor, 845/838-8200, www.swfny.com). Among the major airlines flying into Stewart are Allegiant, American Airlines, Delta, and JetBlue.

TRAIN AND BUS

The region is easily reached by **Amtrak** (800/872-7245, www.amtrak.com) or the **Trailways bus service** (800/858-8555, www.trailwaysny.com) departing New York City.

CAR

From **Albany International Airport,** the drive to Saratoga Springs is 30 miles

(48 km) and takes about 45 minutes. Hop on I-87 North. Take the exit for NY-9P North. Follow NY-9P North to East Avenue. Turn right and take East Avenue to Lake Avenue. Turn left and follow Lake Avenue into Saratoga Springs.

Getting Back

It's 205 miles (330 km) to drive from New York City back to Saratoga Springs. The drive will take four hours. From New York City, follow NY-495 West to New Jersey. Merge onto NJ-495 West, taking it to I-95 North. Follow I-95 North to I-80 West. Continue on I-80 West, then merge onto NJ-17 North. Use NJ-17 North to connect with I-287 North. Take this to I-87 North and continue on I-87 North. Take the exit for NY-9P North. Follow NY-9P North to East Avenue. Turn right and take East Avenue to Lake Avenue. Turn left and follow Lake Avenue into Saratoga Springs.

Another option is to fly into Albany and out of New York City, using **John F. Kennedy International Airport** (JFK, 718/244-4444, www.jfkairport.com) or **LaGuardia Airport** (LGA, 718/533-3400, www.laguardiaairport.com), both of which are located in Queens. It's 190 miles (305 km) and takes a little less than four hours to get from Saratoga Springs to **Queens.** Use NY-9P South out of Saratoga Springs to access I-87 South. Follow I-87 South to NY-7 East. Follow NY-7 East to I-787 South to I-90 East. Continue on I-90 East to merge onto Taconic State Parkway South. This becomes Sprain Brook Parkway and then Bronx River Parkway. While on Bronx River Parkway heading south, take I-295 South. Follow I-295 South into Queens.

CONNECT WITH

• At New York City: **Hudson River Valley** (PAGE 540)

• At Port Henry: **Lake Champlain Scenic Byway** (PAGE 510)

HUDSON RIVER VALLEY

WHY GO: Farm-to-table cuisine, sprawling estates, pastoral countryside, fall foliage, antiques browsing, quaint villages

TOTAL DISTANCE: 120 miles/ 195 kilometers

NUMBER OF DAYS: 2

SEASONS: Early summer and fall

START: New York City, New York

END: Rhinebeck, New York

▾ KYKUIT, THE ROCKEFELLER ESTATE

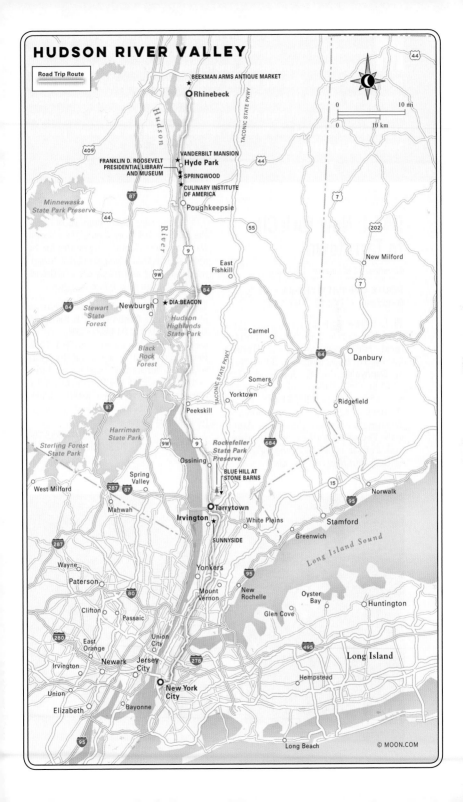

More than 400 years ago, Henry Hudson explored this 315-mile (510-km) waterway, a river carving between high peaks and deep valleys covered by forested woodlands, and running south from the Adirondacks to the Atlantic Ocean. Starting in New York City, this road trip leads you north through the tranquil Hudson River Valley, where orchards and quaint villages share green space with historic sites and opulent estates. You'll soon understand why artists and creatives are so enamored of the swooning, pastoral beauty of this region.

DAY 1: New York City to Tarrytown

45 miles/72 kilometers | 2 hours

ROUTE OVERVIEW: NY-9A • US-9/ Broadway • NY-117 • NY-448

❶ Let **New York City** recede in your rearview mirror and take in the pastoral, rural rhythms of the Hudson Valley. In **Irvington,** stop for a tour of **Sunnyside** (3 W. Sunnyside Ln., 914/366-6900, www.hudsonvalley.org, hours vary seasonally, $12 adults, $6 children 3-17), the historic home of Washington Irving—known as "America's Founding Father of Literature" and author of *The Legend of Sleepy Hollow* and *Rip Van Winkle.*

> From Lower Manhattan, you'll follow the Hudson River's east bank. Take NY-9A N out of the city, continuing on this for 24 miles (39 km) until you get to US-9/Broadway. Turn right and follow US-9 N/Broadway for 2 miles (3 km) into Irvington.

❷ Once you get into **Tarrytown,** splurge for a room at **Castle Hotel & Spa** (400 Benedict Ave., 914/631-1980, www.castlehotelandspa.com, $569-1,005). Perched on a hill overlooking the Hudson, this authentic castle was built near the turn of the 20th century by the son of a Civil War general. Check in, leave your bags, and head out to explore the charms of Tarrytown.

> Continue on US-9 N/Broadway for 2.5 miles (4 km) into Tarrytown.

SUNNYSIDE, THE HOME OF WASHINGOTN IRVING

Top **3** HUDSON RIVER VALLEY

1. Tour **Sunnyside,** the historic home of legendary author **Washington Irving** (PAGE 542).

2. Walk the miles of carriage paths laid out by John D. Rockefeller at **Rockefeller State Park Preserve** (PAGE 544).

3. Savor a meal at **The Culinary Institute of America,** the acclaimed proving grounds for top chefs (PAGE 544).

BLUE HILL AT STONE BARNS

❸ Take an afternoon walk through the well-kept 750-acre **Rockefeller State Park Preserve** (125 Phelps Way, Pleasantville, 914/631-1470, http://parks.ny.gov, 7am-dusk daily, parking $6). Explore meadows and thick woodlands that thread throughout 45 miles (23 km) of wide, level paths made from crushed stone and laid out by John D. Rockefeller in the early 20th century.

> *Continue north for another 2.5 miles (4 km) on US-9 N/Broadway, then turn right and continue east for less than a mile to reach the entrance to the preserve.*

❹ Make sure to book ahead for dinner at one of the area's many excellent restaurants, such as the farm-to-table **Blue Hill at Stone Barns** (630 Bedford Rd., Pocantico Hills, 914/366-9600, www.bluehillfarm.com, tasting menu $188-278), a luxe culinary experience in a beautifully restored barn.

> *To reach the restaurant from the preserve, follow NY-117 (2 mi/3 km), then turn right onto NY-448 and continue for 1.5 miles (2.5 km). To return to Castle Hotel & Spa, continue south on NY-448 for 2 miles (3 km) until you're back in Tarrytown.*

KEY RESERVATIONS

- A dinner at **Blue Hill at Stone Barns** in Tarrytown is not to be missed. The restaurant offers only a tasting menu, and advance reservations are required.

- Call at least **a day** ahead for a reservation to tour **Springwood,** Franklin D. Roosevelt's Hudson River mansion in Hyde Park.

DAY 2: Tarrytown to Rhinebeck

75 miles/121 kilometers | 2.5-3 hours

ROUTE OVERVIEW: US-9 • US-202 • NY-9D • US-9

❶ Head north to **Dia:Beacon** (3 Beekman St., 845/440-0100, www.diabeacon.org, 11am-4pm Fri.-Mon. Jan.-Mar., 11am-6pm Thurs.-Mon. Apr.-Oct., 11am-4pm Thurs.-Mon. Nov.-Dec., $15 adults, $12 children) and explore the experimental and modern-art collection housed in a nearly 300,000-square-foot former printing plant.

> *Depart Tarrytown via US-9 N/Broadway. Follow this for 17 miles (27 km) to US-202, continuing on US-202 E for 4 miles (6 km) to NY-9D. Turn right and follow NY-9D N for 16 miles (26 km) to Dia:Beacon.*

❷ Continue to **Hyde Park,** where the renowned **Culinary Institute of America** (1946 Campus Dr., 845/452-9600, www.ciachef.edu, tours daily, $6)—the training grounds for the most influential and talented chefs in the world—offers a tasty lunch at its signature restaurants.

> *Continue north on NY-9D for 9 miles (15 km) to US-9. Take US-9 N for 11 miles (18 km), then turn right onto St. Andrew Rd. and follow it for 1 mile (1.6 km) to Hyde Park.*

❸ Nearby, you'll find FDR's home, **Springwood** (4079 Albany Post Rd./US-9, 845/229-5320, reservations 800/967-2283, www.nps.gov/hofr, 9am-5pm daily, $18 adults, free for children under

- **Sunnyside, Tarrytown** (3 W. Sunnyside Ln., 914/366-6900, www.hudsonvalley.org, hours vary seasonally, $12 adults, $6 children 3-17): Writer Washington Irving's former abode, full of gables and towers, sits beside a pond with swans. Guides in period dress take you back to the mid-19th century during a house and grounds tour.

- **Lyndhurst, Tarrytown** (635 S. Broadway, 914/631-4481, www. lyndhurst.org, noon-5pm Mon., 10am-5pm Fri.-Sun. May-Oct., $16): This magnificent Gothic Revival estate, designed by the great Alexander Jackson Davis in 1838, was home to a mayor, a merchant, and a railroad magnate. You can take a guided tour of the house and grounds.

- **Philipsburg Manor, Sleepy Hollow** (381 N. Broadway, 914/631-3992, www.hudsonvalley.org, hours vary seasonally, $12 adults, $6 children 3-17): This reconstructed 17th- and 18th-century manor house, which relied heavily upon slaves for its operation, is complete with a functional water-powered gristmill and guides in period dress.

- **Kykuit, The Rockefeller Estate, Sleepy Hollow** (visitors center at Philipsburg Manor, 381 N. Broadway, 914/631-8200, www.hudsonvalley. org, admission and hours vary): This former Rockefeller estate is famed for its magnificent grounds and collection of art, including works by Picasso and Calder. Staff offer guided tours.

- **Van Cortlandt Manor, Croton-on-Hudson** (525 S. Riverside Ave., 914/631-8200, www.hudsonvalley. org, hours vary seasonally, $12 adults, $6 children 3-17): This 18th-century stone-and-clapboard house is not as well known as the Tarrytown mansions, so it's a good place to visit on summer weekends. Guides show visitors one of the largest and best-equipped 18th-century kitchens in the United States, as well as colonial and Federal period furniture.

- **Locust Grove, Poughkeepsie** (370 South Rd./Rte. 9, 845/454-4500, www.lgny.org, May-Nov., hours vary seasonally, $11 adults, $6 children 6-10): This romantic octagonal villa was once the summer home of artist-scientist-philosopher Samuel Morse, inventor of the telegraph. It is now a museum and 200-acre nature preserve.

- **Springwood, Hyde Park** (4079 Albany Post Rd./US-9, 845/229-5320, www.nps.gov/hofr, 9am-5pm daily, $18 adults, free for children under 16, advance reservations required): Perhaps the most interesting of the Hudson River estates, Springwood is FDR's former home. Nearby is Eleanor Roosevelt's Val-Kill. Together, they comprise the Franklin D. Roosevelt National Historic Site.

- **Vanderbilt Mansion, Hyde Park** (119 Vanderbilt Park Rd., 845/229-9115, www.nps.gov/vama, 9am-5pm daily, $10 pp): This was the most extravagant Hudson River estate, built in a posh beaux arts style. Go here to drool over lavish furnishings, gold-leaf ceilings, and Flemish tapestries.

- **Staatsburgh State Historic Site, Staatsburg** (75 Mills Mansion Rd., 845/889-8851, www.parks.ny.gov, 11am-5pm Thurs.-Sun., $8 adults, $6 children): The vast 65-room mansion sits on a hill overlooking the Hudson River and Catskill Mountains. Edith Wharton based the Trenor estate in *The House of Mirth* on this place.

- **Wilderstein, Rhinebeck** (330 Morton Rd., 845/876-4818, www. wilderstein.org, noon-4pm Thurs.-Sun. May-Oct., $11 adults, $10 children): This whimsical, all-wooden Queen Anne mansion with interiors by Tiffany and grounds designed by Calvert Vaux is one of the smaller estates. Enjoy a house tour and explore the three miles of trails crisscrossing the estate.

VANDERBILT MANSION IN HYDE PARK

16, reservations suggested), a Georgian-style mansion along the Hudson. To learn more about the president, visit the adjacent **Franklin D. Roosevelt Presidential Library and Museum** (4079 Albany Post Rd./US-9, 845/486-7770 or 800/337-84142, www.fdrlibrary.marist.edu, $18 adults, free for children under 16), which offers a self-guided tour.

> *It's less than a mile north on US-9 to Springwood from the St. Andrew Rd. turnoff for Hyde Park.*

❹ Afterward, stroll the lovely paths overlooking the Hudson on the grounds of the Gilded Age **Vanderbilt Mansion** (119 Vanderbilt Park Rd., 845/229-7770, www.nps.gov/vama, 9am-5pm daily, mansion $10 pp, grounds free) before hitting the road.

> *Continue north on US-9 for another 2 miles (3 km) to reach the mansion.*

❺ Spend the rest of the day exploring **Rhinebeck,** a picturesque village that has shady streets lined with restored Victorian buildings. It's known for its antiques stores and art galleries, many of which are located along Route 9 and Market Street. Start with **Beekman Arms Antique Market** (Beekman Square at the Beekman Arms, 845/876-3477, 11am-5pm daily), which houses more than 30 vendors in an old red barn.

> *Follow US-9 N for another 9 miles (15 km) to reach Rhinebeck.*

Getting There

AIR

To get to New York City, travelers can fly into either **John F. Kennedy International Airport** (JFK, 718/244-4444, www.jfkairport.com) or **LaGuardia Airport** (LGA, 718/533-3400, www.laguardiaairport.com), both of which are located in Queens.

Other options include **New York Stewart International Airport** (SWF, 1180 1st St., New Windsor, 845/838-8200, www.swfny.com) and **Albany International Airport** (ALB, Albany Shaker Rd., Colonie, 518/242-2200, www.albanyairport.com). Among the major airlines flying into Stewart are Allegiant, American Airlines, Delta, and JetBlue; those flying into Albany are American Airlines, Delta, Southwest, and United.

RHINEBECK

TRAIN AND BUS

Many towns along the east bank of the Hudson River and some in Westchester's Harlem Valley are reached by trains that depart from Grand Central in Manhattan. Taxis are usually available at the villages' railroad stations. **Amtrak** (800/872-7245, www.amtrak.com) provides rail service between New York City and more than 40 stations in the Hudson Valley.

Adirondack-Pine Hill-New York Trailways (800/225-6815, www.trailwaysny.com) and **ShortLine Bus** (800/631-8405, www.coachusa.com/shortline) offer daily bus service between Manhattan's Port Authority Bus Terminal and many Hudson Valley communities.

CAR

Driving from **Queens** to Tarrytown runs 50 miles (80 km) and will take about two hours. Traffic will be heavy no matter the season or time of day. Take I-278 East to FDR Drive in Manhattan. Take exit 14 from FDR Drive. Follow East 97th Street through Central Park to NY-9A North. Turn right to get on NY-9A North. Follow NY-9A North out of the city, continuing on this until you get to US-9/Broadway. Turn left and follow US-9 North to Irvington. Continue on US-9 North to Tarrytown.

Getting Back

It's 105 miles (165 km) to drive the two-hour trip back to **Queens** and the New York-area airports from Rhinebeck. The fastest route is via the Taconic State Parkway. From Rhinebeck, take E. Market Street due east to Violet Hill Road. Turn right on Violet Hill Road, following it to NY-9G South. Turn right and drive NY-9G South to Slate Quarry Road. Turn left. Continue on Slate Quarry Road to Taconic State Parkway. Turn right and merge onto Taconic State Parkway South. This becomes Sprain Brook Parkway and then Bronx River Parkway. While on Bronx River Parkway heading south, take I-295 South. Follow I-295 South into Queens.

▶ *Playlist*

HUDSON RIVER VALLEY

SONGS

- **"Autumn in New York" by Billie Holiday:** Even if this song wasn't about one of the most beautiful seasons in New York, Holiday's emotional voice captures the sensibility of this part of the country: classic, iconic, historic, and resonant.

- **"Strangers in the Night" by Frank Sinatra:** No vocalist is associated with New York more than Sinatra. And while "New York, New York," might be the obvious song to play while driving north from the city, "Strangers in the Night" is better. Let the sweeping romance overtake you.

- **"Take the A Train" by Duke Ellington:** What is it about the rambling elegance of New York's Hudson River Valley that begs for jazzy accompaniment? As the river curves along beside you, let this sprightly song energize you.

CONNECT WITH

- At New York City: **Adirondacks and Catskills** (PAGE 530)

THE JERSEY SHORE

WHY GO: Bustling boardwalks, midway games, Atlantic City, seaside strolls, saltwater taffy, lighthouses, charming inns, fresh seafood

TOTAL DISTANCE: 195 miles/ 315 kilometers

NUMBER OF DAYS: 4

SEASONS: Late spring through early fall

START: Cape May, New Jersey

END: Long Branch, New Jersey

▼ LONG BEACH ISLAND

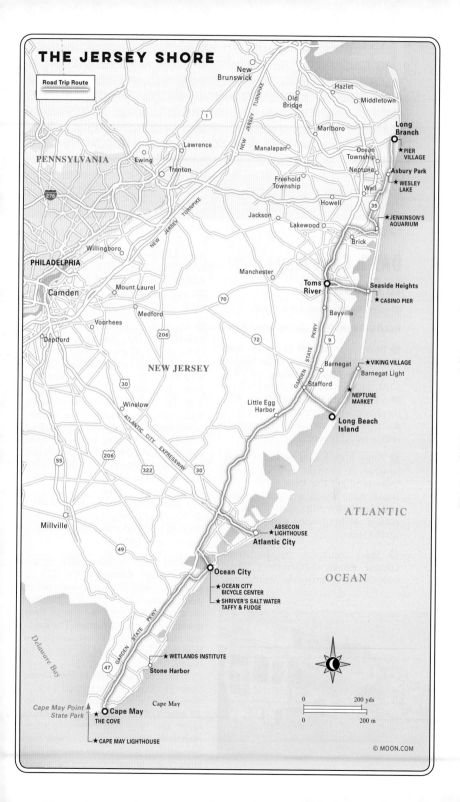

THE JERSEY SHORE

Road Trip Route

New Brunswick

Hazlet

Old Bridge

Middletown

Marlboro

Long Branch
★ PIER VILLAGE

Ocean Township

PENNSYLVANIA

Lawrence

Ewing

Trenton

Manalapan

Neptune

Asbury Park
★ WESLEY LAKE

Freehold Township

Wall

35

Howell

★ JENKINSON'S AQUARIUM

Jackson

Lakewood

Brick

Willingboro

PHILADELPHIA

Camden

Manchester

Toms River

Seaside Heights
★ CASINO PIER

Mount Laurel

70

Bayville

Medford

206

72

Voorhees

NEW JERSEY

9

Barnegat
★ VIKING VILLAGE

Deptford

Barnegat Light

30

Winslow

Stafford

★ NEPTUNE MARKET

Little Egg Harbor

Long Beach Island

Millville

55

206

322

30

ATLANTIC CITY EXPRESSWAY

49

ATLANTIC

GARDEN STATE PKWY

★ ABSECON LIGHTHOUSE
Atlantic City

Ocean City

OCEAN

★ OCEAN CITY BICYCLE CENTER

★ SHRIVER'S SALT WATER TAFFY & FUDGE

47

Delaware Bay

★ WETLANDS INSTITUTE

Stone Harbor

Cape May

Cape May Point State Park ▲
★ THE COVE
Cape May

★ CAPE MAY LIGHTHOUSE

0   200 yds
0   200 m

© MOON.COM

In terms of distance, the Jersey Shore is only an hour or two from Philadelphia and New York City. But in spirit, it's a world away, a place where brightly lit boardwalks line sandy beaches and stately lighthouses perch at the ocean's edge. During this trip, which starts in the seaside town of Cape May and then ventures north along the Atlantic Ocean, you'll dine on catch-of-the-day in a fishing village, play arcade games at a boardwalk midway, see sharks at an aquarium, and spend the night in luxe accommodations that range from B&Bs to resorts. The best part: The Jersey Shore comprises a series of barrier islands, which means you'll enjoy lovely views over the water of both sunrise and sunset.

DAY 1: Cape May to Ocean City

40 miles/64 kilometers | 1-1.5 hours

ROUTE OVERVIEW: Garden State Pkwy.

1 Start your trip off in quaint **Cape May.** Climb the 199 steps to the top of the **Cape May Lighthouse** (609/884-5404, $10 adults, $5 children) in **Cape May Point State Park** (Lighthouse Ave., no phone, www.state.nj.us, dawn-dusk daily, free) and take in the views of the surrounding peninsula.

2 Cape May has a series of lovely beaches. A favorite with locals and tourists alike, **The Cove** (west end of Beach Ave., $6) is a popular, pretty, and family-friendly spot. Watch the surfers catching waves while you soak up the sun.

3 Have lunch at the harborside **Lobster House** (Fisherman's Wharf, 609/884-8296, http://thelobsterhouse.

com, 11:30am-3pm and 4:30pm-9pm daily Jan.-Mar., 11:30am-3pm and 4:30pm-10pm daily Apr.-Dec., $21-35)—or nab a table on the schooner that's docked right outside.

4 It's a short jaunt north to **Stone Harbor.** At the **Wetlands Institute** (1075 Stone Harbor Blvd., 609/368-1211, http://wetlandsinstitute.org, 9:30am-4:30pm daily late May-late Sept., 9:30am-4:30pm Sat.-Sun. late Sept.-late May, $8 adults, $6 children 3-12), you can wander along an elevated walkway over the surrounding marshlands and hang out on the dock, watching for birds and other wildlife. Inside the institute are fun learning stations and exhibits that explore the area's flora and fauna.

> *Take the Garden State Pkwy. north for 10 miles (16 km), then turn right and follow Stone Harbor Blvd. for 4 miles (6 km) to Stone Harbor.*

5 Head north to **Ocean City.** At the family-owned **Osborne's Inn** (601 E. 15th St., 609/398-4319, www.osbornesinn.com, $145-215), the hospitable owners will welcome you to their guesthouse with open arms. The inn is two blocks from the water, so you can lounge away the rest of the day on the beach.

> *Retrace your path to the Garden State Pkwy. via Stone Harbor Blvd. (4 mi/6 km). Follow the parkway north for 15 miles (24 km). Take the exit for Roosevelt Blvd. and turn right onto Roosevelt. Follow this for 2 miles (3 km), then turn left onto Bay Ave. and continue for 3 miles (5 km) to reach Ocean City.*

CAPE MAY

Top ③ THE JERSEY SHORE

① Watch surfers ride the waves at The Cove in **Cape May** (PAGE 550).

② Stroll **Atlantic City's** famous **boardwalk** (PAGE 552).

③ Ride the Tilt-a-Whirl at Casino Pier in **Seaside Heights** (PAGE 553).

DAY 2: Ocean City to Long Beach Island

60 miles/97 kilometers | 1.5-2 hours

ROUTE OVERVIEW: Stainton Memorial Causeway • surface streets • US-9 • Atlantic City Expy. • US-9 • NJ-72

❶ In the morning, walk down the 2.5-mile **boardwalk**—or pedal its length after renting a bike from **Ocean City Bicycle Center** (8th St. and Atlantic Ave., 609/399-5550, http://oceancitybicyclecenter.com, 7am-3pm Mon.-Thurs., 7am-5pm Fri.-Sun. Memorial Day-Labor Day, call for off-season hours, from $7 per hour).

❷ Pop into a few of the many shops that line the boardwalk, such as long-standing **Shriver's** (boardwalk at 9th St., 609/399-0100, http://shrivers.com, 10am-5pm daily), which sells saltwater taffy, including a chocolate-covered variety, and homemade fudge.

❸ It's about a half-hour drive from here to reach **Atlantic City.** After you've walked along the famous boardwalk, try your hand at the slot machines or poker tables at the luxe **Borgata Hotel Casino & Spa** (1 Borgata Way, 609/317-1000, www.theborgata.com, 24 hours daily).

> Take the Stainton Memorial Causeway to Shore Rd. (2 mi/3 km). Turn right on Shore Rd., make a left on Bethel Rd., then turn right on US-9. Follow US-9 for 6 miles (10 km) to Atlantic City Expy. Turn right and follow this to Atlantic City (6 mi/10 km).

LONG BEACH ISLAND

❹ Just a few blocks in from the boardwalk, visit **Absecon Lighthouse** (31 S. Rhode Island Ave., 609/449-1360, www.abseconlighthouse.org, 10am-5pm daily July-Aug., 11am-4pm Thurs.-Mon. Sept.-June, $10 adults, $6 children 4-12), the tallest lighthouse in the state. You'll get awesome views of the shore and the endless ocean from the top.

❺ Continue north and bed down for the night at the boutique **Daddy O** (4401 Long Beach Blvd., Brant Beach, 609/494-1300, www.daddyolbi.com, from $350) on **Long Beach Island.** Once you've checked in, head up to the rooftop bar for a cocktail.

> Use the Atlantic City Expy. to reach US-9. Turn right and drive US-9 for 26 miles (42 km) to NJ-72. Turn right and follow NJ-72 to Central Ave. (5 mi/8 km). Turn right and follow Central for 1 mile (1.6 km) to Long Beach Island.

THE BOARDWALK IN OCEAN CITY

DAY 3: Long Beach Island to Toms River

60 miles/97 kilometers | 1.5-2 hours

**ROUTE OVERVIEW: Surface streets •
NJ-72 • Garden State Pkwy. • NJ-37**

❶ Spend the morning strolling the beach, then head to **Neptune Market** (8014 Long Beach Blvd., 609/494-2619, http://neptunemarketlbi.com, 7am-7pm daily, $10-17) for lunch. Try a Philly-style cheesesteak or go for their famed half-pound Nooney Burger.

❷ Head to the northern tip of Long Beach Island to visit the town of **Barnegat Light.** There, check out the historic **Viking Village** (19th St. and Bayview Ave.), a small fishing village that's also home to a pocket of cute shops and restaurants.

> *Drive Long Beach Blvd. north for 8 miles (13 km) to reach Barnegat Light.*

❸ You'll need to backtrack south a few miles, head inland, then go north again to reach **Seaside Heights.** This town was once the setting of MTV's *Jersey Shore,* and its boardwalk saw major damage from Hurricane Sandy in 2012. The town has since bounced back, drawing young revelers and families alike to its boardwalk. The rebuilt **Casino Pier** (Grant Ave. at Ocean Terr., 732/793-6488, www.casinopiernj.com, noon-midnight daily mid-June-Labor Day, shorter hours Labor Day-mid-June) boasts amusement rides, a water park, and arcades

KEY RESERVATIONS

- During summer, the Jersey Shore's high season, hotels book up. It's wise to make advance reservations for **all lodging** on this trip.

- For most restaurants, you don't need reservations (and often they don't take them), but at **Mar Belo** in Long Branch, you should book a table **a week** prior to your arrival.

aplenty. Once you've worked up an appetite, chow down at one of the boardwalk's many eateries.

> *Leave Barnegat Light via Long Beach Blvd., taking it back to Long Beach Island. At 24th St., turn right, then make a quick left on Central Ave. Drive Central for 2 miles (3 km) to 8th St. Turn right and follow 8th St. as it turns into NJ-72. Stay on NJ-72, driving west for 7 miles (11 km) to the Garden State Pkwy. Go north for 18 miles (29 km). Take the exit for NJ-37 and head east for 7 miles (11 km) to Seaside Heights.*

❹ For a peaceful night's sleep, head inland to **Toms River.** Nab a room at **Mathis House** (600 Main St., 732/818-7580, www.mathishouse600main.com, from $179), a Victorian-era bed-and-breakfast with beautifully manicured grounds and an on-site tea room.

> *Head inland for 7 miles (11 km) on NJ-37 W, exiting at Washington St. to reach Toms River.*

DAY 4: Toms River to Long Branch

35 miles/56 kilometers | 1-1.5 hours

ROUTE OVERVIEW: Garden State Pkwy. • surface streets • NJ-35 • surface streets • NJ-71

❶ After breakfast at your B&B, hit the road and head to the town of **Point Pleasant Beach.** Spend some time at **Jenkinson's Aquarium** (300 Ocean Ave., 732/892-0600, http://jenkinsons.com/aquarium, 10am-10pm daily late

BARNEGAT LIGHT

▶ Playlist

THE JERSEY SHORE

ALBUMS

- *Greetings from Asbury Park, N.J.* by Bruce Springsteen: Cue up this entire album for the trip. You're in for nine songs jam-packed with riveting stories, funny asides, lively characters, and vivid imagery, all from Asbury Park's hometown hero, Bruce Springsteen. The 1973 debut studio album from The Boss draws from his personal experiences growing up on the Jersey Shore.

June-Labor Day, shorter hours Labor Day-late June, $14 adults, $8 children 3-12), set on the town's boardwalk. You'll see sharks, penguins, and sea otters up close and personal.

> *Merge onto the Garden State Pkwy. via US-9, driving it for 9 miles (15 km) to Burnt Tavern Rd. Turn right and stay on Burnt Tavern until Ocean Rd. (3 mi/5 km).*

Turn left and follow Ocean Rd. to Cincinnati Ave. (2 mi/3 km). Take Cincinnati Ave. to Point Pleasant Beach.

2 Next stop is **Asbury Park,** which is the hometown of Bruce Springsteen. Today, thanks to its diversity, culture, and incredible live-music scene, it's fondly known as "Brooklyn on the beach." Get your legs working by pedaling your way around **Wesley Lake** in a **swan boat** (Asbury Park Pedal Boats, Wesley Lake between Grand Ave. and Heck St., 732/228-0466, www.asbury-parkpedalboats.com, 11am-sunset May-Sept., $20 for 30-minute ride). Afterward, walk north up the coast to check out the town's abandoned casino, a beautiful work of beaux arts architecture.

> *Head north on Cincinnati Ave. as it becomes NJ-35, following it for 8 miles (13 km) to Memorial Dr. Make a slight right on Memorial. Head north for 2 miles (3 km) to Asbury Park.*

3 Head north to **Long Branch** for some upscale window-shopping. **Pier Village** (bounded by Landmark Pl., Laird St., Ocean Ave., and Chelsea Ave., no phone, http://piervillage.com, hours vary by merchant) is a collection of high-end boutiques, a gourmet market, and even a luxury spa.

> *Leave Asbury Park by taking Main St. north for less than a mile to Deal Lake Dr. Turn right and then make a quick left on NJ-71. Drive north on NJ-71 for 4 miles (6 km) to Cedar Ave. Turn right, then go left on Norwood Ave. Stay on Norwood for 1.5 miles (2.5 km) to Long Branch.*

LONG BRANCH

❹ Splurge on a nice dinner at **Mar Belo** (611 Broadway, 732/870-2222, www.marbelorestaurant.com, 11am-11pm Tues.-Sun., $24-36), an intimate spot that serves Spanish and Portuguese dishes. Advance reservations are a good idea. Raise a toast to the Jersey Shore.

❺ Spend your last night on the shore, listening to the waves crash, at the ritzy beachfront **Ocean Place Resort & Spa** (1 Ocean Blvd., 732/571-4000, www.oceanplace.com, from $550).

Getting There

AIR

The largest airport closest to Cape May is **Philadelphia International Airport** (PHL, 215/937-6937, www.phl.org). PHL offers seven terminals, four runways, and daily departures to more than 120 cities. It's served by about a dozen airlines. The airport is located 95 miles (155 km) from Cape May, a drive that takes about 1.5-2 hours.

In New Jersey, there's **Atlantic City International Airport** (ACY, 609/645-7895, http://sjta.com/acairport), a smaller airport that offers flights on Spirit Airlines from Denver, Las Vegas, Dallas, New Orleans, Atlanta, and Orlando, among others.

TRAIN

No trains run to Cape May, but New Jersey's public transportation system, **NJ Transit** (973/275-5555, www.njtransit.com), has a commuter rail line between Atlantic City and Philadelphia. If you fly into Philadelphia, you can take the train to Atlantic City, then rent a car in Atlantic City or take a bus from Atlantic City to Cape May.

BUS

NJ Transit (973/275-5555, www.njtransit.com) buses run from Philadelphia, New York, and several other locations in New Jersey, into Cape May via Atlantic City. From Atlantic City, buses run directly to Cape May. Cape May is on the 552 Atlantic City-Cape May bus route, which drops off passengers at the Welcome Center in the middle of town.

CAR

Cape May is an island, accessible by one of two main bridges that cross the canal waterway linking the Delaware Bay with the Atlantic Ocean.

Philadelphia International Airport is located 95 miles (155 km) from Cape May, a drive that takes about 1.5-2 hours depending on traffic. From the airport, take the Ben Franklin Bridge to I-676 South. Follow the signs to RT-42 South and Atlantic City Expressway. From the Expressway, take Exit 7S and merge onto the Garden State Parkway, following it into Cape May.

From **Atlantic City International Airport,** it's a straight shot south on the Garden State Parkway from the airport to Cape May, a 45-mile (72-km) drive that takes 45 minutes to an hour.

Getting Back

It's a two-hour, 115-mile (185-km) trip back to **Cape May** from Long Branch. Get on the Garden State Parkway and drive south to NJ-109, following it into Cape May.

Another option is to book a one-way flight out of any of the New York City-area airports: **John F. Kennedy International Airport** (JFK, Queens, New York, 718/244-4444, www.jfkairport.com), **Newark Liberty International Airport** (EWR, 3 Brewster Rd, Newark, New Jersey, 973/961-6000, www.newarkairport.com), or **LaGuardia Airport** (LGA, Queens, New York, 718/533-3400, www.laguardiaairport.com).

From Long Branch to **JFK,** the drive takes a little over an hour (65 mi/105 km) via the Garden State Parkway, NJ-440/NY-440, I-278, and the Belt Parkway. To **Newark,** it's a 45-minute drive of 40 miles (65 km) going north on the Garden State Parkway, then connecting to I-95 North. To reach **LaGuardia,** the 70-mile (115-km) trip on the Garden State Parkway and I-95 takes about 90 minutes. Because all three of these airports are located within the New York City metro area, traffic will be heavy, and notably worse during morning and evening rush hours.

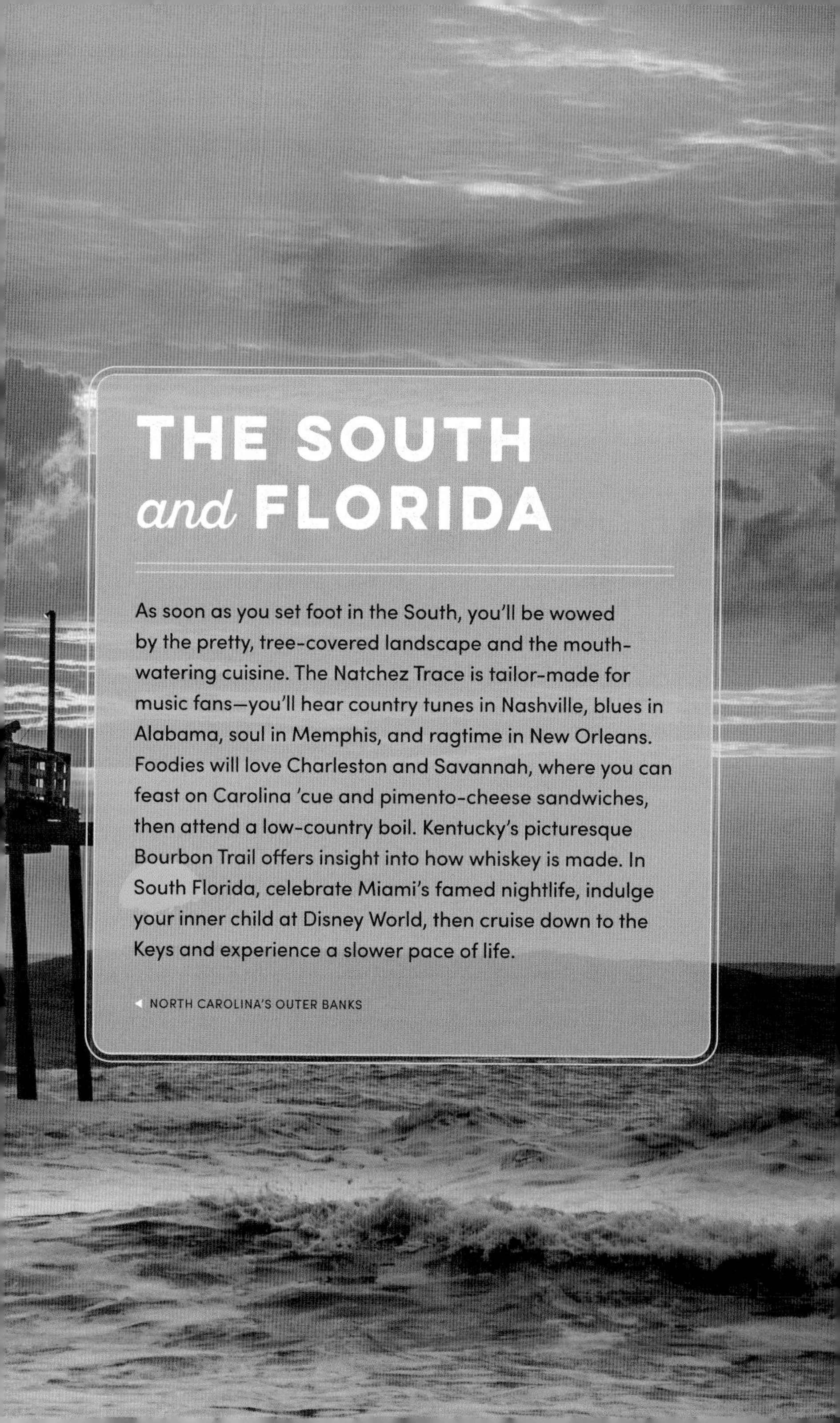

THE SOUTH
and FLORIDA

As soon as you set foot in the South, you'll be wowed by the pretty, tree-covered landscape and the mouth-watering cuisine. The Natchez Trace is tailor-made for music fans—you'll hear country tunes in Nashville, blues in Alabama, soul in Memphis, and ragtime in New Orleans. Foodies will love Charleston and Savannah, where you can feast on Carolina 'cue and pimento-cheese sandwiches, then attend a low-country boil. Kentucky's picturesque Bourbon Trail offers insight into how whiskey is made. In South Florida, celebrate Miami's famed nightlife, indulge your inner child at Disney World, then cruise down to the Keys and experience a slower pace of life.

◀ NORTH CAROLINA'S OUTER BANKS

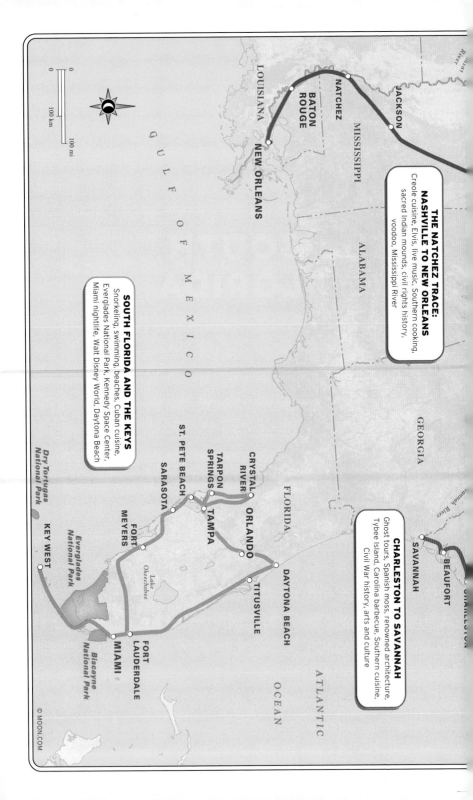

THE NATCHEZ TRACE: NASHVILLE TO NEW ORLEANS

Creole cuisine, Elvis, live music, Southern cooking, sacred Indian mounds, civil rights history, voodoo, Mississippi River

SOUTH FLORIDA AND THE KEYS

Snorkeling, swimming, beaches, Cuban cuisine, Everglades National Park, Kennedy Space Center, Miami nightlife, Walt Disney World, Daytona Beach

CHARLESTON TO SAVANNAH

Ghost tours, Spanish moss, renowned architecture, Tybee Island, Carolina barbecue, Southern cuisine, Civil War history, arts and culture

JACKSON

NATCHEZ

BATON ROUGE

LOUISIANA

NEW ORLEANS

MISSISSIPPI

ALABAMA

GEORGIA

SAVANNAH

BEAUFORT

CHARLESTON

FLORIDA

Lake Okeechobee

CRYSTAL RIVER

TARPON SPRINGS

ORLANDO

TAMPA

ST. PETE BEACH

SARASOTA

FORT MEYERS

TITUSVILLE

DAYTONA BEACH

FORT LAUDERDALE

MIAMI

Everglades National Park

Biscayne National Park

KEY WEST

Dry Tortugas National Park

G U L F   O F   M E X I C O

A T L A N T I C   O C E A N

0   100 km
0   100 mi

© MOON.COM

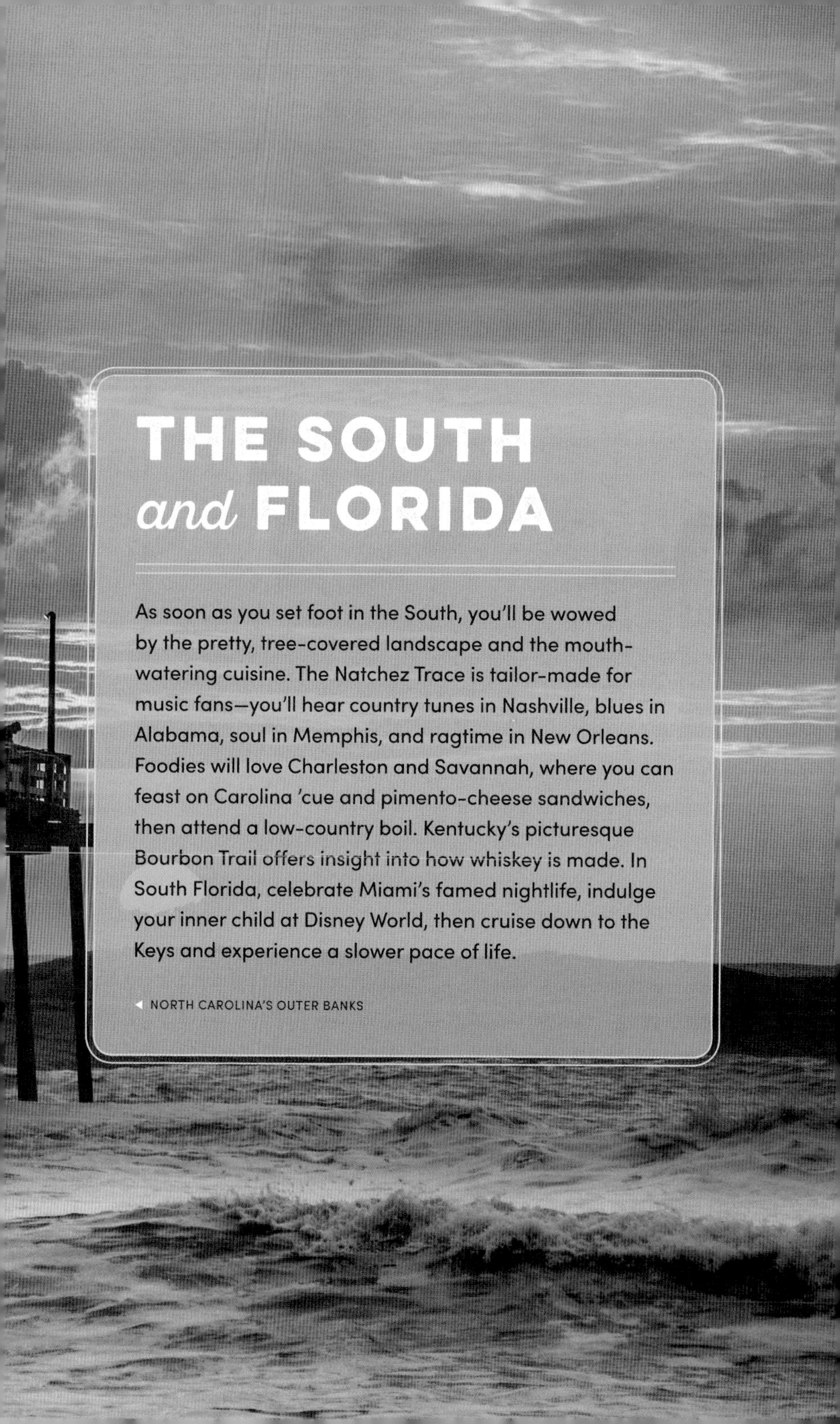

THE SOUTH
and FLORIDA

As soon as you set foot in the South, you'll be wowed by the pretty, tree-covered landscape and the mouth-watering cuisine. The Natchez Trace is tailor-made for music fans—you'll hear country tunes in Nashville, blues in Alabama, soul in Memphis, and ragtime in New Orleans. Foodies will love Charleston and Savannah, where you can feast on Carolina 'cue and pimento-cheese sandwiches, then attend a low-country boil. Kentucky's picturesque Bourbon Trail offers insight into how whiskey is made. In South Florida, celebrate Miami's famed nightlife, indulge your inner child at Disney World, then cruise down to the Keys and experience a slower pace of life.

◀ NORTH CAROLINA'S OUTER BANKS

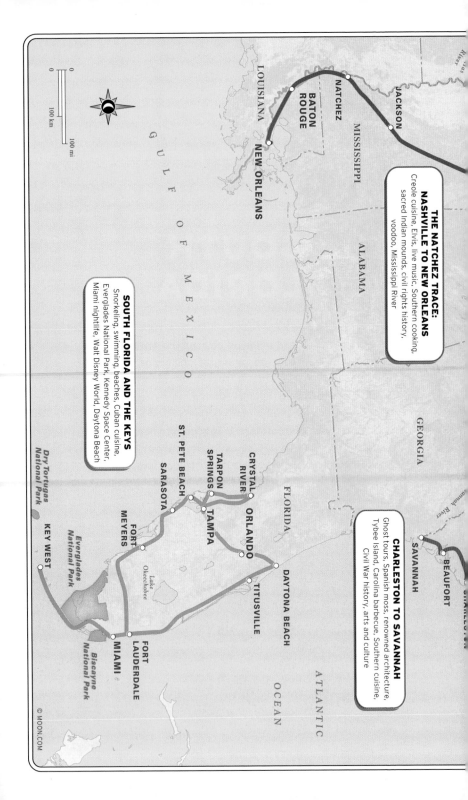

THE NATCHEZ TRACE:
NASHVILLE TO NEW ORLEANS
Creole cuisine, Elvis, live music, Southern cooking, sacred Indian mounds, civil rights history, voodoo, Mississippi River

SOUTH FLORIDA AND THE KEYS
Snorkeling, swimming, beaches, Cuban cuisine, Everglades National Park, Kennedy Space Center, Miami nightlife, Walt Disney World, Daytona Beach

CHARLESTON TO SAVANNAH
Ghost tours, Spanish moss, renowned architecture, Tybee Island, Carolina barbecue, Southern cuisine, Civil War history, arts and culture

LOUISIANA

MISSISSIPPI

ALABAMA

GEORGIA

FLORIDA

JACKSON

NATCHEZ

BATON ROUGE

NEW ORLEANS

GULF OF MEXICO

SAVANNAH

BEAUFORT

CHARLESTON

CRYSTAL RIVER

TARPON SPRINGS

TAMPA

ST. PETE BEACH

SARASOTA

FORT MEYERS

ORLANDO

TITUSVILLE

DAYTONA BEACH

Lake Okeechobee

Everglades National Park

MIAMI

FORT LAUDERDALE

Biscayne National Park

KEY WEST

Dry Tortugas National Park

ATLANTIC OCEAN

0   100 km
0   100 mi

© MOON.COM

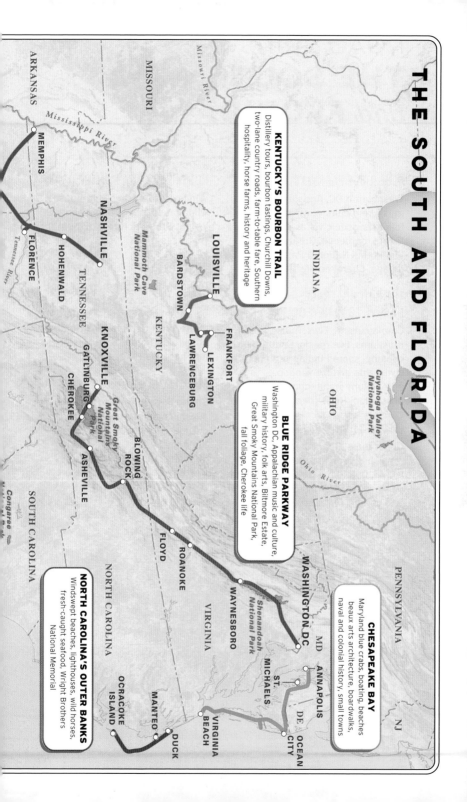

THE SOUTH AND FLORIDA

KENTUCKY'S BOURBON TRAIL
Distillery tours, bourbon tastings, Churchill Downs, two-lane country roads, farm-to-table fare, Southern hospitality, horse farms, history and heritage

BLUE RIDGE PARKWAY
Washington DC, Appalachian music and culture, military history, folk arts, Biltmore Estate, Great Smoky Mountains National Park, fall foliage, Cherokee life

CHESAPEAKE BAY
Maryland blue crabs, boating, beaches, beaux arts architecture, boardwalks, naval and colonial history, small towns

NORTH CAROLINA'S OUTER BANKS
Windswept beaches, lighthouses, wild horses, fresh-caught seafood, Wright Brothers National Memorial

ARKANSAS

MISSOURI

Missouri River

INDIANA

OHIO

PENNSYLVANIA

NJ

Mississippi River

MEMPHIS

NASHVILLE

FLORENCE

HOHENWALD

TENNESSEE

Tennessee River

Mammoth Cave National Park

LOUISVILLE

BARDSTOWN

FRANKFORT

LEXINGTON

LAWRENCEBURG

KENTUCKY

Cuyahoga Valley National Park

Ohio River

WASHINGTON, DC

MD

DE

ANNAPOLIS

OCEAN CITY

ST. MICHAELS

KNOXVILLE

GATLINBURG

CHEROKEE

Great Smoky Mountains National Park

ASHEVILLE

BLOWING ROCK

FLOYD

ROANOKE

WAYNESBORO

Shenandoah National Park

VIRGINIA

VIRGINIA BEACH

DUCK

MANTEO

OCRACOKE ISLAND

NORTH CAROLINA

SOUTH CAROLINA

Congaree National Park

ROAD TRIPS OF
THE SOUTH
and FLORIDA

BLUE RIDGE PARKWAY

Washington DC, Appalachian music and culture, military history, folk arts, scenic vistas, Biltmore Estate, barbecue, Great Smoky Mountains National Park, fall foliage, Cherokee life (PAGE 562)

THE NATCHEZ TRACE: NASHVILLE TO NEW ORLEANS

Creole cuisine, Elvis, music museums, live music, Southern cooking, sacred Indian mounds, civil rights history, voodoo, antebellum architecture, Mississippi River (PAGE 582)

CHARLESTON TO SAVANNAH

Ghost tours, Spanish moss, renowned architecture, Tybee Island, Carolina barbecue, Southern cuisine, Civil War history, arts and culture (PAGE 600)

CHESAPEAKE BAY

Maryland blue crabs, boating, beaux arts architecture, beaches, boardwalks, naval and colonial history, charming inns, small towns (PAGE 612)

NORTH CAROLINA'S OUTER BANKS

Windswept beaches, lighthouses, wild horses, fresh-caught seafood, Wright Brothers National Memorial (PAGE 620)

KENTUCKY'S BOURBON TRAIL

Distillery tours, bourbon tastings, Churchill Downs, chocolate-covered bourbon balls, two-lane country roads, farm-to-table fare, Southern hospitality, horse farms, history and heritage (PAGE 628)

SOUTH FLORIDA AND THE KEYS

Snorkeling, swimming, beaches, sunshine, palm trees, Cuban cuisine, Everglades National Park, Kennedy Space Center, Miami nightlife, Walt Disney World, Daytona Beach, impressive art (PAGE 638)

LEFT TO RIGHT: FLORENCE, ALABAMA; THE BATTERY IN CHARLESTON; MIAMI BEACH

1 Drive the vista-studded **Newfound Gap Road** in **Great Smoky Mountains National Park** (PAGE 579).

2 Honor the King's legacy at the **Elvis Presley Birthplace** in Tupelo and at **Graceland** in Memphis (PAGE 590).

3 Take a ferry to **Fort Sumter National Monument,** site of the battle that started the Civil War (PAGE 604).

Great Smoky Mountains National Park

Graceland, Memphis

Fort Sumter National Monument

wild horses in the Outer Banks

Little Havana, Miami

4 See wild ponies frolicking in the surf on a **wild horse tour** in North Carolina's **Outer Banks** (PAGE 624).

5 Order a *café cubano* in Miami's **Little Havana,** the heart of the Cuban community (PAGE 64?).

BLUE RIDGE PARKWAY

WHY GO: Washington DC, Appalachian music and culture, military history, folk arts, scenic vistas, Biltmore Estate, barbecue, Great Smoky Mountains National Park, fall foliage, Cherokee life

TOTAL DISTANCE: 980 miles/ 1,580 kilometers

NUMBER OF DAYS: 14

SEASONS: Spring and fall

START: Washington DC

END: Knoxville, Tennessee

▼ EARLY OUTUMN IN THE BLUE RIDGE MOUNTAINS

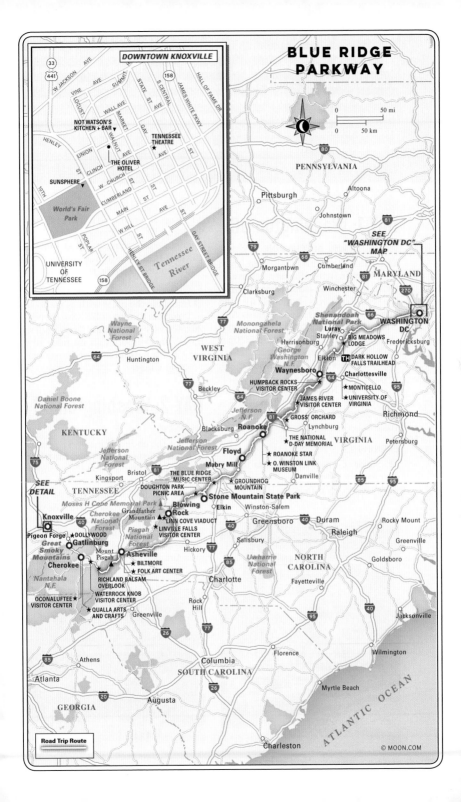

The Blue Ridge Parkway leads you down a road where mist hovers and a canopy of trees arches overhead. It meanders past u-pick orchards where plump fruit tempts you to stop. It curves through the mountains of a national park and climbs spiny ridges to 360-degree sunset views. As this road trip twists and turns through Virginia, North Carolina, and Tennessee, vibrant traditions come to life. You'll never know what to expect—from a bear crossing the road ahead to a town rife with artisan-crafted treasures—but it's in the unexpected where those moments of magic are found.

DAY 1: Washington DC

MORNING AND AFTERNOON

① Settle into your hotel room, then spend the rest of the day at any of DC's stellar museums. Don't miss the Smithsonian's **National Air and Space Museum** (Independence Ave. and 6th St. SW, 202/633-2214, www.airandspace.si.edu, 10am-5:30pm daily, free), **National Portrait Gallery** (8th St. and F St. NW, 202/633-8300, www.npg.si.edu, 11:30am-7pm daily, free), or the **National Museum of Natural History** (10th St. and Constitution Ave., 202/633-1000, www.mnh.si.edu, 10am-5:30pm daily, free).

EVENING

② Savor dinner at **Sfoglina** (4445 Connecticut Ave. NW, 202/450-1312, www.sfoglinadc.com, 4pm-10pm Mon., 11:30am-10pm Tues.-Thurs., 11:30am-10:30pm Fri., 10:30am-10:30pm Sat., 10:30am-9pm Sun., $19-24), among the best Italian restaurants in the city, with handmade pasta, regional dishes, and big, shareable plates.

③ Conclude the night with a jazz show at **Columbia Station** (2325 18th St. NW, 202/462-6040, 5pm-2am Tues.-Thurs., 5pm-3am Fri.-Sun.), an intimate and cozy space with great live music and no cover charge.

DAY 2: Washington DC

MORNING

① Visit the enlightening and powerful **National Museum of African American History and Culture** (1400 Constitution Ave. NW, 844/750-3012, www.nmaahc.si.edu, 10am-5:30pm daily, free). There's only one problem with the popular museum: Tickets can be difficult to procure. Timed passes are released online for visits 3-4 months out. This museum is well worth the effort.

NATIONAL MUSEUM OF NATURAL HISTORY

NATIONAL MUSEUM OF AFRICAN AMERICAN HISTORY AND CULTURE

Top **5** BLUE RIDGE PARKWAY

1. Pay your respects at **Arlington National Cemetery**, which was established during the Civil War (**PAGE 567**).

2. See **Monticello**, the sprawling grounds of Thomas Jefferson's home (**PAGE 568**).

3. Learn about the origins of bluegrass at the **Blue Ridge Music Center** (**PAGE 572**).

4. Eat traditional North Carolina barbecue at **Buxton Hall Barbecue** (**PAGE 575**).

5. Drive the vista-studded **Newfound Gap Road** in **Great Smoky Mountains National Park** (**PAGE 579**).

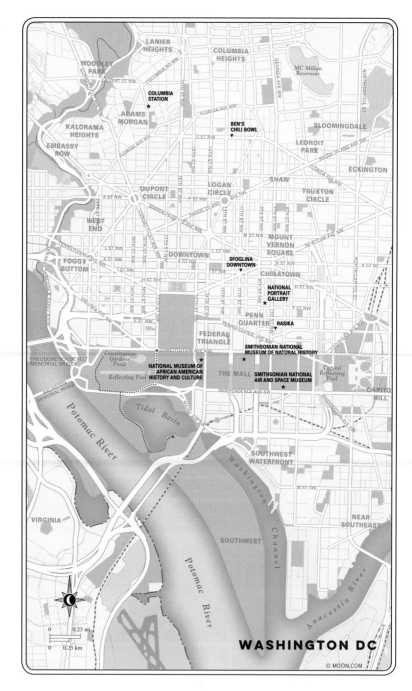

WASHINGTON DC

© MOON.COM

BEN'S CHILI BOWL

AFTERNOON

❷ Cross the river to **Arlington National Cemetery** (across Memorial Bridge from the Lincoln Memorial, Arlington, Virginia, 877/907-8585, www.arlingtoncemetery.mil, 8am-7pm daily Apr.-Sept., 8am-5pm daily Oct.-Mar., free, parking $2/hour). The second-oldest national cemetery contains the Tomb of the Unknown Soldier and the gravesite of JFK, among its monuments to patriotic sacrifice.

EVENING

❸ For dinner, head to **Rasika** (633 D St. NW, 202/637-1222, www.rasikarestaurant.com, 11:30am-2:30pm and 5:30pm-10:30pm Mon.-Thurs., 11:30am-2:30pm and 5pm-11pm Fri., 5pm-11pm Sat., $20-28), which will transform the way you look at Indian cuisine.

DAY 3: Washington DC to Shenandoah National Park

125 miles/201 kilometers | 3-4 hours

ROUTE OVERVIEW: I-66 • VA-55 • Skyline Dr.

❶ Check out iconic monuments along the **National Mall,** like the **Washington Monument** (2 15th St. NW, 877/444-6777 or 877/559-6777 for tickets, www.nps.gov/wamo, 9am-10pm daily Memorial Day-Labor Day, 9am-5pm daily Labor Day-Memorial Day, free, tickets required), **Lincoln Memorial** (2 Lincoln Memorial Circle NW, 202/426-6841, www.nps.gov/linc, 24 hours daily, free), and the **Vietnam Veterans Memorial** (5 Henry Bacon Dr. NW, 202/426-6841, www.nps.gov/vive, 24 hours daily, free).

❷ Have lunch at **Ben's Chili Bowl** (1213 U St. NW, 202/667-0909, www.benschilibowl.com, 6am-2am Mon.-Thurs., 6am-4am Fri., 7am-4am Sat., 11am-midnight Sun., $4-9), a DC institution, before hitting the road.

❸ Head to **Shenandoah National Park** (540/999-3500, www.nps.gov/shen, 24 hours daily, $25 vehicles, $10 pedestrians and cyclists) and cruise the beautiful **Skyline Drive.** The 105-mile vista-to-vista ridge-top drive carries you through Shenandoah National Park from Front Royal to Rockfish Gap. Along Skyline, 75 overlooks in the park give a sense of the vast wilderness that once blanketed the countryside.

> *Head west on I-66 for 62 miles (100 km). Exit onto VA-55 W and follow that for 5 miles (8 km) toward Front Royal, Virginia. Turn left onto Remount Rd./US-522, then make a right shortly after that onto E. Criser Rd. In less than a mile, turn left onto US-340 S. Follow signs for Skyline Dr.*

SHENANDOAH NATIONAL PARK

DARK HOLLOW FALLS

LURAY CAVERNS

④ Off of Skyline Drive, stop for a short hike along **Dark Hollow Falls Trail** (1.4 mi/2.3 km round-trip, 1.5 hours, moderate-strenuous) to see a beautiful 70-foot waterfall. The trail is all downhill on the way to the falls and a 440-foot elevation gain on the way back up. It's a thigh-burner, for sure. Find the trailhead at MP 50.7.

> *Continue south down Skyline Dr. for 50 miles to reach the parking area for the trailhead.*

⑤ Spend the night inside the park at **Big Meadows Lodge** (MP 51.2, 877/847-1919 or 877/247-9261, www.goshenandoah.com, $125-206). Built in 1939 of native stone and chestnut wood paneling, the lodge is listed in the National Register of Historic Places.

> *Back on Skyline Dr., take a right onto Big Meadows after less than a mile. Follow Big Meadows for about a mile to reach the lodge.*

DAY 4: Shenandoah National Park to Waynesboro, Virginia

170 miles/275 kilometers | 4-5 hours

ROUTE OVERVIEW: Skyline Dr. • US-211 • US-340 • US-33 • Skyline Dr. • I-64 • surface streets • I-64

❶ Head outside the park to the spectacular **Luray Caverns** (101 Cave Hill Rd., Luray, 540/743-6551, www.luraycaverns.com, from 9am daily, tours depart every 20 minutes, final tour times vary by season, $27 adults, $15 children 6-12), one of the best cave systems in the nation. On the guided tour you'll see chambers as tall as 10-story buildings and tiny stalagmites no bigger than a dime, which formed before the founding of our nation.

> *Go north on Skyline Dr. for 20 miles (32 km) to US-211, then head west on US-211 for 10 miles (16 km). Turn right on Cave Hill Rd. to reach Luray Caverns.*

❷ When you're finished, drive down to **Waynesboro,** near the end of Skyline Drive and the start of the Blue Ridge Parkway, and check in at **Iris Inn** (191 Chinquapin Dr., 540/943-1991, www.irisinn.com, $229-339). Every room has fabulous views and is decorated in a contemporary style.

> *Head back to US-211/US-340 and drive southwest for 6 miles (10 km). Turn left to continue south on US-340. In 17 miles (27 km), merge onto US-33 E and continue for 6 miles (10 km). Get on Skyline Dr. headed south. Continue for 40 miles (64 km), then get onto US-250 W. Drive for 4 miles (6 km) to reach Waynesboro.*

❸ Head east to **Charlottesville** where you can tour **Monticello** (931 Thomas Jefferson Pkwy., 434/984-9800, www.monticello.org, 8:30am-6pm daily, $28

UNIVERSITY OF VIRGINIA

adults, $16 children 12-18, $9 children 5-11). Thomas Jefferson's home is one of the most beautiful and historic sites in the region. Spend time exploring the gardens and outbuildings, which include slave quarters, a sobering reminder of the cruelty underneath the beauty of the plantation.

> *Take US-250 E for 2 miles (3 km), then merge onto I-64 E. Continue for 22 miles (35 km). Take the exit for VA-20 S and follow this road for less than a mile. Turn left onto VA-53 E; continue for 2 miles (3 km), following signs for Monticello.*

❹ Walk the grounds of the **University of Virginia** (434/924-0311, www.virginia.edu), which was founded by Jefferson and bears his architectural mark.

> *Retrace your path along VA-53 (2 mi/3 km), then turn right to take VA-20 N. Continue for 1 mile (1.6 km), then turn left onto Elliott Ave. Continue for 2 miles (3 km), then turn onto Roosevelt Brown Blvd., which leads to the eastern edge of the campus in less than a mile.*

❺ Try dinner at creative, French-influenced **C&O Restaurant** (515 E. Water St., 434/971-7044, www.candorestaurant.com, 5pm-1am daily, $12-37). The restaurant has six distinct dining areas, from a barnwood-paneled bar to a cozy brick patio to a mezzanine warmed on cool nights by a woodburning stove. Head back to Waynesboro for the night.

> *Take I-64 W for 21 miles (34 km), then take exit 96 and turn right onto Delphine Ave. This road will lead to the southern edge of Waynesboro in about a mile.*

DAY 5: Waynesboro to Roanoke, Virginia

160 miles/260 kilometers | 4-5 hours

ROUTE OVERVIEW: US-250 • Blue Ridge Parkway • VA-43 • Blue Ridge Parkway

❶ Start your journey south along the **Blue Ridge Parkway.** Make your first stop the **Humpback Rocks Visitor Center** (MP 5.9, 540/377-2377, 10am-5pm daily May-Nov.). Take the **Humpback Rocks Trail** (2 mi/3.2 km round-trip, 1.5 hours, moderate-strenuous) to the eponymous rocks. From your perch atop the rocks, the view is simply spectacular.

> *Take US-250 E out of Waynesboro. In 2 miles (3 km), veer right to get onto the Blue Ridge Parkway heading south. In 6 miles (10 km), the parking area for the visitors center will be on the right.*

THE VIRGINIA COUNTRYSIDE NEAR WAYNESBORO

❷ Stop at the **James River Visitor Center** (MP 63.6, 10am-5pm Wed.-Sun. late May-late Oct.), the lowest point on the Parkway, and stretch your legs on one of the short walks that detail the history of the river or the diverse plant life here.

> Continue south on the Blue Ridge Parkway for 58 miles (93 km). The visitors center is on the left side, just before the James River.

❸ At Milepost 86, detour off the Parkway for lunch in **Bedford.** Spend the afternoon taking a free docent-led tour of the **National D-Day Memorial** (3 Overlord Circle, 866/935-0700, 10am-5pm daily Mar.-Nov., 10am-5pm Tues.-Sun. Dec.-Feb., $10 adults, $6 children 6-18). The memorial stands on a hilltop overlooking Bedford and tells of the planning and preparation for Operation Overlord (commonly known as D-Day), then leads you through the storming of the beachheads at Normandy, and the eventual Allied victory.

NATIONAL D-DAY MEMORIAL

> Continue south on the Blue Ridge Parkway for 22 miles (35 km). Turn left onto VA-43 S/Peaks Rd. and continue for 10 miles (16 km) to reach Bedford.

❹ Head to one of the many orchards around Bedford for some fruit picking. **Gross' Orchard** (6817 Wheats Valley Rd., 540/586-2436, www.grossorchards.com, 8am-6pm Mon.-Sat., free) has been family owned and operated since the late 1800s, so these folks know their apples.

> Retrace your path back to VA-43 and head north for 5 miles (8 km). Turn right on VA-643; in less than a mile, turn left onto VA-640. Continue for 2 miles (3 km) to reach the orchard.

❺ Continue south to **Roanoke.** Enter the city via the Mill Mountain Parkway at Milepost 120 and pass by the famous, 88.5-foot-tall **Roanoke Star.** Then rest up at one of the B&Bs in

WITH LESS TIME

WAYNESBORO TO FLOYD

2-3 days; 199 miles/320 kilometers

If you only have a **long weekend** to drive the Blue Ridge Parkway, head straight for the Parkway's starting point in **Waynesboro, Virginia.** This is a driving-heavy itinerary for **two or three days,** but you'll enjoy the beautiful sights and scenic views the Parkway is renowned for, plus a relaxing overnight in **Roanoke.** See *Days 4-6* for more details.

ASHEVILLE TO KNOXVILLE

4-5 days; 170 miles/274 kilometers

In **four days,** you can go from **Asheville,** North Carolina, along the Blue Ridge Parkway to **Knoxville,** Tennessee, with enough time to explore both cities, as well as take your time driving the Parkway. See *Days 11-14* for more details; if you have time, tack on **an extra day** of exploration in Knoxville.

ORCHARD NEAR BEDFORD

town before heading to **River and Rail Restaurant** (2201 Crystal Springs Ave. SW, 540/400-6830, www.riverandrail-restaurant.com, 11am-2pm and 5pm-10pm Tues.-Sat., 11am-2pm Sun., $12-28), which works closely with a network of farmers, ranchers, and fishers from the Roanoke Valley and the region to put the best of the area's bounty on every plate.

> *Retrace your path by heading south to get back on VA-43. Turn right and drive north for 5 miles (8 km), then rejoin the Blue Ridge Parkway by turning left. Continue for 43 miles (69 km) to Mill Mountain Pkwy. Turn right and follow this road for 2.5 miles (4 km), then veer left onto Mill Mountain Spur to reach the base of the star. Double back on this road and turn left onto J. P. Fishburn Pkwy. This road will lead into Roanoke proper in 1.5 miles (2.5 km).*

DAY 6: Roanoke to Floyd, Virginia

50 miles/81 kilometers | 1-2 hours

ROUTE OVERVIEW: Blue Ridge Parkway • VA-637 • VA-615

① For breakfast, have a crazy good biscuit at **Scratch Biscuit Company** (1820 Memorial Ave., 540/855-0882, 6am-1pm Mon.-Fri., 7am-2am Sat., $2-8).

② Wander over to the **Market Square** (1 Market Sq., 540/342-2028, www.down-townroanoke.org, 8am-5pm Mon.-Sat., 10am-4pm Sun.), where the farmers market will be in full swing any day of the week. It's the oldest continuously operating open-air market in Virginia and one of the oldest such markets in the nation.

③ Check out the **O. Winston Link Museum** (101 Shenandoah Ave., 540/982-5465, www.roanokehistory.org, 10am-5pm Tues.-Sat., $6 adults, $5 children 3-12), which displays the work of Brooklyn photographer Winston Link, who captured the end of the steam locomotive era.

④ Head south and have lunch in Floyd. Check into **Ambrosia Farm Bed & Breakfast** (271 Cox Store Rd., 540/745-6363, www.ambrosiafarm.net, $90-135), which is made up of two cabins built from hand-hewn logs and a 200-year-old log farmhouse. Surrounded by pastures and hills, the farm is truly a retreat.

> *Head south on Mill Mountain Pkwy. for 2 miles (3 km) to Blue Ridge Parkway. Turn right and follow Blue Ridge Parkway to VA-860 (39 mi/63 km). Turn right, then make a quick left on VA-637. In 2 miles (3 km), turn right on VA-615 and follow that for 2 miles (3 km) to Floyd.*

DAY 7: Floyd to Stone Mountain State Park

115 miles/185 kilometers | 3-4 hours

ROUTE OVERVIEW: VA-8 • Blue Ridge Parkway • US-21 • surface streets

① Enjoy the drive from Floyd to the **North Carolina state line,** one of the most beautiful sections on the Parkway. Stop at **Mabry Mill** (MP 176.1),

MARKET SQUARE

MABRY MILL

one of the top places to photograph in any season. Take a look at the working waterwheel-powered gristmill and sawmill.

> *Drive south on VA-8 to Blue Ridge Parkway (6 mi/10 km). Turn right onto the Parkway and follow it for 11 miles (18 km) to Mabry Mill.*

❷ At **Groundhog Mountain** (MP 188.1), enjoy spectacular views from the observation tower. Views from here are sweeping, to say the least. You can see the Dan river valley and the mountains easing into Piedmont as well as Pilot Mountain's odd quartzite peak jutting upward.

> *Continue south on the Parkway for 13 miles (21 km) to Groundhog Mountain.*

❸ Learn how country and bluegrass music originated in these very hills at the **Blue Ridge Music Center** (700 Foothills Rd., Galax, 276/236-5309, www.blueridgemusiccenter.org, 10am-5pm daily May-Oct., free) at the state line. In this museum, video and audio displays help tell the story of the development of old-time and bluegrass music and show how this distinct sound has influenced other genres throughout the years.

> *Keep going south on the Parkway for 24 miles (39 km) to Music Center Rd. Turn left and continue less than a mile to Blue Ridge Music Center.*

❹ Set up camp at **Stone Mountain State Park** (3042 Frank Pkwy., Roaring Gap, 336/957-8185, reservations: www.northcarolinastateparks.reserveamerica.com or www.ncparks.gov, $15-52). Spend a few hours hiking the **Stone Mountain Loop Trail** (4.5

mi/7.2 km loop, 3-3.5 hours, strenuous) to the top of the namesake bald granite dome. The trail eventually gets steep enough that there are a few cables along the way to help you climb. Don't stray far from the trail—it's marked with orange dots—as the granite can be slick.

> *Return to the Parkway and continue south to US-21 (17 mi/27 km). Turn left onto US-21 and in 5 miles (8 km), turn right onto Oklahoma Rd./Stone Mountain Rd. Follow this for 3 miles (5 km) to Frank Pkwy. Turn right and follow signs for Stone Mountain State Park (1 mi/1.6 km).*

❺ Head into nearby **Elkin** for dinner at **Southern on Main** (102 E. Main St., 336/258-2144, www.southernonmain.com, 11am-9pm Tues.-Thurs., 11am-10pm Fri.-Sat., $6-23), which dishes up Southern favorites like fried green tomatoes, blackened catfish, and shrimp and grits.

> *Leave the park via Frank Pkwy. to Traphill Rd. (3 mi/5 km). Turn right, then make a quick left and follow Traphill for 12 miles (19 km). Continue straight onto Elk Spur St. and drive into town (2 mi/3 km). Return to the park via the same route.*

DAY 8: Stone Mountain State Park to Blowing Rock, North Carolina

80 miles/129 kilometers | 2-3 hours

ROUTE OVERVIEW: US-21 • Blue Ridge Parkway • US-221

❶ North Carolina's High Country is no joke. The mountains are steep, and the road grows aggressively curvy, making for otherworldly views as you round corners with nothing but space and the Blue Ridge Mountains in front of you. Stretch your legs on a few of the 30 miles of trails in **Doughton Park** (MP 238.5, 336/372-1947, sunrise-sunset daily), which is one of the best places for wildlife viewing in High Country. The **Cedar Ridge Trail** (4.4 mi/7.1 km one-way, 2 hours, moderate) starts near **Brinegar Cabin** (MP 238).

STONE BRIDGE ON BLUE RIDGE PARKWAY

BRINEGAR CABIN

> Leave Stone Mountain via Oklahoma Rd. and drive 3 miles (5 km) to US-21. Turn left and follow US-21 N to Blue Ridge Parkway (5 mi/8 km). Merge onto the Parkway, heading south for 9 miles (14.5 km) to reach the cabin.

❷ Stop at the turn-of-the-20th-century manor house in **Moses H. Cone Memorial Park** (MP 294.1, 828/295-7938, 9am-5pm daily Mar. 15-Nov., free). More commonly called Flat Top Manor, it's a wonderfully crafted house—a huge white, ornate mountain palace built in 1901. Today it's home to the gift shop of the **Southern Highland Craft Guild** (828/295-7938, www.southernhighlandguild.org, 9am-5pm daily mid-Mar.-Nov.), a place to buy beautiful textiles, pottery, jewelry, furniture, and dolls handmade by some of the best craftspeople of the Appalachian Mountains.

> Continue south on the Parkway for 55 miles (89 km) to reach the manor house.

❸ **Blowing Rock** is just a few miles away, and so are your accommodations at **The New Public House & Hotel** (239 Sunset Dr., 828/295-3487, www.thenewpublichouse.com, $175-250). The combination of comfy rooms, an outstanding restaurant, and a charming neighborhood make this a relaxing getaway.

> Double back on the Parkway for less than a mile. At US-221, turn left and drive 2 miles (3 km) to the hotel in Blowing Rock.

DAY 9: Blowing Rock to Asheville, North Carolina

105 miles/169 kilometers | 3.5-4 hours

ROUTE OVERVIEW: Blue Ridge Parkway • US-70

❶ Back on the Parkway, prepare yourself for one of the road's most striking stretches: the **Linn Cove Viaduct** (MP 304.4), a bridge-like structure hanging from the side of the mountain in a dizzying S-curve. A pair of viewing areas about a quarter mile from either

LINN COVE VIADUCT

GRANDFATHER MOUNTAIN

end of the viaduct give you the chance to stretch your legs and snap a few pictures of this amazing part of the road.

> *Head south on the Blue Ridge Parkway to the Linn Cove Viaduct (10 mi/16 km).*

② On the other side of the viaduct, drive to the top of **Grandfather Mountain** (2050 Blowing Rock Hwy./US-221, 828/733-4337, http://grandfather.com, 8am-7pm daily summer, 9am-6pm daily spring and fall, 9am-5pm daily winter, weather permitting, $20 adults, $9 children 4-12) and take the **Mile High Swinging Bridge** to one of its lower peaks for 360-degree views of the Blue Ridge.

> *Drive 1 mile (2 km) southwest on the Parkway to US-221. Turn right and drive 1 mile (2 km) to Grandfather Mountain Entrance Rd. to reach the top of the mountain (2 mi/3 km).*

③ Continue down the Parkway to the entrance to the **Linville Falls Visitor Center** (MP 316.3). Hike the **Erwins View Trail** (1.6 mi/2.8 km round-trip, 1 hour, moderate) to reach several overlooks providing the best views of the falls and the Linville Gorge.

MILE HIGH SWINGING BRIDGE

> *Return to the Parkway via US-221 (3 mi/5 km). Once on the Parkway, drive 11 miles (18 km) south, then take a left onto Linville Falls Rd. Follow it for 1.5 miles (2.5 km) to the visitors center.*

④ Then continue to the **Folk Art Center** (MP 382, 828/298-7928, www.southernhighlandguild.com, 9am-5pm daily, free), just outside Asheville. Part gallery, part store, the center displays works like woven baskets and wood carvings by master craftspeople from the southern Appalachians.

> *Return to the Parkway (1.5 mi/2.5 km) and continue south for 65 miles (105 km) to the Folk Art Center.*

⑤ In Asheville, spend the night downtown at the swank **AC Hotel by Marriott Asheville Downtown** (10 Broadway, 828/258-2522, www.marriott.com, $166-410). It's an easy walk to just about any restaurant, brewery, cocktail lounge, or music venue in town. Spend a late night downtown checking out the breweries and bars and listening to a little music.

> *Head south on the Parkway for less than a mile, then turn right onto Tunnel Rd./US-70. In 2 miles (3 km), merge onto I-240 W and drive into Asheville (3 mi/5 km).*

DAY 10: Asheville

MORNING AND AFTERNOON

① Start the day in Asheville with breakfast downtown, then head over to the **Biltmore Estate** (1 Approach Rd., 800/411-3812, www.biltmore.com, 8:30am-6:30pm daily, $55-65 adults,

BILTMORE ESTATE

$27.50-32.50 children 10-16, additional fees for activities). Asheville's most popular attraction is not only an awe-inspiring palace and symbol of the Gilded Age, it's also a collection of great little restaurants, shops, and a popular winery, all in a beautiful riverside setting. Spend the day touring the home, walking the gardens, and doing some wine-tasting.

EVENING

❷ For excellent barbecue, head to **Buxton Hall Barbecue** (32 Banks Ave., 828/232-7216, www.buxtonhall.com, 11:30am-3pm and 5:30pm-10pm daily, $5-16), which celebrates North Carolina traditions in every delicious bite.

❸ Enjoy late-night cocktails at **Sovereign Remedies** (29 N. Market St., 828/919-9518, www.sovereignremedies.com, 4pm-2am Tues.-Thurs., 10am-3pm and 4pm-2am Fri.-Mon.). Between the bartenders and local foragers, the bar stays stocked with wild herbs, berries, fruit, and roots used to make cocktails or bitters, infuse or macerate various liquors, and create shrubs (drinking vinegars).

ASHEVILLE

▶ Playlist

BLUE RIDGE PARKWAY

SONGS

- **"My Tennessee Mountain Home" by Dolly Parton:** Dolly Parton is a music icon. Her voice dances light as air while her words ground stories in place and time. Born in a small town in the Great Smoky Mountains, Parton penned this 1973 song about her upbringing in rural Tennessee.

- **"Swing and Turn Jubilee" by Jean Ritchie:** Known as the Mother of Folk, Ritchie made a name for herself as an Appalachian musician. She often sang without accompaniment, but when she did use an instrument, she played the Appalachian dulcimer. Hear how its steady hum lifts Ritchie's pure voice high and clear on this lovely song.

PODCASTS

- ***Down the Road:*** These episodes showcase North Carolina bluegrass music and the stories, performers, and traditions that comprise the spirit of the Blue Ridge.

- ***Dolly Parton's America:*** This nine-part series covers Dolly Parton's life and career, her unique outlook on the world, and her enduring legacy as one of the greatest icons of the United States.

Best HIKES

SKYLINE DRIVE

- **Mary's Rock Trail** (2.6 mi/4.2 km round-trip, 2-3 hours, moderate; trailhead at MP 33.5): Views from Mary's Rock are some of the best along Skyline Drive, with full panoramas of the mountain chain stretching off into the distance.

- **Dark Hollow Falls** (1.4 mi/2.3 km round-trip, 1.5 hours, moderate-strenuous; trailhead at MP 50.7): This short but taxing trail in Shenandoah National Park leads to a beautiful 70-foot waterfall.

BLUE RIDGE PARKWAY

- **Linville Falls Trail** (2 mi/3.2 km round-trip, 1-1.5 hours, moderate; trailhead at MP 316.3): Take in three views of one of the most beautiful waterfalls in what's called the "Grand Canyon of the East."

- **Craggy Gardens Trail** (1.6 mi/2.6 km round-trip, 1 hour, moderate; trailhead at MP 364.6): Venture out on this moderate hike through rhododendron tunnels reminiscent of a fairy-tale forest

GREAT SMOKY MOUNTAINS NATIONAL PARK

- **Andrews Bald** (3.5 mi/5.6 km round-trip, 3 hours, moderate; trailhead at Clingmans Dome parking area): Wildflowers abound in this bald, a high meadow in Great Smoky Mountains National Park.

- **Alum Cave Bluff to Mount LeConte** (5 mi/8 km one-way, 3-3.5 hours, strenuous; trailhead at Alum Cave): This hike has a huge payoff as you take in the views from the top.

- **Hen Wallow Falls Trail** (4.4 mi/7.1 km round-trip, 3.5 hours, moderate; trailhead at Gabes Mountain): A short trail leads you to a photogenic 90-foot waterfall that starts out only 2 feet wide but spreads to 20 feet at the base.

▽ DARK HOLLOW FALLS IN SHENANDOAH NATIONAL PARK

DAY 11: Asheville to Cherokee, North Carolina

95 miles/153 kilometers | 3-3.5 hours

ROUTE OVERVIEW: I-26 • NC-191 • Blue Ridge Parkway • US-441

❶ The winding section of the Parkway between Asheville and the southern terminus in Cherokee is quite beautiful. Before you hit the road, down a giant biscuit at **Biscuit Head** (733 Haywood Rd., 828/333-5145, www.biscuitheads.com, 7am-2pm Mon.-Fri., 8am-3pm Sat.-Sun., $3-10).

❷ Continue down the Parkway and take in the view of **Mount Pisgah** (MP 408.6). If you're feeling ambitious, hike the **Mount Pisgah Summit Trail** (2.6 mi/4.2 km round-trip, 2-2.5 hours, moderate-strenuous) for views that are well worth the effort.

> Go west on I-240 to I-26 (2 mi/3 km). Continue on I-26 for 5 miles (8 km), then take exit 33 for NC-191. In 3 miles (5 km), get on the Blue Ridge Parkway and head southwest for 14 miles (23 km) to Mount Pisgah.

❸ **Richland Balsam Overlook** (MP 431.4) is the highest point on the Blue Ridge Parkway, at 6,047 feet, so stop here and mark your trip with a selfie.

> Continue on the Parkway for 24 miles (39 km) to reach the overlook.

❹ Stop at the **Waterrock Knob Visitor Center** (MP 451.2, 828/298-0398, 10am-5pm daily May-Sept.) for a panorama of the Great Smoky Mountains. The view at sunset is especially fabulous.

> Continue on the Parkway for 20 miles (32 km) to the visitors center.

AUTUMN VIEW OFF THE BLUE RIDGE PARKWAY

WATERROCK KNOB OVERLOOK

❺ In Cherokee, spend the night at **Harrah's Cherokee Casino Resort** (777 Casino Dr., 828/497-7777, www.caesars.com, 24 hours daily, $130-510), where you can gamble, visit the spa, and grab a bite in one of the casino's restaurants. From the higher floors, the view of the mountains is spectacular.

> Continue for another 18 miles (29 km) on the Parkway to US-441. Here, turn left and follow it south for 3 miles (5 km) into Cherokee.

DAY 12: Cherokee to Gatlinburg, Tennessee

35 miles/56 kilometers | 1.5 hours

ROUTE OVERVIEW: US-441/Newfound Gap Rd.

❶ Start the day with a visit to Cherokee's **Qualla Arts and Crafts Mutual** (564 Tsali Blvd., 828/497-3103, http://quallaartsandcrafts.com, 8am-7pm Mon.-Sat., 8am-5pm Sun. June-Aug., shorter hours Sept.-May). The gallery's high standards and the community's thousands of years of artistry make for a collection of very special pottery, baskets, masks, and other traditional art.

❷ As you enter **Great Smoky Mountains National Park** (GSMNP, 865/436-1200, www.nps.gov/grsm, 24 hours daily, free), stop at the **Oconaluftee Visitor Center** (1194 Newfound Gap Rd., 828/497-1904, www.nps.gov/grsm, 8am-4:30pm daily Dec.-Feb., 8am-5pm daily Mar. and Nov., 9am-6pm daily Apr.-Oct.) for a park map. Be sure to check out the adjacent **Mountain Farm Museum** (sunrise-sunset daily, free),

FABULOUS FALL *Foliage*

As you cruise along Skyline Drive and the Blue Ridge Parkway during October, the height of autumn color, be prepared for two things: a slower pace and a feast for the eyes. You can pull over at any **overlook** for a frame-worthy photo, but check out the list below for the best lookouts, hikes, and vantage points for fall color on the rolling and wrinkled hills of the Blue Ridge and Smoky Mountains.

SKYLINE DRIVE

- **Range View Overlook (MP 17.1):** From here, look down a long stretch of the Blue Ridge with Stony Man Mountain at the far end, and see why the valley adjacent was once called "the Great Wagon Road."

- **Big Run Overlook (MP 81.2):** This iconic view is breathtaking, and offers horizon-to-horizon leaves in fall. On the best days, you'll see veins of quartz twinkling on Rocky Top Ridge across the valley.

- **Crimora Lake Overlook (MP 92.6):** Crimora Lake shines from the middle of a sea of fall colors, a gorgeous reminder of what was once a manganese mining operation.

BLUE RIDGE PARKWAY

- **Rockfish Valley Overlook (MP 2):** Start your trip down the Parkway with a stop looking over the Rockfish River.

- **James River Visitor Center (MP 63.6):** The lowest point on the Parkway showcases fall leaves reflected in the placid James River and makes a lovely place for a picnic.

- **Peaks of Otter (MP 85.9):** Abbott Lake reflects Flat Top and Sharp Top, the Peaks of Otter, near Bedford.

- **Mabry Mill (MP 176.1):** See for yourself why this millhouse and waterwheel is one of the most-photographed places on the Parkway.

- **Chestoa View (MP 320.8):** The sweeping views of Linville Gorge are just a short walk from the parking area.

- **Orchard at Altapass (MP 328.3):** Admire the views as you pick apples in this historic orchard.

- **Looking Glass Rock Overlook (MP 417):** The slick stone face of Looking Glass Rock makes quite the contrast to the green, red, and yellow ridges around.

- **Graveyard Fields (MP 418.8):** The view is lovely from the overlook, but it's even better on the hike to Lower Falls or through the color-studded fields.

- **Devil's Courthouse (MP 422.4):** A great view from the overlook only improves when you take the short, steep hike to the knob of rock that is Devil's Courthouse.

FALL FOLIAGE IN THE SMOKY MOUNTAINS

which showcases some of the finest farm buildings in the park.

> *Drive northeast on US-441 to the visitors center (3 mi/5 km).*

❸ The famous **Newfound Gap Road** (US-441, from Cherokee to Gatlinburg) is the perfect introduction to the park. Contour-hugging curves, overlooks with million-dollar views, and easy hikes right off the roadway give you a great overview of these mountains and this spectacular park. As you drive, keep your eyes peeled for bears, who sometimes cause traffic jams as they cross the road.

> *Once inside Great Smoky Mountains National Park, take US-441 N for 31 miles (50 km) to Gatlinburg.*

❹ Check into a hotel in **Gatlinburg,** then take a walk down the main drag of this tourist haven. Grab some moonshine at **Sugarlands Distilling Company** (805 Parkway, 865/325-1355, www.sugarlandsdistilling.com, 10am-10pm Mon.-Thurs., 10am-10:30pm Fri.-Sat., noon-6:30pm Sun.) before getting dinner in town.

DAY 13: Gatlinburg to Knoxville, Tennessee

45 miles/72 kilometers | 2 hours

ROUTE OVERVIEW: US-321/US-441 • city streets • US-441

❶ Grab breakfast at the **Pancake Pantry** (628 Parkway, 865/436-4724, www.pancakepantry.com, 7am-4pm daily June-Oct., 7am-3pm daily Nov.-May, $6-10), the oldest pancake house in town. There are 24 varieties of pancakes and crepes, as well as waffles, omelets, and French toast.

❷ Head straight to **Dollywood** (2700 Dollywood Parks Blvd., Pigeon Forge, 800/365-5996, www.dollywood.com, Apr.-Dec., $79-109, parking $11-17). Ride roller coasters and get a taste of southern Appalachian music, history, and culture at this theme park owned by country music legend Dolly Parton. One of the best-known spots in the park is **Showstreet,** where stages and theaters are always busy with musicians, square dances, and storytellers. There's also a bevy of master craftspeople practicing their Appalachian arts for all to see: blacksmiths, basket weavers, candlemakers, and woodworkers.

> *Head north on US-321/US-441 for 6 miles (10 km). Turn right onto Dollywood Ln. and continue for 2 miles (3 km), following signs for the theme park.*

❸ Grab the best burger in **Pigeon Forge** at **Local Goat** (2167 Parkway, 865/366-3035, www.localgoatpf.com, 11am-11pm Mon.-Thurs., 11am-midnight Fri.-Sat., 11am-10pm Sun., $8-26), where the beef is ground fresh and the buns are baked daily.

> *Retrace your path back down Dollywood Ln. toward Pigeon Forge, turning right at Teaster Ln. after 1.5 miles (2.5 km). Follow this road for 2.5 miles (4 km), then turn right onto Parkway to reach the restaurant.*

❹ Head to **Knoxville** for the night and cozy up in a room at **The Oliver Hotel** (407 Union Ave., 865/521-0050, www.theoliverhotel.com, $216-410). The

PANCAKE PANTRY, GATLINBURG

DOLLYWOOD

service is impeccable and the rooms amazing—everything is done to a luxurious, but not ostentatious, level.

> *Get onto US-441 toward Sevierville (4 mi/6 km). Continue west on US-441 for 25 miles (40 km) until Knoxville.*

DAY 14: Knoxville

MORNING AND AFTERNOON

❶ Start your day with a walk in the **World's Fair Park** (963 World's Fair Park Dr., www.worldsfairpark.org, 6am-midnight daily). This 10-acre park has walking paths, a small lake, open grassy spaces, soccer fields, fountains, and a gorgeous stream running right down the middle.

❷ Also in the park is the **Sunsphere** (810 Clinch Ave., 865/215-8160, www.worldsfairpark.org, 9am-10pm daily Apr.-Oct., 11am-6pm daily Nov.-Mar., free), a 266-foot-tall tower topped by a huge golden ball. Climb to the top for the best view in town.

EVENING

❸ Take in a concert at the historic **Tennessee Theatre** (604 S. Gay St., 865/684-1200, www.tennesseetheatre.com, box office 10am-5pm Mon.-Fri., 10am-2pm Sat., showtimes and ticket prices vary). The exterior features a classic marquee, and the Spanish-Moorish-style interior puts any contemporary movie theater or music hall to shame.

❹ Have dinner at **Not Watson's Kitchen + Bar** (15 Market Sq., 865/766-4848,

TENNESSEE THEATRE

www.notwatsons.com, 11am-10pm Mon.-Thurs., 11am-11pm Fri.-Sat., 11am-9pm Sun., $9-22), in the center of downtown. Afterward, explore the city center to your heart's content.

Getting There

AIR

While most visitors drive to the Blue Ridge Parkway, Shenandoah National Park, or Great Smoky Mountains National Park, it's convenient to fly into a nearby city, rent a car, and hit the road at any point along the route.

Three airports serve the Washington area: **Dulles International Airport** (IAD, 1 Saarinen Circle, Dulles, Virginia, 703/572-2700, www.flydulles.com), **Reagan National Airport** (DCA, 2401 Smith Blvd., Arlington, Virginia, 703/417-8000, www.flyreagan.com), and **Baltimore/Washington International Airport** (BWI, 7050 Friendship Rd., Baltimore, 410/859-7111, www.bwiairport.com).

SUNSPHERE IN WORLD'S FAIR PARK

TRAIN

Amtrak (800/872-7245, www.amtrak.com) service is dependable through this region. Amtrak pulls into Washington DC's **Union Station** (50 Massachusetts Ave. NE, 24 hours daily), with trains coming from and going to destinations all over the Eastern Seaboard. Amtrak services include the Acela Express, Northeast Regional, Silver Service/Palmetto, Cardinal/Hoosier State, Crescent, Vermonter, Capitol Limited, and Carolinian/Piedmont.

Amtrak also serves **Charlottesville** (CVS, 810 W. Main St., 434/296-4559, www.amtrak.com, 6am-9:30pm daily), where the Cardinal/Hoosier State, Crescent, and Northeast Regional Lines pass through daily. The Amtrak station in **Roanoke** (101 Norfolk Ave., 800/872-7245, www.amtrak.com) serves passengers on the Crescent and Northeast Regional lines.

BUS

You can take a **Greyhound bus** (800/231-2222, www.greyhound.com) to every major city and most of the larger towns on or near the Blue Ridge Parkway. The most useful routes are those that take you to Washington DC's **Union Station** (WAS, 50 Massachusetts Ave. NE, 24 hours daily); the **Charlottesville Greyhound station** (310 W. Main St., 434/295-5131, www.greyhound.com, 8am-10pm daily); the **Roanoke Greyhound station** (26 Salem Ave. SW, 540/343-5436, midnight-2am and 9am-5pm daily); or the **Knoxville Greyhound station** (100 E. Magnolia Ave., 865/525-9483, www.greyhound.com, 4:30am-1:30am daily), because they put you in places where it's easy to get started on the Parkway.

CAR

From **Dulles Airport** to Washington DC, it's a 28-mile, 40-minute drive east on VA-267 to I-66. From Reagan Airport, it's 15 minutes (5 mi/8 km) to Washington DC. Take George Washington Memorial Parkway to I-395 N.

It's 33 miles (53 km) to reach Washington DC from the **Baltimore airport.** Drive northwest on I-195 to MD-295 S, continue onto Baltimore-Washington

Parkway, and then merge onto US-50 toward Washington.

Two major interstates—I-64 and I-77—intersect the Blue Ridge Parkway at the northern and southern ends, and I-81 provides easy access as it runs diagonally up the western border of Virginia, parallel to the Parkway.

I-66 connects Washington DC with the beginning of Skyline Drive in northern Virginia. **I-64** passes by Shenandoah National Park and is the de facto dividing line between Skyline Drive and the Parkway, providing easy access to both at Rockfish Gap just outside Waynesboro.

In North Carolina, the Parkway goes right by Asheville and ends in Cherokee. In Tennessee, Knoxville (touched by both **I-40** and **I-75**) is the nearest city to Great Smoky Mountains National Park, though the towns of Gatlinburg and Pigeon Forge are nestled close to the park's borders.

Getting Back

You'll definitely want to make better travel time on the return drive from Knoxville back to **Washington DC.** Get on I-40 E from Knoxville and drive for 33 miles (53 km) to I-81. Go north on I-81 through Tennessee and Virginia (375 mi/604 km) to I-66 E. Hop on I-66 and head straight into DC (75 mi/121 km). This **487-mile (784-km) route** takes about **seven hours** and is doable in a day.

There's a closer airport if you want to fly back home from Knoxville, rather than drive back to DC. **McGhee Tyson Airport** (TYS, 2055 Alcoa Hwy., Alcoa, 865/342-3000, www.tys.org) in Alcoa is about 20 minutes south of Knoxville. Airlines serving McGhee Tyson include Allegiant, American, Delta, Frontier, and United.

CONNECT WITH

● At Washington DC: **The Appalachian Trail** (PAGE 494), **Chesapeake Bay** (PAGE 612), and **The Loneliest Road** (PAGE 36).

THE NATCHEZ TRACE: NASHVILLE TO NEW ORLEANS

WHY GO: Creole cuisine, Elvis, music museums, live music, Southern cooking, sacred Indian mounds, civil rights history, voodoo, antebellum architecture, Mississippi River

TOTAL DISTANCE: 1,070 miles/ 1,725 kilometers

NUMBER OF DAYS: 12

SEASONS: Spring and fall

START: Nashville, Tennessee

END: New Orleans, Louisiana

▼ NEW ORLEANS

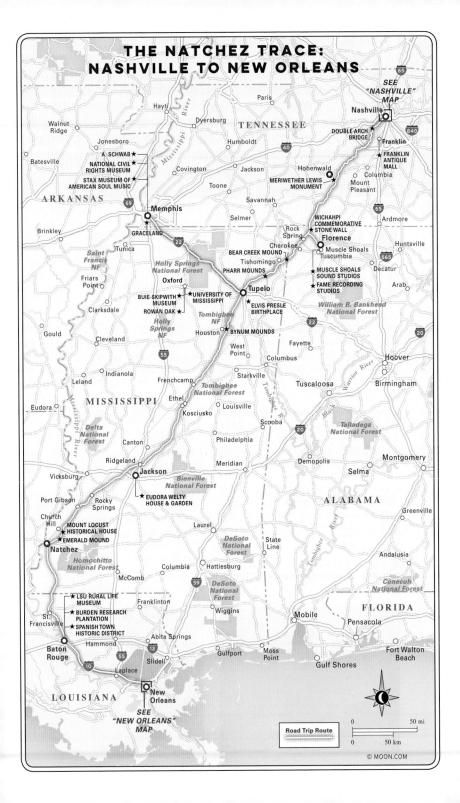

THE NATCHEZ TRACE:
NASHVILLE TO NEW ORLEANS

Road trips that take you on a 10,000-year-old journey are few and far between. The Natchez Trace Parkway is one of those expeditions. Even though it clocks in at 444 miles—not epic in terms of overall distance—the Parkway reaches deep into the past, to when early Native Americans used it to travel. European explorers, traders, and soldiers followed the route in later years, and some of our country's cultural icons were born and raised in towns along the way. From the Appalachian foothills to the lower Mississippi River, the Trace bisects four ecosystems, winds through scenic landscapes, and provides you with an immersive experience.

DAY 1: Nashville

MORNING

1 Arrive in **Nashville** and check into a downtown hotel, such as **Union Station** (1001 Broadway, 615/726-1001, www.unionstationhotelnashville.com, $234-274). The 125-room hotel is located in what was once the city's main train station and boasts high ceilings, lofty interior balconies, magnificent ironwork and molding, and an impressive marble-floored great hall.

2 Walk to the **Tennessee State Capitol** (600 Charlotte Ave., 615/741-0830, tours 9am-3pm hourly Mon.-Fri., free), which strikes a commanding pose overlooking downtown Nashville. Ask at the information desk for a printed guide that identifies each of the rooms and many of the portraits and sculptures both inside and outside the building.

AFTERNOON

3 Feast on Indian street food at **Chauhan Ale & Masala House** (123 12th Ave. N., 615/242-8426, http://chauhannashville.com, 11am-2:30pm and 5pm-10pm Sun.-Thurs., 11am-2:30pm and 5pm-11pm Fri., 5pm-11pm Sat., $12-28) for lunch. The vibe is fun and friendly, the cocktails go down easy, and there is even an interpretation of a Nashville hot chicken dish.

4 Visit the **Civil Rights Room at the Nashville Public Library** (615 Church St., 615/862-5782, www.library.nashville.org, 9am-6pm Mon.-Fri., 9am-5pm Sat., 2pm-5pm Sun., free), a powerful exhibit on the movement for civil rights that took place in Nashville in the 1950s and 1960s.

EVENING

5 Grab dinner at **Pinewood Social** (33 Peabody St., 615/751-8111, www.pinewoodsocial.com, 7am-1am Mon.-Fri., 9am-1am Sat.-Sun., $7-25) before heading to **Lower Broadway,** the official entertainment district of Nashville. Enjoy dancing at the honky-tonks on your first night in town.

TENNESSEE STATE CAPITOL BUILDING IN NASHVILLE

DOWNTOWN NASHVILLE

Top ⑤ THE NATCHEZ TRACE

① See a show at the legendary **Grand Ole Opry** in Nashville (PAGE 587).

② Visit the **Wichahpi Commemorative Stone Wall**, a powerful tribute to the Trail of Tears (PAGE 588).

③ Honor the King's legacy at the **Elvis Presley Birthplace** in Tupelo and at **Graceland** in Memphis (PAGE 590).

④ Take a tour of **Emerald Mound,** one of the largest Native American mounds in the United States (PAGE 594).

⑤ Eat an authentic Creole dinner at **Commander's Palace** in New Orleans (PAGE 598).

DAY 2: Nashville

MORNING

① Visit the **Country Music Hall of Fame and Museum** (222 5th Ave. S., 615/416-2001, www.countrymusichalloffame.org, 9am-5pm daily, $25 adults, $15 children 6-12) in the morning and learn about the genre's complex roots.

AFTERNOON

② Grab an early lunch at **Arnold's Country Kitchen** (605 8th Ave. S., 615/256-4455, www.arnoldscountry-kitchen.com, 10:30am-2:45pm Mon.-Fri., $7-10) to fuel up. No haute or fusion cuisine here—this is some of the best Southern cooking in town.

③ Poke around the **Johnny Cash Museum** (119 3rd Ave. S., 615/256-1777,

COUNTRY MUSIC HALL OF FAME AND MUSEUM

JOHNNY CASH MUSEUM

www.johnnycashmuseum.com, 9am-7pm daily, $19 adults, $15 children). The collection was amassed by one fan-turned-collector, and it features interactive listening booths, the jumpsuit the Man in Black wore when he flipped the bird in public, and other memorabilia from a varied and lauded career.

EVENING

❹ Spend your evening attending a show at the iconic **Grand Ole Opry** (2804 Opryland Dr., 615/871-6779 or 800/733-6779, www.opry.com, $37-77). Even if you think you don't like country music, you'll love this place. For more than 90 years this weekly radio showcase of country music has drawn crowds to Nashville, and each show is carefully balanced to include bluegrass, classic country, popular country, and, sometimes, gospel or rock.

> From downtown, take US-31/James Robertson Pkwy. across the river. In 1 mile (1.6 km), merge onto US-31E heading north. Continue for 4 miles (6 km), then join TN-155 E. In 5 miles (8 km), take the exit for Opry Mills Dr. and continue for 1 mile (1.6 km), following signs for the Grand Ole Opry.

DAY 3: Nashville to Hohenwald

90 miles/145 kilometers | 2.5-3 hours

ROUTE OVERVIEW: TN-100 • Natchez Trace Parkway • TN-96 • Natchez Trace Parkway

❶ As you head to the Natchez Trace Parkway the next morning, drive by **Centennial Park** and see **The Parthenon** (2500 West End Ave., 615/862-8431, www.nashville.gov/parthenon, 9am-4:30pm Tues.-Sat., 12:30pm-4:30pm Sun., $6 adults, $4 children). This

THE PARTHENON IN CENTENNIAL PARK

life-size replica of the Greek Parthenon, complete with a statue of Athena, is a gathering place, a museum, and one of the reasons Nashville is called "the Athens of the South."

> From downtown, follow Church St. southwest for 1.5 miles (2.5 km), then continue for less than a mile onto Ellison Pl. to Centennial Park.

❷ Fill up your stomach with fluffy biscuits from **The Loveless Cafe** (8400 TN100, 615/646-9700, www.lovelesscafe.com, 7am-9pm daily, $7-17), then fill up the tank with gasoline from a nearby station. It's the last place you'll pass before getting on the Natchez Trace Parkway.

> Take US-70S to TN-100 (3 mi/5 km). Continue onto TN-100, traveling southwest for 8 miles (13 km) to the café.

THE LOVELESS CAFE

DOUBLE ARCH BRIDGE

❸ Your first stop on the Natchez Trace is a prime photo spot: the **Double Arch Bridge** (MP 438). This bridge is a feat of engineering and design, with arches that flow with the rolling hills of the countryside.

> *Join the Natchez Trace and drive south for 4 miles (6 km) to reach the bridge.*

❹ Exit the scenic parkway to find good options for food, drink, and entertainment in **Franklin.** In the self-proclaimed New Antiques Capital of Tennessee, take the opportunity to browse the **Franklin Antique Mall** (251 2nd Ave. S., 615/790-8593, www.franklinantiquemall.com), located in the town's old icehouse. The mall is a maze of rooms, each with different goods on offer. Possibilities include books, dishware, quilts, furniture, knickknacks, and housewares.

> *Go east on TN-96 into Franklin (8 mi/13 km).*

❺ Back on the Trace, stop at the **Meriwether Lewis Park and Monument** (MP 385.9, Meriwether Lewis Park Rd., Hohenwald, www.nps.gov/natr, 800/305-7417, free), a somber memorial to a man who helped the country expand. This is also where to camp (free, no amenities) for the night before crossing into Alabama.

> *Double back on TN-96 heading west to return to the Trace (8 mi/13 km). Follow the Trace south for 52 miles (84 km) to Meriwether Lewis Park and Monument.*

DAY 4: Hohenwald to Florence, Alabama

75 miles/121 kilometers | 2-2.5 hours

ROUTE OVERVIEW: Natchez Trace Parkway • AL-20

❶ You'll be covering fewer miles on the Trace today, but there's still plenty to see. Cross into Alabama and stop at the **Wichahpi Commemorative Stone Wall** (MP 338, Florence, 256/764-3617, 8am-4pm daily, free). Known to locals as Tom's Wall, it's named for the late Tom Hendrix, the man who spent more than 30 years building what has become the largest unmortared wall in the country. The mile-long wall is a monument to Hendrix's great-great grandmother, Te-lah-nay, and her journey on the Trail of Tears. Each stone, hand-placed by Hendrix (or visitors) beginning in 1988, symbolizes a single step Te-lah-nay took. Today the wall includes stones from more than 120 different countries.

> *Return to the Trace and head south to Wichahpi Commemorative Stone Wall (48 mi/77 km).*

❷ Take a side trip to the **Quad Cities** region, where the namesake cities of Muscle Shoals, Florence, Sheffield, and Tuscumbia offer myriad opportunities. **Muscle Shoals** is home to important music sites like **3614 Jackson Highway** (256/978-5151, www.msmusicfoundation.org, 10am-4pm

MUSCLE SHOALS SOUND STUDIOS

Mon.-Sat.), also known as **Muscle Shoals Sound Studios.** In addition to nabbing a requisite selfie in front of the famous door, you can also take a tour (hourly 10:30am-3:30pm Mon.-Sat., $12, free for kids under 6).

> *Continue on the Trace for 2 miles (3 km) to AL-20. Follow AL-20 E to the Quad Cities (14 mi/23 km). Turn right onto US-72 and drive 2 miles (3 km) south to Muscle Shoals Sound Studios.*

❸ Nearby is **Fame Studios** (603 Avalon Ave., 256/381-0801, http://fame-studios.com, tours 9am-10am and 4pm-6pm Mon.-Fri., 10am-2pm Sat., $10). Etta James, the Osmonds, Aretha Franklin, Cher, Alicia Keys, the Civil Wars, Otis Redding, and Jamey Johnson are all part of the long list of performers who have recorded here.

❹ Shop for unique clothing or souvenirs in **Florence,** then tuck in for the night at the area's most luxurious hotel, the **Marriott Shoals Hotel & Spa** (10

FAME STUDIOS IN FLORENCE

Hightower Pl., 256/246-3600, www.marriott.com, $124-154). The 360-degree views from the top of the hotel are unparalleled.

> *Retrace your path on US-72 to return to Florence.*

WITH LESS TIME

NASHVILLE TO THE QUAD CITIES

4 days; 191 miles/307 kilometers

For music-loving travelers seeking a short trip, this **four-day** drive starts in **Nashville,** the nation's country-music capital. After spending **two days** here, you'll then head south to the start of the Natchez Trace Parkway and continue along the Trace to Alabama's **Quad Cities.** Spend two days visiting and touring the world-famous recording studios that call this region home.

NASHVILLE TO MEMPHIS

6 days; 531 miles/854 kilometers

A **six-day** trip along the Trace gives you plenty of time to hit the big sights in **Nashville,** visit Elvis Presley's birthplace in **Tupelo** and his mansion at **Graceland,** learn about the civil rights history of **Memphis,** explore the origins of soul and R&B music in the South, and see many of the **sacred Indian mounds** along the parkway. Follow *Days 1-7,* skipping the side trip to the Quad Cities.

NATCHEZ TO NEW ORLEANS

3 days; 172 miles/277 kilometers

Weekend warriors can spend **three days** exploring **Baton Rouge** and **New Orleans.** Start at the Natchez Trace's southern terminus in **Natchez,** admiring the town's antebellum architecture on your first day. Baton Rouge is a short drive away, and it's a great spot to spend a few hours poking around Louisiana State University before heading into New Orleans for the rest of your second day. Cram as much food, drink, and music as you can into your **last day** in the Crescent City.

DAY 5: Florence to Tupelo, Mississippi

100 miles/161 kilometers | 2-2.5 hours

ROUTE OVERVIEW: AL-20 • Natchez Trace Parkway

❶ Don't forget to get gas in the Quad Cities before heading back to the Trace. Head south on the Trace, where you'll cross into **Mississippi.** Stop at **Bear Creek Mound** (MP 308.8), a square, flat-topped mound of earth that was likely once a temple or chief's house circa AD 1100-1300.

> *Drive northwest on AL-20 to return to the Trace (14 mi/23 km). Turn left onto the Trace and head south to Bear Creek Mound (28 mi/45 km).*

❷ One of the best-known and most significant stops on the Natchez Trace is **Pharr Mounds** (MP 286.7), a complex of eight burial mounds that comprise the largest archaeological site in northern Mississippi, and one of the largest in the region.

> *Continue on the Trace to Pharr Mounds (21 mi/34 km).*

❸ Once you arrive in **Tupelo,** sample the blueberry doughnuts at **Connie's Fried Chicken** (821 S. Gloster St., 662/842-7260, 7am-8:30pm Mon.-Sat., 7am-2pm Sun., $8), often referred to as the Café Du Monde of Tupelo.

> *Continue south on the Trace to I-22 (25 mi/40 km). Turn left to merge onto I-22 E. In 1 mile (1.6 km), get on US-45 S and follow it for 1 mile (1.6 km) into Tupelo.*

❹ Then head to the **Elvis Presley Birthplace** (306 Elvis Presley Dr., 662/841-1215, http://elvispresleybirthplace.com, 9am-5pm Mon.-Sat., 1pm-5pm

ELVIS PRESLEY BIRTHPLACE

Sun., $17 adults, $7 children 7-12), where you'll honor the King's legacy and learn how he got to be who he was.

❺ Catch a show at the **Blue Canoe** (2006 N. Gloster St., 662/269-2642, www.bluecanoebar.com, 3pm-midnight Mon.-Thurs., 3pm-1am Fri., 2pm-1am Sat., $8-13), a bar and restaurant with live music and a better-than-bar-food menu.

DAY 6: Tupelo to Memphis, Tennessee

135 miles/217 kilometers | 2.5-3 hours

ROUTE OVERVIEW: I-22 • I-269 • I-55 • I-69

❶ From Tupelo, head to **Memphis.** Check into **The Peabody Memphis** (149 Union Ave., 901/529-4000, www.peabodymemphis.com, $300-410), the city's most famous hotel. Even the ducks in the fountain get the red-carpet treatment at this landmark.

> *Follow US-45 N to I-22 (1 mi/1.6 km). Drive west on I-22 for 74 miles (119 km), then merge onto I-269 and continue west for 16 miles (26 km) to I-55. Go north on I-55 for 15 miles (24 km), continuing onto I-69. Follow I-69 for 4 miles (6 km) into Memphis.*

❷ Head to **Graceland** (3717 Elvis Presley Blvd., 901/332-3322 or 800/238-2000, www.graceland.com, 9am-5pm Mon.-Sat., 9am-4pm Sun. Mar.-Oct., shorter hours Nov.-Feb., tours from $39 adults, $17 children) to immerse yourself in the world of the King. High points include watching the press conference Elvis gave after leaving the

BEAR CREEK MOUND

army, witnessing firsthand his audacious taste in decor, and visiting the meditation garden where Elvis, his parents, and his grandmother are buried.

> *Get back on I-69, this time heading south to Elvis Presley Blvd. (5 mi/8 km). Follow this for 1 mile (1.6 km) to Graceland.*

❸ Visit **Mud Island** for the afternoon to remind yourself that you are just steps away from the great Mississippi River. There you can visit the **Mud Island River Park and Mississippi River Museum** (125 N. Front St., 901/576-7241, www.mudisland.com, 10am-5pm Tues.-Sun. Apr.-Oct., $10 adults, $7 children), which has exhibits about early uses of the river, steam- and paddleboats, floods, and much more.

> *Retrace your path north once again on I-69 for 5 miles (8 km) to get back into central Memphis.*

❹ Go treasure-hunting at **A. Schwab** (163 Beale St., 901/523-9782, http://a-schwab.com, noon-6pm Mon.-Thurs., noon-8pm Fri.-Sat., 11am-5pm Sun.), a souvenir shop that focuses on odd and hard-to-find items.

❺ For dinner, try some of the delicious poultry at **Gus's World Famous Fried Chicken** (310 Front St., 901/527-4877, http://gusfriedchicken.com, 11am-9pm Sun.-Thurs., 11am-10pm Fri.-Sat., $6-12).

DAY 7: Memphis to Tupelo

120 miles/193 kilometers | 2.5-3 hours

ROUTE OVERVIEW: City streets • I-69 • I-55 • I-269 • I-22

❶ Go to the **National Civil Rights Museum** (450 Mulberry St., 901/521-9699, www.civilrightsmuseum.org, 9am-5pm Mon. and Wed.-Sat., 1pm-5pm Sun., $15 adults, $12 children 4-17). For years, the Lorraine Motel represented merely the tragic assassination of Martin Luther King Jr. Today, it tells the story of the African American struggle for civil rights.

❷ Explore the **Stax Museum of American Soul Music** (926 E. McLemore Ave., 901/942-7685, http://staxmuseum.org, 10am-5pm Tues.-Sat., 1pm-5pm Sun.-Mon. Apr.-Oct., 10am-5pm Tues.-Sat., 1pm-5pm Sun. Nov.-Mar., $13 adults, $10 children 9-12), which tells the story of the city's legendary soul music. Exhibits bring to life the work of Otis Redding, the Staple Singers, Isaac Hayes, and more.

❸ Head to dinner at **Soul Fish** (862 S. Cooper St., 901/725-0722, http://soulfishcafe.com, 11am-10pm Mon.-Sat., 11am-9pm Sun., $9-16). The atmosphere is open and cheerful, with a few touches of subtle sophistication.

MUD ISLAND, MEMPHIS

STAX MUSEUM OF AMERICAN SOUL MUSIC

Best OF SOUTHERN CUISINE

Honey-baked hams, biscuits, and pecan pies: A trip through the Deep South is tasty. Here's where to eat some regional specialties.

- **The Loveless Cafe** (8400 TN100, Nashville, 615/646-9700, www.lovelesscafe.com, 7am-9pm daily, $7-17): They may not be the best biscuits in Nashville, but they are the most iconic, and they're at the northern terminus of the Trace.

- **FloBama Music Hall** (311 N. Court St., Florence, 256/764-2225, 11am-2am Mon.-Sat., 11am-10pm Sun., $7-10): Whole smoked chicken, ribs, and live music. There's nothing more Southern than that.

- **Connie's Fried Chicken** (821 S. Gloster St., Tupelo, 662/842-7260, 7am-8:30pm Mon.-Sat., 7am-2pm Sun., $8): This is the place to stop for fried chicken, biscuits, and blueberry doughnuts.

- **Ajax Diner** (118 Courthouse Sq., Oxford, 662/232-8880, www.ajaxdiner.net, 11:30am-11pm Mon.-Sat., $8-15): The turnip green dip, po'boys, and fried catfish are said to be favorites of football legend Eli Manning.

- **The Biscuit Shop** (104 S. Washington St., Starkville, 662/324-3118, www.thebiscuitlady.com, 6:30am-2pm Tues.-Sat., $1.50-2.50): A good biscuit isn't hard to find in the South, but these are some of the best, with varieties you never imagined.

- **Carriage House Restaurant** (401 High St., Natchez, 601/445-5151, 11am-2pm Wed.-Sun., $15): Fried chicken and blue-plate specials are served in the antebellum mansion Stanton Hall.

▼ THE BISCUIT SHOP, STARKVILLE

④ Hang out for a drink or two at **Young Avenue Deli** (2119 Young Ave., 901/278-0034, www.youngavenuedeli.com, 11am-3am daily), a friendly neighborhood bar that books occasional live acts. Head back to **Tupelo** this evening.

> Take I-69 S from Memphis for 5 miles (8 km), then continue onto I-55. Follow this south for 15 miles (24 km), then merge onto I-269 heading east. Continue for another 15 miles (24 km), then exit onto I-22 and follow this southeast for 75 miles (121 km) to reach Tupelo.

DAY 8: Tupelo to Jackson

270 miles/435 kilometers | 5-6 hours

ROUTE OVERVIEW: US-278 • MS-41 • Natchez Trace Parkway • I-55

① Gas up the car for the hour-long drive to **Oxford,** home of Ole Miss. Wander the **University of Mississippi campus** (123 University Circle, 662/915-7211, http://olemiss.edu), where you can tour the **University Museum** and several of the campus's historic civil rights sights.

> Take US-45 S for 3 miles (5 km) to US-278. Turn right and head west on US-278 for 49 miles (79 km) to Oxford.

② Get lunch at **City Grocery** (152 Courthouse Sq., 662/232-0808, http://citygroceryonline.com, 11:30am-2:30pm and 6pm-10pm Mon.-Thurs., 11:30am-2:30pm and 6pm-10:30pm Fri.-Sat., 11am-2:30pm Sun., $10-30) in **The Square** (Jackson Ave. and Courthouse Sq., http://visitoxfordms.com), the historic center of all things Oxford.

③ Visit **Rowan Oak** (916 Old Taylor Rd., 662/234-3284, www.rowanoak.com, grounds dawn-dusk daily, house 10am-4pm Tues.-Sat., 1pm-4pm Sun. Aug.-May, 10am-6pm Mon.-Sat., 1pm-6pm Sun. June-July; grounds free, house $5), William Faulkner's home. The Greek Revival-style house, sitting on 29 acres, offers insight about the Nobel and Pulitzer Prize winner, as well as his creative process.

④ You have about an hour on the road to hook back up with the Trace. Continue south to the six Indian burial mounds at **Bynum Mounds** (MP 232.4). These significant archaeological sites were built between 100 BC and AD 100 (known as the Middle Woodland period). Just two of the mounds, the two largest, have been restored to their original appearance and are available for public viewing. This is a sacred space, so be sure to stay on the path and treat the site with respect.

> From Oxford, go east on US-278 for 23 miles (37 km), then exit at Oxford St. Follow this for 7 miles (11 km) to MS-15. Continue on MS-15 for 2 miles (3 km), then get onto MS-41 and go south for 13 miles (21 km), then rejoin the Trace. Continue for 15 miles (24 km) to reach Bynum Mounds.

⑤ Make for **Jackson** to spend the night at the **Fairview Inn** (734 Fairview St., 601/948-3429, http://fairviewinn.com, $199-339). This former 1908 Colonial Revival mansion is Jackson's only small luxury hotel. Amenities include a library, bar, restaurant, spa, and lovely gardens in which to stroll. The rooms are large, some with parlors and fireplaces and giant soaking tubs.

> Continue south on the Trace for 129 miles (208 km) to I-55. Go south on I-55 into Jackson (9 mi/14 km).

DOWNTOWN OXFORD, MISSISSIPPI

DOWNTOWN JACKSON, MISSISSIPPI

DAY 9: Jackson to Natchez

105 miles/169 kilometers | 2.5-3 hours

ROUTE OVERVIEW: I-20 • Natchez Trace Parkway

EMERALD MOUND

① You have many museums from which to choose in Jackson, Mississippi's capital city. The perfectly preserved **Eudora Welty House and Garden** (1119 Pinehurst St., 601/353-7762, http://eudorawelty.org, tours 9am, 11am, 1pm, and 3pm Tues.-Sat. and by appointment, $5 pp) feels like the author has just run out to lunch. Look at her paintings, photographs, and thousands of books. Walk her garden and see what inspired her. The gift shop has many of Welty's books for sale (as well as some of her photographs); you'll likely be motivated to read them after your visit.

② Head back on the Trace for the last piece of your Natchez Trace drive. Appreciate the leisurely pace as you drive, stopping to read historical signs. Allocate some time at **Mount Locust Historic House** (MP 15.5, no phone, 8:30am-5pm daily, free), an 1800s building and grounds with cemeteries, walking trails, and more.

> To get back to the Trace, use I-20 W, following it for 8 miles (13 km). Turn left onto the Trace and continue south for 72 miles (116 km) to Mount Locust.

③ Drive on to **Emerald Mound** (MP 10.3), because while you may have seen a lot of Indian mounds on this trip, this is one on which you can climb. Emerald Mound is, at 80 acres,

the second-largest ceremonial mound in the United States. Built between AD 1250 and 1600 by the Natchez people, this is the largest mound along the Trace.

> Continue south to Emerald Mound (5 mi/8 km).

④ You've made it to the southern terminus! **Natchez** is known for its antebellum architecture. Don't miss the opportunity to stay in one of these sweet, restored homes. At **Devereaux Shields House** (709 N. Union St., 601/304-5378, www.dshieldsusa.com, $135-188), you'll get a wine reception at night. Check in and wander the manicured garden.

> Follow the Trace south to its terminus in Natchez (10 mi/16 km). Drive into Natchez via Liberty Rd. (1 mi/1.6 km).

⑤ Order flatbread and beer at **King's Tavern** (613 Jefferson St., 601/446-5003, www.kingstavernnatchez.com, 11:30am-9pm Sun. and Thurs., 11:30am-10pm Fri.-Sat., $15-28) for dinner. The restaurant, which may be haunted, is in the oldest building in the state.

MOUNT LOCUST HISTORIC HOUSE

NATCHEZ, MISSISSIPPI

Best HIKES

The Natchez Trace Parkway isn't just a great drive. It also offers access to great walks—some short, some long. Here are a few of the best.

- **Garrison Creek** (up to 24 mi/39 km one-way, 1-2 days, moderate; trailhead at milepost 427.6): As the northern terminus of the Highland Rim Trail, this is the place serious hikers go to escape the hubbub. Make it long and strenuous, or just do a quick section.

- **Wichahpi Commemorative Stone Wall** (1 mi/1.6 km, 30 minutes, easy; trailhead at milepost 338): Meditate and contemplate while walking along this mile-long unmortared wall, which honors those who walked the Trail of Tears.

- **Rock Spring** (0.5 mi/0.8 km loop, 20 minutes, easy; trailhead at milepost 330.2): Take a 20-minute hike to a bubbling brook, sheltered from the sun under a canopy of trees.

- **Bailey's Woods Trail** (0.6 mi/ 1 km, 20 minutes, easy; trailhead at Rowan Oak, Oxford): Though doing this 20-minute wooded walk means taking a side trip to Oxford, Mississippi, it's worth it for the chance to visit William Faulkner's home, which connects to the trail.

- **Cypress Swamp Loop Trail** (0.4 mi/ 0.6 km loop, 20 minutes, easy; trailhead at milepost 122): Less than a half mile long, this boardwalk stroll spans a serene swamp of water tupelos and bald cypress.

- **Natchez Trace Multi-Use Trail** (10 mi/16 km; access at mileposts 105-100): A paved path winds next to the parkway and is great for walkers, strollers, hikers, and bikers.

▼ ONE OF MANY TRAILS ACCESSIBLE FROM THE NATCHEZ TRACE PARKWAY

DAY 10: Natchez to Baton Rouge, Louisiana

95 miles/153 kilometers | 2-2.5 hours

ROUTE OVERVIEW: US-61 • I-110

❶ Continue to **Baton Rouge,** the capital of Louisiana. Only a short drive southeast of downtown, the **LSU Rural Life Museum** (4560 Essen Ln., 225/765-2437, www.lsu.edu/rurallife, 8am-5pm daily, $10 adults, $8 children 6-11) is a living-history museum on the 450-acre **Burden Research Plantation.** The museum comprises numerous buildings and exhibits that show different aspects of early Louisiana living. The plantation quarters constitute a complex of authentically furnished 19th-century structures, including a kitchen, schoolhouse, and slave cabins.

> Take US-61 S to I-110 (80 mi/129 km). Head south on I-110 into Baton Rouge (9 mi/14 km).

❷ Drive through **Spanish Town** (bounded by State Capitol Dr., 5th St., North Ave., and 9th St., http://spanishtownbr.org), the city's oldest neighborhood, dating to 1805. Listed in the National Register of Historic Places, the neighborhood is characterized by bright, colorful homes and an offbeat character. It's best to visit Spanish Town during daylight hours.

❸ Order boudin balls and fried green tomatoes at **Beausoleil Restaurant and Bar** (7731 Jefferson Hwy., 225/926-1172, www.beausoleilrestaurantandbar.com, 11am-9pm Tues.-Thurs., 11am-10pm Fri.-Sat., 11am-3pm Sun., $17-38) for dinner.

❹ Spend the night at **Hilton Baton Rouge Capitol Center** (201 Lafayette St., 225/344-5866 or 877/862-9800, www.hiltoncapitolcenter.com, $149-199), which is in the National Register of Historic Places. The pool deck overlooks the Mississippi River.

DAY 11: Baton Rouge to New Orleans

80 miles/129 kilometers | 2-2.5 hours

ROUTE OVERVIEW: I-10

❶ Drive to **New Orleans** and start your day in the French Quarter with some warm café au lait and sugar-covered beignets at the world-famous **Café Du Monde** (800 Decatur St., 504/525-4544, www.cafedumonde.com, 24 hours daily), part of the historic **French Market,** a collection of eateries, gift stores, and praline shops.

> Take I-10 E for 80 miles (129 km) to New Orleans.

❷ After breakfast, stroll through picturesque **Jackson Square** (Decatur St. and Chartres St. between St. Peter St. and St. Ann St., 504/658-3200, www.experienceneworleans.com, 8am-7pm daily summer, 8am-6pm daily winter, free), the heart and soul of the French Quarter and the perfect place to get your bearings. Tour the stunning structures that surround this well-landscaped park and promenade.

❸ Visit the **New Orleans Historic Voodoo Museum** (724 Dumaine St., 504/680-0128, www.voodoomuseum.com, 10am-6pm daily, $7 adults, $3.50 children under 12) for a chance to dive into the city's colorful past, with tales of voodoo priestesses and zombies, ritual art, and a stroll through St. Louis Cemetery No. 1.

❹ At night, don your finest attire for a quintessential French Creole dinner at **Galatoire's Restaurant** (209 Bourbon St., 504/525-2021, www.galatoires.com, 11:30am-10pm Tues.-Sat., noon-10pm Sun., $24-42) on Bourbon Street.

JACKSON SQUARE, NEW ORLEANS

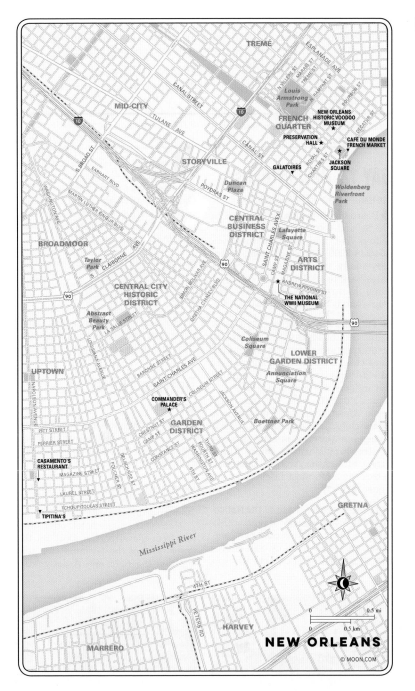

TREMÉ

ESPLANADE AVE

N VILLERE ST
MARAIS ST
TREMÉ ST
RAMPART ST
BOURBON ST
DECATUR ST

Louis
Armstrong
Park

CANAL STREET

MID-CITY

TULANE AVE

FRENCH
QUARTER

NEW ORLEANS
HISTORIC VOODOO
MUSEUM ★

CANAL ST

PRESERVATION
HALL ★

CAFE DU MONDE
FRENCH MARKET
★

S BROAD ST

STORYVILLE

GALATOIRES ▽

ROYAL ST
CHARTRES ST

JACKSON
SQUARE

EARHART BLVD

POYDRAS ST

Duncan
Plaza

MARTIN LUTHER KING JR BLVD

WASHINGTON AVE

Woldenberg
Riverfront
Park

CENTRAL
BUSINESS
DISTRICT

SAINT CHARLES AVE
CAMP ST
MAGAZINE ST

Lafayette
Square

BROADMOOR

Taylor
Park

S CLAIBORNE AVE

ARTS
DISTRICT

ANDREW HIGGINS ST ★

CENTRAL CITY
HISTORIC
DISTRICT

SIMON BOLIVAR AVE
ORETHA CASTLE BLVD

THE NATIONAL
WWII MUSEUM

Abstract
Beauty
Park

LA SALLE STREET

Coliseum
Square

LOWER
GARDEN DISTRICT

LOUISIANA AVENUE

BARONNE STREET

Annunciation
Square

UPTOWN

NAPOLEON AVENUE

SAINT CHARLES AVE

COLISEUM STREET

JACKSON AVENUE

Boettner Park

PITT STREET

COMMANDER'S
PALACE ★

PERRIER STREET

CHESTNUT ST
CAMP ST

GARDEN
DISTRICT

CASAMENTO'S
RESTAURANT
▽

MAGAZINE STREET

CONSTANCE ST

PRYTANIA ST
FOUCHER ST

FOURTH ST
THIRD ST
WASHINGTON AVE
6TH ST

LAUREL STREET

TCHOUPITOULAS STREET

▽ TIPITINA'S

GRETNA

Mississippi River

4TH ST

PETERS RD

0   0.5 mi

0   0.5 km

HARVEY

MARRERO

NEW ORLEANS

© MOON.COM

⑤ Afterward, walk to the world-famous **Preservation Hall** (726 St. Peter St., 504/522-2841, www.preservationhall.com, 8pm-11pm Mon.-Wed., 6pm-11pm Thurs.-Sun., cover $15-20) for a short jazz concert. Get here early, as the line forms quickly for these nightly concerts (8pm, 9pm, and 10pm Mon.-Wed., 6pm, 8pm, 9pm, and 10pm Thurs.-Sun.).

DAY 12: New Orleans

MORNING AND AFTERNOON

① Board the **St. Charles streetcar** (Canal St. and Carondelet St. to S. Carrollton Ave. and S. Claiborne Ave., 504/248-3900, www.norta.com, hours vary daily, $1.25 one-way), which dates back to 1835 and has been featured in numerous films over the years, and head to the **Garden District.**

② Pop into **Casamento's** (4300 Magazine St., 504/895-9761, www.casamentosrestaurant.com, 11am-2pm Tues.-Sat., 5:30pm-9pm Thurs.-Sat., $10-20) for oysters and then explore the antiques shops, galleries, and boutiques along the funky six-mile **Magazine Street.** Secondhand clothiers, music clubs, java joints, and historic homes line the way, but it's the lower stretch of Magazine—from Canal Street to Jackson Avenue—that possesses the city's most fascinating antiques district.

③ In the afternoon, head to **The National WWII Museum** (945 Magazine St., 504/528-1944, www.nationalww2museum.org, 9am-5pm daily, $26 adults, $16.50 children 5-17), where you can watch an immersive documentary and experience exhibits pertaining to the Allied victory in World War II.

EVENING

④ Splurge on a modern Creole dinner at the classic **Commander's Palace** (1403 Washington Ave., 504/899-8221, www.commanderspalace.com, 11:30am-1:30pm and 6:30pm-10pm Mon.-Fri., 11am-1pm and 6:30pm-10pm Sat., 10am-1:30pm and 6:30pm-10pm Sun., $39-45). Nestled in a blue-and-white Victorian mansion in the Garden District, this local landmark is a terrific place to try turtle soup, griddle-seared Gulf fish, and bread pudding soufflé.

⑤ Afterward, catch live rock, funk, jazz, and blues music at well-loved Uptown joints like **Tipitina's** (501 Napoleon Ave., 504/895-8477, www.tipitinas.com, hours and cover vary depending on show). Anybody looking for an introduction to the city's eclectic music scene should head here.

Getting There

AIR

The **Nashville International Airport** (BNA, http://flynashville.com) brings back some of the pleasure to air travel. It is easy to navigate and only overwhelmingly crowded during big events like the CMA Music Festival. BNA is about 10 miles east of downtown, a 20-minute drive in average traffic.

Many of the major hotels offer shuttles from the airport; a kiosk on the lower level of the terminal can help you find the right one. A designated

ST. CHARLES STREETCAR

TOURING THE GARDEN DISTRICT OF NEW ORLEANS

▶ *Playlist*

THE NATCHEZ TRACE

SONGS

- **"Black Bottom Stomp" by Jelly Roll Morton:** This New Orleans-born pianist claimed to have invented jazz. Whether or not that's true, nobody disputes the fact that Morton was the first musician to arrange jazz compositions. This song, composed in 1925, bears hallmarks of New Orleans-style ragtime.

- **"Ain't That a Shame" by Fats Domino:** Born in New Orleans, the French-Creole Domino pioneered rock-and-roll music. On this song, the blues piano plays fast and loose and Domino's vocals ooze warmth.

- **"Jailhouse Rock" by Elvis Presley:** In 1957, this rock screamer became a huge hit for Presley. You probably already know all the words, making the tune a perfect road-trip sing-along for your visit to Graceland.

- **"Wild Horses" by Rolling Stones:** There's a little place in Alabama where big musicians go to record. It's called Muscle Shoals Sound Studios, and the Rolling Stones are just one of many music legends that have laid down tracks here. In 1969, the Stones recorded this emotional and beautiful song for their 1971 album *Sticky Fingers*.

PODCASTS

- ***Voices of the Movement:*** Pulitzer Prize-winning journalist Jonathan Capehart hosts this insightful podcast that tells the stories of the heroes of the civil rights movement.

ride-sharing area is on the ground floor where hotel shuttles wait, past the taxi stand. Taxis are also a feasible option for ground transport from BNA. Rates start at $7 plus $2.10 per mile. To downtown or Opryland, the flat rate is $25.

BUS

Greyhound (709 5th Ave. S., 615/255-3556, www.greyhound.com) fully serves Nashville, with daily routes that crisscross the state in nearly every direction. The environmentally friendly depot has a restaurant, a vending area, and ample space for buses coming and going. Service goes to major cities in most directions. Budget-friendly **Megabus** (http://us.megabus.com) leaves from the same station.

CAR

Driving is the most popular way to get to Nashville. The city is 250 miles (405 km) from Atlanta, 330 miles (530 km) from St. Louis, 400 miles (645 km) from Charlotte, 530 miles (850 km) from New Orleans, and 670 miles (1,080 km) from Washington DC.

The 9-mile (14.5-km) drive from the **Nashville airport** to downtown takes 20 minutes. Take I-40 W into town.

Getting Back

It's close to an eight-hour drive from New Orleans back to **Nashville,** totaling 530 miles (850 km). Take I-10 E to I-59 N and continue to I-65, which leads into Nashville.

If you want to return home directly from New Orleans, **Louis Armstrong New Orleans International Airport** (MSY, 900 Airline Dr., Kenner, 504/303-7500, www.flymsy.com), 15 miles west of downtown New Orleans via I-10, is a massive facility with service on several airlines.

CHARLESTON TO SAVANNAH

WHY GO: Ghost tours, Spanish moss, renowned architecture, Tybee Island, Carolina barbecue, Southern cuisine, Civil War history, arts and culture

TOTAL DISTANCE: 200 miles/ 320 kilometers

NUMBER OF DAYS: 6

SEASONS: Year-round

START: Charleston, South Carolina

END: Tybee Island, Georgia

▼ SAVANNAH, GEORGIA

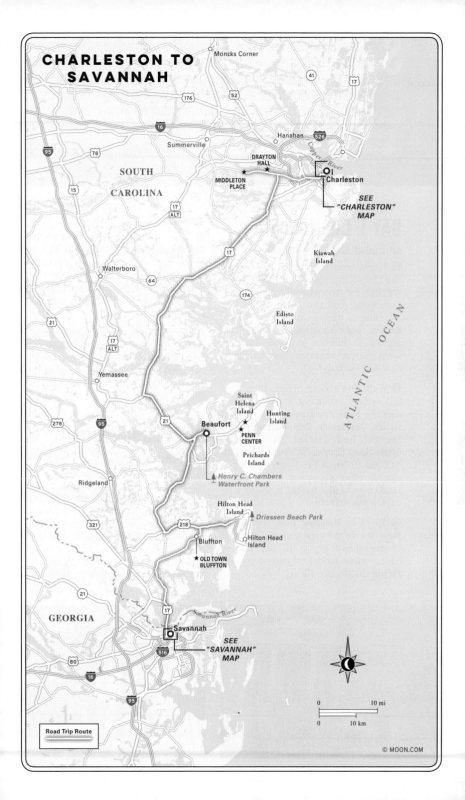

CHARLESTON TO SAVANNAH

Moncks Corner

41

17

176

52

16

SOUTH

78

Summerville

Hanahan

526

DRAYTON
HALL

Charleston

95

CAROLINA

MIDDLETON
PLACE

15

SEE
"CHARLESTON"
MAP

17
ALT

17

Kiawah
Island

Walterboro

64

174

21

Edisto
Island

17
ALT

278

Yemassee

ATLANTIC OCEAN

21

Saint
Helena
Island

Hunting
Island

Beaufort

PENN
CENTER

95

Prichards
Island

Ridgeland

Henry C. Chambers
Waterfront Park

321

Hilton Head
Island

Driessen Beach Park

218

Hilton Head
Island

Bluffton

21

OLD TOWN
BLUFFTON

17

Savannah River

GEORGIA

Savannah

516

SEE
"SAVANNAH"
MAP

80

16

95

0   10 mi

0   10 km

Road Trip Route

© MOON.COM

602

Lo named for the low-lying marshlands that lead to the Atlantic Ocean, the Low Country—bookended by Charleston, South Carolina, and Savannah, Georgia—packs a lot into a geographically small area. Live oaks drip with Spanish moss and Gothic Revival mansions sport colors of mint and pink. History seeps from every cobblestone. Stop to listen to the katydids. Walk through a cemetery that's hundreds of years old. Bite into crispy fried chicken. Watch shrimp boats trawl and chat it up with the locals. In short, take this trip nice and slow to soak it all in.

DAY 1: Charleston

MORNING AND AFTERNOON

❶ Begin your journey in **Charleston,** the Holy City, named not for its piety but for the steeples in its skyline. First, feel the pulse of the city by going to its bustling heart, **Marion Square** (between King St. and Meeting St. at Calhoun St., 843/724-5003, www.charlestonparksconservancy.org, dawn-dusk daily).

❷ Walk down King Street, then turn left onto Market Street. Here you'll find the pedestrianized and air-conditioned **Charleston City Market** (Meeting St. and Market St., 9:30am-5pm Sun.-Thurs., 9:30am-5pm and 6:30pm-10:30pm Fri.-Sat.), where you can do some shopping. Buy a handmade sweetgrass basket made by a local Gullah artisan.

❸ Head to **Rainbow Row** (79-107 E. Bay St.) to admire one of the most photographed sights in the United State: nine pastel-colored mansions facing the Cooper River.

EVENING

❹ Take a sunset stroll around **The Battery** (Water St. and E. Bay St.), an iconic city spot. Tranquil surroundings combine with beautiful views of Charleston Harbor, historical points key to the Civil War, and amazing mansions.

❺ For dinner, head up Meeting Street to dive right into a great meal at **Home Team BBQ** (126 Williman St., 843/225-7427, www.hometeambbq.com, 11am-10pm daily, $12-17), an outpost of Charleston's favorite barbecue chain.

DAY 2: Charleston

MORNING

❶ Put your historian hat on and visit one of Charleston's great house museums, the rambling **Aiken-Rhett House** (48 Elizabeth St., 843/723-1159, www.historiccharleston.org, 10am-5pm daily, last tour 4:15pm, $12 adults, $5 children). There are certainly more ostentatious house museums in Charleston, but none that provide such a virtually

CHARLESTON CITY MARKET

RAINBOW ROW, CHARLESTON

1. Take a ferry to **Fort Sumter National Monument,** site of the battle that started the Civil War (PAGE 604).

2. Walk the streets of **Savannah,** considered the most haunted city in the country, on a spooky ghost and cemetery tour (PAGE 607).

3. Feast on a **low-country boil**—shrimp, corn, potatoes, and sausage—at **The Crab Shack** on Tybee Island (PAGE 610).

THE AIKEN-RHETT HOUSE

intact glimpse into real antebellum life. Take the self-guided audio tour to get the most out of your visit.

AFTERNOON

❷ Take an afternoon ferry trip to **Fort Sumter National Monument** (843/883-3123, www.nps.gov/fosu, hours vary by season, free) to see where the Civil War began. You can only visit by boats run by the approved concessionaire **Fort Sumter Tours** (843/881-7337, www.fortsumtertours.com, $21 adults,

$13 ages 6-11). For many, the highlight is the boat trip itself, with beautiful views of Charleston Harbor and the islands of the Cooper River estuary. Ferries leave from Liberty Square at Aquarium Wharf on the peninsula three times a day during the high season (Apr.-Oct.).

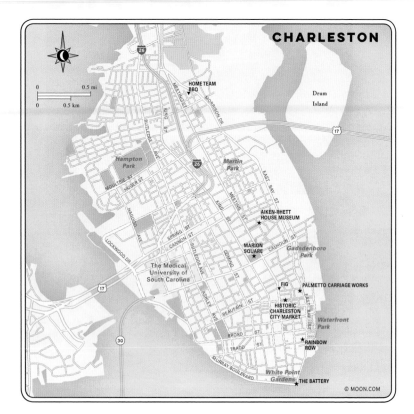

CHARLESTON

FRENCH QUARTER, CHARLESTON

EVENING

❸ Have dinner at **FIG** (232 Meeting St., 843/805-5900, www.eatatfig.com, 6pm-11pm Mon.-Thurs., 6pm-midnight Fri.-Sat., $30-36), an intimate bistro with a stylish bar. FIG is one of Charleston's great champions of the Sustainable Seafood Initiative, and the kitchen staff strives to work as closely as possible with local farmers and anglers in determining its seasonal menu.

❹ Take a carriage ride through the **French Quarter** to close the evening. There's not a lot of difference in service or price among the carriage companies, but the oldest and one of the best is **Palmetto Carriage Works** (40 N. Market St., 843/723-8145, www.palmettocarriage.com, $18-28). Typically, rides take 1-1.5 hours.

DAY 3: Charleston to Beaufort

105 miles/169 kilometers | 2.5-3 hours

ROUTE OVERVIEW: SC-61 • US-17 • US-21 • Sea Island Pkwy.

❶ Make the 20-minute drive over the Ashley River to gorgeous **Middleton Place** (4300 Ashley River Rd., 843/556-6020, www.middletonplace. org, 9am-5pm daily, $28 adults, $10-15 children, guided house tour $15 extra). The grounds contain a historic restored home, working stables, 60 acres of breathtaking gardens, and the Inn at Middleton Place, a stunning piece of modern architecture.

> Take SC-30 over the Ashley River to SC-61. Drive north for 12 miles (19 km) on SC-61 to Middleton Place Rd. Turn right and take it to Middleton Place.

❷ Then stop at adjacent **Drayton Hall** (3380 Ashley River Rd., 843/769-2600, www.draytonhall.org, 9am-5pm Mon.-Sat., 11am-5pm Sun., tours on the half hour, $22 adults, $6-10 children, grounds only $10) and see one of the oldest and best-preserved plantation homes in the nation.

> Retrace your path south on SC-61 for 4 miles (6 km) to reach Drayton Hall.

❸ Make the hour-long drive into **Beaufort** and spend the afternoon exploring the beautifully preserved historic

PALMETTO CARRIAGE WORKS

MIDDLETON PLACE

ST. HELENA ISLAND

BEAUFORT INN

district. Be sure to stroll through the **Henry C. Chambers Waterfront Park** (843/525-7054, www.cityofbeaufort. org, 24 hours daily), a tastefully designed and well-maintained green space with wonderful marsh views.

> *Head south on SC-61 for 2 miles (3 km). Turn right onto Bees Ferry Rd. In 5 miles (8 km), the road becomes US-17. Continue west for 43 miles (69 km) to US-21. Go south on US-21 for 12 miles (19 km), then take US-21 BUS for 3 miles (5 km) to reach Beaufort.*

④ Go over the bridge to **St. Helena Island** and visit historic **Penn Center** (Penn Center Circle W., 843/838-2474, www.penncenter.com, 9am-4pm Tues.-Sat., $7 adults, $3 children), the center of modern Gullah culture and education—and a key site in the history of the civil rights movement. The Gullah are African Americans of the Sea Islands of South Carolina and Georgia. Gullah culture is the closest living cousin to the West African traditions of the people brought to this country as slaves.

> *Cross the Woods Memorial Bridge to St. Helena Island. Continue on Sea Island Pkwy. for 6 miles (10 km), then turn right onto Martin Luther King Dr. to reach Penn Center.*

⑤ Back in Beaufort, spend the night at the **Beaufort Inn** (809 Port Republic St., 843/379-4667, www.beaufortinn. com, $152-425), consistently voted one of the best B&Bs in the nation. It comprises not only the 1897 historic central home, but also a cluster of freestanding historic cottages, each with a charming little porch and rocking chairs.

> *Retrace your path along Sea Island Pkwy. to return to Beaufort (7 mi/11 km).*

DAY 4: Beaufort to Savannah, Georgia

70 miles/113 kilometers | 2-2.5 hours

ROUTE OVERVIEW: SC-170 • US-278 • SC-46 • SC-170 • US-17

① From Beaufort, drive to **Hilton Head Island,** where you can spend a few hours sunning and playing at the family-friendly **Driessen Beach Park** (64 Bradley Beach Rd., www.hiltonhead-islandsc.gov, 6am-9pm daily Mar.-Sept., 6am-6pm daily Oct.-Feb., parking $0.25/30 minutes).

> *Take US-21 BUS to get onto SC-170, then drive southwest for 20 miles (32 km). At US-278, head east for 13 miles (21 km) to reach Hilton Head Island.*

PENN CENTER

HILTON HEAD ISLAND

2 A half hour away, make a late-afternoon stop in **Old Town Bluffton** to shop for art and see the beautiful **Church of the Cross** (110 Calhoun St., 843/757-2661, www.thechurchofthecross.net, free tours 10am-2pm Mon.-Sat.) on the May River.

> *Retrace your path by going west on US-278 for 3 miles (5 km). Get on Bluffton Pkwy. and drive to Burnt Church Rd. (3 mi/5 km). Turn left and drive into Old Town Bluffton.*

3 Have some cut-above pub food at the popular and friendly **Old Town Dispensary** (15 Captains Cove, 843/837-1893, www.otdbluffton.com, 11am-2am daily, $15-25).

4 Another half hour's drive puts you in **Savannah** to relax for the night. Stop in a pub for a pint, then get one to go—Savannah is one of the few U.S. cities with an open-container policy. Check into the circa-1896 **Foley House Inn** (14 W. Hull St., 912/232-6622, www.foleyinn.com, $244-374). The location on Chippewa Square is pretty much perfect: well off the busy thoroughfares but in the heart of Savannah's theater district and within walking distance of anywhere.

> *Take SC-46 W to SC-170 (10 mi/16 km). Continue onto SC-170, then SC-315, and drive south for 6 miles (10 km) to US-17. Turn left and follow US-17 S for 6 miles (10 km) to Savannah.*

DAY 5: Savannah

MORNING

1 Hit downtown Savannah hard today, starting with a walk down **River Street** (Barbard St. to E. Broad St.). Despite the street's tourist tackiness, there's nothing like strolling the cobblestones amid the old cotton warehouses, enjoying the cool breeze off the river, and watching the huge ships on their way to the bustling port.

2 Choose from the aesthetic charms of the two adjacent **Telfair Museums** (912/790-8800, www.telfair.org), one

CHURCH OF THE CROSS IN BLUFFTON

JEPSON CENTER FOR THE ARTS

OWENS-THOMAS HOUSE MUSEUM

modern and one traditional: The **Jepson Center for the Arts** (207 W. York Ln., noon-5pm Sun.-Mon., 10am-5pm Tues.-Sat., $12 adults, $5 students) has a rotating assortment of late 20th-century and 21st-century modern art, a surprising juxtaposition to this traditional city. The **Telfair Academy of Arts and Sciences** (121 Barnard St., noon-5pm Sun.-Mon., 10am-5pm Tues.-Sat., $12 adults, $5 students) features an outstanding collection of primarily 18th- and 20th-century works.

AFTERNOON

❸ Have an authentic Southern lunch at **Mrs. Wilkes' Dining Room** (107 W. Jones St., 912/232-5997, www.mrswilkes.com, 11am-2pm Mon.-Fri., $25 adults, half-price for children). Eat at a communal table in a convivial atmosphere and enjoy what many consider the finest fried chicken in the South, among other classic dishes.

© MOON.COM

There's so much to learn about these historically significant cities, and so many different perspectives to get on them. Here are some picks for the best tours in each city.

CHARLESTON

- One of the best walking tours in the city is from **Ed Grimball's Walking Tours** (Waterfront Park, Concord St., 843/813-4447, www.edgrimballtours.com, $22 adults, $8 children), led by a longtime local expert with a vast knowledge of the city. Advance reservations are a must.

- For a unique perspective of Charleston, check out **Bulldog Tours** (18 Anson St., 843/722-8687, www.bulldogtours.com, $25 adults, $15 children), which has exclusive access to the Old City Jail through the Haunted Jail Tour.

- **Carriage tours** are particularly conducive to Charleston, with its narrow avenues and cozy neighborhoods. All the companies are equally good and their humane practices are regulated by the city of Charleston. **Palmetto Carriage Works** (40 N. Market St., 843/723-8145, www.palmettocarriage.com) and **Old South Carriage Company** (14 Anson St., 843/723-9712, www.oldsouthcarriage.com) are both good options.

SAVANNAH

- **Old City Walks** (E. Jones Lane, 912/358-0700, www.oldcitywalks.com, prices vary) offers a range of personally guided tours by engaging local experts.

- For a culinary adventure that includes food and drink, look no further than **Savannah Taste Experience** (meeting points vary, 912/221-4439, www.savannahtasteexperience.com, prices vary).

- **Ghost tours** are a popular way to see the city and enjoy a scary story or two. There are a number of companies that offer ghost and cemetery tours, but **6th Sense World** (912/292-0960, http://6thsenseworld.com, $25, reservations required) offers three themed walking tours, plus Fireside Tales, a storytelling event held by the fireplaces of various inns throughout Savannah.

---

❹ Tour the exquisite **Owens-Thomas House Museum** (124 Abercorn St., 912/233-9743, www.telfair.org, noon-5pm Sun.-Mon., 10am-5pm Tues.-Sat., last tour 4:30pm, $20 adults, $15 students). Savannah's single greatest historic home is one of the country's best examples of Regency architecture and a fine example of state-of-the-art historical preservation.

EVENING

❺ Cap off the day with a drink or two at **Rocks on the Roof** (The Bohemian Hotel, 102 W. Bay St., 912/721-3800, www.marriott.com, 11am-midnight Sun.-Thurs., 11am-1am Fri.-Sat.), one of the best hotel bars in the city. In good weather the exterior walls are opened up to reveal a large wraparound seating area with stunning views of downtown on one side and of the Savannah River on the other.

DAY 6: Savannah to Tybee Island

25 miles/40 kilometers | 1 hour

ROUTE OVERVIEW: US-80

❶ On your way out to **Tybee Island**, stop to explore the moss-bedecked **Bonaventure Cemetery** (330 Bonaventure Rd., 912/651-6843, 8am-5pm daily, free). To do a self-guided tour, go by the small visitors center at the

BONAVENTURE CEMETERY

TYBEE ISLAND LIGHT STATION AND MUSEUM

entrance and pick up one of the free guides to the cemetery. Be sure visit the famed monument to little Gracie in Section E, Lot 99.

> *Take Wheaton St. for 1 mile (1.6 km) to Skidaway Rd., then turn left after 1 mile (1.6 km) onto Bonaventure Rd. Follow this for less than a mile to reach the cemetery.*

❷ A half-hour drive takes you to scenic and historically important **Fort Pulaski National Monument** (U.S. 80 E., 912/786-5787, www.nps.gov/fopu, 9am-5pm daily, $7 adults, free under age 16). Take the steep corkscrew staircase up to the ramparts and take in the jaw-dropping view of the lush marsh, with the Savannah River and Tybee Island spreading out in the distance. There's no railing on the inboard side of the ramparts, so keep the kids well back from the edge.

> *From the cemetery, drive south to get onto US-80. Continue east for 10 miles (16 km) to reach Fort Pulaski.*

FORT PULASKI NATIONAL MONUMENT

❸ Scoot on into Tybee and climb to the top of the **Tybee Island Light Station and Museum** (30 Meddin Ave., 912/786-5801, www.tybeelighthouse.org, 9am-5:30pm Wed.-Mon., last ticket sold 4:30pm, $9 adults, $7 children) for a stunning view of Tybee, the Atlantic, and Hilton Head Island.

> *Continue east on US-80 for 3 miles (5 km) to get to central Tybee Island. Make a left onto Polk St., then a right onto Fort Ave. The light station is less than a mile from US-80.*

❹ For dinner, grab a table at **The Crab Shack** (40 Estill Hammock Rd., 912/786-9857, www.thecrabshack.com, 11:30am-10pm Mon.-Thurs., 11:30am-11pm Fri.-Sun., $15-29), a favorite local seafood place set in a former fishing camp. The emphasis here is on mounds of fresh, tasty seafood, heavy on the raw-bar action.

❺ Spend the night at **The Georgianne Inn** (1312 Butler Ave., 912/786-8710, www.georgianneinn.com, $210-400), the best B&B-style experience on Tybee. It's just a short walk off the beach and close to most of the island's action.

Getting There

AIR

Way up in North Charleston is **Charleston International Airport** (CHS, 5500 International Blvd., 843/767-1100, www.chs-airport.com), served by American, Delta, JetBlue, and Southwest. As in most cities, taxi service from the airport is regulated. This translates to about $30 for two people from the airport to Charleston Place downtown.

WATER

One of the coolest things about the Charleston and Savannah area is the presence of the **Intracoastal Waterway,** a combined artificial and natural sheltered seaway from Miami to Maine. Many boaters enjoy touring the coast by simply meandering up or down the Intracoastal, putting in at marinas along the way.

TRAIN

Charleston and Savannah are both served by the New York-Miami Silver Service route of the national rail system, **Amtrak** (www.amtrak.com), which is pretty good, if erratic at times. Amtrak stations are in light industrial parts of town, nowhere near the major tourist centers. Charleston's station is at 4565 Gaynor Street (843/744-8263), while Savannah's is at 2611 Seaboard Coastline Drive (912/234-2611).

CAR

There are two main routes into Charleston: I-26 from the west-northwest (which dead-ends downtown) and US-17 from the west (called Savannah Highway when it gets close to Charleston proper), which continues east over the Ravenel Bridge into Mount Pleasant and beyond.

It'll take about **20 minutes** to make the **12-mile drive** from the **Charleston airport** to downtown via I-26.

Getting Back

To return to **Charleston** from Tybee Island, the 124-mile (200-km) route takes about 2.5 hours. Drive west on US-80 to Islands Expressway, cut through Savannah, and merge onto US-17 N. Follow US-17 to I-95. From I-95, at exit 33, merge back onto US-17, heading north into Charleston.

To return home directly from **Tybee Island,** the most centrally located airport for the region is **Savannah/Hilton Head International Airport** (SAV, 400 Airways Ave., 912/964-0514, www.savannahairport.com), directly off I-95 at exit 104. The 33-mile (53-km) trip from Tybee Island to SAV takes about 45 minutes. Take US-80 to Islands

Expressway, then cut through Savannah and head north on Augusta Road/GA-21. The airport is off of Gulfstream Road.

▶ **Playlist**

CHARLESTON TO SAVANNAH

SONGS

- **"C'est Si Bon" by Eartha Kitt:** The formidable talents of South Carolina-born Kitt range from singing and dancing to acting and writing. This 1940s-era French song has enjoyed numerous recordings over the years, but Kitt's 1953 version showcases her unique voice—bewitching and husky with a distinctive vibrato.

- **"Try a Little Tenderness" by Otis Redding:** Born and raised in Georgia, soul singer Redding revolutionized the 1960s R&B genre. This song's lyrics border on the maudlin, but the instrumentation and Redding's vulnerable, throaty vocals build suspense in dramatic musical fashion. You'll want to put this one on repeat.

PODCASTS

- *Southern Mysteries:* Both Charleston and Savannah are known for their haunted buildings and chilling ghost stories. Tune in to these episodes that explore the mysteries and legends of the American South.

CHESAPEAKE BAY

WHY GO: Maryland blue crabs, boating, beaux arts architecture, beaches, boardwalks, naval and colonial history, charming inns, small towns

TOTAL DISTANCE: 315 miles/ 510 kilometers

NUMBER OF DAYS: 4

SEASONS: Spring through fall

START: Annapolis, Maryland

END: Virginia Beach, Virginia

▼ ANNAPOLIS, MARYLAND

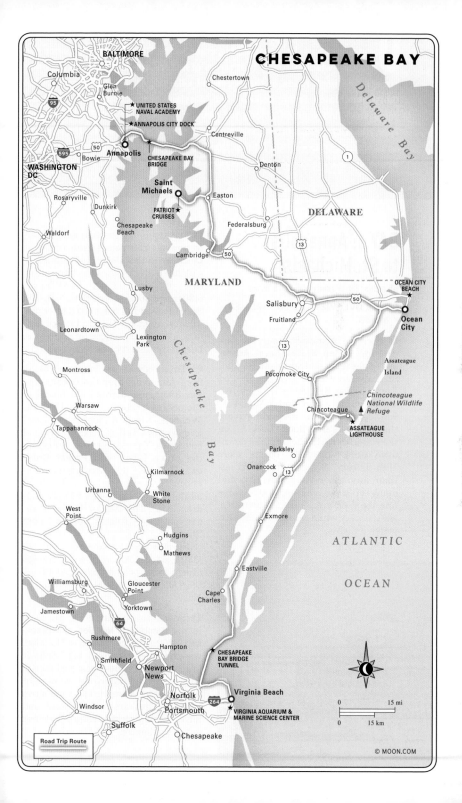

Our country's founding fathers raised a pint in the pubs of Annapolis and watermen have been harvesting crabs in the Chesapeake Bay since the 1600s—which is to say that layers of history are embedded in the brick streets and back roads of these coastal villages. As you travel south from the sophisticated sailing capital—and Maryland state capital—of Annapolis, you'll soon find yourself among the bucolic greenery of the Eastern Shore. Then the cornfields, farms, and produce stands give way to the seaside amusements of Ocean City. From there, it's a quick jaunt to sunny Virginia Beach, an oceanside retreat so relaxing that you might never leave.

DAY 1: Annapolis to St. Michaels

55 miles/89 kilometers | 1-1.5 hours

ROUTE OVERVIEW: US-50 • MD-322 • MD-33

❶ Start in **Annapolis**. Tour the fascinating **United States Naval Academy** (pedestrian entrance on Randall St. between Prince George St. and King George St., photo ID required, 410/293-8111, 9am-4pm Mon.-Fri., 9am-5pm Sat.-Sun., free) and explore the **Annapolis City Dock** (Dock St. on the waterfront), the heart of the downtown area. Annapolis boasts more 18th-century beaux arts buildings than any other American city, and many of these charming structures line the dock area. Take in the waterside scenery while ogling the many expensive yachts.

❷ For lunch, try the seasoned-to-perfection quarter-pound crab cakes at **Chick & Ruth's Delly** (165 Main St., 410/269-6737, www.chickandruths.com, 6:30am-11:30pm Sun.-Thurs., 6:30am-12:30am Fri.-Sat., $6-29). Specialty sandwiches named after politicians augment the traditional deli fare, along with seafood, pizza, wraps, burgers, and tasty ice-cream treats.

❸ Drive about an hour southeast from Annapolis over the **Chesapeake Bay Bridge** and across Kent Island to the quaint Eastern Shore town of **St. Michaels.** Stroll through the historic downtown full of restaurants and boutiques. Take a narrated cruise up the Miles River with **Patriot Cruises** (410/745-3100, www.patriotcruises.com, early spring-late fall, $26.50 adults, $12.50 children 12-17, $5 children 3-11). The two-level, 49-passenger boat leaves from 301 North Talbot Street.

> Follow US-50 southeast to MD-322 (38 mi/61 km). Turn right and in 2 miles (3 km) make another right onto MD-33. Drive MD-33 W into St. Michaels (9 mi/14 km).

❹ Spend the night in St. Michaels in the **Hambleton Inn Bed and Breakfast** (202 Cherry St., 410/745-3350, www.hambletoninn.com, $220-805). It arguably has the best location in town, with wonderful waterfront views right in the historic district. The home's two large porches are a focal point and have inviting rocking chairs that look out to the harbor.

THE WATERFRONT IN DOWNTOWN ANNAPOLIS

Top **3** CHESAPEAKE BAY

1 Visit the historic **United States Naval Academy** on the banks of the Severn River in Annapolis (PAGE 614).

2 Climb to the top of the **Assateague Island Lighthouse** in Virginia (PAGE 617).

3 Ride a bicycle along the shores of the Atlantic Ocean at the **Virginia Beach Boardwalk** (PAGE 617).

DAY 2: St. Michaels to Ocean City

90 miles/145 kilometers | 2 hours

ROUTE OVERVIEW: MD-33 • US-50

1 Drive southeast to **Ocean City** and join the excitement at the bustling **Ocean City Boardwalk** (2nd St. to 27th St.). It's a 24-hour hub of activity, lined with dozens of hotels, motels, shops, restaurants, arcades, and entertainment venues.

> Take MD-33 E for 9 miles (14 km) to Easton Pkwy. Turn right and follow Easton Pkwy. to US-50 (3 mi/5 km). Merge onto US-50 and head east to Ocean City (73 mi/117 km).

2 You can't visit Maryland and not indulge in boardwalk fries. They're crispy, hand-cut French fries drizzled in apple cider vinegar and tossed in salt and Old Bay Seasoning. Get a cup at **Thrasher's French Fries** (410/289-7232, www.thrashersfries.com, 10am-10pm daily Memorial Day-Labor Day, 10am-5pm daily Labor Day-Memorial Day). You'll have to wait in line, but it's worth it; Thrasher's has been making fries on the boardwalk since 1929.

3 Spend the rest of your day relaxing on the white sands of the expansive **Ocean City Beach** (5am-10pm daily). Brightly colored umbrellas are lined up in front of most hotels and are available for rent. In peak season, the beach and water can get very crowded, so be prepared for company. You'll find beach access nearly everywhere along the 10-mile shoreline, but the main entrance is at Division Street and Baltimore Avenue.

4 Tuck into the 1927 **Atlantic House Bed and Breakfast** (501 N. Baltimore

OCEAN CITY BOARDWALK

Ave., 410/289-2333, www.atlantic-house.com, $190-270) for the night. The owners at this family-run hotel treat you with morning coffee in the sunroom, along with a home-cooked breakfast. Find a seat on the wonderful front porch to watch the bustle of tourist activity on the street.

DAY 3: Ocean City to Chincoteague Island, Virginia

60 miles/97 kilometers | 1-1.5 hours

ROUTE OVERVIEW: US-50 • US-113 • US-13 • VA-175

1 Drive to **Chincoteague Island** in Virginia. Explore the **Chincoteague National Wildlife Refuge** (8231 Beach Rd., 757/336-6122, www.fws.gov, 5am-10pm daily May-Sept., shorter hours Oct.-Apr., $20 vehicles, free for pedestrians and cyclists), which consists of beach, dunes, marsh, and maritime forest on the Virginia end of Assateague Island. Look for signs of the wild ponies that live here, and keep an eye out for various species of waterfowl, shorebirds, songbirds, and wading birds.

> Head east on US-50. In 6 miles (10 km), turn left onto Old Ocean City Blvd. In less than a mile, turn left onto US-113.

OCEAN CITY FISHING PIER

WILD PONIES OF CHINCOTEAGUE ISLAND

Drive south on US-113 to US-13 (29 mi/47 km). Turn left onto US-13 and in 9 miles (14 km), turn left onto VA-175. Follow VA-175 E to Chincoteague Island (11 mi/18 km).

❷ At the refuge, you can take a short hike to the 142-foot-tall, red-and-white **Assateague Island Lighthouse** (0.4 mi/0.6 km loop, 20 minutes, easy). The lighthouse is open for climbing (free) spring-fall, but the days when it is open change seasonally and with the weather; call ahead for the current schedule.

❸ Spend the night on the island at the adorable **Miss Molly's Inn** (4141 Main St., 757/336-6686, www.miss-mollys-inn.com, $180-240). This beautiful Victorian B&B offers seven delightful guest rooms and five porches with rocking chairs.

DAY 4: Chincoteague Island to Virginia Beach

110 miles/177 kilometers | 2.5-3 hours

ROUTE OVERVIEW: VA-175 • US-13 • US-60

❶ Continue down the scenic Eastern Shore and through the famous **Chesapeake Bay Bridge-Tunnel** (www.cbbt. com). The four-lane bridge-and-tunnel system spans 20 miles (32 km), taking vehicles over, through, and under the shipping channels. Five-acre artificial islands are located at each end of the two tunnels.

> *Head west on VA-175 to US-13 (11 mi/18 km). Turn left on US-13 and drive south for 74 miles (119 km) to the Chesapeake Bay Bridge-Tunnel.*

❷ Keep going until you reach **Virginia Beach**. Visit the **Virginia Aquarium & Marine Science Center** (717 General Booth Blvd., 757/385-3474, www. virginiaaquarium.com, 9am-6pm daily, $25 adults, $20 children 3-11). With its more than 800,000 gallons of aquariums, live animal habitats, numerous exhibits, and a six-story 3D movie screen ($8), you could spend several hours here and not get bored. More than 300 species are represented in the educational exhibits, and there are many hands-on experiences, including a touch pool of friendly animals.

> *Once you cross the bay, drive southwest on US-13 to US-60 (10 mi/16 km). Go left on US-60 and follow it east into Virginia Beach (12 mi/19 km).*

❸ Walk the famous **Virginia Beach Boardwalk** (1st St. to 42nd St.), which runs parallel to the ocean for 3 miles (4.8 km). The boardwalk is adorned with benches, grassy lawns, play areas, amusement parks, arcades, hotels, restaurants, and shops. There is also a large fishing pier at 15th Street. There are public restrooms at 17th, 24th, and 30th Streets.

VIRGINIA BEACH

CHESAPEAKE BAY

SONGS

- **"This Must Be the Place" by Talking Heads:** Lead singer David Byrne was born in Scotland, but raised in Maryland. He formed the Talking Heads in New York City in the 1970s, and while the band may be more notable for hits like "Burning Down the House" or "Psycho Killer," it's this 1983 song—whimsical, fluty, repetitive—that best accompanies long drives.

- **"Space Song" by Beach House:** When this dreamy song plays through your open car windows, and the wind swirls around your face, and your gaze is trained at the Atlantic Ocean crashing in the distance, you'll feel like you're starring in a music video. Cue up the tune by this Baltimore band for your drive through Ocean City.

- **"My Girls" by Animal Collective:** This experimental-pop band from Baltimore breaks music rules in playful ways. From verse to verse, guitar thrum to keyboard plink, this song surprises in delightfully pleasing ways—just like the tiny towns and seascapes of Maryland's Eastern Shore.

BIKES ON THE VIRGINIA BEACH BOARDWALK

❹ Enjoy fresh seafood at **Catch 31** (3001 Atlantic Ave., 757/213-3472, www.catch31.com, 6am-2am Mon.-Fri., 7am-2am Sat.-Sun., $14-49). Located inside the Hilton Virginia Beach Oceanfront, this is one of the finest restaurants along the main strip. They offer at least 15 types of fresh fish, and their signature dish is the seafood tower with crab legs, mussels, lobster, and shrimp. If the weather is nice, dine outside on their beachfront terrace.

❺ Spend the night right on the ocean at the **Belvedere Beach Resort** (3603 Atlantic Ave., 800/425-0612, www.belvederebeachresort.com, Apr.-early Oct., $209-297). The light-filled, wood-paneled rooms offer private balconies with views of the beach. This is a pleasant, comfortable choice in a fantastic location. Check ahead to see if a minimum stay is required.

Getting There

AIR

Annapolis is around 20 miles (32 km) from **Baltimore/Washington International Thurgood Marshall Airport** (BWI, 410/859-7040, www.bwiairport.com). This busy regional airport is a hub for **Southwest Airlines** and offers some of the best fares in the Washington DC/Baltimore area. Most other major airlines offer flight service to BWI as well. Car rentals are available at the airport from numerous national car rental companies.

Washington DC, about an hour away by car from Baltimore and Annapolis, also has two major airports. The first is **Ronald Reagan Washington National Airport** (DCA, 703/417-8000, www.metwashairports.com), just outside Washington DC in Arlington, Virginia. Taxi service is available at the arrivals curb outside the baggage claim area of each terminal. Rental cars are available on the first floor in parking garage A. The shuttle to the rental car counter is available outside each baggage claim area. The second is **Washington Dulles International Airport** (IAD, 703/572-2700, www.metwashairports.com), about 30 miles (48 km) west of Washington DC in Dulles, Virginia. Most major airlines serve these airports.

TRAIN

Amtrak runs dozens of trains through Baltimore's **Penn Station** (1500 N. Charles St., 800/872-7245, www.amtrak.com) daily from all corners of the country. They offer ticket discounts for seniors, children, students, veterans, and conference groups.

BUS

Just south of downtown Baltimore in an industrial section of the city is the **Greyhound** bus station (2110 Haines St., 410/752-7682, www.greyhound.com). Bus service runs daily from multiple destinations. It is advisable to take a cab from the station to points around Baltimore. Walking near the station is not advisable after dark.

CAR

Most people arrive in Annapolis by car. The city is a quick 45-minute drive east from **Washington DC** (32 mi/51 km) via US-50 and about 30 minutes (26 mi/42 km) south of the Inner Harbor in **Baltimore** (via I-97).

From the **Baltimore airport,** it's 24 miles (39 km) to Annapolis, a 30-minute drive. Take I-97 S, then jump on US-50. Take the exit for Rowe Boulevard and follow it into town.

It's 36 miles (58 km) from **Reagan airport** to Annapolis, a 45-minute drive. Go north on I-395, east on I-695,

north on DC-295, and then drive east on US-50 to Rowe Boulevard.

The 62-mile (100-km) trek from **Dulles airport** takes 90 minutes. Drive east on VA-267 to I-495 N. Continue north on I-495 to US-50. Stay on US-50 E to Rowe Boulevard. Exit at Rowe Boulevard for Annapolis.

Getting Back

It's 243 miles (391 km) to return to **Annapolis** from Virginia Beach. The trip takes close to **four hours.** Depart Virginia Beach by traveling west on I-264. Get on I-64 W and head north. Merge onto I-295 and drive north to I-95. Continue on I-95, then join I-495 E. Stay on I-495, then take US-50, following it to Rowe Boulevard, which takes you into Annapolis.

You can skip the trip back to Annapolis and fly home from the **Norfolk International Airport** (ORF, 2200 Norview Ave., Norfolk, www.norfolkairport.com). Daily flights are available through multiple commercial carriers. The airport is approximately 17 miles (27 km) from Virginia Beach, which takes 25 minutes. To get there, go west on I-264, then merge onto I-64 W. Follow I-64. Take exit 281 and follow signs for the airport.

Located 102 miles (164 km) from Virginia Beach is another airport option: **Richmond International Airport** (RIC, 1 Richard E. Byrd Terminal Dr., 804/226-3000, http://flyrichmond.com). American, Southwest, United, Delta, and JetBlue offer service to destinations such as Atlanta, Boston, Charlotte, Chicago, Dallas, Denver, Detroit, Nashville, New York, and Philadelphia. From Virginia Beach, drive west on I-264. Get on I-64 W and go north. Take exit 197B, turn left onto VA-156, and continue to the airport.

CONNECT WITH

- At Ocean City: **The Loneliest Road** (PAGE 36) and **The Jersey Shore** (PAGE 548)
- At Washington DC: **Blue Ridge Parkway** (PAGE 562)

NORTH CAROLINA'S OUTER BANKS

WHY GO: Windswept beaches, lighthouses, wild horses, fresh-caught seafood, Wright Brothers National Memorial

TOTAL DISTANCE: 180 miles/ 290 kilometers

NUMBER OF DAYS: 3

SEASONS: Year-round

START: Manteo, Roanoke Island

END: Ocracoke village, Ocracoke Island

▼ WILD HORSES IN COROLLA

NORTH CAROLINA'S OUTER BANKS

Road Trip Route

Corolla
★ COROLLA WILD HORSE TOURS

ATLANTIC

Duck
Southern Shores

OCEAN

Elizabeth City

Kitty Hawk

Kill Devil Hills
★ WRIGHT BROTHERS NATIONAL MEMORIAL

Albemarle Sound

ELIZABETHAN GARDENS
FORT RALEIGH NATIONAL HISTORIC SITE

Nags Head

Columbia

Manteo
Manns Harbor
Roanoke Island
Wanchese

BODIE ISLAND LIGHTHOUSE

Aligator River

Pamlico Sound

Swanquarter

Avon

Hatteras
HATTERAS FERRY

Ocracoke Island

0   5 mi
0   5 km

© MOON.COM

This two-lane coastal drive starts on tiny Roanoke Island and takes you over bridges, through charming villages, beside beaches where the swells of the Atlantic Ocean crash, and to historic sites like the Wright Brothers National Memorial. The route follows NC-12, a flat and straight path up the coast—easy to navigate and with plenty of options to pull over and snap seaside photos. From climbing nineteenth-century lighthouses and discovering the lore of maritime history to soaking up the sunrise at an oceanfront resort, this road trip is a journey into the seafaring life, both past and present.

DAY 1: Manteo

AFTERNOON

1 Plan to arrive on **Roanoke Island** around lunchtime, and grab a bite to eat at **Poor Richard's Sandwich Shop** (303 Queen Elizabeth St., 252/473-3333, www.poorrichardsmanteo.com, 11am-3pm Mon.-Sat., bar 5pm-2am Mon.-Sat., $4-8) in **Manteo.** Their burgers and sandwiches are legendary.

2 After lunch, take US-64 to visit the **Fort Raleigh National Historic Site** (1401 National Park Dr., 252/473-2111, www.nps.gov/fora, 9am-5pm daily, free) where the Lost Colony, the first English settlement in the New World, mysteriously disappeared in the 1580s.

3 Within the historic site, don't miss the **Elizabethan Gardens** (1411 National Park Dr., 252/473-3234, http://elizabethangardens.org, 9am-6pm Apr.-Sept., shorter hours Oct.-Jan. and Mar., $9 adults, $6 children 6-17, $2

children 5 and under). This 10.5-acre garden holds many treasures, including an ancient live oak so huge that many believe it has been standing since the colonists' days.

EVENING

4 Your last stop in the historic site should be the Waterside Theater, where you can take in the longest-running outdoor drama in the United States, ***The Lost Colony*** (1409 National Park Dr., 252/473-6000, http://thelostcolony.org, 7pm Mon.-Sat. late May-late Aug., from $20 adults, from $10 children 6-12). An impressive list of actors has performed in the play, including Andy Griffith.

5 Drive back down to Manteo to spend the night at the **Tranquil House Inn** (405 Queen Elizabeth Ave., 800/458-7069, www.tranquilhouseinn.com, from $219 summer, from $109 off-season). Enjoy dinner in-house at 1587, widely regarded as one of the best restaurants in this part of the state.

FORT RALEIGH NATIONAL HISTORIC SITE

ELIZABETHAN GARDENS

Top 3 NORTH CAROLINA'S OUTER BANKS

1. See wild ponies frolicking in the surf on a tour with the **Corolla Wild Horse Fund** (PAGE 624).
2. Solve the mysterious disappearance of the first English settlement at **Fort Raleigh National Historic Site** (PAGE 622).
3. Eat fresh-as-can-be oysters caught on the shores of the Outer Banks at **Howard's Pub & Raw Bar Restaurant** (PAGE 626).

1

2

3

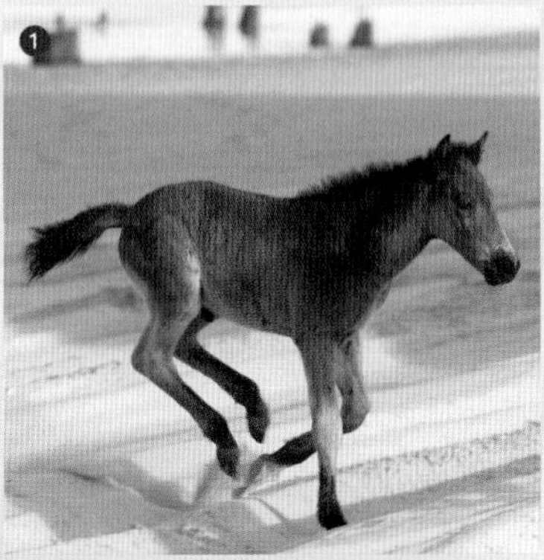

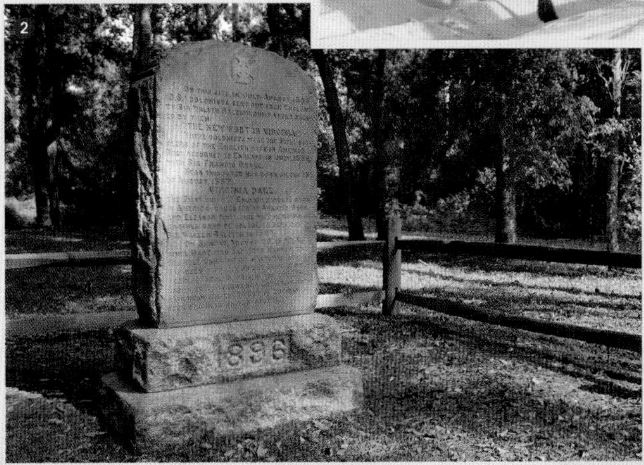

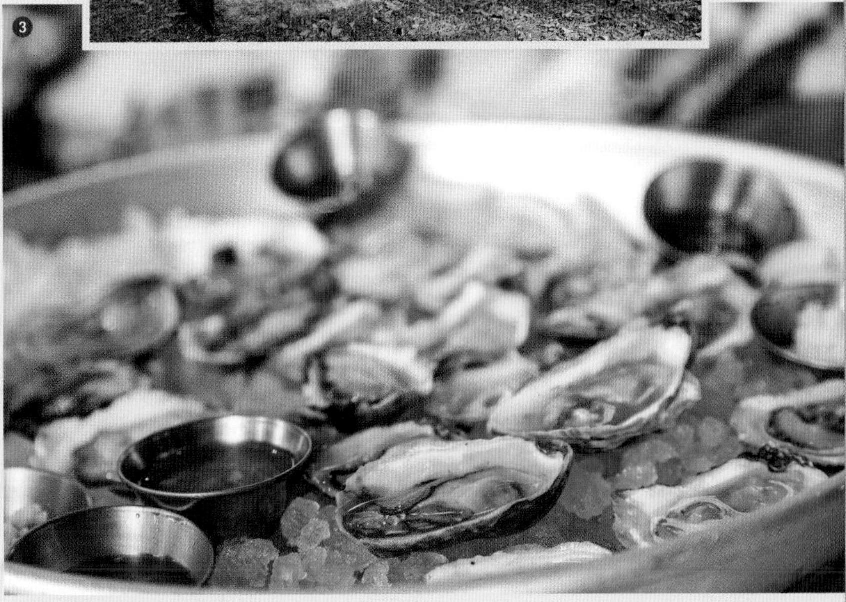

DAY 2: Manteo to Duck

75 miles/120 kilometers | 2-2.5 hours

ROUTE OVERVIEW: US-64 • NC-12 • US-158 • NC-12

❶ Pack up and head east across the sound toward the beach. Grab breakfast at **Sam & Omie's** (7728 S. Virginia Dare Tr., 252/441-7366, www.samandomies.net, 7am-9pm Mon.-Sat., 7am-4pm Sun., $6-26), an Outer Banks classic, in **Nags Head**, then walk across the street to **Jennette's Pier** for some beach time.

> *Go east on US-64 for 6 miles (10 km) to Nags Head.*

❷ Detour south to the **Bodie Island Lighthouse** (6 mi/10 km south of Whalebone Junction, 252/473-2111, www.nps.gov/caha, visitors center 9am-5pm daily, $8 adults, $4 children 11 and under) and climb to the top for a breathtaking view of the Outer Banks.

> *Take NC-12 south for 7 miles (11 km) to the lighthouse.*

❸ Take NC-12 north toward Duck. On the way, stop at the **Wright Brothers National Memorial** (Milepost 7.5 US-158/1000 N. Croatan Hwy., Kill Devil Hills, 252/473-2111, www.nps.gov/wrbr, 9am-5pm daily year-round, $10 adults, free for children 15 and under) and see a replica of the brothers' famed flying machine and the site where those historic first flights took place.

> *Head back north on NC-12 for 6 miles (10 km), then continue for 9 miles (13 km) on US-158 to the Wright Brothers National Memorial.*

❹ Continue north to the village of **Duck.** Have a late lunch before checking in to luxe accommodations at the oceanfront **Sanderling Resort** (1461 Duck Rd., 855/412-7866, www.sanderling-resort.com, $299-729).

> *Continue north on US-158 for 6 miles (10 km), then follow NC-12 N for 10 miles (16 km) to the resort.*

❺ Take an excursion to **Corolla,** the next town up from Duck, for a **wild horse tour** on the beach with the **Corolla Wild Horse Fund** (1129 Corolla Village Rd., 252/453-8002, www.corollawildhorses.com, $45 adults, $20 children). See ponies frolic in the dunes, along the shore, and even in the surf. Return to Duck for dinner.

> *Continue north on NC-12 for 12 miles (19 km) to reach Corolla. Retrace your path south to return to Duck.*

BODIE ISLAND LIGHTHOUSE

WILD HORSE IN COROLLA

DAY 3: Duck to Ocracoke

105 miles/170 kilometers | 3 hours

ROUTE OVERVIEW: NC-12 • US-158 • NC-12 • ferry to Ocracoke Island • NC-12

❶ It's about three hours from Duck to Ocracoke Island, so strike out early, following NC-12 south through **Cape Hatteras National Seashore.** This stretch of beach is wild, and you'll find just a handful of small towns. Close to the southern tip is the **Cape Hatteras Lighthouse** (near Buxton,

CAPE HATTERAS LIGHTHOUSE

Fishing villages dot the coast of North Carolina, and many restaurants offer fresh-caught seafood on their menus. To dine like a local, pick restaurants like the favorites listed below, which use local seafood, meat, and produce while paying homage to the culinary traditions that make coastal culture distinct. Check out **Outer Banks Catch** (www.outerbankscatch.com) for more restaurants serving local seafood in the region.

- **Basnight's Lone Cedar Café** (7623 S. Virginia Dare Tr. on the Nags Head-Manteo Causeway, 252/441-5405, www.lonecedarcafe.com, 4:30pm-9pm Mon.-Sat., 11am-3pm and 4:30pm-9pm Sun., $14-32) serves the freshest seafood in a dining room surrounded by water.

- Enjoy an oyster stout with your dinner at the **Outer Banks Brewing Station** (Milepost 8.5, 600 S. Croatan Hwy., Kill Devil Hills, 252/449-2739, www.obbrewing.com, 11:30am-2am Mon.-Fri., 11am-2pm Sat., 11am-midnight Sun., $15-31), where fresh seafood plays a prominent role. This restaurant enjoys the distinction of being the country's first wind-powered brewery.

- **Sam & Omie's** (7728 S. Virginia Dare Tr., Nags Head, 252/441-7366, www.samandomies.net, 7am-9pm Mon.-Sat., 7am-4pm Sun., $6-26) opened in 1937 to feed hungry fishermen, and the concept stuck. Try a platter of broiled or fried seafood the way the first patrons ate it—hot and fresh.

- In Duck, **AQUA Restaurant** (1174 Duck Rd., Duck, 252/261-9700, www.aquaobx.com, 11:30am-9pm daily, $18-32) serves a small menu of exquisitely prepared dishes that take advantage of the abundant seafood harvested right on the Outer Banks.

ENTRANCE TO CAPE HATTERAS LIGHTHOUSE

252/473-2111, www.nps.gov/caha, 9am-5pm daily, $8 adults, $4 children, children under 42 inches tall not permitted) with its iconic black and white spiral paint job. Snap a photo or climb to the top. In the warmer months, tickets are sold on the premises beginning at 9am, and climbing tours run every 10 minutes starting at 9am.

> Take NC-12 S for 10 miles (16 km), then join US-158. Follow this south for 15 miles (24 km), after which it becomes NC-12 once again. Continue south for another 47 miles (76 km) to reach the lighthouse.

❷ A few miles to the southeast in **Hatteras,** board the **Hatteras-Ocracoke Ferry** (800/368-8949, www.ncdot.gov/ferry, frequent departures 5am-midnight daily, free) and take the hour-long journey to **Ocracoke Island.** The village of Ocracoke is walkable, and golf cart and bicycle rentals are available. Once on the island, park your car at your hotel, and opt for one of these modes of transportation instead.

> Continue on NC-12 S for 12 miles (19 km) to reach the ferry landing. On Ocracoke, it's about 14 miles (23 km) southwest on NC-12 to the village.

LOCAL SEAFOOD

❸ Once on Ocracoke Island, spend the day relaxing on the 16 miles of shell-strewn beach, pausing for lunch at **Eduardo's Taco Stand** (252/588-0202, 8am-3pm and 5pm-9pm Mon.-Sat., 8am-3pm Sun., $7-12). Order up a crab, *carne asada,* or *pollo* taco, then dine at the picnic tables or just a few blocks away at the water's edge.

❹ In the evening, head to the harbor for oysters on the half shell at **Howard's Pub & Raw Bar Restaurant** (1175 Irvin Garrish Hwy., 252/928-4441, www.howardspub.com, 11am-10pm daily, $15-26). Spend the night on Ocracoke, taking time for stargazing, which is especially good outside of town.

Getting There

It's not possible to reach the Outer Banks by train or bus. Most visitors will arrive via air or car.

AIR

From **Wilmington International Airport** (ILM, 1740 Airport Blvd., Wilmington, 910/341-4125, www.flyilm.com), the 225-mile drive to Manteo takes four hours. Follow NC-133 to I-140, then pick up US-17 to NC-171. This links up with US-64, which you'll follow east for 77 miles to Manteo.

It's about 100 miles (160 km), a two-hour drive, to Manteo from Virginia's **Norfolk International Airport** (ORF, 2200 Norview Ave., Norfolk, 757/857-3351, www.norfolkairport.com). Allegiant, American, Delta, Frontier, Southwest, and United operate flights to destinations such as Denver, Las Vegas, San Diego, Miami, Boston, New York City, Nashville, and Atlanta. From the airport, drive east on I-64 to VA-168 (which becomes NC-168 when you cross the border), then continue onto US-158 E and US-64. Follow US-64 W to Manteo.

Raleigh-Durham International Airport (RDU, 2400 W. Terminal Blvd., Morrisville, 919/840-2123, www.rdu.com), located about midway between Raleigh and Durham, is inland from the coast. It will take you 3.5 hours on US-64 to reach the Outer Banks from Raleigh-Durham.

In addition to the Wilmington airport, there are several smaller airports with regularly scheduled domestic passenger service. **Pitt-Greenville Airport** (PGV, 400 Airport Rd., Greenville, 252/902-2025, www.flypgv.com) is about 2 hours from Manteo; **Coastal Carolina Regional Airport** (EWN, 200 Terminal Dr., New Bern, 252/638-8591, www.newbernairport.com) is 2.5 hours from Manteo; and the **Albert J. Ellis Airport** (OAJ, 264 Albert Ellis Airport Rd., Richlands, 910/324-1100, www.flyoaj.com) is about 3.5 hours from the coast.

You can take your pick of **car-rental agencies** at Raleigh-Durham; there are fewer choices at smaller regional airports. There are also car-rental pickup and drop-off offices in many towns.

CAR

Manteo is 225 miles (4 hours) northeast of **Wilmington.** Follow NC-133 to I-140, then pick up US-17 to NC-171. This links up with US-64, which you'll follow east to Manteo. From **Norfolk,** it's 90 miles (2 hours) south via VA-168, NC-168, US-158, and US-64. It's 190 miles (3 hours) from **Raleigh** to Manteo, a straight shot on US-64.

From mainland North Carolina, you first reach the town of Mann's Harbor on the inland side of the Croatan Sound. Take **US-64/US-264** and you'll cross the sound to the north, arriving in Manteo.

Getting Back

A three-hour ferry ride from Ocracoke Island puts you back on the Inner Banks at the **Swan Quarter Ferry Terminal** (748 Oyster Creek Rd., Swan Quarter, 800/293-3779, http://ferry.ncdot.gov, $15 per vehicle), where you're three hours from the airport in Raleigh via US-264.

A two-hour ferry ride from Ocracoke Island lands you at the **Cedar Island Ferry Terminal** (3619 Cedar Island Rd., Cedar Island, 800/293-3779, http://ferry.ncdot.gov, $15 per vehicle), which is closer to Wilmington International Airport, a three-hour drive on US-17.

▶ **Playlist**

NORTH CAROLINA'S OUTER BANKS

SONGS

- **"Coast of Carolina" by Jimmy Buffett:** This low-key tune perfectly complements an alfresco meal of fresh seafood.

- **"It's Called: Freefall" by Rainbow Kitten Surprise:** Originating in Boone, North Carolina, this band has taken the indie scene by storm. Their folk-pop melodies and jangly guitars are best enjoyed among cool sea breezes.

- **"A Rockin' Good Way" by Dinah Washington and Brook Benton:** A warm, fuzzy, 1960s song that'll remind you of timeless romance. Why? It was featured in the Outer Banks-set love story *Nights in Rodanthe,* based on the book by Nicholas Sparks.

PODCASTS

- **"The Lost Colony of Roanoke":** This episode from the *Stitcher Rejects and Revolutionaries* podcast delves into the mysterious outcome of America's first colony.

- *The Maritime History:* This podcast discusses the legends and lore of mariners and their adventures at sea.

KENTUCKY'S BOURBON TRAIL

WHY GO: Distillery tours, bourbon tastings, Churchill Downs, chocolate-covered bourbon balls, two-lane country roads, farm-to-table fare, Southern hospitality, horse farms, history and heritage

TOTAL DISTANCE: 195 miles/ 315 kilometers

NUMBER OF DAYS: 7

SEASONS: Spring and fall

START: Louisville, Kentucky

END: Lexington, Kentucky

▶ BARDSTOWN, KENTUCKY

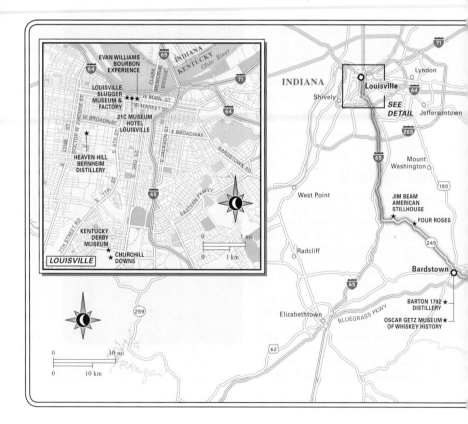

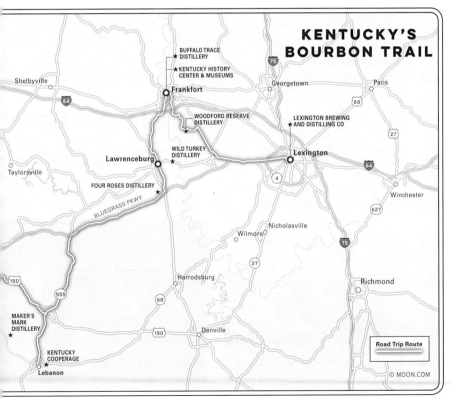

KENTUCKY'S BOURBON TRAIL

Shelbyville

BUFFALO TRACE DISTILLERY

KENTUCKY HISTORY CENTER & MUSEUMS

Frankfort

Georgetown

Paris

WOODFORD RESERVE DISTILLERY

LEXINGTON BREWING AND DISTILLING CO

WILD TURKEY DISTILLERY

Lawrenceburg

Lexington

Taylorsville

FOUR ROSES DISTILLERY

Winchester

BLUEGRASS PKWY

Nicholasville

Wilmore

Harrodsburg

Maker's Mark Distillery

Kentucky Cooperage

Lebanon

Danville

Richmond

Road Trip Route

© MOON.COM

You don't have to be a bourbon connoisseur to appreciate the Kentucky Bourbon Trail. In fact, if you're a booze newbie, you might get more out of this trip than anyone else thanks to the educational and enlightening distillery tours. Because of the limestone-filtered water and locally grown grains, this region has made our country's bourbon for generations. Today, there are 17 signature distilleries and 20 craft distilleries throughout Kentucky's bluegrass country. Meet the passionate makers and taste bourbon made with care, precision, and time-tested recipes. In between, enjoy the most scenic road-tripping around, from horse farms wrapped by white fences to winding back roads haloed by trees.

DAY 1: Louisville

MORNING

1 Start your day at **Churchill Downs,** which brims with atmosphere as the most historic thoroughbred racetrack in the world. The adjoining **Kentucky Derby Museum** (704 Central Ave., 502/637-1111, www.derbymuseum. org, 8am-5pm Mon.-Sat., 11am-5pm Sun. Mar. 15-Nov., 9am-5pm Mon.-Sat., 11am-5pm Sun. Dec.-Mar. 14, $16 adults, $10 children 5-14) lets you experience the thrill of the races even when the track is dark.

AFTERNOON

2 Head to the **Evan Williams Bourbon Experience** (528 W. Main St., 502/272-2623, www.evanwilliams-bourbonexperience.com, 11am-5:30pm Mon.-Thurs., 10am-6pm Fri.-Sat., 1pm-5:30pm Sun., tours daily, $15 adults, $12 children 11-20), located in an old Whiskey Row building, to officially begin your exploration of the Bourbon Trail. You'll be immersed in bourbon history as you take a guided tour through this distillery with museum-style exhibits. A tasting is included with the one-hour tour. Afterwards, grab lunch at any of the many nearby choices downtown has to offer.

3 Walk to the **Louisville Slugger Museum & Factory** (800 W. Main St., 877/775-8443, www.sluggermuseum. com, 9am-5pm Mon.-Sat., 11am-5pm Sun., $16 adults, $9 children 6-12), where you can witness the transformation of a piece of ash wood into an iconic Louisville Slugger baseball bat.

EVENING

4 Have dinner downtown before staying the night at the nearby **21C Museum Hotel** (700 W. Main St., 502/217-6300, www.21chotel.com, $170-558), the most modern, artsy, and innovative hotel around.

CHURCHILL DOWNS

LOUISVILLE SKYLINE

Top **3** KENTUCKY'S BOURBON TRAIL

Top 3 KENTUCKY'S BOURBON TRAIL

1. Discover the history of thoroughbred horse racing at the **Kentucky Derby Museum** (PAGE 630).

2. Swing for the fences at the **Louisville Slugger Museum & Factory** (PAGE 630).

3. Sample the fine bourbon at **Buffalo Trace Distillery,** the oldest continually operating distillery in the United States (PAGE 635).

DAY 2: Louisville to Bardstown

45 miles/72 kilometers | 1-1.5 hours

ROUTE OVERVIEW: I-65 • KY-245 • KY-1604 • KY-245 • KY-1430

1 Grab breakfast and then cruise down to Clermont for a tour of the **Jim Beam American Stillhouse** (526 Happy Hollow Rd., 502/543-9877, www. americanstillhouse.com, 9am-5:30pm Mon.-Sat., noon-4:30pm Sun. Mar.-Dec., tours daily, $14 adults, $7 children 10-20). The 90-minute guided tour begins at the natural limestone water well and doesn't end until you've seen every part of the process, from mashing to distilling, barreling, storing, and bottling. Tours end with your choice of 2 tastings from a selection of 15 options. Afterwards, walk over to **Fred's Smokehouse,** the on-site café that serves Kentucky favorites with a Jim Beam twist.

> Drive south on I-65 to KY-245 (23 mi/37 km). Turn left and follow KY-245 southeast to the Jim Beam American Stillhouse (2 mi/3 km).

2 Visit the nearby **Four Roses Warehouse and Bottling Facility** (624 Lotus Rd., Cox's Creek, 502/543-2664, http:// fourrosesbourbon.com, tours daily, by reservation only, $10). Although the distillery is located in Lawrenceburg, you can tour this bottling facility and warehouse. Unique among bourbon distilleries, Four Roses uses single-story warehouses to age its bourbon, believing this helps minimize temperature fluctuations to create a more consistent taste. The tour ends with a tasting.

> Continue southeast on KY-245 to KY-1604 (4 mi/6 km). Turn left and in less than a mile, you'll reach Four Roses Warehouse and Bottling Facility.

3 From Clermont, follow KY-245 to Bardstown. Make a stop at **My Old Kentucky Home State Park** (501 E. Stephen Foster Ave., 502/348-3502, http://parks.ky.gov, 9am-4:45pm daily Mar.-Dec., 9am-5pm Wed.-Sun. Jan.-Feb., tours $14 adults, $9-10 children), which is where you'll find the home that was the inspiration for Stephen Foster's famous song of the same name. Costumed tour guides lead visitors through the house, doling out information and anecdotes about the Rowan family, who originally lived here. After the tour, wander around the grounds to best admire the beautiful landscaping.

> Return to KY-245 via KY-1604 (4 mi/6 km), then follow KY-245 S for 8 miles (13 km) to KY-1430. Turn right and drive 2 miles (3 km) into Bardstown.

4 Spend the night in the slammer at the **Jailer's Inn Bed and Breakfast** (111 W. Stephen Foster Ave., 502/348-5551, www.jailersinn.com, $120-175). While the back jail remains preserved, the front jail has been renovated to contain six guest rooms. Plenty of ghost stories surround the property, so a stay here might not be for the faint of heart.

JIM BEAM AMERICAN STILLHOUSE

JAILER'S INN BED AND BREAKFAST

BARDSTOWN, KENTUCKY

HEAVEN HILL DISTILLERY

DAY 3: Bardstown

MORNING

❶ Start with a tour of **Barton 1792 Distillery** (300 Barton Rd., 866/239-4690, www.1792bourbon.com, 9am-4:30pm Mon.-Sat., tours Mon.-Sat., free), which is one of the few distilleries that still offer complimentary tours and tastings. The one-hour tours are quite comprehensive, and the guides are both friendly and knowledgeable. Each tour ends with a tasting of Very Old Barton and 1792 bourbons.

❷ Head to the **Oscar Getz Museum of Whiskey History** (114 N. 5th St., 502/348-2999, www.whiskeymuseum.com, 10am-5pm Mon.-Fri., 10am-4pm Sat., noon-4pm Sun. May-Oct., 10am-4pm Tues.-Sat., noon-4pm Sun. Nov.-Apr.), which bursts with whiskey-related paraphernalia. You'll find clever advertising art, moonshine stills, Abraham Lincoln's liquor license, antique distilling vessels, and more.

AFTERNOON

❸ Opt for one of the tours at **Heaven Hill Distillery** (1311 Gilkey Run Rd., 502/337-1000, http://heavenhilldistillery.com, 10am-5:30pm Mon.-Sat., noon-4pm Sun. Mar.-Dec., 10am-5pm Tues.-Sat. Jan.-Feb., tours Tues.-Sun., from $10), an attractive building loaded with museum-quality exhibits on the history of bourbon. The tastings, which take place in the barrel-shaped tasting room at the end of the tour, are very professionally done, with the guide leading you through a discussion of the taste, smell, and feel of the bourbons.

EVENING

❹ Spend your evening at one of Bardstown's historic taverns. **Old Talbott Tavern** (107 E. Stephen Foster Ave., 502/348-3494, www.talbotts.com, 11am-8pm Sun.-Thurs., 11am-9pm Fri.-Sat., $15-29) serves a menu of Kentucky favorites—such as bourbon barbecue ribs, country-fried steak, and beef pot roast—in a welcoming stone building that dates back to 1779.

DAY 4: Bardstown to Lawrenceburg

85 miles/137 kilometers | 2-2.5 hours

ROUTE OVERVIEW: US-150 • KY-55 • KY-429 • KY-152 • KY-555 • Bluegrass Pkwy. • US-127

❶ Rise early to continue through the countryside to **Lebanon** to see where most of Kentucky's bourbon barrels are made. Take the morning tour of the **Kentucky Cooperage** (712 E. Main St., 270/692-4674, www.independentstavecompany.com, tours at 9am, 10:30am, and 1pm Mon.-Fri., free). Because this is a factory tour, closed-toe shoes are required and cameras are not permitted.

BARRELS OF BOURBON AT MAKER'S MARK

> *Follow US-150 E to KY-55 (15 mi/24 km). Turn right on KY-55 and drive south to Lebanon (10 mi/16 km).*

❷ Drive to **Maker's Mark** (3350 Burks Spring Rd., 270/865-2099, www.makersmark.com, 9:30am-3:30pm Mon.-Sat., 11:30am-3:30pm Sun., tours daily, $14 adults, $5 children) to join one of their tours. Set on a village-like campus, it wins the award for most picturesque distillery. The buildings feature cut-out bourbon bottles on every window shutter. One of the tour stops is the area where the bottles are dipped in their famous red wax. The finale is a well-conducted tasting of bourbon at four different stages, complemented with a bourbon ball. Enjoy a farm-to-table lunch at the distillery's **Star Hill Provisions** ($11-15).

> *Go north on KY-429 to Burks Spring Rd. (5 mi/8 km). Turn left on Burks Spring and drive 3 miles (5 km) to Maker's Mark.*

❸ From Lebanon, head to **Lawrenceburg,** where you can spend the night at the **Lawrenceburg Bed & Breakfast** (643 N. Main St., 502/930-8242, http://lawrenceburgbb.com, from $169). Guests are treated to wine and cheese in the afternoon and home-baked desserts in the evening, which can be enjoyed on the large and inviting front porch.

> *Take Burks Spring Rd. back to KY-429 (3 mi/5 km). Turn left on KY-429 and follow it north for 4 miles (6 km) to KY-152. Turn right and drive 2 miles (3 km) to Bardstown Rd. Turn right, then make a left on KY-555. Go north on KY-555 for 15 miles (24 km). At Bluegrass Pkwy., turn right. Follow this to US-127 (17 mi/27 km). Head north on US-127 into Lawrenceburg (5 mi/8 km).*

DAY 5: Lawrenceburg

15 miles/24 kilometers | 30-45 minutes

ROUTE OVERVIEW: US-62 • US-127 BUS

❶ Get up early so that you can fit in two tours today. Start with the **Wild Turkey Distillery** (1417 Versailles Rd., 502/839-2182, www.wildturkeybourbon.com, 9am-5pm Mon.-Sat. and 11am-4pm Sun. Mar.-Dec., 9am-5pm Mon.-Sat. Jan.-Feb., tours daily, from $11), which provides one of the most in-depth looks at the process by which raw grains are turned into smooth bourbon. The tour ends with a tasting flight.

> *Take US-62/Versailles Rd. east from town for 2 miles (3 km) to reach the Wild Turkey Distillery.*

❷ Have a lunch break at the classic stop along the Bourbon Trail, **Heavens to Betsy** (116 S. Main St., 502/859-9291, 11am-8pm Mon.-Sat., $6-10), where the sandwiches are enormous and made with the finest ingredients.

> *Retrace your path back into town to reach Heavens to Betsy (2 mi/3 km).*

❸ Head to your second tour of the day at **Four Roses Distillery** (1224 Bonds

WILD TURKEY DISTILLERY

The best way to enjoy the Bourbon Trail is safely and comfortably. These working distilleries are legally limited by how much alcohol they can give to guests, plus they cannot sell alcohol to consume on the premises. If you plan to sample any bourbon, it's a good idea to have a designated driver. For more information about the Kentucky Bourbon Trail visit http://kybourbontrail.com.

- **Don't drink and drive.** Samples are small, but the cumulative effect of many samples can be an impairment, and the roads between distilleries are often windy. Have a **designated driver** or opt for a tour. **Mint Julep Tours** (www.mintjuleptours.com) and **Pegasus Distillery Experiences** (www.takepegasusdistilled.com) offer a selection of Bourbon Trail tours.

- **Book a ride.** Ride-hailing services are available to transport you safely along the route. **Lyft** offers rides to and from any distillery on the Kentucky Bourbon Trail, while **Uber** offers rides within the city limits of Louisville and Lexington. The website for the Kentucky Bourbon Trail often has promo codes for Lyft and Uber.

- **Pack comfortable and safe shoes.** Some tours require participants to wear closed-toe shoes, and with all the walking involved, it's a good idea to opt for a pair that's comfortable to boot.

- **Bring a photo ID.** You must be of legal drinking age to partake in bourbon tastings. All distilleries require proper identification

- **Hydrate.** Alcohol consumption dehydrates. Bring a reusable bottle with you and ask where you can fill it with water.

- **Time it right.** The distilleries shut down production during the high heat of summer, so plan to visit at a different time of year if you want to see bourbon being made.

Mill Rd., 502/839-3436, http://fourrosesbourbon.com, tours daily, $10). Because the aging warehouses and bottling facilities are located in Clermont, the tour is shorter than those offered at other distilleries, but it does end with a tasting of three different bourbons. Return to Lawrenceburg once you're done.

> *Take US-127 BUS/Main St. south for 4 miles (6 km), then take KY-513 west for 1 mile (1.6 km) to reach Four Roses Distillery. Retrace your path to get back to Lawrenceburg (5 mi/8 km).*

DAY 6: Lawrenceburg to Frankfort

15 miles/24 kilometers | 30 minutes

ROUTE OVERVIEW: US-127

❶ Drive to Frankfort, the state capital, to do some sampling at **Buffalo Trace Distillery** (113 Great Buffalo Trace, 502/696-5926, www.buffalotracedistillery.com, 9am-4pm Mon.-Sat., noon-3pm Sun., tours daily, free). Thanks

FOUR ROSES DISTILLERY

BUFFALO TRACE DISTILLERY

Playlist

KENTUCKY'S BOURBON TRAIL

SONGS

- **"Coal Miner's Daughter" by Loretta Lynn:** Born in the coal-mining town of Butcher Hollow, Kentucky, Loretta Lynn is the most awarded female country recording artist of all time. This 1970 song serves as her autobiography, telling the story of Lynn and her seven siblings growing up in rural Kentucky.
- **"Where to Begin" by My Morning Jacket:** Louisville native Jim James heads up My Morning Jacket, an alt-country rock band that built a loyal following thanks to their energetic live performances. You can hear the band's country roots on this track, a heartfelt, slow-like-honey song that appeared in Cameron Crowe's 2005 Kentucky-based film, *Elizabethtown*.
- **"Swing and Turn Jubilee" by Jean Ritchie:** Affectionately named the Mother of Folk, Jean Ritchie was a singer, songwriter, instrument maker, author, folklorist, and teacher. She often sang her bluegrass tunes without accompaniment, but when she did, it was usually the Appalachian dulcimer. On this song, hear how this instrument quietly backs Ritchie's clear, bell-like, lyrical voice.
- **"The End of the World" by Skeeter Davis:** Both Dolly Parton and Tammy Wynette have cited Davis—born Mary Frances Penick—as inspiration. Country-music elements always tinged Davis's pop songs, especially during the bridge of this 1960s chart-topper about lost love.

to the fact that it was allowed to remain open during Prohibition as one of four distilleries authorized to produce "medicinal" liquor, Buffalo Trace owns the title of the oldest continually operating distillery in America. The tour, which ends with a tasting, is free.

> *Go north on US-127 for 15 miles (24 km) to Frankfort.*

❷ Trace the history of Kentucky back through thousands of years by way of interactive exhibits and performances at the **Kentucky History Center & Museums** (100 W. Broadway, 502/564-1792, http://history.ky.gov, 10am-5pm Tues.-Sat., $8 adults, $6 children 6-18).

❸ Try the bourbon balls at **Rebecca Ruth Candy** (116 E. 2nd St., 502/223-7475, www.rebeccaruth.com, 10am-noon and 1pm-5pm Mon.-Sun.), but not before taking the interesting 20-minute tour of this small facility that produces three million bourbon balls a year.

❹ Have dinner at **Serafini** (243 W. Broadway, 502/875-5599, www.serafinifrankfort.com, 11am-2:30pm Mon.-Fri. and 4:30pm-11pm Mon.-Sat., $12-39), where at least one of the nearly 90 bourbons on offer ought to satisfy. This is Frankfort's nicest restaurant, serving up an excellent selection of pastas and meat and fish dishes to accompany your drink.

DAY 7: Frankfort to Lexington

35 miles/56 kilometers | 1 hour

ROUTE OVERVIEW: KY-1659 • US-60

❶ Head east to join the one-hour tour at **Woodford Reserve** (7785 McCracken Pike, Versailles, 859/879-1812, www.woodfordreserve.com, 10am-3pm Mon.-Sat. Jan.-Feb., 10am-3pm Mon.-Sat., 1pm-3pm Sun. Mar.-Dec., tours daily, $16-$20). Enjoy an in-depth look at the process by which this premium

LEXINGTON BREWING AND DISTILLING CO.

liquor, the official bourbon of the Kentucky Derby, is made. After the tasting that caps off the tour, grab lunch at the on-site café.

> Go east on US-60/Main St. for 1 mile (1.6 km) to MLK Jr. Blvd. Turn right and follow this for 1 mile (1.6 km), then continue onto KY-1659. Follow KY-1659 southeast for 10 miles (16 km) to Woodford Reserve.

❷ Make the drive to **Lexington.** Tour the unique **Lexington Brewing and Distilling Co.** (401 Cross St., 859/255-2337, www.lexingtonbrewingco.com, 9:30am-5:30pm Mon.-Wed., 9:30am-6pm Thurs.-Sat., 11:30am-5:30pm Sun., tours daily, $12), which produces beer as well as bourbon. The tasting at the end allows you to pick between beer and bourbon.

> Continue southeast on KY-1659 for 1 mile (1.6 km) as it turns into KY-2331. In 1 mile (1.6 km), make a slight left on Steele Rd. Continue for 1 mile (1.6 km) to US-60. Turn right and take US-60 E to Lexington (17 mi/27 km).

❸ Indulge in a genteel Southern dinner at **Merrick Inn** (1074 Merrick Dr., 859/269-5417, www.themerrick-inn.com, 4pm-11pm Mon.-Thurs., 4pm-midnight Fri.-Sat., $25-55). This esteemed restaurant was built before the Civil War and served as the manor house for a horse farm. The menu straddles the line between fine, traditional Southern fare and innovative takes on the classics.

Getting There

AIR

The **Louisville Muhammad Ali International Airport** (SDF, 600 Terminal Dr., 502/368-6524, www.flylouisville.com) is conveniently located about five miles south of downtown, and it's notably simple to navigate, with two terminals, each branching off from the main hall and each easily reached on foot. Airlines offer nonstop flights to 20 destinations and a slew of connecting flights to cities around the world. To get to or from the airport, you can take a taxi, rental car, hotel shuttle, or bus.

BUS

Greyhound (www.greyhound.com) services Louisville with a downtown station (720 W. Muhammad Ali Blvd., 502/561-2805).

CAR

Lying at the intersections of I-65, I-64, and I-71, Louisville is 80 miles (129 km) and a 1.5-hour drive from **Lexington** via westbound I-64. Louisville is 115 miles (185 km) and two hours south of **Indianapolis** via I-65; 100 miles (161 km) and 1.5 hours southwest of **Cincinnati** via I-71; and 175 miles (282 km) and 2.5 hours north of **Nashville** via I-65.

To get to downtown Louisville from the **airport,** it's a 7-mile (11-km) drive that takes 15 minutes via I-65. Take the exit for Broadway/Chestnut Street. When you exit the freeway, go left on Jacob Street, right on 2nd Street, left on Broadway, and then right on 5th Street into downtown.

Getting Back

It's 75 miles (121 km) to return to **Louisville** from Lexington, and it takes a little over an hour. Head northwest on US-421 to I-64, then go west on I-64 to Lexington.

If you choose to fly home from **Lexington,** there are five major commercial carriers (Allegiant Air, American Eagle, Delta, United, and US Airways) that serve Lexington's **Blue Grass Airport** (LEX, 4000 Terminal Dr., 859/425-3114, www.bluegrassairport.com).

CONNECT WITH

● At Lawrenceburg: **The Loneliest Road** (PAGE 36)

SOUTH FLORIDA AND THE KEYS

WHY GO: Snorkeling, swimming, beaches, sunshine, palm trees, Cuban cuisine, Everglades National Park, Kennedy Space Center, Miami nightlife, Walt Disney World, Daytona Beach, impressive art

TOTAL DISTANCE: 1,380 miles/ 2,230 kilometers

NUMBER OF DAYS: 14

SEASONS: Year-round

START: Miami, Florida

END: Fort Lauderdale, Florida

▼ BAHIA HONDA STATE PARK

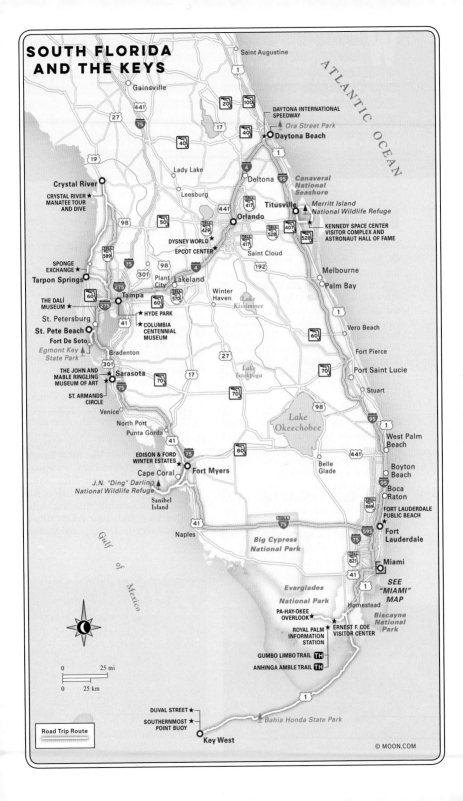

SOUTH FLORIDA AND THE KEYS

Saint Augustine

ATLANTIC OCEAN

Gainsville

DAYTONA INTERNATIONAL SPEEDWAY
Ora Street Park
Daytona Beach

Canaveral National Seashore

Crystal River
CRYSTAL RIVER ★ MANATEE TOUR AND DIVE

Lady Lake

Leesburg

Deltona

Titusville

Merritt Island National Wildlife Refuge

KENNEDY SPACE CENTER VISITOR COMPLEX AND ASTRONAUT HALL OF FAME

Orlando

DYSNEY WORLD ★
EPCOT CENTER ★

Saint Cloud

Melbourne
Palm Bay

SPONGE EXCHANGE ★
Tarpon Springs

Plant City
Lakeland

Winter Haven

Lake Kissimmee

THE DALÍ MUSEUM ★
Tampa

★ HYDE PARK

St. Petersburg

★ COLUMBIA CENTENNIAL MUSEUM

St. Pete Beach
Fort De Soto

Egmont Key State Park

Bradenton

Vero Beach

Fort Pierce

Port Saint Lucie

THE JOHN AND MABLE RINGLING MUSEUM OF ART ★
Sarasota

ST. ARMANDS CIRCLE ★

Stuart

Venice

North Port
Punta Gorda

Lake Istokpoga

Lake Okeechobee

West Palm Beach

EDISON & FORD WINTER ESTATES ★
Cape Coral
Fort Myers

J.N. "Ding" Darling National Wildlife Refuge

Sanibel Island

Belle Glade

Boyton Beach

Boca Raton

FORT LAUDERDALE PUBLIC BEACH

Naples

Big Cypress National Park

Fort Lauderdale

Miami

SEE "MIAMI" MAP

Everglades National Park

Homestead

Biscayne National Park

PA-HAY-OKEE OVERLOOK ★

ROYAL PALM INFORMATION STATION
ERNEST F. COE VISITOR CENTER ★

GUMBO LIMBO TRAIL TH
ANHINGA AMBLE TRAIL TH

0 ——— 25 mi
0 ——— 25 km

DUVAL STREET ★
SOUTHERNMOST ★ POINT BUOY

Bahia Honda State Park

Key West

Road Trip Route

© MOON.COM

Whether you're here for sun and sand, arts and culture, or music and nightlife, South Florida brims with sights to see, things to do, and people to meet. This trip originates in vibrant Miami, where Cuban culture meets art deco style. You'll then venture into Florida's tropical lands and wildlife refuges before stumbling upon arts-centric seaside towns where renowned museums rub shoulders with offbeat galleries and artists' colonies. Thrills await in Orlando at Walt Disney World Resort and Epcot Center. Daytona Beach and Fort Lauderdale offer festive fun and big beaches.

DAY 1: Miami

MORNING

① Spend your first morning walking around **Little Havana.** The heart of Little Havana is **Calle Ocho** (SW 8th St.), a 23-block-long stretch that serves as Main Street for Miami's Cuban community. Grab a *café cubano* at **Versailles** (3555 SW 8th St., 305/444-0240, www.versaillesrestaurant.com, 8am-2am Mon.-Thurs., 8am-3am Fri., 8am-4:30am Sat., 9am-1am Sun., from $5).

AFTERNOON

② Leave the mainland to explore **South Beach,** snapping photos of the beautiful art deco architecture along **Ocean Drive** (15th St. to South Pointe Dr.). This part of town is as beautiful during the day as it is decadent at night, when the nightclubs housed in the art deco buildings come to life. Soak up some rays on the beach at **Lummus Park** (Ocean Dr. between 5th and 15th Sts., 305/673-7730, www.miamibeachfl.gov), which is also great for people-watching.

> Go north on 37th Ave. for 1.5 miles (2.5 km), then turn right onto FL-836 E. After 3 miles (5 km), the road becomes I-395. In less than a mile, keep right to continue on MacArthur Causeway. In 4 miles (6 km), the road leads to South Beach.

EVENING

③ Hopefully by now you've worked up enough of an appetite to dig into the modern soul food on offer at **Yardbird Southern Table & Bar** (1600 Lenox Ave., 305/538-5220, www.runchickenrun.com, 11:30am-11pm Mon.-Thurs., 11:30am-midnight Fri., 10am-midnight Sat., 10am-11pm Sun., from $20).

④ Indulge in South Beach's legendary nightlife at clubs like **Nikki Beach** (1 Ocean Dr., 305/538-1231, www.nikkibeachmiami.com, 11pm-5am Wed.-Sun.), which comes complete with beds to lounge on while enjoying high-priced drinks. (Advance reservations and bottle service are required for the beds.)

KEY RESERVATIONS

- In Miami, advance reservations and **bottle service** are required for the beds at **Nikki Beach.**
- Make dinner reservations **two weeks early** at **Café L'Europe** in Sarasota.
- It's wise to **buy tickets online** and in advance of a visit to Orlando's **Walt Disney World Resort** and **Epcot Center.**

OCEAN DRIVE, SOUTH BEACH

Top ⑤ SOUTH FLORIDA AND THE KEYS

① Order a *café cubano* in Miami's **Little Havana,** the heart of the Cuban community (PAGE 640).

② Immerse yourself in the wild flora and fauna of **Everglades National Park** (PAGE 644).

③ Snap selfies with your favorite Disney characters at **Walt Disney World Resort** (PAGE 652).

④ Rev your engines at the legendary **Daytona International Speedway** on the **Richard Petty Driving Experience** (PAGE 653).

⑤ Discover space flight at the **Kennedy Space Center Visitor Complex and Astronaut Hall of Fame** (PAGE 655).

© DISNEY

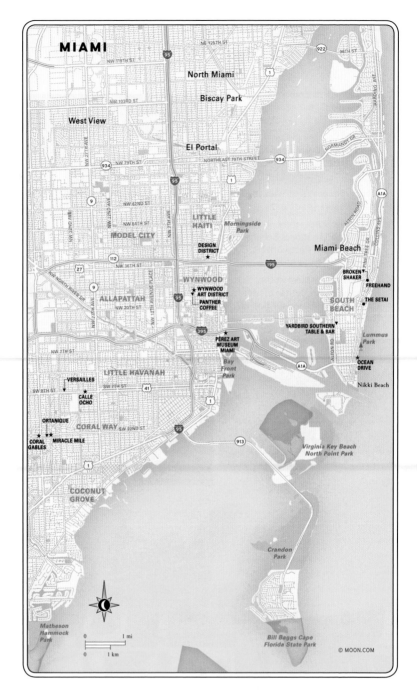

MIAMI

NW 119TH ST
North Miami
Biscay Park
NE 125TH ST
96TH ST
West View
NW 103RD ST
El Portal
NORTHEAST 79TH STREET
NW 79TH ST
NORMANDY DR
NW 62ND ST
NW 22ND AVE
NW 7TH AVE
LITTLE HAITI
Morningside Park
ALTON ROAD
COLLINS AVE
PINE TREE DR
HARDING AVE
NW 64TH ST
MODEL CITY
DESIGN DISTRICT ★
Miami Beach
NW 32ND AVE
NW 27TH AVE
NW NORTH RIVER DR
NW 36TH ST
BROKEN SHAKER ▼
WYNWOOD
FREEHAND
ALLAPATTAH
WYNWOOD ART DISTRICT ★
THE SETAI •
NW 20TH ST
PANTHER COFFEE ★
SOUTH BEACH
NW 12TH AVENUE PLACE
YARDBIRD SOUTHERN TABLE & BAR ▼
Lummus Park
NW 7TH ST
PÉREZ ART MUSEUM MIAMI ★
LITTLE HAVANAH
Bay Front Park
OCEAN DRIVE ★
VERSAILLES ▼
SW 7TH ST
SW 8TH ST
CALLE OCHO ★
Nikki Beach
ORTANIQUE ★
CORAL WAY
SW 22ND ST
CORAL GABLES ★
★★ MIRACLE MILE
Virginia Key Beach North Point Park
COCONUT GROVE
Crandon Park
Matheson Hammock Park
0   1 mi
0   1 km
Bill Baggs Cape Florida State Park
© MOON.COM

MIAMI BEACH

⑤ Spend the first of two nights at up-scale hostel **Freehand** (2727 Indian Creek Dr., 305/531-2727, www.thefree-hand.com, dorms from $45 pp, private from $200), which is just a block from the ocean in **Miami Beach.** The on-site bar, the **Broken Shaker** (786/671-8927, 6pm-2am Mon.-Thurs., 6pm-3am Fri., 1pm-3am Sat., 1pm-2am Sun.), is one of the best craft cocktail bars in town. Miami Beach is just 2 miles (3 km) north of South Beach.

DAY 2: Miami

MORNING

① In the morning, head to the **Wyn-wood Art District** (between NW 20th St. and NW 36th St.) and fuel up at **Panther Coffee** (2390 NW 2nd Ave., 305/677-3952, www.panthercoffee.com, 7am-9pm Mon.-Sat., 8am-9pm Sun.). Spend some time browsing the neighborhood's 40-plus art galleries.

② Head a few blocks south to the **Design District** (NE 36th St. to NE 42nd St. between NE 2nd Ave. and N. Mi-ami Ave., 305/722-7100, www.mi-amidesigndistrict.net) to window-shop for budget-busting decor. This oldest of Miami's neighborhoods is also one of its premier spots for contemporary art and furnishings.

AFTERNOON

③ Next, check out the **Pérez Art Muse-um Miami** (PAMM, 101 W. Flagler St., 305/373-5000, www.pamm.org, 10am-6pm Tues.-Wed. and Fri.-Sun., 10am-9pm Thurs., $12 adults, $8 children). This world-class museum has a robust and forward-looking collection of mod-ern art.

EVENING

④ Hit **Coral Gables** for an excellent dinner of Caribbean fusion fare at **Ortanique** (278 Miracle Mile, Cor-al Gables, 305/446-7710, http://or-taniquerestaurants.com, 6pm-10pm Mon.-Wed., 6pm-11pm Thurs.-Sat., 5:30pm-9:30pm Sun., from $31). After-ward, take in a theater show on Coral Gables's **Miracle Mile.**

> To get to Coral Gables from the De-sign District, take I-395 W. In less than a mile, continue on to FL-836 W. In 2.5 miles (4 km), take the NW 37th Ave. exit. Keep left, then merge onto NW 14th St. Continue for less than a mile, then turn left onto FL-953 S/NW 42nd Ave. In 2.5 miles (4 km), you'll reach the Miracle Mile.

MIAMI'S DESIGN DISTRICT

PÉREZ ART MUSEUM MIAMI

DAY 3: Miami to Key West

215 miles/345 kilometers | 5 hours

ROUTE OVERVIEW: I-395 • FL-836 • FL-826 • FL-874 • Ronald Reagan Turnpike • FL-9336 • US-1

❶ Slather yourself in sunscreen and bug spray and head south to **Everglades National Park** (305/242-7700, www.nps.gov/ever, 24 hours daily, $30 vehicles, $15 pedestrians and cyclists). Make your first stop at the convenient **Ernest F. Coe Visitor Center** (40001 SR-9336, Homestead, 305/242-7700, 9am-5pm daily mid-Apr.-mid-Dec., 8am-5pm mid-Dec.-mid-Apr.). This is the park's main visitors center and its main entrance. This is an ideal place to get tips from a ranger on how to navigate the park, and there are also some excellent exhibits that detail the flora, fauna, and history of the Everglades.

> From Miami Beach, take the MacArthur Causeway west into Miami proper (4 mi/6 km). Follow I-395 W for 1 mile (1.6 km) to FL-836 W. Continue for 7 miles (11 km), then get onto FL-826 S/Palmetto Expy. Continue for another 4 miles (6 km), then take FL-874 S for 8 miles (13 km) to Ronald Reagan Turnpike. Follow the turnpike for 17 miles (27 km), then take FL-9336/SW 344th St. into Everglades National Park (10 mi/16 km).

❷ Continue to the **Royal Palm Information Station** (4 mi/6.4 km west of park entrance on Main Park Rd., 305/242-7237, 9am-4:15pm daily, admission included with park entrance fee). This is the starting point for two of the park's most popular walking trails: the **Anhinga Amble Trail** (0.8 mi/1.3 km

EVERGLADES SWAMP

round-trip) and the **Gumbo Limbo Trail** (0.4 mi/0.6 km round-trip). Both trails manage to be easily navigable while taking hikers through the stunning Everglades terrain. Even during the hottest summer months, you're likely to see a decent array of wildlife (especially alligators).

❸ Go farther west into the park to reach the **Pa-hay-okee Overlook** (12.5 mi/20 km west of park entrance off Main Park Rd.). This elevated boardwalk offers magnificent and expansive vistas of the Everglades and is wheelchair accessible.

❹ Say goodbye to the park and point your car south for a three-hour drive to **Key West.** Once you've checked into your hotel, whoop it up in the clubs and bars of **Duval Street**. The open-air bar at **Willie T's** (525 Duval St., 305/294-7674, www.williets.com, 10am-4am Mon.-Sat., noon-4am Sun.)

DUVAL STREET, KEY WEST

ANHINGA AMBLE TRAIL

Best BEACHES

Between the peninsular coastlines, barrier islands, and the archipelago of the Florida Keys, you're never more than a couple of hours away from an afternoon of castle building, shell collecting, or simply whiling away worries.

- **Bahia Honda State Park** (36850 Overseas Hwy./US-1, Big Pine Key, 305/872-2353, http://bahiahonda park.com, 8am-sunset daily, $6 vehicles): This is one of the best beach areas in the state, with three gorgeous beaches and snorkeling just a few hundred feet offshore.

- **Bill Baggs Cape Florida State Park** (1200 S. Crandon Blvd., Key Biscayne, www.floridastateparks. org, 8am-sunset daily, $8 vehicles): There's a mid-19th-century lighthouse at this park. Despite the allure of historical exploration, most visitors to this Key Biscayne park head directly for the calm blue waters and mile-long beach.

- **Blind Creek Park** (5500 S. State Rd. A1A, Hutchinson Island, sunrise-sunset daily): There's a 335-foot beach here that boasts tropical blue waters and a wide stretch of sand—and it's usually empty.

- **Caladesi Island State Park** (727/469-5918, ferry 727/734-1501, www.floridastateparks.org, ferry $9 adults, $4.50 children, plus admission to Honeymoon Island State Park): The four miles of beaches on Caladesi Island are only accessible by boat. Such limited access would make it a prime beach-going spot even if those four miles weren't some of the most beautiful and pastoral stretches of white sand you'd ever seen.

- **Canaveral National Seashore** (212 S. Washington Ave., Titusville, 386/428-3384, www. nps.gov/cana, 6am-6pm daily Nov.-Feb., 6am-8pm daily Mar.-Oct., $10 vehicles): There are 24 miles of undeveloped beach in this government-owned park. Kennedy Space Center's launch pads are visible from the southernmost beach.

- **Cayo Costa State Park** (north of Captiva Island, Fort Myers, 941/964-0375, 8am-sunset daily, $2): This beach consistently pops up on state and national "best beach" lists. The soft white sand and crystal-blue Gulf waters are only accessible by boat.

- **Crescent Beach** (western end of Point of Rocks Rd., Siesta Key, sunrise-sunset daily, free): The curving coastline of Crescent Beach at Siesta Key is legendary for its white sand and wide and spacious stretches. It's quite popular thanks to those expanses of sand and blue Gulf waters that are shallow and calm.

- **Fort Lauderdale Public Beach** (State Rd. A1A between 17th St. and E. Sunrise Blvd., Fort Lauderdale): With broad stretches of sand, blue-green Atlantic waters, and ample facilities, the city's oceanfront draws crowds, but they don't detract from the beauty.

▲ FORT LAUDERDALE PUBLIC BEACH

- **Fort Myers Beach** (Estero Blvd., Fort Myers, sunrise-sunset daily, free): Enjoy the casual and welcoming atmosphere at Fort Myers Beach, which couples large and accessible swaths of white sand with a laid-back, beach-bum vibe.

is a good option to watch the parade of humanity traipse by. The atmosphere here is personable and a little ramshackle. The bar serves great mojitos and even has a decent food menu.

> *Retrace your path east out of the park back to the Ernest F. Coe Visitor Center (12.5 mi/20 km). Take FL-9336 for 10 miles (16 km) to US-1 S. Follow US-1 S for 123 miles (198 km) to reach Key West.*

DAY 4: Key West to Miami Beach

170 miles/275 kilometers | 4 hours

ROUTE OVERVIEW: US-1 • Ronald Reagan Turnpike • FL-874 • FL-826 • FL-836 • I-395 • MacArthur Causeway

① Spend the early morning strolling the sidewalks of **Key West,** exploring the historic buildings and soaking up the tropical vibe before the sun makes the heat and humidity unbearable. Take the requisite photo at the brightly painted **Southernmost Point Buoy** (South St. and Whitehead St.). You're at the southernmost point in the continental United States—and only 90 miles from Cuba.

SOUTHERNMOST POINT BUOY, KEY WEST

BAHIA HONDA STATE PARK

② Have lunch at the vegetarian-friendly **Blue Heaven** (729 Thomas St., 305/296-8666, www.blueheavenkw.com, 8am-10:30pm daily, from $8). With its whimsical painted picnic tables and an upstairs "tree house" dining room, this spot is quintessential Key West.

③ Make your way about an hour north to **Bahia Honda State Park** (36850 Overseas Hwy./US-1, 305/872-2353, http://bahiahondapark.com, 8am-sunset daily, vehicles $6) to take in the rustic oceanfront scenery. The three white-sand beaches here—Sandspur, Loggerhead, and Calusa—are the best in the Keys. There are ample snorkeling opportunities just a few hundred feet from the shore of all three beach areas. Bahia Honda also has plenty of opportunities for bird-watching and hiking along two fantastic nature trails, one of which takes visitors up to the ruins of the old Bahia Honda Bridge, a vantage point that provides fantastic views of the deep-blue ocean.

> *Follow US-1 N for 35 miles (56 km) to reach the state park.*

④ From here, it's about a three-hour drive back to Miami. Indulge by spending the night at the luxe **Setai** (2001 Collins Ave., 305/520-6500, www.thesetaihotel.com, from $599).

> *Take US-1 N for 91 miles (147 km). Follow signs for FL-821 to get onto the Ronald Reagan Turnpike. Continue north for 17 miles (27 km), then get onto FL-874 N. Continue for 7 miles (11 km), then merge onto FL-826 N. In 3 miles (5 km), get onto FL-836 and continue east for 7 miles (11 km). Continue to I-395, then the MacArthur Causeway to reach Miami Beach (5 mi/8 km).*

DAY 5: Miami Beach to Fort Myers

210 miles/340 kilometers | 5 hours

ROUTE OVERVIEW: I-195 • I-95 • Florida's Turnpike • I-595 • I-75 • surface streets • FL-867

❶ Get up early for the three-hour drive to **Sanibel Island,** which has some of the most beautiful beaches in Florida. Explore the island's **J. N. "Ding" Darling National Wildlife Refuge** (1 Wildlife Dr., 239/472-1100, www.fws.gov/ding-darling, wildlife drive 7:30am-sunset Sat.-Thurs., $5 vehicles). The refuge's Wildlife Drive, a 5-mile (8-km) circuit that's open to automobiles, is quite popular, especially during the winter. It allows visitors a leisurely route through the park's mangrove forests and mudflats in their own vehicles. The **visitors center** (9am-5pm daily Jan.-Apr., 9am-4pm daily May-Dec.) is also an impressive sight, with exhibits that cover the variety of wildlife within the refuge.

> Take I-195 W for 4 miles (6 km) into Miami proper. Get onto I-95 N and continue for 8 miles (13 km). Get onto Florida's Turnpike and continue north for 12 miles (19 km). Get onto I-595 W and continue for 8 miles (13 km), then continue on I-75 N for 109 miles (175 km). Take the exit for Alico Rd., continue for 4 miles (6 km), then turn right onto US-41/Tamiami Trail. Continue for 3 miles (5 km), then

⏱ WITH LESS TIME

MIAMI, THE KEYS, AND THE EVERGLADES

4-6 days; 398 miles/641 kilometers

Take **1-2 days** in **Miami** to soak up the colorful architecture, art museums, and bustling nightlife, then take **3-4 days** to spot wildlife and walk the trails in **Everglades National Park** and bask in the tropical, laid-back lifestyle of the **Florida Keys.**

turn left onto Gladiolus Dr. In 1 mile (1.6 km), merge onto Summerlin Rd. After 2.5 miles (4 km), the road becomes McGregor Blvd. Continue for 2 miles (3 km), then cross the Sanibel Causeway to reach Sanibel Island.

❷ On nearby Captiva Island, grab a bite and a beer at **The Mucky Duck** (11546 Andy Rosse Ln., 239/472-3434, www.muckyduck.com, noon-10pm Mon.-Sat., 3pm-9pm Sun., from $24), where the high-quality pub grub is made that much better by the gorgeous waterfront views.

> Take Sanibel Captiva Rd. north for 5 miles (8 km), then take Blind Pass Bridge onto Captiva Island.

❸ It's about a half hour to **Fort Myers,** where you can spend a few hours exploring the **Edison & Ford**

J. N. "DING" DARLING NATIONAL WILDLIFE REFUGE

FORT MYERS

Winter Estates (2350 McGregor Blvd., 239/334-7419, www.edisonfordwinterestates.org, 9am-5:30pm daily, $12 adults, $5 children). Here, you can get a feel for the genius that drove industrial titans Thomas Edison and Henry Ford by visiting Edison's house and labs, as well as a museum filled with various inventions and memorabilia from both men's pasts.

> Retrace your path back to the mainland via Sanibel Island (20 mi/32 km). After you've crossed the Sanibel Causeway, follow McGregor Blvd. for 3 miles (5 km) to FL-867. Continue north on FL-867 to reach Fort Myers.

❹ Continue the theme by having dinner downtown at **Ford's Garage** (2207 1st St., 239/332-3673, www.fordsgarageusa.com, 11am-11pm Mon.-Thurs., 11am-midnight Fri.-Sat., 11am-10pm Sun., from $10), a popular burger joint decorated to look like a Model T garage.

DAY 6: Fort Myers to Sarasota

80 miles/129 kilometers | 2 hours

ROUTE OVERVIEW: US-41 • I-75 • FL-780

❶ Hit the road for the 90-minute drive to **Sarasota.** After a morning on the beach, make your way to the northern part of town. Walk through the galleries of the **John and Mable Ringling Museum of Art** (5401 Bay Shore Rd., 941/359-5700, www.ringling.org, 10am-5pm Fri.-Wed., 10am-8pm Thurs., $25 adults, $5 children), home to one of the best-curated collections of masterworks in the state. Keep an eye out for works by El Greco, Diego Velázquez, Titian, Peter Paul Rubens, and many more.

> Head north on US-41 to Tuckers Grade (17 mi/27 km). Turn right to reach I-75 (1 mi/1.6 km). Turn left and follow I-75 to FL-780 (52 mi/84 km). Turn left on FL-780 and follow it for 5 miles (8 km) into Sarasota.

❷ Head downtown for more local and contemporary art at the **Towles Court Artist Colony** (Adams Lane, between S. Links Ave. and Washington Blvd., 941/374-1988, www.towlescourt.com, most galleries open noon-4pm Tues.-Sun.). Originally part of a golf course, the property was turned into a residential district in the 1920s. Many of the bungalows from that era have been transformed into galleries, studios, and restaurants. With most of the establishments reliably open noon-4pm, afternoons are the best time to visit.

❸ It's a quick drive over the Ringling Causeway to **St. Armands Circle** (John Ringling Blvd. and Blvd. of the Presidents, Lido Key, 941/388-1554, www.starmandscircleassoc.com), where you can browse tony boutiques and jewelry shops galore.

❹ You won't have to go far to treat yourself to dinner. Upscale **Café L'Europe** (431 St. Armands Circle, 941/388-4415, www.cafeleurope.net, 11:30am-3pm and 5pm-10pm daily, from $35) has been a St. Armands mainstay since the 1970s. With white-linen service, an extensive wine list, and a menu of French and Italian classics, the intimate and romantic environment is as perfect for a date night as it is for a luxurious vacation splurge.

❺ Crash at the vintage beachfront **Gulf Beach Resort Motel** (930 Ben Franklin Dr., 941/388-2127, www.gulfbeachsarasota.com, from $160). It's the oldest hotel on Lido Beach, located on a beautiful, quiet stretch of sand.

JOHN AND MABLE RINGLING MUSEUM OF ART

Whether it's the heat, the humidity, or just the constant influx of people from around the country and around the world who are determined to make the peninsula their own peculiar paradise, Florida is home to quite a few weird sights.

- **Bubble Room** (15001 Captiva Dr., Captiva Island, 239/472-5558, http://bubbleroomrestaurant.com, 11am-3pm and 4:30pm-10pm daily, from $10): Inside the Bubble Room on Captiva Island, the 1930s, '40s, and '50s are brought back to life in garish, outsized fashion. The restaurant, complete with dishes like the "Duck Ellington," is packed with pop-culture memorabilia and a kitschy attitude.

- **Coral Castle** (28655 S. Dixie Hwy., Homestead, 305/248-6345, www.coralcastle.com, 8am-6pm Sun.-Thurs., 8am-9pm Fri.-Sat., $15 adults, $7 children): This architectural oddity, about a half hour south of downtown Miami, was handcrafted out of local materials by a lovesick Latvian as a tribute to his one true romance.

- **Jules' Undersea Lodge** (51 Shoreland Dr., Key Largo, 305/451-2353, www.jul.com, from $675): Here, guests swim to their rooms, which are located some 21 feet beneath the surface in an underwater research facility. A "mer-chef" delivers subsurface gourmet food, and you'll see fish swimming right outside your bedroom.

- **Stiltsville** (Key Biscayne, www.nps. gov/bisc, access by permit only): There are seven houses in the waters of Biscayne Bay, near Miami. In the 1920s, Miamians seeking a refuge from the mores (and, occasionally, the law enforcement) of the mainland began constructing shacks—on stilts—in the bay. Although there are only a handful remaining of the dozens that originally composed the makeshift village, you can still get a sense of the site's singular weirdness.

DAY 7: Sarasota to St. Pete Beach

55 miles/89 kilometers | 2 hours

ROUTE OVERVIEW: US-301 • US-41 • US-19 • I-275 • Pinellas Bayway • FL-679 • FL-682

❶ Before you hit the road, start your day at **The Breakfast House** (1817 Fruitville Rd., 941/366-6860, 7am-2pm Mon.-Sat., 9am-2pm Sun., from $7). With morning dishes that nod both to a Gulf Coast heritage (shrimp and grits) and the tropical weather (pancakes with pineapple, coconut, and macadamia nuts), the menu here is a great combination of tradition and innovation.

❷ Make for the isolated **Egmont Key State Park** (727/644-6235, www.floridastateparks.org, 8am-sunset daily,

free). This island refuge is only accessible by **ferry** (Tampa Bay Ferry & Taxi, Fort De Soto Bay Pier, 727/398-6577, http://tampabayferry.com, daily spring-summer, fewer departures fall-winter, $25 adults, $12.50 children 11 and under) from the town of **Fort De Soto.** Excellent snorkeling can be found just offshore of this

EGMONT KEY STATE PARK

wildlife refuge. There's a good chance that you'll wind up swimming alongside one of the pods of dolphins that frequent the area. Note that there are no restrooms or running water on the island.

> Drive north for 14 miles (23 km) on US-301, then continue on US-41 for 2 miles (3 km). Veer slightly left to get on US-19. In 3 miles (5 km), merge onto I-275 N. Stay on I-275 to Pinellas Bayway (12 mi/19 km). Turn left and follow Pinellas Bayway 2 miles (3 km) to FL-679/Pinellas Bayway. Turn left and follow this to Fort De Soto (7 mi/11 km).

❸ Spend the night on **St. Pete Beach** at the gorgeous, historic, and shell-pink **Don CeSar** (3400 Gulf Blvd., 866/728-2206, www.doncesar.com, from $359). Be sure to check out the on-site ice cream shop.

> Take FL-679/Pinellas Bayway north to FL-682 (7 mi/11 km). Turn left on FL-682 and drive 1 mile (1.6 km) to Gulf Blvd. Turn right on Gulf and in 2 miles (3 km), you'll reach St. Pete Beach.

DAY 8: St. Pete Beach to Tampa

35 miles/56 kilometers | 1 hour

ROUTE OVERVIEW: City streets • I-275

❶ Spend the morning on St. Pete Beach, where there's public beach access on almost every block. From here, it's about a half hour to **St. Petersburg** proper, where you can take in **The Dalí Museum** (1 Dali Blvd., 727/823-3767,

ST. PETE BEACH

www.thedali.org, 10am-8pm Thurs., 10am-5:30pm Fri.-Wed., $25 adults, $18 children 13-17, $10 children ages 6-12), an essential stop for even the most casual art lover. The museum houses the largest collection of the famous surrealist's paintings in the United States.

> Go northeast on Pasadena Ave. for 2 miles (3 km) to 1st Ave., then turn right and follow 1st Ave. into St. Petersburg.

❷ Take the hour drive to **Tampa**. Explore the shops and restaurants of **Hyde Park,** being sure to grab some modern diner fare for lunch from **Daily Eats** (901 S. Howard Ave., 813/868-3335, www.ilovedailyeats.com, 11:30am-10pm Tues.-Fri., 8:30am-10pm Sat.-Sun., $7).

> Take I-275 N for 23 miles (37 km) to reach Tampa.

❸ Next, check out the historic district of **Ybor City**. It's known mainly for its numerous nightclubs and bars, but you can get a rich sense of

THE DALÍ MUSEUM

HISTORIC YBOR CITY

history from walking around during the day. The **Columbia Centennial Museum** (2117 E. 7th Ave., 813/248-4961, www.columbiarestaurant.com, 10am-5pm Mon.-Sat., noon-6pm Sun., free) is filled with small, artifact-heavy exhibits about the history of Ybor City.

4 Grab dinner in Ybor City. If you still have energy afterward, dig into the neighborhood's decadent late-night club culture at **Club Prana** (1619 E. 7th Ave., 813/241-4139, www.clubprana.com, 9pm-3am Wed.-Sat.). A night in Ybor is perfect for sampling as many venues and cocktails as possible.

DAY 9: Day Trip to Crystal River and Tarpon Springs

170 miles/275 kilometers | 4.5 hours

ROUTE OVERVIEW: FL-589 • US-98/US-19 • US-19 ALT • surface streets • FL-589 • FL-60 • I-275

1 Wake up early for the drive to **Crystal River,** a small rural town on the Gulf Coast with a network of warm freshwater springs that are favored by manatees. Spend the morning with **Crystal River Manatee Tour and Dive** (36 NE 4th St., 888/732-2692, www.manateetouranddive.com, manatee swim tours $55 adults, sightseeing boat tours $40 adults), who will help you to commune with the gentle giants from the top of the water or by snorkeling alongside them. The company conducts tours year-round and also offers rentals of canoes and kayaks.

> Take FL-589 N for 42 miles (68 km), then join US-98/US-19. Continue driving north for 17 miles (27 km) to reach Crystal Springs.

2 Heading back toward Tampa, the small fishing village of **Tarpon Springs** is about an hour away. There you can be immersed in the village's rich Greek history, which includes the legacy industry of sponge diving. Park at the **Sponge Exchange** (735 Dodecanese Blvd., 727/934-8758, www.thespongeexchange.com, 10am-9pm Mon.-Sat., 10am-7pm Sun.) to browse through the shops selling everything from tourist trinkets and candy by the pound to Greek fashion and Peruvian ceramics. From there you can make your way to the sponge docks, where you'll be invited by numerous touts to take a sponging excursion.

CRYSTAL RIVER

> Take US-19 S for 53 miles (85 km). Make a slight right onto US-19 ALT and follow it into Tarpon Springs (3 mi/5 km).

③ Of the many Greek restaurants on the main drag, **Hellas Bakery & Restaurant** (785 Dodecanese Blvd., 727/943-2400, www.hellasbakery.com, 11am-10pm Sun.-Thurs., 11am-11pm Fri.-Sat., $9-22) is the best. Don't be fooled by the garish neon and mirrored walls—this is a solid dining experience with a menu that includes authentic Greek dishes as well as fresh seafood entrées and an excellent bakery next door. Spend the night back in Tampa.

> Take Tarpon Ave./Keystone Rd. east out of Tarpon Springs. In 8 miles (13 km), turn right onto Boy Scout Rd. Continue for 4 miles (6 km), then take Race Track Rd. for less than a mile. Turn right onto Gunn Hwy. In 3 miles (5 km), join FL-589 S and continue for 9 miles (14 km). Take FL-60 E for 1.5 miles (2.5 km), then merge onto I-275 N. This will lead you to downtown Tampa in 5 miles (8 km).

DAY 10: Tampa to Orlando

70 miles/113 kilometers | 1.5 hours

ROUTE OVERVIEW: I-4

① Depart Tampa as early as possible and head for the **Walt Disney World Resort** (407/939-5277, http://disneyworld.disney.go.com, from $109), which is only about an hour to the east. Spend the day exploring the fairy-tale fantasies of the **Magic Kingdom** (generally 9am-10pm daily, hours vary seasonally).

> Drive east on I-4 for 66 miles (106 km). Take exit 65 for Osceola Pkwy. and in less than 1 mile (1.6 km) you'll reach Walt Disney World Resort.

② When people think of Walt Disney World, they almost immediately envision **Fantasyland,** the emotional heart of the resort. It's an essential stop on any Disney itinerary, whether or not you are traveling with young children. For the classic Disney experience, get in line for the slow-moving boats of **It's a Small World.**

MAGIC KINGDOM, WALT DISNEY WORLD RESORT

③ Next, make your way to **Tomorrowland,** the retro-futuristic part of the park. The most popular ride here is **Space Mountain.** Opened in 1975, the 2.5-minute-long, 28-mph indoor roller coaster is far from the fastest, but the combination of quirky futurism, quick turns, and darkened thrills is irresistible. Lines stack up quickly here, so during high season a FastPass+ reservation is essential.

④ If Tomorrowland is all about retro-futurism, then **Frontierland** is all about retro-retro-ism, evoking a halcyon vision of the Mild West. There are thrills to be found, most notably at **Big Thunder Mountain Railroad,** a clickety-clacking coaster that takes riders on a high-speed run through an abandoned mining town. The careening coaster dips into dark caves and plummets down mountains, tossing you from side to side as it makes its way along the track.

⑤ In the evening, head to **Disney Springs** (Buena Vista Dr., off FL-535, www.disneysprings.com, hours vary by merchant), a shopping, dining, and entertainment complex. Peruse the shops, then pick a spot for dinner and rest your weary feet.

EPCOT CENTER

DAY 11: Epcot Center

① Today is all about the international food-and-drink possibilities of **Epcot Center** (generally 9am-9pm daily, hours vary seasonally). Epcot has taken a while to shake off its early identity crisis as the Disney park that doesn't seem like a Disney park. Today, though, the park stands quite well on its own.

② There are very few actual rides or attractions in Epcot's **World Showcase,** but the charming tourist-brochure image of each of its 11 represented countries makes for a fantastic way to spend an afternoon.

③ In the **China Pavilion,** watch the **Jeweled Dragon Acrobats** (20 minutes, multiple times daily). During the performances, the acrobats use props and sheer feats of flexibility to wow the audience.

④ Next, take one of the few rides in Epcot. **Frozen Ever After,** in the **Norway Pavilion,** is a briefly exhilarating boat ride that interpolates the location-agnostic Arendelle of the film *Frozen* into Norway. Be ready to sing along with your favorite songs with Anna and Elsa. Continue strolling around the lake and complete your tour around the world. Once your appetite strikes, you're in luck: In Epcot, you'll have no problem finding something to eat.

DAY 12: Orlando to Daytona Beach

75 miles/121 kilometers | 2 hours

ROUTE OVERVIEW: I-4 • US-92/ International Speedway Blvd.

① **Daytona Beach** is about 90 minutes away from Walt Disney World. The city's legendary Daytona 500 race kicks off the stock car season every year. Because there can't be a stock car race every day or even every month, the **Daytona International Speedway**

DAYTONA INTERNATIONAL SPEEDWAY

(1801 W. International Speedway Blvd., 386/681-6800, www.daytonausa.com) offers behind-the-scenes tours (from $19 adults, $13 children) of the legendary racetrack on non-racing days throughout the year. True gearheads can undertake the **Richard Petty Driving Experience** ($150), which puts them in the passenger seat as a professional driver takes you out for three laps around the track. Specific tour dates depend on track availability, so call ahead.

> *Drive northeast on I-4 for 65 miles (105 km) to US-92 E. Go east on US-92/ International Speedway Blvd. into Daytona Beach (5 mi/8 km).*

② It's time to hit the beach. Your best bet is to head for **Ora Street Park** (800 Ora St., near the Daytona Beach Bandshell), which is reasonably accessible and often uncrowded.

③ If you're hungry, get away from the bustle of the tourist strip at **Martini's Organic** (1821 S. Ridgewood Ave., 386/763-1090, http://martinisorganic.com, 5pm-10pm Tues.-Thurs., 5pm-11pm Fri.-Sat., from $18). This restaurant is a sedate and sumptuous respite from the buzzing beachside. With sophisticated interiors providing a complementary atmosphere for the decadently sized slabs of meat served, Martini's thrives as one of the few truly high-end restaurants in Daytona.

④ Once you've had enough sun, check into the **Plaza Resort & Spa** (600 N. Atlantic Ave., 386/255-4741, http://plaza-resortandspa.com, from $159). The hotel's location in the heart of the tourist district and proximity to the convention center guarantees a near-constant hum of activity. Rooms are spacious and well appointed, with classy understated wood furnishings and modern amenities.

DAY 13: Daytona Beach to Titusville

105 miles/169 kilometers | 2.5 hours

ROUTE OVERVIEW: US-1 • FL-402 • US-1 • FL-405 • US-1

① Point the car toward **Titusville.** About an hour south of Daytona, via a scenic drive, is **Merritt Island National Wildlife Refuge** (entrance at east side of Max Brewer Causeway Bridge, Titusville, www.fws.gov/merrittisland, sunrise-sunset daily, visitors center 8am-4:30pm Mon.-Fri., 9am-5pm Sat., 9am-5pm Sun. Nov.-Mar., $10 vehicles). The natural surroundings still look pretty much the same today as they did millennia ago. The well-marked trails provide plenty of chances for spotting endangered turtles, scrub jays, or any of the other

MERRITT ISLAND NATIONAL WILDLIFE REFUGE

hundreds of species of birds, mammals, and plants within the refuge's boundaries. Pick up a trail map at the park gate.

> Take US-1 S for 46 miles (74 km). Turn left onto Garden St., then continue across the A. Max Brewer Bridge for 3 miles (5 km). At FL-402, make a slight right and drive 3.5 miles (5 km), then turn right and drive 2 miles (3 km) to Merritt Island National Wildlife Refuge.

❷ Cool off at the beautiful beaches of nearby **Canaveral National Seashore** (southern entrance at 212 S. Washington Ave., Titusville, 386/428-3384, www.nps.gov/cana, 6am-6pm daily Nov.-Feb., 6am-8pm daily Mar.-Oct., $10 vehicles). Although quite a few people pass through the gates during the summer, even the busiest day at Canaveral never feels crowded. You will encounter the easily accessible **Playalinda** via the Titusville entrance. There are 13 parking areas, each of which has rudimentary toilet facilities, trash and recycling containers, and boardwalks to cross over the dunes.

> Retrace your path to FL-402, then head east for 6 miles (10 km) until you reach the parking areas.

❸ Grab lunch and a craft beer at **Playalinda Brewing Company's Brix Project** (5220 S. Washington Ave., Titusville, 321/567-5974, www.playalindabrewingcompany.com, 4pm-10pm Mon.-Wed., 4pm-11pm Thurs., 3pm-midnight Fri., 11:30am-midnight Sat., 10am-9pm Sun., from $9). Make sure you try the signature burger (locally farmed beef topped with brisket, beets, blue cheese, and more) or the blackened red drum fish.

> Head back to FL-402 (6 mi/10 km), then continue west for 5 miles (8 km). Cross the A. Max Brewer Bridge, then make a left onto S. Hopkins Ave. In 1 mile (1.6 km), the road becomes US-1. Continue south for 4 miles (6 km) to reach Brix Project.

❹ Nerd out at the **Kennedy Space Center Visitor Complex and Astronaut Hall of Fame** (FL-405 E, Titusville, 866/737-5235, www.kennedyspacecenter.com, 9am-5:30pm daily, $50 adults, $40 children; includes admission to Astronaut Hall of Fame). This as close as you'll get to extraterrestrial action. NASA has translated the challenges and glory of spaceflight into something more than a museum. Stand next to a full-sized rocket in one of the exhibit halls and you can't help but be astonished and amazed. The insightful guided tours of the complex and the virtual-reality launch simulator bring things to life. Be sure to seek out the $100 million exhibit featuring the shuttle *Atlantis*.

> Take US-1 S for 1.5 miles (2.5 km), then merge onto FL-405 E. Continue for

KENNEDY SPACE CENTER VISITOR COMPLEX

2.5 miles (4 km), after which the road becomes NASA Pkwy. Continue for 4 miles (6 km) to Kennedy Space Center.

⑤ Lodging options are limited in Titusville. Your best choice is the cute and tidy **Casa Coquina del Mar Bed & Breakfast** (4010 Coquina Ave., 321/268-4653, www.casacoquina.com, from $99), a nine-suite house with great views of the Indian River.

> Take NASA Pkwy. west for 6 miles (10 km), crossing back into Titusville. Take US-1 N for 3 miles (5 km) to the B&B.

DAY 14: Titusville to Fort Lauderdale

195 miles/315 kilometers | 4 hours

ROUTE OVERVIEW: I-95

① Head south to **Fort Lauderdale,** one of Florida's most popular tourist destinations. Leave your bags at the **Riverside Hotel** (620 E. Las Olas Blvd., 954/467-0671, www.riversidehotel. com, from $229), one of Fort Lauderdale's nicest hotels since it opened in the 1930s. Luxurious touches are present throughout, from the marble bathroom countertops and beautiful furnishings to the high-end dining options and cocktail lounge.

> Go south on I-95 for 185 miles (300 km) to reach Fort Lauderdale.

② You won't have to go far to enjoy the next activity: Spend a few hours shopping the boutiques along **Las Olas Boulevard.** While Las Olas is decidedly fancy, it feels less like an exclusive enclave than a well-to-do Main Street.

③ While away some hours at the **Fort Lauderdale Public Beach** (State Rd. A1A between 17th St. and E. Sunrise Blvd.). The beach is as large as it is beautiful, and it can often get incredibly crowded. The atmosphere here is festive and generally family-oriented.

④ Have dinner at **The Foxy Brown** (723 E. Broward Blvd., 754/200-4236, www. myfoxybrown.com, 11:30am-10pm Mon.-Fri., 9:30am-10pm Sat.-Sun., from $12), which splits the difference between upscale neighborhood diner and locavore foodie spot. A tightly curated wine list and craft-beer selection complement the creative menu that changes frequently.

Getting There

AIR

Miami International Airport (MIA, 4200 NW 21st St., 305/876-7000, www.miami-airport.com) is not only served by multiple daily flights by all major low-cost and cut-rate American carriers but is also the primary point of entry for travelers entering the United States from South America and the Caribbean. The airport, a hub for American Airlines, is located only about 8 miles (13 km) from downtown Miami. **Taxis** (flat rate, $32 to South Beach, $26.50 to North Miami

FORT LAUDERDALE PUBLIC BEACH

Beach, $21.70 to downtown and Coconut Grove) and **shuttles** (from $10 pp to hotels) are available in the ground transportation area. Ride-share services like Lyft and Uber also operate from MIA, but their legal status seems to be constantly in flux.

Many travelers use **Fort Lauderdale-Hollywood International Airport** (FLL, 320 Terminal Dr., Ft. Lauderdale, 866/435-9355, www.broward.org/airport) to reach Miami. Less than an hour away from downtown Miami, FLL caters to low-cost carriers and is far easier to navigate than MIA. Taxis can run upwards of $75 to Miami, but shuttle services are available in the ground transportation area from around $40.

TRAIN

Amtrak (www.amtrak.com) runs its Silver Star and Palmetto services between Miami and Jacksonville, Orlando, and Tampa. Service terminates at the **Miami Central Station,** at Miami International Airport.

BUS

The Miami **Greyhound station** (4111 NW 27th St., 305/871-1810, www.greyhound.com) is open 24 hours.

CAR

From the **Miami airport** to downtown, it's a 20-minute drive (8 mi/13 km). Follow FL-836 E to I-95. Go south on I-95 into the city.

To get to downtown Miami from the **Fort Lauderdale airport,** it's under an hour's drive (26 mi/42 km). Take FL-818 West from the airport to I-95, then drive south on I-95 to Miami.

Getting Back

The drive from Fort Lauderdale back to **Miami** is 29 miles (47 km) along I-95 S and takes about 45 minutes, depending on traffic.

You can also fly home out of **Fort Lauderdale-Hollywood International Airport.** It's 4 miles (6 km) from downtown Fort Lauderdale going south on US-1 from town.

▶ Playlist

SOUTH FLORIDA AND THE KEYS

SONGS

- **"Conga" by Gloria Estefan:** Many influential singers, rappers, and musicians have come out of Miami, but arguably the best known is Havana-born Estefan. She exploded onto the scene with this 1985 song, which became a worldwide hit. It's a flood of joyous sound, a dance-party anthem with an irresistible beat and lyrics.

- **"In the Air Tonight" by Phil Collins:** Few television shows are as intrinsically linked to South Florida as the Don Johnson vehicle *Miami Vice*. Played during the show's pilot episode, this moody, dark song—with a famous killer drum break at the end—captures the style of Miami in the 1980s.

- **"Give Me Everything" by Pitbull:** Miami-born, Cuban-American rapper Pitbull launched his career in Latin hip-hop and club-friendly crunk music before crossing over into danceable pop. This powerhouse of a song keeps you moving, whether you're on the dance floor or the beach.

PODCASTS

- *Retro Disney World:* This nostalgia-filled podcast brings Disney World's rich past to life with interviews with former cast members and looks at decades-old parades and rides.

ALASKA and *HAWAI'I*

Alaska and Hawai'i have more in common than you might think at first. Both offer breathtaking natural beauty. Both boast tall mountains and endless ocean vistas. Both are home to people whose cultures have been influenced by the sea. See for yourself by driving Maui's Road to Hana, where each curve reveals yet another astonishing view. Bear witness to nature's power and majesty as you tour Alaska's Kenai Peninsula, where you'll have countless opportunities to spot wildlife and glaciers alike.

◄ ROAD TO HANA, MAUI

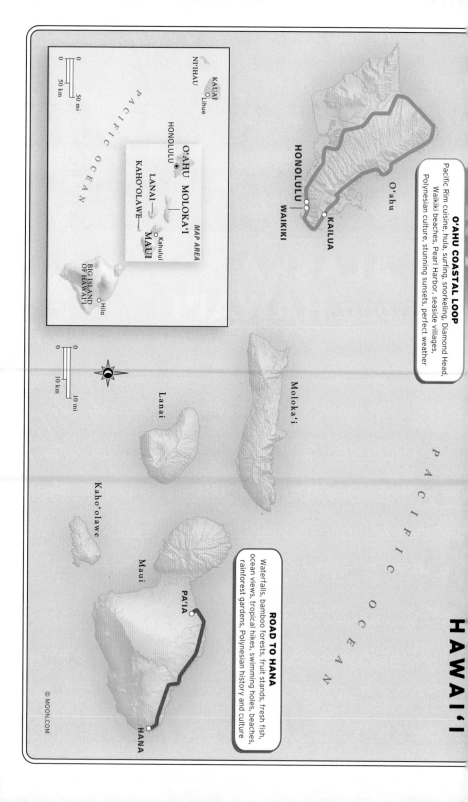

HAWAI'I

O'AHU COASTAL LOOP
Pacific Rim cuisine, hula, surfing, snorkeling, Diamond Head, Waikiki beaches, Pearl Harbor, seaside villages, Polynesian culture, stunning sunsets, perfect weather

ROAD TO HANA
Waterfalls, bamboo forests, fruit stands, fresh fish, ocean views, tropical hikes, swimming holes, beaches, rainforest gardens, Polynesian history and culture

HONOLULU

WAIKIKI

KAILUA

O'ahu

Moloka'i

Lanai

Kaho'olawe

Maui

PA'IA

HANA

PACIFIC OCEAN

PACIFIC OCEAN

0 — 10 mi
0 — 10 km

© MOON.COM

NI'IHAU

KAUA'I
Lihue

HONOLULU

O'AHU   MOLOKA'I
LANA'I
KAHO'OLAWE
MAUI
Kahului

MAP AREA

BIG ISLAND OF HAWAI'I
Hilo

PACIFIC OCEAN

0 — 50 mi
0 — 50 km

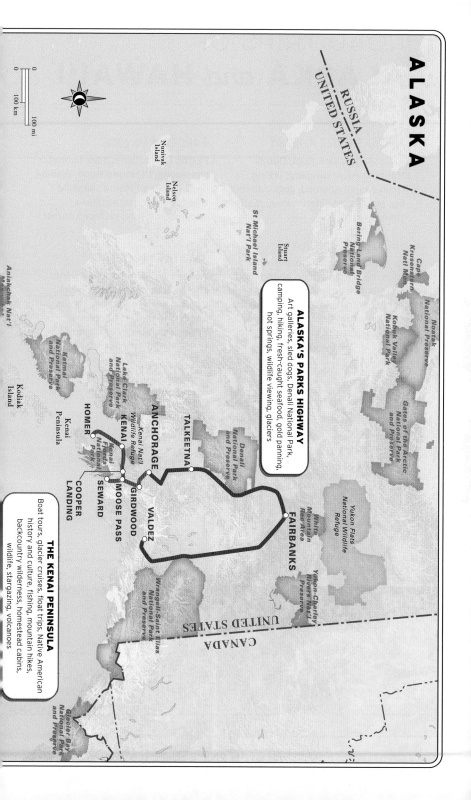

ALASKA

RUSSIA
UNITED STATES

0   100 km
0   100 mi

Nunivak
Island

Nelson
Island

Stuart
Island

St. Michael Island
Nat'l Park

Noatak
National Preserve

Cape
Krusenstern
Nat'l Mon.

Kobuk Valley
National Park

Bering Land Bridge
National
Preserve

Gates of the Arctic
National Park
and Preserve

Yukon Flats
National Wildlife
Refuge

ALASKA'S PARKS HIGHWAY

Art galleries, sled dogs, Denali National Park,
camping, hiking, fresh-caught seafood, gold panning,
hot springs, wildlife viewing, glaciers

Denali
National Park
and Preserve

White
Mountain
Rec Area

Yukon-Charley
Rivers Nat'l
Preserve

TALKEETNA

FAIRBANKS

Lake Clark
National Park
and Preserve

Kenai Nat'l
Wildlife Refuge

ANCHORAGE

KENAI

GIRDWOOD

VALDEZ

Katmai
National Park
and Preserve

Kodiak
Island

Aniakchak Nat'l
Monument

HOMER

Kenai
Peninsula

Kenai
Fjords
National
Park

COOPER
LANDING

SEWARD

MOOSE PASS

Wrangell-Saint Elias
National Park
and Preserve

UNITED STATES
CANADA

Glacier Bay
National Park
and Preserve

THE KENAI PENINSULA

Boat tours, glacier cruises, float trips, Native American
history and culture, fishing, mountain hikes,
backcountry wilderness, homestead cabins,
wildlife, stargazing, volcanoes

ROAD TRIPS OF
ALASKA *and* HAWAI'I

ALASKA'S PARKS HIGHWAY

Art galleries, sled dogs, Denali National Park, camping, hiking, fresh-caught seafood, gold panning, hot springs, wildlife viewing, glaciers (PAGE 664)

THE KENAI PENINSULA

Boat tours, glacier cruises, float trips, Native American history and culture, fishing, mountain hikes, backcountry wilderness, homestead cabins, wildlife, stargazing, volcanoes (PAGE 674)

O'AHU COASTAL LOOP

Pacific Rim cuisine, hula, surfing, snorkeling, Diamond Head, Waikiki beaches, Pearl Harbor, seaside villages, Polynesian culture, stunning sunsets, perfect weather (PAGE 688)

ROAD TO HANA

Waterfalls, bamboo forests, fruit stands, fresh fish, ocean views, tropical hikes, swimming holes, beaches, rainforest gardens, Polynesian history and culture (PAGE 698)

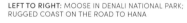

LEFT TO RIGHT: MOOSE IN DENALI NATIONAL PARK; RUGGED COAST ON THE ROAD TO HANA

1 Explore the remote expanse of Alaska's **Denali National Park and Preserve** (PAGE 666).

2 Brave the steep climb up to the 150-foot face of **Exit Glacier** (PAGE 679).

3 Join a **deep-sea fishing charter** in **Homer,** the halibut fishing capital of the world (PAGE 686).

Denali National Park and Preserve

Exit Glacier

halibut in Homer, Alaska

Diamond Head Summit Trail

Pools of 'Ohe'o

4 Climb to the top of an extinct volcano on O'ahu's **Diamond Head Summit Trail** (PAGE 690).

5 Hike to the **Pools of 'Ohe'o,** also known as Maui's **Seven Sacred Pools** (PAGE 704).

ALASKA'S PARKS HIGHWAY

WHY GO: Art galleries, sled dogs, Denali National Park, camping, hiking, fresh-caught seafood, gold panning, hot springs, wildlife viewing, glaciers

TOTAL DISTANCE: 950 miles/ 1,535 kilometers

NUMBER OF DAYS: 6

SEASONS: Summer through early fall

START: Anchorage, Alaska

END: Valdez, Alaska

▼ DENALI NATIONAL PARK

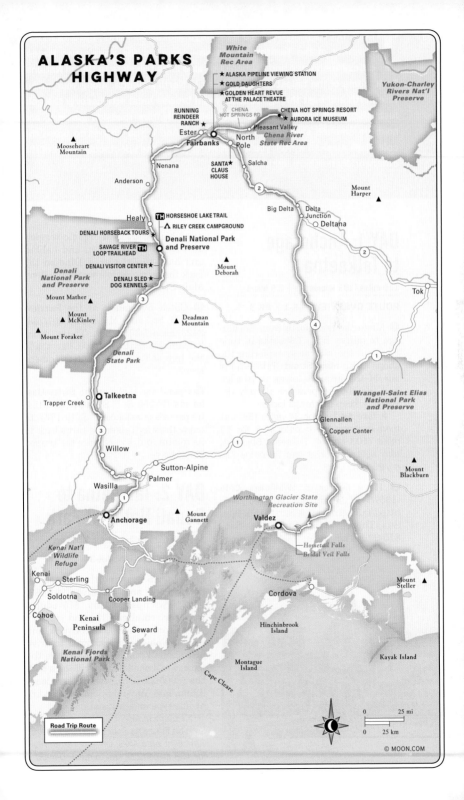

he Parks Highway—named for George Alexander Parks, the 1925-1933 governor of the Territory of Alaska—connects the state's two largest cities, Anchorage and Fairbanks. It also links travelers to Denali National Park, home of the tallest mountain peak in North America. Along your adventure north and east through Alaska, you'll browse local art, discover the gold rush history of Fairbanks, see waterfalls gush from roadside glaciers, and nosh on smoked salmon and wild seafood. And if you choose to brave the cold, dark Alaskan winter, you'll be rewarded with the spectacular sight of the otherworldly northern lights.

DAY 1: Anchorage to Talkeetna

120 miles/193 kilometers | 2.5 hours

ROUTE OVERVIEW: AK-1 • AK-3

❶ Make the trek north from Anchorage to quirky little **Talkeetna** in time to spend the afternoon exploring the shops along **Main Street.** Talkeetna is one of the artsiest towns in Alaska, and the shopkeepers are fiercely devoted to keeping things local.

> Take AK-1 N for 34 miles (55 km), then continue north onto AK-3 for 64 miles (103 km). At Talkeetna Spur Rd., turn right and drive into Talkeetna (14 mi/23 km).

❷ Have dinner at **Wildflower Cafe** (13578 E. Main St., 907/733-2695, http://talkeetnasuites.com, 11am-9pm Sun.-Thurs., 11am-10pm Fri.-Sat., $15-30). The menu features salads piled high with local organic veggies, as well as fresh salmon and halibut and hand-tossed pizzas. Dine on the deck for prime people-watching along Main Street.

❸ Catch live music at the **Fairview Inn** (D St. and Main St., 907/733-2423, noon-1:30am Sun.-Thurs., noon-2:30am Fri.-Sat.), a dive bar that's the hub of Talkeetna's entertainment scene.

❹ Spend the night at the **Swiss-Alaska Inn** (22056 S. F St., 907/733-2424, http://swissalaska.com, $119-170) to enjoy the way Talkeetna turns back to its quaint, quirky self once the tourist buses leave.

DAY 2: Talkeetna to Denali National Park

155 miles/250 kilometers | 3.5 hours

ROUTE OVERVIEW: AK-3

❶ Drive 2.5 hours north to **Denali National Park and Preserve** (907/683-9532, www.nps.gov/dena, $15 adults, free for children 15 and under). There's only one road in the park, and private vehicles are allowed to drive just a small part of it. To explore the park, you'll need to get a ride on a **park bus** (800/622-7275, www.reservedenali.com, late May-mid-Sept., rates vary by bus type and destination).

> Return to AK-3 by going south out of town on Talkeetna Spur Rd. (14 mi/23 km). Turn right onto AK-3. Drive north on AK-3 for 138 miles (222 km) to reach Denali.

MAIN STREET, TALKEETNA

Top ③ ALASKA'S PARKS HIGHWAY

① Explore the remote expanse of **Denali National Park and Preserve** (PAGE 666).

② Walk among a herd of reindeer at **Running Reindeer Ranch** (PAGE 670).

③ Witness the centuries-old beauty of glaciers at **Worthington Glacier State Recreation Site** (PAGE 672).

DENALI NATIONAL PARK VISITORS CENTER

❷ Acquaint yourself with the park (and pay your entrance fee) by stopping at the **Denali Visitor Center** (Mile 1.5 Park Rd., 8am-6pm daily mid-May-mid-Sept.). The visitors center has many ranger-led activities, an Alaska Geographic bookstore and gift shop, a luggage check, the only restaurant in the park, and beautiful exhibits showcasing Denali's landscapes, wildlife, and natural history.

❸ Denali is the only national park with working sled dogs. Visit the **sled dog kennels** (off Denali Park Rd., 9am-4:30pm daily mid-May-mid-Sept.) to get a free 30-minute tour and watch a fun demonstration with the dogs. Parking is very limited, so plan to walk 1.5 miles (2.4 km) or take a shuttle from the Denali Visitor Center.

❹ From the visitors center, you're close to the **Horseshoe Lake Trail** (3.2 mi/5 km loop, 1.5 hours, easy-moderate).

To get to the trailhead from the visitors center, walk along the bike path or Taiga Trail. Keep an eye on the lake and you might spot a beaver or moose.

❺ Camp right in the park at **Riley Creek Campground** (Mile 0.5 Park Rd., 907/683-9532, year-round, $15-30). It offers both tent and RV sites. It's close to the park entrance and a trail connects it to the Denali Visitor Center.

DAY 3: Denali National Park

25 miles/40 kilometers | 1 hour

ROUTE OVERVIEW: AK-3

❶ Hop on a bus to venture down the park road. Make sure you have your binoculars and camera ready for great

VIEW OF DENALI

SAVAGE RIVER LOOP

wildlife and landscape photo ops. Hike the mostly level **Savage River Loop** (1.7 mi/2.7 km round-trip, 1 hour, easy), which starts from the Savage River Day Use Area.

2 To cover more ground, join a horseback riding tour with **Denali Horseback Tours** (907/322-3886, http://denalihorsebacktours.com, $110-265). Located in Healy, this is the closest outfitter to the park. They offer one-, two-, and four-hour rides in small groups and can accommodate most experience levels, from "never ridden" to "bona fide horse person." After booking, you'll be sent detailed driving directions to the tour starting point.

> *Healy is 12 miles (19 km) north of the park entrance via AK-3.*

3 Jump just outside the park to have dinner at **Alpenglow** (Mile 238 Parks Hwy./AK-3, 855/683-8600, www.denalialaska.com, 5am-3pm and 5pm-9pm daily, $40), the restaurant in the Grande Denali Lodge. This is the best fine dining in the area, specializing in freshly caught wild seafood. Head back to your campsite and turn in.

> *From the park, go north on AK-3 for 1 mile (1.6 km). Follow Grande Dr. for 1 mile (1.6 km) to reach the restaurant.*

DAY 4: Denali to Fairbanks

160 miles/260 kilometers | 4 hours

ROUTE OVERVIEW: AK-3 • surface streets • AK-2 • surface streets

1 Continue north to **Fairbanks.** Stop by **Gold Daughters** (1671 Steese Hwy./AK-2, 907/347-4749, http://golddaughters.com, 10am-6pm daily Memorial Day-mid-Sept., $20 pp) to try your hand at Fairbanks's most authentic gold-panning experience. You'll scoop panfuls of the real deal: pay dirt that's hauled here by a mining company. When you want a break, explore the largest collection of historical mining artifacts in the state in the outdoor mining museum or browse the rustic gift shop.

> *Take AK-3 N for 117 miles (188 km) to reach Fairbanks. Take the exit for Geist Rd./Chena Pump Rd. and turn left. After 1.5 miles (2.5 km) Geist Rd. turns into Johansen Expy. Continue for 4 miles (6 km), then turn left to join AK-2. Continue for 6.5 miles (10.5 km) to reach Gold Daughters.*

SAVAGE RIVER IN THE FALL

➋ Visit the **Pipeline Viewing Station** (Mile 8 Steese Hwy./AK-2, 24 hours daily, free), which is just across the highway from Gold Daughters, for an up-close-and-personal view of one of the state's most impressive engineering accomplishments. There's no charge, no staff, and no entrance gate; you can walk right up to the pipeline and its H-shaped support/cooling stanchions, which help keep the permafrost underneath frozen and create a safe surface the pipeline can slide around on in case of an earthquake.

➌ Spend a couple of hours on a nature walk among a herd of reindeer at **Running Reindeer Ranch** (907/455-4998, http://runningreindeer.com, $70-100 adults, $40 children 4-12). It's an eye-opening, magical experience; there's something surreal about seeing a herd go leaping through the forest or walking placidly within arm's reach.

> Follow AK-2 W for 1 mile (1.6 km), then turn left onto Goldstream Rd. Follow this for 11 miles (18 km). Turn right onto Murphy Dome Rd., then make another right onto Ivans Alley, driving for less than a mile to reach the ranch.

➍ Drop your bags at the **Wedgewood Resort** (212 Wedgewood Dr., 800/528-4916, www.fountainheadhotels.com, from $165), where you'll be spending the next two nights. The property is on a large swath of land and is close to a migratory waterfowl refuge.

> Retrace your path to Goldstream Rd., then turn right onto Sheep Creek Rd.

and continue for 5 miles (8 km). This road will become Tanana Dr., Alumni Dr., and then College Rd. as you continue east for 2 miles (3 km) back into central Fairbanks. The resort is accessible from College Rd.

➎ Cap off the evening at the hilarious **Golden Heart Revue dinner show** (2300 Airport Way, 907/452-7274, www.akvisit.com, 8:15pm daily mid-May-Sept., $25 adults, $13 children) in the Palace Theatre at Pioneer Park Plaza. This musical comedy is a polished, locally written send-up of Fairbanks's history and the eternal question: Why would anybody want to live here?

DAY 5: Day Trip to Chena Hot Springs

125 miles/201 kilometers | 3 hours

ROUTE OVERVIEW: AK-2 • Chena Hot Springs Rd. • AK-2

➊ Have breakfast at **The Crepery** (523 2nd Ave., 907/450-9192, 7am-7pm Mon.-Fri., 9am-6pm Sat., 11am-5pm Sun.), a hole-in-the-wall serving excellent savory and sweet crepes.

➋ Hit the road for **Chena Hot Springs Resort** (Mile 56.5 Chena Hot Springs Rd., 907/451-8104, http://chenahotsprings.com). This luxurious resort is powered by geothermal hot springs. Here, you'll have plenty of time to lounge in the adults-only **hot springs rock pool** (age 18 and over, day pass $15). Visit the on-site **ice museum**

CHENA HOT SPRINGS RESORT

The enchanting phenomenon known as the northern lights, or aurora borealis, is caused by charged particles from the sun striking Earth's atmosphere. The lights are unpredictable and only visible when skies are dark and clear (**October through April** are the best months), so there's no guarantee you'll see them while you're here—but if you take three or four days and use the following tips, you'll have great odds.

- **Plan your visit in Fairbanks.** It's at a high enough latitude to see the lights overhead. You might still see the lights in more southerly parts of Alaska, but they're more likely to shine low on the horizon and may even be blocked by mountains.

- **Get as far away as you can from the city lights and any other light pollution.** The darker the sky, the clearer your view of the lights will be. **Chena Hot Springs** (Mile 56.5 Chena Hot Springs Rd., 907/451-8104, http://chenahotsprings.com) is a good place for viewing the northern lights. It's 60 miles out of town and offers heated viewing areas where you can watch for the lights all night long.

- **Ask for a wake-up call.** Most hotels under the "aurora oval" (the latitude at which the aurora shines overhead) will happily let you know if the aurora comes out. You can also check the University of Alaska Fairbanks Geophysical Institute's aurora forecast at www.gi.alaska.edu/auroraforecast.

- **Be patient.** The northern lights don't shine every night, but if you spend three nights under the aurora oval—when it's dark enough to see them, and you're actively looking for them—you have at least an 80 percent chance of seeing them.

NORTHERN LIGHTS

Want to take a great photo of the northern lights? Set your camera to the longest exposure possible, choose an object to be silhouetted in the foreground (it adds interest), and use a tripod. Bonus points if you have a remote shutter release or can set the shutter to a two- or three-second delay, so the motion of your pushing the button doesn't blur the image.

($15 adults, $10 children 6-11), a spectacular building carved from ice by husband-and-wife world champion ice carvers, Steve and Heather Brice.

> *Follow AK-2 W for 3 miles (5 km). Take the exit for Chena Hot Springs Rd. Turn right and drive 56 miles (90 km) to the resort.*

❸ Drive back to Fairbanks in time for a late dinner at the casual **Brewster's Northgate** (354 Old Steese Hwy./AK-2, 907/374-9663, 11am-10pm Sun.-Thurs., 11am-11pm Fri.-Sat., $11-20). It's a bar, it's a pub, it's a brewery—and it's the home of excellent halibut-and-chips.

> *Retrace your path by heading west on Chena Hot Springs Rd. for 56 miles (90 km), then taking AK-2 E for 3 miles (5 km) back into Fairbanks.*

DAY 6: Fairbanks to Valdez

365 miles/590 kilometers | 7 hours

ROUTE OVERVIEW: AK-2 • AK-4

1 In the morning, get an early and delicious start with an enormous cinnamon roll from **The Cookie Jar** (1006 Cadillac Ct., 907/479-8319, http://cookiejarfairbanks.com, 6:30am-8pm Mon.-Sat., 8am-3pm Sun., $7-29). They also serve diner-style food if you want a more balanced breakfast.

2 Head east from Fairbanks to visit the gleefully kitschy **Santa Claus House** (101 St. Nicholas Dr., 907/488-2200 or 800/588-4078, www.santaclaushouse.com, 9am-8pm mid-May-mid-Sept., shorter hours mid-Sept.-mid-May) in **North Pole, Alaska,** where it's all Christmas, all the time.

> Drive east on AK-2 for 13 miles (21 km) to North Pole and the Santa Claus House.

3 You've got a long drive to Valdez ahead of you. Along the route, you'll come across the beautiful **Worthington Glacier State Recreation Site** (Mile 28.7 Richardson Hwy./AK-4), which showcases one of the most spectacular roadside glaciers in Alaska. Take an hour to do a short, paved hike to a viewing platform with pedestal binoculars, where you can watch waterfalls gushing out of the glacier and down granite walls.

> Continue east on AK-2 for 81 miles (130 km) to AK-4. Make a slight right onto

BRIDAL VEIL FALLS

AK-4 and venture south for 235 miles (380 km) to Worthington Glacier State Recreation Site.

4 As you near **Valdez,** stop to marvel at **Bridal Veil Falls** (Mile 14 Richardson Hwy./AK-4) and **Horsetail Falls** (Mile 13.5 Richardson Hwy./AK-4), two of the most beautiful waterfalls in Alaska, right off a paved road.

> Continue south on AK-4 for 15 miles (24 km) to reach the waterfalls.

5 Once you arrive in town, you'll likely be ready for a hearty dinner. You can't possibly do better than **The Fat Mermaid** (143 N. Harbor Dr., 907/835-3000, www.thefatmermaid.com, 7am-11:30pm daily summer, reduced winter hours, $18-33). The pizzas are stellar and creative—don't miss the smoked salmon—and the salads are enormous.

> Continue following AK-4 for another 17 miles (27 km) into Valdez.

Getting There

AIR

The easiest way to reach Anchorage is by air. **Ted Stevens Anchorage International Airport** (ANC, 5000 W. International Airport Rd., www.dot.state.

WORTHINGTON GLACIER STATE RECREATION SITE

ak.us) receives year-round service from Alaska Airlines, Delta, United, and Iceland Air, with seasonal service from an ever-expanding list of airlines that includes JetBlue, Lufthansa, and Condor. That said, Alaska Airlines has the most flights here far and away, including nonstop options from Seattle, Portland, Chicago, Phoenix, Los Angeles, and sometimes Salt Lake City. If you're coming from another Alaska community, both **Alaska Airlines** (800/252-7522, www.alaskaair.com) and **Ravn Air Group** (907/266-8394 or 800/866-8394, www.flyravn.com) have extensive intrastate flight networks.

TRAIN

Alaska Railroad passenger trains (800/544-0552, alaskarailroad.com) are not connected to lines from Canada or the Lower 48. However, if you're starting out from the Alaska communities of Seward, Whittier, Talkeetna, or Fairbanks, the train is a great way to get to Anchorage, and vice versa. The train is slower than driving, but offers occasional glimpses of wild scenery you won't see from the car.

CAR

It's possible to drive the beautiful Alaska-Canada, or Alcan, Highway—1,390 miles of mind-blowing scenery and wildlife sightings—through Canada to Anchorage. Most people take at least a week to make the drive. If you don't want to drive both directions, you can always take the ferry back to Washington or Canada. Just book your ferry ticket early, because vehicle slots fill up very quickly.

From the **Anchorage airport** to Talkeetna—the first stop on the itinerary—it's 2.5 hours (120 mi/193 km). Take AK-1, then continue north onto AK-3. At Talkeetna Spur Road, turn right and follow it to Talkeetna.

Getting Back

The 298-mile (480-km) drive from Valdez back to **Anchorage** takes about 5.5 hours. Head north on AK-4 to AK-1. Turn left onto AK-1 and follow it south to Anchorage.

▶ Playlist

ALASKA'S PARKS HIGHWAY

SONGS

• **"Run Red" by Young Fangs:** This song embodies an Alaskan adventure: It's a little wild, a little serious, and it's big and wide and open. The guitars shimmer, the melody hooks, and the backbeat keeps everything in line. If you get a chance to see this Fairbanks indie band live, do it.

• **"Alaska" by Dr. Dog:** The city of Philadelphia—where this rock group hails from—sits about as far from Alaska as you can get in the Lower 48. And yet, the mysterious draw of Alaska's remote lands inspired the lyrics for this song.

PODCASTS

• *The Homer Alaska Podcast:* Weekly episodes feature interviews with locals in Homer, Alaska. Story topics range from homesteading and fishing to food and family heritage.

CONNECT WITH

• At Anchorage: **The Kenai Peninsula** (PAGE 674)

THE KENAI PENINSULA

WHY GO: Boat tours, glacier cruises, float trips, Native American history and culture, fishing, mountain hikes, backcountry wilderness, homestead cabins, wildlife, stargazing, volcanoes

TOTAL DISTANCE: 665 miles/ 1,075 kilometers

NUMBER OF DAYS: 10

SEASONS: Summer through early fall

START/END: Anchorage, Alaska

▼ PORTAGE GLACIER

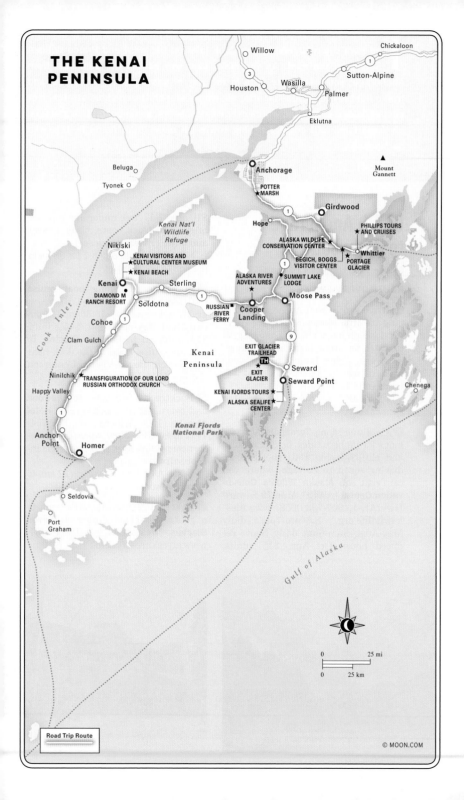

THE KENAI PENINSULA

Chickaloon

Willow

Sutton-Alpine

Houston

Wasilla

Palmer

Eklutna

Beluga

Tyonek

Anchorage

Mount Gannett

POTTER MARSH ★

Girdwood

Hope

PHILLIPS TOURS AND CRUISES ★

Nikiski

ALASKA WILDLIFE CONSERVATION CENTER ★

KENAI VISITORS AND CULTURAL CENTER MUSEUM ★

BEGICH, BOGGS VISITOR CENTER ★

Whittier

★ KENAI BEACH

PORTAGE GLACIER ★

Kenai

Sterling

ALASKA RIVER ADVENTURES ★

SUMMIT LAKE LODGE ★

DIAMOND M RANCH RESORT ■

Soldotna

RUSSIAN RIVER FERRY ■

Moose Pass

Cohoe

Cooper Landing

Clam Gulch

Kenai Peninsula

EXIT GLACIER TRAILHEAD

Ninilchik

TH

Seward

TRANSFIGURATION OF OUR LORD RUSSIAN ORTHODOX CHURCH ★

EXIT GLACIER ★

Seward Point

Happy Valley

KENAI FJORDS TOURS ★

Chenega

ALASKA SEALIFE CENTER ★

Anchor Point

Homer

Kenai Fjords National Park

Seldovia

Port Graham

Gulf of Alaska

Kenai Nat'l Wildlife Refuge

Cook Inlet

0   25 mi

0   25 km

Road Trip Route

© MOON.COM

The Kenai Peninsula extends 150 miles (240 km) across, and is separated from the mainland by the Cook Inlet on the west and Prince William Sound on the east. As you make your way across the peninsula from Anchorage, you'll see very little in the way of gas stations, billboards, and traffic lights. This is Alaska, after all, where star-cluttered skies stretch over mist-shrouded peaks and watch over whales, bears, and moose. Blue glaciers, icy waterfalls, and coastal fishing towns all make their home in this wild backcountry.

DAY 1: Anchorage to Girdwood

65 miles/105 kilometers | 2 hours

ROUTE OVERVIEW: AK-1

❶ Drive south from Anchorage, stopping at **Potter Marsh** (off Seward Hwy./AK-1, no phone, www.adfg.alaska.gov) to watch for arctic terns and trumpeter swans. Bring binoculars for your walk along the boardwalk that extends into the marsh.

> Take AK-1 S for 6 miles (10 km) to Potter Marsh.

❷ Continue along **Turnagain Arm,** famous for its bore tides, beluga whales, and cliff-traipsing Dall sheep. Keep driving south to **Portage,** where you can visit the **Alaska Wildlife Conservation Center** (AWCC, Mile 79 Seward Hwy./AK-1, 907/783-0058, www.alaskawildlife.org, 8:30am-7pm daily May-Aug., 9am-6pm daily Sept., reduced hours Oct.-Apr., $15 adults,

$10 ages 7-17, free under age 7) to see brown and black bears, bison, moose, and other critters up close.

> Continue south on AK-1 for 38 miles (61 km) to reach Portage.

❸ Take an hour-long **boat cruise** (907/783-3117 or 888/425-1737, www.graylinealaska.com, 10:30am-4:30pm daily mid-May-mid-Sept., $45 adults, $25 children) to **Portage Glacier.** To join the cruise, head to the dock near the Begich, Boggs Visitor Center on Portage Lake Loop.

❹ Backtrack a few miles to **Girdwood** and overnight at the luxurious **Hotel Alyeska** (1000 Arlberg Ave., 907/754-1111 or 800/880-3880, www.alyeskaresort.com, $359-399). Don't miss the indoor saltwater pool.

> Take AK-1 N for 11 miles (18 km) to reach Girdwood.

❺ Take the Alyeska Resort's tram to a gourmet seafood dinner at **Seven Glaciers Restaurant** (907/754-2237, www.alyeskaresort.com, 5pm-10pm

TURNAGAIN ARM

HOTEL ALYESKA

Top ⑤ THE KENAI PENINSULA

① Sip a glacier-ice cocktail aboard a glacier cruise with **Phillips Tours and Cruises** near Whittier (PAGE 678).

② Brave the steep climb up to the 150-foot face of **Exit Glacier** (PAGE 679).

③ Spot marine wildlife on a boat trip with **Kenai Fjords Tours** (PAGE 680).

④ Dine on halibut fish-and-chips at the old-school **Thorn's Showcase** in Seward (PAGE 680).

⑤ Join a deep-sea fishing charter in **Homer,** the halibut fishing capital of the world (PAGE 686).

daily mid-May-late Sept., noon-3pm and 4pm-9:30pm daily late Nov.-mid-Apr., $42-59), high above Turnagain Arm. Sitting on a crag at 2,303 feet above sea level, you'll have one of the finest views you're ever likely to get while dining. Reservations are required.

DAY 2: Girdwood to Moose Pass

80 miles/129 kilometers | 2.5 hours

ROUTE OVERVIEW: AK-1 • Portage Glacier Rd. • AK-1 • AK-9

❶ Return to **Portage** and pass through the 2.5-mile tunnel to the little town of **Whittier,** a popular port for cruise ships and day tours. Join a boat tour to the spectacular glaciers of western Prince William Sound with **Phillips Tours and Cruises** (907/276-8023, www.26glaciers.com). On the five-hour 26-Glacier Cruise ($159 adults, $99 children

GLACIER IN PRINCE WILLIAM SOUND

2-11), you'll get plenty of time to linger at several actively calving glaciers. A hot lunch is included, there's a bar on board (glacier-ice margaritas!), and the lounges provide plenty of room inside should the weather be less than perfect.

> Take AK-1 S for 11 miles (18 km), then turn left onto Portage Glacier Rd. Continue for 11 miles (18 km) to reach Whittier.

❷ Double back through the tunnel and head south, stopping for a pleasant dinner at **Summit Lake Lodge** (Mile 46, Seward Hwy./AK-1, 907/244-2031, www.summitlakelodge.com, 11am-8pm Mon.-Thurs., 11am-9pm Fri.-Sun., $22-32). Save room for the memorable Fruit of the Forest pie à la mode.

WHITTIER HARBOR

> *Retrace your path back to AK-1 by heading west on Portage Glacier Rd. for 11 miles (18 km). Take AK-1 S for 33 miles (53 km) to reach the lodge.*

❸ Overnight at **Inn at Tern Lake** (Mile 36, Seward Hwy./AK-1, 907/288-3667, www.ternlakeinn.com, $200-225), a large and exquisite B&B near **Moose Pass.**

> *Continue south on AK-1 for another 8 miles (13 km), then keep left to follow AK-9 for 1.5 miles (2.5 km) to reach the inn.*

DAY 3: Moose Pass to Seward

60 miles/97 kilometers | 2 hours

ROUTE OVERVIEW: AK-9 • Exit Glacier Rd. • AK-9

❶ Once you arrive in the town of **Seward,** get a latte and check out the artwork at **Resurrect Art Coffeehouse Gallery** (320 3rd Ave., 907/224-7161, www.resurrectart.com, 7am-6pm daily summer, 7am-5pm daily winter).

> *Head south on AK-9 for 35 miles (56 km), through Moose Pass, to reach Seward.*

❷ Make the quick trek north to **Exit Glacier.** In an hour or two you can explore the country around this fast-retreating glacier. A short **nature trail** (1 mi/1.6 km round-trip, 30 minutes,

⏱ **WITH LESS TIME**

ANCHORAGE TO SEWARD

4 days; 201 miles/323 kilometers

Take **four days** to drive from Anchorage through **Portage** and **Moose Pass** to Seward. This affords you astonishing views of the Alaskan landscape and plenty of opportunities for wildlife encounters, specifically at the **Alaska Wildlife Conservation Center** and the **Alaska SeaLife Center.** You'll have enough time to enjoy a **glacier cruise** or a **glacier hike,** as well as dining on fresh halibut.

easy) provides a quiet forest walk. Two paths break off from it: **Glacier's Edge Trail** climbs a steep 0.25 mile up to the 150-foot face of Exit Glacier; a second path, **Toe of the Glacier Trail,** crosses the rocky outwash plain where you'll probably need to wade an icy-cold creek or two (use caution) to reach the end of the glacier. Don't get too close, since the glacier can calve without warning. Note that cell phones will not work in the Exit Glacier area.

> *Take AK-9 N for 4 miles (6 km), then turn left onto Herman Leirer Rd. After 1 mile (1.6 km), the road becomes Exit Glacier Rd. Continue for 8 miles (13 km) to reach the parking lot for the trailhead.*

EXIT GLACIER

③ Back in Seward, reward yourself with a farm-to-table dinner at **The Cookery** (209 5th Ave., 907/422-7459, www.cookeryseward.com, 5pm-10pm daily mid-May-early Sept., reduced hours early Sept.-mid-May, $12-27). Save room for cream cheese ice cream with fresh strawberries.

> Retrace your path back to Seward via Exit Glacier Rd. and AK-9 S (13 mi/21 km).

④ Check in to one of the two rooms at **Alaska Paddle Inn** (13745 Beach Dr., 907/362-2628, www.alaskapaddleinn.com, Mar.-Oct., $199), just south of town on Lowell Point. Both units include kitchenettes stocked with breakfast ingredients, gas fireplaces, and private baths. There's a two-night minimum here.

> Follow Lowell Point Rd. south for 2 miles (3 km) to reach the inn.

DAY 4: Seward

MORNING AND AFTERNOON

① Take a half-day wildlife boat tour with **Kenai Fjords Tours** (907/224-8068 or 888/478-3346, www.alaskacollection.com, mid-Mar.-early Oct., $109 adults, $55 children) around **Resurrection Bay.** This is *the* cruise for seeing marine wildlife. On a good day, you can spot humpbacks and orcas, plus porpoises, seals, sea otters, sea lions, hundreds of puffins, kittiwakes, auklets, and the occasional bald eagle and oystercatcher.

② In the late afternoon, visit Seward's **Alaska SeaLife Center** (301 Railway Ave., 907/224-6300 or 888/378-2525, www.alaskasealife.org, 9am-9pm daily mid-May-late Aug., shorter hours late Aug.-mid-May, $25 over age 12, $13 ages 4-12, free under age 4), where enormous tanks house puffins, seals, and playful sea lions.

EVENING

③ Enjoy a "bucket of butt" (halibut, that is) at **Thorn's Showcase Lounge** (208 4th Ave., 907/224-3700, 10am-11pm Sun.-Thurs., 10am-midnight Fri.-Sat., $13-36). This old bar serves the best fish-and-chips in town. It's hard to miss the lounge's remarkable collection of 525 historic Jim Beam bottles covering the walls; it's said to be one of the largest in existence. Head back to Alaska Paddle Inn for the night.

ALASKA SEALIFE CENTER

VIEW FROM KINGFISHER ROADHOUSE

DAY 5: Seward to Cooper Landing

50 miles/81 kilometers | 1.5 hours

ROUTE OVERVIEW: AK-9 • AK-1

① Today, visit the tiny settlement of **Cooper Landing** along the Kenai River. Take the day to relax with a float trip on the Kenai River with **Alaska River Adventures** (Mile 48, Sterling Hwy./AK-1, 907/595-2000, www.alaskariveradventures.com, May-Sept., $55-65 adults, $30-45 children).

> Take AK-9 N for 36 miles (58 km) to AK-1. Turn left and follow AK-1 for 12 miles (19 km) to Cooper Landing.

② For dinner, enjoy a delicious Alaskan meal in a rustic setting at **Kingfisher Roadhouse** (Mile 47, Sterling Hwy./AK-1, 907/595-2861, www.kingfisheralaska.com, 5pm-10:30pm daily late May-mid-Oct., $16-36).

③ Settle in for an angelic night at **Alaska Heavenly Lodge** (Mile 49, Sterling Hwy./AK-1, 907/595-2012 or 866/595-2012, www.alaskaheavenly.com, $196). This homey lodge overlooks the Kenai River and surrounding mountains.

DAY 6: Cooper Landing to Kenai

65 miles/105 kilometers | 2.5 hours

ROUTE OVERVIEW: AK-1 • Skilak Lake Loop Rd. • AK-1 • Kenai Spur Hwy.

① Along the Sterling Highway, stop at Mile 55 to ride the self-propelled **Russian River Ferry** (Mile 55, Sterling Hwy., 907/522-8368, www.alaskarm.com, $11 adults, $6 children) across the river where salmon anglers stand shoulder to shoulder for "combat fishing" during the peak of the sockeye run. If you want to try your hand, you'll need hip waders, and you can only use flies, not lures. Local fishing shops have the correct flies and often rent out rods and boots.

> Go west on AK-1 for 6 miles (10 km) to reach the ferry landing.

② Take the scenic route from here by turning onto **Skilak Lake Loop Road**. This pretty dirt road crosses the

KENAI NATIONAL WILDLIFE REFUGE

heart of **Kenai National Wildlife Refuge** (907/262-7021 or 877/285-5628, http://kenai.fws.gov). Take one of the many hikes scattered throughout the refuge. The **Bear Mountain Trail** (1 mi/1.6 km round-trip, 30 minutes, easy) is a short hike with dramatic views from a rocky promontory.

> Continue west on AK-1 for 4 miles (6 km), then turn left onto Skilak Lake Loop Rd. Continue for 5 miles (8 km) to reach the trailhead.

❸ Back on the Sterling Highway, continue west to **Soldotna.** At the **Kenai Spur Highway** junction, turn north and head to the small city of **Kenai.** Order fish tacos at the festive and colorful **Playa-Azul Mexican Restaurant** (12498 Kenai Spur Hwy., 907/283-2010, 11am-9pm daily, $14-16).

> Follow Skilak Lake Loop Rd. west for another 14 miles (23 km). Go west on AK-1 for 18 miles (29 km) to reach Soldotna. Take the Kenai Spur Hwy. northwest for 11 miles (18 km) to reach Kenai.

❹ Spend the night a few miles south of Kenai at the **Diamond M Ranch Resort** (48500 Diamond M Ranch Rd., 907/283-9424, www.diamondmranchresort.com, tents $65, RVs $70-95, rooms and cabins $85-209), a full-service resort with lodging options that range from tent camping to B&B rooms to an authentic homestead cabin with a sod roof and outhouse.

> Follow Bridge Access Rd. south for 3 miles (5 km), then turn left on Kalifornsky Beach Road. In less than a mile, follow signs for the ranch.

DAY 7: Kenai to Homer

85 miles/137 kilometers | 2.5 hours

ROUTE OVERVIEW: Kalifornsky Beach Rd. • AK-1

❶ In the morning, visit the **Kenai Visitors and Cultural Center Museum** (11471 Kenai Spur Rd., 907/283-1991, www.kenaichamber.org, 9am-6pm Mon.-Fri., 10am-5pm Sat., noon-5pm Sun. late May-early Sept., shorter hours early Sept.-late May, free). This museum and visitors center houses cultural artifacts from Kenaitze Native peoples, an amazing collection of

TRANSFIGURATION OF OUR LORD RUSSIAN ORTHODOX CHURCH, NINILCHIK

walrus ivory, and art exhibits. The centerpiece is an enormous scale model of a Cook Inlet oil production platform.

❷ Wander over to **Kenai Beach** (end of Spruce St.) at the mouth of the Kenai River; it's one of the best and most easily accessible beaches in Alaska. In July you'll see hundreds of **dipnetters** catching salmon from the riverbanks. Dipnetting is only open to Alaskan residents, but makes a great spectator sport for all. Special nets with 15-foot metal handles are used to catch fish as they head upriver to spawn.

❸ Drive south from Kenai to **Kasilof.** As you're driving, look across the inlet for views of snowy mountains and active volcanoes. A short distance south of Kasilof is **Ninilchik,** home to the **Transfiguration of Our Lord Russian Orthodox Church** (Orthodox Ave., off Sterling Hwy./AK-1), located on a hilltop facing the volcanic summit of Mount Iliamna.

> Take Kalifornsky Beach Rd. south for 15 miles (24 km) to Kasilof. Continue south on Kalifornsky Beach Rd. for 1 mile (1.6 km) to AK-1. Drive south for 25 miles (40 km) on AK-1 to Ninilchik.

❹ Continue south to the small city of **Homer,** where the Sterling Highway ends. Stop at the big hilltop overlook just before you reach town for an all-encompassing vista across Kachemak Bay. Check into the **Driftwood Inn** (135 W. Bunnell Ave., 907/235-8019, www.thedriftwoodinn.com, $119-155 shared bath, $124-199 private bath), where you'll be spending the next three nights. The historic main building has a common room with a stone fireplace, comfortable chairs for relaxing, and inexpensive breakfast and snack items.

> *Continue south on AK-1 to reach Homer (36 mi/58 km).*

5 Keep it laid-back with a casual dinner at **Captain Pattie's Fish House** (4241 Homer Spit Rd., 907/235-5135, www.captainpatties.com, 11am-9pm daily, $15-30). The seafood-centric menu features fresh bounty, such as Alaskan king crab, salmon, and local oysters, plus a nice roundup of Alaska-brewed beers.

STICKY BUNS AT TWO SISTERS BAKERY IN HOMER

DAY 8: Homer

MORNING

1 Have an enticing breakfast at **Two Sisters Bakery** (233 E. Bunnell Ave., 907/235-2280, www.twosisters-bakery.net, 7am-5pm Mon.-Tues., 7am-8:30pm Wed.-Sat., under $10), a

Homer institution that should not be missed. Two Sisters is always fragrant with the scent of fresh-baked pastries, daily breads, roasted veggie focaccia sandwiches, sticky buns, and ham and cheese savories from the wood-fired brick oven.

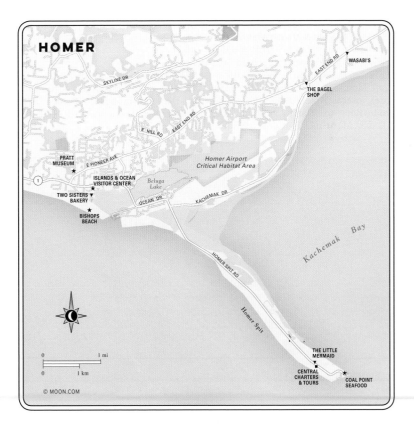

HOMER

© MOON.COM

BISHOPS BEACH IN HOMER

ANGLERS ON THE HOMER SPIT

2 Head down the street to **Bishops Beach** (off Beluga Ave.). This is a delightful spot for a low-tide walk, with extraordinary views of the mountains, volcanoes, and glaciers lining Kachemak Bay.

AFTERNOON

3 At the **Islands & Ocean Visitor Center** (95 Sterling Hwy., 907/235-6961, www.islandsandocean.org, 9am-5pm daily early May-early Sept., 10am-5pm Mon.-Sat. early Sept.-late May, free), interactive exhibits offer an introduction to the 4.9-million-acre Alaska Maritime National Wildlife

Refuge, some 2,500 islands, spires, and coastal headlands scattered from southeast Alaska to the Arctic. These remote islands comprise the largest seabird refuge in the United States, with millions of the birds nesting on rugged cliffs.

4 Explore the **Pratt Museum** (3779 Bartlett St., 907/235-8635, www.prattmuseum.org, 10am-6pm daily mid-May-mid-Sept., noon-5pm Tues.-Sat. mid-Sept.-Dec. and Feb.-mid-May, $10 adults, $5 ages 6-18, free under age 6), one of the finest small museums in Alaska, with interesting historical and cultural pieces, artwork, and wildlife displays.

EVENING

5 Homer's most-loved destination is the four-mile-long **Homer Spit.** This natural peninsula extends into Kachemak Bay, with a busy boat

HOMER SPIT

With millions of acres of wild country in all directions, it's easy to find great hikes in Anchorage and along the Kenai Peninsula.

ANCHORAGE

- **Flattop Mountain Trail** (3 mi/4.8 km round-trip, 1.5 hours, moderate) in Chugach State Park near Anchorage

- **Tony Knowles Coastal Trail** (11 mi/17.8 km one-way, 4.5 hours, easy) in downtown Anchorage

- **Turnagain Arm Trail** (9.5 mi/15.3 km one-way, 4 hours, moderate) in Chugach State Park south of Anchorage

- **Crow Pass Trail** (23 mi/37 km one-way, 9-10 hours, moderate-difficult) in Chugach State Park near Girdwood

- **Portage Pass Trail** (5.4 mi/8.7 km round-trip, 2.5 hours, moderate) in Chugach National Forest near Whittier

KENAI PENINSULA

- **Resurrection Pass Trail** (38 mi/61 km one-way, 2-3 days, moderate-difficult) in Chugach National Forest between Hope and Cooper Landing

- **Summit Creek Trail** (8 mi/12.9 km one-way, 3.5 hours, moderate) in Chugach National Forest near Summit Lake

- **Lost Lake Trail** (13.8 mi/22 km round-trip, 5.5 hours, moderate) in Chugach National Forest north of Seward

- **Skilak Lookout Trail** (5 mi/8 km round-trip, 2 hours, moderate) on Kenai National Wildlife Refuge near Cooper Landing

- **Glacier Spit Trail** (4 mi/6.4 km round-trip, 1.5 hours, easy) in Kachemak Bay State Park near Homer

- **Grace Ridge Trail** (8.3 mi/13.4 km round-trip, 5 hours, moderate-difficult) in Kachemak Bay State Park near Homer

GRACE RIDGE TRAIL

harbor and a cluster of shops, galleries, restaurants, campgrounds, and lodging at the end. Enjoy dinner on the Spit at the cozy and friendly **The Little Mermaid** (Homer Spit, 907/399-9900, www.littlemermaidhomer.com, 11:30am-9pm Thurs.-Tues. May-mid-Sept., $14-40, reservations required).

THE KENAI PENINSULA

SONGS

- **"Morning Song" by Jewel:** Better known for her radio-friendly hits, such as the '90s-era "Who Will Save Your Soul," it's Jewel Kilcher's quieter songs that pack an emotional punch. Simply arranged to allow her vocals to ring clear as a bell (the Homer-raised singer was trained as a yodeler), this song cuts through the cold Alaska air.

- **"Doors and Windows" by Bearfoot:** With their roots firmly planted in traditional bluegrass, this Anchorage band brings a modern sensibility to the genre. In this song, from the 2009 album of the same name, the band's trio of female vocalists weave a captivating tale with a bewitching melody.

PODCASTS

- **The Firn Line:** Created by an Anchorage man who once led guiding and climbing trips around the world, this podcast features interviews and stories about the adventures of mountain climbers.

The food is artful and fun, including a wonderful Montreal-inspired poutine with hand-cut fries, brown gravy, and white cheddar.

DAY 9: Homer

MORNING AND AFTERNOON

❶ Homer calls itself the Halibut Fishing Capital of the World. Sportfishing attracts droves of enthusiasts every day of the summer, not only for halibut but also for king and silver salmon. Join an early-morning halibut and salmon fishing charter through **Central Charters & Tours** (907/235-7847, www.centralcharter.com, half-day charters from $175 pp) to see what all the fuss is about. Wear warm, layered clothing, and don't forget rain gear and soft-soled shoes. Binoculars are a definite plus—seabirds, otters, and whales are often viewable.

❷ Once the trip is over, bring your catch over to **Coal Point Seafood** (4306 Homer Spit Rd., 907/235-3877 or 800/325-3877, www.welovefish.com). They will process, freeze, and ship your catch directly to your home.

EVENING

❸ For dinner, check out **Wasabi's** (59217 East End Rd., 907/226-3663, www.wasabisrestaurant.com, 5pm-10pm Wed.-Sun. late May-early Sept., 5pm-9pm Wed.-Sat. early Sept.-late May, $28-48) for Asian fusion cuisine. There's a good choice of fresh sushi (try the Tutka Bay roll with shrimp, avocado, and masago), along with fresh halibut, Thai coconut curry rockfish, Muscovy duck, and tempura prawns. Get a window seat for bay vistas.

DAY 10: Homer to Anchorage

260 miles/420 kilometers | 5.5 hours

ROUTE OVERVIEW: AK-1 • Hope Hwy. • AK-1

❶ It's a long drive back to Anchorage, but if you get going early enough, you can still have fun along the way. This will be a long day, so start with a best-in-Alaska bagel at **The Bagel Shop** (3745 East End Rd., 907/299-2099, www.thebagelshopalaska.com, 7am-4pm Tues.-Fri., 8am-4pm Sat.-Sun. Mar.-Aug. and Oct.-Jan., $3-14) before leaving town.

2 It takes around 1.5 hours to get to **Soldotna.** Browse the wares at **Dragonfly Gallery** (183 S. Soldotna Ave., 907/260-4636, www.chellinelarsen. com, 11am-6pm Tues.-Sat.), which displays silk scarves, quilted wall hangings, and prints by Chelline Larsen, plus the works of more than 20 other artists.

> *Drive north on AK-1 for 75 miles (121 km) to reach Soldotna.*

3 Drive northeast to the historic town of **Hope,** with its quaint log buildings. Stretch your legs by walking the dirt street down to the tidal flats. Note: The flats are dangerous, so don't walk on them. Have lunch at **Creekbend Café** (19842 Hope Hwy., 907/782-3274, www.creekbendco.com, 8am-4pm daily mid-May-mid-Sept., shorter hours mid-Sept.-mid-May, $10-17).

> *Continue north on AK-1 for 76 miles (122 km) to Hope Hwy. Turn left and head northwest for 17 miles (27 km) into the town of Hope.*

4 Finish the drive to Anchorage, grabbing dinner from one of the many spots downtown. Bed down for your last night in Alaska at the **Dimond Center Hotel** (700 E. Dimond Blvd., 907/770-5000 or 866/770-5002, www. dimondcenterhotel.com, $260). The luxurious rooms feature plush beds and big soaking tubs.

> *Retrace your path back to AK-1 by taking Hope Hwy. south for 17 miles (27 km). Turn left on AK-1 and drive for 70 miles (113 km) to Anchorage.*

Getting There

AIR

Almost everybody who flies into Alaska from the Lower 48 lands at **Ted Stevens Anchorage International Airport** (ANC, 907/266-2525, www.anchorageairport.com), 6 miles (10 km) southwest of downtown. Many of the big domestic carriers fly into and out

of Anchorage from the Lower 48, including Alaska Airlines, American, Delta, JetBlue, Sun Country Airlines, and United.

Several companies offer nonstop international service to Anchorage: **Air Canada** from Vancouver, **Condor** from Frankfurt, **Iceland Air** from Reykjavik, and **Yakutia Airlines** from Petropavlovsk-Kamchatsky in Russia. **Alaska Airlines** flies from destinations across Mexico, and even as far as Costa Rica.

The **People Mover bus 40** (907/343-6543, www.peoplemover.org, 7am-11pm Mon.-Fri., 9am-9pm Sat., 11am-7pm Sun., $2 adults, $1 ages 5-18 and seniors) runs from the airport's lower level and into downtown Anchorage. There's always a line of cabs ($20-25 to downtown) waiting out front as you exit the baggage claim area.

TRAIN

Anchorage is a major stop for the Alaska Railroad, with service north all the way to Fairbanks and south to Seward and Whittier. The **Alaska Railroad train depot** (411 W. 1st Ave., 907/265-2494 or 800/544-0552, www.alaskarailroad. com) is just down the hill from the center of Anchorage.

CAR

It's 11 miles (18 km) from the **Anchorage airport** to Potter Marsh, the first stop on the trip. Take AK-1 to reach Potter Marsh.

One essential for Alaskan drivers is *The Milepost,* a thick annual book that's packed with mile-by-mile descriptions for virtually every road within or to Alaska. The book is sold everywhere in Alaska and is easy to find in Lower 48 bookstores or online at www.themilepost.com.

For current road conditions, construction delays, and more, contact the **Alaska Department of Transportation** (dial 511 toll-free anywhere in Alaska or 907/465-8952, http://511. alaska.gov).

CONNECT WITH

• At Anchorage: **Alaska's Parks Highway** (PAGE 664)

O'AHU COASTAL LOOP

WHY GO: Pacific Rim cuisine, hula, surfing, snorkeling, Diamond Head, Waikiki beaches, Pearl Harbor, seaside villages, Polynesian culture, stunning sunsets, perfect weather

TOTAL DISTANCE: 145 miles/ 235 kilometers

NUMBER OF DAYS: 7

SEASONS: Year-round

START: Waikiki, O'ahu

END: Honolulu, O'ahu

▼ WAIKIKI BEACH AND DIAMOND HEAD

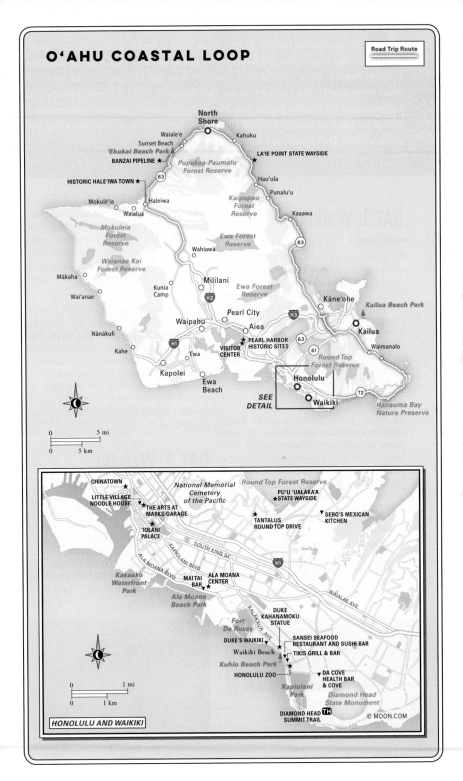

O'AHU COASTAL LOOP

Road Trip Route

North Shore

Waiale'e
Sunset Beach
Kahuku
'Ehukai Beach Park ★
BANZAI PIPELINE ★
LA'IE POINT STATE WAYSIDE ★

Pupukea-Paumalu
Forest Reserve

HISTORIC HALE'IWA TOWN ★

Haleiwa
Hau'ula
Punalu'u

83

Mokulē'ia
Kaipapau
Forest
Reserve

Waialua
Kaaawa

Mokuleia
Forest
Reserve

Ewa Forest
Reserve

Wahiawā
83

Waianae Kai
Forest Reserve

Mākaha

Mililani
Ewa Forest
Reserve

Kunia
Camp
H2

Kāne'ohe

Kailua Beach Park ▲

Wai'anae

Pearl City
H3

Waipahu
Kailua

Nānākuli
Aiea
63

Kahe
VISITOR
CENTER
PEARL HARBOR
HISTORIC SITES ✈
Waimanalo
61

Ewa
Round Top
Forest Reserve

Kapolei

Honolulu
72

Ewa
Beach
SEE
DETAIL
Waikiki

Hanauma Bay
Nature Preserve

0   5 mi
0   5 km

National Memorial
Cemetery
of the Pacific
Round Top Forest Reserve

CHINATOWN ★

LITTLE VILLAGE
NOODLE HOUSE ★
THE ARTS AT
MARKS GARAGE ★

PU'U 'UALAKA'A
★ STATE WAYSIDE

★ SERG'S MEXICAN
KITCHEN

'IOLANI
PALACE ★

★ TANTALUS
ROUND TOP DRIVE

SOUTH KING ST

KAPIOLANI BLVD

H1

ALA MOANA BLVD

WAIALAE AVE

Kakaako
Waterfront
Park

MAI TAI
BAR ★
ALA MOANA
CENTER ★

Ala Moana
Beach Park

KALAKAUA AVE

DUKE
KAHANAMOKU
STATUE ★

Fort
De Russy

DUKE'S WAIKIKI ▼
SANSEI SEAFOOD
RESTAURANT AND SUSHI BAR

Waikiki Beach
▼ TIKIS GRILL & BAR

Kuhio Beach Park
HONOLULU ZOO

DA COVE
▼ HEALTH BAR
& COVE

Kapiolani
Park
Diamond Head
State Monument

DIAMOND HEAD ⊤ℍ
SUMMIT TRAIL

© MOON.COM

HONOLULU AND WAIKIKI

0   1 mi
0   1 km

This meandering coastal drive takes you from the tourist-thronged sidewalks of Waikiki to the quiet towns of the North Shore, where sometimes the only sound is the pounding of the ocean's surf. You'll encounter tropical forests, local wildlife, historic sites, tree-covered parks, and, perhaps most importantly, the spirit of aloha, the Hawaiian word for love, peace, and compassion. No matter where you find yourself on this journey—whether it's dining on poke or toasting a mai tai—you're never far from the sparkling turquoise water that surrounds the island of O'ahu.

DAY 1: Waikiki

MORNING

❶ Spend your first day getting acquainted on foot with the surroundings right outside your hotel. Follow the self-guided **Historic Waikiki Trail** (http://waikiki.com), which covers fascinating historical, geological, and cultural sights with tidbits about Waikiki past and present. Along the way, stop at **Waikiki Beach** (from the Royal Hawaiian to the Moana Surfrider) for a swim.

AFTERNOON

❷ Stroll down Waikiki's main drag, **Kalakaua Avenue,** and check out the **Duke Kahanamoku Statue** (along Kalakaua Ave., by Kuhio Beach), where you can pay homage to the original ambassador of aloha, the man who grew up in Waikiki and brought the sport of surfing to the world.

EVENING

❸ Enjoy *pau hana* (happy hour) on the upstairs deck at the locally owned **Tiki's Grill & Bar** (Aston Waikiki Beach Hotel, 2570 Kalakaua Ave.,

808/923-8454, http://tikisgrill.com, 10:30am-2am daily). Catch Hawaiian Hula Nights every Thursday (5pm-11pm), featuring traditional and contemporary Hawaiian music, hula, and food and drink specials on the open lanai.

❹ After freshening up back at your hotel, head out for dinner at **Sansei Seafood Restaurant and Sushi Bar** (2552 Kalakaua Ave., 808/931-6286, www.sanseihawaii.com, 5:30pm-10pm Sun.-Thurs., 5:30pm-1am Fri.-Sat., from $8). With its handful of award-winning sushi creations, the à la carte menu is perfect for sampling the gamut.

DAY 2: Waikiki

MORNING

❶ Start the day by hiking the **Diamond Head Summit Trail** (1.6 mi/2.6 km round-trip, 1.5-2 hours, moderate) inside the Diamond Head crater, an extinct tuff cone volcano that erupted about 300,000 years ago. It's part of **Diamond Head State Monument** (www.hawaiistateparks.org, 6am-6pm

WAIKIKI BEACH

DIAMOND HEAD

Top 3 O'AHU COASTAL LOOP

1. Climb to the top of an **extinct volcano** on the **Diamond Head Summit Trail** (PAGE 690).

2. Surf the waves at **Canoes** in Waikiki (PAGE 692).

3. Sample the shave ice at **Matsumoto's** in **Hale'iwa** (PAGE 694).

daily, $5 per vehicle, $1 pedestrians, cash only). The historic trail, built in 1908, climbs 560 feet from the crater floor to the summit in just 0.8 miles (1.3 km). To reach the trailhead, follow Kalakaua Avenue to Monsarrat Avenue, then continue on Diamond Head Road.

AFTERNOON

❷ Have lunch at **da Cove Health Bar & Cove** (3045 Monsarrat Ave., 808/732-8744, www.diamondheadcove.com, 9am-8pm Mon. and Fri.-Sat., 9am-11pm Tues.-Thurs. and Sun., $5-13), a small juice and kava bar famous for its hearty and healthy acai bowls.

❸ Walk under the flowering canopy trees in the oldest public park in Hawai'i, **Kapi'olani Park,** to the **Honolulu Zoo** (151 Kapahulu Ave., 808/971-7171, www.honoluluzoo.org, 9am-4:30pm daily, $19 adults, $11 children 3-12). There you can see the animals of the African savannah, Asian and American tropical forests, and Pacific Islands.

EVENING

❹ For live music during happy hour, make your way to **Duke's Waikiki** (2335 Kalakaua Ave., 808/922-2268, www.dukeswaikiki.com, 7am-midnight daily, $15-33) and hang out in the **Barefoot Bar.** Request a table for dinner here and enjoy a beachside drink as you wait, watching the sun set over Waikiki Beach.

DAY 3: Waikiki

MORNING

❶ Spend the morning **surfing at Canoes** (in front of Duke Kahanamoku Statue, Kuhio Beach Park). No stay in

CANOES SURF BREAK

KUHIO BEACH PARK

Waikiki is complete without surfing, whether it's your first time getting your feet on the wax or you've been surfing your entire life. Become a part of the legacy.

AFTERNOON

❷ Relax at **Kuhio Beach Park** (from the Moana Surfrider to the concrete pier at the intersection of Kapahulu and Kalakaua Aves.), the thumping heart of Waikiki. It has a snack bar, two lagoons for sheltered swimming, grassy knolls for relaxing in the shade under a palm tree, and ample beach services.

EVENING

❸ Take a sunset **catamaran cruise** off the Waikiki coast for a fresh perspective. There are many options to choose from; the 44-foot *Maita'i* **Catamaran** (808/922-5665, www.leahi.com) is a good one, with the Sunset Mai Tai Sail ($39 adults, $19 children) departing at 5pm.

DAY 4: Waikiki to Kailua

25 miles/40 kilometers | 1.5 hours

ROUTE OVERVIEW: I-H-1 • HI-72

❶ Head to the windward shores, where there are a lot of ocean-related activities to consider. Start out by snorkeling **Hanauma Bay Nature Preserve** (7455 Kalanianaole Hwy./HI-72, 808/395-2211 or 808/396-4229, www.hanaumabaystatepark.com, 6am-7pm Wed.-Mon., $7.50 admission, $1 parking). The first marine protected area in the state of Hawai'i, this unique, circular bay lies within an extinct

HANAUMA BAY NATURE PRESERVE

volcanic cone, protected from wind and waves. Live coral reef, 400 species of fish, and endangered sea turtles call it home. You'll need to get there before 9am to find a parking spot.

> Go east on I-H-1 for 2.5 miles (4 km), then join HI-72. Continue east for 6 miles (10 km) to reach the preserve.

❷ Drive up to **Kailua** for a relaxing afternoon. Have a *kiawe* charcoal-broiled burger for a late lunch at **Buzz's Lanikai** (413 Kawailoa Rd., 808/261-4661, http://buzzssteakhouse.com, 11am-9:30pm daily, $19-44). Don't forget to order the signature mai tai, a mix of rum with a cherry on top.

> Get back on HI-72 and drive to Kailua Rd. (12 mi/19 km). The road will wind east and then curve north. Turn right on Kailua Rd. and drive into Kailua (2 mi/3 km).

❸ Cross the street and bask on the fine white sand of **Kailua Beach Park** (Kawailoa Rd.). There are outfitters within walking distance if you want to try stand-up paddling or kayaking.

❹ Stay the night at **Sheffield House Bed & Breakfast** (131 Kuulei Rd.,

808/262-0721, www.hawaiisheffield-house.com, $129-194), just steps away from Kailua Beach.

DAY 5: Kailua to North Shore

40 miles/64 kilometers | 2 hours

ROUTE OVERVIEW: HI-630 • HI-83

❶ It's time to head for the North Shore. Drive up Kamehameha Highway to **La'ie Point State Wayside** (eastern end of Naupaka St., no phone, http://hawaiistateparks.org). A dramatic offshore, wave-battered sea arch sits just off a rugged point jutting sharply out into the Pacific. It's a great place to pull up and enjoy a quiet lunch. There's a cliff-jumping spot on the south side—if you dare.

> Take HI-630 for 3 miles (5 km) to Kamehameha Hwy./HI-83, then head north for 23 miles (37 km) to Anemoku St. Turn right, then make another right on Naupaka St. to reach La'ie Point State Wayside.

❷ Continue north to **Kahuku Superette** (56-505 Kamehameha Hwy./HI-83, 808/293-9878, 6am-10pm daily) for some of the best *poke* on the island. The market also has alcohol and beverages, beach gear and fishing supplies, and a limited assortment of snacks and groceries.

> Continue north on HI-83 to Kahuku Superette (3 mi/5 km).

❸ Spend the rest of the afternoon at **'Ehukai Beach Park** (Kamehameha Hwy./HI-83, across from Sunset Beach Elementary School, 5am-10pm daily).

BEACH AT KAILUA

BANZAI PIPELINE AT 'EHUKAI BEACH PARK

Here you'll find the world-famous **Banzai Pipeline,** where expert surfers attempt to ride the barrel at one of the most dangerous breaks in the world. Swimming is great up and down the beach, which is lined with palms and shrubs offering midday shade. During the summer, the snorkeling is better on the Pipeline side of the park, where there is a wide shelf of reef, canyons, and caves to explore.

> Follow HI-83 northwest for 8 miles (13 km) to 'Ehukai Beach Park.

❹ Check into **Ke Iki Beach Bungalows** (59-579 Ke Iki Rd., 808/638-8829, http://keikibeach.com, $160-230), located on Ke Iki Beach, just to the north of Sharks Cove and not far from Pipeline.

> Continue on HI-83 for 1 mile (1.6 km) to reach the bungalows.

DAY 6: North Shore to Honolulu

40 miles/64 kilometers | 1.5 hours

ROUTE OVERVIEW: HI-83 • Kamehameha Hwy. • Kaukonahua Rd. • HI-803 • I-H-2 • I-H-201

❶ For shopping, sightseeing, and dining, stop in **Historic Hale'iwa Town.** Visit the art galleries and get a quintessential Hawaiian treat at popular **Matsumoto's Shave Ice** (66-111 Kamehameha Hwy., 808/637-4827, www.matsumotoshaveice.com, 9am-6pm daily). Be prepared to wait quite a while, especially on the weekends and during the summer.

> Take HI-83 W for 6 miles (10 km) to Hale'iwa. Note that HI-83 and Kamehameha Hwy. diverge in Hale'iwa.

❷ Continue on to Honolulu, where you can visit the city's **historic district.** In addition to the state capitol building, you can see **'Iolani Palace** (364 S. King St., 808/522-0822, www.iolanipalace.org, 9am-5pm Mon.-Sat.), the only royal residence in the United States. The palace served as the official residence of the monarch of Hawai'i until the overthrow of the Hawaiian kingdom in 1893. Be sure to check out the east side of the building, which houses

'IOLANI PALACE

the large and opulent Throne Room, the scene of formal meetings and major royal functions.

> Take Kamehameha Hwy. south for 1 mile (1.6 km). Continue south on Kaukonahua Rd. for another mile, then turn left to get on HI-803. In 8 miles (13 km), the highway becomes I-H-2. Continue south for 8 miles (13 km), then merge onto I-H-1. In 5 miles (8 km), merge onto I-H-201 and drive for another 6 miles (10 km) to reach Honolulu.

❸ Spend the rest of the day in **Chinatown.** Stroll through fine art galleries like **The ARTS at Marks Garage** (1159 Nuuanu Ave., 808/521-2903, www.artsatmarks.com, 11am-6pm Tues.-Sat.), the heartbeat of Chinatown's art scene. With 12 major exhibits and performances, lectures, screenings, and workshops, Marks has transformed the Chinatown community through the arts.

HONOLULU'S CHINATOWN

Best SURFING

The sport of surfing was born in Hawai'i. Legendary Olympic gold-medal swimmer, original beachboy, and ambassador of aloha Duke Kahanamoku introduced surfing to the world on the sands of Waikiki and through traveling exhibitions in California and Australia. Be a part of that legacy and get on a board during your stay on O'ahu. Whether it's your first time or you're a lifelong surfer, there is year-round surf and the perfect wave to suit your skill level.

BEGINNERS

- **Populars and Paradise, Waikiki:** Once you're comfortable with your feet in the wax, paddle out to Populars and Paradise for longer rides on Waikiki's outer reefs.

- **Canoes, Waikiki:** No stay in Waikiki is complete without surfing famous Canoes surf break. A slow, rolling wave, it's fun whether it's your first time or you can hang ten. Surfing Canoes is being part of the history of Waikiki.

- **Chun's Reef, North Shore:** A beautiful point on the North Shore, the slow-breaking wave is perfect for beginners and even has small waves occasionally during the summertime.

- **Turtle Bay, North Shore:** Slow, rolling white-water breaks along the rugged point at Turtle Bay. With board rental and surf instructors on-site, it's a great place to give surfing a try and have your friends or family snap some pictures from the cliff.

EXPERTS

- **Ala Moana Bowls, Waikiki:** Some of the best waves on the south shore are along a strip of reef in front of the Ala Moana Small Boat Harbor. Ala Moana Bowls is a long, fast left that local surfers keep under lock and key, coveting every barrel.

- **Laniakea, North Shore:** Just past Hale'iwa town on the North Shore, Laniakea is a long, right point break. On the right swell, fast, perfect waves grind down the point. Lani's, as it's often called, is surfable up to 20 feet on the face.

- **Banzai Pipeline, North Shore:** One of the most dangerous and deadliest waves on the planet, the Banzai Pipeline is a heavy, barreling left that detonates over shallow reefs and offers some of the best and biggest barrels in the world.

- **Sunset Beach, North Shore:** This powerful and unforgiving wave, no matter what size, is famous for separating the experts from the herd. The right boards, the right frame of mind, and stamina are a must to paddle out and surf the heaving walls of water that break along Sunset Beach.

- **Makaha, Leeward Coast:** Makaha is a predominant right-hand point break, famous for its powerful surf, the characters in the lineup, and its backwash close to shore. Makaha breaks nearly all year long, on south, west, and north swells, and sees gigantic waves during the winter; it's the biggest surfable break on the leeward side.

▲ TURTLE BAY, NORTH SHORE

Playlist

O'AHU COASTAL LOOP

SONGS

- **"Ipo Lei Manu" by Gabby Pahinui:** Born in Honolulu, Pahinui is beloved for his mastery of the traditional Hawaiian slack-key guitar and his soulful vocals. His influence on Hawaiian music and culture is so renowned, a medley that he recorded in 1947 was inducted into the U.S. National Recording Registry for its cultural, historical, and aesthetical significance.

- **"While My Guitar Gently Weeps" by Jake Shimabukuro:** If you hung around a coffee shop in Honolulu during the late '90s, you might have caught a performance by this ukulele prodigy. His virtuoso finger-work elevates this Beatles song in ways never dreamed possible.

- **"Times Like These" by Jack Johnson:** There's something about Johnson's music that makes you want to kick off your shoes and dig your toes in the sand. A professional surfer-turned-musician, Johnson is from the North Shore of O'ahu. When it comes to capturing the vibe of Hawai'i, he gets it. This song appeared on his 2003 album *On and On,* which was recorded in his studio on O'ahu.

④ For Chinatown's premier Chinese restaurant, visit **Little Village Noodle House** (1113 Smith St., 808/545-3008, http://littlevillagehawaii.com, 10:30am-8pm daily, $13-50). With over 100 menu items covering meat, poultry, seafood, rice, and noodle dishes, the family-friendly restaurant has every palate covered.

DAY 7: Honolulu

40 miles/64 kilometers | 2 hours

ROUTE OVERVIEW: I-H-1 • I-H-201 • HI-99 • I-H-201 • Round Top-Tantalus Dr. • city streets

① Strike out early and be at the front of the line to see the **Pearl Harbor Historic Sites** (808/454-1434, www.pearlharborhistoricsites.org, free). Once you arrive and find free parking in one of several designated lots, you'll see the **visitors center** (7am-5pm daily). From there, you can tailor your experience to your liking, visiting different memorials, museums, and sites.

> Take I-H-1 W to I-H-201 (2 mi/3 km). Continue for 5 miles (8 km). Take the exit for Stadium Aiea, then continue onto Moanalua Rd. to Aiea Access Rd. Turn left. Stay on this for less than a mile, then make a slight right onto HI-99. In less than a mile, turn right on Arizona Memorial Pl. and follow this to Pearl Harbor.

② Head to **Ala Moana Center** for lunch and shopping. The lively, open-air **Mai Tai Bar** (1450 Ala Moana Blvd., 808/947-2900, 11am-1am daily) is a

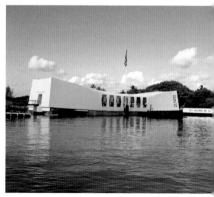

PEARL HARBOR

good option, serving appetizers and entrées with a local flair.

> Follow HI-99 to I-H-201; drive east for 5 miles (8 km) to I-H-1. Continue east for 3 miles (5 km) to exit 22. Continue straight on Kinau St. to Ward Ave. Turn right on Ward and in 1 mile (1.6 km), turn left on Ala Moana Blvd. to Ala Moana Center.

❸ Now that you're rested up, it's time to hit the road for the scenic **Tantalus-Round Top Drive.** The leisurely drive passes hillside homes along a route that's narrow and thick with vegetation. Follow Round Top Drive to the **Pu'u 'Ualaka'a State Wayside** (2760 Round Top Dr.). There, you'll have reached the top of a cinder cone, offering amazing views of Honolulu, from Diamond Head to Pearl Harbor. A round-trip on the winding roads is about 20 miles.

> Drive north for less than a mile on Piikoi St. to King St. Make a right on King and a left on Ke'eaumoku St. Follow Ke'eaumoku to Wilder Ave., turn right, and then turn left on Makiki St. Stay on Makiki for 2 miles (3 km), then take a left to start the Tantalus-Round Top Drive. Follow Round Top Dr. for 2.5 miles (4 km) to the wayside. Complete the 20-mile (32-km) drive by continuing north on Round Top. On the north side of the cinder cone, the road becomes Tantalus Dr. Continue southwest on Puowaina Dr. to reach downtown Honolulu.

❹ Have dinner at the long-established **People's Cafe** (1300 Pali Hwy., 808/536-5789, 10am-8pm Mon.-Sat., 10am-5pm Sun., $6-12). Look for the bright red neon sign for this small restaurant serving all the favorite Hawaiian combos plus some extras like salted meat and kimchi.

Getting There

AIR

All commercial flights to O'ahu are routed to the **Honolulu Daniel K. Inouye International Airport** (HNL, 300 Rodgers Blvd., 808/836-6411, http://hawaii.gov/hnl), as are most other flights with neighbor islands as final destinations. HNL has three terminals, and there is a free intra-airport shuttle service for getting around. Ground transportation is available just outside the baggage claim areas on the lower level, along the center median. The airport is a mere 9 miles (14 km) from Waikiki, and 6 miles (10 km) from downtown Honolulu.

BUS

TheBus (808/848-4500, www.thebus. org) provides island-wide transportation, including from the airport. If you're planning on riding the bus from the airport to your hotel, keep in mind that your bags have to be able to fit under the seat or on your lap without protruding into the aisle. There are several bus stops on the second level of the airport on the center median. Fares are $2.75 for adults, $1.25 children ages 6-17, and children 5 and under are free if they sit on an adult's lap. Call 808/848-5555 for route information or download TheBus's smartphone app **DaBus2,** which provides real-time information.

CAR

There are six on-airport car rental agencies and several off-airport companies. If you haven't booked a rental car online prior to your arrival, the registration counters are located in the baggage claim area.

From the airport, drive east on I-H-1 to **Waikiki.** Take exit 23 and follow Punahou Street south to Beretania Street. Turn right, then make a quick left onto Kalakaua Avenue and follow Kalakaua into the city. The 9-mile (14-km) trip from the airport takes about 20 minutes.

Getting Back

It's a short 3-mile (5-km) trip to return to **Waikiki** from Honolulu, although in traffic it can take about 15 minutes. Plan accordingly. Take Kapiolani Boulevard southeast to Kalakaua Avenue. Turn right and follow Kalakaua into Waikiki.

To get to the **Honolulu airport** from Waikiki (6 mi/10 km), follow Ala Wai Boulevard northwest to McCully Street. Turn right. Drive McCully to I-H-1, then head west on I-H-1 to the airport.

ROAD TO HANA

WHY GO: Waterfalls, bamboo forests, fruit stands, fresh fish, ocean views, tropical hikes, swimming holes, beaches, rainforest gardens, Polynesian history and culture

TOTAL DISTANCE: 75 miles/ 120 kilometers

NUMBER OF DAYS: 1

SEASONS: Year-round

START: Pa'ia, Maui

END: Hana town, Maui

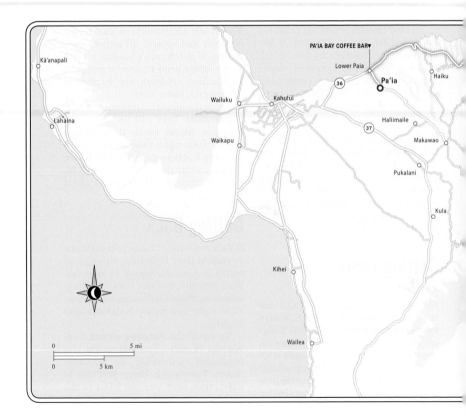

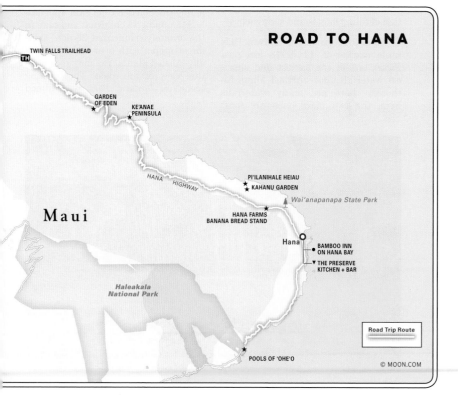

ROAD TO HANA

TWIN FALLS TRAILHEAD

GARDEN
OF EDEN

KE'ANAE
PENINSULA

HANA HIGHWAY

PI'ILANIHALE HEIAU
KAHANU GARDEN

Wai'anapanapa State Park

Maui

HANA FARMS
BANANA BREAD STAND

Hana

BAMBOO INN
ON HANA BAY

THE PRESERVE
KITCHEN + BAR

Haleakala
National Park

Road Trip Route

POOLS OF 'OHE'O

© MOON.COM

ana, a tiny town of 1,300 souls, remains one of the most isolated spots in Hawai'i. The only way to visit is with a leisurely drive along the Hana Highway (HI-360). This legendary road hugs Maui's eastern coastline, sweeping past lush valleys, inching over one-lane bridges, curving around hairpin turns, and bestowing travelers with ocean vistas stretching to the horizon. Take your time. Pull over often. Stop to hike to a waterfall or dunk in a swimming hole. Fill up on banana bread from a roadside farm stand. Or simply roll down your windows to breathe in the fresh sea air. Whatever you do, remember: Hana is a journey, not a destination.

MORNING: Pa'ia to Ke'anae Peninsula

30 miles/48 kilometers | 2 hours

ROUTE OVERVIEW: Hana Hwy.

❶ Fuel up for your early-morning start at **Pa'ia Bay Coffee Bar** (115 Hana Hwy., 808/579-3111, www.paiabaycoffee.com, 7am-5:30pm daily), a local favorite in a hidden tropical courtyard. In addition to coffee, there's a selection of filling bagels and sandwiches.

❷ Your first excursion is **Twin Falls** (mile marker 2, 11 mi/18 km past Pa'ia), one of the easiest and shortest waterfall hikes in East Maui. Although there are many waterfalls here, the two main ones are most accessible via a 1.3-mile (2.1-km) trail. Go in the early morning to avoid the crowds. Before you leave, stop at the **Twin Falls Farm Stand** (808/463-1275, www.twinfallsmaui.net, 8am-3:45pm daily) in the parking lot to grab a coconut or sugarcane juice.

> *From Pa'ia, turn right onto Hana Hwy. and drive east for 12 miles (19 km) to Twin Falls.*

❸ Head to the **Garden of Eden** (mile marker 10.5, 808/572-9899, www.mauigardenofeden.com, 8am-4pm daily, $15 adults, $5 children) and take in the ornately manicured 26-acre rainforest utopia with over 600 individually labeled plants. You may recognize this view of the coast: The opening scene of *Jurassic Park* was filmed here.

TWIN FALLS

Top 3 ROAD TO HANA

1. Stand in awe before **Pi'ilanihale Heiau,** the **largest remaining temple** in the state (PAGE 702).

2. Bite into the famous banana bread at **Hana Farms Banana Bread Stand** (PAGE 702).

3. Hike to the **Pools of 'Ohe'o,** also known as the **Seven Sacred Pools** (PAGE 704).

> *Continue east on Hana Hwy. to the Garden of Eden (9 mi/14 km).*

4 Stop at **Ke'anae Peninsula** (mile marker 16.6), where you can get a glimpse into one of the last holdouts of an ancient way of life. The peninsula is a mosaic of green taro fields, vital to the livelihood of Ke'anae village. Watch the powerful surf crash onto the rugged volcanic shore.

> *Follow the highway east for another 6 miles (10 km) to Ke'anae Rd., then continue straight for less than a mile to Ke'anae Peninsula.*

AFTERNOON:
Ke'anae Peninsula to Wai'anapanapa State Park

20 miles/32 kilometers | 1.5 hours

ROUTE OVERVIEW: Hana Hwy.

1 Visit the **Kahanu Garden** (turn-off at mile marker 31 to 'Ula'ino Rd., 808/248-8912, www.ntbg.org, 9am-4pm Mon.-Fri., 9am-2pm Sat., $10, free under age 13). The sprawling gardens focus on species integral to Polynesian culture. A self-guided tour details the history of the plants and their uses. Within the gardens, the towering **Pi'ilanihale Heiau,** a massive multi-tiered stone structure, is the largest remaining *heiau* (temple) in Hawai'i. The walls stretch 50 feet high in some places, and the stone platforms are the size of two football fields.

> *Follow Hana Hwy. for 14 miles (23 km) to 'Ula'ino Rd. Turn left and in 2 miles (3 km), you'll reach Kahanu Garden.*

2 Only a few miles before the town of Hana, the legendary **Hana Farms Banana Bread Stand** (mile marker 31.2, 808/248-7371, 8am-6:30pm Mon.-Thurs., 8am-8pm Fri., 8am-6:30pm Sat.-Sun.) features six types of banana bread as well as a full range of fruits, coffee, sauces, and flavorings. There are other fruit stands, but none are like this.

> *Retrace your path to Hana Hwy. (2 mi/3 km). Head south; in less than half a mile you'll reach the Hana Farms stand.*

3 **Wai'anapanapa State Park** (mile marker 32, http://dlnr.hawaii.gov), also known as Black Sand Beach, has an overlook with one of the most iconic vistas along this drive and the chance to swim inside hidden caves. If you spend the night in Hana, be sure to get up early and come back for sunrise here.

> *Continue for less than a mile on Hana Hwy., then turn left onto Honokalani Rd. You'll reach the beach in less than a mile.*

WAI'ANAPANAPA STATE PARK

BLACK SAND BEACH, WAI'ANAPANAPA STATE PARK

Driving Tips for THE ROAD TO HANA

One of the most beautiful activities on Maui is driving the Road to Hana. Weaving around 600 curves and 56 one-lane bridges, it's the most loved and loathed stretch of road on the island. Here's how to plan a visit to Hana that will leave you poring over a photo album instead of searching for a divorce lawyer.

- **Enjoy the journey.** Visitors who race to the sleepy village of Hana are left saying, "This is it?" Remember, Hana is a place where you can get away from it all.

- **The Road to Hana doesn't end at Hana.** The famous Road to Hana is the 52-mile (84-km) stretch between Kahului Airport and the town of Hana, but many of the natural treasures are in the 10 miles (16 km) beyond Hana town. Hamoa Beach, consistently voted one of the top beaches in the country, is a few miles past Hana, as is Waioka Pond, a hidden pool on the rocky coast. Thirty minutes beyond Hana town are the Pools of 'Ohe'o (the Seven Sacred Pools), with a series of cascading waterfalls falling directly into the Pacific.

- **Don't drive back the way you came.** Your rental car contract may tell you the road around the back of the island is for 4WD vehicles only, but that's not true. Parts are bumpy,

and a few miles are dirt road, but unless there's torrential rain, the road is passable with a regular vehicle. Following the back road all the way around the island grants new views as the surroundings change from lush tropical rainforest to arid, windswept lava flows.

- **Don't make dinner reservations.** Too many people try to squeeze Hana into half a day or end up feeling rushed. Hana is a place to escape the rush, not add to it. If you're planning a day trip to Hana, block off the entire day, leave early (7am), and see where the day takes you.

- **Stop early and stop often.** Take a break for a morning stroll or for breakfast at a tucked-away café. Pick up some snacks and watch the waves. Stop and swim in waterfalls, hike through bamboo forests, and pull off at roadside stands for banana bread or locally grown fruit. If the car behind you is on your tail, pull over and let it pass—there isn't any rush.

EVENING: Waiʻanapanapa State Park to Hana Town

25 miles/40 kilometers | 2 hours

ROUTE OVERVIEW: Hana Hwy.

1 If there's enough time before sunset, go past **Hana** to visit the fabled **Pools of ʻOheʻo** inside **Haleakalā National Park** (parking at mile marker 42.1, 808/248-7375, www.nps.gov/hale, 24 hours daily, $15 per vehicle). The pools are also known as the Seven Sacred Pools, but locals appreciate you using the real name, which is pronounced oh-HEY-oh. From the visitors center, take the Kuloa Point Loop Trail to the famous pools. Along the 10-minute walk, you'll go through groves of *hala* trees and past a number of historic sites. Eventually the trail emerges at a staircase down to the pools and one of the most iconic vistas in Hawaiʻi. The three main pools are open most days for exploring and swimming, although they're closed during heavy rains. Reaching the uppermost pools requires some rock scaling; it's worth the effort, but be careful on the slippery rocks.

> Follow Honokalanai Rd. back to Hana Hwy., turn left, and drive 13 miles (21 km) to the Pools of ʻOheʻo.

2 Head back to Hana and enjoy fresh regional cuisine at **The Preserve Kitchen + Bar** (5031 Hana Hwy., 808/359-2401, 7:30am-9pm daily, $20-48). Housed in the Travaasa Hana hotel, this restaurant has fine dining rivaling the best on the island. Take the server's suggestion for the evening and order the fish of the day, which was likely caught in waters just off Hana.

> Retrace your path on Hana Hwy. for 10 miles (16 km) to reach Hana town.

3 Spend the night in town at the funky, ultra-relaxing **Bamboo Inn** (off Uakea Rd., 808/248-7718, www.bambooinn.com, $195-265), where three oceanfront rooms look out over the water toward Waikoloa Beach.

Getting There

AIR

You'll likely land at **Kahului Airport** (OGG, 1 Kahului Airport Rd., 808/872-3830, www.hawaii.gov), which is 30-45 minutes by car from the resort areas

AERIAL VIEW OF THE ROAD TO HANA

of Wailea and Ka'anapali. Kahului has direct flights to a host of mainland cities and a handful of international destinations, and it's served by most major carriers.

Other than Kahului, there are two small airstrips in Kapalua and in Hana. They have no direct flights to the mainland, but there are seven flights per day between the **Kapalua Airport** (JHM, 4050 Honoapi'ilani Hwy., 808/665-6108, www.hawaii.gov) and Honolulu on neighboring O'ahu.

BUS

The **Maui Bus** provides regular service between Pa'ia, Ha'iku, the Kahului Airport, and Queen Ka'ahumanu Center in Kahului, where you can connect with buses to anywhere else on the island. The rate is $2 per boarding or $4 for a day pass, and pickups begin daily in Pa'ia in the early morning headed toward Ha'iku and Kahului. The route also makes stops at the Ha'iku Marketplace and Ha'iku Community Center, with the final bus going from Ha'iku to Kahului departing the Ha'iku Marketplace.

CAR

From **Kahului Airport**, it's 20 minutes (8 mi/13 km) to Pa'ia. Take HI-36, then turn right on Baldwin Avenue and into Pa'ia.

Getting Back

From Hana to **Kahului Airport**, the trip is 51 miles (82 km), which takes about two hours. Head west on HI-360 to HI-36, then turn right on Airport Road. In 1 mile (2 km), go left on Lanui Circle and follow Lanui Circle to the airport.

To reach **Kihei** from Hana, head west on HI-360 to HI-36 (34 mi/55 km). At Hansen Road, turn left. In 2 miles (3 km), turn left on HI-311. Drive south on HI-311, then continue onto HI-31, following it into Kihei.

It's 72 miles (116 km), or a 2.5-hour drive, from Hana to **Lahaina**. Drive west on HI-360 to HI-36, then turn left on Airport Road. Take HI-380, then go left on HI-30. Follow HI-30 south to Lahaina.

▶ *Playlist*

ROAD TO HANA

RADIO STATIONS

- **KPOA 93.5:** This radio station broadcasts from Maui and plays contemporary Hawaiian music. Think: a mix of rock, reggae, and country songs tinged with slack-key and steel guitars, ukulele, and the guitar-like *machete:* Tune in either on your car's radio or via the station's streaming service.

SONGS

- **"Even After All" by Finley Quaye:** The son of an African jazz musician, Quaye pulls musical influences from jazz, reggae, and rock. This song appeared on the 2000 surf documentary *Thicker Than Water,* and is the kind of chill tune that sways like palm fronds, sinks like a setting sun, rolls like a crashing wave, and makes you want to slow way, way down.

- **"Kauanoeanuhea" by Keali'i Reichel:** To hear a powerful blend of modern Hawaiian music and traditional Hawaiian chanting, add this Maui-born and -raised musician to your playlist. In addition to performing at Carnegie Hall and opening for the likes of Sting and LeAnn Rimes, Reichel also founded a hula school to help keep Hawaiian language and culture alive for younger generations.

ESSENTIALS

PASSPORTS AND VISAS

If you are visiting from another country, you must have a **valid passport** and a **visa** to enter the United States. As of 2020, U.S. citizens will need a passport or REAL ID-compliant driver's license to travel domestically. For more information, visit www.dhs.gov/real-id#.

The U.S. government's Visa Waiver Program allows tourists from many countries to visit without a visa for up to 90 days. To check if your country is on the list go to http://travel.state.gov. To qualify, you must apply online with the **Electronic System for Travel Authorization** (www.cbp.gov) and hold a return plane or cruise ticket to your country of origin dated less than 90 days from your date of entry. Even with a waiver, you still need to bring your passport and present it at the port of entry.

Holders of **Canadian passports** don't need visas or waivers. In most countries, the local U.S. embassy can provide a **tourist visa.** Plan for 2-3 weeks for visa processing. More information is available at http://travel.state.gov.

If you lose your passport, visit the **U.S. Department of State** (www.usembassy.gov) to find an embassy from your home country to help.

DRIVER'S LICENSE AND DOCUMENTATION

All drivers need to have a **government-issued license** or **permit** to operate a vehicle and need to be older than 16 years of age.

International visitors who wish to drive in the United States need to obtain an **International Driving Permit,** available from the country that issued their driver's license. This permit cannot be obtained once in the United States.

Regardless of whether you're an international driver or a United States citizen, make sure all documentation is up to date and located in an accessible place within the vehicle.

VEHICLE RENTALS

Most car rental agencies are located on-site at international, national, and regional airports. Airport locations usually have large fleets from which to choose and often offer unlimited mileage. It's best to reserve a car in advance of your arrival.

To rent a vehicle, you must have a valid driver's license and be at least 25 years old. Some companies rent to drivers under the age of 25 as long as they pay the underage driver fee and meet all other requirements. Adding other drivers may incur an additional charge of $5-7 per day.

RENTING A CAR

The average cost of a rental car is $35-50 per day; rates vary by season, location, vehicle type, and distance traveled. Weekend rentals cost more. If you plan to drop off the vehicle in a different city or state from where you picked it up, you'll likely pay a "one-way" fee.

RENTING AN RV, CAMPERVAN, OR TRAILER

This option affords you lodging and dining flexibility while on the road, since most RVs provide sleeping quarters and small kitchens. Many campgrounds offer hookups and sites for RVs, campervans, and trailers, or you can use designated RV parks. It's important to note that these are big vehicles, which can be tricky to maneuver and park. They're also expensive to rent ($1,200 per week) and expensive to refuel.

VEHICLE AND TRAVEL INSURANCE

Not all states require drivers to have auto insurance, but all 50 states do require drivers to provide proof of financial responsibility should something happen to them or the vehicle. **Auto insurance** is the most common way to obtain this proof.

When renting a car, you can opt to purchase insurance from the rental agency for the duration of the vehicle rental. If you already have private auto insurance, check with your carrier to see if the policy covers rentals. During the trip, keep all insurance and vehicle-related paperwork in a secure place.

Depending on the type of coverage you buy, **travel insurance** reimburses medical expenses, lost luggage, flight cancellation, and other losses incurred while traveling. Do your due diligence when researching travel insurance policies, as coverage varies.

WHAT TO BRING

It can be tempting to bring everything you own, but it'll make your life easier if you pack light. Here are a few things you should bring with you:

- Driver's license, vehicle registration, insurance documents
- Wireless or hands-free option for your phone
- Cell phone charger and/or USB cord
- Road atlas
- Cash; coins for road tolls
- Clothing you can layer, including a waterproof jacket
- Sunglasses; sunscreen
- Travel-sized toiletries; towel; toilet paper
- Camera
- Day pack for hikes

- Small cooler for snacks; nonperishable foods such as beef jerky and nuts; potable water, ideally one gallon per person
- Reusable water bottle; travel coffee mug
- Blanket; pillow
- First aid kit; Swiss Army knife; flashlight and batteries; waterproof matches

HOW TO PACK THE CAR

Pack important items first so you don't forget them. These include vehicle registration, insurance documents, and driver's license; store these in the glove compartment.

Next, pack emergency items, such as the first aid kit, water, and flashlight. Whether you're renting a car or driving your own, ensure that there's a spare tire, tire repair kit, flares, and jumper cables.

Put clothes in soft duffel bags rather than hard suitcases, and make sure to have an overnight bag with toiletries and a fresh change of clothes stowed in an easily accessible spot.

Stash the cooler with drinks and snacks on the floor behind the passenger's or driver's seat, and toss the pillow and blanket in the backseat for easy access.

Keep loose change and cash in the center console along with a travel mug and reusable water bottle. Slip the road atlas between the console and the passenger seat.

Store as many of your items as possible in the trunk to keep the inside of the vehicle as clutter-free as possible.

ROAD RULES

In the United States, motorists drive on the right side of the road, distance and speed is measured in miles, road signs display miles, and vehicle speedometers display both miles and kilometers. Drivers should be familiar with the road regulations and laws for each state they visit. More information can be found at www.usa.gov/motor-vehicle-services.

CELL PHONES

Many states prohibit drivers from using hand-held cell phones while operating a vehicle, and outright ban the use of a cell phone by teen drivers. If you're caught breaking one of these laws, there could be steep fines. Always have a hands-free option available. Find state-by-state rules here: www.ncsl.org/research/transportation/cellular-phone-use-and-texting-while-driving-laws.aspx.

MOTORCYCLES

Motorcycle drivers must hold a valid license to operate a motorcycle and have current registration. Motorcyclists adhere to the same road laws as other vehicles, although there are rules that apply specifically to motorcycles. These include wearing a helmet, sitting astride the seat facing forward, keeping at least one hand on the handlebars at all times, and keeping both feet on the foot pegs. **EagleRider** (877/557-3541, www.eaglerider.com) offers road-trip tours and also rents Harleys, Indians, Hondas, Yamahas, and BMWs.

SPEED LIMITS

Speed limits vary from state to state, and are posted in increments of five miles per hour. Maximum speed limits tend to be higher (75-80 miles per hour in some areas) in the West as opposed to rates of 65-70 in states east of the Mississippi River.

CONSTRUCTION ZONE LAWS

Road maintenance requires construction crews to share the road with vehicles. In order to keep crews safe, each state has laws that increase penalties for speeding or committing traffic violations while in a construction zone. In some states, the penalty is applicable only when workers are present; in other states, workers do not have to be present in the work zone for penalties to apply. All construction work zones along roadways will have visible signage. Keep an eye out for these and adhere to them closely.

CROSSING STATE LINES

While it's fairly easy to drive from state to state, there are some things to keep in mind. There are **six time zones** in the United States: Hawaii, Alaska, Pacific, Mountain, Central, and Eastern. Each is separated by one hour. Arizona and Hawaii don't observe daylight saving time.

In general, the rules of the road throughout the country are the same. Notable exceptions relate to **speed limits, motorcycle helmet laws, seat belts,** and **child restraints.** Get specific state road rules at www.dmv-department-of-motor-vehicles.com.

Take special care when driving on **Native American lands.** Each community has its own guidelines, rules, and judicial system.

Drivers entering California must stop at **Agricultural Inspection Stations.** You don't need to present a passport, visa, or a driver's license, but be prepared to present fruits and vegetables, even those purchased within neighboring states. Other items that may be illegal to transport across state lines include **fireworks, exotic animals,** and **certain plants.**

Federal law allows travelers who can legally carry **firearms** under federal, state, and local laws to bring a gun across state lines. However, states have their own laws governing the transportation of firearms, so be sure to comply with the legal requirements in each state. When in doubt, carry firearms unloaded, locked in a case, and stored in the trunk. Store ammunition in a separate, locked container.

VEHICLE MAINTENANCE

It helps to have a basic knowledge of how to check tire pressure and oil levels, and be aware of how many miles your vehicle can travel on a tank of gas.

If you're driving your own vehicle and not renting one, have a mechanic examine the belts, lights, and turn signals before you take off. Check fluid levels, such as oil, brake fluid, coolant, and power steering fluid, as well as tire pressure. Tires should have at least 2/32-inch (0.2-cm) tread.

FUEL

There are remote areas within the country where **service stations** are few and far between, specifically along Route 66 and Route 50 (aka the Loneliest Road). A good rule of thumb for road-tripping is to keep the gas tank level above the **half-full** line, and fuel up in major towns whenever possible.

WI-FI AND GPS

Wi-Fi is available at most accommodations, attractions, restaurants, and welcome centers throughout the country.

Cell phone service is widely available around the country, with the exception of remote areas of the Pacific Crest Trail in Oregon and Washington; parts of North and South Dakota; West Texas; northern New Mexico; the Mojave Desert in California; and several of the larger national parks.

Never rely solely on GPS for navigation. Always have a **printed map** or a **road atlas** in the vehicle to use as a backup.

MONEY AND CURRENCY EXCHANGE

Nearly all attractions, lodging, and restaurants accept major **credit cards** and **bank debit cards.** Bring **cash** for smaller businesses, as well as for emergencies and tipping. How much to bring depends on the time and distance of your road trip, but a useful standard is $100 per week. There are **bank ATMs** located in cities and small towns, so you'll be able to access cash at most destinations on the routes listed in this guide.

If you're traveling to the United States from a foreign country, you'll need to exchange your currency at the airport, bank, or currency exchange. Businesses within the United States only accept U.S. currency.

STREAMING MUSIC SERVICES AND RADIO STATIONS

Tune in to local **radio stations** to indulge in regional flavor, but note that in rural parts of the country, reception can be spotty.

Streaming music services or **satellite stations** are more reliable forms of entertainment. You can buy a subscription to these for a nominal fee. If you rent a vehicle, it might come with satellite radio or a streaming service as part of the rental package; if not, inquire about purchasing it for an additional fee.

With **Spotify**, you can listen for free (with ads) or upgrade to a premium package to download songs for offline play and create playlists. Rates run $10/month for an individual, $15/month for families, and $5/month for students. You can also try it free of charge for three months.

Apple Music is a streaming service that offers 60 million songs, all available via playlists, online radio stations, and as downloads. A subscription costs $10/month for an individual, $15/month for families, and $5/month for students.

Sirius XM is a satellite service that offers dozens of stations that play ad-free music, entertainment, and news.

EMERGENCY PREPAREDNESS

For emergencies in the United States, including Alaska and Hawaii, **dial 911** on your phone for immediate assistance.

Make sure your vehicle has a first aid kit, 3-5 gallons of potable water, jumper cables, a spare tire or tire-repair kit, flashlight, new batteries, blanket, emergency flares, and waterproof matches. In the event that you have to wait for assistance, pull your vehicle off to the right side of the road and put on your hazard lights.

ROAD CONDITIONS

The routes in this guide generally follow well-traveled, paved, maintained routes. However, it's not uncommon for road conditions to be affected due to closures, accidents, traffic jams, construction, and weather. Most states provide real-time road conditions, construction updates, and road closure information via the **U.S. Department of Transportation's Federal Highway Administration.** To access this information on the road, **dial 511.** Of the 50 states, 11 do not have active 511 access. These are: Michigan, Indiana, Illinois, Texas, Oklahoma, Missouri, Arkansas, Alabama, Rhode Island, Connecticut, and Delaware.

WEATHER

Check the weather forecast every day, and monitor it at least 2-3 days out. That gives you plenty of time to alter your itinerary in case of bad conditions.

If driving in **snow,** turn on the headlights, go slowly, and keep a safe distance between your vehicle and the one in front of you. If it's too difficult to see, pull off to the side of the road, turn on the hazard lights, and wait until the storm subsides. If you're caught in a blizzard, don't panic. Preserve the heat in the vehicle, preserve the car battery, and bundle up warmly. Then phone 911 and tell the dispatcher where you are.

With heavy **rainfall,** turn on the headlights and drive slowly to avoid the risk of hydroplaning. As with snow, make sure you maintain a safe distance between you and the vehicle ahead of you. Most importantly, avoid flooded roadways. The depth of water is not always obvious, and the road may be washed out under the water.

For severe **thunderstorms,** pull onto the shoulder of the road and make sure the vehicle is clear from trees or other objects that could fall. Stay in the car, turn on the hazard lights, and wait until the storm subsides. If there is lightning, you are safest inside your vehicle.

Driving in **fog** requires you to slow down, use your headlights—but not high-beam or bright headlights—and stay focused on the road.

WILDLIFE ON THE ROAD

If you see signs indicating that wildlife is nearby, slow down and be alert. Give yourself more time to brake in case an animal darts in front of you.

Animals are more active at **dusk and dawn,** especially in the fall and spring. If you see one deer, there will likely be more; they travel in herds.

Use your **horn** to alert a deer standing in the middle of the road. They are mesmerized by headlights, so a few bursts of the horn will startle them.

If a collision is unavoidable, don't swerve. Instead, maintain control of the car, press on the brakes firmly, then let off the brakes at the moment of impact. Lean toward the door, not the center of the car; when animals are hit head-on, they may roll over the vehicle, crushing the center of the windshield and roof. Pull off to the side of the road, call the police, and don't touch the animal.

HIGHWAY SIGNS *Defined*

The United States is a big place with a rich variety of geography, wildlife, culture, and weather. This means that highway signage can vary greatly by region. Check out a full list of highway signs and their meanings at: www.trafficsigns.com. Here are a few to get you started.

- **Animal crossing:** A silhouette of an animal—a deer or moose—is depicted, sometimes followed by "x-ing". Watch for wildlife crossing the road.

- **Camping:** Looking for a campsite for the night? Keep your eye out for an image of a triangular tent.

- **Flash flood area:** Written out clearly, this sign informs you to use caution during heavy rains.

- **Photo enforcement:** If you see a picture of a camera, slow down. It means photo radar enforces the speed.

- **Picnic areas:** This picture of a picnic table lets you know there's a place to stop and eat lunch nearby.

- **Tractor crossing:** Look for a silhouette of a tractor, usually found in rural farming communities.

- **Slippery when wet:** You'll see an image of a car with curving tire tracks. Use caution when driving in stormy conditions.

- **Tram or light-rail:** An image of a train indicates public transport.

- **Falling rocks:** Found on mountainous roads, this sign depicts falling boulders, and warns drivers of the potential danger from the surrounding cliffs.

- **Winter recreation:** A simple snowflake indicates that winter fun is to be had close by.

- **Scenic overlook:** This clearly written sign tells you about a beautiful view ahead. Stop and check it out!

DRIVING AN RV, CAMPERVAN, OR TRAILER

Remember that RVs, campervans, or vehicles pulling a trailer are heavy pieces of machinery. This means they will take longer to slow down, so give yourself time to **brake** and maintain a greater distance between you and other vehicles.

To **park** safely, use a spotter, use your mirrors, and take your time. Try to park in designated RV spots whenever possible; these are larger and often let you pull in straight on.

Slow down when driving on hills and mountains. Use **low gears** going uphill and downhill, and always stay in the right lane.

Make **turns** long and wide, especially right turns. Make good use of your side and rearview mirrors. Keep as close to the center lane as possible.

Pay attention to **height clearances** for parking garages, overpasses, and bridges. Know the maximum height of your vehicle.

Whether you're road-tripping alone or with friends, there are certain safety precautions to keep in mind.

Know your limits. Driving long distances can take a physical and mental toll on solo travelers. Before you set out, have an idea of how long you're comfortable driving each day, and don't push it.

Set a schedule. This doesn't have to be a live-or-die itinerary, but it helps to have a list of must-see highlights for each day. That way you won't miss anything and you'll be able to plan drive-time efficiently.

Remember where you parked your car. You don't want to be wandering around in an unknown place searching for your vehicle. Make a note in your phone or on a notepad.

Book accommodations in advance. When you're traveling alone, this saves you the hassle of trying to book while on the road.

Consider travel insurance. It covers medical expenses, including the cost of transporting loved ones to your side in the event of an emergency.

Get a membership to AAA. This automobile association provides nationwide roadside assistance, maps, travel tips, itineraries, and more.

Start each day's drive early. This ensures you're fresh and alert and that you arrive at your destination before dark.

Lock your vehicle doors. Always. Even if it seems like you're in a safe, friendly spot.

Have entertainment cued up. As a solo driver, you want to pay attention to the road, not the radio. Set up your music playlists, podcasts, and audio books before you start driving.

Stay in touch with loved ones. A simple text or email to let trusted friends or family know where you are and where you plan to be takes just a few minutes.

Don't pick up strangers or hitchhikers. Also, don't stop for someone stranded on the side of the road.

Instead, find a safe place and then dial 911 for them.

LGBTQI RESOURCES

When driving through rural communities in the United States, you might find a lack of establishments that cater to LGBTQI visitors.

A few good LGBTQI travel resources include **The Advocate** (www.advocate.com/travel), **Mister B&B** (www.misterbandb.com), **Out Traveler** (www.outtraveler.com), and **Purple Roofs** (www.purpleroofs.com).

SENIOR TRAVELERS

Nearly all of the road trips in this guide take motorists off the major highways and on safe and leisurely drives with plenty of places to stop and sightsee. Most attractions, restaurants, and accommodations offer **senior discounts,** so have a photo ID or an AARP card in hand.

TRAVELERS WITH DISABILITIES

The Americans with Disabilities Act (ADA) requires public places to provide facilities to accommodate disabled patrons. Most major restaurants and accommodations are wheelchair accessible, but small businesses located in older properties were grandfathered in and do not have to abide by the new laws. Chain motels generally have rooms with larger doors for wheelchair access, but it's best to call ahead and reserve the room you need.

U.S. citizens with permanent disabilities are eligible for a lifetime **Access Pass** (www.store.usgs.gov/pass/access.html) with free entry to the country's national parks. You can obtain an Access Pass in person at any federal recreation site or by submitting a completed application by mail.

The pass does not provide benefits for special recreation permits or concessionaire fees. Passes generally take 3-5 days to process and about one week to ship.

CYCLISTS

Road rules for bicyclists vary from state to state. Get a complete list here: www.bikeleague.org/statebikelaws. Another great resource for road-trippers traveling by bicycle is **Adventure Cycling Association** (www.adventure-cycling.org). This nonprofit organization offers cycling routes, maps, guided trips, and information on safe cycling in the United States.

SEASONALITY

Seasonal weather throughout the United States differs drastically from north to south, east to west. Take this into consideration when planning your road trip. For the purposes of this guide, **fall** is defined as September-November, **winter** is December-February, **spring** is March-May, and **summer** is June-August.

FALL

In New England, the Mid-Atlantic states, the Rocky Mountains, and the Great Lakes region, fall means cool, crisp temperatures and autumn colors. There may be early snowfall in November, especially in New England and the Rockies. In the Southwest, Texas, Southern California, Florida, and parts of the South, temperatures will start to cool off, but will still be warm compared to the rest of the country. The Pacific Northwest offers cool, damp temperatures and beautiful foliage. Fall colors peak in Alaska, although the days are short and the weather is cold. Hawaii is sunny and temperate.

WINTER

Heavy snowfall, shorter days, and cold—often freezing—temperatures reflect winter weather in Alaska, New England, the Rockies, the Great Lakes, and the Mid-Atlantic. Winter is considered the rainy season in Hawaii and parts of the Southwest, although the temperatures remain mild. Texas and certain regions of the South can experience ice storms, but these are infrequent. Southern California enjoys mild temperatures and sunny days. The Pacific Northwest is rainy and cold; snow and ice are rare outside of the mountains.

SPRING

In the Southwest, Texas, Southern California, the South, and Florida, spring is near perfect: sunny, warm, very little rainfall, and very little humidity. New England, the Great Lakes, the Mid-Atlantic, and the Midwest can still experience some snow and cold days, but as the weather warms up, it brings more rainfall than snowfall. The Rockies also get snow in the early spring. The Pacific Northwest's temperatures warm slightly, although the region still gets quite a bit of rain. Spring in Hawaii is sunny and warm.

SUMMER

New England, the Pacific Northwest, the Rocky Mountains, the Great Lakes, the Midwest, and Alaska enjoy sunny days, warm temperatures, and light rainfall. The Midwest and New England can be humid. The South and Florida are very hot, humid, and rainy, while the Southwest and Texas experience extreme heat and little to no rainfall. Hawaii experiences its warmest temperatures of the year, but these are still fairly moderate. Early summer can bring tornadoes to the Midwest and the South. In Florida and the Southern states on the East Coast, hurricane season kicks up in late summer. Late summer is also monsoon season in Arizona. Many of the western states are at risk for wildfires during late summer.

HIGH SEASON

Prepare for busy crowds, higher costs, and advance reservations. On the upside, high season means nicer weather, longer business hours, and more available services.

- **Pacific Northwest and Northern California:** summer, June-September
- **Southern California:** year-round
- **Southwest and Texas:** winter, December-February
- **Rocky Mountains:** summer, June-September
- **Great Lakes:** summer, June-August
- **New England, New York, and Pennsylvania:** summer and fall, June-November

- **The South and Florida:** fall and winter, December-April
- **Alaska:** summer, June-August
- **Hawaii:** winter, December-March

LOW SEASON

You'll enjoy crowd-free access, cheap lodging and airfare, and a local vibe. But you might also encounter limited hours and poor weather.

- **Pacific Northwest and Northern California:** winter, November-March
- **Southwest and Texas:** summer, May-August
- **Rocky Mountains:** April-June, October-November
- **Great Lakes:** winter, November-March
- **New England, New York, and Pennsylvania:** spring, April-May
- **The South and Florida:** summer, May-September
- **Alaska:** winter and spring, October-March
- **Hawaii:** summer, April-June, and fall, September-November

SUSTAINABLE TRAVEL

VEHICLE ENERGY EFFICIENCY

Get a pre-trip tune-up to aid in better fuel efficiency. Plan your route so you don't waste gas by backtracking. Use cruise control to maintain efficient speeds. Check your tire pressure. Tires that are not operating at the optimum pressure use more fuel.

If you're not driving your own car, rent an electric car or a hybrid.

REUSE AND RECYCLE

Pack reusable water bottles to fill up at hotels, welcome centers, rest areas, campsites, and parks. Bring reusable food containers.

Buy cans instead of bottles. They're easier to crush, thus saving space.

Use fabric grocery bags for shopping. If you have to use plastic grocery bags, save them to reuse.

Keep recyclables separate. Stop at retailers with recycling bins or at rest stops to recycle. Access Google Maps to locate recycling centers wherever you are.

FOOD AND WATER

To create less food waste, plan out your meals. If you have food in the cooler, eat it instead of ordering at a restaurant or fast-food joint. Buy in bulk when it's feasible.

Bring reusable water bottles to avoid wasting plastic. If you must buy water, purchase gallon-size containers rather than individual bottles, then fill your reusable water bottle.

WATER CONSERVATION

Do a full load of laundry instead of several small ones. Rewear clothes, or wash single items in your hotel sink.

Shower, don't bathe. Use dry shampoo to extend the time between hair washings.

ACCOMMODATIONS

HOTELS

From luxury to budget, small to sprawling, hotel accommodations span coast to coast. The benefits of properties owned by major brands (Marriott, Hilton, Best Western, etc.) is that you can find them anywhere; they usually have room availability or can refer you to a sister property that does; and they offer consistent amenities.

MOTOR LODGES AND MOTOR COURTS

Vintage and full of charm, these retro gems are often found on scenic byways and in tiny towns. Because they are older, they may offer small guest rooms, no Wi-Fi, and limited amenities. But for travelers who desire one-of-a-kind accommodations, a motor lodge or court is the way to go.

BED-AND-BREAKFASTS

Plan to reserve a bed-and-breakfast well in advance, especially during peak season, as they usually offer only a few guest rooms. The benefit is a white-glove experience in a thoughtfully appointed home, complete with a gourmet breakfast.

CAMPING

National parks provide a safe—and beautiful—way to camp. Book campsites months in advance during the summer, except for in the Southwest, when many campsites shut down because of extreme heat. Always check with park rangers about campfire regulations, information on local wildlife, and **Leave No Trace** (www.lnt.org) policies.

VACATION RENTALS

Short-term rentals, such as **Airbnb** (www.airbnb.com), **VRBO** (www.vrbo.com), and **HomeAway** (www.homeaway.com), or regional companies that manage privately owned properties, let you lease a private home or room. These tend to offer affordable options in highly desirable areas, such as big cities or beach towns. Homeowners provide essentials, such as toilet paper, linens, and basic kitchen and pantry staples; you're responsible for everything else.

HOSTELS

For the budget-friendly traveler, hostels are a great option. Typically found in major metropolises, hostels offer a bed in a shared room or single room in a dorm-like setting. You might also share bathrooms, showers, and a community kitchen with other guests. **American Hostels** (http://americanhostels.us) lets you search by region within the United States.

BOOK AHEAD, OR
On the Road?

....

You don't have to book lodging weeks in advance when on the road. In fact, the flexibility to change your mind is part of the beauty of a road trip. But a little forethought goes a long way. Within each chapter, any accommodations that require advance reservations are noted. These include places that offer a limited number of rooms or hotels that book up quickly in high tourist seasons. No matter where you choose to stay, at the very least, try to phone ahead each day to make same-day reservations.

HOMESTAYS

During a homestay, you'll share a residence with the homeowner in exchange for a small fee, gift, or housekeeping or work on the property. You and the host agree to the exact terms of the homestay in advance. Food is usually provided as is use of utilities, but there may be rules related to curfew, smoking, and drinking. A good resource is **Homestay:** www.homestay.com.

FARMSTAYS

Farmstays are similar to homestays except that your accommodations are on a working farm, ranch, or vineyard. **FarmStay USA** (http://farmstayus.com) lets you search by what type of work you're interested in doing.

TRAVEL COMPANIONS

WHO DOES WHAT

If you're road-tripping with a friend, partner, or spouse, the division of responsibilities goes beyond switching off who drives and who naps.

DRIVER

As the one behind the wheel, you should be aware of local road rules and speed limits. Monitor the vehicle's dashboard instruments (speedometer, fuel gauge, odometer) and note important alerts, such as low tire pressure, low oil, or engine temperature. Before getting on the road, adjust the seat height and distance from steering wheel to your comfort level, and adjust the rearview mirror and both side mirrors. Also, it's smart to have snacks or drinks handy, such as in the center console.

PASSENGER

Think of the passenger as the driver's copilot. The primary duty is navigation. Using either GPS or a road atlas, you should make sure the driver knows where to turn, what exit to take, and what's coming up next in the route. Other duties include booking hotel or restaurant reservations for upcoming stops, adjusting music playlists and volume, getting snacks and drinks for the driver, and in general, keeping the driver company on long stretches.

TRAVELING WITH KIDS

Road trips with children can be fun-filled or patience-testing. The trick is to stop often to let little ones stretch their legs and run off excess energy; maintain a well-stocked supply of water, juice, and snacks; and keep kiddos entertained with car games.

Most of the expeditions in this guide include family-friendly attractions, interactive museums, restaurants with children's menus, easy hikes, national parks with Junior Ranger programs, and cities with parks, zoos, and playgrounds. A road trip offers surprises around every corner, so engage kids by involving them in the planning process.

All states require child-safety seats for infants and children fitting specific criteria, but requirements vary based on age, weight, and height. Here is a **complete list of laws by state**: https://drivinglaws.aaa.com/tag/child-passenger-safety.

Many laws require all children to ride in the rear seat of a vehicle whenever possible, and most states permit children over a particular age, height, or weight to use an adult safety belt. All states, except for South Dakota, require booster seats or other appropriate devices for children who have outgrown child-safety seats but are too small to use an adult seat safely. This law also includes Washington DC. The following states require children younger than two to sit in a rear-facing child seat: California, Connecticut, Nebraska, New Jersey, New York, Oklahoma, Oregon, Pennsylvania, Rhode Island, South Carolina, and Virginia.

TRAVELING WITH DOGS

Dogs make everything better, including road trips, although taking them requires some extra planning—and extra stops for potty breaks. Before you decide to bring along your dog, be sure they don't get carsick.

Pack the following items for your four-legged companion: dog food in a sealed container, reusable water bottle that you can refill with fresh water, dog leash, dog-waste bags, towel, dog bed, food and water bowls, and your pup's favorite ball or toy.

Store the leash, food, bowls, and dog-waste bags in an accessible place in the vehicle so when you stop, you can easily get to them. Make sure your dog is wearing a collar at all times with an ID tag that displays your name and phone number.

CAR GAMES
and Activities

- **The Alphabet Game:** Choose a category, then starting from the letter A, go through the alphabet naming things that fit into the category. For example, if the category is "movies," a good start would be *Ant-Man*.

- **20 Questions:** A classic game where one person thinks of an object and the other players in the car determine the object by asking questions—up to 20, of course.

- **License Plate Bingo:** Print customizable bingo sheets that list state names. When a player sees a vehicle on the road with a license plate from a different state, mark each one on the bingo sheet. First one to hit bingo wins!

- **I Spy:** One player chooses an object that they see (a tree or a billboard). That player describes it in one word and the other players in the car try to guess the object.

- **Don't Say It!:** Pick a few words (3-5) that nobody in the car is allowed to say. If someone says one of the words, they get a point. Lowest score wins.

Most attractions and accommodations allow leashed animals, including national parks, forests, and monuments; hotels such as Red Roof Inn, La Quinta, Kimpton, and Best Western; independently owned hotels and motor courts; and many restaurants. Even rest stops offer dog runs and dog parks. Pet-friendly travel resources include **Go Pet Friendly** (www.gopetfriendly.com) and **Bring Fido** (www.bringfido.com).

SUGGESTED READING

- *On the Road* by Jack Kerouac: The epic novel about friends searching for meaning on a cross-country road trip.

- *Wild: From Lost to Found on the Pacific Crest Trail* by Cheryl Strayed: A memoir of one woman on her trek along the Pacific Crest Trail. The book was made into an Academy Award-nominated movie starring Reese Witherspoon.

- *A Walk in the Woods: Rediscovering America on the Appalachian Trail* by Bill Bryson: A story of the Appalachian Trail from Georgia to Maine.

- *The Wangs vs. The World* by Jade Chang: This story details an immigrant family's cross-country journey.

- *America for Beginners* by Leah Franqui: A Indian man travels from New York to California, making friends along the way.

- *Station Eleven* by Emily St. John Mandel: In a postapocalyptic America, a woman embarks on a dangerous journey.

SUGGESTED MOVIES

- *Thelma & Louise:* The ultimate road-trip movie, starring Susan Sarandon and Geena Davis.

- *Easy Rider:* Peter Fonda and Dennis Hopper play motorcyclists bound for New Orleans.

- *Little Miss Sunshine:* A 2006 film featuring a family on their trip to California to support a little girl in a beauty contest.

- *Planes, Trains, and Automobiles:* A 1987 classic. Steve Martin and John Candy play two very different men traveling together on the way home for the holidays through a dangerous snowstorm.

- *Into the Wild:* This beautiful and sad movie tells the story of a man who ventures into the wilderness on a solo journey.

- *Dumb and Dumber:* This classic 1994 comedy features Jim Carrey and Jeff Daniels as two dim-witted best friends on the run.

- *Zombieland:* A comedy with Emma Stone, Jesse Eisenberg, Woody Harrelson, and Abigail Breslin, a ragtag group of survivors who survive the zombie apocalypse—on a road trip, of course.

PHOTOGRAPHY *Tips*

- Always have your camera ready.
- Keep your eye out for weird signage or funny moments.
- Shoot in the early morning or early evening for the best light.
- Capture a sense of place with a shot of an iconic site or something indicative of the region.
- Take lots of photos. You can always delete the not-so-great pics later.
- Review your photos each night to filter out what you don't want and to keep what you like.
- Take photos of people or places that are meaningful to you.

RESOURCES

ROAD CONDITIONS AND WEATHER

Most smartphones include apps that offer weather forecasts and updates on road conditions, as do these organizations.

U.S. Department of Transportation's Federal Highway Administration
Dial 511 or visit www.fhwa.dot.gov/about/webstate.cfm.

National Weather Service
www.weather.gov

The Weather Channel
http://weather.com

AUTOMOBILE ORGANIZATIONS

The American Automobile Association (AAA) provides roadside assistance, typically within 60-90 minutes of reaching out to them. If you rented a vehicle, you can also call your rental-car agency for assistance.

American Automobile Association
800/222-4357, www.aaa.com

CAR RENTAL COMPANIES

Advantage
800/777-5500, www.advantage.com

Alamo
844/354-6962, www.alamo.com

Avis
800/230-4898, www.avis.com

Budget
800/218-7992, www.budget.com

Dollar
800/800-5252, www.dollar.com

Enterprise
855/266-9289, www.enterprise.com

Hertz
800/654-3131, www.hertz.com

National
844/382-6875, www.nationalcar.com

Payless
800/729-5377, www.paylesscar.com

Thrifty
800/847-4389, www.thrifty.com

RV, CAMPERVAN, AND TRAILER RENTALS

Cruise America
800/671-8042, www.cruiseamerica.com

Escape Campervans
877/270-8267, www.escapecampervans.com

Outdoorsy
855/664-6740, www.outdoorsy.com

MAPS

Never embark on a road trip without an up-to-date printed map or guide, preferably a road atlas. Do not rely solely on GPS or smartphone navigation.

American Automobile Association
www.aaa.com

National Geographic
www.natgeomaps.com

Rand McNally
www.randmcnally.com

U.S. STATE TOURISM BUREAUS

Each of these tourism bureaus offers travel-planning tools, trip itineraries, calendars, maps, and more.

Alabama
http://alabama.travel

Alaska
www.travelalaska.com

Arizona
www.visitarizona.com

Arkansas
www.arkansas.com

California
www.visitcalifornia.com

Colorado
www.colorado.com

Connecticut
www.ctvisit.com

Delaware
www.visitdelaware.com

Florida
www.visitflorida.com

Georgia
www.exploregeorgia.org

Hawaii
www.gohawaii.com

Idaho
http://visitidaho.org

Illinois
www.enjoyillinois.com

Indiana
http://visitindiana.com

Iowa
www.traveliowa.com

Kansas
www.travelks.com

Kentucky
www.kentuckytourism.com

Louisiana
www.louisianatravel.com

Maine
http://visitmaine.com

Maryland
www.visitmaryland.org

Massachusetts
www.massvacation.com

Michigan
www.michigan.org

Minnesota
www.exploreminnesota.com

Mississippi
https://visitmississippi.org

Missouri
www.visitmo.com

Montana
www.visitmt.com

Nebraska
http://visitnebraska.com

Nevada
http://travelnevada.com

New Hampshire
www.visitnh.gov

New Jersey
www.visitnj.org

New Mexico
ww.newmexico.org

New York
www.iloveny.com

North Carolina
www.visitnc.com

North Dakota
www.ndtourism.com

Ohio
http://ohio.org

Oklahoma
www.travelok.com

Oregon
http://traveloregon.com

Pennsylvania
http://visitpa.com

Rhode Island
www.visitrhodeisland.com

South Carolina
http://discoversouthcarolina.com

South Dakota
www.travelsouthdakota.com

Tennessee
www.tnvacation.com

Texas
www.traveltexas.com

Utah
www.visitutah.com

Vermont
www.vermontvacation.com

Virginia
www.virginia.org

Washington
www.experiencewa.com

West Virginia
https://wvtourism.com

Wisconsin
www.travelwisconsin.com

Wyoming
http://travelwyoming.com

All interior photos © Dreamstime.com, except: pages 3 bottom, 301, 303, © Tim Hull; pages 13, 34 left & middle, 37, 40, 47 top, 49, 50, 51 top, 53 bottom, 54, 58, 62 top, 64, 67, 69, 70, 73, 74 right, 75, 76 top, 348 right, 351, 512 right, 513 middle, 514 top, 515 top, 516, 706 © Jessica Dunham; pages 35 top, 41, 44, 215 bottom-right, 407 middle, 409 top, 427, 428, 448 top, 568 left, 667 photo 1, 668-669, 671 © National Park Service; pages 56 bottom, 564 left © James Di Loreto / Smithsonian Institution; page 81 photo 2 © Gary Halvorson, Oregon State Archives; photo 3 © Sean and Julie Chickery; pages 81 bottom, 82, 83, 84 left, 85, 86 left, 91 left, 94 top, 95, 98, © Katrina Emery; pages 106 middle, 165, 170, 171 top, 216 bottom-left © Kayla Anderson; pages 111 photos 2 & 5, 116, 164, 175 © Stuart Thornton; pages 126, 128, 129, 135, 138 bottom, 180, 181 bottom, 189 top, 190-191, 199, 200, 241 right, 242 bottom, 243 bottom-left, 244, 245, 246, 248-249 © Ian Anderson; pages 130, 173 © Monterey Bay Aquarium; page 133 © Darren Alessi; pages 142, 144, 145, 146, 147 top, 150-151 © Caroline Hinchliff; pages 204, 206, 208-209 © Elizabeth Veneman; page 205 bottom © National Hotel & Restaurant; page 214 left © Kit Anderson; pages 214 right, 266, 268, 270-271, 273 © Matthew Lombardi; page 219 top © Ana Minnix; pages 219 photo 3, 291 photo 2, 443 photos 1 & 3, 453 photo 3, 585 photo 4, 701 photo 2 © Shutterstock; pages 220, 221, 223 left, 227, 228 top, 231, 233, 238 right, 241 left © Allison Williams; page 230 © Portland Art Museum; pages 253 bottom, 255 top, 256 left, 257-261, © Caroline Hinchliff; page 269 © Two Mountain Winery; page 276, 279, 293 top, 294, 332, © Judy Jewell; pages 286 left, 292 bottom, 295 left, 328, 331 © Paul Levy; pages 286 right, 338 top, 339 photos 1 & 3, 340, 342 bottom, 343, 344 © Justin Marler; pages 287 photo 5 and 349 photo 1 © Ramon Arguelles; page 296 top © Bill McRae; pages 299, 306, 309 right © Steven Horak; page 321 photo 2 © NCNHS/Humboldt Museum; page 348 left © David Solce/Unsplash; page 349 photo 2 © Texas Historical Commission; pages 358 right, 406, 407 photos 1 & 3, 408, 409 bottom, 410 bottom, 411 © Laural Bidwell; page 371 © Tino Woodburn; page 377 © Carter G. Walker; pages 392 bottom, 395 © Terri Cook and Lon Abbott; pages 399 top, 400-401, © Dana Hopper-Kelly; pages 419 photo 5 and 463 photo 2 © Al Johnsons Swedish Restaurant; page 422 right © Tricia Cornel; pages 434 top, 442, 454, 456 top © Paul Vachon; page 463 top © White Gull Inn; pages 463 bottom, 466-469 © Thomas Huhti; pages 482, 485 bottom, 491 © Jen Rose Smith; page 496, 499, 501, 504, 506, 507 © Timothy Malcolm; page 497 photo 5 © Michael Shake/123RF; page 513 photo 1 © Woodchuck Hard Cider; page 565 photo 4 © Andrew Thomas Lee; pages 567 top, 569 bottom, 570-572, 573 top, 575 bottom, 579 left, 580, 622 right © Jason Frye; page 585 photo 2 © Meg McKinney/Alabama Tourism Department; page 589 top © Art Maripol/visitflorence.com; page 589 bottom © Chris Granger/visitflorenceal.com; pages 592, 594 top, © Margaret Littman; pages 604, 605 bottom right, 606, 607 top, 608, 610 © Jim Morekis; page 631 photo 2 & 3, 634 left, 635 © Theresa Dowell Blackinton; page 643 bottom left and right, 646, 647 right, 650 top & bottom-right, 651, 653 top © Jason Ferguson; pages 652, 641 © Disney; pages 667 photo 2, 672 © Lisa Maloney; pages 676, 677 photo 3, 678-680, 682-685 © Don Pitcher; pages 690 right, 692-695 © Kevin Whitton

TEXT CREDITS

Cross-Country Routes

Text for the Oregon Trail adapted from *Moon Oregon Trail Road Trip,* first edition, by Katrina Emery.

California

Text for the Best of the Golden State adapted from *Moon California Road Trip,* third edition, by Stuart Thornton.

Text for the Pacific Coast Highway adapted from *Moon Pacific Coast Highway Road Trip,* second edition, by Ian Anderson.

Text for the Pacific Crest Trail adapted from *Moon Drive & Hike Pacific Crest Trail,* first edition, by Caroline Hinchliff.

Text for the Northern California Loop adapted from *Moon Northern California Road Trips,* first edition, by Stuart Thornton & Kayla Anderson.

Text for the Southern California and Route 66 Loop adapted from *Moon Southern California Road Trips,* first edition, by Ian Anderson.

Text for the California Deserts adapted from *Moon California,* first edition, by Elizabeth Linhart Veneman.

Text for the Gold Country Ramble adapted from *Moon Northern California,* eighth edition, by Elizabeth Linhart Veneman.

Pacific Northwest

Text for the Best of the Pacific Northwest adapted from *Moon Pacific Northwest Road Trip,* second edition, by Allison Williams.

Text for the Pacific Coast Highway adapted from *Moon Pacific Coast Highway Road Trip,* second edition, by Ian Anderson.

Text for the Pacific Crest Trail adapted from *Moon Drive & Hike Pacific Crest Trail,* first edition, by Caroline Hinchliff.

Text for the Columbia River Gorge and Wine Country adapted from *Moon Washington,* eleventh edition, by Matthew Lombardi.

Text for High Adventure in Bend adapted from *Moon Oregon,* thirteenth edition, by W.C. McRae & Judy Jewell.

The Southwest and Texas

Text for the Best of the Southwest adapted from *Moon Southwest Road Trip,* second edition, by Tim Hull.

Text for Santa Fe, Taos, and the Enchanted Circle adapted from *Moon Santa Fe, Taos & Albuquerque,* fifth edition, by Steven Horak.

Text for the Apache Trail adapted from *Moon Arizona,* fourteenth edition, by Tim Hull.

Text for Reno to the Rubies adapted from *Moon Nevada,* first edition, by Scott Smith.

Text for Salt Lake, Park City, and the Wasatch Range adapted from *Moon Utah,* thirteenth edition, by W.C. McRae & Judy Jewell.

Text for Austin, San Antonio, and the Hill Country adapted from *Moon Austin, San Antonio & the Hill Country,* fifth edition, by Justin Marler.

Rocky Mountains

Text for Yellowstone to Glacier National Park adapted from *Moon Yellowstone to Glacier National Park Road Trip,* first edition, by Carter G. Walker.

Text for Wild Wyoming adapted from *Moon Montana & Wyoming,* fourth edition, by Carter G. Walker.

Text for Denver, Boulder, and Rocky Mountain National Park adapted from *Moon Colorado,* tenth edition, by Terri Cook.

Text for Idaho's Rivers and Mountains adapted from *Moon Idaho,* seventh edition, by James P. Kelly.

Text for Mount Rushmore and the Black Hills adapted from *Moon Mount Rushmore & the Black Hills,* fourth edition, by Laural A. Bidwell.

Great Lakes

Text for Minneapolis to Voyageurs National Park adapted from *Moon Minnesota,* fourth edition, by Tricia Cornell.

Text for Michigan's Upper Peninsula adapted from *Moon Michigan's Upper Peninsula,* fourth edition, by Paul Vachon.

Text for Michigan's Gold Country adapted from *Moon Michigan,* sixth edition, by Paul Vachon.

Text for Wisconsin's Door County adapted from *Moon Wisconsin,* eighth edition, by Thomas Huhti.

New England, New York, and Pennsylvania

Text for Best of New England adapted from *Moon New England Road Trip,* first edition, by Jen Rose Smith.

Text for the Appalachian Trail adapted from *Moon Drive & Hike Appalachian Trail,* first edition, by Timothy Malcolm.

Text for Philadelphia, Pittsburgh, and Pennsylvania Dutch Country adapted from *Moon Pennsylvania,* sixth edition, by Rachel Vigoda.

Text for the Adirondacks and Catskills and the Hudson River Valley adapted

from *Moon New York State,* seventh edition, by Julie Schwietert Collazo.

The South and Florida

Text for the Blue Ridge Parkway adapted from *Moon Blue Ridge Parkway Road Trip,* second edition, by Jason Frye.

Text for the Natchez Trace adapted from *Moon Nashville to New Orleans Road Trip,* first edition, by Margaret Littman.

Text for Charleston to Savannah adapted from *Moon Charleston & Savannah,* eighth edition, by Jim Morekis.

Text for Chesapeake Bay adapted from *Moon Chesapeake Bay,* first edition, by Michaela Riva Gaaserud.

Text for North Carolina's Outer Banks adapted from *Moon North Carolina Coast,* third edition, by Jason Frye.

Text for Kentucky's Bourbon Trail adapted from *Moon Kentucky,* second edition, by Theresa Dowell Blackinton.

Text for South Florida and the Keys adapted from *Moon South Florida & the Keys Road Trip,* first edition, by Jason Ferguson.

Alaska and Hawai'i

Text for Alaska's Parks Highway adapted from *Moon Alaska,* second edition, by Lisa Maloney.

Text for the Kenai Peninsula adapted from *Moon Anchorage, Denali & the Kenai Peninsula,* third edition, by Don Pitcher.

Text for the O'ahu Coastal Loop adapted from *Moon Honolulu & O'ahu,* eighth edition, by Kevin Whitton.

Text for the Road to Hana adapted from *Moon Maui,* eleventh edition, by Greg Archer.

ACKNOWLEDGMENTS

I owe a debt of gratitude to the writers who contributed their regional expertise. Without their tireless research and road-trip insights, this book would not exist.

Thank you to Nikki Ioakimedes for her creativity, collaboration, and vision as we outlined the book in the early stages.

I'd be lost without my editor, Leah Gordon. She offered thoughtful edits and wise guidance—all while keeping me on deadline—to deftly steer this project from inception to completion.

Big thanks to Cassidy Horan for her fact-checking and research assistance.

I want to thank my sister, Rebekah Dunham, who was my first road-trip partner on our family expeditions, during which we spent hours playing games and listening to Dad-selected radio tunes.

To Katie Cappello: best friend, driving buddy, Google maps navigator, and playlist deejay. The Loneliest Road was a little less lonely because of you.

Thank you to my mom, Donna Dunham, who always jumps at the chance to hit the road, whether it's a mother-daugther trip on Route 66 or a spur-of-the-moment drive to San Diego.

My husband, Jason Wilson. Not only is he an endless source of love, support, and encouragement, he's also the most fun person to bring on a road trip. Every year, we load up our dogs (hats off to Daisy and Nora for being seasoned canine travel companions) and drive 5,200 miles from Arizona to Vermont and back again. And there's nobody else on earth I'd rather make that journey with than him.

I'd like to dedicate this book to my father, Ross Dunham. Your enthusiasm, spontaneity, curiosity, and zeal are what epic adventures—on the road and in life—are made of.

MAP SYMBOLS

══════ Expressway	○ City/Town	✗ Airport	⚓ Golf Course
─────── Primary Road	◉ State Capital	✗ Airfield	🅿 Parking Area
········ Secondary Road	⊛ National Capital	▲ Mountain	🏛 Archaeological Site
░░░░░ Unpaved Road	✪ Highlight	✛ Unique Natural Feature	🍾 Church
─ ─ ─ Trail	★ Point of Interest		🔌 Gas Station
············ Ferry	• Accommodation	🖋 Waterfall	◯ Glacier
╼╼╼╼ Railroad	▾ Restaurant/Bar	⬆ Park	Mangrove
▦▦▦ Pedestrian Walkway	■ Other Location	TH Trailhead	Reef
▥▥▥ Stairs	Λ Campground	✗ Skiing Area	Swamp

CONVERSION TABLES

°C = (°F - 32) / 1.8
°F = (°C x 1.8) + 32
1 inch = 2.54 centimeters (cm)
1 foot = 0.304 meters (m)
1 yard = 0.914 meters
1 mile = 1.6093 kilometers (km)
1 km = 0.6214 miles
1 fathom = 1.8288 m
1 chain = 20.1168 m
1 furlong = 201.168 m
1 acre = 0.4047 hectares
1 sq km = 100 hectares
1 sq mile = 2.59 square km
1 ounce = 28.35 grams
1 pound = 0.4536 kilograms
1 short ton = 0.90718 metric ton
1 short ton = 2,000 pounds
1 long ton = 1.016 metric tons
1 long ton = 2,240 pounds
1 metric ton = 1,000 kilograms
1 quart = 0.94635 liters
1 US gallon = 3.7854 liters
1 Imperial gallon = 4.5459 liters
1 nautical mile = 1.852 km

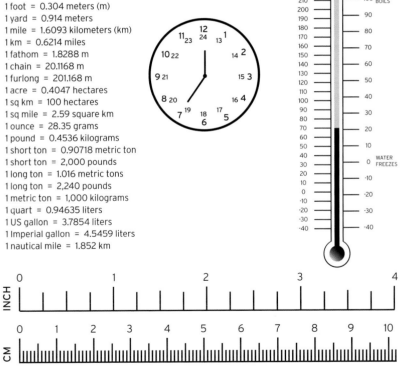

THE OPEN ROAD
Avalon Travel
Hachette Book Group
1700 Fourth Street
Berkeley, CA 94710, USA
www.moon.com

Editor: Leah Gordon
Acquiring Editor: Nikki Ioakimedes
Copy Editor: Brett Keener
Graphics and Production Coordinator: Lucie Ericksen
Cover Design: Erin Seaward-Hiatt
Interior Design: Megan Jones Design
Moon Logo: Tim McGrath
Map Editor: Mike Morgenfeld
Cartographer: Karin Dahl
Editorial Assistance: Rachael Sablik
Proofreader: Ashley Benning
Indexer: Rachel Kuhn

ISBN-13: 978-1-64049-930-0

Printing History
1st Edition — October 2020
5 4 3 2 1